VOICES OF MY COMRADES

AMERICA'S
RESERVE OFFICERS
REMEMBER
WORLD WAR II

VOICES OF MY COMRADES

EDITED BY CAROL ADELE KELLY

FORDHAM UNIVERSITY PRESS

New York 2007

Library of Congress Cataloging-in-Publication Data

Voices of my comrades : America's Reserve officers
remember World War II / edited by Carol Adele
Kelly.—1st.

    p. cm.—(World War II—the global, human, and
ethical dimension ; 13)
  Stories originally submitted by members of the
Reserve Officers Association of the United States and
published in a monthly feature of The officer, Dec.
1991–Sept. 1995.
  Includes bibliographical references and index.
  ISBN 978-0-8232-2823-2 (cloth : alk. paper)
  1. World War, 1939–1945—Personal narratives,
American. I. Kelly, Carol Adele. II. Reserve Officers
Association of the United States. III. Officer.
D769.V64 2007
940.54′8173—dc22

                2007037890

Printed in the United States of America
09 08 07   5 4 3 2 1
First edition

To the men, women, and families of World War II
who preserved the world from tyranny, and especially
to our nation's citizen-soldiers who from our country's
founding have taken up arms in defense of liberty.

They had come not to conquer or terrorize but to
liberate. . . . They prevailed and thereby saved us all. . . .
They brought more freedom to more people around
the world than any other generation in history.
—Stephen E. Ambrose

CONTENTS

FOREWORD

Senator Ted Stevens and Senator Daniel K. Inouye

We share more than a common connection with the men and women whose stories fill the pages of this book. We share a history and a bond as comrades in the deepest sense of the word.

These accounts, from members of the Reserve Officers Association who served in World War II, cover terrain with names inseparable from the historic events which occurred there: Pearl Harbor, Bataan, Midway, Guadalcanal, Algeria, Normandy, Burma, Ardennes, Iwo Jima, Dachau, Tokyo Bay. Terrain personally familiar to us is recalled in accounts from northern Italy and China.

Here, too, are events from lesser-known territories that proved this conflict to be a *world* war: Greenland, Fiji, Ascension Island, Iceland, Iran, Chad, Australia, Aruba. Indeed, of particular interest to us, this book has extensive accounts of "the Forgotten War" in the Aleutian Islands, where Japanese troops occupied Alaskan territory, and it shows Hawaii to be a vital player in the Pacific campaigns after the devastating attack on Pearl Harbor.

You'll recognize the famous generals many of these soldiers encounter: Patton, MacArthur, Eisenhower. You'll witness profound events, including the liberation of concentration camps. And you'll find an account of the D-Day invasion from our late colleague Senator Strom Thurmond, then a young Army paratrooper.

But, more than putting the reader into a well-known time and place in history, these veterans' accounts share the personal, singular experiences of going to war. This book covers the breadth of "combat." You'll feel what it was like to pilot through flak-filled skies while fending off enemy fighters and mechanical failure, to save your merchant marine ship after it was hit by a Kamikaze, to fight hedgerow to hedgerow and house to house through Normandy, and to pilot a glider into a chaotic landing zone behind enemy lines.

You'll also experience equally important but much less glamorous missions—a reserve unit that created an airstrip on an isolated volcanic island, finance officers getting soldiers' pay ashore after D-Day, combat engineers building a bridge over the Rhine, and a Jewish chaplain who conducted, in sequence, a Catholic, a Protestant, and a Jewish service for troops on the eve of battle.

In times of war, personal discomfort is often as great a concern as the actions of the enemy. This book features harrowing accounts of battle, but we also empathize with those beleaguered by sand-clogged engines in North Africa, nagging mosquitoes in the South Pacific, and government bureaucracy upon returning home. Food is another common theme in this book. We now take our access to this most basic of necessities for granted, but in the following pages, you'll read how isolated soldiers treated K-rations as gourmet food, and how prisoners of war were delighted to receive fresh lemons one day.

While we share many of the experiences and feelings our fellow veterans relate in this book, there are also pages here describing a heroism we have never known: that of POWs, from the Bataan Death March to the Stalags of Germany. These pages contain accounts of successful escapes, near escapes, and prisoners merely surviving to see the next day in the face of starvation, forced labor, and torture.

Years after the end of World War II, President Ronald Reagan would observe, "Perhaps you and I have lived with this miracle too long to be properly appreciative. Freedom is a fragile thing and is never more than one generation from extinction. It is not ours by inheritance; it must be fought for and defended constantly by each generation, for it comes only once to a people."

These are the stories of a generation which risked everything to defend our freedom. In *Voices of My Comrades*, we are reminded of the heroism and dedication to duty which carried American men and women to victory in World War II. And we remember also our current generation of Reservists, who today carry these same attributes into battle all across the globe as they continue to protect this nation.

Senator Daniel K. Inouye of Hawaii served in the U.S. Army's 442nd Regimental Combat Team, the legendary "Go for Broke" regiment of Japanese-American soldiers. He was wounded in combat in North Italy, and was awarded the Medal of Honor, the nation's highest award for military valor, for his actions there.

Senator Ted Stevens of Alaska was stationed in the China–Burma–India Theater, where he flew C-46s and C-47s for the Army Air Corps in support of General Claire Chennault's 14th Air Force Flying Tigers. He received two Distinguished Flying Crosses, two Air Medals, and the Republic of China's Yuan Hai medal for his service.

PREFACE

These voices, these quiet words, these footsteps . . . behind me recall me at a bound from the terrible loneliness and fear of death. . . . They are more to me than life, those voices . . . and more than fear . . . they are the voices of my comrades.

—Erich Maria Remarque

Here they are by the hundreds, those voices: World War II accounts from men and women of the Reserve Officers Association of the United States (ROA). Their stories were submitted for the series "Remembrances of the War Years," featured monthly in ROA's magazine, *The Officer*, from December 1991 through September 1995, to coincide with fiftieth anniversaries of the events described.

The idea for the magazine's World War II commemoratives was that of Colonel Norman S. Burzynski, USAF (Ret.), editor of *The Officer* from 1976 to 1995. Since I was freelancing for the magazine at the time, Colonel Burzynski asked me to serve as editor of the series.

In late 1990, when *The Officer* first began soliciting material for the series—challenging ROA's WWII veterans to provide accounts of their most memorable moments and to "tell it as it was"—neither the colonel nor I had any idea what the response would be. Slowly at first, and then steadily, the material began to arrive. More than 350 ROA members responded, with their own reminiscences and photos or with diaries, letters, or stories from family members. A sampling from that outpouring is reprinted in this volume.

Among the first communiqués to arrive was a postcard from Major Michael H. Quinn, USAR, of Columbus, Ohio, asking whether we might be interested in the POW diary of his late father, Colonel Michael A. Quinn, AUS (Ret.), who served as chief of motor transportation on the staff of Lieutenant General Jonathan Wainwright in the Philippines and became a prisoner of the Japanese with the fall of Bataan in April 1942. For forty months as a POW, Colonel Quinn kept detailed, near-daily accounts of his life in seven POW camps, written as letters to his wife and seven children.

Along with Colonel Quinn, those quiet voices of his comrades include the twenty-two-year-old ensign who escapes from the USS *Cassin* minutes before it explodes at Pearl Harbor, 7 December 1941; the nurses who minister from napa huts on Bataan, from aboard the hospital ship *Shamrock* in the Mediterranean, and from field hospitals behind frontlines in France; eight of the D-Day invaders of Normandy, including then–Lieutenant Colonel J. Strom Thurmond, paratrooper; and the twenty-five-year-old officer who loses 117 of his men in one day at Bitburg, Germany.

Among their other stories, contributors describe involvement with around-the-clock repair of aircraft at Burtonwood, England; the early days of the Women Airforce Service Pilots (WASP); construction of Wideawake Field on a lava rock called Ascension Island in the Atlantic; work of the Railway Operating Battalion in the European Theater of Operations and of the Seabees in the Pacific Theater. They write of the sinking of the *Leopoldville* when 750 men die on Christmas Eve 1944 in the English Channel; of marching fifty miles through snowstorms and sub-zero temperatures while being transferred as a POW of the Germans; of the horrific discovery of the extermination camps in Germany; and of the bombing of unmarked Japanese ships transporting U.S. POWs from the Philippines to camps closer to Japan near war's end. Stories range the globe from the Aleutians and Australia to Normandy and Guadalcanal, from the Bulge and Burma and Iran, to Berlin and Tokyo, with most points in between and all of the military services represented.

In the introductions that precede their stories, contributors are identified by their latest rank in the military. In the index, they are further identified by branch of service and last known place of residence. In cases where published books or an unpublished manuscript were provided, material is excerpted from these sources. Those authors and their works are acknowledged at the back of this volume.

Chapters usually begin with an introductory story featuring the most significant event, the most interesting story, or a theme for that month of the war (holiday, victory celebration, et cetera). If for the European Theater, for example, this introduction is followed by recollections from that theater, then from the Pacific Theater and, in last place, from the States, with each group in near-chronological order. To assist readers in easily perusing the Colonel Quinn diary in sequence, his entries, when included, are usually placed at or near the end of chapters.

As you read the WWII recollections, please consider the following:

- If a significant battle or event was not written about by a contributor, a summary at the beginning of chapters provides that information, besides giving an overview of the all-inclusiveness of the war.
- The use of certain appellations is retained in letters, journals, and retrospectives, reflective of writers' rage at the enemy they fought. To censor their words would be unpardonable revisionism.

- Military style for date and time is retained for the purpose of simplicity.
- While reasonable efforts have been made to ascertain accuracy of facts and figures, dates and spellings, each story is essentially the contributor's own, and written from his or her point of view.

As you read, take note also of certain themes that echo from among the contributors: Their youthfulness (average age of WWII participants was nineteen); longevity of service (average length of WWII service was thirty-three months); familial history of military service, as sons and daughters follow parents' paths; and their devotion to military service. By the nature of this volume, the contributors were U.S. Reserve officers. This means that after years of commitment during World War II, they also chose to dedicate additional years in service to their country as members of our nation's Reserve forces.

To all of the ROA members who generously shared their WWII stories, first in the magazine and now in this compilation, and to friend and colleague Norm Burzynski who entrusted the series to me: my heartfelt appreciation for this extraordinary privilege. As the title to one WWII song says, "Bless 'Em All."

As yet another of their war songs suggests, those valiant men and women of World War II who "did it before" in wartime duty will now give you a small idea of how they managed to preserve freedom for an entire world as they "do it again" by recounting their stories and by sharing with you the voices of their comrades.

—Carol Adele Kelly

The Reserve Officers Association of the United States (ROA) was founded 2 October 1922, when several hundred military officers met with General of the Armies John Joseph Pershing in Washington, D.C., to discuss the general's concerns about losing the officer corps, plus growing isolationism and post–World War I complacency. Public Law 595 of the 81st Congress chartered ROA to "support and promote the development and execution of a military policy for the United States that will provide adequate National Security." The charter was signed 30 June 1950 by President Harry S. Truman, an early member of ROA.

ROA's national headquarters is located at 1 Constitution Avenue NE, Washington, D.C.

WORLD WAR II CHRONOLOGY

1939

1 September	Germany invades Poland: World War II begins.
3 September	Great Britain and France—also Australia, Canada, India, South Africa, and New Zealand—declare war on Germany.
27 September	Warsaw surrenders to Germany.

1940

9 April	Germany occupies Denmark and Norway.
10 May	Germany invades Luxembourg, Belgium, and the Netherlands.
12 May	Germany invades France.
10 June	Italy declares war on Britain and France.
11 June	Italy invades France.
14 June	Germany enters Paris.
13 August	Eagle Day begins Germany's air offensive against Great Britain. The Blitz continues until 10–11 May 1941, killing 40,000 British.
13 September	Italy invades Egypt.
27 September	Tripartite Pact signed by Japan, Germany, and Italy: each to declare war on any party that wars against one of the others.
28 October	Italy invades Greece.

1941

6 April	Germany invades Yugoslavia and Greece.
22 June	Germany invades USSR.
7 July	U.S. Marines begin arriving in Iceland, replacing British forces.
24 July	Japan occupies French Indo-China.
9–12 August	Atlantic Conference, Newfoundland: Roosevelt, Churchill, and military staffs meet; Roosevelt extends escorts in Atlantic to Iceland to protect shipping against U-boats; Atlantic Charter signed, describing war/peace principles of Great Britain and United States.

4 September	USS *Greer* attacked by U-boat off Iceland.
8 September	Germany lays siege to Leningrad.
17 October	USS *Kearny* hit by torpedo in North Atlantic; 11 sailors die.
31 October	USS *Reuben James* torpedoed by U-boat in North Atlantic; 115 perish, 45 are rescued.
7 December	Japan attacks U.S. at Pearl Harbor; on the same day (8 December, west of international date line), Japan attacks Wake Island, Guam, and the Philippines and invades Hong Kong, Thailand, and Malaya.
8 December	United States and Britain declare war on Japan.
9 December	Japan invades Gilbert Islands.
10 December	Japan takes Guam; makes first landings on Luzon in Philippines.
11 December	Japan invades Burma. Germany and Italy declare war on the United States, which takes reciprocal action.
16 December	Japan invades Borneo.
22–28 December	Arcadia Conference begins: Churchill, Roosevelt, chiefs of staff, and political leaders meet in Washington, D.C.
23 December	Japan captures Wake Island.
25 December	Hong Kong falls to Japanese.
31 December	Japan occupies Manila, the Philippines.

1942

1 January	United Nations Declaration signed in Washington, D.C.
1–5, 11–14 January	Arcadia Conference resumes. Combined Chiefs of Staff established; "Germany First" set as strategy before war on Japan.
7 January	Siege of Bataan begins in Philippines.
11 January	Japan invades Netherlands East Indies.
31 January	First U.S. Expeditionary Force in Europe arrives in Ireland.
1 February	U.S. planes bomb Japanese bases in Marshall and Gilbert Islands.
15 February	Singapore surrenders to Japanese.
22 February	First U.S. air headquarters in Europe established in England.
27–28 February	Battle of Java Sea.
28 February	Japan invades Java.

1–31 March	Nazis begin large-scale transport of Jews to extermination camps.
8 March	Japanese land in New Guinea.
12 March	17,500 U.S. troops, with first Seabees, arrive at New Caledonia.
13 March	Japanese land on Solomon Islands, Southwest Pacific.
14 March	U.S. troops begin arriving in Australia.
30 March	Douglas MacArthur appointed Supreme Commander Southwest Pacific (SWPA); Nimitz, Commander in Chief Pacific (CINPAC).
9 April	U.S. forces on Bataan fall to Japanese.
18 April	Sixteen B-25s take off from carrier USS *Hornet* for raid on Tokyo.
22 April	U.S. forces land in India.
2–8 May	U.S. defeats Japanese in Battle of the Coral Sea.
6 May	Corregidor surrenders, along with all U.S. forces on Philippines.
8 May	Germans begin preliminary offensives in USSR.
26 May	Rommel's Afrika Korps goes on offensive in Libya; U.S. forces arrive in Espiritu Santo, New Hebrides.
3–6 June	Battle of Midway, turning point of Pacific War; Japanese lose 17 ships, 275 planes, and 4,800 men.
6–7 June	Japan invades Kiska and Attu in the Aleutian Islands, Alaska.
9 June	Japan completes conquest of the Philippines.
13 June	Four German spies land from submarine off Long Island, New York; detected and captured by U.S. Coast Guard and FBI.
18–25 June	Roosevelt and Churchill meet at Hyde Park, New York, and Washington, D.C.: discuss second front in Europe, development of atomic bomb.
21 June	Japanese submarine I-25 shells Fort Stevens, Oregon.
25 June	Army establishes European Theater of Operations under Major General Dwight D. Eisenhower.
26 June	Germany announces unrestricted submarine warfare off U.S. Atlantic coast.
7–8 August	U.S. Marines and Army land on Guadalcanal and other sites in Solomon Islands, marking the first U.S. land offensive of the war.

17 August	U.S. Eighth Air Force makes first all-American attack on European target, Rouen-Sotteville, northern France.
17–18 August	U.S. Marines conduct raid on Makin Island, Gilbert Islands.
24–25 August	Battle of the Eastern Solomon Islands.
1 September	German units reach Stalingrad.
12 September	Eisenhower assumes post as Commander in Chief, Allied Expeditionary Force for Northwest Africa.
12–14 September	Battle of Bloody Ridge: Marines repulse Japanese on Guadalcanal.
15 September	U.S. Army lands in New Guinea.
11–12 October	Battle of Cape Esperance, Guadalcanal.
8 November	Operation Torch begins: Allies invade Algeria and French Morocco, North Africa.
12–15 November	Naval Battle of Guadalcanal.
11 December	U.S. troops arrive in Iran and Iraq.
14 December	American forces capture Buna, New Guinea.

1943

14–24 January	Casablanca Conference, Morocco: Roosevelt, Churchill, chiefs of staff discuss U-boat offensive; Pacific operations; moves to Sicily and Italy after North Africa; preparations for a landing in Europe; Roosevelt calls for unconditional surrender of Germany, Italy, and Japan.
22 January	Battle of Papua, New Guinea, ends with first decisive defeat of Japanese on land.
27 January	U.S. Eighth Army Air Force bombs Wilhelmshaven in its first attack on Germany.
2 February	Last German troops in Stalingrad surrender.
9 February	U.S. forces complete Guadalcanal campaign; Japanese lose approximately 10,000 soldiers; U.S. loses 1,600.
19–28 February	Battle of Kasserine Pass, Tunisia.
21 February	U.S. 43rd Division seizes Russell Islands.
2–4 March	Battle of the Bismarck Sea: Japanese suffer heavy losses.
14–20 March	War's largest convoy battle in Battle of the Atlantic: 20 U-boats, from pack of 40, destroy 21 of 100 ships.
7 May	Allied 18th Army Group captures Tunis and Bizerte, Tunisia.

11 May	Canadian forces/U.S. Army 7th Division attack Japanese on Attu.
11–26 May	Roosevelt and Churchill meet at White House and Shangri-la (now Camp David): set May 1944 for cross-Channel operation; resolve to share information on development of atomic bomb.
30 May	Americans complete the capture of Attu.
13 June	African campaign ends with defeat of Axis in Tunisia.
21 June	4th Marine Raider Battalion lands on New Georgia.
22 June	German U-boats withdraw from North Atlantic.
30 June	Solomon Islands operations begin at Rabaul, New Britain.
9 July	Allies invade Sicily in Operation Husky; victorious 17 August.
24 July–2 August	Allies saturation-bomb Hamburg, Germany.
25 July	Mussolini overthrown and arrested; succeeded by Pietro Badoglio.
1 August	In Operation Tidal Wave, U.S. B-24s bomb Ploesti, Romania.
6 August	Japanese defeated in naval battle of Vella Gulf, Solomon Islands.
17 August	U.S. B-17s raid Schweinfurt and Regensburg, Germany.
17–24 August	Roosevelt and Churchill meet in Quebec, Canada: discuss invasion of Europe (Operation Overlord) and impending collapse of Italy.
3 September	Allies invade Italy.
8 September	Italy surrenders to Allies.
9 September	Allies land at Salerno, Italy.
10 September	German forces take over Rome and much of Northern Italy.
13 October	Italy declares war on Germany.
14 October	U.S. B-17s suffer heavy losses in raid on Schweinfurt; of 291 planes, 60 are lost; 140 damaged.
1 November	U.S. Marines land on Bougainville, Solomon Islands.
20 November	2nd Marine Division lands on Tarawa in Gilbert Islands.
22–26 November	Allied Cairo Conference begins: Roosevelt, Churchill, and Chiang Kai-shek discuss Allied operations in Asia.

28 November– 1 December	Teheran Conference begins: Roosevelt, Churchill, and Stalin discuss invasion of France; Stalin to join war against Japan after Germany's defeat.
2–7 December	Allies resume Cairo Conference: Eisenhower named Supreme Commander of Allied Forces for invasion of Europe.
26 December	1st Marine Division lands on Cape Gloucester, New Britain.

1944

11 January	Allies begin air offensive against German aircraft industry/air force.
22 January	U.S. Army lands at Anzio, Italy.
31 January	U.S. forces land on Kwajalein, Marshall Islands.
15 February	Allies bomb Monte Cassino, Italy.
18–25 February	German V-1 bombs hit Great Britain in the Little Blitz.
20 February	"Big Week" of air attacks begins against German aircraft industry.
6 and 8 March	U.S. Eighth Air Force makes first U.S. bomber attacks on Berlin.
5 April	U.S. Air Force bombers raid Ploesti oil fields, Romania.
13 April	Allies begin attacks on German coast defenses in Normandy.
11 May	U.S. Fifth/British Eighth Armies launch offensive in central Italy.
18 May	Monte Cassino, Italy, falls to Allies, ending four-month struggle.
23 May	Large-scale U.S. and British offensive begins at Anzio, Italy.
24 May	Navy aircraft attack Wake Island in North Pacific Ocean.
5 June	Allied forces enter Rome.
6 June	D-Day: Allies land at Normandy in Operation Overlord.
13 June	Germans begin V-1 rocket attacks on London.
15 June	U.S. bombs Tokyo.
15 June	2nd/4th Marine Divisions invade Saipan, Mariana Islands; reinforced by Army's 27th Infantry Division 16 June; complete capture 9 July.

19–20 June	Japanese fleet defeated in Battle of Philippine Sea.
27 June	Cherbourg, France, surrenders to VII Corps.
18 July	U.S. XIX Corps liberates Saint-Lo, northwest France; Japanese general Tojo falls from power.
21 July	1st and 3rd Marine Divisions land on Guam, Mariana Islands.
24 July	4th Marine Division lands on Tinian, Mariana Islands.
25 July	Northern France campaign begins with Operation Cobra.
10 August	U.S. retakes Guam.
15 August	Allied forces invade Southern France in Operation Dragoon.
25 August	Paris is liberated: General Charles de Gaulle returns on 26 August.
2 September	First Army enters Belgium.
8 September	Ninth Army assaults Brest, France; first German V-2 rocket lands in London.
10 September	First Army takes Luxembourg.
11 September	First Army units cross into Germany.
11–16 September	Roosevelt and Churchill meet for Quebec Conference: America agrees to extend Lend-Lease and to give postwar aid to Britain; principals discuss occupation of Germany and Italy and keeping atomic project secret while working in "full collaboration."
15 September	1st Marine Division lands on Peleliu, Caroline Islands.
17 September	Allied Airborne Army units dropped in the Netherlands.
20 October	U.S. Sixth Army lands on Leyte, the Philippines.
21 October	First German city, Aachen, falls to U.S. troops.
23–26 October	Battle for Leyte Gulf.
24 November	B-29s begin air attacks on Tokyo from bases in the Mariana Islands.
13 December	U.S. Army completes capture of Metz, France.
15 December	U.S. Army lands on Mindoro, the Philippines.
16 December	Germans attack in Adrennes, beginning Battle of the Bulge.
21 December	Germans besiege Bastogne in eastern Luxembourg.
25 December	Allies launch counteroffensive in the Ardennes.
31 December	New Guinea campaign ends.

1945

Mid-January	Battle of Bulge ends with German defeat.
4 February	1,000 U.S. bombers attack Berlin.
4–12 February	Big Three Yalta Conference, South Crimea, Ukraine: Roosevelt, Churchill, and Stalin plan occupation zones in Germany.
19 February	U.S. Marines land on Iwo Jima, completing capture 26 March: losses are heavy, with 6,000 Americans dead; 17,200 wounded; of 20,700 Japanese involved, about 200 survive.
25 February	B-29s drop incendiary bombs on Tokyo.
26 February	1,200 U.S. bombers strike Berlin.
2 March	U.S. Airborne troops recapture Corregidor, the Philippines.
3 March	Japanese resistance in Manila ends.
7 March	U.S. Third Army crosses Rhine on bridge at Remagen, Germany.
9–10 March	279 Superfortresses firebomb Tokyo, killing 80,000 to 120,000.
11 March	U.S. Eighth Army units land on Mindanao, the Philippines.
1 April	U.S. forces land on Okinawa, securing it 21 June.
12 April	Roosevelt dies; Harry S. Truman succeeds him as U.S. president.
25 April	U.S. and Soviet troops meet at the Elbe.
28 April	Mussolini is executed by partisans.
29 April	German forces in Italy surrender; American troops enter Dachau concentration camp, liberating more than 32,000 prisoners.
30 April	Hitler commits suicide in bunker; Donitz chosen head of state.
2 May	Berlin surrenders to Soviet forces.
2 May	German surrender in Italy effective at noon.
7 May	Germany signs surrender at Eisenhower Headquarters, Reims, France.
8 May	V-E Day proclaimed.
26 June	San Francisco Conference: U.N. Charter signed.
5 July	The Philippines Islands are liberated.

16 July–2 August	Potsdam Conference: Truman, Churchill, and Stalin discuss peace plans for Europe and terms of surrender for Japan.
16 July	Atomic bomb successfully tested at Alamogordo, New Mexico.
26 July	Potsdam Declaration issued, detailing surrender terms for Japan.
6 August	Atomic bomb dropped on Hiroshima, Japan; estimates of number killed range from 80,000 to 119,000.
8 August	Soviet Union declares war on Japan.
9 August	Atomic bomb dropped on Nagasaki, Japan; estimates of number killed range from 40,000 to 74,000. Soviet forces invade Manchuria.
14 August	Japan surrenders, ending World War II.
15 August	Nations celebrate V-J Day.
2 September	Japan signs surrender documents aboard battleship USS *Missouri* in Tokyo Bay.
20 November 1945– 1 October 1946	War crimes trials conducted in Nuremberg, Germany; of 21 tried, 10 are hanged in October 1946.
December 1945	U.S. military commission condemns to death General Tomoyuki Yamashita, former Japanese commander in the Philippines.

1946–47

May 1946– November 1947	War crimes trials held in Tokyo; General Hideki Tojo and four others are sentenced to death.

PROLOGUE

While 7 December 1941 is the date officially associated with the entry of the United States into World War II, there was involvement for certain service members even before the bombing of Pearl Harbor. Among those who would definitely consider themselves part of the war effort, pre–Pearl Harbor, were the crew of the old four-stacker destroyer, the USS *Dickerson*, patrolling the Caribbean and Atlantic for German subs by mid-1941; members of the Electronics Training Group working with the British on radar in England by September 1941; Coast Guardsmen aboard the U.S. Coast Guard cutter *Northland*, which captured the German-controlled Norwegian sealer *Buskoe* in Mackenzie Bay, north of Yukon Territory, 12 September 1941, in what is designated the first naval capture of World War II; and the crew of the USS *Reuben James*, which was torpedoed by a German U-boat in the North Atlantic, 31 October 1941, and is considered the first U.S. warship sunk in World War II.

Four servicemen describe their involvement in these prewar scenarios, with stories that exemplify the courage and fortitude typifying all of the accounts in *Voices of My Comrades*.

Mid-1941–December 1944
Caribbean, Atlantic, Philippine Sea

Chief Warrant Officer Clifford A. Roberts describes his experience on board the USS Dickerson *(DD-157).*

"Prior to WWII, approximately six months before we entered the war, we were on assignment in the Caribbean, hunting and tracking German submarines," Mr. Roberts writes. "We were not allowed to attack them, but we reported them to the English navy. When we entered the war, we were allowed to attack and were sent to find a fleet of subs headed for U.S. waters. We found them and went to General Quarters thirteen times during the night and dropped depth charges twelve times. We were given credit for sinking four that night, with an unknown number damaged.

"I was a second-class fire controlman, the only one on the destroyer with a striker [a person in apprenticeship to his mentor's job]. Later, we went to the North Atlantic run, then to escort the first convoy to Casablanca, Morocco, during the invasion of North Africa [8 November 1942]."

Mr. Roberts was transferred to the USS *Hobby* (DD-610) and then to the USS *Luce* (DD-522). He was aboard the *Luce,* on the other side of the island from Manila when his brother Hugh was killed 15 December 1944 by U.S. bombs that struck an unmarked Japanese ship transporting POWs to Japan. Lieutenant Roberts' one comprehensive letter to his family is reprinted in this volume, divided chronologically into the appropriate monthly chapters.

September 1941–1943
England

Colonel Louis P. Goetz was with the Electronics Training Group (ETG), which worked with the British on RADAR (Radio detecting and ranging).

In his preface to *Electronics Training Group World War II,* a history of ETG through recollections of former members, Colonel Goetz explains that members "were mostly company grade officers throughout Word War II, trained by the British army and the Royal Air Force (RAF) in England, many serving as commanding officers of British units, and all working on radar. Eight members were killed during training while flying with the RAF and probably represent the first American soldiers killed in the European Theater of Operations." This should dispel any doubts "that we were truly neutral prior to 7 December 1941 with respect to the European war and, further, that our Army was prepared technically to successfully employ radar operationally in 1941," he writes.

Quoting from Terret, Tompson, and Harris's *United States Army in World War II: The Technical Service,* Colonel Goetz describes ETG as "an application of the principle of lend-lease," with men rather than property or materiel as the resources. The idea for its formation was proposed to President Franklin D. Roosevelt in April 1941 after a return from England by Dr. James B. Conant, president of Harvard University and member of the National Defense Research Committee.

Recruitment began 30 June 1941 via newspaper, magazine, and radio announcements. This was followed by tours of cities and Army camps by the Military Personnel Division, Office of the Chief Signal Officer. From an initial 2,000 applications, 400 were considered for this select group of technical volunteers. Colonel Goetz notes that his recruitment to ETG came from the National Roster of Scientific Personnel.

"Though not generally known, nearly all graduates with degrees in science or engineering in the United States were listed with this government group . . . ; Big Brother had started making lists before WWII. Many of us were commissioned directly from civilian life and had very little military training. I arrived at

Fort Monmouth, New Jersey, 8 August 1941, and was in England in mid-September."

After three weeks of basic training, Second Lieutenant Goetz and thirty-four other ETG second lieutenants left for Montreal on 12 September and sailed for England three days later aboard the transformed Canadian Pacific ship *Empress of Asia*. The new officers docked in Liverpool where they were divided into two groups, seventeen to be trained by the RAF and eighteen by the British army, with Lieutenant Goetz in the latter group.

On 1 October 1941 he started school at Bury Lancashire at the British Military College of Science. For three months, six days a week, the men were taught by instructors from the British Broadcasting Company and British colleges. Four-hour morning sessions were followed by a tea break and then lab work in the afternoons—"first, working problems, learning about English test equipment; then learning about the Anti-aircraft (AA) Radar and the Search Light Radar (ELSIE). . . .

"The operations of this group were one of the best-kept secrets of WWII," Colonel Goetz says. "The atom bomb project cost the United States an estimated $2 billion. Three billion dollars was spent on radar, yet this entire operation was maintained in a high state of secrecy until after WWII."

Terret, Tompson, and Harris report that ETG, from its inception until its close in December 1943, brought the Signal Corps 2,200 electrical engineers, 900 of whom were trained in England. Of this latter group, there were eighteen separate units of about fifty members each. The first four groups were in England on 7 December 1941; the fifth group was en route and learned upon arrival of the attack on Pearl Harbor.

"On 31 December 1941, the Bury ETG 1 was sent to London to be assigned to its British units," Colonel Goetz recalls. He was assigned to Royal Army Ordnance Corps outside of Sittingbourne, Kent, about forty miles from London. The unit—consisting of five officers, including him, and about 100 enlisted men—was part of an anti-aircraft division positioned north and south of the Thames River, which the Germans used as a compass to get to London for night-time bombings.

Colonel Goetz describes their duties: "We were responsible in American terms for the third and fourth echelon maintenance of anti-aircraft and searchlight radar. . . . The part of the unit I was with tried to keep slightly over 100 radars in operation, mostly searchlight radars and about a dozen anti-aircraft radars. The unit also repaired the guns and the mechanical computer, which provided firing information to the guns. . . .

"The ELSIE radars provided guidance for the RAF interceptor aircraft. The ELSIE was a simple radar; when the eight-man unit was alerted by radio-telephone to turn on its radar, and general coordinate data was given, the men found a target and turned on their searchlight, which tracked the target and blinded the pilot. Intelligence reports state that the German pilots were much disturbed to suddenly be blinded by the searchlights."

According to a joint report from the War and Navy Departments: "America's entry into the war accelerated the return of some of the ETG officers, and by March 1942 a total of fifty-eight had been brought back for reassignment to aircraft warning duties with the RAF fighter commands along the coast of the Continental United States and at overseas bases. Many of those remaining in England took over active positions in the British aircraft warning service as well as on airborne radar patrols against German submarines."

September 1941–August 1942
Mackenzie Bay to Greenland

Chief Warrant Officer Second Class Albert F. Courter served aboard the Coast Guard cutter Northland *(WPG-49) 1940–1943, patrolling off northeastern Greenland.*

When he enlisted in 1939, Mr. Courter says his goal was to become a radioman, but "that all changed as soon as I saw the main engine-room on the *Northland* and immediately fell in love with all types of engines."

As flagship of the Greenland Patrol, the icebreaker *Northland* served with the *North Star* and the *Bear.* Commander Edward H. (Iceberg) Smith, who later became rear admiral, commanded the patrol; Captain Carl Christian von Paulsen commanded the *Northland.*

"Our main job was to keep the Germans from establishing radio weather stations in Greenland," Mr. Courter writes. "This was an ongoing effort from September 1941 until the end of the war. Many stations were destroyed and enemy ships were captured or destroyed. Also during WWII, the *Northland* engaged enemy U-boats, did convoy duty and weather patrol, carried out search-and-rescue missions, and rescued a frozen-in U.S. Army base, a mission that took nine weeks of continuous icebreaking.

"My job in all this was to help keep the engines running and to make fresh water out of salt water. We were able to make about 200 gallons per four-hour watch, not much by today's standards," he admits. Some of his other duties included "being a qualified small-boat engineer, first-loader on a three-inch .50

gun if necessary, pulling starboard stroke oar in the lifeboat, and being ready to go ashore with a landing party when called upon."

On 12 September 1941 the *Northland* was sent to investigate a suspicious "fishing vessel," the German-controlled Norwegian sealer *Buskoe*, which had reportedly landed a party in a fjord. The *Northland* followed the *Buskoe* into Mackenzie Bay (north of Yukon Territory and northwest of the mainland portion of the Northwest Territories, Canada), boarded it and, according to the *Northland*'s fiftieth-anniversary brochure, "discovered personnel and equipment to establish a German radio station on the Greenland coast. A night raiding party from the *Northland* surprised and seized the station [on 14 September], taking prisoner three Nazis, as well as German plans for other radio stations in the far north."

Serving on board the *Northland* with Mr. Courter was Chief Warrant Officer Ira A. Beal, gunner's mate second class. "We deposited him and a companion in Greenland with six months' stockpile of food and supplies and didn't get back to pick them up until about eleven months later!" Mr. Courter exclaims.

After his *Northland* duty, Mr. Courter served on the *Planetree*, FS-199, F-74, and the *General Greene*. He credits the 8,000 Coast Guard members of 1939 and 1940 with being "the trainers" of those who came in during the war. For example, when assigned to the FS-199, he says, "I was the only man aboard who had any military experience. Of the twenty-five men in the crew, only two others had even been to sea. . . . The process took a lot of training and drills but in the end we had a real good crew, and so we headed out to the Asiatic Pacific area." The *Northland* performed weather patrols until it was decommissioned 27 March 1946.

31 October 1941
USS *Reuben James*, North Atlantic

George F. Giehrl was a fireman second class aboard the USS Reuben James *(DD-245), sunk 31 October 1941 by German U-boat 552.*

The *Reuben James* was commissioned 24 September 1920 and served a variety of assignments before joining the Neutrality Patrol in January 1939, guarding Atlantic and Caribbean approaches to the American coast at the outbreak of war in Europe, Mr. Giehrl writes. "In March 1941, the *Reuben James* joined convoy escort forces to promote the safe arrival of supplies to Britain. In June, she provided support in setting up the first weather station by American forces in Greenland."

Commenting that "the summer of 1941 was the beginning of undeclared warfare between American warships and German U-boats," he adds: "Our escort force guarded convoys as far as Iceland, after which the British navy took on that duty."

The *Reuben James* was on "her second assignment to convoy escort duty when she sailed from Argentia, Newfoundland, on 23 October. With four other destroyers, she joined in . . . an immense convoy of ships, and its size must have alerted the German U-boats. Not too many days later, contact was being made with the U-boats, and depth charges were being dropped."

Mr. Giehrl records the torpedoing as follows: "On 31 October 1941, sailing in harm's way, the destroyer USS *Reuben James* engaged in escort duty to protect convoy HX-156 carrying supplies to Great Britain. At approximately 0525, two torpedoes fired by the German submarine U-552 found their mark. The ship's magazine exploded, blowing away three-quarters of the forward and midship section. Within fifteen minutes, the stern section sank into the North Atlantic Ocean. Of the crew of 147 men, 102 perished, including the captain and all commissioned officers and all chief petty officers but one. Upon abandoning ship, 45 of the crew were saved.

"In all of these years, those of us who survived have never forgotten the emotional experience of this tragedy," Mr. Giehrl acknowledges, as he continues his saga: "Leaderless, without the guidance of officers, the men cut loose the life rafts and jumped into the frigid sea. There were a few who were able to climb aboard the three rafts but most had to cling to the sides . . . [or to] empty ammunition cases and other pieces of wreckage. Covered with fuel oil and tossed about by the waves, we found ourselves alone in the vastness of the ocean. With the ship gone, we realized our great loss and the fear of what the future would hold."

Nothing, however, could have prepared them for what happened next! With subs in the area the previous day, Mr. Giehrl explains, the *Reuben James* had prepared for attack by setting two depth charges, one to explode at fifty and the other at seventy-five feet. "Somehow, after General Quarters were secured, the depth charges were not reset at the safe position and still remained armed."

As the sinking *Reuben James* reached the fifty-foot level, "a tremendous undersea explosion took place. The first charge had detonated and, as that tremendous force pushed upward, sending a geyser of water cascading into the air, the men and rafts beneath the geyser were picked up and flung about. As the water began to fall back to the sea, it struck the rafts and men with such force that their life jackets were torn from their bodies.

"Momentarily, there was a calm," he recalls, "and as we gasped for breath, suddenly the second depth charge let loose and again we went through the same terrifying ordeal. By now, most of us were in a state of shock. The cries of the injured could be heard and prayers for rescue were said out loud."

Suddenly, out of the shadowy darkness, the destroyer *Niblack* appeared on the scene. It rescued twenty-eight men, one of whom died. Later, the destroyer HP *Jones* rescued another seventeen men.

And just as composer and folk-singer Woody Guthrie memorialized the men and their ship with his 1941 ballad, "The Sinking of the *Reuben James*," so, too, tribute was again paid fifty years later, at a reunion of the eighteen remaining survivors, by President George H. W. Bush, by representatives of the British Embassy and the U.S. Department of Navy, by a former captain of the guided-missile frigate USS *Reuben James*, and by crewmen from the two ships that rescued survivors.

DECEMBER 1941

1

It was the best of times—military duty in the Territory of Hawaii and in the Philippines in the late 1930s and in the earliest years of the 1940s.

"We were greeted by hula dancers and a band, and everyone received a lei," says Colonel Cy Felheimer, recalling his mid-October 1941 welcome to the Island of Oahu in Hawaii. Major General Henry Mohr remembers Sunday morning breakfasts of "hot pancakes, fresh pineapple, and the works," served against a backdrop of breathtaking scenery.

In the Philippines, "America's outpost in the Far East," there was the aura of "the magic of the Orient" that "captured the imagination of the tourists and the American servicemen with consuming curiosity," says Lieutenant Colonel Mariano Villarin. Servicemen stationed with him described the Philippines as "a paradise in the Far East."

General Mohr was newly promoted to private first class on 6 December 1941, anxious to celebrate his first Saturday-night pass in six weeks. He recalls the scene, as he took the short road from Schofield Barracks to Honolulu, past Pearl Harbor, where most of the Pacific Fleet was at anchor: "Ablaze with lights from major fighting ships, the harbor was an unforgettable sight. There were 94 to 96 ships in all; 70 were combat vessels. Eight battleships were in the harbor; most were lined up at the famous Battleship Row. Fortunately, most of the American aircraft carriers were out to sea."

By morning, those *best of times* had become *the worst of times*! An air armada of 351 Japanese fighters and bombers blasted Pearl Harbor and an entire nation out of its apathy and into World War II. "The Pearl of the Pacific" became the pearl of great price: 2,403 Americans killed and 1,178 wounded; 18 U.S. naval vessels and 300 aircraft destroyed or disabled; and the lives of almost every person living at that time dramatically changed forevermore. The bombardment was launched in two waves of 183 and 168 planes, respectively, which took off from 33 ships about 200 miles offshore. The attack lasted two hours.

In the Philippine Islands, across the international dateline, it was already 8 December. About nine hours after news of Pearl Harbor hit the Philippines, so too did Japanese planes and troops: attacking and landing on the Island of Batan, north of the island of Luzon; attacking Luzon by midday—destroying 100 planes at Clark Field while simultaneously attacking Iba Field; striking Camp John Hay at Baguio in northern Luzon and Nichols Field near Manila a short time later—and blasting Mindanao in the evening from 22 planes. Also on that Day of Infamy, as President Roosevelt noted in his speech on 8 December, the Japanese government attacked Malaya, Hong Kong, Guam, Wake Island, and Midway.

From men and women of the Reserve Officers Association who were there, here are some of the stories, describing 7 December and the beginning of the war years, as the United States was catapulted into World War II.

7 December 1941, 0740-plus hours
Schofield Barracks, Oahu, Territory of Hawaii

Major Maurice J. Herman was a corporal with HQ and HQ Battery,
13th Field Artillery Battalion, 24th Infantry Division.

Twenty-one-year-old Corporal Herman had just received word on 6 December of his appointment as Army Aviation Cadet, scheduled for immediate return to the States.

"We got back from our night on the town to our quadrangle at about 0740 hours on Sunday, 7 December," he recalls. "I was already down to my shorts, getting ready to head for the showers, when I observed—through the window next to my bunk—a formation of aircraft heading my way through Kolekole Pass . . . and the markings were the Rising Sun insignia of the Japanese Empire."

"I ran downstairs to the second deck, in my shorts," to sound the hand-cranked air-raid siren mounted on the porch railing. But first, he says, "I had to get the siren handle." This was kept in the office "to avoid alcohol-induced, soldierly tom-foolery." While Corporal Herman cranked away, an aircraft swept over and raked the men in the chow lines below. Scattering, they raced for their guns: Colt .45s, Springfield '03s, and Browning automatic rifles, while "our unit was the only battalion in the whole U.S. Army equipped with British 75s of WWI vintage."

7 December, 0750
Upper Schofield Barracks, Oahu, Territory of Hawaii

Colonel Joseph B. Moore was with the 98th Coast Artillery Regiment (AA).

Walking back to the barracks from breakfast, he hesitated when he heard plane engines. "Looking toward Kolekole Pass, just up the mountain behind our barracks, I saw the approaching aircraft. There were thirteen torpedo planes, carrying the biggest torpedoes I have ever seen," he recounts. Colonel Moore says he remembers looking at his watch; it read 0750.

"The fighter bombers were attacking Wheeler Field to eliminate our P-40 fighters, and you could see smoke and flames rising from the area" and "massive clouds of smoke above the harbor as the bombers pressed their attack on the fleet."

7 December, 0755
Aboard USS *Cassin*, Pearl Harbor, Territory of Hawaii

Captain Wesley P. Craig was a twenty-two-year-old ensign who, as officer of the deck, sounded General Quarters on the USS Cassin *(DD-372) at 0759 on that Day of Infamy.*

In a letter to his fiancée Ruth, dated 24 December 1941, Ensign Craig describes what happened after he heard "loud explosions around 0755" and saw the sky "covered with huge Japanese bombing planes and torpedo planes":

"The first wave of green Japanese bombers did tremendous damage to our heavy forces. They launched their torpedoes and bombs at our battleships. It was horrible watching the ships roll over and sink. We started to open fire and put up a barrage of machine-gun fire. The captain said to get our five-inch .38 guns going, but when we started we couldn't fire them because lots of the parts were in the yard being fixed and overhauled. That didn't stop us. We manned our four 5-caliber machine guns and opened fire at 0807. The Japanese were diving down and machine-gunning men in the yard and in the water. It was ghastly. They were helpless."

At 0845, "a terrific explosion nearby" trapped Ensign Craig and seven others between the galley and pantry. Turning to run, they found the wardroom blazing and steel flying everywhere. Ensign Craig continues: "A terrific bomb hit us amidship. . . . Now the whole starboard side was in flames. . . . Loose shells on the deck from our guns started to explode from the heat. . . . Flames started to get hotter and hotter. The paint on the deck started to melt and it became very slippery and warm. We could hear the screaming bombs coming down all around us. There were twelve bombs that exploded around us and one was a direct hit that did 'hell' to us. . . . Three of the seamen right next to me were hit. The fire became terrific, almost unbearable. I thought any moment was going to be the end."

Dashing through fire a minute later, he and some shipmates reached the bridge, then jumped across the gangway to the yard. As they ran, they were machine-gunned, but no one was hit. From a warehouse two minutes later, Ensign Craig watched the *Cassin* blow up, when "its magazine and the warheads exploded."

"An hour and a half later, the last plane disappeared," he adds.

"Being blown from a bomb and being machine-gunned twice, I feel terribly lucky to come out the way I did. All I ask of you, darling, is just wait for me and remember I love you very much. You are very nice," the letter ends. He closes with "love" and signs it "Wesley Posey Craig."

After twenty-two months overseas, Lieutenant Junior Grade Craig returned to marry Ruth, that "nice" lady to whom he had sent his letter. At the time that he submitted his story, the couple was celebrating their forty-eighth anniversary on 7 July 1991.

7 December, about 0756
Ewa Marine Barracks, Oahu, Territory of Hawaii

Chief Warrant Officer Fourth Class John W. Hanson was a PFC, with HQ Squadron MAG 2.

Private First Class Hanson was in his barracks when camp bugler Sergeant Wiley sounded off at 0755 for the guard mount, held with the changing of the guard at 0800. About three or four minutes before 0800, "the bugler stopped and then started blowing assembly; at the same time planes started strafing our airfield," Mr. Hanson recalls.

Admitting that he probably "took lightly" his Marine basic rifleman's training, he declares that he was a complete believer as he reached for the rifle "that was tied on strings under my bunk, and put on my helmet and ammo belt. One of the ordnance men, Sergeant Scarbrough, ran to our ordnance area, carrying two boxes of ammo as he dashed amid the strafing.

"We were allowed a half bandoleer for our rifle," he says. "I had a hard time getting my first round off, knowing I was trying for the first time in my life shooting to kill or injure someone. After the first shot, the rest came easy.

"One of the sad sights was seeing Major Ira Kimes, commanding officer of our VMBS Squadron, with tears running down his face as his planes were burning and he stood on the edge of the runway using an '03 Springfield rifle just like the rest of us."

7 December, before 0800
Schofield Theater, Oahu, Territory of Hawaii

Colonel George D. Zahner was a staff sergeant, 34th Engineers, Schofield Barracks.

With orders for morning duty with the Haleiwa Beach Convoy, Sunday, 7 December 1941, Sergeant Zahner was waiting in the open-air lobby of Schofield

Theater when he heard a loud explosion shortly before 0800 that seemed to shake the building and then, within a few seconds, another explosion.

"Excitement was at a fever pitch by the time I got back to our regiment," Colonel Zahner recalls, and the high priority was "an effort to locate the man with the keys to the locked rack where our new M-1 rifles were stored, delivered so recently we hadn't yet been out on the firing range with them."

7 December, before 0800
Schofield Barracks, Oahu, Territory of Hawaii
Lieutenant Colonel John G. Starr was a young first lieutenant at Schofield.

He was looking forward to Sunday, 7 December, "when our football team was to meet one of the infantry teams for championship of the Hawaii department.

"As I was dressing to inspect the guard before 0800, the commotion started: explosions, smoke, and the sound of gunfire," Colonel Starr says. After strafing and bombing Wheeler [Field], "the Japanese pilots left their calling card on the engineer area. Our only defense was to stay under cover, as we had no ammunition available for the weapons we did have."

7 December, about 0800
Schofield Barracks, Oahu, Territory of Hawaii
Major General Henry Mohr, former chief, U.S. Army Reserve, had just completed six weeks of recruit training with Battery A, 11th Field Artillery Battalion, 24th Infantry Division, on 6 December. He was a full-fledged private, with a monthly pay of $30.

Of that December morning, General Mohr writes: "At about 0800, all hell broke loose. An explosion shook the building. Then more earth-shaking explosions, machine guns, and heavier 20mm cannon fire. It appeared that the southern half of the island was erupting and on fire. Flames and smoke from bombs, exploding warships, and aircraft were billowing into the sky from Pearl Harbor, Hickam and Wheeler Fields. U.S. P-40 fighter planes were trying to take off from Wheeler; only a few succeeded.

"From the north, a Japanese fighter-bomber swooped between the barracks at Schofield. On the plane's next pass, bullets from its machine guns etched twin lines in the pavement and sidewalks, as the pilot tried to hit men standing in the street.

"An hour after the attack started, a bugler appeared in Battery Street and sounded the alert! The war raging around us was now official."

7 December, about 0800
Schofield Barracks, Oahu, Territory of Hawaii

Brigadier General James L. Carroll was a ten-year-old, having breakfast with his family at their Schofield Barracks quarters. His father, Major James V. Carroll, was with the 89th Field Artillery Battalion, 25th Infantry Division.

Hearing noise from the bombing at Wheeler Field, young James Carroll went out to the front yard and saw a Japanese aircraft strafing the house next door. "Next, I looked up and observed other Japanese aircraft flying over our block. At that point, my mother made me return to the house," he recalls.

Since their quarters were built of wood, they were sent to the enlisted barracks, considered safer because of concrete construction.

General Carroll continues: "That night, we were evacuated with other dependents to a school in Honolulu for approximately three days. . . . We returned to Schofield Barracks and had a wonderful time, since school did not resume. Everyone was issued a gas mask, which we were required to take along with us at all times. Trenches were dug for air-raid shelters in the parade ground across the street from our quarters. A curfew was established, as well as a blackout. Armed sentries patrolled our streets each night."

7 December
Camp Malakole, Oahu, Territory of Hawaii

Lieutenant Colonel Kenneth K. Little was a sergeant and three-inch-gun commander, Battery B, 251st Coast Artillery Regiment (AA) (Mobile).

Sergeant Little awoke to "a lot of racket—the sound of machine guns and low-flying aircraft—that Sunday morning."

Though section leaders gathered crews and equipment, "our guns could not be fired until deployed," but "we returned fire with small arms and were officially credited with four downed aircraft," he notes. "I did see a young kid with a water-cooled .30-caliber machine gun on an AA-mount shoot one down. No water in the jacket, the smoke was so heavy. I don't know how he could see to shoot, but hit the aircraft he did.

"During the afternoon, several survivors from the overturned battleship USS *Oklahoma* arrived; we helped clean them up and gave them clothes and some food. They augmented our short crews," Colonel Little says.

He recalls that a collect telegram was sent to his mother on 15 December. His battery commander had gathered messages from the men to send to families on the mainland. Sergeant Little's read: "Safe and well. Will write soon."

7 December 1941
USS *Castor*, Mary's Point, Pearl Harbor, Territory of Hawaii

Commander Stanley W. Dilloway and his brother Joe were aboard the USS Castor *(AKS-1), which was tied up at Mary's Point, with Battleship Row astern of it.*

"During the battle, I was on the deck relaying orders to four 20mm anti-aircraft guns," as the Japanese planes were passing overhead "and dropping their torpedoes just astern of us," Commander Dilloway recalls. "Since we were firing at them, they returned fire, strafing our decks."

7 December 1941
Aboard USS *Case*, Pearl Harbor, Territory of Hawaii

Captain Fred S. Bertsch Jr. was a newly commissioned ensign, the only engineering officer on board the USS Case *(DD-370), outboard the USS* Whitney *for a week of destroyer-tender upkeep on the morning of 7 December.*

"The 1.1-inch anti-aircraft gun directly over my head began firing at the same time that the general alarm sounded," Captain Bertsch writes. As he ran toward the engine-room hatch, "a Val [the Japanese Aichi D3A1 dive bomber] flew past our fantail at an altitude of about 100 feet. Our after-.50-caliber machine guns were firing at it. . . . The nest of destroyers at Berth X-7 was credited with shooting down six of the twenty-nine Japanese planes lost that day—not bad, since the .50s and the 1.1s were the only effective armament we had," he explains.

At the beginning of the attack, all utilities, including electricity, steam, and water, were cut off to ships alongside the tender, "leaving us on 'cold iron' and working by light of battle lanterns" and "below decks, with bombs exploding in the non-compressible water around." All hands helped to carry back and re-install eight auxiliary steam-line valves and other pieces of engineering equipment and to put back together pumps, valves, and flushing water lines. Meanwhile, he recalls, the first-class watertender in the forward fireroom was singing "Elmer's Tune" and "Why Don't We Do This More Often?"

Soon after the *Case* got up steam shortly after noon, Captain A. M. Bledsoe, commodore of Destroyer Division 6, "informed me that a Japanese midget submarine had been hit by the USS *Curtiss* (AV-4), that bubbles were coming to the surface from the sub, and that we had been ordered to drop a depth charge on it."

Captain Bledsoe disapproved of the first plan that would have had Ensign Bertsch, as junior officer, drop a 250-pound depth charge from a motor whaleboat just as soon as he was over the area of bubbles. Captain Bledsoe's alternate plan was to cut through the nipple of the depth-charge fuse cover, place the charge on top of the stern depth-charge racks with a wire attached, place Ensign Bertsch and the whaleboat crew over the bubbles; and then, as the *Case* made a high-speed approach down the west side of Ford Island, sound the boat's whistle when the captain could see the bubbles, as signal that the whaleboat could depart and that the depth charge could be rolled off the stern rack and the wire paid out and jerked.

"When the charge went off, we in the whaleboat had not gone more than fifty to sixty yards," Captain Bertsch relates. "It appeared that the whole bottom of Pearl Harbor erupted and towered above us. Amazingly, the jury-rigged charge was apparently very effective, for when the sub was raised it was mangled as though a giant had crumpled it."

7 December, 1941
Hospital Ship *Solace*, Pearl Harbor, Territory of Hawaii

Captain Henry F. Page joined the Hospital Ship Solace *as a junior medical officer on 27 October 1941.*

His unit's project was to build and establish a Fleet Mobile Base Hospital overlooking Pearl Harbor. This was accomplished and operative on 6 December. "We had worked feverishly seven days a week and were looking forward to our first day off," but . . .

"First came the high-altitude bombers, dropping what we interpreted as smoke bombs on the airfield at Ford Island. Next came the low-altitude torpedo bombers, so close we could almost touch the red ball on the wings. Then came a mixture of everything, including our own wayward anti-aircraft shells—one of which killed the sailor standing next to me. Then ensued a blazing inferno, with even the water alive with burning oil," Captain Page reports.

"The doctors and I manned the boxing arena, with mattresses between the rows for beds. Nurses and corpsmen plus the wives of naval personnel constituted the staff. We maintained full activity for three days. The great majority of injuries were burns."

7 December at 1030
Navy Yard, West Loch, Pearl Harbor, Territory of Hawaii

Lieutenant Commander William E. Eaton was an ensign, age twenty-six, in charge of the degaussing barges in West Loch near the ammunition depot.

Checking on his crew at dry dock at 1030 hours, Commander Eaton recalls the scene: "Smoke from the *Arizona*, reaching to the sky, and a great confusion across the channel, where Ford Island had been hit drastically."

The morning after the bombing, at the site of the *Cassin* and the *Downes*, a crane with large hook and canvas sling was in operation over the *Downes*. "They were hoisting bodies out of the vessel from the forward end that had been hit very badly. They never had a chance. Nearby, I found a Navy wool blanket that had been discarded for [use as] a number-one oil blot. I still have it."

◼ As ROA contributors recount their Pearl Harbor experiences, certain themes recur: stories of strafing and the extremely low altitude of Japanese attack planes, comments on the state of unpreparedness, references to fear of further attack.

Generals Mohr and Carroll, Colonels Little and Denver D. Gray, Major Herman, and Captains Page and Bertsch all comment on planes flying so low that the Rising Sun symbol or the face of a pilot was clearly visible.

Major Herman tells of "supply sergeants requiring each soldier to sign for the weapon and ammo he withdrew." Others recite their litanies of M-1 rifles being locked away, no ammunition available for weapons on hand, and guns that could not be fired until deployed. The night of 7 December was "very long," as Colonel Starr remembers it, with gunfire erupting "at the slightest sound of movement." "Miserable and frustrating" is the way Colonel Little describes the balance of the day and night of 7 December, with the "conflicting and false reports of enemy invasions by air, boat, or whatever."

Colonel Gray tells of "little rest after dark because of the return to Ford Island of some USS *Enterprise* naval planes. They were mistaken for Japanese planes and several were shot down by our own ground fire." Major Herman describes another incident of "friendly fire" from the height above Waialua Bay, where his battalion positioned itself just before 1100 hours in its preplanned island-defense site: "The only ship sighted was a submarine that surfaced in midafternoon. Its response to our colors of the day was incorrect, so we opened fire. . . . Fortunately, none of our shells hit the U.S. Navy sub that hadn't as yet got word that Oahu had been attacked by the Japanese. Its white flag got our attention and an immediate cease-fire."

"A very big concern was whether the attacking naval force had included amphibious landing troops for a full-scale invasion," Colonel Moore comments. But Captain Bertsch probably best sums up the feelings of those who were there on 7 December 1941: "We all expected that Japanese surface forces would arrive the next morning and finish us off." ◼

7 December at 2030
Midway Islands

Colonel William P. Spencer was with the 7th Defense Battalion, FMF, when news of Pearl Harbor reached Midway.

"About 2030, we began to hear loud cracks, and soon shells were hitting the island," Colonel Spencer writes. "D Battery and others opened fire. About forty to sixty 5-inch shells hit the island. The two Japanese destroyers raced away to southwest about 2130 and the shelling stopped. The command post, power house, and fuel-storage tanks were hit. Seven to nine Marines and sailors were dead, and others wounded."

8 December (7 December in Hawaii)
Clark Field, the Philippines

Lieutenant Colonel Mariano Villarin was a second lieutenant with the 2nd Regular Division, Philippine Army, U.S. Army Forces, Far East.

"A few hours after Pearl Harbor, Japanese planes attacked Clark Field. Half of General Douglas MacArthur's Air Force, consisting of Flying Fortresses and P-40s, was destroyed on the ground," Colonel Villarin writes.

"On 22 December, the enemy landed in the Lingayen Gulf area and began moving south into Manila. On 24 December, another task force landed on the Tayabas coastline and began moving north into Manila. U.S. forces were retreating into the Bataan Peninsula, where the 'last-ditch stand' would be made."

8 and 25 December
Clark Field/Fort Stotsenberg, the Philippines

Lieutenant Colonel Garry J. Anloff Jr. was assistant, Adjutant General's HQ, Philippine Division, at Fort Stotsenberg, north of Manila.

"I stood and watched about eight bombers salvo their bombs on Clark Field, destroying our bomber force of B-17s," Colonel Anloff writes.

"We abandoned Fort Stotsenberg (Clark) on Christmas Day. We withdrew, delaying as much as we could, into Bataan. Some of us knew that Bataan held no food, no buildings, little ammunition, no roads, very few people. Not a happy thought."

9 and 25 December
Cavite Navy Yard and Corregidor, the Philippines

Captain Daniel Roberdeau Dorsey was a lieutenant junior grade, with the Civil Engineering Corps at Cavite Navy Yard and Sangley Point Naval Air Station.

As he listened to President Roosevelt's Pearl Harbor address, originating from the States on 8 December, "our air-raid siren began to wail," Captain Dorsey writes. "I went outside and looked up. There was the beautiful and spectacular formation of sixty-three silver-bellied twin-engine bombers that was to strike a quick and violent end to Cavite and the Navy Yard. It was later estimated that casualties exceeded 1,000."

Toward sundown, as the area was being evacuated, "I watched from across Canacao Bay the funeral pyre of the second great naval activity to succumb to the onslaught of the Japanese war bird."

On Christmas Day, Lieutenant Dorsey hitched a ride on the destroyer *Peary* to Corregidor, the Rock, to join up with the Navy contingent in Queen Tunnel. "Under air attack, and with her ship's company at General Quarters, she zig-zagged out into the bay and somehow negotiated the twenty-five miles of open water between Cavite and Corregidor without being hit. Months later, we learned that the gallant little *Peary* had gone down fighting, in the vicinity of Darwin, Australia.

"Lugging what personal gear we had, we trudged topside into the tunnel that was to be subterranean quarters, shelter, and home for two months," he recalls. Other caves on Corregidor included the Navy's five concrete tunnels of varying size and length, the Army's main Malinta tunnel, a honeycomb of tunnels for storing ammunition, and mazes of tunnels where doctors and nurses ministered to casualties.

"My experiences on Corregidor began with a delicious and much unexpected Christmas dinner" in the dimly lighted Queen Tunnel, headquarters of Rear Admiral Francis W. Rockwell, USN, commandant, 16th Naval District. "It was a happy and touching reminder that Uncle Sam could hesitate in the business of waging war to provide this token of Christmas Day," he notes. In addition to being served turkey, dressing, cranberry sauce, all the trimmings, and pie, he remembers gifts of "tooth paste, razors, chewing gum, candy, and many other little items most of us had nearly forgotten about, or at least had never expected to see again."

24 and 25 December

Field Hospital #1, Bataan, the Philippines

Lieutenant Colonel Hattie R. Brantley was a second lieutenant in the Army Nurse Corps in the Philippines in 1941.

Colonel Brantley remembers going by bus with her nurses to Bataan on 24 December—"dressed in white, starched, duty uniforms, complete with white hose and shoes," as "the big Jap bombers and some smaller planes zoomed in and we hit the ditches many times before reaching Camp Limay.

"On Christmas Day, nurses, doctors, corpsmen, and all hands uncrated and distributed old iron cots—rusty and dirty—setting up thirty to forty in each of the eighteen nipa buildings. Soon those wards were overflowing. Surgery was from first light until too dark to continue. At dark, we'd sit on the beach and watch for that convoy that was coming!" Colonel Brantley recalls.

. . . and in the States, 7 December 1941

LaGuardia Field, New York

Captain James L. Zock was on duty with another newcomer, George Netherton, at LaGuardia's airline terminal.

"Sunday afternoon tranquility was shattered by the noisy teletype at American's counter," Captain Zock relates. "The tape read tersely 'Pearl Harbor being bombed by Japanese Naval Aircraft.'"

At 1900 the previous day, the two airline novices had assisted a contingent of twenty-one Japanese requesting an immediate charter flight to Mexico City, carry-on luggage only, with payment in cash. Unaware that peace talks had just ended, but suspicious nevertheless, Netherton notified the FBI. Captain Zock adds in tribute: "George did his part."

Washington, D.C.

Colonel George R. Norris was with the Navy Department in the old WWI Army/Navy Munitions Building, 17th and Constitution, in December 1941.

On 7 December, Colonel Norris says, he was listening to the Redskins game "when it was rudely interrupted" by the attack on Pearl Harbor. "My first reaction was to try on my old uniform, Sam Brown belt, cavalry boots, et cetera. On 8 December, all military wore uniforms and the whole city smelled like mothballs for a week. My most urgent official problem was to find and ship underwater welding rods to repair ships at Pearl Harbor."

Washington, D.C.

Major Allen Early was a civilian with the War Department, also located in the WWI Munitions Building in Washington, D.C.

"On Sunday," he says, "orders went out for military personnel to report in uniform the next day. On Monday, some wore military shirts; others, military pants; some wore old WWI uniforms. However, things soon became more 'uniform.'"

Washington, D.C.

Lieutenant Colonel Roland L. Stewart Jr. was on pass in D.C., with Sergeants Roland Young and Jerome Litvin from Coast Artillery Enlisted Specialist School, Fort Monroe, Virginia.

"Passing the Japanese Embassy about noon, we noticed smoke rising from what we assumed was the back-yard incinerator," Colonel Stewart writes. Driving back to classes, "we were thunderstruck" by news on the radio: "Pearl Harbor in Hawaii under attack. . . . All military personnel return to stations."

Fort MacArthur, California

Lieutenant Colonel Mark Finley reported for duty as a first lieutenant at Fort MacArthur on 7 December.

"The sergeant handed me a doughboy helmet, a pair of woolen wrap leggings, and an aluminum mess kit," Colonel Finley relates. "'It's all I have. We're not prepared for war,' the sergeant explained."

Camp McCoy, Wisconsin

Colonel Jean W. Christy was a second lieutenant, at camp for service practice with the 50th Field Artillery Battalion.

"Sent for more ammunition, Second Lieutenant Kenny Sears soon roared back into camp and yelled: 'The Japs just bombed Pearl Harbor.' We all stood in stunned silence," Colonel Christy recalls, "then someone yelled back at Sears: 'You're crazy as hell. Go get the ammunition.'"

JANUARY 1942

2

They lived on hope in the Philippines in the early days of World War II. There was not much else. "No food, no buildings, little ammunition, no roads, very few people," Lieutenant Colonel Garry J. Anloff Jr. says of Bataan. Lieutenant Colonel Hattie R. Brantley, in her recollection of Christmas Eve 1941, tells of sitting on the beach at Bataan with her nurses from Fort McKinley, staring across at Manila, the city they left behind that morning, and wondering "what was happening to us." However, she adds: "Let me quickly say, the main theme then, there, and forever after was: 'Help is on the way!' We evidenced faith, hope, and trust: in God, in General MacArthur, in FDR, and in the USA."

Helping to fortify such optimism, a Voice of Freedom broadcast from Corregidor told of a large convoy that had left San Francisco for the Philippines, says Lieutenant Colonel Mariano Villarin. "It was only a seven-ship convoy carrying troops, dive bombers, light artillery, and ammunition that was en route when war broke out. Because of the untenable situation in the Philippines, the convoy was diverted to Australia, arriving there 22 December," he explains, pointing out that "a strong Japanese naval blockade in the Dutch East Indies prevented American convoys from reaching Bataan and Corregidor. What kept the defenders' spark alive was the reassuring message from MacArthur to his troops on 15 January that 'help is on the way.' It never came."

From his perspective with the Civil Engineering Corps on Corregidor, Captain Daniel Roberdeau Dorsey was able to see the damage and destruction and "knew only too well there was little cause for confidence." The Corregidor tunnel-dwellers, however, "had little idea of actual conditions on Corregidor and the Bataan Peninsula. Most of their information came from rumor or from daily bulletins published by Army and Navy headquarters," he says. "These were cheerful and confident, as though our forces were actually holding their own against the swarming Japanese on Luzon."

"At night, we saw flashes of artillery over on the peninsula, and we noted with dismay that each night the field of battle was closer to that 'prepared position' at the tip end of Bataan," Captain Dorsey relates. The siege of Bataan by the Japanese began 7 January 1942.

January 1942
Bataan, the Philippines

Lieutenant Colonel Mariano Villarin was a second lieutenant with the 2nd Regular Division, Philippine Army (PA), U.S. Army Forces, Far East (USAFFE).

"The American garrison in the islands consisted of only 19,000 troops, plus 12,000 Philippine Scouts who were part of the U.S. Army officered by Americans. It was a boost for morale when nearly 100,000 troops from the PA were sworn in to the USAFFE under General MacArthur. Most of the inducted PA troops had just completed six months of training and were scantily equipped," Colonel Villarin writes.

"From 7 December 1941 until 9 April 1942, the Japanese were in the driver's seat and we knew it. We had no aerial or naval support and the enemy staged one breakthrough after another. We kept retreating and tightening our belts. There was no way for further retreat unless we swam the shark-infested channel to Corregidor Island, our command headquarters. Thousands of sick, starving, and demoralized soldiers kept pouring into the rear lines. Wounded men were limping their way back toward Mariveles, at the southern tip, in the hope of getting a boat ride to Corregidor, three miles away.

"War correspondent Frank Hewlett referred to the defenders as the 'Battling Bastards of Bataan . . . no mama, no papa, no Uncle Sam.' As a matter of fact, Uncle Sam had written off the Philippines. We were, in effect, Orphans of the Pacific."

June 1941–April 1942
Bataan, the Philippines

Lieutenant Colonel Garry J. Anloff Jr. was a captain, assistant, Adjutant General's Department, Headquarters Luzon Force, the Philippines.

"In June 1941, the military in the Philippines was told by the War Department that 10,000 tons of mixed ammunition was en route to Manila. Where to put it?" Colonel Anloff ponders. "Ordnance OFF forced them to send it to Bataan, with not even a wharf to unload on, so it was barged to the shore. That brought on building the road from Limay to Mariveles.

"In October, I took our War Plan (WPO-3) up to G-2 (Intelligence) and asked: 'Please update me on the roads to Bataan.' The officer in charge took a pencil and scratched out the main road, saying, 'This road does not exist. There are no supplies, no food, some ammunition. I doubt that any American officer has been there. Some may have flown over the peninsula.'"

"He was totally correct," Colonel Anloff affirms.

In the final days of the war on Bataan, in April 1942, when the Americans recognized that Japanese victory was a fait accompli, then-Captain Anloff escorted a Japanese captain to headquarters. "We walked in. His eyes fell on the map we had made of Bataan and he asked: 'You use *this*?'"

"It is the best we have," Captain Anloff replied.

"I have better," the Japanese captain responded.

"He opened his map case and handed me a beautiful four-color coast and geodetic-type contour map! His map showed our Trail 20 as complete. It was completed only three weeks before," Colonel Anloff recalls. He adds: "We fought the war with oil-company road maps."

Describing another incident with the Japanese captain he escorted to headquarters—located between Hospitals #1 and #2—Colonel Anloff says he informed the officer that there were twenty-three Japanese POWs at Hospital #1, to which the Japanese captain replied: "You cannot have POWs. Japanese die first." Later, when the captain inspected them, the Japanese POWs reported on their good treatment, stating that "they ate when we ate and even got cigarettes when we did." Colonel Anloff adds: "This must have done some good."

January 1942
Corregidor, the Philippines

Captain Daniel Roberdeau Dorsey continues his Civil Engineering Corps saga.

After hitching a ride on the destroyer *Peary* to Corregidor, the Rock, on Christmas Day, he joined up with the Navy contingent in Queen Tunnel, "our impregnable bastion of defense at the entrance to Manila Bay."

"After one of our more serious raids . . . I was approached by an Army runner from Malinta, the main Army tunnel that was being used as a field hospital," he recalls. Advised that all power had been knocked out, he recruited a Navy electrician and a civilian mechanic. Together, they crept through the newly dug lateral shaft to the tunnel where they found "confusion, terror, and darkness—dead and wounded lying everywhere, as more were carried in." While doctors and nurses hurried about with flashlights, the threesome rigged and started up two salvaged Navy generators. The light initially flickered on, and then off.

"I passed in and out among the laterals of the hospital tunnels, unscrewing every unnecessary bulb. Then Mac and Williams spun the generators again. This time, the lights stayed on. Life on Corregidor quickly became routine," he says. "We worked, we were bombed and shelled, and we went to work again."

He lists his "most important and certainly most spectacular assignment [as] the installation of a salt-water supply from Manila Bay to the southern escape

entry to Queen Tunnel." Commander J. D. Wilson "managed to locate an electrically driven, submarine water-pump that might be used to supply much-needed
wash, flush, and bath water to the tunnels. We recovered a bomb-wrecked International station wagon, the motor of which was substantially intact, and we
rigged up, to our own amazement and satisfaction, a workable pump driven by
a gasoline engine.

"One evening, late in January, three or four of us sitting in the darkness of
south dock suddenly noticed a strange blinking of lights offshore in Manila Bay.
After a while, the blinking took on the regularity of signals and Ensign Jimmy
Mullins, a communications man, was able to decode, 'Where shall we land?'. . .
From the officers and crew of the submarine, we learned that she had come from
Pearl Harbor, submerging by day and running on the surface by night. And we
now got our first official and authentic news to the effect that Pearl Harbor had
been struck so cruel a blow that there was virtually no such thing as a Pacific
Fleet—the fleet we had been so hopeful of seeing arrive off the China Sea. There
was no fleet.

"The sub's mission was highly secret. She was to remove certain strategic personnel, along with the gold and silver bullion of the Treasury of the
Philippines. . . . Under the direction of Public Works, working parties spent all
that night and the next loading the bullion aboard—but only after the sub had
been stripped of all torpedo gear to make room. During the day, she had to pull
out into Manila Bay and submerge."

Captain Dorsey notes that it was necessary to substitute sufficient dead weight
to compensate for the loss of the submarine's torpedo racks and fittings. "It was
feared that without this bullion, the sub could not have submerged until loaded.
But the job was accomplished even though some of the bullion (approximately
350 pounds per 'pig') and a few torpedo warheads had to be placed on the deck
before the undersea depository shoved out to its bay-bottom hideout in the last
few minutes before dawn."

Completing Captain Dorsey's story, Colonel Villarin adds, in his book: "On
the night of February 4, the submarine _Trout_, carrying $10 million in gold and
silver weighing twenty tons, slipped away from the dock and headed for Pearl
Harbor."

January 1942

Cabcaben and Little Baguio, Bataan, the Philippines

Lieutenant Colonel Hattie R. Brantley was a second lieutenant, Army Nurse Corps.

Lieutenant Brantley and her nurses had spent Christmas Day setting up Field Hospital #1, the hospital that was to have been "all set" and waiting for them at Cabcaben. "The hours were endless, the situation was definitely growing worse, the food was inadequate, the casualties kept coming, but the *esprit de corps* was high and the very best of medical and nursing care was given as was possible under the existing conditions," Colonel Brantley writes.

"Something was always cropping up, and now it was shoes," she says. "Our white oxfords didn't serve long in the dusty, dirty conditions, and so the call went out for shoes. They came from all directions and soon the GI shoe was a part of our uniform." For Josie Nesbitt, who finally found her size-twelve men's shoe, it meant that "for the first time in her life, her feet didn't hurt. How she took care of those shoes—like a mother cat does her newborn kitten. They got TLC. And, would you believe, she wore those shoes through the combat period, the imprisonment [until February 1945], and in 1972 donated them to the Armed Forces Institute at Walter Reed Hospital for a special exhibit.

"In mid-January, I think it was, the lines fell back and our position was endangered at Limay, so Hospital #1 was moved farther south to Little Baguio, an old motor-pool site with a few frame buildings, a huge shed, corrugated roofing, and a concrete floor. It was built in three levels, and each level was an ideal place and size for a ward. Again, we set up beds and we continued to run a hospital and vice versa (that is, and it ran us!). . . .

"Ambulances came off the road; a tent marked the sorting area. One of our first acts here was to use a number of white sheets (which we really couldn't spare, as there was always a shortage) and fasten them with wooden stakes out on the hillside in the form of a huge white cross. This was to plainly mark our site as a hospital and non-combatant facility.

"Soon we also had a Japanese prisoner ward and, although the census was never high, they were given care and treatment as human beings in need, just as our own GIs were. We settled down to the two-meal routine. Hard work, long hours, and hunger became our constant companions."

23 January–8 February 1942
Bataan, the Philippines

Captain Kermit Lay was on Bataan in January 1942 when "bumped up" from private to second lieutenant and asked to train the 724th Aviation Ordnance Company in infantry basics.

"At Aglaloma Point, the Japanese made a landing [of 600 men at 0300 on 23 January, according to Colonel Villarin] and holed up in the caves and ledges. Because the Air Force's provisional infantry was having a hard time getting rid of them, they called on the 724th for assistance," Captain Lay relates.

"Sergeant Beus took twenty of us, with a load of thirty-pound fragment bombs, and we went to work . . . While the provisional infantry was entrenched on the beach with .50-caliber machine guns, and the P-40s were strafing the barges, Sergeant Beus and company made cluster bombs for six to eight of the thirty[-pound] frag bombs, with an electric charge in the middle bombs, and we swung them over the cliff edge. In addition, we put fuses on single bombs and rolled them over the cliff side. It was a two-and-one-half-day mission and it worked. We killed a lot of Japanese."

January 1942
Fort Dix, New Jersey

Colonel Tommy R. Gilliam was a platoon leader, Company B, 1st Battalion, 2nd Infantry Regiment, 5th Infantry Division, Fort Custer, Michigan.

He confesses to being "so green that I reported for active duty with my gold bars crossway on my 'shoulder straps' instead of parallel with them. After the trauma of Pearl Harbor and regimental missions in late December—ranging from protection of the tunnel to Canada at Detroit to the protection of Wright-Patterson Air Field, Ohio—we were alerted for overseas movement and on 6 January 1942 departed for a secret destination. It was so secret that many of the wives preceded us to Fort Dix, New Jersey, and were waiting when our troop train pulled in," Colonel Gilliam says.

"The best-kept secret that the entire division was privy to was that we and the 11th Infantry Regiment and all other units of the division were following our sister regiment, the 10th Infantry Regiment, to Iceland, where they had landed in September, relieving the Marine units already there." U.S. Marines began arriving in Iceland 7 July 1941, replacing British forces there since May 1940 with that country's consent.

FEBRUARY 1942

3

From Pearl's Harbor, the waves of war lash out quickly in all directions after 7 December 1941. By February 1942, according to contributors' stories, bombs are falling on Australia, on Aruba, and on ships in the Timor Sea near Java; the valiant defenders of the Philippines continue their struggle; and "unidentified aircraft" are being fired upon over Los Angeles.

Also during February 1942, German U-boats sink eighty-five ships in the Atlantic; the Japanese attack an Allied squadron of sixteen ships in the Java Sea; Singapore surrenders to the Japanese 15 February; President Roosevelt on 22 February orders General MacArthur to leave the Philippines; and U.S. naval forces, led by Admiral William Halsey, attack the Marshall and Gilbert Islands and Wake Island.

January–February 1942
Bataan, the Philippines

Lieutenant Colonel Mariano Villarin was a second lieutenant with the 2nd Regular Division, Philippine Army, U.S. Army Forces in the Far East (USAFFE).

In his book *We Remember Bataan and Corregidor*, Colonel Villarin describes the Battle of the Points—Caibobo Point, Aglaloma-Quinauan Points, and Lapiay-Longoskawayan Points—as "one of the bloodiest on Bataan," lasting from 22 January to 13 February 1942. "It was not until 13 February that Anyasan-Silaim Points were cleared of the enemy. The task force losses were 96 killed and 142 wounded. An undetermined number of Japanese drowned at sea trying to escape. The 20th Infantry lost two battalions." One of the heroes of the battle was Captain José Tando, 1st Battalion, who was awarded the Distinguished Service Cross for his 9 February action when he "crept forward . . . to the enemy gun emplacement and personally put the weapon out of action by a direct grenade hit."

In the Battle of the Pockets—the Big Pocket at Tuol, the Little Pocket at Cotar, and the Upper Pocket—fought 28 January to 17 February, "the heroic exploits of the Fil-American boys paid off and individual acts of gallantry in action were duly recognized." Among them were 1st Lieutenant Willibald Bianchi, 45th Infantry,

Philippine Scouts, who was awarded the Medal of Honor, and three Distinguished Service Cross awardees: Major Alfredo M. Santos, 1st Infantry, 1st Battalion; First Lieutenant Napoleon Mangonon, 1st Infantry; and 2nd Lieutenant Aureo Capili, 11th Infantry.

Praising the courage of the Igorot tribesmen of the 11th Infantry in the 12 February battle of the Upper Pocket, Colonel Villarin writes: "Hoisted to the tops of tanks . . . and oblivious to all danger of being exposed to enemy fire, they cleared the entangling foliage with their bolos and indicated to the American tankers the enemy positions by pounding on the right or left side of the tanks with their rifle butts." Their action merited kudos from General MacArthur, who said that he had "never known the equal of those Igorots riding the tanks."

14–16, 19 February 1942
Australia to Netherlands East Indies to Australia

Lieutenant Colonel Robert F. Casemore, with Battery C, 1st Battalion, 148th FA Regiment, 41st Infantry Division, was ordered to the Philippines to support the Army garrison in Luzon.

The 1st Battalion sailed from San Francisco 22 November 1941 aboard the *Willard A. Holbrook*, a former Pacific luxury liner converted to troopship; reached Pearl Harbor 27 November; set sail three days later with several other ships, and while on the high seas learned of Pearl's 7 December fate. No longer headed for the Philippines, the ship on 23 December put into port at Brisbane, Queensland, "the first American troops to arrive in Australia. The cheering Aussies gave us a hearty welcome that I'll never forget," Colonel Casemore writes.

The 1st Battalion spent Christmas in Brisbane, then the *Holbrook* left them in Darwin in early January. "We were in Darwin and the Australian bush for about six weeks, 'lost' American troops under temporary Australian command. Then, on 14 February 1942, we set sail once more as part of the Sparrow Expeditionary Force, heading for Timor—the tail-end island in a chain extending eastward from Java—to help in the defense of Netherlands East Indies troops. We Americans were on two, small, stinking Dutch vessels, the *Tulagi* and the *Portmar*. My battery was on the latter. Two other ships carried Australian units. We were escorted by the destroyer *Peary* and the cruiser *Houston*, as well as some Australian ships. We had no air cover, but on the decks of the *Portmar* and the *Tulagi* we had .50-caliber machine guns.

"Unknown to us, the Japanese were converging on Singapore, Java, and Papua, New Guinea, and, of course, the island of our destination. On 16 February, on the Timor Sea, we were attacked by a Japanese plane that dropped bombs upon our little convoy. It missed the *Portmar* by what appeared to me to be just a few yards. I was a young soldier. I was uncomfortable as hell at sea, to say nothing of scared. . . .

"Then, through the blue skies, came nearly forty Japanese Mitsubishi bombers. Never before had I heard the sound of whistling bombs. When they missed my ship, as they did, the shock of underwater explosions made the *Portmar* bob like a cork. All the while, the *Houston* sent up flak. . . . The exec officer of my battery said that our convoy and our lives were saved by the anti-aircraft action of the *Houston*, that heroic ship that went on to the Battle of the Java Sea where the Japanese sank it.

"We learned that the enemy had landed on Timor, and so we were ordered back to Darwin. A respite? Fat chance! The Japanese aircraft dogged us back to Darwin Harbor. The Aussies had debarked from their ships; the 148th FA Battalion had not. We were sitting ducks. On 19 February, Japanese fighter planes and land-based dive bombers set out systematically to pattern-bomb the harbor and Darwin itself.

"In that first Japanese attack on the Australian mainland, my ship, the *Portmar*, with her filthy hull riddled with scores of holes, sank in the harbor. So did other ships, as well as the destroyer *Peary*. Hundreds were wounded and many killed, both on ship and shore, among them two of my buddies, Basil Skelton and Jim Wafford. I went over the side, into the water and, GI by GI, we somehow made it to dry land. Darwin was leveled. It was put under martial law immediately, as hordes of civilian refugees fled the burning city.

"The 148th went deep into the bush again and we established camps until we could regroup. The Aussies fed us, clothed us, and gave us tent shelters from the monsoons. At long last—and by then a corporal—I came under American command again."

16 February 1942
Aruba, Netherlands West Indies

Lieutenant Colonel Dwight M. Gowdey was with U.S. Army Force Aruba, stationed at Camp Savaneta, near St. Nicholas.

Colonel Gowdey tells of "the first attack, and one of very few such attacks, on the American Continent after Pearl Harbor" that took place 16 February when the Germans attacked Aruba, source of a large share of the oil for the Allied war effort.

"In accordance with Rainbow 5—the initial WWII plans—American forces were sent to the Netherlands islands of Aruba and Curacao, off the coast of Venezuela, by M-45 to relieve British units that were to participate in the North Africa invasion. Forces Aruba and Curacao left New Orleans on 6 February, but their departure was a poorly kept secret, and later a lengthy inquiry was made into this lack of security. . . . The Germans had learned of this movement and hoped to catch the troop transports as they arrived or as the British troops left on 14 February by the same transports. . . . Fortunately, the two Caribbean cruise ships that had been taken over for this movement—under escort by two destroyers—arrived on 11 February before the Germans got there.

"Since the Germans were unable to intercept the transports, they proceeded to do as much damage as possible, aiming for the shallow-draft lake tankers filled with oil from Lake Maracaibo, Venezuela, that were waiting to unload at St. Nicholas. At about 0100 on 16 February, the *Pendernales* and the *Orangestad* were torpedoed and sunk. The SS *Arkansas* was heavily damaged at the dock but did not sink.

"The oil released from the tankers caught fire and there was a spectacular ten-mile wall of flame and smoke along the island. Attacking the tankers first was a mistake by the Germans because when they surfaced and tried to shell the refinery, they could not see where they were shooting. As a result, their only hits were on an empty oil tank and a local school.

"Since the American forces had just arrived, their only weapons to counter the attack were small arms and some small AA guns. Moreover, like the Germans, they could not see where to shoot because of the smoke and fire."

Colonel Gowdey recalls that he was awakened by the alarm, went to his post, and from there saw the results of the attack. "The wall of fire and smoke from the torpedoed tankers extended from the refinery to past the camp, and it was an awesome sight to behold. The security at the refinery was reinforced and the troops were ready for movement if a landing had been attempted, but nothing developed. The alert continued until the morning and then regular duties were resumed."

That night, another lake tanker was sunk off Willemstad, Curacao, as well as two others in the general area, he reports. "On 20 April, a few shells landed on Curacao but without any effect. Other attempts were made to shell the refinery at Aruba, but by then the American forces had an SCR-268 (radar) in place that picked up any submarine that surfaced, and so the defense forces were alerted."

20–28 February 1942
Corregidor, Island-Hopping, and Cebu, the Philippines
Captain Daniel Roberdeau Dorsey continues his Civil Engineering Corps saga.

"Life went along—busy, exciting, and discouraging, sometimes almost to the point of despair. Then it happened!" Captain Dorsey exclaims. On the evening of 20 February, his name appeared on a list of sixty officers who were to be evacuated "to relieve the seriously increasing food shortage."

"February twenty-first, my last day on Corregidor, was just another day of hard work," he recalls. "I had been working on a piece of paving at the entrance to tunnel nine. The job was essential and, since I had the grades and forms already set, I wanted to see the thing through. We completed the pour at about 1500 hours, and I had just enough time to eat evening chow, grab my gear, and report at the mouth of Queen Tunnel."

The men whose names were on the list were herded into several trucks, handed twenty-peso notes each, along with private messages to be forwarded to loved ones, and offered the best wishes of Admiral Francis W. Rockwell, commandant of 16th Naval District, "for a safe journey" to wherever they might be going. From the trucks, they transferred to steam launches that took them to the *Legaspi*, the Philippine inter-island motorship that periodically ran the blockade in and out of Corregidor with much-needed supplies.

"We moved slowly through the mined fields. . . . Aboard, our group of naval officers found a sizeable contingent of American and Philippine Army pilots headed south in hopes of finding a spot to which planes might be flown in from Australia. Then they might fight again," Captain Dorsey continues. "Our plan was to run by night, lay-to and hide in coves by day."

The ship dropped anchor off Mindoro, opposite Batangas Province; the port of Romblon; and Capiz, on the island of Panay, where the men unloaded gear and left the *Legaspi*, which took on supplies for the return trip to Corregidor and Bataan.

Then, via "transportation furnished by Army forces, which were scattered throughout these islands," the entourage was hauled by buses overland to Iloilo, central city of the Visayas, where the party split up—some to remain there, others to be distributed throughout the Central Visayas, and Lieutenant Dorsey's group to continue south by launch, bus, boat, and bus again until they "screeched into Cebu City, tired, shivering, hungry, and disheveled after a hectic trip of four nights and three days." On the morning of 25 February, Lieutenant Dorsey's group of forty naval officers, representing different corps and ranks, reported for duty to the senior officer in command, Headquarters Cebu Brigade, USAFFE.

Lieutenants Dorsey and Jim Davis immediately set about building air-raid shelters, and continued to do so. "Since Cebu had been bombed in the opening days of the war, with specific attacks and considerable damage to oil-storage installations on neighboring islands, we felt that the targets were too important to be long-neglected by the Japanese. And we were right. . . . At the crack of dawn on Sunday morning, three days after our arrival, a Japanese cruiser stood off the city and blasted away with her guns. Fires were started and several small ships were hit. There were no defenses, and the man-of-war banged away at leisure until, apparently satisfied with the damage inflicted, it steamed arrogantly away.

"From that day on, these visits by warships became more frequent than air raids. . . . These raids became annoying, but damage was superficial and casualties were very light."

25 February 1942
Los Angeles, California

Major Henning B. Dieter was a self-described "sixteen-year-old Army brat," son of Captain H. B. Dieter at Greenville Flying School, Mississippi, when he received four letters from men previously under his father's command.

Major Dieter says that the men who sent the letters—Privates First Class Charles Patrick and Charles J. Young, Corporals J. A. Driscoll and J. (Swede) Zeisler—were all responsible members of Battery B, 122nd Coast Artillery, AA Battalion, New Jersey National Guard, stationed at Downey, California. The attack "by unidentified aircraft" was also confirmed by the Western Defense Command, the 4th Interceptor Command, and the Los Angeles Police Department, Major Dieter points out. Additionally, in the 26 February 1942 issue of the *New York Times*, the incident is simultaneously described by reports (on pages 1 and 3) and then denied (by Secretary of War J. Frank Knox, on page 3). The front page headline reads: "Los Angeles Guns Bark at the Air 'Enemy.'" The continuation headline reads: "Los Angeles Pounds Unseen Foe in Reported Aircraft Invasion."

In his letter that begins, "Dear Dieter II," Corporal Driscoll writes: "The main purpose of this letter is to straighten you out on this 'firing affair over L.A.' I know neither you nor your 'Pop' would want to go thru life not knowing the real story. Here it is. When the call to arms was sounded and the distant booming of the AA guns around L.A. was heard, the boys were at their guns itching for the command to fire. . . . The searchlights had the sky lit up like a pattern with their crossbeams. They had the planes right in the center—and they *were* planes (not gigantic sea gulls) but they were out of our range. Well, the planes kept coming in our direction. . . . D Battery let go a barrage of fire at the planes, which were flying at about 6,000 feet, using a seven-and-one-half fuse. . . . The shrapnel was showering all around Battery C. They fired about 160 rounds; it sounded like the Fourth of July. Then for a split second they came within our range—then we let loose, our guns pounding away. We fired thirty-two rounds and they must have been effective because the planes scattered after our fire. I'll bet 'Pop' wishes he was with us as much as we wish he were here."

Private First Class Patrick writes: "Well, Hen, here is the lowdown on that attack 25 February. . . . When we dashed out, we saw that about fifty searchlights were concentrated on a spot in the sky and I could barely see the planes, but they were up there alright. I could see six planes, and shells were bursting all around them. Naturally, all of us fellows were anxious to get our two-cents' worth in and, when the command came, everybody cheered like a son of a gun. We fired about twenty rounds at them and then the formation broke up but returned about five minutes later and we opened fire again. All in all, we fired forty rounds. . . . We received the credit from Brigade Headquarters for forcing the formation to scatter." He adds: "Do you know, this is the first time we ever fired at night and only the second time we have ever fired the guns."

"When we opened fire, they broke formation and hightailed it home, wherever that may be," Corporal Zeisler writes, after also pointing out that B Battery received full credit for turning away the planes.

"Well, kid, I'll try to answer all of your questions truthfully—I mean it," Private First Class Young begins in his letter. "It was about 0255 that the call to arms was blown. . . . Then we got the all-clear. Ten minutes later, call to arms was again blown. . . . I hear *boom—boom—boom*! Saw the searchlights and the H. E. *Burstory*. Got to the gun in nothing flat. Was at the gun about five minutes when we got the order to open fire. Funny, too, 'cause they were at all times out of fuse range. I guess the idea was to throw up a barrage to keep 'em high. . . . At first I thought the planes (there were at least five, according to the flightfinder crew and director crew) were bombing Vultee. . . . Most of the men believe that they weren't bombers but were reconnaissance planes." In his postscript, he cautions the teenager: "All this is off the record. Don't forget!"

In the opening paragraphs of its story, the *New York Times* reports the incident as follows:

Anti-aircraft batteries protecting airplane factories and oil deposits in the Los Angeles metropolitan district directed barrage after barrage in the pre-dawn darkness today against planes which late in the afternoon were still unidentified.

Residents from Santa Monica southward to Long Beach, covering a thirty-nine-mile arc, watched from rooftops, hills and beaches as tracer bullets, with golden-yellowish tints, and shells like skyrockets offered the first real show of the second world war on the United States mainland.

Police throughout the area said that planes, ranging in number from one to 100, were overhead, but no bombs fell during the five-hour blackout and no aircraft was shot down.

Under the headline "Knox Calls It 'False Alarm,'" the Knox story begins: "Secretary Knox said today that advices from the Pacific Coast indicated that the raid scare in Los Angeles was 'a false alarm.'"

Having saved his letters for fifty years, Major Dieter comments: "I long expected that after the war, the airlines, the U.S. Navy, Mexico, or Japan would eventually reveal where these unidentified aircraft came from and what they were up to. However, if the information was ever revealed, I did not hear about it. I continue to save these letters until someone, somewhere, someday may reveal the truth."

EDITOR'S NOTE: *Brigadier General Cullen Gulko responded to Major Dieter's story with a Letter to the Editor of* The Officer *that "may shed additional light on the Great Los Angeles air raid of 25 February 1942." He provides the following information:*

My best friend in high school and my roommate at USC was a straight arrow of unquestioned honesty, and I learned from Haig Arakelian when our paths crossed in Finschhafen, New Guinea, in 1944 that, on that eventful night, Haig was a section chief in an AAA battery stationed in Alondra Park. He recalled that the person who was on duty that night evidently was fiddling around and inadvertently fired off a round from one of his section's guns. As he hurriedly dressed, he said he had visions of beginning a new career as a shoemaker-trainee at Leavenworth. Fortunately, virtually all of the guns in the Park opened up, evidently firing for effect. This obscured the trail to what we must now acknowledge as "the first gun to fire a round in defense of the continental United States in WWII."

Haig had advanced to captain when we met and was adjutant for a triple-A group.

As to my own WWII record, it is noteworthy in that I was someplace that never was. One day in April 1942, I was in a group of thirty casual fillers who detrained at Charleville, about 600 miles due west of Brisbane, Australia. We were welcomed by the CO of the 45th Air Base Group, Lieutenant Colonel Charles H. Kruse, who told us that the mission of the group, which included the 8th Materiel Squadron, was to expand the nearby airstrip because this was, he said clearly and distinctly, 'the west flank of the Brisbane Line.' It was not until I saw the motion picture *MacArthur* some forty years later that I realized there never could have been such a place.

MARCH 1942

4

Fighting was sparse, and food even more sparse, on Bataan, in the Philippines in late February and March 1942.

Lieutenant Colonel Mariano Villarin attributes the lull in fighting to the fact that only one-third of Japanese General Masaharu Homma's force was in combat condition, with 13,000 of his men in hospitals between 1 January and 31 March. "Having failed to subdue the USAFFE within the allotted time of fifty days . . . Homma swallowed his pride and asked for reinforcements. The Tokyo warlords sent the 4th Division, which reached Luzon on 15 March."

As for the scarcity of food, he says, "severe wartime rationing drastically cut our rations to two meals a day," consisting mainly of a rice gruel called *lagao*.

"And later, we were down to half-rations," writes Captain Kermit Lay. It got so bad, both men relate, that pack-train mules and then the 26th Cavalry's horses were slaughtered for food. After that, the mess sergeants went looking for monkeys and iguanas. Colonel Villarin says that in a 1982 meeting with Dr. Herbert Ott, the veterinarian who oversaw the butchering of the cavalry horses, the doctor spoke of General Jonathan Wainwright's "painful decision . . . to tell me to go ahead and slaughter his favorite prize jumper, Joseph Conrad."

In other war-related events in March, General Claire Chennault's Flying Tigers in Burma move on 1 March to the RAF base at Magwe, from where both forces withdraw on 27 March; General Joseph W. Stilwell establishes U.S. China Headquarters at Chunking 3 March; Admiral William Halsey's task force attacks Marcus Island in the Central Pacific 4 March; Rangoon is evacuated by the British on 7 March and Java by the Dutch on 9 March; and American forces, with the first Seabees to see active service, arrive 12 March to build a base in New Caledonia.

Vowing to return, General MacArthur leaves the Philippines for Australia on 11 March. General Wainwright assumes his command. On 30 March, MacArthur is appointed commander in chief, Pacific Ocean Zone.

4 March–June 1942
Pearl Harbor, Territory of Hawaii

Captain Wesley P. Craig, who escaped the USS Cassin *7 December 1941, was on temporary duty by 11 December with the staff of the commander in chief, U.S. Pacific (CINCPAC).*

At CINCPAC, he was on duty in the operations room the night of 4 March when "suddenly reports came in around 0100 of 'bogies,' unidentified enemy planes, from the northwest."

"I immediately notified the operations duty officer who notified the admiral. Ten minutes later, Admiral Chester Nimitz sat down next to me at our plotting table as I relayed reports . . . on planes coming from the sea," Captain Craig writes. "Condition Red went out to all ships and stations in Hawaii. Everything was blacked out. It was extremely tense. We were using coded words, so anyone listening in on the phones could not understand our conversations.

"Around 0130, the admiral turned to me and said, 'Let's send up six night-fighter planes.' Then at 0145, the admiral said, 'Let's send out another six night-fighters.' I passed the orders to our air bases. Then we waited for the bombing attack. . . . Several bombs were dropped by the Japanese planes at around 0230—not on Pearl Harbor this time but at the Punch Bowl, our military cemetery where we buried our dead of 7 December 1941. There was only minor damage. . . . Our night-fighter planes never could see the two big Japanese bombers. This incident was later elaborated by our naval Intelligence.

"This incident was on 4 March, two months prior to the elaboration of the final Midway Plan, with the Japanese utilizing for the first time Operation K: two large flying boats taking off from Wotje, Marshall Islands, putting down at French Frigate Shoals [about 500 miles northwest of the Territory of Hawaii], refueling from three submarines waiting there, flying on to Oahu to make a night reconnaissance of Pearl Harbor, and then dropping their bombs and heading back to their base at Jaluit in the Marshall Islands.

"Since our admiral now knew that Japanese submarines were off the coral reef, Admiral Nimitz sent a couple of our destroyers to patrol French Frigate Shoals before our task force headed for the Battle of Midway. That kept the Japanese subs down deep in the water where they could not see anything. Then we sent three of our aircraft carriers up for the Midway Battle—fooling the Japanese admiral (who did not know that we had three carriers for the Battle of Midway) and thus winning a tremendous victory in June 1942."

December 1941–March 1942
Oahu, Territory of Hawaii

Colonel Philip A. Grimes was battery exec with Battery B, 89th FA Battalion, 25th Infantry Division, assigned to defend the southern half of the east coast of Oahu.

"The battalion was armed with badly worn World War I British 75mm howitzers, pulled by 1934 commercial Chevrolet trucks, painted the GI olive-drab color. Our battalion commander was Lieutenant Colonel William P. Bledsoe, a veteran Regular Army officer. In anticipation of a Japanese landing attack, the battalion built two bunkers on the beach, in which two howitzers were placed. The bunkers were built with logs and sand, and were fully enclosed and concealed as well as possible, except to the front facing the beach," Colonel Grimes writes.

"Colonel Bledsoe felt terribly insecure because of the limited area that could be covered by the beach guns. All of the battery guns were in the battery positions, most of which had been dug-in and were difficult to move. . . . In February 1942, the new 2¹/₂-ton modern and powerful trucks arrived and were distributed within the battalion. Within a week or two, Colonel Bledsoe came to me and inquired whether or not I thought a British 75mm howitzer could be mounted in the back of the truck for easy movement as a mobile weapon that could move up and down the coast and cover the entire area. This was discussed with the non-commissioned officers and it was decided that it could be done. Colonel Bledsoe asked that I take on the project.

"We reinforced the front of the bed of the truck to absorb the recoil by using big timbers, earth, and sandbags. The howitzer was secured so that it would not bounce around. We attempted to get armor plate from the Navy, as protection, but after firing at it . . . we found that [it] was not heavy enough to turn the fire. The howitzer was then mounted and secured and ready for test-firing.

"About this time, a major from the island ordnance office showed up, looking for Colonel Bledsoe, incensed that he was going to mount a howitzer in one of his trucks. The major said that it would totally destroy the truck, that it was not an authorized use, and that he had come down as a representative of ordnance to stop its use. This was all Colonel Bledsoe really needed to turn on his adrenalin. After listening to the major, he looked him in the eye and said, 'Major, we're at war, and we're anticipating a possible attack, and we need a mobile gun. We have one mounted and ready to use, and we're going to use it.'

"This was the artillery's first such mounted gun. Later, 'Bledsoe's Mobile Gun' was used throughout the battalion for service practice from many positions up and down the coast. It worked very successfully. When the 105mm howitzers arrived, Bledsoe's mobile gun was retired, but everyone was proud of him and his determination."

3 March 1942
USS *Asheville*, Java Sea

Major Kenneth Blake was a buck sergeant who had been on his way back from Carolina maneuvers to Fort George G. Mead, Maryland, when Pearl Harbor was attacked.

"Not having any great exploits of my own," he explains, "I submit this tribute to an old sailor who had a long Navy career and a very short war." The sailor was Chief Electrician's Mate William F. Carlin, "possibly the ranking enlisted man on the ill-fated USS *Asheville*."

Major Blake describes Electrician's Mate Carlin as "a 'China sailor' of the old school, who spent most of his twenty-two-year service with the Asiatic Fleet." Upon retirement, he was assigned to the USS *Augusta*, flagship of the fleet at the time, then immediately recalled as a Reservist and assigned to the USS *Asheville*, where he was listed as chief petty officer.

On 3 March 1942, the *Asheville* was engaged in action south of Java in the Java Sea when it was bombed by Japanese planes. All on board were first declared missing, and then, later, dead. Major Blake reports that his brother-in-law Richard Carlin, brother of William, "remembers a report that one *Asheville* survivor made it to shore and was taken prisoner, only to die in Japan. The story was never confirmed, however."

An Associated Press story describes the *Asheville*, a 1,270-ton gunboat, as the nineteenth American combat ship acknowledged lost since the war began. With a normal complement, the ship would have had 185 aboard. A September 1942 military call-up in Asheville, North Carolina, however, requested that 160 men come forward to enlist to replace those lost in the sinking of that city's namesake ship. The AP story concludes: "From Chief Jarrett Blythe, head of the Eastern band of Cherokee Indians, came word that he would bring in from the reservation at the foot of the Great Smoky Mountains, ten young men to wear the Navy's blue."

January–March 1942
Flights from Fiji Islands

Lieutenant Colonel Leonard W. Frame was a second lieutenant, assigned to 35th Pursuit Group, 70th Pursuit Squadron.

When the attack on Pearl Harbor delayed the squadron's departure to the Philippines, Lieutenant Frame found himself over the skies of San Francisco, protecting the West Coast in one of two single-engine advanced-training planes, an AT-6—with "an inexperienced corporal in the back seat and two .30-caliber machine guns, neither of which we could fire." The twenty-five P-40s that were supposed to be available per squadron were being disassembled for shipment overseas. When the 70th finally sailed on 12 January 1942, Colonel Frame recalls, it was part of the newly formed 347th Fighter Group, along with the 67th, 68th, and 339th Squadrons. Their new destination: the Fiji Islands.

The squadron arrived 25 January at Suva Harbor, Fiji, with twenty-five P-39s, all unassembled and in boxes. These were "loaded on barges, floated up a river, and set out in a 3,000-foot grass strip about 10 miles from Suva. We set up tents, and the mechanics—most of whom had never seen a P-39—started putting the airplanes together." When the work was completed, "we folded our tents and moved across the island to Nandi."

After the planes were checked out, it was time to check out the thirty-five pilots: ten with 100 or more hours of flight time in P-40s; twenty-five with zero to fifteen hours; Lieutenant Frame with six hours and ten minutes in a P-40 pursuit plane.

At this point, the men put in four hours of cockpit time "just sitting in the plane, looking at where everything was." And then it was time "to crank it up and go." Since the planes were not two-seaters, "the first time you flew, you flew solo." Describing the P-39 fighter bomber, Colonel Frame says it was powered by one 1,150 horsepower Allison V-1710–35, 12-cylinder Vee, liquid-cooled engine. "As we began to do a little flying, we started doing some gunnery," most of it, ground firing with ammunition "a little bit old," he recalls. "Some of the .50-caliber ammunition would hang fire," firing when a propeller blade was in front of it. This left the squadron with "a few airplanes all ready to fly except for a propeller." Soon, however, there were four planes on alert each morning patrolling the area. "As we built up our time in our P-39s, we were doing a lot of formation flying, ground gunnery, simulated combat, and some navigation," the colonel says.

About the time their first mail arrived on 1 March, word also came of promotions. With thirty-two of the pilots becoming first lieutenants and three being named captains, "some Indian silversmiths had extra work making insignias. In fact, U.S. servicemen bought so much silver jewelry that local silversmiths took too many of the silver coins out of circulation and melted them down. The Fijian government printed paper shillings as replacements."

In March, new neighbors began arriving west of them in New Caledonia: members of the 67th Fighter Squadron, the first Army Air Force troops to be committed to the invasion of Guadalcanal. By now, the 70th was operating off "what we called the main base. It is the same runway that commercial airlines now use in landing at Nandi."

30 March–10 July 1942
Wideawake Field, Ascension Island

Colonel W. A. Chapman was platoon commander of F Company when the 38th Combat Engineer Regiment of Fort Jackson, South Carolina, departed Charleston 14 March 1942.

Sixty-four officers and 1,460 enlisted men—slightly above the 38th's regiment strength—comprised Task Force Agate. After refueling at Recife, Brazil, and departing easterly on 27 March, the task force was finally advised of its secret mission and destination: to construct a 6,000-foot paved runway, complete airport, and fueling facilities on Ascension Island in ninety days, as a base "urgently needed to provide a mid-Atlantic fuel- and rest-stop for U.S. military aircraft en route to the Africa Campaign," Colonel Chapman writes.

"We of Task Force Agate first saw Ascension Island on 30 March 1942 from the deck of the USAT *Coamo*. The island seemed to rise from the waters of the South Atlantic Ocean as we steamed toward it." He describes the British possession of Ascension as an inhospitable island with no native material for construction except rock in abundance; roughly 34 square miles of barren lava rock, with 2,000-foot-high Green Mountain; situated eight degrees south of the equator, midway between the west coast of Africa and Brazil, and about 5,000 miles southeast of Florida.

"Everything we used was brought with us on the troop transport and the two freighters, the *Luckenback* and the *Pan Royal*," with D Company constructing the access road from the pierhead to the airport site while the ships were unloading. When the convoy departed, "we felt very lonely, having to complete the mission and survive until the job was done.

"Living conditions were harsh, physically and psychologically. Fresh water was the critical element and was used only for drinking (two canteens per man per day), cooking, and equipment radiators. Sea water was used even for concrete. Food was less than gourmet, with lots of Spam and powdered eggs." There was no recreation and no mail, in or out, for about four months. "There was nothing but wind, dust, rock, and work." And on Ascension Island, "the wind is eternal." Equally eternal was the work: "The project proceeded twenty-four hours a day, seven days a week. The shift for all was twelve hours, seven days a week."

Officers of the 38th included those "recently graduated from Southern colleges and universities, with their shiny, new gold bars earned via the land-grant college ROTC programs" and "a smattering of older, experienced Reserve officers, the company commanders who had worked in civilian engineering jobs before being called to active duty."

As for the draftees, "you never saw such men as these: farmers, butchers, tradesmen, a bootlegger, and even a powderman from Brooklyn who had worked on the big New York tunnel jobs. With the Army's reputation for misfitting men to jobs, how did the powderman ever become assigned to an outfit with the destiny of the 38th Engineers? There were clerks, an FBI man, construction equipment operators, truck drivers, and mechanics. They were all there! Was this staffing providential or did the Army just get it right once? Whatever the basis, Wideawake Field, Ascension Island, still in service today, attests to the skills of these men of the 38th.

"The greatness of the men stood out in contrast to the inadequacy of the construction equipment of the Army Engineers of that era. Improvisation, determination, and 75,000 pounds of dynamite were the ingredients of success. Dynamite was required even to dig latrines. All of the explosive was used in the excavation, one-third of which was employed in two grand-finale shots. Even so, there was not enough explosive to construct a level runway. Wideawake Field, as the base was named, has a hump in the middle where it is cut through the base of a cinder cone on one side and a lava flow on the other.

"The runway was completed in the ninety days allotted and the first U.S. Army Air Force plane, a B-24, the *Kissin' Cousin*, landed on 10 July 1942. . . . When the field was finished, the 38th departed, leaving the 898th Engineer Aviation Company (Separate) to provide engineer support to the new base. Barely enough equipment had survived the ordeal to outfit the company. The rest had been completely expended on the ninety-day project. The 38th was completely resupplied and outfitted at its next station, even down to shoes and sox."

APRIL 1942

5

For the defenders of the Philippines, the war was over but new battles were just beginning when Bataan fell on 9 April 1942. Ahead of them lay the ignominious Death March and, for survivors, the horrors of life as "Japanese captives, not prisoners of war," as differentiated at the time by their captors.

"It was the most humiliating defeat in American military history when Major General Edward King surrendered his 12,000 American and 66,000 Filipino troops to the enemy," says Lieutenant Colonel Mariano Villarin. "Of the 78,000 troops who surrendered on Bataan, only 54,000, including 9,300 Americans, reached Camp O'Donnell. Some 2,000 escaped to Corregidor, including seventy nurses who had priority in being evacuated to Corregidor. Several thousand escaped along the Death March route, including dozens of Americans, most of whom were later recaptured and executed. The few lucky ones organized guerrilla units and harassed the Japanese, surviving until the liberating Americans landed on Luzon Island in January 1945."

And as the Bataan defenders marched on to imprisonment at O'Donnell, the Doolittle Mission flew on to Tokyo, almost as if to say, "Here's one for Pearl Harbor and for the men in the Philippines." Taking off from the USS *Hornet* (CV-8), 800 miles from Japan, sixteen B-25 bombers set out on 18 April 1942. The bombers took off one day earlier and 400 miles farther out than originally planned, expecting that they had lost their element of surprise when the *Hornet* convoy sighted and fired upon a Japanese patrol boat on the horizon. The planes met little resistance, however, as they bombed selected military targets in Tokyo, Yokohama, Osaka, Kobe, and Nagoya. Of the raid, the *World Almanac of World War II* notes: "The effect on the morale of both sides is enormous."

April 1942
Bataan, the Philippines

Lieutenant Colonel Mariano Villarin continues his Philippine story as follows:
"It was during the Holy Week in April that the Japanese commander, General Masaharu Homma, with 15,000 fresh troops, 140 pieces of artillery, and eighty

bombers, unleashed his catastrophic devastation of Bataan. . . . The defenders fought with tenacity but the enemy kept coming. And then it was over. . . .

"They told us in no uncertain terms, 'You surrendered. You deserve no mercy. You are not prisoners of war. You are captives.' That's why on the march from Bataan to an unknown destination, we were subjected to the most incredible and unimaginable forms of atrocities. It was to be known later as the infamous Bataan Death March, when an estimated 7,000 to 10,000 prisoners died from starvation, disease, dehydration, beatings, and executions. Estimates by U.S. historians of the Americans who died on this march vary from 650 to 2,330. . . .

"In the first day of the march, there was considerable roughing up and a lot of faces were slapped, mainly because we didn't understand what the Japanese were saying. A Japanese soldier would pick a POW that struck his fancy from among the marchers and toss him around to the amusement of fellow Japanese soldiers. . . . The Japanese preferred to pick on Americans, especially the six-footers, to impress their fellow countrymen that the bigger the POWs were, the harder they fell. The Japanese took everything they could get their hands on; they took our watches, our rings, and money. By the time we reached San Fernando, most of us had nothing but the clothes on our backs.

"On two occasions, I saw the enemy drive his truck deliberately into a marching column, killing one or two POWs and injuring several others. And the Japanese soldiers riding in the rear who witnessed the incident would laugh at us sadistically. The Japanese would not allow the prisoners to get water from streams or from artesian wells along the road. The guards warned us to stay away from those who could barely march. It was survival of the fittest. Those who were lagging behind or could not make it were clubbed, shot, or bayoneted. Thousands of petrifying, bloody corpses littered the main road to San Fernando. There were headless corpses, too—one American for every five Filipino corpses.

"We finally reached San Fernando after a six-day march under the broiling sun, and on practically empty stomachs. Some groups made it in ten days, depending on the guards. The average distance traveled by the POW was sixty-five miles. For four days we saw nothing but ruins in Bataan Province. When we entered Pampanga Province at San Fernando on the fifth day, we finally got our first food from the townsfolk who lined each side of the road. There were tears streaming down their faces, as they asked for their loved ones. They risked their lives as they threw all kinds of food to the American and Filipino POWs marching in captivity. The Japanese guards would swing their rifles at them, some shooting. At San Fernando, we were herded into boxcars as though we were cattle heading for the slaughterhouse. Our destination was the Camp O'Donnell prison camp.

"Our starvation diet consisted of a ball of rice, sometimes with a sweet potato and a leafy vegetable, twice a day. Nearly everyone was a walking skeleton suffering from malaria and dysentery. Our medics were helpless without medical supplies and the so-called camp hospitals were filled to capacity. POWs were dying in their shacks, the sick living with the able-bodied. Flies, mosquitoes, and human filth dominated the area. Those with advanced cases of dysentery just lay there or sat there in their miserable plight, filthy, half-naked, looking at each other, waiting to die."

April 1942

Bataan and Camp O'Donnell, the Philippines

Colonel Michael A. Quinn served as chief of transportation under General Jonathan Wainwright at the time of the fall of Bataan. While in captivity, he kept a near-daily journal, written as letters to his wife Mike and seven children.

In the introduction to his journal, Colonel Quinn explains: "To keep the Japs from confiscating my notes, I removed the bottom from a British water bottle or canteen after having taken off the cloth cover. The notebooks were crammed inside the empty canteen and the cover replaced. The Japs picked up the canteen innumerable times, but they did not discover the contents."

The first entry, datelined "POW Camp O'Donnell, Capas Tarlac, P.I., April 26, 1942," explains that this was his first chance "to jot a line in my diary." He begins: "General King had been making preparations for the surrender. He had ordered the ammunition dumps destroyed. . . . Just before the explosion was due, we had the most severe earthquake I have ever experienced. . . . The people on Corregidor that night saw the most beautiful pyrotechnic display of their lives if they were on the watch. The air was full of scrap metal and the ground was vibrating from the concussions. Floyd Marshall was in the foxhole with me, and his description of the explosions was that they reminded him of something Sibelius might have written. . . . That bombardment went on for thirty-six hours at least. . . .

"About daylight on the morning of the 9th . . . General King started on his fateful journey between eight and nine o'clock. I saw the Old Man as he was going down to get in his car to go to Limay. I felt sorry for him. . . . The road between Mariveles and Limay was jammed with refugees the night of 8–9 April. Civilians seeking safety, soldiers lost from their outfits, mingled in confusion. All of them wandered up and down the road aimlessly and hopelessly. They had no more notion of what they were supposed to do than a bunch of zombies. I have seen moving pictures of the refugee-clogged roads in Europe, but I believe none equaled this misery of that lost mob on the Mariveles–Limay Road that night. There were about 35,000 refugees inside our lines, from babes in arms to very old men and women. Children, lost from their parents, were crying hysterically. No one was able to help them. . . .

"At ten o'clock in the morning of the 10th, we were notified that we would leave for Hospital #1 at Little Baguio. . . . When in Little Baguio, I ran into Father [William T.] Cummings. He was a Maryknoll missionary who . . . had been badly wounded in a Jap bombing raid on Hospital #1, but he stood his ground taking care of the wounded during the bombing and after. Everybody around the hospital thought he was about the best thing they had ever met. . . .

"Thousands of Philippine Army troops were trudging along the road on which we were traveling [north toward Stotsenberg]. Apparently, they had been marching all day. They reported that many of their men had been shot or bayoneted, and others had been beaten with clubs. . . . I fell asleep and was awakened when the car stopped. We were at Camp O'Donnell. . . . About half-completed, it was to have been a training center for a Philippine Army division. The headquarters area had been set up and quite a number of nipa shacks had already been built. The camp originally had been designed to hold about 10,000 men. It soon was to be the concentration point for almost 50,000 prisoners. . . .

"The entire water supply for the area was one artesian well. Its water was distributed in a 5/8-inch main throughout the camp. The main was on top of the ground . . . and by the time we drew water it was too hot to drink. We didn't get a meal until five o'clock that afternoon. It consisted of a bowl of rice. . . .

"After General King's arrival [the following day], other prisoners began pouring in. They were not as fortunate as we were. They had been compelled to march. . . . Men came into O'Donnell raving maniacs. Some were being carried by their comrades. Some were being carried on litters that had been improvised from bamboo poles, clothing, or rope, and an occasional blanket. . . .

"Our hospital is a large shack with bamboo floors. In it, there is no water, no bedding, and no beds. The ill lay naked on the floor in utter filth. There are no sanitary facilities. When the victims die, they are buried naked. Their clothing and shoes are needed for the living. We who appear to be well watch our men dying, and wonder if their next breath will be the last. . . .

"This whole episode up to now has been a nightmare. The Japs so far have given no indication that they intend to recognize the Geneva Convention or the Articles of War. . . ."

In his 27 April entry, Colonel Quinn reports: "Eight or ten deaths in the American camp. Father Curran, a Dominican, said the rosary last night. . . . No new arrivals today, so there seems to be no doubt that many of our friends are missing. The camp now holds approximately 8,200 Americans. There are about 40,000 Filipinos. . . . All we hear from each other is about something to eat, and our own dreams about a home and a plot of ground of our own, where each of us can let the rest of the world go by. If I have that and you [addressing his wife], that's all I want."

April 1942
Bataan, the Philippines

Captain Kermit Lay was a second lieutenant serving as assistant provost marshal, Headquarters, 1st Philippine Corps.

Captain Lay writes: "On 9 April 1942, Bataan surrendered and the Death March began, and the Japs really put us through our paces. We were in no condition to make it even under normal conditions. . . . While on this horrible Death March, if anyone fell out to relieve himself, or to get a drink from an occasional artesian well, the Japs would shoot or bayonet them. . . . One day I saw a soldier who had to relieve himself so badly, he pulled off his trousers, threw them over his shoulder, and relieved himself while walking, with the waste running down his legs and into his shoes.

"Captain David Miller of the 26th Cavalry and Captain Lee Miles and I from 1st Corps Headquarters were in this particular group on the march. As we got near a Jap artillery position, it opened up fire on Corregidor, and Corregidor returned fire. Everyone was running off the road, hitting the ground. I happened to look up and saw Corregidor hit a truck loaded with Jap soldiers and they went everywhere. The Japs were mad; we were sick and exhausted. They got us back on the road and marching again. Captain Miller was not only sick and exhausted, his feet were badly blistered from his cavalry boots, which he had cut down. Captain Miles was on one side of him and I was on the other trying to help him. Someone yelled, 'Guard,' and as I turned around, a Jap rammed a bayonet right through Captain Miller.

"The next day they got us marching again, then had us get off the road and took us to a rice paddy. They told us there was going to be a shakedown, to empty our pockets, turning them inside out, and to lay our possessions on the ground in front of us for inspection. I had a New Testament in my left shirt-pocket that had some pesos and a ten-yen bill in it. . . . The Jap was within one person in front of me, looking at the captain's things, taking his jewelry and other valuables, putting them in his pockets. I cannot figure out to this day why I picked up the ten-yen bill, folded it up into an inch-square, and stuck it behind my belt. After the inspection was over, they took three officers and five enlisted men out

behind a rice-straw stack and shot them. We learned that they were shot for having Jap money."

5–9 April 1942
Bataan and POW Camp O'Donnell, the Philippines

*Lieutenant Colonel Garry J. Anloff Jr. was a captain and assistant in the Adjutant
General's Department, Headquarters Luzon Force.*

"It had been a different kind of war! From the time I stood and watched about
eight bombers (each with a red ball on the side) salvo their bombs on Clark Field,
destroying our bomber force (B-17s), to the day that I met a Nip tank captain at
the main road and escorted him to Luzon Force HQ on Bataan to meet our chief
of staff, it was as if a movie were being shown at twice normal speed. Everything
was 'emergency'—with little time to eat," Colonel Anloff writes.

"In our 122-day war, I lost thirty-one pounds, 'gained' malaria, and felt that I
was better off than most. . . . On 5 April 1942, the chief of staff called me, told
me I was to be HQ commandant security, that I would alter trails around headquarters so that no stragglers would come in. . . . I happened to be at the main
road when a Nip light tank drove up."

After first taking the captain to headquarters, "later that day I took him to our
guest quarters, a canvas cot, blanket, pillow, under a tent fly. . . . His comment
surprised me. 'This will be great. I have not slept in a bed in seven years.' Seeing
my face, he explained, 'I have been in China.'

"The next day I arranged with him to move sedans from Bataan to where they
might be needed and, incidentally, take us to wherever they wanted us to go. We
had thirty-seven sedans and two Ford 1½-ton stakeside trucks. . . . We went to
Camp O'Donnell, a Philippine Army camp where we became 'captives,' not
POWs. It was not until December that the Nips reported us as prisoners of war.
This fact has caused every POW serious problems ever since. Why? Because one-
third of us die as killed in action, not as a POW. The published statistics convey
erroneous impressions!"

April 1942
Bataan and POW Camp O'Donnell, the Philippines

*Chief Warrant Officer Clifford A. Roberts submitted the POW diary-letter of his
brother, First Lieutenant Hugh H. Roberts, written from Bilibid Prison, Manila,
26 November 1944.*

The 1944 letter from Lieutenant Roberts was the only one his family ever
received from him. It was written in quadruplicate and given to others to mail,

with the explanation to his family: "If anything happens to me, they will be delivered to you and you will know that I stood up morally and physically this far."

Of his brother Hugh, Mr. Roberts writes: "He was promoted to captain but never got word." He was killed 15 December 1944 "when our bombers sank unmarked Japanese ships" leaving Manila Harbor with "all of the prisoners the Japs could pack on three freighters to send to Japan to work camps." Mr. Roberts was on the other side of the island on the destroyer USS *Luce* (DD-522) when his brother's prison ship was sunk.

"I hope you can read this," Lieutenant Roberts begins his letter. "I can't because I am partially blind due to malnutrition. . . . During the Bataan Campaign, I had charge of the MP Station at Limay on the east coast, the nearest station to the front lines, where I was bombed and shelled regularly but was never under rifle fire. . . .

"On April 7, we withdrew to Little Baguio and surrendered on the 9th. The Japs robbed us of nearly everything we had, would not feed us, and kept us along the road in hopes that Corregidor would not shell them while they brought up their guns. Some prisoners were even forced to carry ammunition to guns that had been set up. I was kept on the Death March out of Bataan five days without food. Many died along the way, among them John Hayes of Portland, my roommate before the war. I walked a total of sixty miles in the five days without food, and twenty-seven of them on the last day. Captain Hutchings, I think of Salem, who came over on the same orders as I and whom I knew at Fort Ord, gave out and died that day or the next.

"We reached San Fernando on the 14th and were fed rice and salt. On the 16th, we were loaded in boxcars and taken to Camp O'Donnell, and I will never forget that ride. The Filipinos robbed themselves to throw food into the cars and carried water to us when the train stopped and suffered being beaten by the guards to get food to us. We got all we could eat.

"Eight thousand five hundred of us reached O'Donnell and were there six weeks. During that time, the death toll increased from two or three a day to fifty per day when I left for Cabanatuan Prison on June 1 [1942]—a total of over 1,400 deaths all due to diet and lack of medicine. They were listed by the doctors as [having had] dysentery, diarrhea, and malaria."

1–10 April 1942
Mactan, the Philippines

Captain Daniel Roberdeau Dorsey continues his Civil Engineering Corps saga.

In March, Lieutenant Dorsey was assigned to a special demolition detail charged with the guarding and ultimate destruction of large stores of oil, gasoline, and coconut oil in the installations on Mactan Island, off the central coast of Cebu.

"On Mactan, our course of action was clear enough," Commander Dorsey writes. "We tightened our communication lines, such as they were, and carefully checked our explosives, detonating apparatus, and wiring. We also took time to check the several outrigger sailing *bancas* the Army had provided us for escape after demolition. . . .

"Early in April came word of the fall of Bataan. To the Filipinos who had been taught from childhood that Bataan was invincible, this was a cruel and terrible blow. . . . At about 0430 (on 10 April), Colonel Edmands notified us that the landings had taken place just south of Cebu. We were to proceed with demolition and get away in any manner we saw fit. . . . Carpenter O'Brien blew up Texaco, the most remote and isolated of our three installations. . . .

"The Texaco blast was also a signal for me, and I quickly made my way in our car to the Standard Oil plant. The percussion of the blast was deafening and overwhelming beyond description. I waited what seemed an eternity for the heat and shock of the blast to subside, then I scrambled up and began a dash of fifty yards back to the car. . . .

"Since there was no further need for blackouts, I flashed on the lights and we sped away to the next demolition station—the Philippine Refinery. I reported our readiness to Slimmon, and we made the electrical contact that blew up the tanks. We quickly set the wires, which were to blow up the power plant and shop later, and then hurried down to the pier and the waiting speedboat. As we pulled away from Mactan, heading cross-channel toward Cebu, there was little cause for doubting that our mission was successfully completed. The raging fires behind us told the story. Texaco was burning the most furiously, belching huge and terrible billows of smoke and flame from the inferno of its furnaces, fed by thousands of gallons each of gasoline, kerosene, diesel oil, and bunker oil. I looked with some pride at Standard, which was burning well but which could not compare with the spectacle of O'Brien's Texaco."

April 1942
Bataan, the Philippines

Lieutenant Colonel Hattie R. Brantley was a member of the Army Nurse Corps
stationed at Field Hospital #1, Bataan. She writes as follows:

"There was a dearth of mail during this time but one of the nurses received a sparkling, shiny, beribboned straw hat—just in time for Easter! Everyone who heard about that hat, and came to the hospital area for any reason, asked if they could see it. The crown jewels of England were never viewed with any more solemnity than was that hat. . . .

"Phosphorus bombs were dropped; we received patients yellow as mustard, with horrible burns. Supplies were dwindling by the day; dressings were not changed until absolutely necessary. . . . We worried about running out of ether. And morphine. . . . The patients were wonderful, never complaining.

"From time to time, bombs fell in the area. . . . We felt secure with the white cross on the hill but one day several bombs fell and the cross was blasted. Dust flooded the place; the wounded moaned. Everybody was numb, frightened. Father Cummings entered the hospital area and climbed upon a big steel desk. (We had some incongruous items in the jungle hospitals and a big steel desk—GI-issue-type—on each ward was one of those items.) Father started praying the Lord's Prayer. The planes were returning, but his voice was lifted over the roar of the plane, and it zoomed overhead without further damage. His voice lent an atmosphere of peace and hope to those of us in this unreal situation.

"The day after Easter, with casualties mounting, and the need for expansion, a load of 100 triple-deck bunks, built by the QM of native materials from the jungle, was being delivered to our hospital. The chief nurse sent me out to arrange a new ward. . . . Planes approached and this time a 500-pound bomb was dropped directly on the hospital. It was a direct hit on the ward I had just vacated. This was the raid in which some nurses received shrapnel wounds; many patients and corpsmen were killed or wounded. Doctor Weinstein cursed in Yiddish and operated all day, doing some spectacular orthopedic procedures, and later he had no memory of that day!

"Then suddenly on the evening of 8 April, about dusk, Colonel Duckworth again told us to take a light bag and pile onto a bus [just as he had done when sending them to Hospital #1]. The doctors and detachment personnel stood by, joking and laughing with us as we reluctantly boarded the scarred old bus. They said: 'The Golden Gate in '48' and 'Help is on the way!' and we moved out. We moved, inching our way, through a scene of unbelievable activity. Ammunition exploded on all sides—the nighttime sky, bright as day. Corregidor's guns roaring over our heads, vehicles jamming the roads, foot soldiers slogging along in the choking dust, dust so thick it clouded the atmosphere and gave a ghostly appearance to the entire landscape.

"And somehow, we got to Mariveles, the cool, clean bay. We sat around, waiting for a boat, talking about many things in hushed whispers, but not about our fear or sorrow at leaving our patients behind, our feeling that we had gone before the job was finished.

"And then a boat was there, and Mariveles was falling away behind us, and Corregidor loomed ahead!"

18 April 1942–May 1943
Tokyo, Japan, and Fresno, California

Colonel Elmer O. Vitous had special reason to enjoy the book Thirty Seconds over Tokyo *by Captain Ted W. Lawson. As a dentist at Hammer Field in Fresno, he treated several of the book's principals as patients after their mission.*

Colonel Vitous notes that the book describes air bases, including McChord near Tacoma, Washington, and others throughout the United States where flyers were encouraged to participate in a secret mission to be led by then-Lieutenant Colonel James (Jimmy) Doolittle.

Providing his recollection of the book, Colonel Vitous writes: "All personnel were eventually stationed at Eglin Air Force Base, Florida, for training. The planes on this mission, B-25 bombers, were to take off from a carrier and drop their bombs. Since the carriers were much shorter than customary landing fields, a white chalk line was placed across the field for practice purposes and the first attempts were made to take off at this point, representing the end of the carriers. The success was virtually zero at first, but on future attempts the planes came closer and closer to a completion of their mission. There was much discussion whether a medical officer was needed and finally it was decided to authorize Lieutenant [Thomas R.] White to make the trip."

On 18 April, the mission headed for Japan, where the bombers were to drop their bombs on selected targets and then head for small Chinese landing fields and on to Chungking. Colonel Vitous points out that author Ted Lawson, who in crash-landing injured his leg, was one of the less fortunate ones. By the time the leg could be treated weeks later, the injury had become "progressively worse and it was determined to amputate his leg."

Around May 1943, then-Captain Lawson was at Hammer to be relieved of active duty and returned to the Los Angeles area to continue in the aircraft industry. "I had him as a patient once and later Lieutenant White [by then, Major White] several times and enjoyed his conversation of experiences in Chinese hospitals," Colonel Vitous says.

General Doolittle was "commended for his efforts," and all returned personnel "were well decorated after their mission."

6

"On 6 May 1942, the American high command on Corregidor with 13,000 troops fell to the enemy. After General Douglas MacArthur was ordered by President Franklin Roosevelt to proceed to Australia to organize a new Army, the generals on Bataan and Corregidor, led by Lieutenant General Jonathan Wainwright, had no choice. They wanted to avoid further bloodshed. With a starvation diet of two meals a day, with malaria and dysentery, and the constant bombings and shellings, it was no wonder that the defense collapsed," Lieutenant Colonel Mariano Villarin writes.

In his POW diary, Colonel Michael A. Quinn records the following concerning the siege of Corregidor, from information provided to him by General George Moore, Corregidor's garrison commander:

"Aerial activity and bombardment increased daily from the 10th [of April]. All vegetation on Corregidor destroyed, also utilities and communication. Searchlights and artillery positions toward Bataan were destroyed, as well as beach defensive position on the north side of the island. Roads were almost totally destroyed and, at the end, only one motor truck was in running condition. With all these conditions, supply was very difficult, so much so that during the last week, troops on the beach got little food or water. Due to the state of the moon and tide, intense artillery fire attack was expected between 3rd and 7th [of May]. . . . The artillery barrages on the east points were very intense, beginning one hour before moonrise on the nights of 3, 4, and 5, but the attack actually started before midnight on 5 May, with the initial landing made at North Point. The landing was opposed but . . . a beachhead was established . . . [and] rapidly expanded despite opposition, and daylight found the Japanese in possession of the tail of the island, east of Kinley Field. . . . Due to the establishment of the Japanese on the east end of Corregidor, the condition of all troops, weapons, communications, and supplies, and also knowing that additional landing of forces on Corregidor would be made in the night with no stopping of them, it was useless to sacrifice human life. The surrender was ordered at twelve noon, 6 May. The dust was so heavy from exploding shells and bombs that all activities had to go on in a continuous cloud. Added to this was a continuous, coordinated fire from Bataan. The operation was a masterpiece of coordination and efficiency."

In other war-related activities in May 1942, the Battle of the Coral Sea is fought 4–8 May; German U-boats continue to operate off the Florida coast, moving south to the Caribbean and Gulf of Mexico; and U.S. forces arrive at Espiritu Santo, New Hebrides.

1942 and October 1944
Bataan, Palawan Island, and Laguna Province, the Philippines

Lieutenant Colonel Mariano Villarin continues his Philippine story.

Of death and massacre in the Philippines, Colonel Villarin writes: "The most notorious massacres during the war occurred on Bataan and Palawan Island. In the first example, some 400 officers and noncoms from the 91st Division Philippine Army (PA) were massacred by decapitation and bayonet thrusts on 12 April 1942. Only four survived by pretending to be dead. I interviewed one of them, a retired PA colonel. He told me, 'It was not until two days later that we received the order to surrender. We had poor communications in the jungle. So we kept fighting and inflicting heavy casualties among the enemy. The Japanese didn't like it.'

"In one Filipino guerrilla attempt to rescue 150 American POWs in Laguna Province in 1942, only one American escaped with the guerrillas," Colonel Villarin writes. "The next day came retribution. Nine of the ten POWs in the group were executed by firing squad. One of the POWs, from Lompoc, California, watched his younger brother die under the palm trees.

"During the first three months at Camp O'Donnell, with aggravated malnutrition and worsening dysentery and malaria, the death rate in the Philippine section went as high as 500 a day. The Americans were losing fifty a day. Conditions improved during the fifth month as Red Cross supplies and medicines, presumably intercepted by Japanese along the line, began to trickle in. But it was too late; the damage had been done.

"The other massacre occurred on Palawan Island in October 1944 when 150 American POWs were herded into air-raid shelters when the air-raid alarm sounded, but there were no American planes. The Japanese then threw buckets of gasoline on the helpless Americans and set them on fire. Those who climbed out of their shelters with their clothes on fire were mowed down by machine-gun fire. Miraculously, eleven survived." Colonel Villarin interviewed two of those survivors, men from the 4th Marine Regiment who had been evacuated from Shanghai just before Pearl Harbor. Details are in his book, *We Remember Bataan and Corregidor.*

May 1942
Camps O'Donnell and Tarlac, the Philippines

Colonel Michael A. Quinn continues his POW journal.

After recording in his entry of 30 April that 104 Filipinos were buried the previous day and that twenty-eight Americans died in the last forty-eight hours, Colonel Quinn begins his May entries. "There were two American deaths last night," he reports on 2 May. "I saw more than 300 Filipino bodies carried out to the burial ground. We hear now that the Japs are radioing the names of all prisoners of war. Hope it is so, for you [his wife] will know that I am alive."

In his 3 and 5 May entries, Colonel Quinn writes: "Went to Mass and Communion today. Father Curran was down to a stone altar, a chalice, napkin, and a paten. . . . Corregidor is still holding out, although I heard bombing last night and about twenty-seven Jap planes flew over toward Mills."

"Corregidor must have taken a beating yesterday, but so far (it's 0930) we've seen no bombers," the colonel writes on 7 May. At 0630, he writes: "Just heard that Corregidor capitulated. . . . No confirmation yet, but there has been no air activity all day. We have been notified that we will leave for Tarlac about 0900 Saturday. Rumors are that we have been held as hostages pending negotiations for repatriation. I am satisfied that if there is any way, the Japs will get us out of the Philippines."

"Deaths among the Americans so far amount to 235. At least twenty-five died yesterday," Colonel Quinn reports on 8 May. After many rumors and postponements concerning the move to Tarlac, it is confirmed on 10 May. Colonel Quinn notes on 11 May that the men were informed that they were "now prisoners of war according to international law." Until this time, they were considered captives. The colonel continues: "The Japs brought out some newspapers and we saw about the fall of Corregidor, about 11:15 P.M., May 6, by assault."

On 14 May, Colonel Quinn recalls: "It is just a year since you [Mike, his wife] sailed away for the States. . . . Thank God I sent you home." In documenting characteristics of other prisoners, he enumerates: "Lack of interest in living; lack of expression on the faces of all men except while eating; and the labor of ordinary walking. . . . Starvation for several months does funny things to a person."

"We had pictures taken today," he writes on 20 May. "I was excused because of sickness, but I stood it anyway, hoping you might see it in some State Department bulletin and know that I was alive and safe. Lacking the opportunity for religious services, my missal [a prayer book] comes in handy for many fellow prisoners. Be they Catholic, Protestants, or Jews, the missal is used by many. . . . O'Donnell is being evacuated at a rate of 500 a day; eighty died there in the last two days."

"We also hear O'Donnell is continuing the closing out of Americans," he writes on 31 May. "Dreamt last night we bought a farm near Kansas City. . . . Every day I sit in a grass shack and dream of the future."

December 1941–May 1942
Midway Islands

Colonel William P. Spencer—who was with 6th Defense Battalion, FMF, on Midway when two Japanese destroyers fired on the island 7 December 1941—is S-1, battalion adjutant, and CO of H&S Battery. He describes activities from 7 December until the battle of Midway, 4 June 1942.

"During this period, we continued to reinforce and improve the defenses of the island. We spent a lot of time playing cards and poker. There wasn't much else to do but watch and wait. We began to get a lot of high-ranking visitors. The airfield was expanded and additional squadrons ordered in. Ships came and went. Planes patrolled out of Midway daily on lookout to the west. . . .

"Along about April 1942, we began to get rumors about a possible Japanese attack on Midway. We did not know at the time that the Japanese codes had been broken and that soon Midway was confirmed as the target. I recall that either Admiral Chester Nimitz or one of his high staff officers came out to see Captain Simmard, USN, and Colonel H. Shannon in April or early May. . . .

"I learned shortly thereafter that Captain Simmard and Colonel Shannon had been asked if they could hold the island if they were given all the reinforcements they wanted. They replied that they thought they could and would do their best. After this, things began to pop fast. Shortly, new 90mm AA guns began to arrive. Two companies of 1st Raider Battalion and a tank platoon came in, and all manner of other guns and supplies. An aircraft carrier stood offshore and additional planes were unloaded, some Army B-26s. Also, the PBYs were increased for patrol. Army B-17s came later. The Navy moved about fourteen PT boats to Midway and soon we heard there were about twenty submarines moved to west of Midway before the battle, out near Kure Island. H&S Battery installed two .50-caliber (for a total of four) machine guns on pedestal mounts near battalion command post and tower. . . .

"In May, James Roosevelt and others came out with their 1st Raider Battalion troops. He was the executive officer of the battalion. . . . James Roosevelt and others ate lunch with us at the tent on one occasion. One company of the Raider Battalion was dug-in in the cable station woods, north of the battalion command post, along with the platoon of tanks. One company of the Raiders went to Eastern Island under Major Benson's command.

"It was now about 15 May, three weeks before the Battle of Midway . . . and the coded information we had was amazing. Midway was now the sure target and the date was 4 June 1942 at dawn from the northwest, and the whole combined fleet of Japan was to be there.

"On about 15 May, Colonel Shannon ordered Captain R. McGlashan, S-3, to call all officers to a conference in the center of Sand Island, west of the battalion command post, and give them all the word. We had the names of ships, landing units, where they would land, and routes of various Japanese fleets. They were to converge on Midway on 4 June with a dawn air-destruction, followed by a combined fleet bombardment and the taking of Midway about 5 or 6 June. We even had the names of some individual ship's commanders. They were loaded for bear and, although we were as ready as we could be—the island was about to sink with guns and planes—we knew that only the Navy and Air Force units stood between us and Midway's destruction and capture."

May 1942
New Jersey to Ireland

Chaplain (Colonel) Harry P. Abbott was a major and regimental chaplain, 13th Armored Regiment, 1st Armored Division, Fort Knox, Kentucky.

Soon after Pearl Harbor, "intensive training became the order of the day and we were placed on 'Alert' or 'Semi-Alert' status. Soon we were on our way to Fort Dix, New Jersey, where increased training, schools, drill, and 'brushing-up' prepared us for what was ahead," Chaplain Abbott writes in his book, *The Nazi "88" Made Believers*. The division was heading overseas for eventual participation in Operation Torch.

After a capacity church service on Mother's Day, 10 May, "we were given our 'marching orders.' Some last good-byes, and we were on our way overseas" on that "beautiful and majestic liner, the *Queen Mary*." Chaplain Abbott describes the trip through submarine-infested waters as "uneventful except for the tenseness aboard, boat drills, organizations affected, and being on alert at all times," and the seasickness.

The troops arrived in Northern Ireland, and were stationed near the Mourne Mountains. "Everyone's life was a busy one here and the chaplain's life was no exception: sending cables, money orders for the men, giving lectures, holding services, having interviews with the men, visiting hospitals, burying the dead, attending conferences, schools, and pinch-hitting." And just as he had sold Liberty Bonds as a Boy Scout in Rockford, Illinois, during World War I, he helped to sell Defense Bonds in Ireland to service members buying them during World War II.

Chaplain Abbott notes that "entertainment was provided by dances, movies, and USOs, all of which helped. Such stars as Al Jolson, Ida Lupino, Merle Oberon, Jimmy Durante, and a host of others brought cheer and gladness to many hearts; but mostly they were welcomed as Americans, ambassadors from home."

JUNE 1942

7

About the time the Japanese were striking Midway in the North Pacific and the Aleutian Islands southwest of the Alaska Peninsula on 4 June 1942, thousands of American troops were boarding the HMS *Queen Elizabeth* in New York Harbor, preparing to cross the Atlantic. Among them was the ground echelon of 1st Pursuit Group, headed immediately for Goxhill, England, and eventually for North Africa and Operation Torch in November 1942. As each man boarded, he was handed a communiqué from his commander in chief, written on the White House letterhead. Lieutenant Colonel Clyde W. Gabler saved his copy of that message to the troops, addressed "To Members of the United States Expeditionary Forces." The text reads as follows:

> You are a soldier of the United States Army.
>
> You have embarked for distant places where the war is being fought.
>
> Upon the outcome depends the freedom of your lives: the freedom of the lives of those you love—your fellow-citizens—your people.
>
> Never were the enemies of freedom more tyrannical, more arrogant, more brutal.
>
> Yours is a God-fearing, proud, courageous people, which, throughout its history, has put its freedom under God before all other purposes.
>
> We who stay at home have our duties to perform—duties owed in many parts to you. You will be supported by the whole force and power of this Nation. The victory you win will be a victory of all the people—common to them all.
>
> You bear with you the hope, the confidence, the gratitude and the prayers of your family, your fellow-citizens, and your President—

And then, at this point, the signature *Franklin D. Roosevelt* appears.

3–7 June 1942
Midway Islands

Colonel William P. Spencer was on Midway when the Japanese opened fire there 7 December 1941; he was there also for the big battle, serving as S-1, battalion adjutant, and CO of H&S Battery.

"On 3 June 1942, Navy patrol planes, PBYs out of Midway, spotted leading ships of the Japanese support and landing force (Kondo, I believe) approaching

Midway from the southwest (300 to 400 miles). The carrier strike force under Nukumo had not yet been sighted, nor had the main battle fleet under Yamamoto, following the carriers by about 450 miles," Colonel Spencer writes.

"However, we had known they were coming—and on schedule—and made final preparations, and were expecting the first attacks early on the morning of 4 June. We were up early, 0300 to 0430, and were at battle stations. Patrol planes were dispatched west and northwest early, before dawn, and at about 0530 one or more reported many planes at 320 about 100 miles out. I remember the first radar report well: 'Many planes, bearing 320, distance 77 miles.' I recall that by this time, patrol planes had spotted one carrier.

"We now knew that the broken code information we had was correct and 'all hell would soon break loose!' And it did! General Quarters was sounded and all planes took off. PT boats left the docks and departed. Colonel Shannon issued his orders to fire on all targets as they came within range and we had acknowledgments from all units. Radar continued the 'many bogies' reports 320 until they were about 25 miles out. (We later heard that there were about 132 Japanese planes.)

"It was at this time that our fighters and SBDs and B-26s, et cetera, intercepted the Japanese formations north of Midway. Reports were coming in to the command post fast from the units, some of which picked them up in their AA directors' scopes at 25 to 27 miles. All was ready.

"The next reports, I recall, were: 'Two planes down in flames north of Midway' and 'Four planes on fire north of Midway,' and finally 'Nine planes on fire or down in water north of Midway.' The AA batteries then reported: 'They are splitting into two groups; one group is heading to Eastern Island, one group to Sand Island. They are dropping their bombs.' 'Bombs on way down.' 'Eastern Island is being bombed.' 'All batteries have opened fire,' et cetera.

"All of this was announced or reported in the CP and all knew and heard it. Mind you, we knew the bombs were on the way down and yet none had hit. We were all sweating. . . . Soon the bombs began to hit. The ground shook and trembled, and sand and gravel came down through the roof of the command post.

"A report came in that the Eastern Island command post had been hit, Major Benson had been killed, and others killed or wounded. We soon received another report that Major Benson had been decapitated. Many reports continued of bombs, strafing, fires, hits. About four to five planes were reported to have crashed on the two Midway Islands or to have gone down in the water off Midway. By about 0700, the Japanese had gone back to their carriers. We could hear part of their talk to one another on one of the network radios as they returned.

"Casualties, I recall, were ten or eleven dead on Midway and unknown wounded. Most Midway air units had heavy casualties and losses and many planes and crews from Eastern Island had not returned. The Japanese had apparently 'fired right through our formations,' and came on in with about 132 planes. We had thought at first that the planes going down north of Midway were Japanese, but it was the other way around. . . .

"We all know the rest of the story. Our Navy carriers located the Japanese four-carrier strike force and sank all four (thanks to the broken codes). About half of our planes were lost or ran out of fuel and did not find the Japanese fleet. The *Yorktown* was hit and on fire.

"About 0730, we got a report at the command post of twelve planes dropping their bombs north of the North Midway reef. We almost opened fire but these planes were identified as friendly, from one of our carriers, and almost out of fuel. They were dropping their armed bombs in water before landing, as they had not found the Japanese fleet. Even so, one or more of these planes went down in the lagoon and Marines helped rescue the crews.

"The Japanese fleet got within 63 miles and then turned around, as they had lost all four carriers and all air power, some 350 planes. I also heard that the PT boats and submarines (fourteen and twenty, respectively) had not been able to close on the retiring fleet and get any hits. It was also reported later that none of the high-altitude bombers (B-17s, et cetera) out of Midway had scored any hits on the Japanese fleet (30,000 feet, many close misses)."

Colonel Spencer credits Gunner's Mate Arnold and ordnance men of H&S Battery with two hits. Manning four .50-caliber guns, which they had improvised on air-cooled pedestal mounts welded to swivel 360, they caught two planes almost head-on, he says. One blew up and crashed about 150 yards northwest of the battalion command post near C Battery; the other crashed in the lagoon north of Sand Island and the cable station woods.

Commending the three Navy carriers and all who "contributed, died trying, and did their part," he adds: "We lost many brave men, both with the Navy and from the Marine and Army air units out of Midway." Though "the entire Japanese combined fleet was out there and by all odds should have succeeded, the Japanese 'surprisers' were themselves surprised."

Mid-May–6 June 1942
Territory of Hawaii and Midway Islands

Lieutenant Colonel Denver D. Gray—at Hickam Field, Hawaii, 7 December
1941—was a lieutenant assigned to Headquarters Squadron 17th Air Base Group.

Two weeks before the Battle of Midway, Major General Tinker, commander Seventh Air Force, called all officers at Hickam to a closed meeting at the base theater. "After putting the men 'at ease,' General Tinker paused and then stated: 'Within two weeks, we will be under attack.'

"You could hear a pin drop," Colonel Gray recalls. Those present already knew that "we had broken the Japanese Code and we did in fact know of the pending Battle of Midway," since P-40s had been sent to supplement Navy and Marine aircraft at Midway.

"PBYs flew search missions from Midway" and "when the initial PBY sighting was made, Hickam Field was bumper to bumper with planes. We had 114. Many had flown from the mainland, some just hours or days before. Four B-26s arrived, had torpedo racks installed on each wing at the Hawaiian Air Depot, and went on to Midway. B-17s departed, overloaded with fuel and bombs, to fly directly to bomb the Japanese fleet. The crews knew when they rolled down the runway that Midway was under attack and that they might not be able to land to refuel, which was critical for them to survive and return to Hickam. . . .

"The naval aircraft first spotted the Japanese troopship convoy coming from the west. The B-17s were ordered to strike the convoy. Then another PBY spotted the main Japanese force to the north. This convoy consisted of the capital ships—battleship, carrier, et cetera. The Army Air Force's B-17s, now in the air, were diverted to the main convoy.

"While the B-17s were bombing the Japanese fleet, the Japanese were strafing and bombing Midway. The Japanese carrier planes had returned to their ships and were being loaded with torpedoes for the expected naval engagement with U.S. naval forces. The Japanese admiral, not knowing from where the Army Air Force planes were originating, assumed that they were all from Midway and that his first carrier strike had not been effective. He ordered all Japanese carrier planes rearmed with bombs for another strike at Midway."

"The four B-26s struck at about the same time as the B-17s from Hickam struck," Colonel Gray explains, with the B-26s going in on the deck in order to drop the torpedoes. "Only one of the four B-26s survived the terrific anti-aircraft fire. While no B-17s were lost, there were some injuries from flak and aircraft fire. Shortly thereafter, our naval forces struck with fury, which resulted in one of the great naval battles of all time. Midway was the turning point of the war in the Pacific. The Japanese, having switched from torpedoes to bombs, played a role in the overall outcome in that it delayed their ability to strike back after our naval forces attacked so vigorously and successfully. This role was not known until after the war." Because the Japanese had planned to occupy the island, they "had not materially damaged the runways." Therefore, "our B-17s were able to land at Midway to refuel and load with bombs."

Adding to the Hickam connection, Colonel Gray says, General Tinker was convinced that the Japanese had numerous planes on the ground at Wake Island. Wanting these destroyed, he flew on a bombing raid from Midway to Wake, a raid from which he never returned. Because of his loss, Colonel Gray says, general officers were thereafter not permitted to fly combat missions. Tinker Field in Oklahoma is named in his honor.

Winter 1941–Summer 1942
With SS *Matsonia* to the Pacific

Captain Alvin P. Chester, Merchant Marine Academy graduate and six-year seafaring veteran, was attending the new Navy Gunnery School at Destroyer Base, San Diego, when Pearl Harbor was attacked.

By mid-December 1941, twenty-five-year-old Ensign Chester was ordered to the Armed Guard Center on Treasure Island, San Francisco, for assignment as CO of the U.S. Naval Armed Guard unit aboard SS *Matsonia*, one of three luxury Matson liners being converted to troop transport. It would carry the first U.S. combat forces to the Pacific, transporting 170,000 troops plus huge amounts of supplies by war's end.

This "beautiful white ship," painted gray in late December, already had the somber look of a troopship. In his book *A Sailor's Odyssey*, Captain Chester writes: "We spent the last days of December installing guns, readying ammunition boxes, magazines, storage rooms, repair facilities, and quarters for our personnel."

In early 1942, on its first excursion as troopship, the *Matsonia* departed for Pago Pago, Samoa, "in company with *Lurline* and *Monterey*, two other Matson liners, accompanied by the carrier USS *Enterprise*, cruisers, and destroyers. With the 1st Marine Division embarked in the three ships, no one was taking any chances with the first high-speed convoy." [These were the Marines who were to land on Guadalcanal 7 August 1942.]

"With little time for instruction prior to sailing, I had to train my people on the job," the captain continues. "Instructions in safety, loading, sighting, firing, and misfiring were carried out with an intensiveness I did not have to force. . . .

"Our escort was unlike any I was to experience again. . . . We would zigzag at times and at other times proceed on a straight course. . . . With a speed in excess of 20 knots, we had little to fear from submarines. . . . Several days prior to our ETA in Pago Pago, we received word the island was being bombarded by a Japanese submarine . . . [but] all was peaceful on our arrival . . . and with farewells to my friends in the 1st Marines, we disembarked our first troops without trouble."

On its next trip, the *Matsonia* sailed independently, transporting Army troops to Australia. "We also started taking survivors from the Philippines back to the States. . . . The main subject of the conversation, with both men and women, was *hate*. I talked with a colonel from the Philippine Scouts and nurses . . . including an Army nurse and an ensign from the MTB Squadron that took MacArthur out . . . and the survivors would sit for hours venting their anger about General MacArthur."

Until mid-1942, Lieutenant Chester sailed back and forth across the Pacific, transporting troops to Australia and New Zealand. In mid-June, he was commissioned lieutenant junior grade and assigned to the Sub-Chaser Training Center in Miami, Florida, at old Pier 2 on Biscayne Boulevard, to train for the Destroyer Escorts, a secret new building project.

24 June 1942–4 February 1945
Santo Tomas Internment Camp, Manila, the Philippines

Lieutenant Colonel Hattie R. Brantley left Field Hospital #1 with her nurses on the evening of 8 April 1942, bound for Corregidor.

"We, our group of nurses from Corregidor, reached Santo Tomas Internment Camp [the former Santo Tomas University] in Manila on 24 June 1942, having been transported across the bay that day. However, we were segregated across the street in [one of the] Santa Catalina School building[s], it having been a school for girls conducted by some Catholic nuns. They still occupied part of the downstairs in the same building, but had no direct contact with us. We had our small area downstairs for eating and playing games (at tables), and slept upstairs in beds so close together there was no privacy even under the mosquito netting, which was a 'must' for each bed.

"We lived under such crowded conditions, a sign in the bathrooms advised: 'If you want privacy, close your eyes!' We were held sort of ' incommunicado' for about six weeks, seeing only the men who brought our food over from the main camp. But we were finally allowed religious services, conducted by a missionary and his wife from the main camp. Otherwise, we played table games, had an hour outside in the 'garden' twice a day, and spent time talking about 'help is on the way!'

"We were finally transferred to the main camp about six weeks later, and the Santa Catalina buildings were utilized for the hospital and clinics conducted for internees, with the nursing care provided by us, Army nurses. The Navy nurses conducted the children's hospital in main camp and the clinics (dispensaries) in the camp.

"But we never gave up hope—living in the belief that any day now the Americans will be returning! And they finally did! We were in the camp until 4 February 1945 when rescued by the 1st Cavalry, under the leadership of a General Chase. That is another dramatic story."

June–October 1942
POW Camp Cabanatuan, the Philippines

First Lieutenant Hugh H. Roberts continues his diary-letter, written from Bilibid Prison, Manila, 26 November 1944, several weeks before his death.

After surviving the Death March from Bataan, Lieutenant Roberts spent mid-April through May 1942 at Camp O'Donnell and June through October 1942 at Cabanatuan. His letter tells little of those first six weeks at O'Donnell but picks up, chronologically, with his first confinement at Cabanatuan. "The total deaths were a little over 2,100 for Cabanatuan; some were from Corregidor," he writes from his 1944 perspective. "The daily death count was between five and ten when I left, with an all-time low of one. Scurvy, pellagra, and beriberi were rampant. Many deaths were due to these and also edema. . . . I had it once for three weeks in my feet. It is commonly called *wet beriberi* and is treated much the same. I got beriberi in early September 1942 . . . went blind with it, and nearly died with it in December 1942, and still have it and badly impaired eyesight now."

Describing the available food, he mentions rice, sweet potatoes, and cang cong, a wandering weed "that grows wild everywhere. . . . A typical Jap trick at Cabanatuan was to issue us chicken, five chickens for 500 men, and put white hats and coats on the cooks and take a picture of them for propaganda," he writes. At Cabanatuan, "I worked on 1,500 calories per day," but "I am living on about 1,000 now, and so weak I can barely get upstairs alone. . . .

"Our food has been reduced so far that the men are breaking down again. We have had very few deaths in the past two years, but half of my company died of starvation the first six months of prison, and if the Yanks don't get here soon it looks like many more will again. We are getting two meals a day. Our ration here is supposed to be 300 grains of dry rice a day but we are always short-changed and receive about 250 grains."

June 1942
POW Camp Tarlac, the Philippines

Colonel Michael A. Quinn continues his POW diary.

In this month's entries, Colonel Quinn writes of the 9 June arrival of General Wainwright and some of his staff at the POW camp and of the general's request on 28 June for a chaplain. The 27 June entry notes that Colonel Ito of the Japanese army "brought in a case of beer for General Wainwright. In addition, there were sardines for the general and some milk. Not enough of anything to go around, but the Old Man certainly can use it; he doesn't look good." On 14 June, he records: "We had to turn in three essays to the Japanese—memories of Bataan and the possible future of the Philippine Islands."

Food or the lack of it is an ever-present concern. "We had chicken at noon today, the first I had had since Easter. The reason for the feast was unknown," he writes on 1 June. And on 14 June, he notes that Colonel Ito "brought candy, fruit, cigarettes, and some other stuff for the mess." An entry on 22 June reads: "Got some canned milk and mangos yesterday and, believe me, they were good. They issued one carabao on hoof and it will have to be used soon. There is no refrigeration around here, so . . . you cook the whole thing and eat it as fast as possible. . . . I don't know whether it is the food we had recently, but the dead feeling in the back of my legs is beginning to ease up a bit."

"I often wonder what the kids are doing these days," he writes on 20 June. "I often think of you [his wife, Mike] suddenly when I am reading or doing something not connected with you or the family. I wonder if there is such a thing as transmission of thought and you are thinking of me. If there be such a thing, I know that you know I miss you and long to be with you."

"Halfway between two Christmas Days," Colonel Quinn observes on 25 June. "Lord, I would love to spend the next one with you!"

8

In their WWII stories for July 1942, and for the past few months, ROA members have described departures from the United States and arrivals in England, Ireland, and Scotland. For many, as they continue to train and to depart across the Atlantic, their future is being decided in late July 1942 conferences in London, where negotiators convey President Franklin Roosevelt's agreement that a Second Front in 1942 is not possible. Following the president's instructions, negotiators agree to "another place for U.S. troops to fight in 1942," which results in resurrecting plans for Operation Gymnast, and renaming it Operation Torch, to invade North Africa.

In other war-related activity during July 1942, the convoy system is extended south, off the coast of Florida in early July, bringing down the number of ship losses and resulting in the final two U-boats being ordered to other areas off the U.S. East Coast by mid-July; six USAAF planes join an RAF attack on airfields in Holland on 4 July in the first U.S. operation over Europe; American bombers attack Tulagi and Guadalcanal; the Navy's women's branch, the WAVES, is established; General Carl 'Tooey' Spaatz is appointed to command U.S. air forces in Europe and Admiral William Leahy is appointed personal chief of staff to President Roosevelt.

9 April–27 July 1942
The Philippines and South Pacific Seas to Australia
Captain Daniel Roberdeau Dorsey concludes his Civil Engineering Corps saga.

Their demolition work completed, after blowing up oil refineries and installations in the Philippines in April, Lieutenant Dorsey and his men race to a native outrigger sailboat, hidden for the occasion and outfitted with canned food and 200 gallons of water. They depart, not to be heard from again until July 1942.

In his 27 July radio broadcast, newscaster Lowell Thomas announces the following: "Five of Uncle Sam's naval officers, whom their friends had given up for dead, are safe in Australia after an amazing adventure. They are Lieutenant Commander Alexander Simmons and Lieutenants Carl Faires, Ellis T. Skolfield, William Lipsett, and Daniel R. Dorsey."

"The only instruments of navigation they had were an alarm clock, an ordinary dollar alarm clock, a compass, and a schoolboy's atlas. Beating against adverse tides and headwinds, it took them twenty days to pass the southern tip of the Philippine Islands. The waters, mind you, were literally crawling with enemy ships," Thomas reported.

"After they were clear of the islands, they lost sight of land for two weeks, until May tenth. Then they met a vessel with a fierce-looking native, but he wasn't as fierce as he looked. He helped put them on their course. Through the Malay Archipelago, they navigated, past Celebes, through the Molucca Sea and the Banda Sea, past the Island of Timor, which the Japs had seized."

Picking up his own story at this point, Commander Dorsey says: "By the Fourth of July, we on the outrigger—without power, and only by miracle, pure luck, 'superb seamanship,' or all three—had found ourselves well down and through the slot delineated on our little map as the 130th meridian. We had survived storms, groundings, doldrums (no wind), scrutiny by enemy ships, shore-based collaborators, illness, injuries, near despair, and gorgeous South Sea Island cruising—to within a couple of miles of the coast of Australia."

One frightening experience occurred when a small, armed boat, manned by uniformed men, appeared out of the early dawn mist. "They quickly boarded us. We were towed to the island of Aru, where officials verified that we were, in fact, Americans, and we were released."

Advised that adverse winds precluded their continuing either east or south, they remained on the island until morning when a friendly Australian trader arrived. "This ship, the *Soedoe*, took us aboard, and on to Thursday Island in the Torres Strait, for a short stay as guests of the Army. We were reported in, and soon were in receipt of orders on 'first available transportation' to General MacArthur's headquarters in Brisbane," Commander Dorsey notes. Next 'available' turned out to be the troopship *Anhui*, to Cairns, and thence by trooptrain to Brisbane and civilization.

"I was flown by Naval Air Transport Liberator bomber to San Francisco via New Caledonia, Fiji, Canton, and Pearl Harbor, where I saw and learned the whole story of the 'War in the Pacific'—thus far. Then, on to Washington, where, after a day or two of Rest and Relaxation, I was detailed to duty at still another off-shore island, Key West, Florida."

In his radio sign-off, Lowell Thomas comments: "What a saga!"

4 and 5 July 1942
POW Camp Tarlac, the Philippines

Colonel Michael A. Quinn continues his POW diary.

"At breakfast, the Fourth of July was celebrated with a rendition of the 'Star-Spangled Banner.' The music may have left much to be desired but the spirit was there. The Japs celebrated by giving us two good meals today. The Jap sergeant of the guard gave each of us a cigarette as a gift," Colonel Quinn writes.

In addressing his wife, he says, "I dreamed last night I talked to you on the phone." And then, ever the parent, even from the confines of a POW camp thousands of miles from home, he addresses their children: "I hope you kids celebrated the Fourth with judgment rather than enthusiasm. That day always has me nervous. . . . Today is General [Edward P.] King's birthday," he adds. "We all wished him the best but he seems to be worried very much about whether he did the right thing or not [in surrendering Bataan to the Japanese]."

Again, on 5 July, he comments to the children: "I hope you kids all have your life and limbs left."

September 1938–July 1942
Baltimore, Maryland, and Washington, D.C.

Lieutenant Colonel August E. Smith salutes his field of service, the Transportation Corps. He served with TC from May 1941 until returning from Europe in June 1946.

Providing background on the Corps' beginnings, Colonel Smith submits a 1938 newspaper article from the *Baltimore Sun*, with a headline that announces: "Call for men to Quartermaster Corps brings steady stream of candidates to headquarters."

For that first class of 1938–39 in Baltimore, 1,000 men applied; 400 were permitted to file applications; 130 were appointed; and 90 graduated, with August E. Smith among them. Recruitment and courses were also conducted in Pittsburgh, Philadelphia, and Washington, D.C.

The *Baltimore Sun* story of 25 September 1938 explains: "The school is being established to fill a considerable shortage of Reserve officers for the Quartermaster Corps, which is under its required strength for junior officers."

"We attended without any remuneration, as civilians. The Army provided text materials only," Colonel Smith says. "On our first night of class, Major General Henry Gibbins, quartermaster general of the Army, addressed the class. Halfway through the course, the Army reduced the time for completion, to meet time schedules to attend training at Fort George G. Meade, Maryland. The course was placed on a self-paced program, to be completed ASAP. . . . I took the oath of office in May 1939 and attended Meade."

For that first training camp at Meade, 28 May–10 June, 300 graduates from the four cities were enrolled. The newly commissioned Smith was ordered to duty in the Traffic Management division, Office of Quartermaster General, Washington, D.C., in May 1941. And "on 31 July 1942, Traffic Management and Transportation Units were organized into the Transportation Corps."

July 1942
Pennsylvania to the *Queen Mary*

Major Joseph S. Frelinghuysen was a first lieutenant, 1st Army, 1st Division, when ordered from Fort Benning, Georgia, to Indiantown Gap Military Reservation in Hershey, Pennsylvania, "the staging area for Army units leaving for Europe."

"The camp was a veritable city. Row upon row of white wooden barracks in rectangular patterns stretched to the rim of mountains on the horizon. Unpaved roads and parade grounds separated buildings. Everywhere, the brown, clinging dust blew in the glare of a roasting July sun," Major Frelinghuysen writes.

"Indiantown was a gloomy place; I felt the doomsday mood, the grim specter hanging over the tens of thousands of men waiting for the sentence of banishment that would come with orders to the port of embarkation. The warnings came in sequence. First, all leaves were canceled. Then wives and families had to go home, and men living off the post moved into barracks.

"In the last week of July, Emily [his wife] had come to Indiantown to stay at the old Hershey Hotel so we could steal a few of the remaining hours together. . . . On my last night with Emily, she wore an evening dress with a full green- and rose-colored skirt, and I put on my best garrison uniform. . . .

"We had California champagne, lobster, and flaming crepes with ice cream. We danced to some old ones: Cole Porter's 'Night and Day' and Irving Berlin's tunes from *Top Hat*. Then they played a new one, slowly, and a young girl sang 'The White Cliffs of Dover.' England had been at war for three years," Major Frelinghuysen notes in explaining the lyrics to the song that speaks of "love and laughter" and "peace ever after." "We finished the dance in an embrace. She took my hand, and we walked out through the lobby onto the terrace for a last look at the gardens in the pale light of a quarter moon. . . .

"On 31 July 1942, the 5th and the rest of the 1st Division, 17,000-strong, went by rail to the New York Port of Embarkation, where we boarded the now battle-gray Cunard–White Star Line *Queen Mary*. And a 'queen' she was, all 100,000 tons of her. . . . The *Queen* would land at Gourock in Scotland, where, after intensive training in England, we would embark on a tiny Ulster Line ship for the 8 November invasion of North Africa."

AUGUST 1942

9

As World War II progresses into its ninth month for the United States in August 1942, the 1st Marine Division lands on Guadalcanal, Tulagi, and Taivu in the Solomon Islands, Southwest Pacific, on 7 August. By 20 August, the first 31 fighters land on the captured Japanese airstrip, renamed Henderson Field. These planes are augmented by 18 more fighters and 12 dive bombers that arrive 31 August. On 28 August, when the Japanese land 1,000 reinforcements on Guadalcanal, there are 10,000 American troops on the island.

In other war-related activity, German U-boats begin operating again on the main convoy routes in the North Atlantic; Americans land reinforcements on Espiritu Santo to support the Guadalcanal campaign; U.S. heavy bombers from the Eighth Air Force make their first independent raids on Rouen–Sotteville targets in Occupied France on 17 August; U.S. Marines raid a Japanese seaplane base on Makin in the Gilbert Islands; the battle of the Eastern Solomon Islands takes place 23–25 August, with damage to the USS *Enterprise*; an Australian and American garrison resists Japanese landing in Milne Bay, New Guinea; the aircraft carrier USS *Saratoga* is damaged by a Japanese submarine; and Roosevelt and Churchill name General Dwight D. Eisenhower to lead Operation Torch.

May–7 August 1942
Territory of Hawaii to Kiska, Aleutian Islands

Lieutenant Commander William R. Tenney Jr. was a young Reserve ensign, communication department of CINCPAC, when the USS Honolulu *(CL-48) stood-in to Pearl Harbor.*

A light cruiser of the Brooklyn class, the *Honolulu* was the ship Ensign Tenney had originally been assigned to. When the *Honolulu* informed CINCPAC in early May that it needed a communication watch officer, he volunteered to carry out his original orders.

"We had recently learned that the Japanese had bombed Dutch Harbor [on 3 and 4 June] and that they had a task force in the North Pacific and had set up a base out in the Rat Islands at the tip of the Aleutian Chain. As the ONI did not know what their intentions were, it was decided to send a Navy force up there to find out and to engage the Japanese navy," Commander Tenney writes.

With the *Honolulu* as flagship, the group headed for its base at Woman Bay, Kodiak, Alaska. When it started to operate from there, the Task Force consisted of his ship plus the USS *St. Louis* and *Nashville* (CLs), the *Louisville* (CA), and a few escorting destroyers (DDs), including some old four-pipers.

"In the four months that the *Honolulu* operated with this force, I believe we were in port three or four times," he says. "We had been patrolling back and forth out of the Aleutian Chain several times without sighting any shipping, including the enemy. It was miserably cold at sea, with rough seas, fog, and a general miasma. Of course, we did not have any winter clothing. It was fortunate that the ship had a large supply of chief's woolen blue shirts, which the officers wore under their 'blues.'"

Task Group 8.6 at this time comprised the heavy cruiser *Indianapolis* as flagship, the four original ships, four DDs—the *Case*, *Reid*, *Gridley*, and *McCall*—and the converted four-piper *Elliot* for minesweeping.

"On 7 August 1942, the group approached the harbor entrance of Kiska from a westerly to easterly direction in an echelon formation. . . . Our SOC [Scout Observation Curtis] float-planes were already up to spot the fire of the group. They were at great risk, as there were no protective fighters for them and reboarding them was going to be very hazardous," the commander notes.

"The bombardment lasted for twenty-three minutes, and was broken off when the *Elliot* reported a submarine contact. Upon retiring, one Japanese bomber came out and tried to hit the *Elliot*, which they evidently thought was our major ship because it was leading and had four stacks. One SOC failed to return to the *Indianapolis* and a very few men were wounded.

"Were the results of this operation worth the effort and danger to the force involved? In the official report of the admiral in command of Task Group 8.6, 'No.'"

23 August 1942–1943

California to New Caledonia and the Solomon Islands

Colonel William K. Snyder was a second lieutenant, assigned to USMC Transport Squadron, VMJ 253, at North Island Naval Air Station, Coronado, San Diego.

VMJ 253 was the Marine Corps' Aircraft Marine Utility Squadron, the corps' first transport squadron. Its mission was to "supply replacement personnel and materiel to the forces of the forthcoming Guadalcanal campaign and evacuate wounded to the rear-area hospitals in the New Hebrides, New Caledonia, and Australia."

As part of a team that, unknown to its members, was labeled *expendable*, fourteen new second lieutenants, ten airline pilots recalled to active duty, and four active-duty officer pilots took off at 1800 hours on 23 August 1942 to begin what Colonel Snyder describes as "the longest mass flight of twin-engine aircraft ever made." The fourteen R4D-1s carried five-man crews, a medical corpsman, and 1,620 gallons of fuel, all of which grossed each plane in excess of 32,500 pounds—or 6,700 pounds more than permitted by federal regulations for commercial airliners at the time, he points out.

"Fifteen and four-fifths hours later, twelve of the fourteen started landing at Marine Corps Air Station Ewa, Hawaii. (Two planes returned to San Diego after one lost an engine, six hours out.) On 27 August, island-hopping started: Hawaii to Palmyra, to Canton, to Nandi in the Fijis, to New Caledonia, the Vichy French island 600 miles southwest of Guadalcanal. This was to be home-operations base for the next three years. Three September 0700 dawned, with the first landing of an unarmed transport plane on Guadalcanal, bearing General Roy Geiger and part of his command staff, and thus the start of many firsts by a little-known unarmed squadron in combat, VMJ 253, mother of South-Pacific Combat Air Support (SCAT)."

Colonel Snyder reports that VMJ 253—which became VMR in late 1943—and its companion squadrons, 152 and 153, flew to the tiny islands in the Pacific loaded with candy bars, toilet tissue, live ammunition, antitank guns, fifty-five-gallon drums of aviation gas to keep fighters in the air, replacement personnel, and Red Cross personnel with supplies. On the return trips, there were shell-shocked troops and wounded Marines on stretchers who were being evacuated to rear-area hospitals as far off as Australia and New Zealand.

"The stench of burnt flesh—with eighteen-year-old corpsmen to tend ten to twelve stretcher cases per plane—never daunted the pilot and crews who were flying around the clock, some logging 130 to 150 hours a month," he recalls. "The haunting cry of 'too little, too late' . . . was never heard in the battle for the Solomon Islands. . . . It is not an exaggeration to say that had these pilots and crews and their R4Ds failed or had the Japanese been able to close off the continuous flow of aerial freight being flown into Guadalcanal, the battle of the Solomons might easily have ended in defeat for the Allies."

In one six-month period, SCAT flew 24 million pounds of freight and mail and transported 130,000 passengers. In 1942's last four months, 3,200 patients were evacuated out of Guadalcanal; in 1943, that figure totaled 24,685. Even with a few attacks by Japanese fighters, not a plane was lost to the enemy, thanks to alert Marine fighter pilots the likes of Joe Foss and Robert Haberman, the colonel reports.

The planes might have been called Skytrains, Blue 'Gooses,' or Gooney Birds but, according to Colonel Snyder, the SCAT pilots were unanimous in stating: "We never flew a Douglas airplane we didn't like."

August 1942

POW Camp Cabanatuan, the Philippines

Captain Kermit Lay went overnight from private to second lieutenant and from active service member to Japanese POW in the Philippines, that area where he had requested he not be sent when re-enlisting in mid-1941.

A survivor of the Bataan Death March, Lieutenant Lay was sent to Camp O'Donnell as a POW and then by August was at the POW camp three miles northeast of Cabanatuan.

Because of the high death rate at O'Donnell, the Japanese began transferring prisoners from there in late June 1942. This allowed American medical personnel to treat the Filipino prisoners who remained behind until their release for repatriation in July 1942 or 1943, according to Captain Lay. Cabanatuan was a former Philippine army mobilization and training base. The compound was 600 x 800 yards, containing barracks constructed of wood, bamboo, and nipa. It was surrounded by a barbed-wire fence and guarded by Japanese sentries in twenty-foot-high towers and in machine-gun pits.

"At Cabanatuan Prison, the Japanese put the prisoners of war in 'Blood Brother Groups' of ten. If one escaped, the other nine would be executed," Captain Lay writes. "We had our own guards, provost marshal, and guardhouse inside the fence to prevent anyone from escaping." Because of this practice of retribution by the Japanese, seventy-eight prisoners at Cabanatuan signed an oath, the text of which follows:

We, the undersigned, on this 18th day of August, 1942 A.D., under the command of Lieutenant Kermit R. Lay, United States Army, do solemnly swear, being in our right minds and without malice toward any member or members of the Second Platoon, Fifth Company, Building 17 [and 19], that in the event of any man or group of men who escape from Cabanatuan Prisoners of War Concentration Camp #1 causing the death or punishment of any remaining member or members, will be apprehended at the expense and effort of the remaining members and most definitely and properly punished by either Army or civilian court as the group sees fit.

"American POWs in Cabanatuan were assigned to work details on a farm in the rear of the prison compound and throughout the islands," Captain Lay writes. "All of the work that was performed was hard labor and the results were that in just a thirty-month period, 3,000 died at Cabanatuan alone. These POWs died from disease, executions, beatings, and starvation. It should be noted that more Americans died at Cabanatuan than any other prison camp since Andersonville in the Civil War."

One month after the signing of the Blood Brother Oath—when Lieutenant Lay had been a POW for almost six months—his mother received a letter from the War Department dated 21 September 1942 informing her that her son had been "serving in the Philippine Islands at the time of the final surrender" and that "a further report regarding your son has not been received." The letter also notified her of his 25 January 1942 promotion to second lieutenant.

In February 1943, Mrs. Lay received word that her son was "one of the American Prisoners of War held by the Japanese." In August 1943, she sent a letter that he received, by then in a POW camp in Japan.

August 1942
POW Camps Tarlac, the Philippines, and Karenko, Formosa
Colonel Michael A. Quinn continues his POW diary.

In August 1942, one of the rumors that had been circulating among prisoners at Camp Tarlac in the Philippines was about to materialize: transfer to another camp.

In his catch-up entry on 19 August from POW camp in Karenko, Formosa, he writes of breakfast by candlelight at 0430 on 11 August and beginning a march in the rain at 0630 from Camp O'Donnell to the train station at Tarlac. "Quite a few of the natives got out to see us go by. . . . It was pathetic to see them holding up the 'V for Victory,'" he says.

The POWs boarded the train for Manila at 0730, arrived about 1330, and were then loaded aboard the *Suzuya Maru* for an "uneventful" trip to Takao Harbor. There, they were transferred on 16 August to the *Nagara Maru*, which pulled into Karenko, Formosa, at noon on 17 August.

Colonel Quinn fills in details as follows: "After we were unloaded from the second transport . . . we were marched about two miles to our present campsite. The road we marched over was crowded with people who were quiet and orderly. As far as I could see, no discourtesy was displayed during the entire hike. Those who were unable to walk were furnished transportation to camp. When we arrived at camp, we were searched, and I mean searched! We were given a pair of wooden shoes, sort of like beach slippers, and that's all we had on. Our knives, shoes, matches, and lighters were taken from us; also all of our books and papers. Eventually everything was returned to us except our shoes, lighters, and matches. . . .

"Rations have been very slim since we arrived here," he writes on 22 August, noting also that they got back their shoes but "must turn them in every night." On 23 August, Colonel Quinn records that he was detailed to run the Catholic services. "I started off by reading the Mass from the missal," he says, adding, "Today is General Wainwright's birthday, and we all offered congratulations."

His observations on 31 August summarize conditions at the new camp at that time: "Karenko is much more pleasant than Tarlac. We are surrounded on the west side by very high mountains and to the east of us we have the sea, which is out of sight except when we go up on the second floor. We can hear the surf pounding. Mosquitoes are rather bad, but we sleep under mosquito bars. . . . For once in our prison life, we have plenty of water. We get two baths a week—Tuesdays and Sundays. The area of our activity is very limited—about 150 yards square. I guess our biggest handicap is sort of mental starvation. We have no books to read and we have had no luck in organizing even a Japanese language class. Playing cards are becoming more and more unavailable."

SEPTEMBER 1942

10

On Guadalcanal, the fighting continues in September 1942. Six hundred Marine Raiders land and attack the Japanese base at Taivu, 7 and 8 September, inflicting damage great enough to interfere with Japanese plans to attack the main American position. From 12 to 14 September, American forces and General Kawaguchi's 35th Brigade battle around Bloody Ridge, but the Marines are able to repulse this second major attack by the Japanese on Guadalcanal. Assisting the cause are the aircraft flown in on 12 September from the carrier *Wasp*, which is torpedoed two days later. Additional supplies and the 7th Marine Regiment arrive via six transports on 18 September, bringing to 23,000 the American troop strength on Guadalcanal.

In other war-related activity in September 1942, the USAAF targets France and the Low Countries; American bombers attack the Japanese-held island of Kiska in the Aleutians; German U-boats continue their attacks off Trinidad but the first support groups are formed to escort the convoys; and American troops arrive in New Guinea 16 and 23 September.

Autumn 1942
USS *SC 981* in the Caribbean

Captain Alvin P. Chester spent the first half of 1942 aboard the SS Matsonia, *transporting troops to the Pacific Theater. By mid-1942, he was assigned to Sub-Chaser Training Center (SCTC) in Miami.*

"And so we started to punch our ticket for an ASW [anti-submarine warfare] qualification. Many of our days and nights were spent at sea on SCs and PCs [sub-chasers and patrol crafts], and the training was rigorous. PCs, 173 feet long, were made of steel. The 100-foot-long SCs were made of wood. . . . It was crowded, rough, and uncomfortable on board SCs. Intermingled with all of this were classes and tests. . . . The four weeks passed rapidly," Captain Chester writes.

"During World War II, 300 PCs and 300 SCs were built. They were no-name ships, just numbers; yet they were commissioned vessels of the U.S. Navy, capable of sailing to any part of the world. SCs rated three officers, but mostly received only two at the time; PCs rated four or five officers. I received orders to command SC 981, being built in the Milford Shipyard in Milford, Delaware. . . .

"SC 981, with a maximum speed of 16 knots, was powered by two General Motors Diesel 500-hp engines. It had a World War I three-inch, .23-caliber gun on the foredeck and two .50-caliber machine guns. We also carried depth charges on the stern, and later a mousetrap—a forward-throwing rocket launcher. . . .

"The vessel was soon completed and ready for fitting-out in the Philadelphia Navy Yard. . . . We finally received orders to sail for Miami and shakedown."

"We had no radar and no gyrocompass," and "practically everything on the ship broke down at one time or another." Additionally, the new type of sonar gear (RCA WEA-1) gave no return signals, bearing, or range, "though it sent out a *ping.*"

After SCTC personnel worked on the gear to no avail, an RCA technician arrived and finally commented: "We told the Navy not to install it because it required more work, but they told us to do so anyway." Informing Command of this, Captain Chester writes, he was told "they needed the ship and I should *ping* even though I got no echo. I soon realized it was an exercise in frustration, but continued work on the WEA-1 and to *ping*, hoping to keep up the morale of the crew and to bluff any submarine in the vicinity. We were constantly at sea, operating independently escorting subs, barges, and nondescript craft. . . .

"The area we patrolled in 1942 was a submarine's happy hunting ground. They were having a field day sinking ships, as the SCs and PCs slowly came on the scene. PCs sank one or two subs, but they also were mostly bluffing. Yet it worked, and the sinking declined. I never lost a ship I escorted.

"The physical and mental strain on the crew was reaching a climax when one day we received orders to escort a Seatrain ship from Key West to the harbor entrance of Havana, then return to Key West for one day's maintenance," he writes. Knowing that his crew was in need of R and R, Lieutenant Chester "discovered" some nonexistent mechanical problems with his ship and managed to get his crew an overnight in Havana.

"Our next job was to escort about twenty ships, tugs, and barges . . . all bound for Curacao, a trip that required only several days with a fast convoy, but was going to take us much longer because the speed of advance would be gauged by the slowest vessel in the group. We hoped for six knots, but averaged less than four. . . .

"By the time we reached Curacao and turned over the convoy to local forces, we were completely out of food, fuel, and other supplies. Ships had been sunk all around us while en route, but our group was not attacked, and none of the escorts had made any contact with a sub. . . . Even though we heard distress signals from numerous sinking ships, SC 981 was never assigned rescue duty. It was a bad year for the good guys and an excellent one for the submarines."

April 1942–February 1943
Pittsburgh to San Francisco, Bora Bora, Efate, and Guadalcanal

Major General John G. Brosky writes that among his experiences "some events are quite ludicrous today which weren't so funny then." He tells his story.

"My entering the service on 26 April 1942 came with exemplary speed. My graduation from the University of Pittsburgh was held in the morning on that date, and that afternoon, being an ROTC cadet, I was sworn in as a second lieutenant in the U.S. Army.

"Months later, I was at a staging area in San Francisco with orders to go aboard ship, a Javanese boat with Java sailors conscripted into service, since the Java boat could not return to its country, which was in the hands of the Japanese. I was assigned seventy-five men to go with me to an island in the South Pacific. I reported to a colonel, sitting behind a field desk in a big tent. I was to draw equipment from him for me and my men.

"When I told the colonel I had seventy-five men, he looked in a light-brown-covered Army manual and said: 'You will receive three machetes, three axes, three Thompson submachine guns,' et cetera. When he ended his list, I respectfully advised the colonel that the jungles in the South Pacific were so dense that each man should have a machete. He leaped to his feet and proceeded to chastise me and said, 'Young man, don't you ever question your superior officers.' So, this was my first lesson. There is no doubt the colonel was following an Army manual prepared before 1917 and apparently he had never heard of guerrilla warfare in the jungles.

"As we went on board the converted troop transport, we were told there would be some delay to await other supplies. There was a great deal of secrecy and speculation about the 'other supplies.' After several days, the supplies came on board—300 of the finest mules from Missouri. They were fat, well fed, and identified with a number branded on their backs.

"In charge of the mules was a full colonel. He had a handful of enlisted men, skilled in caring for mules. But mules had to be fed each day and their stalls had to be cleaned. The colonel approached me and said, 'At 1600 hours, report to me with your men for duties in caring for the mules.' Having learned Lesson Number One, I smartly saluted and said, 'Yes, sir.'

"Of course, I never tried to figure out why a young second lieutenant was responsible for the lives of seventy-five men while a full colonel was put in charge of 300 mules. I suppose the policy was set forth in that light-brown-covered Army manual. On board ship, our seventy-five men were stacked on bunks in one hold of the ship. Everywhere else there were stalls for the mules whose heads were popping through every door, opening, and porthole.

"We did our duty for about ten days when our transport was redirected to pull into the lagoon at Bora Bora, Society Islands. I was told this island was only a temporary stop for me and my men. We cheered when told the mules were to go to some other island. Months went by. Finally, orders came to depart, a boat arrived, and we were on our way to Efate, New Hebrides, where I was given a full complement of men to complete an artillery battery with 155mm guns, the 'Long Tom.'

"The unit was put through a vigorous training program in preparation of an amphibious landing in the Solomon Islands. It was Guadalcanal. Our unit came ashore at Kokumbona, Cape Esperance. We weren't the first, however [U.S. Marines landed 7–8 August 1942]. The Marines and Army infantry did their duty and drove the Japs back into the interior. Our area was littered with abandoned or destroyed Jap equipment, vehicles, clothing, and ammunition.

"While setting up the area for the battery, a call came from the landing site that there were still supplies for me. Amidst all the commotion going on at the landing site, the major who had called for me handed me a manifest list of the supplies assigned to me—300 mules or what was left of them.

"It seems the colonel in charge of the mules secured a transfer to a combat unit; and according to the light-brown-covered Army manual, if a senior officer leaves an organization, he must assign all government property to the next senior officer. I presume there was no other senior officer on board the ship that brought me to the South Pacific, so the colonel assigned all the mules to me. When I explained the situation to the major, after a good laugh, he said he would assign the mules to himself. To my knowledge, the animals were never used by the Army.

"In kicking this subject around, the last I heard about the mules, as we left Guadalcanal for Russell Island, was that they were sold to a plantation owner for one dollar a head. However, that was not the case of the Missouri farmer who sold the mules to the U.S. government. It was said he collected $300 per mule. I'm sure the transaction was in accordance with the light-brown-covered Army manual."

September 1942–December 1944
With the WASP

First Lieutenant Faith B. Richards, who joined the Women Airforce Service Pilots (WASP) in February 1943, pays tribute to her branch of service, the first organized group of U.S. women military pilots.

Faith's interest in aviation began as a child, "when my parents took me to many of the air shows at the old Curtis Wright Airfield in Chicago. I remember one in particular where there was a woman pilot in one of the races. I thought at that time—I was about ten—that if she could do it, so could I. Thus, when the opportunity was given to me, I jumped at the chance to take the Civilian Pilot Training program offered to college students between 1939 and the start of the war.

"I did not get into the WASP training until the fourth class" in Houston, Texas, she says. Because weather was a handicap in training, "the decision was made to move the school to Sweetwater, Texas. Jacqueline Cochran started another, fourth class at Avenger Field, Texas. This meant that our class was the largest when the two groups were combined."

Lieutenant Richards says that the idea of women pilots in the military was first proposed in 1939 by Jacqueline Cochran, pioneer pilot who, at the time of her death in 1980, was said to have held more records—for speed, altitude, and distance—than any pilot, male or female.

In early 1942, with the approval of General Henry "Hap" Arnold, commander of the U.S. Army Air Force, Jackie recruited twenty-five women pilots to serve under an eighteen-month contract to the British Transport Auxiliary. According to a 1991 WASP brochure, they were the first American women pilots to fly military aircraft for the Allies in World War II and were known as ATA girls, the acronym for American Transport Auxiliary.

As demands for pilots escalated in 1942, General Arnold asked Jackie to "come home and put her plan into action." In September 1942, she returned and organized a military pilot-training program for twenty-eight women at Municipal Airport, Houston. Simultaneously, a group of twenty-eight women was organizing as the Women's Auxiliary Ferrying Squadron (WAFS) at Castle Army Air Base near Wilmington, Delaware. They were assigned to Air Transport Command and commanded by Nancy Harkness Love.

After graduation, Lieutenant Richards was assigned to the 4th Ferrying Division in Wilmington. Shortly after her arrival on 5 August 1943, the commanding officer announced the change of names and command for the women pilots.

"He said, 'Gentlemen, look out. As of today, the WAFS have developed stingers. They are now officially WASPs.'

"In December 1943, Jackie expanded her field of operation and I was sent to a basic training school as an engineering test and utility pilot. What that really meant: I was a go-fer. I did the odd jobs that no one else wanted to do—flew the flight surgeon, the safety officer, and any non-flying personnel. WASPs ferried planes, towed targets, flew tracking and simulated bombing missions. They did radio control flying, flight-tested aircraft, and gave instrument instructions. . . ."

Their 1991 brochure notes: "The WASP flew more than 60 million miles in seventy-eight different types of military aircraft, nearly every plane in the Army Air Force inventory at the time—trainer, utility aircraft, pursuits (known today as fighters), transports, cargo ships, and bombers, from the smallest to the largest, including the B-29 Superfortress."

Of the 25,000 women who applied to enter the WASP, 1,830 were accepted and 1,074 won their wings. The WASP was disbanded 20 December 1944, with the ever-increasing return of male pilots.

Because WASPs had civil-service status rather than military, Lieutenant Richards says, this meant that the thirty-eight who lost their lives during service had neither military nor civilian insurance. However, more than thirty-five year later, WASPs were finally recognized as veterans, thanks to Public Law 95–202 of November 1977, promoted by Senator Barry Goldwater and Colonel Bruce Arnold, son of General Arnold.

September 1942
POW Camp Karenko, Formosa

Colonel Michael A. Quinn continues his POW journal.

In the States, September usually brings with it thoughts of children and school. It is no different even in the POW camp at Formosa, as Colonel Quinn thinks of his seven children who will be returning to classes. On 8 September, he writes: "I picture the kids back in school today. I wonder if Dick has started yet; he will be six in December. Mike, you ought to have a little time to yourself now that all are away for a few hours a day. . . . Well, kids, study hard and get good grades for me to read when I get home."

And, in what must be a bittersweet picture to witness, he records on 11 September: "Right back of our enclosure is a primary school for Japanese children. From the port of the second floor, we can see them playing at recess period. They just shout at games like the kids do at home. While they are at school, I can hear them singing their lessons in unison."

On 1 September, he writes: "We got paid according to the Geneva Convention. I received fifteen days' pay at the rate of 10 yen a day or Y150. [According to Colonel Quinn in a later document, the prewar value of the yen was about thirteen cents in U.S. currency.] We all chip in 1 percent to the American enlisted men who get no pay. We paid 1 yen for wooden shoes, 60 sen for grass slippers, and then deposited 15 sen with the PX for possible purchases of tea and other items, leaving a balance of 141.90 of which 120 yen is deposited in the Japanese Bank to be paid when we leave here. We will be allowed 30 yen for spending money. We may ask for more, for clothing, et cetera, and if approved, we may purchase it from our bank deposits."

September diary entries on various dates concerning food mention getting four bananas apiece; a six-day supply of "badly needed" vitamins and some more bananas, with the price doubled; a one-month sugar ration of eighty-five cubes; an increase in rations to one ounce of meat per prisoner; some salt and tea; and about four ounces each of duck at 2.70 apiece.

"Here's what our ration consists of, with very slight variations," he writes on 14 September: "Breakfast is a bowl of steamed rice and a 'soup' made with *mizu*, which is sort of bean curd with some vegetables such as lettuce, celery, and radishes, which they call *dikon*. . . . Altogether, the solid matter of the soup would fill about a tablespoon. We have the same thing for lunch and the same thing for supper, except there is no bean curd in the soup for lunch or supper."

In a plaintive note on 28 September, he says: "Lord, I have been hungry for so long, I don't know when I ate last."

And then, in one P.S. entry, he seems to sum up his survival philosophy: "One thing I always remember every day—I am one day closer to you."

OCTOBER 1942

11

For the United States in October 1942, it is month eleven of World War II. On 1 October, General Douglas MacArthur orders the Allied advance on Gona and Buna, New Guinea; on 2 October, President Franklin Roosevelt is empowered to order a freeze on salaries and agricultural prices to take effect 1 November.

A Lend-Lease agreement between the United States and the USSR on 6 October designates 4,400,000 tons of supplies for the Soviet Union between October 1942 and July 1943. While 75 percent of the material will go by sea route, 25 percent will be shipped through Iran by what Lieutenant Colonel A. George Mallis calls the original Persian Gulf Command, which he describes in May 1943, chapter 18.

In other October war-related events, the Battle of Cape Esperance, Guadalcanal, is fought 11 and 12 October; the Army 164th Infantry Regiment reinforces Marines on Guadalcanal 13 October; the Battle of Santa Cruz Islands checks the immediate Japanese threat to Henderson Field on Guadalcanal 26 October but the USS *Hornet* (CV-8)—which launched Doolittle's Tokyo raid in April 1942—is bombed and sinks 27 October; and the Japanese land a second force at Attu, Aleutian Islands, Alaska, 30 October.

Allied shipping losses increase during this month as escorts are diverted to cover ten convoys sailing for Operation Torch, North Africa.

October 1942
England, en Route to North Africa
Chaplain (Colonel) Harry P. Abbott was a major serving as senior chaplain for Company B, 1st Armored Division.
Chaplain Abbott describes preparations for Operation Torch: "Suddenly, there was increased activity, long marches, vehicles to waterproof, a tense atmosphere, and leaves being canceled. . . . Instructors visited us and there were more lectures and more schools. Something was up. We were alerted. . . . Soon we were in England . . . with its dark nights, with its fog. . . . I remember I stopped by a window in one of the towns and saw some peaches. I inquired the price, which was six shillings each, or $1.20 in our money. I asked about bananas. They were

surprised. They said when they could get them, which they could not, they were one dollar each. Again, I thanked God for America! . . .

"We were settling down to the grim tasks of war and we knew it; we could feel it and sense it. Soon we were waiting our chance to load and take off. We held Communion Services, and many took advantage of them; some made decisions for Christ; many were thinking of loved ones, others of what lay ahead. We were to be the invaders. We did not know where we were going, but we were soon on our way. For days and days we traveled the waves. There were hundreds of ships, a sight one never expects to see twice.

"The many liners (I was on the *Durbin Castle*) ploughed majestically on their mission like crusaders of old. . . . The next days were filled with drills, maps, schools, commando tactics, night-unloading practices, and climbing Jacob's ladder with full pack. . . . Protestant, Catholic, and Jewish services were held. It was necessary to have three Protestant and three Catholic services on Sunday. Jewish services were held on Fridays. Men were beginning to think seriously, some perhaps for the first time in their lives. . . .

"We held games, gave away Red Cross kits containing cards, gum, razors, soap. . . . They also had magazines and a few books, not nearly enough of either, and with 'sings,' impromptu programs arranged by the chaplains, et cetera, the time passed slowly on as we approached the zero hour. Soon we were told that we were going to North Africa and were in the biggest convoy ever assembled at one time. . . . As senior chaplain on the boat and chaplain for Combat Command B, I had some necessary planning to do, for I had been assigned the additional task of graves-registration officer for the command."

October–December 1942
Australia and New Guinea

Chief Warrant Officer George R. Woltman underwent basic training at Fort Dix, New Jersey, with the 813th Military Police Company soon after the attack on Pearl Harbor.

By February 1942, Mr. Woltman and the other MPs shipped to the Pacific Theater aboard the *Santa Clara*, a former South American banana boat, in a convoy of six or eight ships. After thirty days at sea, "we arrived in Melbourne on 6 April 1942 and took over the Seaman's House in Melbourne for our MP headquarters," Mr. Woltman recalls. Soon after settling in, the unit was assigned to the headquarters of General Douglas MacArthur, supreme commander of the Southwest Pacific Theater. Assignments included foot patrols, motor patrols, and jail duty, as members worked in conjunction with the office of the provost marshal general.

"Whenever the general returned to his headquarters in the Menzies Hotel, two of us were on duty at the entrance. We always received the same greeting after the salute, 'Good morning (or 'good afternoon'), soldiers.'

"In October 1942, our headquarters was advised that the general and his staff were to establish new headquarters in Brisbane, Australia, approximately 1,500 miles to the north." With five others, then-Private First Class Woltman was recruited from 101st Military Police Battalion to be one of General MacArthur's bodyguards, a position that he would hold during the movement north and for three and one-half more years—through Australia, New Guinea, and finally back to the Philippines. Serving as bodyguards with him were Sergeant Arthur C. Hensman, Privates First Class Arthur M. Tangel and John I. Link, and Privates Anthony Bocchino and John E. Gieseke.

During the move to Brisbane, "two of us with .45-caliber Thompson submachine guns were there wherever the general moved. One of us was right up on line with him, and the other in the rear with his son Arthur and wife, Jean. Our instructions were: 'Safety off; finger on trigger.'" While generals usually don't have personal bodyguards assigned to them, "we were told by G-2 that, in this instance, if he moved his headquarters north, the Japanese would assassinate him.

"On the movement, during dusk hours, I was in the rear of the train looking out and waving to all the Australian police stationed at all the railway bridges en route, seeking out bombs, et cetera, at each crossing. The general came into the Pullman car from his room and as soon as I saw him, he waved his hand to me and said, 'Sit down, soldier,' and he continued to pace up and down for at least an hour, with his hands behind his back. Someone told me later that he was planning his next military move in New Guinea."

At the end of the trip, the general's entourage was taken to Lennons Hotel, his new headquarters in Brisbane, where authority was turned over to the 814th MP Company, sister outfit to the 813th. "In December 1942, the general's field headquarters was moved to Milne Bay, New Guinea, where our outfit was stationed."

26 October 1942
Espiritu Santo, New Hebrides

Lieutenant Colonel Louis M. Wheeler was in command of a rifle company, 172nd Infantry Regimental Combat Team, 43rd Infantry Division, aboard the SS President Coolidge.

It was a sunny Monday morning as the converted luxury liner *Coolidge* sailed into Segund Channel at Espiritu Santo, 26 October. Serving as troopship on its seventh voyage of World War II, it carried 5,440 men, most of whom were with the 43rd Infantry. The ship was also bringing arms and equipment, along with much-needed atabrine for treatment of malaria, to Allied troops on Guadalcanal.

"Almost everyone was on deck watching the ship glide into the channel," Colonel Wheeler recalls, when suddenly at 0935 hours, the *Coolidge* struck U.S. chain mines that had been placed in Segund Channel as protection. "Everyone felt the jolt of the mines as they struck the ship. We were near enough to the shore that no one thought the ship could sink, so there was no panic."

At this point, the Merchant Marine "ship's captain beached the bow of the ship on the coral reefs that made up the shoreline." 'Abandon ship' was sounded and, by 1050, one hour and fifteen minutes later, the *Coolidge* was totally submerged. "It went down stern first, almost vertically."

There were not nearly enough lifeboats, the colonel says, but everyone had life-jackets. He was able to wade ashore through oil-covered water while others, oil-soaked and swimming toward shore, were picked up by harbor boats and Seabees who were stationed on Espiritu Santo, a staging area for Guadalcanal. It was estimated that the loss of the *Coolidge* delayed operations on Guadalcanal by weeks; it delayed the 43rd Infantry until March 1943, when they were finally resupplied and ready for combat.

Five men lost their lives in the accident, including the ship's captain, Elwood Euart.

"At the time, some speculated that it was sabotage and we never learned the disposition of any investigation of the captain's failure to wait for a pilot to guide the ship through the mined channel," Colonel Wheeler writes.

The April 1988 issue of *National Geographic* carries a story and pictures of the SS *Coolidge*, resting like a brown-green ghost of wartime-past under 135 feet of waters in the Southwest Pacific Ocean. Covered with coral and furry-like marine growth are the supplies that troops on Guadalcanal desperately needed: rifles, gas masks, tires, trucks, artillery pieces, even typewriters.

October–November 1942
POW Camps Cabanatuan and Davao, the Philippines
First Lieutenant Hugh H. Roberts continues his diary-letter, written from Bilibid
Prison, Manila, 26 November 1944, several weeks before his death.

Lieutenant Roberts had survived the Bataan Death March in April; imprisonment at Camp O'Donnell, mid-April through May 1942; and Camp Cabanatuan, June through October 1942. By October's end, it was time for another transfer, this time to the Davao Penal Colony on Mindanao. In his letter, Lieutenant Roberts describes going to his third camp within six and one-half months:

"We were loaded in boxcars on 27 October and taken to Manila and loaded on a small freighter called *Erie Maru*. It had been sold to Japan by England for junk. Luckily for us, it was clean and we were now kept below decks, so that by men sleeping on the booms, winches, and in the scuppers, everyone could lie down or sit down to sleep. Not so coming back [on return to Cabanatuan in June 1944]. We stopped at Iloilo from 30 October to 1 November, but did not leave ship, and the same at Cebu on 2 and 3 November, and at Davao on 5 and 6 November.

"We unloaded at Lisnad, north of Davao, on the 7th and walked about eighteen miles to the Davao Penal Colony, Dexacol [probably Dapecol, abbreviation for the name of the penal colony]. It is a plantation established by the Philippine Penitentiary and was a wonderful and paying proposition, but under the Japs it has sure gone to ruin."

The plantation, 6 miles long and 2$^1/_2$ miles wide, was cut out of the jungle in 1927. Initially, when worked by the 2,000 to 3,000 convicts, its sawmill provided lumber and its orchards and farms provided tons of fruit and vegetables to Manila, realizing a good profit for the colony, Lieutenant Roberts writes. About one-third of the plantation had been planted in rice and one-fourth in abacá (manila kemp), large bananas, breadfruit, coconut, coffee, and papaya groves.

"They had thousands of chickens and hundreds of hogs, carabao, and brahmas, and had a dairy ranch. They raised pineapple, peppers, and a few other things under the banana trees. They had an orchard of sixty or eighty acres of avocados, jackfruit, oranges, guava, santos, and several other fruits that I don't know the names of. Lemons grow wild by the ton and it is not uncommon to see a bush three or four feet high with three or four big lemons on it as large as grapefruits. They are thick-skinned and not as good as ours but when the guards would permit us to pick and eat them, they were more appreciated than any fruit ever was in the States."

Into this setting, "we were combined with 900 prisoners who were captured on Davao, making a camp of nearly 2,000 Americans. We were fed nearly one pound of rice and one-half pound of cassava a day, and only twenty men died there in one and one-half years. Also, twenty escaped," he notes.

Describing the Japanese as the "world's worst farmers," Lieutenant Roberts sums up the situation: "Dexecol is a natural garden spot; we could have eaten everything we raised but under their interference, they would not let us have even that. The fruit either rotted or was fed to hogs. Coconut, the same; and the bananas rotted and the trees died. Squash, pechay, cassava, sweet potatoes, et cetera, that we raised, produced but little and was hauled out to the Jap army or rotted in the warehouse.

"When we first arrived, there were about twenty acres of cassava eighteen months old and everyone thought it would last forever, so nothing was planted. When it ran out, all we had besides rice was cang cong, which grows wild everywhere. We get a teacup of thin cang cong soup twice a day.

"I only worked a few days till my beriberi got so bad I had to quit and I was in quarters for nine months."

October 1942
POW Camp Karenko, Formosa

Colonel Michael A. Quinn continues his POW diary.

"Received word that no priest may come into camp. Well, that's that. I can see no reason why we can't have a priest come in at least once a month, since we offered to pay all expenses incident to his trip," Colonel Quinn writes on 1 October.

On 8 October, he notes: "The Japs announced that the Imperial Rescript which opened up the war would be read on the 8th of every month. . . . Then they gave us a speech of the terrible treatment their internees had received in camps in the States, which, of course, I cannot believe. They reminded us that we owed our lives and safety solely to the benevolence and indulgence of His Imperial Highness. The Geneva Convention apparently does not matter."

Colonel Quinn devotes his 15 October entry to birthday greetings to son Jim, one of the Quinns' seven children: "Just eight years ago you came to us at Fort Banks. . . . I hope that neither you nor any of the other children will have to go to war under the same circumstance that I did. We have only ourselves to blame. We had forgotten our duties in so many respects both to God and ourselves and, I might as well say, to humanity as a whole. No doubt we are too self-sufficient and too pleasure-seeking for our own good, and now we must pay for our stupidity. May we never get into that shape again. I believe the idea of living to live forever and living as though you were going to die tomorrow is not a bad one.

Must close now, Jimmy. I wish you many, many prosperous birthdays in the future. I hope to spend the next one with you. As ever, your Dad."

"Today is a big day," Colonel Quinn observes on 20 October. "We received a quarter-pound of tea, which will be plenty for almost a month. There also is half a pound of sugar, a quarter of a pound of peanuts (raw), and five bananas. We were weighed today and I hit the scales at 121 pounds. December 7, 1941, I weighed 179 pounds—fifty-eight pounds net loss. . . . Any effort exhausts us. We expect to get something from the stock farm, but so far nothing has come through."

NOVEMBER 1942

12

In the dark of the moon, a few miles off the shores of northwestern Africa, three blacked-out Allied task forces lay dead in the water. Every man aboard was waiting in taut, brittle silence for the command, "All hands to invasion stations."

Just before midnight of 7 November 1942, thousands of heavily armed troops scrambled down from their transports, on cargo net, into landing craft. Organized in waves, they sped away to assault the beaches of French Morocco and Algeria along a 1,000-mile front and begin a drive deep into the coastal plain. In a matter of hours the troops, the first massive American commitment in World War II, had secured beachheads in the Casablanca area in the western sector, at Oran and Arzew in the center, and, along with a powerful British force, at Algiers in the east.

—Major Joseph S. Frelinghuysen, *Passages to Freedom*

In addition to Operation Torch, which Major Frelinghuysen continues to describe in this chapter, other war-related events in November 1942 include authorization of the U.S. Marine Women's Reserve, 7 November; lowering of the draft age from twenty to eighteen, 12 November; the Naval Battle of Guadalcanal, 13 to 15 November; establishment of the Coast Guard women's branch, SPARS, 23 November; attacks by American and Australian forces on Japanese positions at Gona, New Guinea, in a ten-day battle; and continuation of fighting on Guadalcanal near the Matanuska River and Koli Point.

November 1942
Arzew and St. Lieu, Algeria, North Africa

Chaplain (Colonel) Harry P. Abbott was senior chaplain, Combat Company B, 1st Armored Division, and regimental chaplain, 13th Armored Regiment, 1st Armored Division.

On board the *Durbin Castle* headed toward North Africa, "we tuned in on the radio and heard a broadcast stating that a huge convoy was now going through the Strait of Gibraltar. It didn't please us at all to have our enemies tipped off," Chaplain Abbott writes. "At zero hour we had reached our places off the coast of North Africa and, guided by previous arranged signals, our convoy had split up and several sections made for their respective beaches. . . .

"Since we had to wait the long night through, preparatory to taking off, many private prayers were said by men who had never known what it was to find solace in prayer. A few nights before, I held the most solemn, memorable Communion Service I ever expect to hold. . . . It was impressive and well-attended (the largest attendance at such a service I've ever held in my life). All participated—officers and men—American, British, Army, Navy, and commandos. . . .

"The time had come! Boats were lowered and the commandos and rangers took off along with others. Soon daylight appeared. I walked out on the deck to watch the firing. Suddenly a shell fell to the starboard side of my position. I decided to go to the other side. As I reached there, another shell dropped harmlessly in the water not far away. . . . The shells seemed to be coming from Fort DuNord near Arzew. The third one did not come, thanks to the rangers who silenced them in the meantime. . . .

"We were in full pack. I had my musette bag filled to its capacity and more, and had it fastened on my back. Field glasses were around my neck, and a well-filled dispatch case, loaded with necessary office supplies, was slung over one shoulder. I carried my portable radio (sealed) over the other. I had on my first-aid belt with sulfa drugs and morphine needles. Of course, I had my Bible. . . . Suddenly, the front of the LCT fell out—or, rather, forward—and we stepped off into the water. My shoes leaked immediately, as the water reached my shoulders, but we soon made it and waited for our luggage. . . .

"Our advance troops had already contacted the opposition, and the shelling could be heard within half a mile of where we were. . . . While only passive resistance was planned, it proved to be more serious than anticipated for the first few days. . . . The hospitals were filled with wounded—one was French, the next German, and the next American. The reality of war was very vivid here.

"I shall never forget my first night spent in the city hall of St. Lieu, which was used as a hospital. This was established by Company B, 47th Medical Battalion. They brought in a soldier of the 16th Infantry who had been wounded in the legs. I talked with him, and that night I lay down on the floor near him. At midnight he passed on to the Great Beyond. We left him there until morning. I didn't sleep much that night. On the next day he was buried with full military honors at an established American cemetery near Arzew. . . .

"Soon tanks were unloaded. The French had surrendered at St. Lieu [8 November] but the battle was on in earnest elsewhere. At Casablanca, the 3rd Infantry Division and other troops were engaged, suffering heavier losses. . . .

"At Oran, the 6th Armored Infantry did not fare so well; nearly one entire battalion sank with their ships and nearly 200 of these drowned. [Oran falls to the Allies on 10 November]. . . . Our command captured St. Cloud, then Tafara-oui Airport [8 November], and followed that by converging and taking the main French airport at LaSenia with about 800 prisoners. . . . While at LaSenia Airport, we (Chaplain Doyle, Corporal Dehrs, Corporal Whipple, and others assigned to us temporarily) established our Graves Registration Office and set ourselves to the task of caring for our dead."

November 1942
Arzew and St. Lieu, Algeria, North Africa

Lieutenant Colonel Clyde W. Gabler was squad commander for 1st Pursuit Group's ground echelon, heading into Operation Torch.

"The 26th of October 1942 found the *Woolton* out on the Atlantic Ocean, where it circled around in big circles for eleven days. The weather was mostly good with only occasionally rough seas. Our unit was assigned a space on deck for an hour each day. There we did exercises in order to keep in shape for the landing we knew lay ahead.

"On 6 November 1942, the convoy stopped circling and headed toward the Strait of Gibraltar at increased speed. We passed through at night and could see the lights of the city of Tangier, Morocco, twinkling in the distance. The next day we were escorted by some destroyers. The convoy was attacked by German U-boats and the destroyers lobbed depth charges, which shook our old ship to the keel," Colonel Gabler writes.

"Our destination was east of Oran at a place called Arzew. Our ship anchored there about a mile offshore on 8 November 1942, together with other ships from the convoy. We could see the town of Arzew from the deck of the *Woolton*. Units of the 1st Infantry Division had landed to secure the beaches. There was a fire-fight going on, because our troops were opposed by units of the French Foreign Legion. They were still under control of the Vichy government in France. . . .

"We waited nearly all day [on the deck in full combat gear], meanwhile briefing our troops how to get off the ladders or nets onto the landing craft. . . . In the afternoon, all units were told to go back to the cabins or holds, as we would not debark 'until tomorrow morning; meanwhile, refill your canteen.'

"Finally, at first light on 9 November 1942, the second echelon of the 1st Fighter Group ground echelon boarded the landing craft and went ashore on the beaches at Arzew. I assembled the unit because we had been briefed while aboard ship to march inland to a vineyard on the south outskirts of the village of St. Lieu. However, while on the beach we came under small-arms and light machine-gun fire. Everybody hit the sand. At that time, a captain of the 1st Infantry Division came over to me and said, 'Captain, get some of your men together and join me in this firefight.' I said, 'These men are Air Force troops, mostly aircraft mechanics and support people, not trained infantry. Sorry, I can't do that. My mission is to get my unit to the town center in St. Lieu, without casualties, and receive further orders.' He said, 'Okay, we will do it ourselves.' Forthwith, he ordered his infantry company to attack the Vichy French on the ridge above the beach. That unit of the 1st Infantry Division drove off the attackers.

"The Navy beachmaster, through a bullhorn, urged us to get going, as there were other units coming ashore. We continued through Arzew to the village of St. Lieu and to the vineyard, where we camped. We had only marched seven miles but it seemed longer. In the vineyard, we joined the 1st Echelon, and the 3rd caught us the next day en route to LaSenia. There were many reunions as the men rejoined their squadrons."

With orders on 9 November to march to Airfield Tafaraoui, the groups were "a curious mixture," Colonel Gabler says. "Several of our super mechanics had found an old truck at the vineyard and started it up. They went to the head of the column, picked up a load of men, took them to the airfield, then came back again for another load. They were joined by two trucks, $2^{1}/_{2}$-ton GI-type, from an engineer battalion at the airfield. This leapfrog operation continued all day until all the ground echelon was at Tafaraoui. . . . The 27th Fighter Squadron came in on 13 November. . . . The 71st and 94th Squadrons came in to Tafaraoui the next day.

"By 17 November, by dint of hard work by all ground personnel, the group was able to fly several local sorties. The living was hard because the airfield water system broke down and fresh water had to be hauled from several miles away. The men were sleeping in pup tents and subsisting on B- and C-rations."

When Tafaraoui became too crowded, and thus a prime target for enemy bombers, the 1st Fighter Group moved on Friday, 20 November, to Nouvion Airfield.

"When the rains came, the grass or earth landing strip at Nouvion turned to a sticky mud, meaning that during the November–December rains, it was almost impossible to take off or land." For this reason, "the 94th Squadron was moved to Youks-le-Bains" and "the 71st Squadron was sent to Maison Blanche Airfield, just outside the city of Algiers."

8–27 November 1942
Arzew and Oran, Algeria, North Africa

*Major Joseph S. Frelinghuysen was a captain, First Army, 1st Division,
commanding Battery D, Fifth Field, for D-Day, Operation Torch.*

Major Frelinghuysen recalls those first moments of the invasion: "Darby's Rangers [the 1st Ranger Battalion led by Lieutenant Colonel Bill Darby] had stormed ashore, scaled the steep cliffs at the harbor's edge, and captured the French guns guarding Arzew. But in the process they had dashed our 5th Field Artillery's landing craft on the rocks, leaving us stranded on the transport and forcing us to attempt a landing direct from ship to shore.

"A gusting wind swung the ship and sent her crunching and scraping against the concrete bulkhead. Burly British sailors quickly flung out heavy hemp lines, looping iron stanchions, winching the ship taut to the quay. Some other men from the 5th, on a different ship, had in the meantime made an assault landing while we were going down a gangplank—an ignominious arrival they would never let us forget.

"Bursts of rifle and machine-gun fire whizzed through the ship's rigging and clanged against her steel superstructure. The men ran for the gangplank. As I scrambled off with them, I caught sight of the action on land: a building disintegrated in reddish dirt; black smoke roiled up from burning trucks; detonating explosives reverberated in the town."

Several days later, on 10 November, Captain Frelinghuysen served as interpreter when a "round-bellied man in a black felt hat and business suit" was brought toward his entourage, "clinging to the top of a tank that carried a yellow star and code insignia of Combat Command B, 1st Armored Division." The captain was told that "this guy wants to make a deal, or somethin'" but the commander couldn't "quite understand what the hell he's talkin' about."

Then the civilian "slid off the tank, brushed himself off, made a bow," and announced his message in French. He was the mayor of Oran and he wanted to surrender his town. As the convoy drove into Oran, "windows and balconies of ten- and twelve-story buildings bulged with people waving French and American flags. Arab men in traditional dress, women in veils, and smartly dressed French civilians thronged the streets, and a deep-throated roar began to swell through the city. . . . The sound became a chant: *Vive la France! Vive l'Amerique!*"

November 1942–January 1943
North Africa

*Lieutenant Colonel Paul H. Campbell was a radio gunner and operator, 32nd
Heavy Bomb Squadron, 301st Bomb Group, in Chelveston, the Midlands, England.*

"Our first mission was on 5 September 1942. In the early missions, if we had
to turn back, we dumped the bombs in the English Channel," Colonel Campbell
recalls.

While on leave in London, "we met one of our people on the street who gave
us our plans to fly to Africa. The flight crew went to Africa. We were sent by train
to Liverpool. We were loaded on the Canadian ship *Richmond*. . . .

"We docked at Oran and went out on the hills to sleep in tents. On 24 December, I was on guard duty. Admiral Jean Francis Darlan [commander in chief of
Vichy French Forces in North Africa] was assassinated in Algiers. [I was] relieved
from guard duty with orders to be ready to move on Algiers if the French and
Arabs would cause a riot, which did not take place."

13 November 1942
USS *Barton* at Guadalcanal

*Major James D. Ferguson submitted a collection of prewar and wartime letters from
his brother Henry, a twenty-three-year-old fire controlman first class, who died when
the USS* Barton *was sunk off Savo Bay, Guadalcanal, 13 November.*

"He was part of what I now realize was a tough segment of our Navy. They're
comparable to the U.S. Army Cavalry that does the screening work for the larger
tactical units," Major Ferguson writes. "I never realized how tough destroyer
duty was until I picked up a Bantam Book called *Tin Cans* that gave details of all
the individual destroyers' activities during WWII." The book by Theodore Roscoe
was originally published by the U.S. Naval Institute Press as *United States
Destroyer Operations in WWII* and reissued in 1953 by Bantam.

In a 1940 Clippergram, written on Pan Am Clipper stationery from Pearl Harbor, Hawaii, Henry gives his own play-by-play of the postal-military version of
baseball's Tinker to Evers to Chance when he recounts the story of why several
letters from his family took from one to two months to reach him. He tells his
parents that the letters went by way of *Hovey* to *Dobbins* to *Downes*, back to *Hovey*
and *Dobbins*, and then to *Smith* before finally going back again to *Dobbins* and
Downes. At the time, the *Hovey* was anchored in San Diego; the *Dobbins*, *Downes*,
and *Smith*, in Hawaii.

In a 3 November 1941 letter from the USS *Hovey* (DMS-11), FPO Pearl Harbor,
Henry writes: "Well, it looks like things are popping on that coast. It sort of gets

the guys riled up because some had shipmates on the *Reuben B.* [referring to the *Reuben B. James*, sunk by a German U-boat in the North Atlantic, 31 October 1941]. Anyhow, the Navy's as ready as possible. There are rumors that the Jap fleet is out and near the Hawaiian area but we've done a lot of traveling and have never seen them. We're ready though. They'll have to be damn good to beat the boys out here."

And then in another prophetic letter that predates the attack on Pearl Harbor, he writes on 25 November 1941: "We are pretty busy, as we have started to change our camouflaging. . . . We fired again last week and sure made the target look sick. Those Japs will have to be damn good (that's the best word to fit what I mean). . . ."

By June 1942, while on leave visiting his family, Henry had been assigned to the *Barton*. "Our home at this time was naval housing called Bellvue, sandwiched into an area surrounded by Bolling Air Base, a naval ammo/weapons station, and the Naval Research Lab," Major Ferguson recalls. "My mother and dad worked at the Washington, D.C., Navy Yard, better known as the Navy gun factory, where they built the 16-inch rifles for our battleships, among other weaponry."

In his last letter to his family in August 1942, Henry writes: "Well, I got here OK. . . . It was swell getting back there. Maybe the next time it won't take so long. The cookies went over big back here but they didn't last long. Tell Margie [his sister] the candy was swell. Both cake and cookies went like hotcakes. . . ."

In describing the battle in which the *Barton* was sunk, Theodore Roscoe writes in *Tin Cans*: "The three-day naval engagement, which came to be called the Battle of Guadalcanal, began on Friday, November 13, 1942. . . . Before it was two hours old, four American destroyers were sunk in combat, with heavy loss of life, and three were barbarously damaged."

Navy historian Samuel Eliot Morison says that "the brand-new *Barton* had exactly seven minutes of life in combat."

Major Ferguson describes the sinking of Henry's ship as follows: "His column of ships passed parallel to a Japanese column moving in the opposite direction in the middle of the night. When they discovered each other, all hell broke loose."

"In the ensuing free-for-all, *Barton* remained in combat for a brief seven minutes," Mr. Roscoe writes. "The first torpedo blasted *Barton*'s forward fireroom. Hitting her a split second later, the second torpedo smashed into the forward engine-room. Torn in two, the ship went down almost instantly, drowning 90 percent of her crew."

Explaining that their mother was a secretary/typist whose job was to handle supply requests for all Navy ships, Major Ferguson adds: "She suffered through about six weeks of anxiety when the supply requests for the *Barton* stopped coming in, as we didn't get the fateful telegram until 4 January 1943."

In a letter received by the family in 1944, one of Henry's shipmates who survived describes Henry at his usual battle station when the ship went into action that tragic night.

"You should be very proud of your son, for he proved himself in many ways. I shall always have fond memories of him and my other shipmates," the friend writes. In his accolades, author Roscoe terms the USS *Barton* "a good ship manned by brave destroyermen."

November 1942
POW Camp Karenko, Formosa

Colonel Michael A. Quinn continues his POW diary.

"Yesterday was another big Jap holiday—the anniversary of the birth of Meiji who, they claim, was the founder of the greater and modern Nippon," Colonel Quinn writes on 4 November. "The camp commander had a formation parade to celebrate the occasion and he tossed in forty pounds of pork fat last night, which is not much for 317 men, but we did get something. Then, on top of that, we each received three bananas and eight vanilla wafers, which, by the way, is the first sweet food since we arrived [at Karenko on 17 August].

On 9 November, he comments: "The big news for today is that we may be able to write home tomorrow, and if I could only get word to you by Christmas, I would feel that I had had a real Christmas present." The 17 November entry, however, records his dashed hopes: "Wrote a long letter to you and, yes, it was returned. It seems that all letters must be translated into Japanese and there were so many that some had to be returned. I am just sick about it."

In another entry concerning communication, he writes on 8 November: "Yesterday we were allowed to prepare a radio [message] to our families and I sent mine in. Hope you get a chance to hear it." His postwar addendum mentions that his wife received eighty-three copies of the message, some written and some recorded, from all states of the United States, around 15 March 1943.

Commenting in 1992 on this passage in their father's diary, Major Michael Quinn and his sister Patricia Marie Quinn Krueger point out that the POW messages were incorporated into programs broadcast by Tokyo Rose and received in the United States by ham radio operators who phoned or wrote to Mrs. Quinn with the information or sent recordings of the message. When the prepared

greeting included the complete litany of all the Quinn children's names—
Thomas Francis, Patricia Marie, Michael Hodes, Mary Ellen, Terence Davey,
James Meiners, and Richard Lawrence—mother and children were convinced
that the message was authentic and that their husband/father was indeed alive.

"We got the papers telling about the landing in North Africa," Colonel Quinn
writes on 22 November. He adds: "Also hear that the U.S. Navy has been working successfully around the Solomon Islands."

"This letter is to Mick. Happy birthday to you, Mick," he writes on 27 November to son Michael. "You can put it to music and I will try to supply the sentiment. Many happy returns of the day this year and I hope to be with you for your
fifteenth birthday."

DECEMBER 1942

13

As the United States enters its second year of World War II in December 1942, American troops span the globe in their worldwide commitment against German, Italian, and Japanese forces—over Abbeville and Rouen, France, as the American Air Force attacks targets; over Naples, Italy, 4 December, as the U.S. Ninth Air Force launches a bombing raid from North Africa; in Iran and Iraq, where U.S. troops arrive 11 December; in New Guinea, where American forces capture Buna on 14 December; on Guadalcanal, where General Patch's XIV Corp relieves the weary 1st Marine Division that heads for Australia.

Recalling his first Christmas overseas, stationed in Iceland, Colonel Jean W. Christy writes: "In December of 1942, we were all aware of the approach of Christmas. It was a melancholy time. The long nights and short days, with only an hour or two of dim sunlight, made their contribution to our depressed spirits. Mainly, however, it was just being away from our families and loved ones at a time when we traditionally looked forward to being with them. It was a hard time for American soldiers all across the island. There were a dozen suicides. It was difficult to be away from home any day, but Christmas was especially hard. Thank goodness that Bing Crosby's new movie, *White Christmas*, with its sentimental theme song of the same name didn't arrive on Iceland until late in January."

From Algeria in Northern Africa on Christmas Day 1942, Lieutenant Colonel Clyde W. Gabler writes: "Not much of a holiday. Everyone packing for the move to Biskra, Algeria."

Writing to his family from Bilibid POW Prison, Manila, in November 1944, First Lieutenant Hugh H. Roberts mentions his 1942 Christmas at Camp Davao in the Philippines, a time when he was hospitalized in extreme pain from beriberi.

From Camp Karenko, Formosa, Colonel Michael A. Quinn writes in his journal: "We had Christmas carols here. They were very beautiful, but I don't know, I think they made us feel our captivity more." On 26 December, he records, "I have been following you folks around the clock, as it is still Christmas at home. I hope you had a good time and didn't worry about me more than you had to. . . .

I think the spirit of Christmas among the prisoners was more pronounced than at home; maybe because we had to use our imagination for so much."

24–25 December 1942–Spring 1943
Reykjavik, Iceland

Colonel Tommy R. Gilliam was a first lieutenant, battalion communications officer, 1st Battalion, 2nd Infantry Regiment, 5th Infantry Division.

"Christmas Eve, I was on the docks with two platoons on the 1600- to 2400-hour shift," Colonel Gilliam writes. "We had Christmas Eve dinner in the quartermaster battalion mess. They served Christmas turkey—only it had been frozen and was not adequately thawed. Then we were unloading a British ship that was carrying a cargo of Black Horse Scotch for the British troops—and when we climbed in our trucks to head for camp at midnight I realized I had two drunken platoons on my hands.

"Nor was that the end of it. The next morning, the camp was surrounded by MPs, since the British claimed we had stolen so much Scotch that Iceland Base Command felt they had to make an effort to recover it. There was snow on the ground and up the sides of our Quonset huts to a level of three or four feet, and the men opened their windows and shoved the contraband bottles out in the snow, retrieving them after the MPs left, empty-handed. But not all were recovered. The next spring, after the thaw, walking across the company area, I kicked up a full unopened bottle of Black Horse Scotch, which apparently had been lost in the snow."

December 1942
Reykjavik, Iceland

Colonel Jean W. Christy continues his recollections of Christmas 1942.

"A Christmas tree was a concern because there were no trees on Iceland, the soil being too shallow to support anything that big. There was a 'Y' in the road out toward the range that had a few hundred square feet of small shrubs of some kind. We referred to it as the Icelandic National Forest. Someone suggested that we go out in the dark and steal one of those, but there was agreement that we shouldn't pull a dirty trick like that at Christmas. There was vague talk about putting together an artificial tree out of scraps of wood. That idea didn't go anywhere either.

"Then, a few days before Christmas, a tree appeared in the Officers Club. Not tall, but a real, live evergreen tree. Our headquarters battery commander, Captain Herman Jost, had learned that some trees had been shipped in from England

and had gone into Reykjavik and bought one with money from the battery fund. Each of the batteries had a tree for their mess hall. The cheery Christmas trees helped morale a lot.

"Christmas Day was, of course, a holiday. There was only a minimum of duty to perform. Time hung heavy on our hands. Full darkness had returned by the time the movie started. By the time it was over, melancholy set in for everyone. There was a card game for some, and others of us read. But it was a long day for all of us."

December 1942
Nouvion and Biskra, Algeria

Lieutenant Colonel Clyde W. Gabler continues his diary notes.

"The war really went into high gear for the 1st Fighter Group" on 2 December 1942, then-Captain Gabler writes. "Under the orders from Twelfth Air Force, many missions were flown from the Nouvion, Maison Blanche, and Youks-le-Bains locations to targets at Bizerte and Tunis. Some were in escort to our bombers and some were to attack ground targets.

"The 2nd to the 7th of December had been a really tough week with everyone working real hard—the ground crews to maintain the planes, the support people to feed and house, the Intelligence section to receive and forward reports to our command action—all this while mourning the loss of some of our pilots and planes. There were some victories to compensate for our losses. The Luftwaffe was feeling the effect of our campaign. . . .

"Higher Headquarters has decided to get us out of the mud at Nouvion. Our new airfield is to be Biskra, the other side of the Atlas Mountains," he writes in his journal. The move began to materialize 26 December when an Algerian railroad siding was located, with "a mixed train, some boxcars, some flatcars, and a few passenger cars," and with a steam engine bearing the nameplate "Made in Belgium 1922." The crew was French; the brakemen were Algerian. As troop-train commander, Captain Gabler assigned a gentleman from Group HQ to serve as interpreter, Sergeant Randall Cloteaux, who "spoke French fluently except with a Louisiana Cajun accent."

Finally, when everything was loaded—boxes, tents, some vehicles on the flatcars and the troops on the train, ready to depart—the engineer balked, saying it was overloaded and would never get over the mountains. He suggested cutting off four flatcars.

"I knew that if we left the cars behind, we would never see them again, so I insisted that the train move as loaded. With much huffing and puffing, the train headed down the track," Captain Gabler records. "There were frequent stops at small stations along the way mostly for water for the engine. Also, we stopped at all the bridges while the brakemen walked up the track to see if the bridge was still intact.

"Finally, we came to the Atlas Mountains; the grade grew steeper, and the train moved slower and slower. Near the top of the last grade, on the second day, the train puffed to a stop. All personnel were ordered off to push the train. We did, and finally reached the top of the grade, slowed down, and everyone got on board again. The old engine and cars made it over the top of the grade. It was all downhill from there."

On 28 December, the train finally rolled in to the marshaling yard in Biskra, was unloaded, and supplies trucked out to the airfield. Biskra was "an oasis town, as well as a French army-garrison town, home of the 6th Spahis Cavalry Regiment, native Algerian troops with French officers. Well-trained and -disciplined, they took up the duty of perimeter guards for the airfield."

While at Biskra, the men were visited by war correspondent Ernie Pyle who interviewed pilots for his book *Here Is Your War.* Another visitor was *Life* magazine photographer and correspondent Margaret Bourke-White, who photographed B-17 crews and P-38 ground crews.

August–December 1942
Florida to North Africa via SS *Florence Nightingale*

Major John A. Ritner was a newly commissioned second lieutenant in August 1942.

"In September 1942, the 560th Signal Aircraft Warning Battalion was formed at Drew Field [and then] moved by rail to Orlando Army Air Base," Major Ritner reports. "I was assigned as commander of a radar platoon of approximately fifty men in Company C. The major technical equipment in this platoon was an SCR-270, a long-range early-warning radar. Training during September to November 1942 was intense.

Alerted for overseas shipment, the battalion moved by train to Camp Kilmer, New Jersey. "On 12 December, the battalion was loaded aboard the SS *Florence Nightingale*, one of the many Liberty Class ships built by the Henry J. Kaiser Corporation during WWII. The convoy passed through the Strait of Gibraltar on Christmas Eve 1942. The British fortress on the Rock of Gibraltar to the north was in blackout condition, while the city of Tangier in Spanish Morocco to the south was ablaze with lights. The convoy sailed northeast along the Spanish coast on Christmas Day, landing at Oran, North Africa, the day after Christmas in a blinding snowstorm.

"The irony of it all came together when the personnel were ready in their combat gear to off-load at Oran. The Navy refused to allow the officers to debark from the ship until they had paid their mess bills. Ashore, the battalion went into bivouac on the south side of Oran in an area that became known, and endeared to all, as Mud Hill."

7–14 December 1942

Aboard the *Queen Mary*, en Route to Scotland

Colonel Robert J. Greenwald, first lieutenant with 326th Ordnance Company, went by rail from Fort Bragg, North Carolina, to Fort Dix, New Jersey, in June 1942, for immediate shipment overseas.

The 326th was sidelined at Fort Dix, awaiting orders, Colonel Greenwald recalls. Finally, on 7 December, they "were surprised and excited to see we were to embark on the HMT *Queen Mary*. "I was a country boy from Ohio—originally from Akron—and had never been on a big ocean liner," the colonel comments. He and the other company officers were given "a beautiful stateroom with three separate single beds." The troops were in three-high canvas bunks in the lower areas of the ship, all in specially designated red, white, and blue sections, with the ship divided laterally into thirds and the troops wearing color-coded badges to correspond to their sections.

A prewar luxury liner designed to carry 2,000 passengers and 900 crew, the *Queen Mary* was redesigned as a troop carrier in 1940 for a maximum load of 15,000 troops or one complete U.S. infantry division. At the time of the 326th's trip, there were 10,389 troops and 950 crew members. "This was the first trans-Atlantic trip for the *Queen* since her disastrous collision on 27 September 1942, in which she struck the British cruiser HMS *Curacao*, killing nearly 338 of 429 aboard," Colonel Greenwald writes.

After repairs to its bow at Boston Navy Shipyard, the *Queen* was ready and left on 8 December. "I did not know what to expect. First day was not bad," he recalls. "After that, the ship started to roll. I lay down on my bed—sick, like never before. I could not go to the officers' mess. I was *sick* sick. I could not get out of my bed. The ship continued to roll from end to end and side to side, but I did not care. I did not realize the desperate situation we might have been in."

The *Queen* arrived in Gourock, Scotland, near Glasgow, 14 December, with a total travel time of six days and thirty-seven minutes. "The normal, good-weather zigzag travel time was five to six days. This was the North Atlantic in December, absolutely the worst time to cross the ocean."

When visiting London twenty-five years after his *Queen Mary* trip, Colonel Greenwald was listening to the British Broadcasting Company. Retired Cunard Lines Captain Bisset was being interviewed, telling of his wartime experiences as skipper of the *Queen Mary*. "I turned pale when he told of his ship on the trip of 8 December 1942. He told how rough it was and told that we were hit broadside by a 'killer wave,' and he had fears that the mighty *Queen* might capsize."

Even fifty years after his trip, the colonel was in for still another surprise. When he submitted this account of his story to William Winberg, historian of the *Queen Mary*, Mr. Winberg forwarded a group of photos, including one "taken from an RAF flight sent to observe the ship after the storm. The reason the Royal Air Force was called to investigate was that Winston Churchill happened to be aboard, one of the occasional passages he made during the war."

"You never know who your shipmates are until fifty years later," the colonel adds.

December 1942
POW Camp Karenko, Formosa

Colonel Michael A. Quinn continues his POW diary.

"Another month gone and another month closer to you," Colonel Quinn writes to wife Mike on 1 December 1942. On that same date, he notes: "We drew clothes yesterday and you should see them: a jumper and a suit of wood pulp, blue in color and uncertain as to size. They also put out some raw silk underwear. I guess they might be considered shorts. They look like baby panties. We also got gray wood-pulp shirts. All told, the stuff costs 80 yen. Today was payday and I have about 800 yen saved up."

"We received our first issue of soap since we have been prisoners of war," he records on 15 December. "The supply is less than a pound and it is to do us for three months—for toilet, laundry, shaving, and other uses. . . . Was weighed today; score about 124 pounds. Picked up a little."

Colonel Quinn's 29 December entry is devoted to his birthday greeting to son Dick: "Just think, you are six years old. That seems like a short time to some people, but it has been a whole lifetime to you. . . . Sorry I am not with you to wish you many happy returns of the day. Anyway, you know I am thinking about you. . . . I am hoping you are just as cute as you were when I saw you last May . . . and that you will remember me. . . . Any of you kids who come into this world at this time have a bigger job than we had, undoing all the mistakes (and, Lord knows, we made plenty). The only thing I can ask of you is that you try to be true to the ideals that Mother is trying to instill in you."

Mid-December 1942
Hartford, Connecticut

Lieutenant Colonel Norman L. Stevens Jr. was a senior in high school in mid-December 1942 when he and buddy Warren Jones came up with a plan to circumvent their school assignment.

It was late on a Friday afternoon when young Norman and his boyhood chum realized that their book reports for senior English were due on Monday. "The time was getting short, and we either had to start reading or go to Plan B," Colonel Stevens recalls. "Warren came up with an excellent idea. He said if we enlisted in the Army Air Force, we wouldn't have to do the book reports. This seemed perfectly logical to me, so we proceeded to go to Hartford and take the Army Air Force's cadet examination."

Keeping in mind the Air Force slogan, 'We only want the cream of the crop,' the two were among about 150 young men taking the written exam. "And after the written examination, there were probably fifty left," Colonel Stevens recalls. "After lunch, we took the physical exam. One of the enlisted men told me that I had passed all of the physical requirements except that I was three-fourths to one pound underweight. I was 5 feet 11³/₄ inches and weighed 129 pounds. He said that I had to weigh 130 pounds in order to meet the physical requirements.

"The enlisted man then told me, 'Mister, why don't you go across the street to that drug store, have yourself a couple of banana splits and two or three milk shakes, and then come back and weigh in.' Warren said, 'I'll go with you.' He had also passed all of the physical requirements.

"After enjoying the banana splits and milk shakes, we came back across the street and I weighed slightly over 130 pounds. About thirty minutes later, there were perhaps about fifteen of us out of that original 125 to 150, sworn into the United States Army Air Force as privates, awaiting entrance into the cadet program. Warren and I stood in a line abreast as an officer swore us in.

"After the ceremony, Warren looked up at me and said, 'Stevens, if this is the cream of the crop, don't ever show me the milk!'"

JANUARY 1943

14

In January 1943, German U-boats continue assaults on Allied ships in the Atlantic, with losses considered moderate at fifty ships of 261,400 tons. In the air over Europe, the USAAF makes its first raid on Germany against Wilhelmshaven on 27 January. Allied air forces are activated under Major General Carl Spaatz in Africa 5 January; General Mark Clark becomes commander of the U.S. Fifth Army, which becomes operational in Tunisia, 5 January; and General Robert L. Eichelberger takes command of troops in New Guinea 13 January. On Guadalcanal, fighting continues against Japanese positions on Mount Austen in early January and near Kokumbona on 22 January. American troops on the island now number 50,000; Japanese troops, 15,000. As the war continues, President Roosevelt and Prime Minister Churchill and their chiefs of staff meet in Casablanca, 14–24 January. On the last day of the conference, President Roosevelt announces that the Allies will fight for the unconditional surrender of Germany, Italy, and Japan.

January–April 1943

Algiers, Algeria

Lieutenant Colonel Carlos E. Dominguez arrived in England 28 October 1942, assigned to the Intelligence Division of AFHQ.

In late December 1942, "a few days after landing in Algiers, I was called in and informed that I was being designated as Eisenhower's official officer courier and was given a list of instructions—also a revolver instead of a pistol, due to the prevailing fine sand-dust; a bottle of high-octane gasoline; matches and a lighter, plus extra ammunition, which I was to carry always with me in case I was ever forced down by the enemy. The extra ammunition was to hold the enemy at bay until I could destroy whatever I was in charge of," Colonel Dominguez recalls.

"I was told that I would be picked up, at my billet, at 0600 every morning, seven days a week, and brought to headquarters, where I would receive various messages, orders, and instructions to deliver to five different airports in the front. I would then be taken to the Maison Blanche Airport, sixteen miles away, where a French plane would be waiting for me, and to *always* leave not later than

0700. The plane was an old, small Air France plane, with no heating or pressure control, flown by French pilots who spoke no English.

"We had to fly at tree-top-level because the German planes were usually above us but afraid to come down because of the anti-aircraft guns. It was over the Atlas Mountains that we had to be very careful, but the French pilots were well-acquainted with the direction of the prevailing winds and knew how to fly very close to the sides of the mountains where it would be difficult for the Germans to approach.

"Only once did we receive impact of a total of sixteen shots, of which one hit one of our two engines and another went through both ankles of the copilot. We immediately contacted Setif, our next landing place, high up on top of a mountain.

"When we landed, a Red Cross crew was waiting for us but by that time the copilot's legs had swollen and his boots had to be ripped open. That pilot, a very nice and friendly person, never walked again.

"The day after this incident, I had a hard time with the replacement pilots who were reluctant to get into the plane. They kept talking about what had happened the day before. After I took out my pistol, pointed at my watch, and cocked the pistol, they did get into the plane but would not talk to me for two weeks until I explained to their commander, a French major, that I took out the gun to prevent having to bring charges for insubordination in time of war."

January 1943
Biskra, Algeria

Lieutenant Colonel Clyde W. Gabler continues his diary notes.

"At night or dusk, the German Ju-88 bombers would attack the airfield at Biskra—a suitable target since B-17s and P-38s were there in considerable numbers," then-Captain Gabler writes. "On 10 January 1943, we were attacked at dusk. You could hear and see them coming in at a very low altitude—even see the bombs being released from under the wings, as we dove for our foxholes. We lost, destroyed on the ground, three P-38s from the 71st Squadron. Also, the Bomb Group lost some B-17s. . . .

"Just after this Ju-88 raid, the base received an anti-aircraft battalion with 90mm guns. There was no radar at Biskra but the anti-aircraft outfit was equipped with searchlights for night-spotting of enemy aircraft. The visits by the Ju-88s ceased.

"In spite of the excellent guard work by the Spahis Regiment, some saboteurs invaded in the nighttime and placed sticky bombs on several aircraft. These were timebombs that went off, destroying some B-17s. The saboteurs were Arabs, hired and trained in a Nazi school in Bulgaria. The Spahis caught three of them. They were hauled into Biskra and court-martialed, sentenced to be shot. . . .

"The rest of January saw many missions escorting B-17s on raids to Bizerte and Tunis, plus pounding the docks at Ferryville. There were victories and losses." Group history reflects forty-nine of their aircraft missing in action and thirty-nine damaged beyond repair between 4 June 1942 and the end of January 1943. "Our claims were forty-seven enemy aircraft destroyed, fifteen damaged, and six probably destroyed."

January 1943
Over the Pacific, New Hebrides Area

Lieutenant Colonel Robert F. Schnier was a first lieutenant, with 98th Bomb Squadron (H), 11th Group, on Espiritu Santo in 1943.

"It was January 1943. General Nathan Twining and his B-17 crew failed to return from a mission and were considered missing," Colonel Schnier writes. General Twining was chief of staff, Army Air Force, South Pacific, 1942–43.

"Search planes had been sent out for six days trying to locate them. On the last day, I was copilot of one of the flights. We left at daylight and were flying 1,000 feet off the water—about 300 to 400 miles southeast of Espiritu Santo, New Hebrides—when the navigator in the nose of our B-17 sighted two rafts in the distance. The pilot turned the ship over to me and went to radio-in the sighting.

"I lowered the ship to 100 feet off the water and passed over the two rafts, with twelve men aboard, including General Twining. I lowered the flaps and slowed the ship as much as I dared and made four passes, each time dropping food and water for them. We then resumed our normal altitude and returned to base. The next day, a Navy PBY picked up General Twining and his crew.

"This was the biggest thrill in all my experiences during the war. Only one sour note remains: our pilot received the Distinguished Flying Cross, but the rest of the crew didn't receive even a thank you. Still, it was a very successful mission with a happy outcome."

29 January 1943
USS *Montgomery*, off Guadalcanal

Commander Warren L. Craig was an ensign at Pearl Harbor, 7 December 1941,
aboard the destroyer minelayer USS Montgomery, *undamaged in the attack. After*
the bombing, he met up with, and shared uniforms with, twin brother Wesley, who
had escaped the USS Cassin.

From April through December 1942, "we were all doing defensive mining in
such areas as Pago Pago, Samoa; Suva, Fiji; Efate, New Hebrides; Nouméa, New
Caledonia; Tonga, Tabu, Society Islands; and Dutch Harbor, Aleutians. We laid
some 2,600 defensive mines, trying to forestall the advancement of the Japanese
fleet on these waters," Commander Craig writes.

"On 29 January 1943, we left from our mine-assembly depot at Nouméa with
a full load of ninety-four Mark VI contact control mines on our first offensive
mission. Our ship was the USS *Montgomery* (DM-17), along with our sister ships,
Tracy (DM-19) and *Gamble* (DM-15).

"The casings from our mines originally came from the North Sea barrage of
World War I. Each mine held 300 pounds of TNT. This would be sufficient to
break the back of any ship exploding the mine."

Explaining that "our Marines at Guadalcanal were having a hard time" stopping the Japanese Tokyo Express that kept coming down from north of the Solomon Islands at night to resupply troops and supplies, Commander Craig adds:
"After all ships got underway, orders were broken out for instructing us to lay
mines off of Guadalcanal. Our task force was camouflaged, with canvas put over
the mines, so peering eyes of the Japanese patrol craft could not recognize us.

"Before going into battle, all hands put on clean clothes. It was a moonless
night as we steamed alongside of Guadalcanal, smelling the pungent, sweet odor
of land. All of a sudden, gunfire opened on us from shore. We were then no
more than 2,000 yards offshore, getting into position to plant our mine field. As
the *Montgomery* was the only ship at this time with radar, we picked up beeps of
the Tokyo Express coming from the slot. We all were closing on the enemy at
forty-two knots.

"We had just fifteen minutes to plant our mines and arm them in the water.
All ships planted their ninety-four mines and did a 180 turn. We mined at fifteen
knots and got out of there at flank speed, twenty-six knots. This was the first
offensive mine field to claim a victory over the Japanese navy. The mission was
a total success. No U.S. Navy personnel were lost in this engagement; however,
the Japanese Tokyo Express, which steamed right over the mine field, lost a
cruiser, a destroyer, and many barges. The enormous explosions in the night had

sent Japanese destroyers in force to the scene, dropping depth charges on the false assumption that their cruiser had taken a torpedo from an American submarine. The mines had caught the destroyer, with more explosions in the night, and by that time a Japanese naval 'utter commando' tried to take his remaining ships out of the area, only to be crippled by more mines exploding in the field."

Too old and too slow to be in the Navy books as a toast of the fleet, the old World War I destroyer minelayers nevertheless still had a dangerous job to perform and, if lucky, would crawl back home, Commander Craig notes. And they were doing just that, after laying the mines, when the task-force skipper was surprised to see "a big, land-based American airplane swoop low, dip its wings in salute, and then came down again and repeat the salute. This was the way it went all the way back to Espiritu Santo. More American planes came over, tipping their wings to the old, relic minelayers. The three minelayers were getting a royal welcome."

Because they were on radio silence, it was not until their ships docked that "the skippers and their crew understood what chaos the mine field had on the Tokyo Express—the dead ships, the great oil slicks of already sunken ships, the hundreds of survivors clinging to an unbelievable mass of floating wreckage drifting across several miles of ocean." Because this was "a great victory for the mine force, throughout the ranks of the fleet, there was a new pride in the destroyers that laid mines."

On the bridges of the newly honored ships, four Japanese flags were painted. All ship members received the Presidential Unit Citation as well as congratulations from COMSPAC.

January–March 1943
POW Camp Davao, the Philippines

First Lieutenant Hugh H. Roberts continues his diary-letter written from Bilibid Prison, Manila, 26 November 1944, several weeks before his death.

"About the first of January, my beriberi was so painful that I was only receiving one or two hours' sleep out of twenty-four. Once I took dope to get some rest. Many of the men became addicts," Lieutenant Roberts writes.

"During February and March, the men who worked out on the wood-cutting, logging, pasture, hog ranch, chicken ranch, fencing, and a few other details ate very good because they worked without guards and harvested fruit and vegetables for themselves. While they were eating good, I was eating extra poor. All beriberi and malaria patients were removed to another compound, and food already cooked was shipped over in boxes, and there was very little of it. At one time, half the camp was unable to work. I went to quarters 1 December 1942 and went back to work about September 1943, three months of it in the hospital. I was in the hospital with asmatic [*sic*] pressure. My tissue would not hold water and it came out through sores around my ankles. My blood pressure dropped 90/60 or lower, as it was that later when I was working.

"In January 1943, before we ran out of cassava, I got scurvy and my mouth got so sore I couldn't chew rice and had to swallow it straight. Some lemons were brought in and issued one per man, but the doctor gave me four. It was painful eating them but they contain more vitamin C than any other food and they cured me.

"Before I got it again, the cassava ran out and we were issued cang cong greens and they contained enough vitamin C. About January first, the Japs shipped in some vitamin B-1 and all beriberi patients received shots of it, and it saved my life. Beriberi is neuritis due to lack of B-1. It is rotting of nerves and starts in the feet."

As he writes in 1944, he says, "I still have beriberi." He adds: "Many big, husky men would sit up holding their feet in their hands and cry like babies from the pain."

January 1943
POW Camp Karenko, Formosa

Colonel Michael A. Quinn continues his POW diary.

"My first correspondence of the year, and appropriately, as all my thoughts are for you, I send it to you," Colonel Quinn writes to wife Mike on 1 January 1943. "I imagine you are celebrating and I hope you are thinking of me as much as I think of you. . . . Last night I went to a phonograph concert. It seemed to be an all-waltz program. The Japs allowed services at 10 o'clock . . . [and] at 8:30 we had a formation and salute for the emperor. It was lucky the Nips didn't hear what the real salutations were," he continues on New Year's Day.

On 2 January, he adds: "We had our party last night with all the old songs (no one knows any new ones) and a few recitations." On 29 January, he writes: "The papers claim that all American phonograph records are to be destroyed, as they are demoralizing and indicate a depraved nature. So I guess those records we have managed to collect will be destroyed."

Though the year is new, much remains the same for the POWs: rumors persist, the amount of food continues to be sparse, and the Japanese taunt that "there will be good news" for them this month. When General Parker asks to be excused from hard work, he is informed: "After February, it might be unnecessary."

"I don't know what that means and neither does anybody else," Colonel Quinn comments, but by 2 February he notes: "We are all waiting for the big news, but so far nothing has happened. . . . Something must have gone wrong because they [the sentries] are certainly raising hell." [There is no further entry referring to the "good news."]

In other January entries, Colonel Quinn writes of adding to their minifarm of ninety chickens and twenty pigs with twenty-two goats; reading *Jane Eyre* and "getting hold of some Sherlock Holmes stories"; serving guard duty at the hospital "because of the serious condition of some of our patients"; and buying a canteen as a birthday gift for son Dick.

"Nuñez Pilet caught it from a sentry for eating after work, which might as well have been any one of us because, strange as it may seem, we try to hold out a little bit to eat between meals, as it takes away that awful craving for food. The rice doesn't last long with you anyway," he records on 15 January.

November 1942–January 1943
Camp Barkeley, Texas

Chief Warrant Officer Edward G. Robertson and First Lieutenant Helene Stewart Robertson served aboard the U.S. Army Hospital Ship Shamrock. *They provide background on the formation of the 202nd Hospital Ship Company.*

"What goes into the organization of a hospital ship before it can sail the seven seas on its errands of mercy?" Second Lieutenant James R. Arata asks and then answers his own question, as editor of *Shamrock News and Views* in March 1943: "It all began last fall—a special order from the War Department—some special correspondence—and presto! On 12 November 1942, three hospital ship companies were activated, assigned to the SOS (Service of Supply), and attached to the 8th Service Command. Something entirely new, the floating Army hospital, was to prove its worth at Camp Barkeley, Texas, and later at sea. From all corners of the United States, men gathered at Camp Barkeley to form the 202nd Hospital Ship Company . . . finally [growing] accustomed to serving a hospital ship without the ship."

The original cadre—seventeen men from Fort Knox, Kentucky, accompanied by Captain Herman L. Watson and including Sergeant Edward G. Robertson—began functioning 7 November 1942, "housed in old Civilian Conservation Corps hutments near the 94th General Hospital in Camp Barkeley." On 28 November, another cadre arrived from William Beaumont General Hospital,

Fort Bliss, El Paso, Texas. They were joined the next day by a group from Brooks General Hospital, Fort Sam Houston, San Antonio, Texas. On 5 and 10 January 1943, newcomers from the Presidio of Monterey, California, arrived.

"Around the beginning of January, the Fort Devens group completed its strenuous basic training and went into technical work. No more night hikes and tent-pitching for a while," the newsletter notes. "On 15 January 1943, a contingent of thirty-two sunny Californians rumbled into camp in four large trucks. . . . They completed their basic training, which included gas attacks, the obstacle course, films, films, and more films, some theoretical bandaging, lectures and more lectures, and had in the meantime one grand time growing acquainted with all the men. Then followed the more serious business of technical training for the California boys, interspersed with frequent trips to Abilene and occasional poker games."

FEBRUARY 1943

15

"Prior to Kasserine Pass in Tunisia, our Army ordnance supplies were becoming exhausted. After cannibalizing what ordnance equipment that we could, we welded parts together. Our 'forward' Ordnance Supply Depot was receiving no supplies and we were instructed not to go back beyond the field depot for supplies. We had to take action." This is the way Lieutenant Colonel Nathan A. Allen Jr. recalls his days as a lieutenant in Algeria and Tunisia, where he served as a supply officer of the 109th Ordnance Company of Major General Lloyd Fredendall's II Corps.

"I heard of an Ordnance Base Depot at Constantine, Algeria, and drove back to it, some 320 miles," he writes. Upon arrival, he came face to face with Colonel Urban Niblo, who knew him. "He quickly reminded me that I had disobeyed orders by coming to the rear, and proceeded to bawl me out. However, I was just mad enough to stand my ground," Colonel Allen states, recalling that he then informed the colonel that they were not receiving ordnance supplies up front; that they were welding parts together; and now that they were "getting low on welding rods, I am going to obtain some before I return to the front to carry out our assigned mission."

"At this point, Colonel Niblo turned and asked another colonel when he had last sent supplies to the front. The colonel replied that he never had been told to send supplies up front. I must say, if I thought I got bawled out, the colonel was chewed out to a fare-thee-well, and was ordered to give me everything I needed," Colonel Allen adds. "I returned to the front with a 2^1/$_2$-ton truck loaded with supplies. This was the same old story: 'Peacetime officers, waiting for detailed instructions.' Thank God for the Reserves who were there to get the job done."

In other war-related activity in February 1943, the USS *Dorchester*, with the Four Chaplains, goes down off Greenland, 3 February; convoy SC-118 in the Atlantic is attacked by twenty U-boats, 4–9 February, losing twenty of sixty-three ships; 77th Indian Brigade, the Chindits, led by General Wingate, makes its first raid in Burma, 8 February; the Japanese evacuate their last forces from Guadalcanal 9 February; Sixth American Army becomes operational in the Southwest Pacific under General Walter Krueger 18 February; U.S. Task Group, under

Admiral C. H. McMorris, shells Japanese on Attu Island, the Aleutians, 18–19 February; and Operation Cleanslate troops occupy Banika and Pavuvi, Russell Islands, the Solomons, 21 February.

February–March 1943

Constantine, Algeria, to Kasserine Pass, Tunisia

Lieutenant Colonel Nathan A. Allen Jr. was in Northern Ireland in May 1942, one month after call-up. By November, he was in North Africa.

In his diary on 9 February 1943, Lieutenant Allen writes: "Thelepte Airport [Tunisia] was bombed again." On 10 February, he notes: "We had a snowstorm all afternoon." And then, "it snowed again" on the 11th.

On 15 February, the date of the beginning of the Battle of Kasserine Pass, Lieutenant Allen writes: "Thelepte Airport was heavily bombed twice. Our Army was retreating, so we moved back thirteen miles, which left a mountain pass in front of us. At noon, Johnson and I went up front to deliver supplies to the 168th Combat Team. We volunteered, as the contact party failed to find the 168th. We contacted the front infantrymen and found that the 168th had been captured."

Providing background, Colonel Allen explains: "General Fredendall had reorganized the divisions of II Corps into combat teams. All the teams were understrength in personnel and in equipment—75 percent equipped was the general rule. Field Marshal Erwin Rommel and his Afrika Korps attacked at Kasserine Pass on 15 February 1943, breaking through easily with his superior force."

Writing in his diary on 17 February, Lieutenant Allen continues: "We retreated again. Moved eight miles northeast of Tébessa. Had another snowstorm. Our old area was strafed just after we moved out." And then on 18 February: "We retreated again. Moved thirty-five miles northwest of Tébessa."

On 22 February, he writes: "At noon, we were told to move back again as the Germans had broken through at Kasserine Pass [on 20 February], and were but a few miles away. . . . We received orders to evacuate. . . . We moved in rain and over a muddy road with narrow bridges, which was very dangerous. Moved ten miles north of Clairfontain."

His 24 February entry notes: "The German army has been stopped, so we moved up to a point twenty-six miles northwest of Tébessa, near Haidra. Our Army is fighting with 75 percent and less of authorized equipment."

Colonel Allen says that a delegate from General Eisenhower visited the front during the attack and found General Fredendall "eighty miles back of the front line and everything in chaos." He was relieved by Major General George S. Patton Jr., who brought additional troops with him. "Patton resulted in a complete change. We suffered no more setbacks and obtained considerably more equipment. Patton didn't go through regular channels, but ordered equipment in the States, sent directly to us and other units. His word carried weight—lots of it!"

In his 26 February diary entry, Lieutenant Allen writes: "I drove up beyond Thala [in Tunisia] and viewed the recent battleground. There are lots of wrecked and burnt German tanks. Two of them still had charred bodies. The American and British armies now have the Germans on the run."

Writing that previously "we saw very few American planes," he records the following for 17 and 21 March, respectively: "We are beginning to see more American planes, especially the last two days" and "[t]oday there was wave after wave of bombers and fighters crossing overhead toward the enemy." Though the 30,000 men of II Corps suffered more than 20 percent casualties in the Battle of Kasserine Pass with 300 dead, 3,000 wounded, and 3,000 missing or taken prisoner Colonel Allen says, "We were really *not defeated*, as Rommel had been stopped." Rommel returned to Germany in March, the Germans surrendered in North Africa on 13 May, and in July "we boarded ship for Sicily, but the campaign there was going so well that we disembarked and stayed in Northern Africa all summer."

February 1943
Kasserine Pass, Tunisia

Lieutenant Colonel Warren E. Huguelet was a major, assistant G-3 with Headquarters, U.S. 1st Armored Division (1AD), when he reported to Headquarters II Corps at Constantine, Algeria, to serve as senior combat liaison officer.

"Saint Valentine's Day will be well remembered by those who tried to stop Rommel on 14 February 1943 and the days to come," Colonel Huguelet notes. "Both sides had personnel problems in the higher echelons. . . . After breaking through Kasserine Pass, Rommel favored Tébessa as his next objective. The U.S. supply dump there was a rich prize, but he also was committed to making a thrust to capture Thala, where the British controlled an important route to northern Tunisia. The prong aimed at Tébessa included Italian armor and was meeting increased resistance as U.S. forces under Combat Command B (CC/B) deployed to intercept it.

"The other prong, moving from Kasserine Pass to Thala, pursued British armor, which finally withdrew to its 'tank harbor' for the night. However, some German crews manned captured U.S. tanks and tailed the British column without detection. The surprised British lost most of their tanks, creating a major crisis."

Back at HQ on the wintry evening of 20 February, II Corps was utilizing some modern buildings of a mining operation at Kouif, the colonel recalls. Soon, Colonel Huguelet says, he was alerted "to make a trip to Thala to contact U.S. officers in charge of the advance detail of the 9th Division Artillery, which was completing a 600-mile forced march from Algeria." He was to "ascertain that they had arrived as ordered, that they had concluded preliminary plans with the British for giving artillery support in the morning, and that there were no new problems."

Recalling that trip, with Private Langham serving as his driver, he writes: "Recent snows and rain had made driving conditions terrible. Vehicles tried to use the center of the road, plus all-wheel drive, to keep moving. The artillery pieces, all towed guns, frequently jackknifed or slid off the road. . . .

"Roadside markers showed where to turn off the road for the CP of 9th Division Artillery. There, I asked for the officer in charge, who appeared a few minutes later, a lieutenant colonel named Westmoreland, I believe. He had just come from the British CP where his mission was reviewed, detailing where to locate his artillery for the expected attack in the morning. As he had no new problems, I left for II Corps to make my report, bucking four battalions of towed artillery heading for Thala. It was a grim and desperate sight."

After making his report to II Corps, Major Huguelet was immediately told to drive to HQ 1AD "to see if they could spare twenty cyclists in the morning. Why they didn't ask by phone, I'll never know," the colonel acknowledges. On the drive to Division CP, he noticed something different: "It was not an *order*, but a *request* that allowed the subordinate unit to make a choice."

En route, he was stopped at an MP post on the eastern edge of Tébessa. He recalls the scene: "One electric light on in the roadway disclosed a 3/4-ton C&R car near the sentry station. The MP explained that he couldn't direct the driver on how to get to HQ 1st Infantry Division, as his information was out-of-date. An Army sergeant was attending a man, resting on a cot, who showed extreme fatigue and frustration after a long, cold blackout ride. He was attempting to rejoin his command in their hour of need. He was Brigadier General Theodore R. Roosevelt of the 1st Infantry Division—son of President Teddy Roosevelt—who had been seeing some of the far-flung units of that division. The needed directions were given to the sergeant, and I proceeded to HQ 1AD, where the cycle request was received by Major General Orlando Ward and Colonel Grant Williams, chief of staff. No mission for the cycles had been stated, so I was asked for my opinion. I turned 'thumbs down,' which became the answer to HQ II Corps.

"It was still dark when I went to bed and slept an hour or so. . . . Seeking an answer for all the vacant rooms, I went to the operations area where the G-3 sat alone behind a table. His words were: 'You are in charge now.' He pointed to a place on his map about fifty miles west of Headquarters British First Army; said, 'We are going there'; then took his maps and walked out of the building to a column of vehicles waiting to depart from Kouif. Apparently, the plan was to use the twenty cycles for traffic control!

"No directive was given to stand fast, withdraw or advance, or to turn over my authority to a ranking general. There was nothing in writing. I hadn't even been provided a sandwich for lunch! The only piece of GI equipment that was left in the building was a telephone."

Realizing that Thala was most vulnerable and that time was an important factor, Major Huguelet phoned and immediately got through to General Ward. "I then authorized him to take command of all 1st Armored Division units and then directed him to attack Kasserine Pass, using the same axis as CC/B. These orders were quickly acknowledged. Then I asked him to stop at II Corps Headquarters, if he could. I wanted him to witness the current situation. He and his G-3, Lieutenant Colonel Hamilton H. Howze, appeared in minimum time, followed by the lead vehicles of Headquarters 1st AD."

"Inherent in the offensive plan was the simple, age-old doctrine of 'cut 'em off at the pass," he explains. "Like Custer, Rommel had divided his force after getting through Kasserine Pass. One prong, which he favored, was aimed at the valuable U.S. dumps located at Tébessa. The other prong went north to Thala, which provided a route to northern Tunisia and was now under British command.

"With CC/B now backed up by the 1st Armored Division itself, the plan should be able to aggravate the Tébessa prong by this increasing pressure. Thus, Rommel's own radio net would be telegraphing these increasing threats for him to add to whatever else needed attention. And if Thala wasn't too important to Rommel, effort in that direction might slack off. Then, of course, as the 1st Armored Division regrouped, it could be the factor that sealed off both prongs at their base, Kasserine Pass.

"Slowly, and with skill, Rommel disengaged and withdrew to the east. He still hadn't cleared Kasserine Pass by 25 February. Headquarters II Corps had survived the trauma of the past week and had 'stayed at home' at Kouif. Now, once again, it was in a relaxed mode. The 'green troops' were now pushing the Afrika Korps eastward."

At midday 25 February, after Major Huguelet had resumed liaison functions at Headquarters II Corps, the captain S-2 of 12th Air Support Command was seeking an operations or intelligence officer to process an incoming tactical message. Unable to locate anyone, he turned to Major Huguelet. The message indicated that a large bomber force, taking advantage of the good weather, had just made a run on Kasserine Pass but, on seeing trucks they believed to be American in the pass, dropped the intended bombs on a secondary target of little tactical value.

Although technically he says the affair might have been out of his jurisdiction, Major Huguelet reacted immediately with the observation that "Americans don't lead an attack with trucks. Our troops haven't even reached the pass. Those are Rommel's trucks. Call for another mission."

The captain went to telephone the order for another mission while Major Huguelet called Headquarters 1AD and talked to Captain Kermut Wilson, on duty in the G-3 section, "who confirmed that our troops had not reached the pass."

"The Air S-2 confirmed that a second mission had been approved and was on the way, which scattered Rommel's trucks all over the pass and made Rommel get out of his vehicle and jump in the ditch, as reported by David Irving in *The Trail of the Fox*."

In summary, Colonel Huguelet adds, "How can some say that Americans suffered a great defeat 14 to 26 February 1943 at the Battle of Kasserine Pass? Too much uncorrected, poor leadership in high places was a heavy, early burden that needs more objective study. It would seem that eliminating the Tébessa and Thala prongs, as well as the retirement of Rommel to Faïd, was a considerable victory in itself."

February 1943
Algeria to Kasserine Pass, Tunisia

Lieutenant Colonel Clyde W. Gabler continues with his diary notes.

"In February 1943, the sirocco winds came across the Sahara Desert to the airfield at Biskra. This just tied up everything. The sand and the dust got into the engines and all other parts of the airplane, making maintenance almost impossible. These windstorms would last two or three days. The only way to breathe was to put a wet towel over your head and hole-up in a tent or bunker," then-Captain Gabler writes.

"Of course, the thing now was to plan another move," he notes. And so, from 8 to 15 February, Headquarters, the 27th, 94th, and 71st Squadrons made their move to Chateau-Dun-du-Rhumel, Algeria. Their new airfield, north of the Atlas Mountains, provided a slightly better climate. It also placed them closer to some of their target areas, such as Tunis Harbor, Sfax Airdrome, and Bizerte.

"The 1st Fighter Group set up business on the edge of town in an area that had been a horse-racing track. Just beyond, a runway had been scraped on the soil by the engineers. . . .

"Down the road that passed our airfield was the HQ 5th Bomb Wing and a few miles more, the 97th Bomb Wing. About twelve miles farther east, the 31st General Hospital had been set up to receive casualties from the impending battles.

"On 19 February 1943, the Germans under General von Arnim hit the Kasserine Pass just to the east of us with a vengeance. They engaged the 1st Infantry Division and the U.S. II Corps in a furious battle that drove our troops back, including the 1st Armored Division.

"Two of our P-38 fighter squadrons were put to work, strafing the short but deadly enemy offensive. Our S-2 section posted the bomb line hourly. Several missions were flown in support of our ground troops. Our pilots did well in adjusting so quickly from escort duty to low-level, close, ground support. Between missions, after refueling and reloading the aircraft, our ground crews could see on the road passing our airfield the long lines of ambulances heading toward the 31st General Hospital to the west."

Winter 1942–43
Sbeitla and Kasserine Pass, Tunisia

Chaplain (Colonel) Harry P. Abbott continues his story of service in North Africa.

Chaplain Abbott tells of being bivouacked for a time at Sbeitla and then being ordered to Maktar. "Here for the first time, American troops operated under command of the French XIX Army Corps, with Combat Command B, under General P. M. Robinett, playing an important and decisive part. Here the chaplains of Command B established a forward cemetery, as had to be done prior to each action in which we participated. A suitable place (for this temporary cemetery) was located directly back of a beautiful church. . . .

"While we were burying our dead, the enemy planes would sometimes strafe the town or drop a bomb here and there, much to our discomfort. It was for service rendered in this area that I was awarded the croix de guerre, with gold star, by the French."

Ordered back to Sbeitla, the chaplains and their drivers moved on in the dark in one of the smaller jeeps, known as *peeps*. With the enemy ahead and since it was late, "we were further persuaded by the offer of some French-fried potatoes" to remain overnight in the quarters of the French chaplain but were awakened about 0200 with news that the Americans were withdrawing.

"After refueling our peep, we kept on going to an ammunition dump at Tébessa. With news reporters Hal Boyle and A. A. Devine, I waited, occasionally hearing enemy planes overhead in the darkness and the chilly rain. Soon we were all together and the chaplains stopped near Tébessa at sight of a Red Cross, . . . the dispensary for the railroad unit nearby. . . . They treated us like kings. We received real, white bread (it seemed like cake) for the first time in months, and coffee, jelly, and meat. . . .

"Soon we reorganized and moved out near Haidra. Even though roads were muddy and it was raining, it did not deter us because we were going in the direction we wanted to go—against the enemy. The forward elements had moved on to Kasserine Pass CP location. Ours was the last vehicle to move across that road before enemy fire was laid on it. . . .

"It was while we were at Kasserine Pass that three enemy planes came over the CP of Combat Command B and strafed the area. I remember flinging myself over the side of a hill and hugging Mother Earth during this brief interlude. Immediately thereafter, a lone plane dived from the clouds above and came down with his guns barking and hit Captain Quentin Roosevelt. I was one of the first to reach him and immediately went for a medico who soon attended his wounds and sent him to a hospital from which he was later evacuated to the United States. I was told he returned to the scene of action as soon as he had recovered. He was an artillery officer and a son of Brigadier General T. R. Roosevelt Jr. [who was son of President Theodore R. Roosevelt]."

Chaplain Abbott writes that during action, "young men took on a different attitude. They seemed to age ten years in a few days. Men who had been eager to get into the fray, after having met the Mark VIs and having had some of their tanks shot out from under them, were a little more sober, more judicious and, if possible, more determined toward ultimate victory."

Recalling one occasion when a reserve tank battalion had requested services, Chaplain Abbott writes: "When the chaplain arrived, all were assembled under the trees. Everyone was there. The chaplain spoke and said, 'Men, how does it happen we have such a large attendance today? Back at Fort Knox, I had to urge some of you to go to church.' One sergeant spoke up and said, 'Chaplain, those German 88s are making believers out of us.'"

1 February 1943–September 1943
Egypt to Algeria

First Lieutenant Jerome A. Freedman was an Army Air Force pilot, aboard the SS Mariposa *that left Norfolk, Virginia, 20 December 1942.*

"We sailed unescorted for forty days before landing in Egypt on 1 February 1943, outfitted with Arctic equipment, including snowshoes!" Lieutenant Freedman reports. Among his duties, he flew supplies and equipment to forward units during Rommel's retreat from Alamein and acted as liaison pilot to members of the Royal Air Force. "After following Rommel's forces across North Africa, we spent some time around 10 March in the mountains near Oran, training British army pilots to fly Horsa gliders for the invasion of Sicily. Later, during the summer months of 1943, we were stationed in the desert, where many of the men lost fifteen to twenty pounds because it was too hot to eat. We also had our water rationed because it had to be hauled in."

On 6 September 1943, Lieutenant Freedman was transferred on TD to Headquarters Twelfth Air Force "to fly General Dwight D. Eisenhower to meetings with Field Marshal H. R. Alexander and Admiral A. B. Cunningham, on whose ship I was billeted. It was my privilege and pleasure to have my 'short-snorter' signed by all three men, as well as by comedian Jack Benny, singer Peter Lind Hays, and many of my close friends." [The "short-snorter" was a form of currency on which autographs were usually collected. At times, it might be a collection of bills, taped together into a long chain, representing all of the countries an individual had visited. At a bar, the person with the shortest short-snorter usually paid for the round of drinks.]

28 February 1943
Mission Down in Sahara Desert, Chad

Lieutenant Colonel John E. Senn was a second lieutenant, assigned as co-pilot to the Africa–Middle-East Wing of the Air Transport Command in Accra, Gold Coast (now Ghana).

Providing background, Colonel Senn writes: "The grand strategy, developed by President Roosevelt and Prime Minister Churchill, was to have United States forces, which had recently invaded North Africa, drive Marshal Rommel's Afrika Korps toward the east and to have the British Eighth Army drive them to the west toward Tunisia. U.S. forces also were supposed to assist the Free French Forces with their part in the grand strategy. General Philippe Leclerc was to command the Free French Camel Corps and to proceed north from Brazzaville, Congo, to Libya to close the gap between the U.S. and British flanks. A good

plan, strategically and politically. Tactically, U.S. forces, operating out of Fort
Lamy (now N'Djamena), Chad, were to provide aerial supply to the Free French
Forces en route to Libya.

"By the time the orders had filtered down to the 12th Transport Group, only
one C-47 and one four-man crew was assigned to the mission (the French did
supply a navigator who spoke no English). Loading up with full fuel tanks, blankets, straw ticks, and food, plus truck engines and a full cargo of gasoline in
drums, we left Fort Lamy and headed north about 1,000 miles to a French desert
outpost, Sabha, Libya. We delivered our cargo of gasoline and truck engines.

"After an overnight camp-out in our C-47, we pulled our own daily inspection,
but were unable to refuel due to lack of local supplies. With aerial cover provided
by one Westland Lysander with two .30-caliber machine guns, we started out
with ten ambulatory wounded Congolese soldiers toward another FFI [French
Forces of the Interior] fort where we expected to refuel. We never found it, due
partially to lack of adequate maps and partly to a harmattan (a desert duststorm
that greatly reduces visibility). We then realized we were lost in the center of the
Sahara Desert.

"In those days, radio was in its comparative infancy; we had no UHF, VHF,
or automatic compass. With our most powerful liaison radio and trailing
antenna, we were barely able to raise the U.S. Air Base at Maiduguri, Nigeria,
and obtain a bearing toward them. We reduced engine power to conserve fuel
and headed in that direction. We were about 500 miles away. By this time, we
had flown more than eight hours on a normal ten-hour fuel supply. We knew we
could not make it.

"As we flew along that bearing, at an altitude where we could barely make out
objects on the ground, we decided that our chances would be better if we could
land while we still had some power. By this time, all four fuel gauges indicated
Empty. When we crossed a trail, we advised Maiduguri that we were turning right
and would attempt a crash-landing as soon as we saw a level spot. (Later, we
learned that if we had turned left, we would have reached a French emergency
field that was not on our charts. It was between Mao and Rig Rig, Chad.) The
landing was made among ten-foot-high scrub brush and was not too bad. The
wings and tail were torn up by thorn bushes.

"During these eight days, crew members made several fruitless forays into the
countryside. We were able to hand-start the left engine to generate electricity to
operate our strongest radio transmitter. Thus, we had occasional contact with
Maiduguri.

"Only one airplane in our part of the world, a C-60, had a Bendix radio compass that could receive on the only frequency we could use. That airplane had been in India for six weeks, but came by Maiduguri in time to join in the search. They found us. We were about 200 miles away from our goal. (The note they dropped is still at the Air Force Museum in Dayton, Ohio.)

"The rest is anticlimax. A C-47 was flown in to the auxiliary field and a jeep drove the fifty miles to evacuate the four-man U.S. crew and the natives; the French navigator walked off and was never heard from again. After a week in the hospital for dehydration, the U.S. crew returned to duty.

"The airplane received a new wing and tail and was flown to Accra for a depot inspection and repair. On it first flight after being returned to service, a new crew flew it into a cliff and it was *finis*."

3–6 February 1943
Fort Eustis, Virginia

Captain James L. Swauger claims that he was "dragged, kicking and screaming into the U.S. Army at the behest of my local Board as of 5 November 1942," surviving "Fort Eustis, Camp David, Camp Stewart, Camp Gordon, England, France, Luxembourg, Belgium, and Germany" before returning "to the bosom of my family on 9 April 1946."

"One might say there were many memorable moments (MMMs)" but the one that he recalls "with most fondness, the height of my military career as I see it," occurred in basic training on the evening of 6 February 1943 at Fort Eustis in the barracks of Training Battery A-14th, 1st Platoon. He recounts that MMM:

"Some person had secreted ten rounds of .50-caliber ammunition under the 3rd Platoon's barracks. In an effort to have him who had 'stolen' and secreted the rounds confess, the battery was condemned to scrub barracks floors until said confession emerged.

"Scrub them we did. The nights of the 3rd, 4th, and 6th, we scrubbed them three times; the night of the 5th, we scrubbed them four times. Our floors had always been very, very clean; now they became bone-white. We stole salt from the mess hall and applied it to the floors. We bought lye. We scrubbed with brushes on long handles, with brooms, with scrub brushes on our hands and knees, with rags, and with squeegees. Our hands became as white as the floors, our knees became sore, and gradually we began to look on the whole thing as a big joke. The men on our floor, the second, began to find amusement in singing. We sang 'Beer, Beer, Beer,' 'The Caissons Are Rolling Along,' 'My Blue Heaven,' and anything else that came to mind.

"About the middle of the second evening's songfest (this would be on the 6th), the noise from A-14th became deafening, for the whole battery was now howling songs, and General Stockton himself, the camp commander, over on the other side of camp, must have heard us. It was too much for First Sergeant Johns. Over the P.A. system, he bawled, 'Cut out that noise.' We heard him, of course, but we paid no attention to him, singing louder than ever. Then came a little squeak over the P.A.—some Battery C.Q. taking his life in his hands for our sakes: 'Johns is on his way to the 1st Platoon.' A moment of silence hit us, a moment during which we heard Johns' running feet as he neared the barracks, heard the screen door slam, heard him hit the stairs to our floor. In a flash of genius, I burst joyfully into 'The Star-Spangled Banner.'

"I can never forget the next few minutes. Johns had made it to the head of the stairs, and there he stood, rooted to the floor, half at attention, chest heaving with effort and rage, glaring at us as we bellowed, '. . . the land of the free and the home of the brave," as we scrubbed. We reached the end of the song and watched his red, red face with its blown-out cheeks; his red, red neck with chords stretched out on it; his red, red hands, clenching and unclenching. I was too near the front of the barracks and Johns to take any initiative, but behind me, lost in the platoon, some brave soul began to hum the national anthem, and all of us took it up. Johns quit. 'Bunch of G.D. wise bastards,' he said and turned to clump down the stairs. We had won.

"I wondered then, and I wonder now, whether his swift exit was occasioned to reach the outside before he burst out laughing, or whether it was to give him time alone to plot revenge. In any event, the floor scrubbing was canceled as of the next morning.

"I believe that was the highlight of my military career, that decision to bellow out 'The Star-Spangled Banner' at a perilous moment as Johns bounded up our barracks stairs. Certainly, nothing that the Nazi hordes ever threw in my direction was as terrifying as the possible action of a Sergeant Johns. The next three years or so were all downhill after the evening of 6 February 1943."

"Soldiers: All of us have been in battle. But due to circumstances beyond the control of anyone, we have heretofore fought separately. In our most battle [*sic*], we shall for the first time on this continent, have many thousands of Americans united in one command—the II Army Corps—in union there is strengnt [*sic*]!"

Thus the memo begins—with typos and style intact—as General George S. Patton Jr. addresses his troops in Africa in General Orders No. 16, dated 12 March 1943. His order continues:

Our duty, as told to us by the great President, is plain. We must utterly defeat the enemy. Fortunately for our fame as soldiers, our enemy is worthy of us. The German is a war-trained veteran—confident, brave and ruthless. We are brave. We are better-equipped, better-fed, and in the place of his blood-glutted *woten* we have with us the God of Our Fathers Known of Old. The justice of our cause, and the greatness of our race makes us confident. But we are not ruthless, and not vicious, not aggressive; there in lies our weakness.

Children of a free and sheltered people who have lived a generous life, we have not the pugnacious disposition of those oppressed beasts, our enemies, who must fight or starve. Our bravery is too negative. We talk too much of sacrifice, of the glory of dying that freedom may live. Of course we are willing to die but that is not enough; we must be eager to kill, to inflict on the enemy—the hated enemy— wounds, death and destruction. If we die killing, well and good, but if we fight hard enough, viciously enough, we will kill and live. Live to return to our family and our girl as conquering heroes—men of Mars.

The reputation of our army, the future of our race, your own glory rests in your hands. I know you will be worthy.

The typed signature and identification reads: *G. S. Patton, Jr., Major General, U.S. Army, Commanding.*

Lieutenant Colonel Nathan A. Allen Jr. had saved the memo, the first order received from General Patton, which he labels "a classic, and typical of General Patton."

In other war-related activity in March 1943, the U.S. Eighth Air Force bombs targets in Wilhelmshaven, Germany; American forces re-enter Sbeitla, Tunisia, 2 March; U.S. forces are victorious over the Japanese in the Battle of the Bismarck Sea, 2–4 March; U.S. cruisers and destroyers bombard Japanese airfields at Munda and Vila, the Solomons; the Chindits and the U.S. Tenth Air Force, demolish railroad sections between Nankan and Bongyaung, Burma, 6 March; the U.S. Fourteenth Air Force is activated 10 March in China under command of Major General Claire Chennault; the U.S. 17th Fleet is formed 15 March to operate in the New Guinea area; and Admiral McMorris's squadron battles Admiral Hosogaya's off the Komandorski Islands in the Bering Sea, 26 March.

March–April 1943
Tunisia, North Africa

Chaplain (Colonel) Harry P. Abbott continues his story of service in North Africa.

"After Kasserine Pass, we pushed on and retook Sbeitla and other points and stopped at Maknassy, where American troops, including a task force under Colonel [C.C.] Benson and one battalion of the famous 13th Armored Regiment, continued their drive on the Germans toward Gafsa, ultimately joining up with the British Eighth Army," Chaplain Abbott writes.

"In the early stages of the campaign, it seemed we were outnumbered in the air, but as the war progressed, our forces grew until we finally had complete domination of the skies. It was a great sight to see American bombers and fortresses (at one time I counted ninety-six Flying Fortresses) in the air on their way to bomb Naples, Sousse, Bizerte, or Tunis. Each time (although the men in planes were unaware of it), cheers arose from the men on the ground, whose morale was materially raised by these welcome sights. Each time they returned, the men would count them and offer prayers that any missing might come on in."

"There were no atheists in the front lines," Chaplain Abbott writes in 1946 in a variation of the oft-quoted line, "There are no atheists in the foxholes," attributed to Chaplain William Thomas Cummings from a Bataan field sermon in 1942. "Yes, the men had church services right up at the front. In fact, they demanded them, and I believe they were better soldiers with the increased fortitude their religion afforded them. Sometimes we improvised the 'peep' hood for an altar, sometimes used a mess table; sometimes only with a group, no music, we held a service with just a talk by the chaplain and the Lord's Prayer. Most of the time, however, we took our folding organ and held regular religious services, which seemed most appreciated by the men."

13 March 1943
Mission to Burma, Near Rangoon

Lieutenant Colonel Felix R. Bailey was a first lieutenant, Tenth Air Force, 7th Bomb Group (H), 9th Bomb Squadron (H).

On the morning of 13 March, Lieutenant Bailey was flying left wing in the flight of four B-24 bombers dispatched to bomb the Pazundaung Railway Bridge, a vital link in the north–south supply line of the Japanese in Burma. Captain Baldwin was leading the flight; First Lieutenant Gordon Wilson was flying right wing; and First Lieutenant Short was flying the number-four position to complete a diamond formation.

While still over the ocean, about forty miles south of the target in Rangoon, the flight was intercepted by approximately fifteen Japanese fighters, both single-engine and twin-engine, Colonel Bailey recalls. "They commenced a fifty-five-minute running battle with determined effort and daring. As the bombers settled down on the bomb run, with bomb-bay doors open, the fighters began to press their attacks even harder, flying through their own anti-aircraft fire."

While the fighters and anti-aircraft fire were successful in knocking out two engines on identical wings of both the lead and the number-four ships, "a good bomb run was nevertheless completed, with an excellent pattern of bombs on the target. After bomb release, the lead ship turned south to get back over the water and reduce the time that the fighters would be able to stay with them. The pilot of the lead ship appeared to be having difficulty maintaining control and started losing altitude. The fighters stayed with them and it was noticed that many of the guns were idle."

With this in mind and the fact that the formation was breaking up because of the crippled ships, Lieutenant Bailey elected to stay with the lead ship while Lieutenant Wilson picked up the number-four ship. For Lieutenant Bailey, the tactic was to maneuver his ship as a foil between the fighters and the crippled ship and to use his guns to help break off the fighter passes.

As the lead ship was ditching at sea, Lieutenant Bailey kept circling, while three fighters kept attacking the crippled ship. "I kept maneuvering my ship between the fighters and the ship ditching at sea. After the ditching was completed, the three fighters kept trying to strafe the survivors and I kept getting between them and the ditched aircraft to foil their attacks until they finally left the scene. Mae West life vests were dropped, and the position of ditching was radioed to Calcutta to speed up the air-sea rescue."

Because of additional time and fuel consumed during these maneuvers, Lieutenant Bailey had to locate a friendly airfield to land his B-24. He found one still under construction, where his crew was fed by the lone British officer on the field. They spent the night, returning to their home field after fuel was flown in the next day.

Though his aircraft had sustained some bullet holes, none of its personnel suffered injury. "During the encounter, gunners on this crew were credited with one enemy fighter destroyed, two probables, and two badly damaged," Colonel Bailey notes.

March 1943
POW Camp Davao, the Philippines

First Lieutenant Hugh H. Roberts continues his diary-letter, written from Bilibid Prison, Manila, 26 November 1944, several weeks before his death.

"In March 1943, ten men escaped and no details went out without guards and we were transferred back to the main compound [from the hospital]," Lieutenant Roberts writes to his family.

"I might mention here that in all camps, the barracks are laid off in bays twelve by fourteen feet, and twelve men usually live in each bay. We have but few clothes and only a blanket for protection. Here [at Bilibid] the bay is fourteen by thirteen feet, and fourteen men live here on a concrete floor. One man has a mattress and half have mosquito bars. At Cabanatuan, we had bamboo slats for floors, while at [Dapecol], we had wood floors.

"About September or October 1943, two more men escaped, so the Japs prohibited anyone from wearing shoes of any kind. I had none since November 1942 but made a pair of wooden mules we call skivvies."

March 1943
POW Camp Karenko, Formosa

Colonel Michael A. Quinn continues his POW diary.

"Another month gone and another month closer to you," Colonel Quinn writes to wife Mike in his first entry for March 1943. He continues: "We received a gift of money from His Holiness, Pope Pius XII. According to the Japanese, it amounted to 267 yen, and we understand it is to be used for the benefit of the mess. [In prewar value, one yen was equal to thirteen cents.]. . . . Ran into a little trouble this morning and got beaten up a little bit. However, nothing serious. Finished planting one garden today, so now we open up another one."

On 3 March, he writes of rain that keeps them from working, of being on room guard duty, and of feeling "so infernally weak." His entry continues, "It has not been decided yet what to do with the pope's money. Pappy Selleck held the bucket, day before yesterday, and today the heat is off. (Note: What was meant by 'holding the bucket': A Jap sentry around the latrine would fill a wooden pail with water and require the victim to hold it at arm's length. When he was exhausted, he would just let the thing drop and usually he would spill water all over himself. The bucket held about five gallons.) We were all wondering what caused the heat to be taken off. It starts and stops just like you handle a faucet back home. . . .

"Goebbels' speech from Germany was partially reported. Sounds hysterical to us, and we are just wondering what is going on. A lot of people around here are getting into economics, and there have been some who refer to the *Rerum Novarum* [papal encyclical on capital and labor issued in 1891] by Leo XIII. That might be interesting study to some of our leaders."

On 8 March, Colonel Quinn notes that it is Ash Wednesday, beginning of the Lenten season of prayer and fasting, and for the first time in his life he ate meat on that day of abstinence. "It was cooked through the rice and in the stew for supper, and it was eating the stuff or eating nothing at all," he explains. "I hope I had made up for that in the past." Also on 8 March, he records: "Colonel Bishop of the British army ran into some difficulty and got beaten up severely."

"Colonel Bunker is in a bad way. Age is not helping him any too much either," the colonel observes on 14 March. "He was an enormously powerful man and will not realize that he is not as he used to be as a cadet at West Point. . . . I had to take the services today, and all of us remembered him in our prayers. He is a grand guy."

After wishing his family "the top of the morning" on Saint Patrick's Day, 17 March, he says that he must convey the unpleasant news that Colonel Paul A. Bunker, age 61, died last night "of several ailments brought to a head by 'war endemia' or malnutrition. We had memorial services for him this morning. He is number three to go from this camp. RIP to a gallant officer and gentleman," Colonel Quinn writes in salute to his comrade.

Rumored about for weeks, the expected Red Cross supplies finally materialize on 24 March, but "nothing can be issued until Tokyo says OK." [Distribution begins on 10 April.] The largesse is recorded by Colonel Quinn as follows: "Cocoa, 456 pounds; corned beef, 10,263 one-half pound tins (Note: I believe I must be wrong there); meat and vegetable rations, 5,809 cans; sugar, 16,500 pounds; salt, 3,000 pounds; individual parcels, 1,722; boots (British marching shoes), 1,179 pairs; 2 cases medical supplies. . . ."

He continues on March 24: "Just finished our sixty-day weighing schedule and I lost three and one-half kilos (8.3 pounds) and am now down to 116 pounds.

Of course, I had dysentery in between times. Weather cold and windy today. I am wearing all the clothes I have and I am still cold. A request has come to release some supplies, but no action has been taken yet. Supplies are what we need—'How long, O Lord, how long?'" Colonel Quinn prays in biblical lament. He ends with, "We hear that the gift the pope has given us has gone to the bank to our account instead of for food or anything else we need. Feel rather gloomy and depressed, so will close."

February–April 1943
Buffalo, New York, to Fort Mead, Maryland

Major Henning B. Dieter Jr. submits the letters and orders of his father, Major Henning B. Dieter, who as S-3 with the 74th Coast Artillery Regiment (Anti-Aircraft) was to arrange for AA defense of Buffalo.

On 18 February, Major Dieter Sr. writes of going "right on to Buffalo as soon as we got our orders. . . . The outfit will follow as soon as I get a mess of 100 leases straightened out. . . . Went over to see the mayor and the commissioner of parks . . . . I am going to chisel gun-battery positions off the state and city right early tomorrow."

"I have plenty of fun on this job talking to politicos and wangling things from them. . . . The chairman of the county board of supervisors has now become educated to the point where he signs everything I put on his desk with promptness and dispatch, which helps me out no end! So far, I have wangled two armories, two city parks, all vacant county property, and half a railroad warehouse," he writes to his wife Frances on 27 February.

In his 3 March letter, he thanks his wife for her "sweet letter" and then sweetly scolds her with, "You ain't supposed to mention 74th C.A. though! Not right now, anyhow. . . . It is supposed to be a deep, dark secret that we are here, but as usual they don't give you the means of keeping a secret. Thus, *all* my real estate dealings *have* to be signed with the regiment number, and I don't see how you can keep them secret when you have some sixty places to negotiate for."

"Most of our leasing, et cetera, is completed, and we are real chesty about it," he acknowledges 16 March. Then on 17 March comes the clincher: "Wound up the 1st Battalion real estate, and we're all ready to tell them to come on up—but got orders to 'hold everything!' I'm disgusted!!"

Back at Fort Meade on 26 March, he writes: "It's a terrible war! Can't tell you where we are going yet because I don't know. . . . Gradually constructing a respectable pile of boxes, all nicely marked with beautiful stencils. Wonder what mess of muck we will be unpacking them in," he ponders on 31 March.

In his 21 April letter, he gives his wife his new address, an APO number, care of Postmaster, New York, New York. "This one is probably good for a long time, so don't lose it," he cautions.

"After completion of all necessary leases for gun positions and billets and arranging for rail transportation from Maryland to Buffalo, the regiment was ordered instead to Oran, Algeria," his son, Major Dieter Jr., points out. "With fifty years' hindsight, it now appears absurd that the War Department was concerned with the Air Defense of Buffalo, New York. Also weird is the fact that they had to lease the gun battery positions before deploying guns."

APRIL 1943

17

On World War II battlefronts around the world in April 1943, about 150 Japanese planes attack Guadalcanal and Tulagi 7 April; the Japanese begin constructing new rail lines in Burma with 60,000 Allied POWs as labor, one-fourth of whom subsequently die due to maltreatment; eighty-four Liberator bombers raid Sardinia 10 April; Japanese planes attack Oro Bay, Port Moresby, and Milne Bay in New Guinea, 11, 12, and 14 April, respectively; USCGC *Spencer* sinks Nazi U-boat U-175 in North Atlantic; 115 B-17s bomb Bremen aircraft factories 17 April; U.S. II Corps attacks Hill 60 in Mousetrap Valley, northeast of Beja, Tunisia, 22 April, completing capture by 1 May; and Admiral McMorris leads American squadron in bombardment of Japanese-held harbors on Attu, 26 April.

Recalling early 1943 as the time he made captain, Colonel George R. Norris writes: "We bought a used car, got a driver's license, and soon became educated in the fine art of gas rationing, which really was done to save rubber, as we had plenty of fuel. The first A-card gave you sixteen gallons per month, which gave the ordinary driver about 3,000 miles per year. Then came the thirty-five-mph speed limit and, finally, in the East, two gallons per week."

Rubber rationing had gone into effect soon after Pearl Harbor, on 27 December 1941; gasoline and metal were also restricted during the war. Gas rationing was instituted for the eastern United States 15 May 1942. By 1 December 1942, it was begun nationally. An A-sticker entitled the driver to four gallons per week; T-stickers for truckers, unlimited gas; B- and C-stickers, for doctors, ministers, and mail carriers, unlimited gas. In an attempt to conserve even further, pleasure driving was banned in January 1943, with drivers losing their gas rations for disregarding the rule. The ban was difficult to enforce, however, and was lifted by September 1943.

On the homefront in April 1943, President Roosevelt freezes wages, prices, and critical-industry job changes. By now, most U.S. citizens are in the wartime mode of rationing. Sugar, which remained in short supply throughout the war, had been the first item rationed, in May 1942. War Ration Book One was released at that time, issued through schools to every person in the United States.

War Ration Book Two was issued in February 1943. That month also brought shoe rationing, with three pairs allowable per year. On 1 March 1943, canned goods were rationed; on 29 March, cheese and fat were added to the list. From the ration books, red stamps were used for meats and cheese; blue for processed foods. The stamps allowed twenty to twenty-five pounds of canned vegetables, ninety pounds of meat, and thirteen pounds of cheese per year.

Rationing remained in effect until after the war: Shoe rationing continued until 30 October 1945; meat and butter until 23 November 1945; and tire rationing until 20 December 1945.

7–18 April 1943

Missions from Guadalcanal, Solomon Islands

Lieutenant Colonel Leonard W. Frame, second lieutenant/pilot, 70th Fighter Squadron, arrived in the Fiji Islands January 1942 and was assigned to Guadalcanal in March 1943.

"On 7 April, the Coast Watchers radioed that a large group of Japanese planes was headed toward Guadalcanal," Colonel Frame writes. "I was sent, leading a flight of about four P-39s to patrol over the Russell Islands. Since the fighters were on the same radio frequency, we heard the big fight going on over Guadalcanal, but nothing came our way. After things settled down, we were ordered back to base.

"On the way back, my wingman called, 'Bogey, nine o'clock (unidentified airplane, off to my left wing),' going in the opposite direction. I whipped around, chasing him. I came behind, a little below him, fired one burst of my guns and he flamed. The pilot bailed out and we went on to home base."

"One of the most famous missions of WWII was flown on 18 April 1943," Colonel Frame says. "Navy Intelligence had been decoding and translating about 25 percent of the Japanese radio traffic. One such message was decoded on 13 April and distributed to Pacific Navy Commands. Commander Air, Solomons, was Rear Admiral Marc Metscher. He received a copy of the message. It was a copy of the itinerary of Admiral Isoroku Yamamoto, commander in chief of the Japanese Navy, to make an inspection tour, leaving Rabaul in New Britain, going to Bougainville. It gave the times of departure and arrival.

"When the message came in, the only planes that could make this trip to Bougainville were the P-38s that had arrived in the area in November 1942. . . . The mission was to intercept Admiral Yamamoto's plane just before it landed at Bougainville. The planes flew within fifty feet of the water, out of sight of land for about 435 miles—a two-hour and twelve-minute flight. The last few minutes,

they started to climb and they sighted land, and then there were two Betty bombers and six Zero fighters. The interceptors were four P-38s for the 'killer flight'
and twelve P-38s for top cover. The killer flight attacked the Bettys and tangled
with some of the Zeros. One of the Bettys, carrying Yamamoto, burned and
crashed into the jungle; the other was shot to pieces and crashed in the water.

"I was walking on the flight line on Fighter Two on Guadalcanal when the
mission returned. I met Tom Lamphier, leader of the killer flight, as he was walking from his plane to the Intelligence dugout for debriefing. I asked, 'How'd it
go, Tom?' He replied, 'We got the SOB.' But there is still controversy over who
shot down which plane."

April 1943
Mission off Cape Bon, Tunisia

*Colonel Jack G. Walker was a member of the 82nd Fighter Group, 97th Fighter
Squadron.*

"The group picked up its new P-38s in Belfast and, in groups of twelve to
sixteen, started off for the war in North Africa," Colonel Walker relates. "My
flight got lost in weather and, as tail-end Charlie, I was low on fuel, so I tried to
land on a short, grassy field in Wales. Ran out of runway, jumped railroad tracks,
and class-26ed one P-38. The results: one twisted ankle and a stiff neck. [Class
26 means 'damaged beyond repair.' The item is written off the inventory by the
Class 26 investigating officer.]

"A lonely second lieutenant, I hitchhiked to an RAF station, St. Eval, near
Land's End. There I was told to deliver a photo reconnaissance P-38 to Lieutenant
Colonel Elliott Roosevelt at Algiers. After eight hours and ten minutes in that
cramped cockpit, I landed in Algiers. There, I turned the official papers and the
P-38 over to the ops officer, jumped into a French airmail plane, and finally
arrived back with the 82nd Group.

"I flew ten quick missions and was credited with a three-engine Italian float
plane destroyed. April 1943 was an unbelievable period for the P-38s," Colonel
Walker says, explaining that this was the start of Operation Flax, code name for
a special effort to patrol, intercept, and destroy Axis air convoys delivering tank
fuel to Rommel for his last stand in North Africa.

"On the 5th, thirty-two P-3s were to escort the 321st Bomb Group (B-25s) on a
sea sweep off Cape Bon. We spotted a huge aerial formation of thirty to forty Ju-
52s heading for Tunis. They had an escort of about thirty mixed German and
Italian aircraft. It was like a Cecil B. DeMille movie in living color. We dropped
our belly tanks, and the P-38s above us dropped their tanks on us.

"I lost my wingman during a wild dive to get to the Junkers. I never saw him again, and later he was listed as KIA. I flamed two Ju-52s and damaged a Stuka. With everybody shooting, including the medium bombers, we had over-claimed and they reduced my claims to one Ju-52."

Winter–Spring 1943

Umnak and Adak, Aleutian Islands

Major Leo J. Miller was second lieutenant, 36th Bomb Squadron (H), Eleventh Air Force, in the Aleutian Theater, July 1942 to August 1943.

When weather conditions were just right in the Aleutians—which was not often—men of the 36th could pick up the British Broadcasting Company and Radio Seattle on Don Gillis's Wave Master Radio. Coming in from Seattle one night, "the sweet voice of a silver-throated nightingale," Kate Smith, serenaded them with "Back in Your Own Back Yard." The other voice they would hear was "a sultry one, Tokyo Rose, spewing her sexy-sounding propaganda. We all got a great kick out of her blatant lies," Major Miller observes, paraphrasing a particular broadcast as follows:

> And to you poor, misguided American people with that figurehead you call a president, do you know, do you realize the tragedies that are happening to your soldiers and airmen who are losing this terrible war that was started by your president and Congress? Do you know that your poor, starving sons, brothers, and sweethearts out there in the miserable fog-bound Aleutians are going crazy in that dismal chain of islands we have conquered, and are fighting each other and killing their commanding officers?

The transmission warbled and faded into squeals and static, which was picked up by the men in their own squeals of laughter and their own brand of static as rebuttal to Tokyo Rose: "See, there, O'Dowd, even Rosie knows you're nuts!" "Hey, whose turn is it to kill Pappy Speer today?"

Finally, "the exasperating weather broke open and our squadrons were scheduled to move to Adak Island," Major Miller recalls. "Our ground crews were going to fly down to Adak on C-47 cargo ships, the beloved, old Gooney Bird. We had room for them in our Forts but Bomber Command did not like putting all its eggs in one basket.

"Major Speer was leading our squadron of B-17s. The 21st and the 404th with their B-24s had already left. Over the base, there were thick, shaggy broken decks of clouds from 1,200 to 1,300 feet on up. A beautiful gray day to fly! That didn't last very long. This was still the Aleutians. By the time our nine B-17s got off and into formation with our leader, the multiple decks of clouds began pressing down on each other, building a layer cake."

"We left Umnak in formation, flying at 1,200 feet. In less than fifteen minutes our altimeters read 200 feet. Then it was down to the water as usual to what we called over- and under-water flying," Major Miller writes. "All of a sudden a bowl suddenly opened up over the island and, looking out my side window, I saw four PBYs, a destroyer, several minesweepers, and half a dozen crash boats all going fast out of the harbor, headed east. That's when Sam hollered over to me: 'Bird Dog went down.'"

When they landed, the weather now unusually clear, they learned that one of the planes, skirting Great Sitkin Island and attempting to avoid the big rock immediately in front of it, went into a tight right turn, scraping four feet from its left wingtip as it did. In this maneuver, the pilot tried to go over the top of Captain 'Bird Dog' MacWilliams's ship, but there was no time.

Turning down an invitation to "tie on the feedbag," Lieutenant Miller headed quickly down the taxiway. Soon, he was away from the base, climbing steep fields of tundra and rock, trudging up hills and down into shallow valleys, and up the steep slopes of more hills. Charging, sullen clouds moved overhead and, in the roar of the ever-present wind, he seemed to hear and see Bird Dog: Bird Dog negotiating with the Navy man guarding the Dutch Harbor warehouse when they flew from Umnak on their Beer Run; Bird Dog expertly guiding the ship back through the snowstorm on their return; Bird Dog flying out with the ceiling at 200 feet to escort-in three novice P-40 crews flying on top of the gunk and running low on gas; and Bird Dog being 'kidnapped' later that night by the grateful crew of those three ships, then brought back and tucked into bed, "royally drunk," five hours later.

Up there on the hills, that same unfriendly wind that grounded them below seemed a freeing wind, as it lashed at Lieutenant Miller in his pain and his grief and his anger. He wandered for hours on this island that was strange to him, finally returning to his squad tent and then locating his buddies in the mess hall. Later, they all busied themselves setting up a wooden frame for the pot-bellied stove they were putting together, and finally settled down to a roaring fire.

When Shamrock, Tommy Gill, suggested that "all we lack is a case of beer," Sam Katz rummaged through his A-3 bag and pulled out a half-full pint of Red Label. To such accolades as "The saints bless and prezarve ya" and "I call down a blessing on thee," Sam offered the flask to his tentmates. "You first," they demurred. "He stared for long seconds at the flask in the flickering light and said so softly we could barely hear the words: 'To them.' As the Red Label went around our little group, we each said softly: 'To them.'"

April 1943
POW Camp Karenko, Formosa

Colonel Michael A. Quinn continues his POW diary.

"No Red Cross supplies, no newspapers, no tobacco, and no PX orders," Colonel Quinn reports, among his 3 April entries. Even his home brew, concocted from rice, "tasted like vinegar." But after reminiscing on 10 April about the surrender of the Luzon Force the previous year, on 9 April 1942, he adds: "On the 6th of this month we received a half pound of sugar and a few cigarettes." He then describes being awakened at 0530 for an emergency roll call after which a missing enlisted man was discovered at the hog pen, stealing food that the Japanese kitchen had discarded. When asked why, he explained that he was "so starved, he had to have food."

"Well, hell broke loose right then," Colonel Quinn continues, with the enlisted man being put in the guard house, and *"mirable dictu* [wonderful to relate], the Red Cross supplies were released." Then he itemizes the list: 1 lb. of sugar, ¹/₂ lb. of cocoa, 1 lb. of salt; plus Red Cross package containing 2 apple puddings, 2 ounces of tea, ¹/₄ lb. of chocolate, ¹/₂ lb. of British biscuits (a sort of sweet cracker), ¹/₂ lb. of margarine, ¹/₂ lb. of creamed rice, two 1-ounce cans of sugar, 2 ounces of cheese, 10 ounces of tomatoes, ¹/₂ lb. of precooked bacon, 1 large can Nestles milk, 8 ounces of syrup, ¹/₂ lb. of gelatin meat, 1 lb. of mutton curry, and 1 cake of soap.

"We all started swapping around for other things. I traded an apple pudding for a chocolate pudding and my syrup for marmalade. Last night I finished my chocolate bar, marked 650 calories, before I went to sleep. I also moved in on the biscuits, and this morning hit the sugar, and this noon and tonight ate the gelatin meat. Today is Gurdon Sage's forty-eighth birthday, so John Rodman is arranging for a feast from our individual gardens. . . . The Japs butchered one of our hogs, so we are to have pork tomorrow with a little grease in the soup at night. Just finished two big cups of cocoa and some more biscuits and felt fairly well satisfied. My home brew blew up today, so I will finish it up tonight. . . ."

Colonel Quinn sums up their April euphoria: "Now with the Red Cross supplies coming in, the whole gang acts like a bunch of children on Christmas morning. Personally, I haven't enjoyed presents as much since Santa Claus quit coming to me."

"Still swapping, so I traded a can of milk for ¹/₂ lb. of cocoa," he notes on 14 April. "Yesterday was Fran Stowell's birthday, so [husband] Al had a cocoa party to celebrate it."

"Red Cross issues on sugar and corned beef yesterday," he notes on 17 April. "A goat will be killed tomorrow, but potatoes are off the menu. All vegetables are short because we are in between seasons. . . . Found out that sugar, cocoa, and rice make a fairly good combination, and I cracked that can of bacon today, which is the first I have had in sixteen months. I ate it cold but, boy, it was good."

On 18 April, after the Dutch officiated in their language at Palm Sunday services, "we had roast pig and roast goat, 80 lbs. and 18 lbs., respectively, for 279 people." Observing that it is "funny how we go after little celebrations to revive memories of what we used to have," he records, on 20 April, celebrating Alec Quintard's twenty-fifth and his own upcoming twenty-fourth wedding anniversaries with "cocoa, vegetable stew, and apple pudding. Ken Hoeffel gave us some cinnamon and, all in all, we had a banquet."

And then, POW Colonel Michael A. Quinn writes his love letter to his wife on the anniversary of their marriage. He begins, on 24 April, with, "Just twenty-four years ago today you came to Manila to marry me. I met you on the *Sheridan*. What a pair of lovesick kids we were. It certainly has been an adventure for us. . . . I guess tomorrow, instead of having you with me, I will have to write you a love letter to keep our memories fresh."

On Easter Sunday, 25 April, their twenty-fourth anniversary date, Colonel Quinn greets his wife: "How do you do, Mrs. Quinn? This is your husband writing to tell you he still loves you and salutes you as our family counselor. . . . Somehow or another, during the entire day I was thinking of our wedding day twenty-four years ago. The only regret is that I couldn't spend this day with you. . . . I guess it sounds silly that a man almost forty-eight years old is moonstruck and lovesick, but that is my condition and I guess I will just have to plead guilty. . . . I wrote a letter to you, Mike, in remembrance of this day. . . . Well, good-bye for this time and hope to be with you for our twenty-fifth anniversary. Thanks for the last twenty-four."

For their observance of Easter, "anyone who had anything like a complete uniform wore it, except for the shoes. The Japs have those. All in the squad room saved food for the day. We all sat at one table for dinner and supper. John brought in an Easter lily and, by the way, that reminds me, this is the second time since I have known you that I haven't sent you Easter flowers. I will try to make it up to you when I see you. . . . For supper, the Japs furnished a fine stew and, of course, with rice, cocoa, and pudding, we fared fairly well. . . . Incidentally, this is about the first time in a year and a half that I can say I have gotten up from the table twice in one day really feeling completely fed."

To cap off the anniversary celebration, "Ken Hoeffel and Alec Quintard each gave me a cigar for a wedding present. Alec also had a tea party. Captain Cikot of the Dutch navy gave me five small pieces of chewing gum."

MAY 1943

18

In May 1943, only six months after the light of Operation Torch began to glow at three landing points on the shores of North Africa, its spark was igniting flickers of hope everywhere. As far off as a Japanese POW Camp in Formosa, where belated stories of victories would filter in to American and Allied prisoners, Torch warmed spirits with optimism. It inspired Colonel Michael A. Quinn to write in his diary on 11 May, his son's nineteenth birthday: "I hope I will be spending your next birthday with you, Tom. From the news about North Africa, it doesn't seem so farfetched. Anyway, here's hoping!"

Noting that the victory gave "a false sense that we could wrap up this little war in a short time," Major A. D. Kuperstein described some of his impressions of 9 May 1943 after the fall of Tunisia: "I watched in awe as thousands of German soldiers in a continuous column of fours marched westward toward the prisoner-of-war enclosures to our rear. These were the cream of Germany's Afrika Korps and even in defeat they marched with undismayed arrogance."

Chaplain Harry P. Abbott writes: "I never again expect to see such a sight as greeted us upon capitulation of the German forces in North Africa. . . . There were so many prisoners that hundreds were unguarded, as they themselves drove their vehicles, loaded beyond capacity, into the prison stockades. Some wore expressions of relief that it was over for them, others were smiling, and some were singing. . . . Many, however, were so full of German propaganda that they still refused to believe that their country's defeat was impending and inevitable."

In action in North Africa, Tunis is captured by the British, and Bizerte by the Americans, 7 May; General Jurgen von Arnim surrenders to the Allies 12 May; and Marshal Meese orders surrender of remaining German and Italian troops in Tunisia 13 May. In other war-related activities during May 1943, the 10th Fleet under Admiral King is created to supervise U.S. antisubmarine operations; USAAF drops bombs on St. Nazaire, Antwerp, and Kiel; the U.S. mines New Georgia, in the Solomons, 7 May; General Brown's 7th Division begins landing on Attu, Aleutians, with support from Admiral Kinkaid's Task Force 16 on 11

May; four cruisers led by Admiral Ainsworth attack Villa and Munda, the Solomons, 12 May.

8–13 May 1943
Near Bizerte, Tunisia

Major A. D. Kuperstein was a first lieutenant, 7th Infantry Regiment, 3rd Division.

"Those of us who had experienced a mere three days of combat at Casablanca just six months before and thought we were hot-shots began to realize how important tough training was to face up to an enemy with a combat record that often preceded our own entry into our armed forces," Major Kuperstein says. He notes that just a few months before, when Major General Lucian K. Truscott took command of the 3rd Infantry Division, he had "instituted just such a rigorous training program, including the famous Truscott trot—a requirement for every man and officer to be able to cover five miles in an hour every day with full pack and rifle. Little did we appreciate how important this toughening program would be until we later had to cover the seventy-five miles in three days across Sicily to capture Palermo.

"Another lesson we amateurs had to learn was the importance of digging a foxhole whenever and wherever we stopped. The veterans of the Tunisian Campaign learned that lesson early, and I was amazed at the sophistication that was exhibited by foxholes dug into the hard, white limestone base of the Tunisian landscape with pickaxes—the entrenching shovel being virtually useless there."

In summation, Major Kuperstein writes, "The fall of Tunisia marked the first real victory over German forces that our soldiers could savor, having captured those huge numbers of enemy pouring down from the hills they had held for the last half-year. It was a blessing that we could not visualize what lay ahead in Sicily and Italy, and beyond."

Winter–Spring 1943
Tunisia

Chaplain (Colonel) Harry P. Abbott continues his story of service in North Africa.

The concern of immediate burial of Americans killed in North Africa, the efforts to properly identify bodies, and the attention to "full burial honors as far as the situation permitted" were some of the chaplains' duties. "Many times Chaplain Carper or Chaplain Doyle, my assistants, and I have toured the hills and traveled though mine-infested fields, which the engineers had not yet reached, to recover the bodies of our men," Chaplain Abbott writes. "Oftimes we worked by the light of the moon, and frequently for periods as long as twenty hours in one day, living mostly on canned C-rations, of which we had a plentiful supply.

"Sometimes the cemeteries were located very close to the front, because we were rushing on so rapidly, and thus we were subject to strafing and enemy bombs. Upon occasions such as these, we would jump in a vacant grave, fling ourselves to the ground, or hide behind any protection that was available. While we were recovering the dead near Hill 609, northeast of Beja, shells (88s) began to drop near us. . . . I told Chaplain Carper I heard one shell twice: once when it passed me and again when I passed it."

For the American as well as the enemy soldier, "every effort was made to ascertain the identity of each," through I.D. tags, fingerprints, and other methods. Additionally, "reports were made of the soldier buried on either side, in order to make sure of no mistake in case of the necessity of reburial in the future."

On one occasion at Medjez el Bab, the chaplain was sent to investigate a plane crash in which six survived and four lost their lives. Chaplain Abbott says, "With the assistance of an Arab lad, I was guided to its position. It was necessary to place all four recovered bodies on our peep, along with four of us who were alive, and travel about fifty miles to the nearest cemetery available for burial. The enemy was in possession of one nearby.

"Upon arrival at the cemetery, one entire company of British troops turned out and, even though it was late at night, they assisted with digging the graves and rendering full military honors to the dead." In this case, Chaplain Abbott traveled 600 additional miles to a hospital in the rear to verify with the six survivors the identity of the four men killed in the crash.

"After the victory in North Africa, memorial services were held in which the entire 13th Armored Regiment participated, including the commanding officer, Colonel Chauncey Benson, together with the regimental band and colors," Chaplain Abbott writes. "After the memorial services, the band withdrew to another section of the park and played various selections. I shall never forget the expressions of the local French populace, as the French 'Marseillaise' was played. Tears were streaming down their faces in gratitude for being liberated and for being able to hear again their own national anthem on their own free soil."

May–June 1943
Mission to Pantelleria, Italy

Lieutenant Colonel Clyde W. Gabler continues with his diary notes.

Allied forces having prevailed, essentially by 7 May, with the capture of both Tunis and Bizerte, "the Group S-2 section enlisted men were put to work pasting together a large mosaic display of the Island of Pantelleria," located off the coast of North Africa, east of Tunis, "since it appeared that we were going to devote much attention to that as a target," then-Captain Gabler writes from Chateau-Dun-du-Rhumel, Algeria .

"On 8 May 1943, the 1st Fighter Group attacked the Island of Pantelleria. . . . After some additional attacks by B-17s and B-26s, the island became the first land objective to surrender to an air force. This was on 11 June 1943."

May 1943–December 1944
Khorramshahr to Kazvin and Zanjan, Iran

Lieutenant Colonel A. George Mallis, a captain with 516th Quartermaster Truck Regiment, served as commanding officer of the 3927th Truck Company.

"We called ourselves 'the FBI,' the Forgotten Bastards of Iran, because hardly anyone knew that the United States had such a command, nor what it did," Colonel Mallis recalls. Though folks in the States may not have known of them, there was at least one person elsewhere who was aware of the group's existence. The Nazis' Axis Sally "greeted us by regiment number on our arrival and wished us a safe swim back to the United States."

World War II's Persian Gulf Command (PGC) had its origins in 1942 when the War Department decided that a trucking outfit was needed to carry war supplies to the Russian border from the Persian Gulf. The American Trucking Association was enlisted to find volunteers for two regiments that would become the 516th and the 517th Quartermaster Truck Regiments. Members trained at Camp Van Dorn, near Centreville, Mississippi, in November and December 1942.

Then-Captain Mallis arrived at Khorramshahr with the 516th by way of New Zealand, Australia, and India, 22 May 1943. The 517th reached Khorramshahr 3 July 1943. As the QM truck regiments were arriving, so too were additional troops: longshoremen, railroaders, ordnance personnel, engineers, medics, MPs, and other technicians.

Describing their route through Iran on the road they built, patched, and maintained, Colonel Mallis writes: "The motor transport service started at the Gulf port of Khorramshahr and traveled to the Russian base at Kazvin or Zanjan. There were four sections of the road, with stops at Andimeshk, Khurramabad, and Hamadan. There were two very treacherous sections, one at Razan Pass at about 7,775 feet, just north of Khurramabad, and the other at Avej Pass, at the same elevation, and located about halfway to Kazvin." At the high elevations, temperatures in winter would drop to 25 degrees below zero.

On the trip from Khurramabad to Kazvin, a distance of 636 miles, "we rode the roads for sixteen to eighteen hours a day going up; laid over for six to eight hours; and then repeated the process coming back for more, to do it all over again. We contended with death from hostile tribesmen, outright brigands, fatal accidents, and sheer exhaustion from the constant pounding on the roads, if one may call them that.

"Our first day of no work came from 1800 hours on 24 December 1943 to 1800 hours on 25 December, when we resumed our schedule."

The Command, under General J. B. Sweet, had its maximum strength in late spring and early summer 1943, with about 30,000 troops, and remained that way until early 1944. The Command's peak number of U.S. Army trucks was 6,000 in September 1944.

"I can assure you that the men and women of Operation Desert Storm in 1991 had a picnic compared to those of the PGC," Colonel Mallis contends. "In the Persian desert, temperatures rose to 125° and 130° most every day in the summer, and we were only allowed one gallon of water per day." At those times, no work was allowed from 1000 to 1600 hours. Much work was done at night.

"Initially, we lived in standard O.D. Army tents, and there was no such thing as air conditioning, even in the field hospital or the base hospital in Ahwaz, which was in the heart of the desert. For four months, we lived on canned rations or we ate the meat of wild boar, gazelle, and antelope that roamed the hills, the only native food we were allowed, except for a limited amount of some vegetables such as scallions. And everybody came down with dysentery, malaria, or some other Eastern disease." Other not-so-favorite things in Iran were the "stinging flies, dust storms that blotted out the sun, and sand-fly fever." On the positive side, the PGC soldiers set up an airplane assembly plant and two truck assembly plants, and operated a railroad and motor-truck service.

In a December 1944 letter to members of the Command, Brigadier General Donald P. Booth, commanding general, Headquarters PGC, Teheran, Iran, commended the men and their mission: "Across the stifling heat and cutting sandstorms of the Iranian Desert and through the mountains . . . , you have helped in transporting enormous quantities of aid-to-Russia war materials made in the plants of America. Through December of 1944, you and your comrades in PGC had helped transport nearly 5,000,000 tons of vital war materiel to the Red Army. All of us know to what good use the Russians have put this material."

"I will not presume to say we won the war, but without our help to Russia, Russia would have fallen to Hitler and our attack on Fortress Europe might have had a different ending," Colonel Mallis adds. After its Persian Gulf assignment, the 517th was sent to the China–Burma–India area, hauling supplies over the Burma Road into China. The 516th was sent into the European Theater, assigned to Patton's Third Army to haul gasoline for Patton's tanks.

17 May 1943–8 May 1945

The Netherlands, Germany, France

Major Robert L. Starr, who got his pilot's license at the age of sixteen, was a second lieutenant when he flew over Ijmuiden, attempting to knock out a power plant.

"The power plant furnished electricity for the trains the Germans used in Holland for moving supplies and troops. We had tried to knock it out several weeks before with high-altitude bombing, but it didn't work," Major Starr says.

On 17 May, the planes were using the skip-bombing method when Lieutenant Starr's plane, flying 100 feet above the ground, collided with another. Of sixty-nine men in ten B-26s on the mission, only Major Starr and his crew of eight survived. They were captured after the crash and sent to Stalag 3 POW Camp in Sagan, Germany.

While at Stalag 3, Lieutenant Starr and other POWs received some very special mail: autographed photos from movie stars Hedy Lamarr, Greer Garson, and others. These arrived after Lieutenant Starr had written to Miss Lamarr, telling her of the crashing of his plane, the *Tondelayo*, named after the character she played in the movie *White Cargo*.

In his treasured letter from her, Miss Lamarr wrote: "I am sorry to hear of the misfortune of the *Tondelayo*, although I hope she lived up to what she stood for." The actress mentions being flattered to receive fan mail from the POW camp and that she hoped Lieutenant Starr would soon be able to enjoy a movie of hers more recent than *White Cargo*. She also informs him that he and the prisoners might expect to receive photos of Lana Turner, Judy Garland, Greer Garson, and of herself, cheesecake-style, from the studio publicity department.

As the war neared its end in 1945, the Germans, fearing arrival of the Russians, marched the Stalag 3 prisoners eighty-five miles in knee-deep snow and −10 temperatures to a camp near Nuremberg. It was prior to this march that Lieutenant Starr lost his *Tondelayo* for a second time: his autographed photo of

Miss Lamarr. Because he could not take the picture with him, he says he burned it rather than leave it for one of the German officers.

As General Patton's Third Army came through, they liberated the camp, "but we had to stay put," Major Starr recalls, because the Third Army was on rations and there was no food for the POWs; nor was there transportation. With this the situation, he and a buddy left camp, hitched a ride to Nuremberg on a supply train, and then caught a plane to Reims, France.

They were at a base near Paris at war's end when he and his friend were informed that they had been selected "to ride with General Eisenhower in his staff car for the V-E Day parade." The general told them that he could think of none more deserving to ride with him. And so the two—who had spent two years sitting in depressing POW camps and recently had to hitch rides—now had seats of honor on the back rim of a convertible, with their commander in chief in the rear seat, traveling the streets of festive Reims on V-E Day, 8 May 1945.

"I got more kisses that day than a man could get in a lifetime," Major Starr reminisces, as he recalls the outpouring of appreciation from a grateful French people after years of war and occupation.

For Major Starr, that triumphant conclusion to his own World War II days just had to be shared in 1987 when he spied General Eisenhower's grandson David, with wife Julie, sitting across the room from him and Mrs. Starr on a tour of the Chocolate Factory at Hershey, Pennsylvania.

"You're the missing link!" an excited David Eisenhower exclaimed upon hearing the story. He informed them that he was working on a book about his grandfather and had a certain picture of the V-E Day parade. "They had identified all the soldiers in the picture except me," Major Starr explains.

In a second distinctive postscript to his story, Major Starr tells of visiting Glacier National Park, Montana, in 1986. Seeing a woman who was wearing dark glasses, he told his wife that he was certain the lady was Greer Garson. Going up and introducing himself and discovering that he was correct, he reminded her of the photos that she and Hedy Lamarr had sent to Stalag 3 during the war.

Ever the sweet and gracious Mrs. Miniver—a role that won her and the movie Academy Awards in 1942—Greer Garson "surprised me when she said, 'I know who you are.' And she did," Major Starr adds. During their conversation, she told Major and Mrs. Starr that if they could remain in the area three more days, they would have the chance to meet Miss Lamarr, who was expected to join Miss Garson at her hotel. Regretfully, they were unable to stay. And so, for the third time in his lifetime, *Tondelayo* would be lost to him yet again!

19

In June 1943, the U.S. Air Force bombs Bremen, Kiel, Wilhelmshaven, and Cuxhaven in Germany; Pantelleria and Lampedusa Islands, Sicily; and Sardinia in the Mediterranean. Near Guadalcanal, there are major air battles 12 June, and fighters from Henderson Field claim ninety-one Japanese aircraft shot down in the Solomons 16 June.

In other war-related events during June, the Italian garrison of 11,000 on Pantelleria surrenders 11 June; the first convoys of Operation Husky depart the United States 16 June for the 10 July invasion of Sicily; General Krueger establishes Sixth Army Headquarters at Milne Bay, New Guinea, 20 June; Marine 4th Raider Battalion, with Army reinforcements, lands at Segi Point, New Georgia, 21 and 22 June, to begin the New Georgia campaign; and Operation Cartwheel is launched at Rabaul, New Britain, 30 June.

With the war's progression come victories and defeats for each side, along with prisoners of war for each side. In a book titled *Stalag: U.S.A*, Judith M. Gansberg tells the story of those German POWs, their camps, and the unique re-education program finally adopted at the urging of Eleanor Roosevelt, wife of the president, that was "a massive multimedia effort to bring about a democratic trend among the prisoners" who would eventually "provide a vanguard for redirecting postwar Germany."

Ms. Gansberg writes: "Of the more than 3,000,000 prisoners of war held by the Allies during World War II, approximately 425,000 were in camps within the continental United States. Of that number, nearly 372,000 were German."

Initially placed in Civilian Conservation Corps (CCC) and National Young Administration camps, prisoners later numbering about three-fifths of the total were quartered at facilities on Army posts, according to Ms. Gansberg. At their peak, the POW camps were located in 42 of the then-48 states.

One prisoner, Helmut, listed the following Sunday menu for POWs at Camp Shelby, Mississippi: "Breakfast: milk, corn flakes (Wheaties), sugar, bread, coffee, marmalade. Lunch: tomato soup, ribs, potatoes, vegetables, pudding, pastry, tea. Supper: cold cuts and vegetable dish, bread, cocoa, one apple." POW Reinhold Pable wrote that the POWs "at first suspected the Yanks wanted to make fun of us" with such a menu. "Never before in our military career had we been served a meal like that," he added.

American POW Captain Joseph S. Frelinghuysen describes his daily menu at Capua, near food-scarce Naples, and at Chieti, Italy: "Two 'meals,' each consisting of a roll, half the size of a hamburger bun, and a small plate of tomato soup with rice."

From POW Camp Shirakawa, Formosa, in June 1943, Colonel Michael A. Quinn repeats his refrain of fourteen months in captivity: "Worst of all, we are constantly hungry and physically weak." On 17 June, he notes, a fellow-prisoner offers $125 for one Red Cross box that would retail for about $2. The offer is accepted. "That gives you an idea of the value of food," he writes.

"This prison life would not be so bad if we could ever hear from home. I haven't heard from you in fourteen months and that was only a radio[gram]," Colonel Quinn writes to his wife in his diary on 11 June.

By May 1943, two letters arrive to lift the spirits of Captain Frelinghuysen, though "the feeling . . . was short-lived. In one letter, all the censor had left was, 'Much love, Dad.' So I was willing to bet that my father had been trying to tell me some important military secrets," he writes.

His second letter is from his wife Emily who informs him that she and the children, Margaret and Joey, are well "but our friend Anna Page . . . was giving Emily problems, and Stan Olson had become completely uncooperative." After puzzling over the message, Captain Frelinghuysen translated this into: "The A&P rationing was getting tough [Ann Page was an A&P product brand] and Stan Olson (for Standard Oil) meant she couldn't get gas for the car." In her letter, Emily also says that she has moved into a large house with three friends and their children, meaning that the little white house he had dreamed of returning to no longer fit into that dream. "Suddenly, I felt lost, betrayed," he recalls.

15 March–22 June 1943
Missions to Bremen and Huls, Germany

Major Maurice J. Herman was the twenty-one-year-old corporal who hand-cranked the alarm at Schofield Barracks, Hawaii, on 7 December 1941.

By March 1943, Maurice was a lieutenant and navigator with 401st Squadron, 91st Bomb Group (H), Eighth AF, at Station 121, Bassingbourn, England. "Our crew considered itself most fortunate on being assigned as replacements to the 91st not only because we were going to a plush base, but also because the 91st had a reputation as being the fighting-est bomb group in the European Theater of Operations, that is, heaviest tonnage of bombs dropped, most enemy fighters shot down, and heaviest losses," Major Herman writes.

"Our crew was split up on our first mission to fly as members of other, experienced crews. The date: 15 March; the mission, the Focke-Wulfe plant at Bremen. The 401st put seven planes up that day. I was aboard the only one to return. Half of our crew, which had trained together in the States, was aboard aircraft that went down. That was the end of our crew."

When new crews were developed "from the remnants of personnel that did not fly that fateful 15th of March," Lieutenant Herman was assigned as navigator of the *Royal Flush*, a B-17F that was vying with the *Memphis Belle* to be first to complete twenty-five missions. My second mission was my first as a crew member of the *Royal Flush*. In the weeks that followed, during April, May, and June, we hit St. Nazaire, Lorient, Antwerp, Hamburg, Bremen, Kiel, and Flensburg. We painted eight more bombs and six more swastikas on her nose. We patched up her holes, replaced her damaged engines and control surfaces, and replaced her wounded crew members."

Of mission nine, he writes: "On 22 June, we flew again. Our target that day: the synthetic rubber plant at Huls, a German city in the Ruhr Valley. Intelligence had told us at briefing that this plant manufactured about one-third of the synthetic rubber being produced in occupied Europe at that time. If we succeeded in destroying that plant, we would severely impede Germany's ability to wage the war. . . .

"Lieutenant Marcel Fountain was the aircraft commander. Lieutenant Oscar Diedring flew the right seat. Sergeant Fred Sneed, flight engineer, occupied the top turret. Norman Williams and I were up front. Norm had the responsibility of putting our bombs on target and I had the responsibility for directing us to the target. I see their faces in my mind, but I can no longer recall the names of the other guys. There were ten of us, the extra man being a photographer.

"The formation formed and crossed the North Sea without incident. The flight from the Zuider Zee into the initial point (IP) was routine—not too much flak, no fighters. Then the situation changed. The run from the IP to the target took us up the north side of the Ruhr River Valley, better known to the Eighth Air Force bomber crews as Flak Alley.

"As each bomb group in the formation made its turn over the IP, they slipped a little farther to the south than the preceding group. The 91st, Wray's Ragged Irregulars, was the last group in the formation. *Royal Flush* was right wing of the last flight in the group, and the farthest south in the bomb run from the IP to the target.

"Flak hit the No.1 engine. We feathered it successfully and went on to drop our bombs on the synthetic rubber plant. Flak found us again coming off the target. Huls was burning and so were we. We were able to put the fire out in No. 3 engine but couldn't feather the prop. No. 2 engine still ran, but only on five or six of the nine cylinders. We fell out of formation as we fought to maintain speed and altitude. That's when the jocks in the Fw-190s and Me-109s spotted us. That's when the firefight for our lives began!

"We were at about 24,000 feet when the fighters hit us. They kept coming in, firing their guns and cannons, fishtailing all the way, and rolling under us. We fired back with our .50s from all stations at each attacker. By the time we ducked into a cloud at about 7,000 feet, maybe five minutes later, we had shot down eight of our attackers. But we had suffered casualties also. Both the tail gunner and the ball turret gunner had been hit. The Plexiglas nose of the bombardier/navigator compartment had been shot out. The hydraulic system had been shot out too. But the *Royal Flush* flew on.

"The German fighters were gone. Now, our problem was to get to the coast before we ran out of altitude. We threw our empty ammo cans and now-useless guns overboard to lighten ship. But Marc and Oscar couldn't maintain altitude. Marc hit the bailout bell switch at 2,500 feet. We started to bail out. When all were gone but Marc, Oscar, and Fred, they found they could maintain altitude. They flew on, to the west and the North Sea."

The threesome was able to make the coast, but anti-aircraft fire hit them once again and they had to ditch. "They got out of the *Royal Flush* and into her dinghy, but were captured by the crew of the German patrol boat that picked them up."

"Those of us who bailed out landed in the vicinity of Wesel at the confluence of the Ruhr River with the Rhine" and "were captured in the area where we landed. I managed to evade capture for ten hours, but that's another story.

"The *Royal Flush* went to the bottom off the coast of Holland. She was a good ship. May she ever rest in peace, for this was the only time a Royal Flush has ever lost."

April–July 1943
North Africa to Pantelleria, Italy

Lieutenant Colonel Paul H. Campbell was a radio gunner and operator with the 32nd Heavy Bomb Squadron, 301st Bomb Group, that arrived in North Africa in late 1942.

One of the highlights early in the North Africa campaign was when "Captain Eddie Rickenbacker came and presented us our medals. We made the 'milk run' to Tunis and Bizerte in April 1943" and one trip to the Sahara Desert in the same month, Colonel Campbell writes. "Made one rest-and-recreation trip to Algeria in June 1943 and visited the French Quarter and the Mosque. We saw the Afrika Korps being shipped to America. They were an impressive unit."

On 11 June, when they raided Pantelleria, "which surrendered as our troops hit the beach, we delayed the landing because of the weather on the island." In June, "we made some raids on Sicily and some on Palermo." On one of these, he flew on the lead ship "and was on the bomb run eleven and one-half minutes. . . ."

When they raided Naples, "we had lost both inboard engines. The 'Old Man' circled back and said we would not reach home base. One box formed a circle around us to keep the enemy aircraft away. With a good tail wind, we made the base.

"We made the Rome Raid. I was at the briefing when the location was announced. . . . Anything that could fly went to Rome. . . . We had a tail-end Charlie slot. I told the young pilot that was no place for us. We found our place in the second box. There were only two shots of flak, and we saw an Me-262. The marshaling yards were 2,000 yards from the hospitals but these were not touched. . . . After completing my fifty missions, I was grounded and ordered home by General Carl Spaatz."

December 1942–June 1943
POW Camps Capua and Chieti, Italy

Major Joseph S. Frelinghuysen was a captain with First Army, 1st Division, in command of Battery D, 5th Field, when he landed at Arzew, Tunisia, 8 November 1942.

On 28 November, he and a group of his men were ambushed on the road to Djedeida and he became a *Kriegsgefangener*, a German prisoner of war in POW camps in Italy. In his book *Passages to Freedom*, Major Frelinghuysen tells of being taken first to an Arab jail in Tunis for two days; transferred to a concentration camp at Capua, twenty miles north of Naples, 1 December; and then moved 12 January to Chieti, an old Fascist prison on the Adriatic, about eight miles southwest of Pescara, Italy.

At Capua, he scrounged scraps of paper from the garbage pile so that he could begin keeping notes for a diary; he heard the failed-escape story of a Britisher named Bucky; and he joined a choir that practiced every day and sang in services on Sundays. Because winter had already set in at Capua, Major Frelinghuysen says it was fortunate that they had been "issued wool uniforms for the landing at Arzew" rather than the cotton being considered. "[T]he International Red

Cross gave us long OD overcoats. I wore mine every day and even slept in it. It was truly a godsend."

In late December, Red Cross parcels began to arrive, and then there were fewer. Guard Russo angrily announced: "I have to inform you that the entire city of Naples is under constant air attack by your B-24 bombers. Surely you know that, from the air-raid sirens blowing all night. We can't get anything through, so this delay is no fault of ours." The air-raid sirens blew, too, on New Year's Day 1943 beginning at 0800, with B-24 sightings and bombings later, and sirens again a third time that day.

Then came the move to Chieti, where, to the west for about three miles, stretched "an open plain beyond which rose rugged mounts, deep purples and gray against the afternoon sunlight. Above them all, the snowcapped Gran Sasso d'Italia, the Apennines' highest peak. . . . Off toward the southwest, the massif of the Maiella, a dark, mysterious mountain, extended down the spine of Italy. . . .

"Chieti boasted nine-foot brick walls topped with barbed wire; every 200 feet, sentries on machine-gun platforms scrutinized the entire prison area, while other guards with rifles patrolled the outermost perimeter within the enclave." Recalling that Bucky's failed escape from Capua was because he was inept in Italian, Captain Frelinghuysen soon began to study the language, memorizing thirty words each day, with help from Frank Gallo, an American medical officer captured in North Africa.

"To combat the cold, I started doing some exercises. But it was a lonely business, so I looked for someone to do them with and came across an American B-26 pilot named Conrad Kreps," who had been "a capable gymnast and weight-lifter before the war. . . . Gradually, I got into good shape and was better able to handle cold, discomfort, poor diet, and that oppressing sense of confinement." And gradually, others joined them until they each had three classes a day.

"By 15 May, Radio Roma could not possibly conceal the magnitude of the German and Italian defeat in North Africa," Major Frelinghuysen writes. On the evening of 11 June, Radio Roma reported that the island of Pantelleria, "a key Axis bastion 110 miles east of Tunis and about seventy miles from the coast of Sicily," had been evacuated by the Italian garrison without a fight. The news was so startling, especially since the official radio had been so frank, that it set off a wild celebration in the camp. The SBO issued an order that in the future any such demonstrations would be met with courts-martial. . . .

"By the 15th, the British had stepped up their tunnel digging to a new level. . . . During this period . . . the level of the camp vegetable garden rose two feet.

Because of the constant replanting, however, the vegetables were not as successful as the deluxe tunnel." *[Major Frelinghuysen's POW story concludes in Chapter
22.]*

June 1943
POW Camps Karenko and Shirakawa, Formosa

*Colonel Michael A. Quinn continues his diary, even as he moves from one camp to
another.*

For the prisoners at Karenko, the much-rumored-about, long-awaited move
finally began on 7 June. "We know so little of what we are supposed to do that
packing is a mystery," Colonel Quinn observes, nevertheless he makes preparations by taking advantage of good weather on 2 June to wash all of his clothes
and to join the others in preparing "all stuff to be shipped." For the move, "the
brigadier generals came back to join us," he writes on 5 June but adds, in disappointment, "Generals Wainwright, King, and Moore of the U.S. Army . . . stayed
at the old camp which was at Tamazato."

After reveille at 0500, breakfast at 0630, and assembly at 0930, the prisoners
depart Karenko at 0955 on 7 June; hike leisurely for one hour, or are trucked, to
the dock; board the *Hozan Maru* at 1130; sail north on the east side of Formosa,
and "came around the head of the island and anchored at a port called Sauy (?)
about 1600." They left the boat, hiked a mile to the train, and pulled out at 2200
hours.

"We arrived at our next halt about 1030 on 8 June. Good Lord, it was hot. We
had hot tea to drink and it was that or nothing, so we drank plenty of it. We were
then taken out a few miles in the direction of our new camp on a narrow-gauge
railroad in gondolas. The cars had been formerly used for carrying stone." At
1430 on 8 June, they reached their new location, Camp Shirakawa, meaning
white water, "on the west side of the island, apparently just opposite our camp at
Karenko."

There is a downpour as they arrive and heavy rains on 9, 11, 12, 18, and 21
June. Colonel Quinn notes that drainage is poor, the ground swampy, and "we
hear that malaria is prevalent." By 30 June, that rumor is validated when "about
30 POWs are down with malaria." On 20 June, he observes: "Profanity is almost
never heard these days, and salacious stories are practically unknown. Can you
imagine that, with a group of 300 men of the U.S. Army?"

When the Red Cross supplies are finally distributed on 24 June, Colonel
Quinn lists the following as his "stock in trade: 100 ounces of corned beef, two

cans of Nestles milk, two cans of meat and vegetable stew, and some miscellaneous supplies." Bananas, too, begin to be issued and Colonel Quinn swaps one
can of cheese for six bananas. Afraid to deplete his food reserve to celebrate his
birthday on 14 June, he decides to, in his words, gorge himself at this point. "No
use doing without it when you have it, as well as when you don't."

On their mutual June 14th birthday, Colonel Quinn wishes his wife "happy
birthday. And I guess you are saying the same thing about me." Then, he adds:
"I hoped against all common sense that I would get a letter today, and common
sense won out." He ends the very detailed entry with, "For lack of anything to
send you for a birthday present, I will send you my love."

He records how prisonmates helped him celebrate his birthday: "Fred Ward
gave me two brand-new Gillette blades. Corporal Wurst of the Marines gave me
a saki cup, and Johnny Cook tossed in a Philippine cigarette. These things may
seem trivial to you when you read these notes, but here they are matters of great
importance. I have used one razor blade over 100 times and am still using it."

20

Winston S. Churchill called it "the greatest amphibious operation so far attempted in history." Scripps-Howard war correspondent Ernie Pyle reported that the invasion fleet on the horizon "resembled a distant city" and "covered half of the skyline." *The World Almanac Book of World War II* records that the "elements of eight divisions" landing were "more than on D-Day." It was Operation Husky, the Allied invasion of Sicily, launched 9 and 10 July 1943.

Of the immensity of the operation, Churchill writes in *Closing the Ring*: "In the initial assault nearly 3,000 ships and landing-craft took part, carrying between them 160,000 men, 14,000 vehicles, 600 tanks, and 1,800 guns." Eventually, 480,000 would be ashore, according to the *World Almanac Book of World War II*.

Major A. D. Kuperstein landed on the western coast at Licata, Sicily, with 7th Infantry Regiment, 3rd Infantry Division. He describes one of his first sights after going ashore: "Above the beachhead on a wooded-hillside dirt trail, the German soldier's body lay face down across his rifle, a pool of drying blood under his head. Since this was Italian territory, the presence of Germans could indicate there was danger of counterattack. Fortunately, after the assault troops had passed across the beach, a newspaper reporter (Mike Chinigo, it turned out to be) picked up a ringing telephone in a building and, in fluent Italian, assured the Italian officer on the other end that nothing was going on down here, in spite of rumors to the contrary. As a result, a dangerous counterattack was avoided, allowing us to consolidate the beachhead."

Lieutenant Colonel Clifton L. Adams was with 7th Troop Carrier Squadron, 62nd Troop Carrier Group. He reports that while he was helping to "deliver the British airborne in gliders" south of the Catania Plain on Sicily's eastern coast, a similar assault by the Americans was simultaneously taking place on the southwest coast. "I will be forever grateful we were working with the British that night," he adds.

"En route to Sicily, the troop carrier planes that were carrying American paratroopers overflew the American Navy, and the Navy opened fire at essentially point-blank range. Before the Navy got its guns silenced, they had shot down thirty-four Gooney Birds (C-47s), complete with their paratroopers. I never heard how many, if any, of the men in those planes were rescued." Listing 11 July as the night of this tragedy, several sources report the figures as 23 planes destroyed and 37 badly damaged, and over 200 MIA, KIA, or wounded from among the 2,000 paratroopers aboard 144 aircraft.

Providing what he believes are reasons for the success of the Sicily attack, Colonel Adams explains: "It seems that the troop carrier planes broke formation, went in far too high, and dropped their paratroopers far too fast. Since they were too high and too fast, there were no two of them together." With the German high command receiving reports of paratroopers dropping inland and all over the southwest coast instead of in concentrated spots, "they could not deploy troops to all of the places. So the American paratroops cleaned up!"

In other war-related events during July 1943, U.S. naval forces bombard Kiska in the Aleutians 9 July; Mediterranean air forces bomb targets in Sicily and the Italian cities of Naples, Bari, and, on 19 July, Rome; Eighth Air Force bombs towns in France and Germany; Fourteenth Air Force targets Hankow, Hainan, and Hong Kong. In the European Theater, Americans in Sicily take Gela, Licata, and Vittoria, as the British on 10 July capture Syracuse; Americans capture Biscani Airfield, Sicily, 14 July; U.S. Seventh takes Palermo, Sicily, 22 July; and Americans capture Nicosia, Sicily, 27 July. In the Pacific Theater, Marines capture Viro, New Guinea, 1 July, and U.S. forces land near Munda, New Georgia.

9 July 1943
South of Catania, Sicily

Lieutenant Colonel Clifton L. Adams deployed to England in September 1942. In mid-1943, he was in North Africa, preparing for the invasion of Sicily.

A few days before the invasion, there was a snafu: The brigadier general who commanded the British airborne troops discovered that American glider pilots had no combat training. "All that they were qualified to do was to sit up there and steer the glider and, hopefully, to land it when they reached the landing zone (LZ)," Colonel Adams explains.

"The brigadier came unglued," protesting that he would not take the American glider pilots. He clicked off his list of reasons. "The solution: our glider pilots would train British airborne troops to steer and to land the gliders!

"By flying literally night and day, we managed to check out enough British airborne troops to provide two pilots for all gliders except one. But we were out of time. The brigadier would either have to delay the invasion or he would have to accept two American glider pilots for the assault. He elected the latter and we called for volunteers. "We selected two," with the brigadier specifying that they fly in separate gliders as co-pilots to the British.

"We took off for Sicily into the blackest night in the history of nights. But we made the transit without opposition from the Germans. All that we saw of them prior to reaching our drop point for the gliders was occasionally two converging orange lines in the sky. They were German fighters who were attacking the British navy, over which we were flying. As soon as the two lines of tracers showed up, a British ship would be completely outlined in orange tracers, answering the fire of the German fighter. In every case, they got him! We would watch as the plane went down in flames, burned for a while even after it was under water, and then all would be black again until another German fighter attacked another British ship. . . .

"We arrived at the point where we were to drop the gliders, which was south of the Catania Plain, and lined up on the promontory for the final run. I was the navigator in the lead plane for that assault and we had to use wind direction and speed given to us before take-off by the meteorologists (Metro, we called them) to compute the distance from the LZ and the direction for release of the gliders, since they have limited maneuverability after we cut them loose from the tow ships.

"Metro had stated that the wind would blow from water to land that night, and I made the calculations and led the attack force in its final run to release the gliders. Our track left us over the water at all times, until we hit the promontory, which I used as a checkpoint.

"As it turned out, the wind was 180 out! It was blowing from land to water rather than vice versa. As a result, 60 percent of the gliders landed in the water, but that does not mean that 60 percent of the troops were lost.

"The Germans must have known that we were going to attack that particular point because they had muzzle-to-muzzle ack-ack and machine-gun fire covering the entire part of the coast where the gliders were to go."

10 July 1943
Licata, Sicily

Major A. D. Kuperstein landed at Casablanca in November 1942, was in Tunisia when it fell in May 1943, and participated in the invasion of Sicily.

For the invasion, the regiment began to assemble in its landing craft in the harbor at Bizerte, Tunisia, on 6 July, Major Kuperstein recalls. "I was assigned to the regimental headquarters craft, which was one of the newer-type landing craft infantry (LCI). As we passed into the ocean and headed for Sicily, the weather changed into a violent windstorm that created high surf and rocked our boats unmercifully. Even though I was not normally seasick, I found it difficult to stay on deck for long, and found it equally difficult in our small quarters into which leaked gasoline and oil fumes.

"Thus, as we reached the beaches of the south coast of Sicily, some few miles west of the small town of Licata, most of the troops were the worse for the wear of several days of seasickness. Almost precisely at 0600 (the assault troops had landed about 0430), my ship struck the beach some fifty yards out in the water.

"I found myself walking in chest-high water toward the beach. Suddenly, my footing disappeared and I realized the ship had stopped on a shoal with deep water between it and the beach, making it impossible to unload the ship. Being a good swimmer, I headed toward the beach [but] my helmet had been swept away in the surf, along with my badly needed eyeglasses!

"I stepped onto the beach, exhausted, realizing that the pack on my back was fifty pounds heavier with seawater. Emptying my pack of water on the beach near a group of amused Italian prisoners huddled under the overhang above the beach, I became suddenly aware of bullets and firing from a concrete pillbox above the left edge of the beach on a high cliff.

"By that time, the landing craft I had left had managed to back off its reef and charge over it to get to the beach. . . . Leaving the beach by a dry creekbed, I found the command post a short distance inland and discovered I had left my dispatch case on the beach. Because it had both a classified-codes instrument in it and a prized picture of my wife, I quickly returned to the beach and luckily found it still lying in the sand in front of the even-more-amused Italian prisoners."

As for his lost items, because the troops were able to discard gas masks, "I remembered the set of gas-mask glasses, which I was forced to use for the rest of the Sicilian campaign." The lost helmet, however, was a more serious problem: "General Patton had ordered that everyone must wear his helmet at all times and have his weapon handy or be subject to dire punishment."

A few days later, hearing enemy fire below the command post, "As I started to aim my carbine, my commander yelled at me to get back into hiding and 'right now!' Only a few minutes later I understood why. General Patton was on his way to congratulate some of us who at that moment were given battlefield promotions. Someone handed me a brand-new helmet and a set of captain's bars."

Summer 1943
Southeast of Tunis, Tunisia

Major Lee E. Ross was an officer-pilot, USAAF, with 316th Troop Carrier Group, 44th Squadron, May 1943–February 1945.

In the summer of 1943, Ross and the 316th were stationed in the North African desert about sixty miles southeast of Tunis, Tunisia, where they lived in British desert tents. During this period, he and members of the 44th Squadron were ready to concur with Walt Kelly's comic-strip philosopher Pogo who said, "We haf met the enemy and it is us" or, if not *us*, at least one of our planes, a C-47 that Ross flew from time to time.

"We called it our RON, *remain overnight*, airplane," he explains, recalling once when "we had to stay overnight in Algiers" during another malfunction. The story of the recalcitrant C-47 even made the *Saturday Evening Post* in a feature called "A *Post* War Anecdote." In its write-up, the *Post* quotes Master Sergeant Zene L. Riley of Onawa, Iowa, whom Ross knew in the 44th. "Everything went snafu," Sergeant Riley states in the article. "The radio would black out when badly needed, and instrument trouble of all kinds tantalized us, while the insulation vanished from brand-new wires."

Since the mission of the Troop Carrier Command is to pick up men and supplies for the front, it serves as the glue holding the war-effort together. When that glue doesn't work, everything and everyone starts to come undone, Major Ross explains. And so, for four months—of searching and sweating and swearing—squadron members worked, trying to track down the problem. Then one day, one of the posse members discovered an opening in the plane where none should have been—in the soundproofing above the pilot's seat. Reaching in, he discovered and pulled out "the enemy," a mouse so small that it fit in its captor's hand.

May–December 1943
Australia to Goodenough Island

Lieutenant Colonel O. T. Duggan was a second lieutenant, cavalry, 104th Antiaircraft Artillery Battalion, Alabama National Guard, who spent thirty-eight months in the South Pacific.

The 104th spent the first year occupying various gun positions in Australia, from Brisbane to Horn Island to Armstrong Paddock, Townsville. Crediting the diary of Technical Sergeant Leonard "Link" Skeleton, battalion S-3, and the notes of Sergeant Major Harold Fiever, battalion historian, Colonel Duggan provides the story of the build-up on Goodenough Island from May through December 1943.

"The battalion began loading equipment aboard the Liberty Ship SS *Key Pittman* on 5 May 1943; arrived at Milne Bay, New Guinea, 18 May; and debarked at Wagga Wagga, awaiting trans-shipment. A and B Batteries loaded on the Dutch ship *Van Swoll* and arrived at Goodenough Island 29 May.

"We, A-Battery, moved to a beautiful campsite near the airfield at the foothills of an 8,000-foot mountain range. There were coconut trees and banana trees, and not far away there was a nice stream. There were few troops on the island when we arrived but that was to change very soon. The fighter strip, made from interlaced metal strips, was completed and P-38 aircraft began arriving. We set up our 40mm Bofors and quad .50-caliber guns around the airfield and at the jetty for protection of ships in the harbor.

"June and July brought extensive build-up of aircraft on the island. Four squadrons arrived—the 76th, 77th, 79th, and 90th—with over 100 fighter planes and bombers, P-38s, P-40s, A-20s, B-17s, and P-47s. Jap recon planes were over us almost every day, and raids were frequently at night."

After the first month, mail began coming regularly, Colonel Duggan says, explaining that when an outfit moved, it took a while for mail to catch up, and then there might be fifteen to twenty letters and packages at once. "I usually arranged mine by postmark dates, so as to get the hometown news in order. Outgoing mail provided some diversion for the officers who had to censor it. It was amusing to see the many ways the men tried to let the folks at home know where we were. For instance, one would write: 'This place is no paradise but it is good enough.'"

August brought with it a small tent-shaking earthquake, a field hospital "with nurses," the arrival of Marines, plus entertainers Ray Bolger and Little Jack Little with a show for the troops. "Afterwards, Ray Bolger came to our tent for a little poker game."

"Reports from our S-2 indicated there would soon be 30,000 troops and eight fighter squadrons on the island. Goodenough was obviously the 'jumping-off' point for an offensive move in New Guinea."

With the Marines' arrival, food that had been "pretty poor" soon became better. "Suddenly, there were fresh eggs for breakfast one morning. When I asked the mess sergeant where they came from, he said a crate floated up on the beach. I later learned that some 'dock commandos' were jumping on supply trucks as they labored up a hill and 'procuring' a few cases of fresh food. Perhaps all *is* fair in love and war."

Along with Marines and food that were welcome, so too was the arrival of the 209th AAA with 90mm guns, "because our 40mm guns were not of much use against high-flying bombers." Raids were frequent and there were some casualties, with the 209th firing about 600 rounds and shooting down a Japanese bomber during one of the large raids, when one Yank was killed and eight injured.

July 1943
POW Camp Shirakawa, Formosa

Colonel Michael A. Quinn continues his diary-journal from new quarters, his fourth since becoming a POW in April 1942.

On 1 July, in his fifteenth month of captivity, Colonel Quinn begins Book III of his POW journals. "I hope the Good Lord will let me bring these letters home to you," he writes in a brief preface to his wife. "I feel sure when I read these notes over the years to come, they will sound silly and insane, but the writing of them is a lifesaver to me now. We cling to almost anything and as I write these letters, the memories of what you have been to me mean so much."

In his official entry for 1 July, he writes: "We have about forty in the hospital altogether with malaria. After quite a long delay, the Japs got the local Boy Scouts to come out and clean the latrines. The cleaning was badly needed."

On the Fourth of July, Colonel Quinn records the following: "We were furnished 15 kilos of pork by prison authorities, six cookies and seven bananas apiece. . . . Art Penrose and I made quite a tea of it, thanks to the Red Cross. Had canned tomatoes for breakfast, chocolate, and butter sauce over the rice, and at 10:30 a quarter of British apple pudding each, about four ounces, with whipped condensed milk. Also a cup of coffee. At noon, we had an issue meal plus one can of meat and vegetable stew and at 3:30 coffee and cakes. For supper, pork in the soup and creamed rice. Not so bad for a prisoner. Colonel Allpress of the British took service this morning and because of the 4th of July we read Archbishop Carroll's prayers for the government after services. . . ."

On 8 July, he writes: "We have rumors that the Allies have landed in Sicily. . . . Under the circumstances, it is surprising how well the morale of the organization keeps up. We are all hoping for an early and successful conclusion of the war. I am hoping that I will get home by April 25, 1944. You know, I have an important engagement that day [twenty-fifth wedding anniversary for the Quinns]."

"A wave of optimism hit the POWs yesterday. O'Connor and Quesenberry bet $100 that the war would be over by January 1, 1944. I even got enthusiastic and took a ten dollar to twenty-five dollar bet we would be freed by Christmas," he writes on 11 July, and then continues: "Officers are now being placed on fatigue duty. Geneva Convention be damned."

"The fatigue duty for officers is on its way very merrily. I spoke to General Parker, senior American officer, asking him to protest against it and, of course, got the runaround. . . . The leadership we have among the Americans is very 'inspiring'!" he complains on 13 July.

Once more, on 14 July, he notes: "Went to see General Parker again about officers having to work and received a worthless reply, which was just what I expected." On 30 July, he writes, "Some of our enlisted men tell us that the local guards are fed up with the war and expressed the idea that everything will be over by Christmas. I was thinking of the reported $250 million a day that the war is costing, whereas two days' expenditure at that rate per year before the war would have kept us out of this. We certainly save money on our military policy, don't we?"

AUGUST 1943

21

On the island of Sicily in August 1943, American, British, and Canadian forces battle to the successful completion of Operation Husky, with the capture of Messina on 17 August. Statistics for the thirty-eight-day campaign reveal 7,000 Americans and British killed and 15,000 wounded; 10,000 Germans killed or captured; 100,000 Italians taken prisoner; and more than 100,000 Germans and Italians having escaped across the Messina Strait to Italy.

In the Aleutians on 15 August, 34,000 U.S. and Canadian troops invade the island of Kiska, seeking to take it back from the Japanese. The Japanese garrison of 5,000 had, however, already evacuated the island late in the day on 28 July. They boarded two cruisers and six destroyers, under cover of fog, in what has been termed "one of the greatest secret-rescue operations of the war."

In other war-related activity during August, U.S. B-24s bomb Ploesti, Romania, setting oil fields ablaze; Americans capture Munda airfield, New Georgia, in the Solomons, 2 August, and New Georgia itself 25 August; Fifth Air Force raids oil fields at Balikpapan, Borneo, 13 August; and Americans bomb Schweinfurt and Regensburg, Germany, 17 August.

25 August 1943
Mission from Tunisia to Foggia, Italy

Lieutenant Colonel Jack D. Pettus was a second lieutenant and pilot with 94th Fighter Squadron, 1st Fighter Group, Mateur No. 3 Air Base in Tunisia, North Africa.

"I flew fifty combat missions with the 94th while based in the Mediterranean area, leading the squadron and sometimes the group of three squadrons on my last eight combat missions," Colonel Pettus writes. He was initiated to incoming enemy fire, he says, on his second mission, 25 August 1943, "the strafing of eight enemy air bases in the Foggia, Italy, area by three P-38 fighter groups based in Africa.

"We prepared for this mission by flying three practice missions in our local area," necessitated because of "the danger involved in trying to line up abreast 140 aircraft in the air after making a couple of 90° turns down on the deck (low altitude)" to be in "line-abreast formation to swoop across the air bases grouped near Foggia. Although very dangerous, the practice missions were accomplished without incident."

As the 1st, 14th, and 82nd Fighter Groups took off for Foggia, "we crossed the Mediterranean on the deck, dropped our external tanks at the west coast of Italy, and continued on across Italy at about 100 feet above the ground to avoid detection by radar. At the east coast of Italy, over the Adriatic Sea, we made a turn to the north, stretching out in trail by squadron, and to everyone's surprise, including the enemy's, we flew right over an armada of Italian warships at just above mast-level. Few shots were fired due to the low altitude and the surprise.

"As we reached the coast east of Foggia, the groups turned in toward land with all the squadrons line-abreast to hit the airfields. When we reached the airfields, which were several miles inland, the enemy was completely surprised. Ground personnel were refueling aircraft and doing their routine work, but the anti-aircraft people were quick to open fire. I was flying wing on my squadron leader, the normal position for novice combat pilots on their first few missions, when the tracers from ground fire began to fly between our aircraft. Luckily, neither of us was hit. When I saw the tracers coming so close in front of me, I pushed back in my seat as hard as I could to try to avoid them. For an instant, I forgot to shoot at anything, but I quickly recovered and started blazing away with my four .50-caliber machine guns and 20mm cannon.

"Trucks, gasoline store, and aircraft were going up in flames, bombs were exploding, and general havoc was being wrought. About 150 enemy aircraft were destroyed, along with other equipment, but out of our 150 P-38s and pilots on the mission, only two were lost—one pilot who parachuted right over the field I was strafing and one who was shot out of the sky by anti-aircraft over Italy as we were returning to base in Africa.

"The only enemy aircraft in the air that we saw was spotted by me as we climbed back up off the target and started back to our base. I called it in to my squadron leader. Before he could react, one of our other four-aircraft flights peeled out of formation, came in on the tail of the bogie—a Ju-52 trimotor transport—and set it on fire. It exploded and burned so fast that it didn't look as though anything reached the ground. No parachutes were seen to open."

In a 3 September letter to his wife that passed the Army censor, Lieutenant Pettus included a clipping from *Stars and Stripes* that described the bombings: "The little P-38 Lightnings stole the spotlight over Foggia, the southeast Italian air and rail center, in the first long-distance low-level strafing attack of enemy airdromes in this theater."

"I took part in that raid, so see what your old man is doing," her "devoted husband Jack" wrote to Veraleigh Pettus. "My fightin' blood has been aroused! I think I'll name my ship *The Naples Daily Express*, and touch it up a bit on the side, in my spare time."

For that Foggia raid, each fighter unit was awarded a Presidential Unit Citation.

August 1943
Missions to Foggia and Aversa, Italy

Lieutenant Colonel Clyde W. Gabler continues his diary notes.

"On or about 3 August, at night, the Luftwaffe attacked Bizerte, our supply port, with twenty-five Ju-88s. We could see the whole show from Mateur. It was like a huge fireworks display with the rays of searchlights crisscrossing the sky, the anti-aircraft fire with tracers following the enemy aircraft, all in time to the *bang-bang* of the guns and the *boom-boom* of the bombs. Our batteries must have hit some of them," Major Gabler records.

"The 25th of August found the S-2 section up early stretching the strings on the briefing map from checkpoint to checkpoint to plot the course to Foggia. The display board was posted with aerial photos of the Foggia airfields. (Little did we know that next year this would be our location.) The mission was to destroy by low-level attack the Luftwaffe aircraft on Foggia airfields.

"Our group operations officer, Major George A. Rush, was chosen to lead the mission. We put up sixty-five P-38s to be joined by seventy-five more from the 14th and 82nd Groups. Distance to the target was 530 miles to be flown at low level. S-2's order of battle listed over 200 enemy aircraft on Foggia. Our swift and sudden attack destroyed most of them. First Fighter Group lost two planes and two pilots. Our Group, 1st Fighter Group, received its first Distinguished Unit Citation for the mission.

"On 30 August, the S-2 and S-3 officers were up early studying the ops order and the latest intelligence annex. . . . The mission was to escort B-6s to the Aversa marshaling yards near Naples. All three squadrons were to participate, so forty-some pilots attended the briefing, making the Intelligence tent somewhat crowded. Shortly after 0700, the group took off to rendezvous with the bomb groups. Now began the long wait by the ground crews, hoping and praying that their planes and pilots would make it back to base.

"Somewhere near Aversa, the group was attacked by seventy-five enemy aircraft, both Italian and German. A terrific air battle ensued. Our pilots destroyed and damaged fourteen of the enemy while we had thirteen missing. Some were later classified as lost. The 1st Fighter Group had done its job. Not a B-26 was lost. For this mission, the group was awarded its second Distinguished Unit Citation."

August 1943
Sicily Mission to an Olive Grove to Malta

Colonel Robert M. Johnston was a new second lieutenant, up from sergeant/pilot, with 340th Group, 488th Squadron, Desert Air Force, operating out of Comiso Airdrome, Sicily.

Colonel Johnston remembers the call from operations officer Homer Howard that alerted him to what was probably the most memorable flight of his career: "R. M., there's some Limey brass on his way. He wants taken up toward the bomb line. Take 8-A!"

"I didn't care who the Limey was. It beat flak and fighters," R. M. recalls and then continues: "Out at 8-A, a staff car and escort slid to a stop. A top-ranking Limey officer jumped out and raced to scramble up the ladder into the aircraft. Since I was to be his chauffeur, I raced to follow, but he had other ideas.

"Before I could get up the ladder, he buckled into the left seat and commented: 'I say, old chap, I haven't flown a Mitchell for years. Do you mind?' Now I ask, how the hell does a second lieutenant say no to an 'old boy' wearin' all that brass?"

As Lieutenant Johnston settled into the right seat of the "war weary" B-25, his high-ranking 'highjacker' had the right engine running. "The moment the left engine fired, he kicked off the brakes and started to roll. Sergeant Mario Vuotto, crew chief and my only crew member, was racing after us when 'my pilot' asked, 'Which way to the strip?' I was struggling to put in the top hatch and just nodded, 'straight ahead.' By then, Mario, panting like a marathon runner, tapped my shoulder and helped me get the hatch closed.

"At the end of the runway, the old boy didn't look for traffic, slow down, or check the mags. On the run, he rammed the throttles to the firewall and let her go. Before I could get booster pumps, manifold pressure, et cetera, cleaned up, he horsed 8-A into the air with no flaps at minimum speed in hot August air. Needless to say, we weren't climbing too well!

"We were a yard behind the power curve, and the town of Comiso was above eye-level on the hill straight ahead. Now, I'm not even Catholic, but I said a Hail Mary and sneaked on some flaps. We roared right up Main Street, level with second-floor windows. The old boy leveled off at 500 feet and wandered north, looking at the sights like a tourist. I didn't mind the tour till we started to draw ground fire."

Less than an hour after commandeering the plane, the pilot "pointed over the nose to a little dirt strip in an olive grove ahead. Letting go the wheel, he motioned, 'Land at that Spitfire strip, old chap.' After a few sweeping circles, he lined up on that short, short, little Spitfire strip in the olive grove, and it was all mine! He slid his seat back and fumbled for his briefcase on the floor . . . ready to get out. Before I got parked, the old boy was in the staff car, motioning for me to hurry. Leaving Mario to shut down and gas up, I rushed for the waiting car.

"After a mile of racing through dusty back roads, we were driven through a couple of British road blocks and through two dozen MPs into a stone-walled olive grove. In front of a caravan was a long table with white linen and full silver service. A dozen white-coated waiters served drinks to about twenty high-ranking British officers and civilians. I watched the old boy being welcomed like a long-lost son, as I, with a warm scotch and water, sniffed the aroma of good food and tried to blend into the hired help.

"Halfway through my second scotch, the mess bell rang. To my amazement, the old boy motioned for me to be seated with all that rank! Me, a second John, needing a shave, wearing an old fifty-mission crush, and in sweaty, dirty suntans with sleeves rolled up! Seated, I recognized General Montgomery. He had briefed us at times before a landing. It was then I gasped! I couldn't believe I was seated with such great men! Leaders right out of history!"

Explaining that a fire in more recent years destroyed many of his records and that "a full list of top-ranking British leaders at that lunch is beyond my memory," he recalls that "Monty, Sinclair, and Wilson" were among those present. And then, "I heard my 'old boy' addressed as *Air Marshal Tedder*! It was then I understood what was going on," Colonel Johnston continues. "I was sitting in on a coordinating meeting of the British high command as they reviewed final plans for Sicily and the tactical and political plans for Italy."

For Operation Husky, the invasion of Sicily, Air Chief Marshal Sir Arthur Tedder served as commander, Mediterranean Air Command, immediately under General Eisenhower, Allied commander in chief. Lieutenant General Sir Bernard Montgomery was commander, British Eighth Army; General Sir Henry Maitland Wilson was British commander, Middle East, who later became British supreme commander for the Mediterranean; Sir Archibald Sinclair was British secretary of state for air.

"The lunch lasted two hours. After one more toast for success, the air marshal and I were roaring back to the aircraft. He was poring through a sheaf of papers and scribbling notes on the margins while I was figuring how to get old 8-A off 1,000 feet of dirt and over the ridge at the end of the strip.

"When the air marshal bounded into the aircraft this time, he settled into the right seat and continued working on his papers. I started the engines. He suddenly looked up as if he had just discovered where he was. Talking to no one in particular, he ordered: 'Take me to Malta, please!'

"With full power and a running 180 turn, I headed down the strip, hauled 8-A into the air at the last moment and—minus charts but using the TAR formula (That's About Right)—we were on our way to Malta. The air marshal, deep in paperwork, probably was planning missions for old 8-A.

"As we made landfall on Malta, I remembered that the IFF [Identify Friend or Foe, an electronic identification system] hadn't been turned on all day! I swung 8-A around and parked beside a batch of MPs at a staff car beside the sand-bagged entrance to operations. He again rushed to get out, but this time the old boy waited in front of the aircraft as the props wound down. I thought, 'Oh-oh!' and hurried out. Walking toward him, I tried to put some words together, but he beat me to it. Hand out, he stepped forward: 'Thank you, old chap. I'll be on my way now. Good luck!'

"I shook hands and managed to say, 'Thank you, sir!' I gave him a typical British highball, and he was on his way in a cloud of dust, just like he had arrived in the morning: MP escort, sirens wailing, and a pennant snapping on the fender.

"I filed a clearance, turned on the IFF, and Mario and I headed old 8-A back to Sicily. With Mario doing the flying and me feeling relieved, I recounted the lunch story and joked, 'Damn! I wish I'd asked all those "old boys" to sign my short-snorter!'"

15 August 1943
Kiska, Aleutians

Colonel Joseph S. Drewry Jr. was a first lieutenant, a battery officer with 602nd Field Artillery Battalion (Pack) at Fort Ord, California.

Orders came to pack, board the troop train to San Francisco, and depart aboard USS *Harris* for destination unknown, but that "rumors galore" and "straight scoops" placed anywhere from the South Pacific to Russia. Several days out at sea, "we were introduced to a terrain model of our destination, Kiska Island in the Aleutian Islands, the closest the Japanese had come to the United States, except for an isolated submarine or two," the colonel writes.

"The invasion began early in the morning of 15 August with a reconnaissance landing in rubber boats, paddled by its occupants, the 1st Special Service Force," assigned to "reconnoiter the island and point out the Jap strongholds and key positions. The report came back as to the locations, including the report that Force scouts had seen and heard the Jap troops.

"After a while, armed with the latest intelligence, we stormed ashore. I went in with the first wave, along with my radio operator to provide artillery support for the 2nd Battalion of the 87th Infantry Regiment. After a thorough naval bombardment, we pressed inland along the corridor. . . .

"In the ensuing movement toward the north-south ridge, we encountered what appeared to be hostile fire. At the instruction of Major Works, S-3 of the infantry battalion we were supporting, I directed artillery fire from our 75mm pack howitzers onto the suspected enemy.

"One of the things we learned in the artillery was *communications*, with radio as the first means, followed by W110 field wire as soon as possible. As soon as the wire was established, the artillery observers and fire-direction center discovered we had a real fight going between two of our friendly infantry battalions.

"Thank God for artillery communications! The fight was quickly stopped and we pressed on toward the high ground." Meanwhile, back on the very narrow beach, "load after load of landing craft were disgorging cargo of personnel, equipment, and supplies," and the beaches "were crawling with 'dozers and Athey trailers, a piece of equipment that had tracks on it instead of wheels for use on the tundra ground cover. . . .

"By noon or early afternoon, it was determined that the Japs had pulled one off on us. They were not there. We had come to call and nobody was at home. Having assured ourselves by patrols and other surveillance that no one was there, we began the task of trying to get settled as best we could. We took no chances, always considering the possibility of a Jap counterattack. We remained in a position where we could cover our entire sector by artillery fire should the need arise, and dug-in our positions.

"Back at the beach, tons of materiel was being dumped on shore. The beachmasters and rear-echelon supply troops had lost complete control. We were later told that the landing could not be stopped because the ships had to get back to the mainland to be loaded for another invasion in the South Pacific."

After several days on the island and several days into K-rations, Colonel Drewry says that he and Charlie Beach, executive officer with B Battery, "decided we needed something better" and began to reconnoiter several nearby ration dumps.

"We carefully timed the routine of the guard and learned his every move. One night we decided to execute our plan. Right after dark, we commandeered a Weasel—a quarter-ton, track-laying vehicle—from the motor park and set out on our adventure. During the night, we hit the dump in four separate places, avoiding the guard at all times and loaded the vehicle."

"Next morning, we examined our booty. Eight cases of canned apricots! We hit the dump in four places and all we got were apricots! Well, we had every form of apricot you can imagine: apricots with rice, apricot pudding, apricot stew, apricot cobbler. You name it, we had it. I never got so sick of apricots in my life. Even today, I shy away from apricots."

August 1943–September 1945
Burtonwood, Near Warrington, England

Lieutenant Colonel G. Henry Van Veen, with Eighth Air Force, served as chief inspector of the overhaul and manufacturing shops, Burtonwood Air Depot, August 1943 until September 1945.

"The most potent weapon the United States had in fighting the war in Europe was its air power. It was the effectiveness of this superior force, combined with that of our Allies, that finally strangled Germany's capability to resist. Few realized the kinds of effort required to keep this force of thousands and thousands of aircraft—heavy bombers, medium bombers, fighter bombers, and fighters—flying for years," Colonel Van Veen writes.

"The place where these aircraft, engines, and airborne equipment were overhauled, repaired, and modified was Burtonwood, officially known as Base Air Depot Number One. It was located near Warrington, England, about halfway between Manchester and Liverpool.

"At Burtonwood, a complement of over 10,000 aircraft- and engine-mechanics, machinists, electronic technicians, and engineers worked twenty-four hours a day, seven days a week for nearly three years to keep 'em flying. Just as an example, the production-line engineer overhaul facility, with its 2,000 technicians, reached a peak capability of overhauling and testing over 2,000 engines per month. Modification kits for each type of aircraft, necessary to meet the changing needs of air combat, were designed and manufactured in Burtonwood's 2,500-man engine shop and then sent to forward-fighter and -bomber bases for installation. In fact, any part of a combat aircraft could be repaired or overhauled at Burtonwood.

"All enlisted personnel for the Burtonwood Project were recruited from among aircraft and engine mechanics and technicians employed at U.S. air depots or the aircraft industry. All of these men were inducted as privates and were shipped, as a unit, to England from Kelly Field, Texas, where they had assembled. I was proud to have been an original member of this organization."

June–August 1943
Missions from Guadalcanal and New Caledonia

Lieutenant Colonel Leonard W. Frame, who arrived in the Fiji Islands in January 1942, was a pilot with 70th Fighter Squadron, part of the newly formed 347th Fighter Group.

Colonel Frame gives the following account of 16 June after Coast Watchers again reported many Japanese planes heading their way: "When the controllers finally scrambled us, it was almost too late. My flight of four P-39s met a flight of six or eight Zeros head-on at 6,000 or 7,000 feet. We were climbing; they were diving. We fired, but didn't see any results, although a Zero crashed near our camp that ground observers said was shot down by a P-39 but no one claimed it.

"After the initial pass, I made about two turns and I couldn't see another airplane in the sky. I made a few more turns, finally looking directly over my left shoulder. There was a Zero with the leading edge of his wings blinking at me. I did a half roll and dove away but just as my wing came up in the roll, one of his cannon shells hit my left wing, right next to the fuselage. My dive got me away from that one; then I picked up a wingman. We found a group of six or eight planes, P-40s and Wildcats, chasing one Zero right over the water. We joined in. We made two passes. On the second one, he was coming head-on and pulled up over us. We fired and, as he went over my lead, I could see he was flaming. He went into the water. We each received credit for one-half Zero.

"As we approached to land, my wheels would not come down. I had to crank them down by hand. When I did land, the left tire was flat. I was able to control it on the ground and just pulled off to the side of the runway. The cannon shell that hit the wing sent a splinter through the side of the cockpit and scratched my ankle. I checked into the medical tent where they cleaned and put a band-aid on it. I went up to camp, took a shower, and washed the band-aid off but I received the Purple Heart for 'wounds received in action.' I didn't say anything to my wife, so when she got a telegram from the adjutant general that read, 'We regret to inform you that your husband has been wounded, not hospitalized,' she was a little concerned."

Captain Frame flew his last missions from Guadalcanal 12 and 14 July, "providing some of the cover for the taking of Munda, considered part of the Northern Solomons Campaign." After concluding his second tour to Guadalcanal, he again went to group headquarters in New Caledonia for about seven weeks and "flew about thirty-five hours in P-39s, P-38s, and UC78, C-61, and L-4 aircraft."

Then one day, at the operations office, the sergeant called out, "Captain, you made the team!" Not recalling any particular team he wanted to make, he says he was told that orders had come, sending him back to the States. "I 'cleared the base' that afternoon," he says, was given twenty-two days' leave, and was soon in Portland, Oregon, with his wife.

August 1943
POW Camp Shirakawa, Formosa

Colonel Michael A. Quinn continues his POW diary-journal.

If ever there can be a good month in a POW camp, August had to be that once-in-a-lifetime month for Colonel Quinn in 1943. For the first time in seventeen months, he finally hears from his wife, and for the first time in sixteen months he attends Mass. At the PX, there is even coffee and "a landslide of tobacco."

Colonel Quinn records his precious news of 16 August as follows: "What a bright day! I received a cable from you and here it is verbatim: COLONEL MICHAEL QUINN TAIWAN [FORMOSA]. QUOTE. FRANCES QUINN REPORTS ALL WELL. WRITING. LOVE FROM ALL. UNQUOTE. Girlie, if you only knew what a relief it was to me to know that you know where I am and that you know that I am alive, you might understand a little of my happiness. This is the first word from you since April 1942, the day before Bataan fell. I am hoping to get some mail soon, but I can be patient now that I know you know. I am here and I know you are all thinking of me as much as I am of you. After that message, almost anything will be an anticlimax. So I won't spoil it by writing anything more today. Thanks a million!"

The celebrant of the Mass on 22 August is a British army chaplain, a Jesuit from Dublin, Ireland, who arrived with 125 new prisoners 21 August, bringing the prison population to 480. Describing Father Kennedy as a brilliant and kindly man, Colonel Quinn writes on 29 August: "The British say he took the worst beating of any man in the former prison camp. He used to go around to the rest of the prisoners to collect a little bit of rice to bring to those who suffered from dysentery in the hospital. The Japanese insisted the only remedy for dysentery was starvation. When the Nips saw him bring food in, they beat him up. So he was beaten two to three times a day."

On 8 August, Colonel Quinn records that he "signed the payroll yesterday, and I have a deposit of 2,837.17 yen. . . . Never had so much money in my life and less use for it."

SEPTEMBER 1943

22

In mid-1943 World War II activity in the Mediterranean, the Allies invade Sicily, 9 and 10 July, and complete their takeover of the island 17 August. Benito Mussolini is deposed as Prime Minister of Italy 24 July and replaced by Field Marshal Pietro Badoglio who signs Italy's surrender terms on 3 September. News of the armistice is withheld until the simultaneous announcements by General Eisenhower in Algiers and Badoglio in Rome on 8 September at 1830 hours. Nine hours later, Operation Avalanche, the invasion of Salerno, begins its tortuous and torturous move across Italy, with landings on 9 September at 0330 hours.

In the Battle for Salerno, 9–16 September, one contemporary source places U.S. Fifth Army KIA at 1,084 and WIA at 3,525.

12–13 September 1943
Sorrentine Peninsula, Italy

Colonel Richard M. Burrage was battalion intelligence officer, 1st Battalion, 143rd Infantry Regiment, when the 36th Infantry Division landed at Salerno 9 September.

Colonel Burrage explains that Colonel Walker was informed on 12 September of General Mark Clark's order of formation of a task force, which was to locate Maiori and Colonel William O. Darby, commander of the 6615th Ranger Force (Provisional), better known as Darby's Rangers. He adds: "We were to reinforce his three Ranger Battalions, which were precariously holding on to the heights on the mountains in the Sorrentine Peninsula, protecting the road and passes through the mountains from the plains of Naples to the seacoast at Maiori."

However, just prior to loading, the original make-up of the task force (TF) was changed to comprise the entire 1/143rd Infantry and Battalion A 1/133rd Field Artillery Battalion. Ordered to precede the battalion, Brigadier General William H. Wilbur, assistant division commander—with road maps in hand—boarded a torpedo boat, handed one of the maps to the skipper, and instructed him to proceed to Maiori. On board with General Wilbur were Colonel Walker, who would serve as task force commander; Major James L. Land, TF executive officer; First Lieutenant John J. Klein of Company D; First Lieutenant James F. Graham, battalion surgeon; and then–First Lieutenant Burrage, TF S-3.

"We stayed close to shoreline to permit the boat captain to identify land features from his road map," Colonel Burrage recalls. "Upon arriving at Maiori, we located Colonel Darby in the San Francisco Hotel, which had been taken over as his headquarters. Colonel Darby greeted us warmly, hoping that the much-needed help had finally arrived. . . .

"It was agreed that 1/143rd would be responsible for the Maiori road through Chiunzi Pass to the plains below. We would also be responsible for the ridges alongside the road. The Rangers, supported by the 83rd Chemical Battalion (4.2 inch) and part of the 319th Field Artillery Battalion, would take the area from the ridge on the west side of the road, across the mountains farther west to Castellammare. Initially, our naval gunfire support was from two British cruisers, HMS *Blankney* and HMS *Loyal*. . . .

"The battalion loaded on landing craft back at Red Beach and departed about midnight for Maiori. The U.S. Navy did an excellent job navigating in dark waters (no running lights), trying to locate Maiori. The battalion landed unopposed at 0500 hours on 13 September in high spirits. . . .

"At 0800 hours, after the company commanders had briefed their troops, the column moved out of Maiori on the road to Chiunzi Pass. About 1000 hours, our column came under hostile small-arms and mortar fire. We had one officer killed, First Lieutenant Orlando D. Greely from Delaware, our first KIA on the peninsula. Colonel Walker ordered a platoon from Company C to rout the enemy, and he sent a platoon of Company A to make a flanking movement to neutralize the enemy fire. Company C, with support from a machine-gun platoon of Company D, led by First Lieutenant Richard W. Dashner of Bellmeade, Texas, moved out and routed the black-uniformed German paratroopers. . . . The column continued the six-mile climb to the top of the mountains without incident. The balance of the day and night was spent in preparing and occupying our positions, making range cards, running telephone lines, and doing many other tasks necessary to defend the high ground.

"Colonel Darby spent much of his time driving up to Chiunzi Pass in his jeep, which was outfitted with a .50-caliber machine gun on a pedestal mount. He was usually up front with his troops, encouraging them and seeing that they were cared for with whatever was available. I well remember one occasion when Darby was in his headquarters in the San Francisco Hotel, conferring with our staff, when his driver rushed into the room and told Darby that one of their men had been badly wounded and that the other Rangers had moved him to the ditch alongside the road down in front of Chiunzi Pass. The driver and Colonel Darby raced to the vehicle and left in a hurry up the road toward Chiunzi Pass.

"Going down the road, Colonel Darby started spraying .50-caliber cartridges on both sides of the road toward suspected enemy positions. They arrived at the area where the wounded Ranger was lying. While Colonel Darby continued his firing, the driver put the Ranger in the back of the jeep. The driver then started in reverse, back up the hill, with Colonel Darby still blazing away with his machine gun. He passed the blockhouse in Chiunzi Pass in a cloud of dust and continued on downhill, still in reverse, to the local monastery in Maiori, where the 10th Medical Unit (British) was located. This was typical of Colonel Darby's support of his troops. They believed in him and knew that if they got in trouble up there in the hills, he could and would come to their assistance."

September 1943
Mission from Catania, Sicily, to Frosinone, Italy

Major David E. Smith graduated from the USAAF Flying School in February 1943, a second lieutenant in the Army Air Force Reserve.

After B-25 training at Columbia Army Air Base, South Carolina, he went overseas, "not in a B-25, but as a passenger, along with about forty other air crewmen on a Liberty ship. After a twenty-one-day, all-expense-paid cruise, we docked at Oran, Algeria, in North Africa and had a few days' R&R before going to Sicily to join the 81st Bomb Squadron, 12th Bomb Group, named the 'Earthquakers' by German POWs in North Africa, who said that our twelve- and twenty-four-plane raids on them were like being in an earthquake."

Then-Lieutenant Smith joined the 81st in September 1943 at its base near Catania, Sicily, and was immediately assigned as co-pilot and scheduled for his first mission: "to bomb one of the main supply routes and to create a series of massive road blocks near the town of Frosinone, Italy."

With five other planes from his squadron and up to eighteen more from the other three squadrons in the group, "we soon took off and headed north over the Tyrrhenian Sea, past Naples and Vesuvius. Flying over the seas was to avoid AA fire, but when we reached a point a little south of Anzio, we turned inland toward our target and almost immediately we observed flak, which was extremely heavy, from German 88mm guns.

"Fortunately, our B-25s were equipped with a most unsophisticated bombsight, which was designed initially for the Tokyo raid. It was known as the sixty-cent bombsight and replaced the Norden bombsight, which required a long, straight, and level approach to the target, employing little or no evasive action. It was also classified as top-secret and they didn't want any of these sights to fall into enemy hands. With our sixty-cent sights, we used violent evasive action to avoid AA fire but even with this, the aircraft received four large holes, though not one of the crew was wounded.

"When we approached the target, we made an erratic dive from 12,000 feet to about 8,000 feet, then leveled out for the bomb run. When we saw the lead ship release his bombs, we released our eight 500-pound bombs. With twenty-four planes releasing 4,000 pounds of bombs, we did not strive for pinpoint accuracy. We did a tremendous amount of damage, created some massive road-blocks, and effectively stalled German traffic for some time. Of course, this dam-age was repaired fairly quickly, but our successful mission slowed down the Germans a bit.

"After dropping our bombs, we turned back toward the seacoast and relative safety, and proceeded to base operations for debriefing. It was a custom after debriefing that all the air crewmen lined up and received a two-ounce shot of bourbon to calm our nerves, and then we went to our tents or to the so-called officers club for rest and relaxation."

September 1943
Missions from Dittaino, Sicily, and Tunisia

Lieutenant Colonel Clyde W. Gabler continues his diary notes.

In early September 1943, then-Major Gabler "went with the flight echelon via C-47 to a small airfield in Sicily—Dittaino, a landing strip south of Catania. We were sent from Mateur, Tunisia, to set up a short-term base."

"Our group was on Dittaino for the purpose of flying air cover for the Salerno landing in Italy on 9 September 1943. The objective was to prevent the Luftwaffe from attacking the Allied landing force on the ground. At first, there were patrols over the invasion beaches, then interdiction missions behind the German lines. These later were accomplished by dive bombing and strafing.

"From 9 through 16 September, we had been running about three missions a day. It was work, work, work, day and night, for the ground crews and support people. Brief, debrief, and send reports to higher headquarters. . . . Finally, on the 16th, we were relieved, and on 18 September packed up the air echelon and returned via C-47s to Mateur. We had been in Sicily some twelve days and while there had used up the mission counts on several of our pilots."

September 1943
USAHS *Shamrock*, Salerno–Bizerte Shuttle

Chief Warrant Officer Edward G. Robertson and First Lieutenant Helene Stewart
Robertson served aboard the U. S. Army Hospital Ship Shamrock.

After Pearl Harbor canceled out his hoped-for 8 December 1941 discharge, Mr. Robertson recalls, "somebody in the Army said, 'Robertson, we're sending you to Texas to train a hospital ship company.'" And that's where the new concept of the floating Army Hospital was born—in Texas, at Camp Barkeley, 12 November 1942, when three hospital ship companies were activated, assigned to the Service of Supply, and attached to the 8th Service Command.

At all times, "it was cold, muddy, and sandy." And at all times, there were rookies—enlisted rookies and officer rookies—"but somehow we made it." In 1943, at Camp Kilmer, New Jersey, "lo and behold, I find more rookies— nurses." Taking over close-order drill one day for Lieutenant Arata, he saw "a Second Lieutenant Stewart (Stewie), a platoon leader, who was drilling the platoon up through a field when all of a sudden she tripped and fell. I guess she was really embarrassed but she pulled herself up and continued on. (I later had the very good fortune of marrying this gutsy rookie!)"

Late in July 1943, then-Sergeant Robertson and two other sergeants were ordered to the Brooklyn Navy Yard, where they got their initial look at the *Shamrock*. "My first impression was, 'She will never make it up the Hudson River.' I remember the C&B (Cleveland & Buffalo) on Lake Erie that was bigger than the *Shamrock*." But, with hospital ship companies aboard, the *Shamrock* departed New York 4 September, making its way far beyond the Hudson and arriving in Sicily 21 September and at Agropoli, Italy, 22 September.

Waking on the morning of 22 September and seeing the mountains of Italy, Army nurse Lieutenant Helene Stewart writes in her diary: "All around us were destroyers, battleships, and troop transports, both English and American. About 0730, . . . we came up close to the beach south of Salerno. . . .

"In the harbor and out around us were over a hundred ships, all men at their battle stations. We are now only fifteen miles from where the heavy fighting is going on. The fleet was on the alert for an air raid and we saw scores of our planes take off. . . . The destroyer next to us had all its anti-aircraft guns pointed to the sky."

Ordered to move from that hotspot for the night, the *Shamrock* left the harbor as the sun was going down. "About two miles off starboard, we saw some flares from depth charges that were released, possibly suspecting enemy subs, and about one minute later we could feel the vibration from their explosion. It sounded as if we had hit a mine and the bottom of the ship was falling out.

"All evening, until eleven o'clock, we watched the glow behind the mountains from all the fires and bombing that silhouetted the mountains along the horizon. Then we went inside and had sandwiches and coffee. I trust to God that he will keep us safe."

The *Shamrock* returned to Sicily 26 September, and "we could see some of the mountains of Africa when the sun came out this morning" on 27 September as they enter Bizerte harbor. "About 200 ambulances came down from one of the hospitals and, in only two and one-half hours, all our patients were unloaded," she writes. "So many of these boys should have gone with us back to the United States. They will never be able to go back to fight and some will not be able to live a normal life due to the mark of war. I feel extremely sorry for these boys and all boys who have to suffer, and their families, as a result of man's unadulterated insanity, war."

In other diary comments on 27 September, Lieutenant Stewart writes of being "dead tired" when she and nurse-friend Nicky [Margory Nichols] come off duty at 0800; of having ice cream brought to them at noon, their first since leaving New York; of being amazed at the "desolation and ruins of war and bombs" in Bizerte where "not one building in the whole city is untouched"; and of dating, WWII-style, when twelve nurses and some boys from the 92nd Flight Squadron "do the town," riding in ambulances during a thunderstorm. Traveling slippery, muddy roads, they view bombed-out countryside and evacuation hospitals set up in tents; troops camped and waiting to be called to the front; truck convoys along the roads; and "camp after camp of troop replacements."

In the corner of a badly wrecked airfield building, outfitted with a bar and radio, plus table and chairs salvaged from Bizerte, they have fun "talking and dancing and sampling some of their beverages," as the nurses bring the boys up to date about the latest songs and movies back home. The newfound friends part at 0300 and Stewie notes in her diary: "They are typical American boys and they seem too happy, but they never know when they will be flying their last plane."

September 1943
Mediterranean Theater

Major Jack K. Leavitt was a private first class, in the Mediterranean Theater with the 97th Provisional, Military Police, Prisoner of War, Escort Guard Detachment.

At that time, "our MP Escort Guard Detachment headed for the States with a shipload of 1,000 Italian prisoners of war, captured in North Africa. Soon after passing through the Strait of Gibraltar, word was received that Italy had surrendered and declared war on Germany. Our POWs had suddenly become our allies.

"When informed of their new status, our charges exhibited a variety of emotions. Some were elated that they were now on the correct side of the war. Others expressed concern for their families with the German army now occupying Italy. The ship pulled out of the convoy to the disappointment of many who were looking forward to their visit to America.

"We returned to Gibraltar and then sailed for Casablanca. There, the Italians were disembarked and organized into supporting service units. These units served the Allied cause for the duration of the war. It was obvious that the Italian soldiers were never very comfortable with Italy's original position in World War II. Their attitude was best exemplified by one ex-prisoner, who put his hand on the shoulder of his American guard and said, 'We don't want to fight Americans. I have an uncle living in Chicago.'"

September–November 1943
Chieti and Sulmona to Foggia, Italy

Major Joseph S. Frelinghuysen was a captain with First Army, 1st Division, in command of Battery D, 5th Field, when ambushed and taken prisoner in Tunisia, 28 November 1942.

After being taken prisoner by the Germans, Captain Frelinghuysen spent one year in POW camps in Capua and Chieti, Italy. His escape story follows, summarized by him and the editor from his book *Passages to Freedom*:

"Two hundred American prisoners, followed by 150 British prisoners, marched out the iron gates of Camp 21 at Chieti. Outside on the road was a long column of trucks. German paratroopers counted us into groups of fifty, and we were ordered to mount up. About noon, we were dumped into a wire camp north of Sulmona. Dick [Rossbach] and I hurried through the crowd to our assigned quarters. 'Like Christmas shopping,' Dick said, 'you got to do your escaping early. Let's go look at the barbed wire.'"

After four trips around the camp to find the "most promising" place, the two decided on an escape at 1700 hours. An American major queried: 'You men going now?' To their affirmation, he replied: 'Tell me when, and I'll start a diversion.'

"Moments later, shouts came from a soccer game between off-duty German troops. There were cheers, some loud cursing; fist fights broke out. As Dick dove into the wire, the tower guard shouted, ordering the American prisoners to shut up and stop fighting. Some of it looked very real."

The two in turn wiggled and crept through three rows of barbed wire, stood up outside, and walked fast along a road between some buildings. "All at once, a man's head and shoulders appeared at a window, shaving soap on one cheek. He spun around, and a bare arm came out pointing a pistol. He shouted in German as I looked down the barrel.

"'He'll shoot us if we don't go back,' Dick translated. 'We go back,' I said. 'OK, but once we get in, we make damn sure they don't throw us in solitary,' Dick replied.

"Inside the gate, propelled by German pointed rifles, we saw trucks of British POWs unloading on the dusty parade ground. They began to shuffle their feet, raising a cloud of dust. Surreptitious glances told us these prisoners were helping us. Dick and I ran into a cloud of dust, and hustled through the British prisoners, who let us pass. 'Next, we'll go after dark,' Dick said. 'The wire's toughest right by their CO's HQ. Germans'll never think we'd try there.'

"In the dusk, opposite the door of the HQ," the twosome begin again: unwinding wire, wiggling under fences one, two, three, and four, and then: "We crawled about twenty yards to fence five: a stone wall with wire on top. I climbed over, trying not to dislodge any rocks, but a couple fell, sounding like a landslide. I jumped up, ran in a crouch for about 300 yards, then crept past a black, silent house. . . .

At about 1300 hours, "we reached Roccacasale, a small town seven kilometers from the prison. Searching for a place to sleep, we found an old cave on the hillside, collapsed on the rocky floor, and slept well into the morning."

Captains Frelinghuysen and Rossbach continue their "great escape" for about five weeks: hiding in caves; being fed by townsfolk along the way and even given aid by a local partisan, a Communist Party boss, who elicited a promise of "guns, ammunition, radios, food and blankets, so he could raise hell with the German supply lines." The two captains climbed 7,000-foot Mount Morrone; were joined by, then lost, three others en route; swam across the Aventino River; heard gunfire and brushed shoulders with German troops along the way; and then came face to face with three German soldiers in a farmhouse, and were again recaptured. Dick, who by then was nursing an injured leg, provided diversionary action to allow Captain Frelinghuysen to escape once more.

"In early November, I teamed up with a British soldier, Bart Pyle, a gutsy, combat-trained sergeant. On 12 November, we left with two Italians who had arranged a guide," the major continues. "After a hairy passage through German gun positions, we forded the Sangro River on horses. Two days later, we met a patrol of the British 4th Indian Division in Castiglione, just west of Tor-rebruna. . . .

"[On 16 November], I delivered the *partigiani* chief's message to the intelligence officer at British VIII Army Headquarters in Foggia. Bart left me there. He had had a bullet through a knee at Halfaya Pass, west of Cairo, but he never complained once in all those weeks of running and climbing. He is no longer with us, nor is Dick Rossbach, who died in 1987. *Requiescant in pace.*"

September–October 1943
Kiska, Aleutians, to Seattle, Washington

Colonel Joseph S. Drewry Jr. was a first lieutenant, battery officer, who had landed on Kiska 15 August 1943 to dispel the Japanese.

"We had come to call and nobody was home," Colonel Drewry exclaims. Though the Japanese were no longer at home on Kiska, the 34,000 U.S. and Canadian invaders *were*—emplanted there with weapons, equipment, and supplies.

"Kiska was quite a place," Colonel Drewry understates. "We had to dig-in the best way we could to keep out of the cold, wet wind" and those occasional high winds called the *williwaws*. They quickly found out that the best way to dig a hole in the tundra and rocks was with dynamite, and in a short time all were experts, with blasting considered "a favorite sport."

"To help relieve the boredom, our battalion commander, Lieutenant Colonel F. G. Stritzlinger, took a page from Hadrian's book," but instead of a wall he built a road. "Actually, the Japs had a trail and we made it into a single-lane road with passing areas."

For recreation, there was the "boiling of socks and underwear" as a Saturday night ritual and fishing for "the most beautiful salmon you have ever seen." The fishing technique was to "throw a hand grenade in a stream, stun the fish with the concussion, and catch them in your hand."

"After a very boring stay on Kiska, we finally received orders to move out," this time traveling by Liberty ship headed for Seattle, Washington. Since it was early in the war, "we were the first conquering heroes to return to the United States. As we approached Seattle, we could see a welcome skyline and calm water as we entered the Sound. As we neared the dock, we heard the music of a military band welcoming us home. What a thrill!

"However, someone forgot to tell the ship's captain about the tides and currents in the Sound. He attempted to dock without a tugboat assisting. As we approached land, I could see the people getting larger and hear the band playing louder. Then, without any warning, we headed straight for the dock. Just as we were about to hit, the bandmaster yelled, 'Get the hell out of here,' and with that the full band went in all directions. The tuba landed in the water and the last member I saw was the piccolo player heading down the dock. So much for the welcome home for the conquering heroes!"

After four hours and several unsuccessful attempts, finally, "with the assistance of a tugboat, we docked. In Seattle, that hero's welcome finally materialized. Signs in car windows beckoned, 'Soldiers, ride with me.' There were free drinks and beer in local bars, reduced or free rates in hotels, and free meals in restaurants."

1942–62
Syracuse, New York, to the Southwest Pacific

Lieutenant Colonel Catherine P. Emig Strong was Catherine Piraino in 1942, employed by the Syracuse Trust Company, when the Army established an Aircraft Warning Center in Syracuse.

Catherine Piraino volunteered "to assist in plotting incoming and outgoing planes for intrusion of foreign objects. When I volunteered, I had no idea that it would change my whole life," Colonel Emig Strong writes.

Soon after signing on, she and others were informed that a Women's Army Auxiliary Corps (WAAC) was being established 14 May 1942 and that applications were being processed. They were told that the Aircraft Warning Center in Syracuse required three women to enlist, to take basic training at Fort Des Moines, Iowa, and then return for duty to Syracuse, for the duration of the war plus six months.

"Since I would be returning to Syracuse, my parents agreed, with much opposition, to allow me to enlist in the service. This meant I would be leaving my position with the bank, paying me $150 per month, to receive only $21 per month.

"At Fort Des Moines, the basic training companies were housed on Stable Row. We were trained by a male cadre, since there were no female officers at that time. After basic training, we were assigned to school for administration, motor pool, and so forth, within Des Moines. Those of us with clerical backgrounds were assigned to the Savery Hotel for a course in administration. Before we could start our classes, we had to scrub and clean stairways, halls, bathrooms, and kitchens, in addition to doing KP duty.

"While on KP duty one day, I had a call from Mary Vitrone, my best friend in Syracuse, who heard that the Navy was taking applications for service in the

WAVES and wondered if she should join. Well, my reply to her was, 'Mary, this is not glamorous duty. Be prepared to get up each morning at 0530, scrub and clean, and do KP.' Despite my warning, Mary joined the WAVES, but never had one day of KP or any other menial task. She also expected to 'join the Navy and see the world.' She was assigned to Washington, D.C., and stayed there for the duration plus six months."

When Catherine Piraino returned to Syracuse from basic training as a WAAC—with no official rank because WAACs were an auxiliary—she discovered that "living at home with my parents and being in uniform was not what I expected, so I applied for OCS."

After commissioning as a WAAC second officer 23 May 1943, she served in personnel and administration in Kentucky and Ohio and then, from 1944 until 1962, in staff positions, usually in Command Headquarters—among them, USAFE, Southwest Pacific, in Australia, New Guinea, and the Philippines; State Department in Washington, D.C., and Paris, France; and USAREUR HQ in Heidelberg, Germany. In September 1943, the WAACs dropped the "auxiliary" portion in its name and became WAC, a part of the U.S. Army.

OCTOBER 1943

23

Major James L. Land stood atop Mount Pendolo, gazed westward toward the Gulf and the city of Naples, and grimly intoned, "See Naples and die." And he did. Major Land was executive officer of 1st Battalion, 143rd Infantry Regiment, 36th Infantry Division. With him on top of the mountain that day, 15 September 1943, was his operations/intelligence officer, then-Lieutenant Richard M. Burrage. Recalling that moment, now-retired Colonel Burrage explains that they were "on an inspection of front-line operations. As we neared our western boundary with the Rangers, we saw that the 4th Ranger Battalion had secured Mount Pendolo. We continued to the top of that mountain. . . . The view was inspiring, but a somber note was struck when Major Land said, 'See Naples and die.' I heard that phrase from him several times later. It was sad when that prophecy became self-fulfilling."

It happened on the morning of 4 October, when "the battalion (minus Company B) continued in the advance into Guigliano. Only scattered resistance was met as we entered the town," Colonel Burrage says. "As the head of the column reached the far side of the local town piazza, which was on our right, we were subjected to an intense barrage of enemy artillery fire. The barrage killed twelve officers and enlisted men. Fourteen officers and enlisted men were severely wounded." Major Land was among those killed.

In other action in Italy during October 1943, the Fifth Army takes Naples on 1 October, and Caserta and Capua on 6 October. Over Germany, the Eighth Air Force suffers heavy losses in the 14 October raid on the ball-bearing works at Schweinfurt, Germany, and the USAAF temporarily discontinues its long-range, unescorted daylight attacks. In the Pacific Theater, Wake Island is shelled and bombed by the Allies, 5 and 6 October, and the Marines land on Bougainville in the Solomons 31 October, beginning the battle of Empress Augusta Bay.

October 1943
USAHS *Shamrock*, Salerno–Bizerte Shuttle

Chief Warrant Officer Edward G. Robertson and First Lieutenant Helene Stewart (who later became Mrs. Robertson) served aboard the U.S. Army Hospital Ship Shamrock.

In her diary of 2 October from Naples Harbor, Lieutenant Stewart writes of "little activity until 1800 hours when we got a load of 125 patients. I went on duty at 2000 hours and my ward was full mostly of positive malaria. They are much sicker than the last group we had. Over a dozen of them ran temps of 104 to 106 with chills, and they kept me running all night. We stayed in the harbor in complete blackout again and it was quiet outside. We got the news today that Naples had fallen."

"At 1700 hours, we sailed away from Italy on our way across the blue again to Bizerte," Nurse Stewart writes on 4 October. "This time, we had only a little over 500 patients. Nicky, Gage, Scotty, and I played bridge until time to go to work. I had some very sick patients. One boy from Pennsylvania had malaria microorganism. He was beyond help and expired at 0400. Two are sick with severe TB and one mononucleosis, besides other bad malarias, so I had a trying thought about how sad it must be for the people at home to lose someone and not be with him."

On 18 October, the *Shamrock* leaves Salerno for Naples, some forty miles away. "We are the first American hospital ship to come into Naples and we feel pretty proud," Lieutenant Stewart notes. "Colonel John L. Davis [hospital ship commander] went ashore and said that in spite of the damage done only two weeks ago, business is going on as usual. . . . We are blacked-out here and the danger of air raids is greater than any place we have been so far."

"At 7 A.M., we took ringside seats in *hell!*" Lieutenant Stewart exclaims in her next diary entry, 21 October. "Six waves of German planes attacked Naples while we sat here in the harbor. The flares were dropped and the 90mm anti-aircraft immediately opened up. The sky became a fireworks display and bombs were dropping all around. The tracer bullets blazed long trails into the heavens and we saw two German planes shot down. Shrapnel was flying wildly and landed on our decks. We blacked-out immediately and I watched awhile from C-deck aft, but went in when the anti-aircraft came from both sides of us. We got our emergency lights ready in case ours got knocked out of commission; had life belts ready to give the patients, and our own ready. Then just waited until it was all over—*forty-five minutes.*"

As the *Shamrock* ran its shuttles—eight roundtrips from Bizerte to Salerno, Naples, and Oran in October—some of its personnel and crew ran their own shuttles: to Sergeant McAtee's Bar & Grill, hidden in the supply room. In the words of Mr. Robertson, who was a staff sergeant on board: "Many an officer and enlisted man (not mentioning names) made their daily trip to McAtee's Bar. When the *Shamrock* landed at Bizerte [27 September], Sergeant McAtee went scrounging the countryside for some of his old Fort Knox buddies who were with the 1st Armored Division—arriving back at the *Shamrock* about 7 P.M. with a drum of ethyl alcohol! We had grapefruit-ethyl drinks for many a month. . . .

"That sure was some happy drinking with some wonderful people. Those were the days," Mr. Robertson declares fifty years later.

October 1943–September 1944
Missions from Sicily

Major David E. Smith was a second lieutenant pilot who flew sixty-four missions with 81st Squadron, 12th Bomb Group, based near Catania, Sicily.

Soon after that first mission near Frosinone, Italy, subsequent missions were made "to hit roads, railroad tracks, airdromes, railroad marshaling yards, docks, and shipping. These were primarily in close support of American and British armies."

On one mission, "we were to bomb some ships in the harbor of Zara, Yugoslavia, but when we arrived, the ships had already departed, so we picked a target of opportunity a strange U-shaped building and thoroughly demolished it. Shortly after, the group received a letter of thanks from Yugoslav Marshal Josip Tito congratulating us for destroying a German headquarters unit."

10–11 October, 1943
Guadalcanal, Solomon Islands

Captain Bernard L. Patterson was a second lieutenant, infantry replacement officer, who sailed for Nouméa, New Caledonia, 8 September 1943.

"After a short stay (eight days) in or around Nouméa twenty of us went aboard the *John Couch*, a new Liberty ship. On 10 October, we arrived at Guadalcanal and began unloading the ship, anchored about one mile offshore. Seabee and Marine details came out to unload the cargo, mainly gasoline (aviation and regular) in fifty-gallon drums. . . .

"We anchored about 0900 local time. The unloading started about 1100 hours. It went on all day and into the night. . . . At about 0200 on 11 October, General Quarters sounded, a shot or two was fired from the aft gun turret, manned by Navy gun crews, but stopped on order by the crew captain. A plane had come by too close to the stern (under 500 yards) without lights. We rushed out and were told by the third mate to get our helmets, as a raid on Henderson Field was likely and anti-aircraft fragments would likely be falling on the deck. We did. One of the other officers in our cabin asked, 'What was it that Zero was dropping in the water?' In about one minute or less, we knew! There was a violent explosion forward to us. Looking out our one porthole, we saw a mass of flames. A torpedo had hit number-two hold.

"Back out on deck, the watch officer (the third mate) announced, 'The next blast will be the ship,' and he went over the side. Most of us soon followed, but went off the stern to avoid the gasoline burning on the water. Some stayed to try to fight the fire, but it was hopeless. This was a new ship, but several hoses burst from the water pressure. We did learn that gasoline in drums didn't explode, but heat would cause the seams of the drums to split and then it would burn.

"As soon as the alarm went off, the Marines and Seabees on shore sent out LCVPs to pick up their unloading details. One of the bravest things I saw that night was a coxswain driving his barge through the burning gasoline to the side of the ship to pick up his detail.

"It was soon decided to get everyone off and abandon the ship. The LCVPs picked up the people in the water and some off the ship. . . . The *John Couch* burned for three days and was finally sunk by a destroyer. Tokyo Rose noted the burning ship on her broadcast. Two torpedo planes torpedoed two ships and had one or two shots fired at them and got away. The other ship hit was loaded with 500-pound bombs, but the torpedo did not explode. This was the only dud torpedo from the Japanese that I ever heard of. This was, I believe, the last air raid on Guadalcanal. So, our orders were changed and we landed on Guadalcanal, where most of us joined the 37th Division and went to Bougainville in November 1943."

October 1943–September 1945
Kweilin, China

Captain James A. Kinder went into uniform after medical school, internship, and Medical Field Service School, assigned to the Third Air Force in Tampa, Florida.
Captain Kinder was attending Flight/Surgeon School at Randolph Field, Texas, in 1943 when assigned as a first lieutenant to the Chinese American Composite Wing (CACW) to begin "two years as a flight surgeon in the Chinese Air Force" shortly after "Madame Chiang Kai-shek spoke to Congress and persuaded

the powers in Washington to initiate the CACW. The idea was to have close association between the Chinese and Americans for better training purposes, under actual combat conditions in China."

He left Miami in August, aboard a C-54 loaded with about thirty-five CACW personnel; they landed five days later at Karachi, India. "After the hurry-up trip, we loafed two weeks in Karachi, and finally were assigned to Malir. After two months of training the Chinese pilots there, a first contingent, with me included, moved toward China [but] when we got to the Assam Valley, the India side of the Hump, nobody knew we were coming. . . .

"The CACW planes were flown across the Himalayas by crews, of course, but we ordinary folks had to hitch rides with the B-24 planes that made frequent trips. . . . We were welcomed by the B-24s, and did finally get to Kweilin (now Guilin) where we were to stay for about ten months before the Jap ground forces ran us out."

The CACW—about two-fifths American and three-fifths Chinese—was made up of the 1st Bomb Group, 3rd Fighter Group, 5th Fighter Group, and all of the Chinese Air Force. Three Chinese doctors and two American doctors were assigned to the B-25 group at the CACW airstrip at Kweilin, with Major Percy Sutley of Maryland serving as group surgeon and Lieutenant Kinder, assistant surgeon.

When the first contingent flew to Kweilin in October 1943, "we suddenly found we had no interpreter among us. Finally, the local air-base commander was found to speak French, being from Indo-China (now Vietnam). One of our pilots, Charley Miles, had grown up in North Africa where his father was a construction engineer. Hence, through Indo-Chinese French and rusty North-African French, we did muddle through."

In another instance during the early days, on "a river sweep down the Yangtze," the language difference proved fatal. Captain Kinder explains: "One B-25 got shot up. The American pilot decided to bail out, and so instructed his bombardier, also an American. The bombardier went back through the plane, explaining as best he could to the three Chinese crew that they should leave the plane. When the crashed B-25 was found, it turned out that all three Chinese had stayed with the plane, being killed due to a lack of understanding. After that, crews were all American or all Chinese.

"Casualties were few, being either minor or a total loss of the entire crew or fighter pilot. . . . There were actually more bail-outs, with the plane being lost, and the crew or pilot walking back. This 'walking back' took anywhere from a few days to a month or two."

During late 1943 and early 1944, "air raids by the Japs were fairly frequent and usually at night—inconvenient and bothersome but not usually heavy damage. The Japs frequently would bomb the runway, which was of crushed stone, and by noon the next day the local Chinese repair crew had all the holes filled in, stomped down, and pulled the huge stone rollers over the repair to pack down even tighter."

10 October 1943
Mission to Mesa-Chiang Bridge, Burma

Lieutenant Colonel Felix R. Bailey was a lieutenant with Tenth Air Force, 7th Bomb Group (H), 9th Bomb Squadron (H).

On the morning of 10 October, Lieutenant Bailey was dispatched with six other B-24s to bomb the Mesa-Chiang Railway Bridge, east of the Chin Hills in northern Burma, "a vital link in the supply line for the Japanese troops fighting hand-to-hand combat with British and Indian troops in the Chin Hills."

Flying number-seven position and the last to take off, he soon discovered that "part of the engine cowling of one engine was flapping loose." He immediately circled the field and landed safely, with a full load of bombs and a full load of fuel, a feat that he says "had never been attempted before with this heavy load of fuel." After Tech Sergeant Robert Baird, engineer, crawled out on the wing and fastened down the loose cowling, a second takeoff was made. "The formation was almost overtaken as it started the bomb run," Colonel Bailey writes.

Observing that two lead bombers had failed in knocking out the bridge, Lieutenant Bailey elected to make a solo bomb run. With a nod from his bombardier, Bailey "decided to drop down to tree-top level." From that height, the pilot could release the bombs, using a toggle switch on the yoke.

"The low-level run was successful and three spans of the bridge were knocked out. . . . Then we noticed a troop train in a railway station. I turned toward the target. It was left burning after strafing by our B-24 gunners."

Archives show that Colonel Bailey and his co-pilot, Lieutenant Edwin R. Davies, developed the low-level bombing technique using a GI bedsheet. On the windscreen, a line was scribed. "By trial and error, we found where the line and sheet should be in register for a hit. That's when a toggled bomb could shred the sheet from fifty feet AGL [above ground level]."

The toggle switch had been installed on 9th Squadron aircraft in anticipation of assignment to the Ninth Air Force in North Africa. This did not materialize, but Ninth Air Force carried out its remarkable low-level oil-field raid in Ploesti, Romania, 1 August 1943.

NOVEMBER 1943

24

On Thanksgiving Day 1943, the HMS *Rohna* sailed from the port of Oran, Algeria, with 2,000 American troops, who observed their holiday with "a dinner of canned chicken and doughy biscuits, instead of the more traditional dinner." The next day, 26 November, as the *Rohna* sailed eastward through the Mediterranean Sea just off the coast of Algeria, the troops "were relaxing in their cramped and crowded quarters below deck" and "complaining to each other about the 'lousy chow' and the overcrowded 'accommodations,' when suddenly a flight of German bombers attacked the convoy. The ships in the convoy scattered quickly so that no direct hits were scored by the German bombs, but some of the ships were damaged by near misses."

These are the words of Major Joseph R. Confer, who was one of those troop members aboard the *Rohna* in that convoy of Allied ships, "carrying Army and Air Corps replacements, equipment, and supplies to the China–Burma–India Theater of Operations." The *Rohna* was a British freighter converted to troopship, manned by 200 sailors from the Royal Indian Navy and commanded by an Australian skipper, Captain T. J. Murphy.

"Escorting the convoy were a British destroyer, the HMS *Athestone*, and a U.S. Navy minesweeper, the USS *Pioneer*. These two ships put up a furious battle with their anti-aircraft guns and succeeded in shooting down four of the bombers and driving the Germans away. On the *Rohna*, the troops below deck were watching the action from every available porthole and opening in the side of the ship. We all cheered when the first flight of German bombers was driven off, and we were still watching a short time later when the second flight flew over," Major Confer recalls.

"Along with eight or ten other GIs, I had squeezed into a small space beside a large porthole that had been left open for ventilation. From our vantage point, we had a perfect view of the second flight, which apparently was being followed closely by a small aircraft that we thought was a fighter. As we watched, we saw a streak of flame shoot out from the tail end of the small aircraft and then it headed down in a steep dive, passing beneath the bomber it had been following. We all groaned because we thought the bomber had shot down the fighter, but a few moments later we learned the awful truth. This was not a fighter aircraft; instead, it was a radio-controlled glider bomb, guided by remote control by an operator in the German bomber. (Allied Forces later learned that this was the first of these radio-controlled glider bombs to be used by the Luftwaffe in combat; and it did its job perfectly.)

"A few hundred feet above the sea, the glider bomb banked to the left and began spiraling down in a large circle. As it completed the circle, it leveled off just above sea level, straightened its course, and headed directly for the *Rohna*. This was the birth of the guided missile.

"The bomb hit the *Rohna* at midship on the port side about 15 feet above the water line, smashed through the outer hull of the ship, and then blew up with a tremendous explosion. Huge holes were blown into both sides of the ship; the engine room was blown to pieces; the aft deck collapsed; and the ship, from the funnel aft, became a mass of smoke and flames. Hundreds of men in their quarters below deck were killed outright by the horrendous blast of the bomb. The *Rohna* was dead in the water and the captain gave the order to abandon ship."

Of the 1,138 men killed that day, 1,015 were American troops, 120 were ship's crew members, and three were Red Cross representatives. Among the Americans were 491 men of the 853rd Aviation Engineer Battalion, according to an August 1993 article written by Don Fortune for the *San Francisco Examiner* and submitted by Colonel Fred E. Bamberger Jr.

Colonel Bamberger describes the sinking of the *Rohna* as "one of the worst naval disasters of WWII," ranking with the torpedoing of the Japanese freighter *Arisan Maru* in the China Sea on 24 October 1944, when 1,800 American POWs were killed and with the bombing of the *Arizona* at Pearl Harbor on 7 December, when 1,177 perished.

The *Rohna* convoy, KMF-26, consisted of seventeen troopships and ten escorts and was "the first in two years of war to venture into the Mediterranean's 'Suicide Alley,'" Mr. Fortune writes. It was en route to India via the Suez Canal when intercepted—at about 1700 hours, approximately fifteen miles north of Djidjelli, Algeria—by Heinkel 177s of the Luftwaffe from bases in France. "The *Rohna*, exposed in the convoy's 'coffin corner,' was hit by a Henschel HS-293 bomb, a forerunner of the German V-1 rocket and today's 'smart missiles,'" Mr. Fortune adds.

"The War Department in Washington shrouded the sinking of the *Rohna* in secrecy," Major Confer contends, "to keep the German Luftwaffe from finding out just how effective their new glider bomb really was." He recalls only two lifeboats being lowered by crew members. One was fouled and left hanging. The second, overloaded with about 100 men, broke halfway down, sinking immediately."

Too late for many family members, public acknowledgment of the sinking of the *Rhona* finally came when the U.S. Senate unanimously passed House Concurrent Resolution #408 on 27 October 2000, nearly fifty-seven years after the tragedy.

26 November 1943
HMS *Rohna*, Mediterranean Sea

Major Joseph R. Confer was a nineteen-year-old PFC, group radio operator, with USAAF, Army Airways Communications Systems, en route to the CBI Theater.

When the captain gave the order to abandon ship, "the sea was rough and the waves were high, as the troops went over the side, down the cargo net, and into the cold Mediterranean." As the fire spread quickly to the upper deck, the two .50-caliber machine guns on each side of the upper deck, pointing downward toward the water, began firing into the midst of those who were already overboard, Major Confer recalls.

"About thirty minutes later, after all those who could get away had left the ship, the *Rohna* gave a final shudder, followed by a loud explosion deep within the bowels of the ship; then the aft end of the ship went down, the prow came up out of the water, the ship stood on end for a moment and then sank silently into the sea. Captain Murphy, several of the ship's officers, and three American soldiers were still on deck and went down with the ship.

"I stayed on board until the last minute, helping injured men off and finding life preservers for some who had lost theirs. Just before the ship gave its final shudder, I went over the side and into the water. Swimming as fast as I could to get away from the ship before it sank, I looked back just in time to see the *Rohna* stand on end and slide beneath the waves.

"The USS *Pioneer* was in the area when the *Rohna* got hit, and it quickly maneuvered in to pick up survivors. Unfortunately, heavy seas caused many more men to die as they were trying to get aboard the *Pioneer*. Several hundred men swam over to the *Pioneer* and crowded around the ship trying to get on board. High waves were causing the *Pioneer* to pitch fore and aft, and when the aft end came up out of the water, dozens of survivors, clustered around that end of the ship, would be sucked in under the fantail. Then the fantail would come crashing down on top of them, killing them instantly. This happened over and over again, according to eyewitnesses, and it was estimated 100 to 200 men were killed in this manner.

"The attack on the convoy had taken place late in the afternoon, and darkness fell while the rescue work was under way, making it even more difficult. Before the night was over, the *Pioneer* had picked up over 500 survivors.

"The HMS *Athestone*, which had stayed with the convoy to make sure it was out of danger, returned about an hour after the *Rohna* sank and assisted in the rescue of survivors. Captain Murphy, as well as two of his ship's officers, survived the sinking and was rescued by the *Athestone*, along with seventy-five members of the ship's crew. . . .

"I too shared an overturned lifeboat with one of the ship's officers, but not the same boat that the captain was on. After swimming around for a while, I had come upon the lifeboat floating upside down and clambered up on top of it. A few minutes later, another man swam up and climbed onto the boat with me. He was one of the ship's officers. The officer had a pocket-whistle that he began blowing in order to attract the attention of any other survivors who might be in the water nearby, but no other men came to our boat.

"At one point, the waves washed both of the lifeboats together for just a minute or so, but long enough for us to find out that Captain Murphy and the other officer were the two men on the other boat. After floating in the sea for about an hour or so, and hanging on for dear life, so that the waves wouldn't wash us off that lifeboat, we were also picked up by the *Athestone*.

"Survivors were taken to a British Army camp near the town of Philippeville, Algeria. When roll call was taken the next day, just a little over 600 American troops were present, but this did not include the wounded who had been taken to nearby hospitals."

At Philippeville, Major Confer says, survivors were cautioned not to discuss the sinking of the *Rohna* with anyone, nor to write about it in letters home to family. "On 29 November 1943, three days after the *Rohna* was sunk, the War Department received official word from the Allied Forces Headquarters in Algiers," the major adds. "The report stated: 'The HMS *Rohna* sank within one-half hour after being hit. The bomb damage, supplemented by heavy seas and gathering darkness, hampered rescue work, the result being that half the personnel became casualties.'"

September–November 1943
Missions in ETO; Life in USA

Colonel Ruth J. Lepschat Forsythe provides her own story, along with that of her late husband, Colonel John A. Forsythe, a B-17 navigator on twenty-five missions, October 1943–13 March 1944.

After arrival in England, 18 September, Lieutenant Forsythe's group is stationed at Kimbolton. "We belong to the 379th Bomb Group, 527th Bomb Squadron," he writes in his diary. Then, on 30 October, he flies his first combat mission over enemy territory in a plane named *Judy*, and records the following: "This mission was originally scheduled to go to Duren, Germany, but because of weather we went to Gilze-en-Rijen airport in Holland. Saw no flak that day but saw seven Fw-190s and Me-109s come through behind us and knock down one Fort. This is first Fort I saw go down. His No. 2 engine was burning and he fell into a spin, catching fire as he went down. I saw no chutes open."

Four days later, Lieutenant Forsythe flies to Wilhelmshaven, Germany. "On way across North Sea going in, saw two Forts collide and blow up. Biggest piece of either plane was whole tail assembly that would spin down and then level off. Other pieces were sheets of aluminum that fluttered down like leaves and would sparkle in the sun. Saw one chute open but it caught fire immediately. No damage to our ship, which was *Pappy*," he writes.

"Very intense and accurate flak all around our ship although we were at 31,000 feet. Ruhr is supposed to have about heaviest and most accurate flak at present," he notes of mission three to Gelsenkirchen in Ruhr (Happy) Valley, 5 November. "Damage to *Pappy* was light—three small flak holes. Several other ships of our squadron were badly hit and several men injured."

"Fifth combat mission. Went to Bremen, Germany," he records 29 November. "Flak was moderate and just fairly accurate. The fighters were fairly numerous even though we had good F-47 and P-38 escort. Just after we left the target our interphone and heated suits as well as the two turrets went out.

"After we returned, we found that the power went out because of several .50-caliber shells that hit us, from a Fort. We were lucky to get home, since a gas line in the bomb bays was creased and almost cut, as well as an oxygen line.

"Lieutenant Malarin and crew went down on this mission. Lieutenants Malarin, pilot; Burdett, co-pilot; Kenny, navigator; and Webb, bombardier, lived in our barracks and came from Bovington at same time we did."

As Lieutenant Forsythe was leaving the United States in early September 1943, the young lady who became his wife twenty-eight years later, Ruth J. Lepschat, was preparing to enter the newly created Cadet Nurse Corps program after having spent her summer working in the Oregon shipyards.

In after-school hours during her last semester of high school, she and two other girls "went to a local garage and were taught to operate the oxyacetylene cutting torch," she explains. "After high-school graduation in June of 1943, we took our certificates as 'burner' to the Boilermakers Union hiring hall and were soon employed at Oregon Shipyard in Portland. We built Liberty ships. I cut many a steel deck section on the construction ways of the yard that summer."

Enrolled at the University of Portland College of Nursing in September, Ruth "started nurses' training at St. Vincent Hospital and became a Cadet Nurse," in the program established 23 June 1943 by the U.S. Public Health Service. "We soon learned that our hospital depended heavily on us for patient care, under the supervision of the smaller staff of RNs," since so many RNs were in the military. "The Cadet Nurse program paid all of our expenses for school and we received a stipend of ten dollars a month for two years and then fifteen dollars. In those years, that was quite nice spending money."

Because they were on the Pacific Coast, their seven-story student-nurse building, built on a hill, was blacked-out. "All windows had heavy black shades that were closed at night. Buckets of sand and shovels were on all floors as well. Neighborhood air-raid wardens patrolled at night. Doors opening to the outside had heavy, dark curtains; you passed through carefully so as not to let light out.

"Automobile headlights were covered with blue cellophane and cat-eye slits. All neon signs were out in the city. After V-J Day, they came back on and it was quite a sight. We wrote lots of V-mail. We had air-raid drills, usually in the middle of the night. . . .

"Our ration books were used by our families, as the hospital had special status for meat, sugar, and other rationed items, and we were part of the staff. We did not have to use our ration stamp for leather shoes either when we bought our white duty-shoe."

November 1943
Makin, Gilbert Islands

Major Edward C. Gessert, a first lieutenant, U.S. Signal Corps, returned from England, early 1943, after working with the Royal Air Force on ground radar.

In the States soon after starting his Radar Siting class, Lieutenant Gessert received orders for shipment overseas, again. This time, it was on to Seventh Air Force Signal Office, Hickam Field, Hawaii. "I learned we would acquire a trailer-mounted Navy SC-2 radar and participate in a landing operation on Nauru in the Central Pacific. This was later changed to Makin in the Gilbert Islands."

From the *Alcyone* on the morning of D-Day, 20 November, "we watched the bombardment and air strikes preceding the landing and then the landing itself. LCVPs from the *Alcyone* participated in landing troops." Anchoring in the lagoon just off the reef the next morning, the ship unloaded ammunition and "just before dusk, our time to land came and we climbed down cargo nets into an LCVP."

Several days after locating their radar equipment, they moved it to its location, "up the road, a single-lane track, that led through a swamp that was almost impassable and set up our SC-2 radar. With the help of some combat engineers, we were able to revet the equipment with fifty-gallon drums filled with coral. . . .

"After the Navy left, we were the island's only warning for air raids. Since there was no airstrip on the island, there was only AA artillery, with its SCR-268 radar and searchlights, for protection while an airstrip was being built. Immediately after the Navy's departure, small nighttime air raids started, with our radar picking up the first one at about 100 miles, and island command at once sounding the air-raid alarm. As a result, all lights were turned off and this stopped airstrip construction. The bombers didn't appear for about thirty minutes and all of this was lost work time. On future raids, the alarm was not sounded until a few minutes before the Japs arrived, so work on the airstrip could continue until the last minute."

Soon the garrison radar arrived, the airstrip was finished, and aircraft also started to arrive—P-39s, P-40s, and A-24s (U.S. Navy SBDs). . . . About this time, the Navy ordered all SC-2 radar returned to Pearl Harbor; "all Signal Corps radar people on Makin transferred to the 759th Signal Aircraft Warning Company, and, in the absence of the company commander who was on detached service elsewhere, I was the CO."

November–December 1943
Bougainville, Solomon Islands

Colonel William M. Enright was a nineteen-year-old corporal when he landed at Empress Bay, to spend the next two years in the Solomons and Philippines.

Via the converted luxury-liner *Lurline,* Corporal Enright arrived in early October in New Caledonia, where 750 troops disembarked and the balance of the 4,000 headed for India. "Two weeks later, we landed on Guadalcanal as replacements for the 37th Ohio National Guard Division," Colonel Enright writes. "I was assigned as squad leader in the Heavy Weapons Company of Company H, 148th Regiment. The division had just returned from the successful campaign in New Georgia in August and was resting up for Bougainville. The 'rest' consisted of training and unloading ships.

"On 5 November 1943, our regiment loaded on the transports *Jackson, Hayes, Adams,* and *Fuller* for our trip north on the Solomon Sea. On 8 November, we saw the towering mountain ranges of Bougainville and the volcano Bagana. Our convoy settled in Empress Augusta Bay at 0830, as the big guns echoed across the water and H-hour began. The Marines had landed 1 November to light opposition by the Japanese and had a perimeter 500 yards long and 400 yards deep.

By 1300 hours, our combat troops were on the beach, and suddenly, zooming undetected out of the sun, a flight of fourteen twin-engine bombers and fifty Zero fighters ripped into the transports and warships. The ships pulled anchors and headed for the Solomon Sea. Our company was about 200 yards inland. We set up our heavy machine guns and began to fire at the attacking planes. One Jap bomber laid a 500-pound bomb on the USS *Fuller.* It perforated two decks but failed to explode. Five men were killed and twenty wounded from rolling bombs.

"Our battalion was attached to the 9th Marine Regiment when we landed. We had to slosh through the swamps and mud to our position in the west sector.

"The next day, a force of 400 Japs landed at the Laruma River just a few miles north of our sector. The Japs later retreated back into the jungle and mountain hideouts. Jap planes continued to attack during the day. The cruiser *Denver* was hit, but no serious damage.

"We set up our division defense area after a general advance of 1,000 yards. Our regiment occupied the northwest side of the beachhead. . . . On 25 November, Thanksgiving Day, the final defense line was formed. We began our long, arduous tasks of completing perimeter defenses, digging-in guns, stretching barbed wire, and laying communications. The rifle companies were on continuous patrols looking for the Japs. We had our first real meal of roast turkey. It sure made up for all the C-rations we had been eating.

"By 4 December, the Torokina Airstrip was completed, and artillery liaison planes arrived for our air observation. On 9 December, we realized that for the first time since our beachhead, no Jap planes visited our area.

"As the end of 1943 approached, we continued to improve our defensive positions and our living quarters. Our quarters were pillboxes that were six feet wide, ten feet long, and five feet deep. Logs were placed over the top for protection against shell fragments. Our executive officer, First Lieutenant Edwin Joseph, was the first to die in our unit when a large tree fell across his dugout, killing him.

"Three months later, March 1944, the battle for Hill 700 would take place. It was to be the bloodiest battle the 37th Division had yet to participate in. We fought and defeated the Jap 6th Division of Nanking of the 17th Jap Army. Yet another year later, the 37th Division would win another battle as the liberators of Manila in February 1945."

Winter 1943
Bougainville, Solomon Islands

Lieutenant Colonel Lester Kurtis was a second lieutenant in 1942, fresh out of tank maintenance school, when transferred to 13th Armored Division, Camp Beale, California.

The call came in August 1943 for replacements to the 754th Tank Battalion, and Lieutenant Kurtis soon found himself "in combat on the island of Bougainville in support of the American Division. Bougainville was another strategic island in the South Pacific used primarily for sources of supply and a jumping-off point toward our main objective of retaking the Philippines. The climate was usually very hot and humid with rain almost every day, which accounted for the thick, jungle terrain.

"Besides the enemy, we encountered malaria and jungle rot." The daily use of atabrine tablets and "our water supply from lister bags with purification tablets was part of our life. While on the island, our battalion commander came up with the brilliant idea of installing flame throwers in place of the bow .30-caliber machine gun on our light tanks in order to flush out the enemy from their foxholes. This proved to be very successful." Though he remembers few prisoners being taken on the island, one who was captured "had on his possession a personal diary in which he referred to a specific movie we had shown in our bivouac area. . . .

"Some of our best friends on the island turned out to be the Seabees, for we were able to barter with them for fresh meat, which was a treat considering that C- and K- rations were the norm. Also, the pilots returning from Australia furnished us occasionally with some warm, dark Aussie beer." And then there was the "homemade 'still' in the thicket where the boys were making what was called 'jungle juice.' Can't recall what the actual ingredients were, but our CO had to confiscate it. Many friendships were made with the infantry units on the island, and I take my hat off to those soldiers who had to face the enemy on foot in jungle warfare."

November 1943
Stateside to the Fiji Islands

Lieutenant Colonel William H. Starke enlisted in the Army the day after Christmas 1941; spent a year working to become a pilot; and made it overseas in November 1943.

After combat-training in P-38s, Lieutenant Starke and eleven others flew on 20 November to Hickam Field, Hawaii, then to Christmas Island and Samoa, where they "became victims of some very poor timing." The colonel elaborates:

"When we left Samoa the next morning, it was Thanksgiving Day and the cooks were preparing a sumptuous turkey dinner complete with all the trimmings. We weren't too concerned because we would be landing in the Fiji Islands in a few hours and would have our Thanksgiving 'feast' there.

"To our dismay, when we arrived in Fiji that same afternoon, we found they were serving turkey hash! During our flight, we had crossed the international date line and it was the day after Thanksgiving in Fiji! Yes, there was much grumbling, but we still had to settle for turkey hash!"

After hashing it out, they flew on to Nouméa, New Caledonia, "for a few days of combat training under the expert guidance of one of the finest pilots in the South Pacific, Captain Bill Harris with the 339th Fighter Squadron."

Lieutenant Starke and three others were then sent to Espiritu Santo, New Hebrides, to join the 44th Fighter Squadron, and "on 19 December, we flew up to Guadalcanal and joined the combat section of the Vampire Squadron just in time for the all-out strikes against Rabaul!"

October–November 1943
Washington, D.C.

Colonel Donald R. Hart Jr., with 380th Field Artillery Battalion on Maneuver Wilderness in Louisiana, got word of his "long-hoped-for escape from the field artillery."

On checking with the clerk at battalion headquarters on 2 October, Lieutenant Hart was handed "a peculiarly worded and garbled telegram" ordering him and Captain Ed Malcom of division headquarters staff to travel by air to Washington, D.C., for fourteen days' temporary duty. He found Captain Malcom equally astonished at the order, but learned that "they were looking for officers with staff experience and a knowledge of French."

Their stay in Washington consisted mainly of grand dinners and infrequent, casual, and leisurely interviews.

The fifty who passed the selection process, from colonels down to second lieu-tenants, spent six weeks in and out of Washington, "going home when not needed in town and phoning to our new headquarters each day to see if some-thing new had developed. We only learned the name of our headquarters after about four weeks in Washington: Office of Strategic Services or OSS. It was a name not to be breathed to a soul.

"And we had no inkling of the work we were being selected for until one day then-Brigadier General William J. Donovan called us in to a conference. . . . Don-ovan told us how radios had been landed in Africa prior to the invasion there, and how firsthand intelligence reports had gotten out under the eyes and ears of the Nazis. He told us about events in Corsica and elsewhere prior to the landings in Sicily. And that was about all he said, but it gave us the idea we would be sent behind enemy lines ourselves. We had all stated our willingness to do so if called upon, and we had volunteered to parachute anywhere at any time, should that become necessary. We were all set to go. . . .

"We became three little staffs composed of operations officers, intelligence officers, and security officers," each of which, with further training in the United Kingdom, would go separately into France on the appointed day—one with the First Army, one with the Third, and one with the Twelfth Army Group Headquarters.

"We had to learn about the whole Underground Resistance set-up in France. We studied all the diverse political elements in control of the Underground net-works. We had to get to know 'who was who' among the important agents con-trolling various regions of France, how many men each group or network possessed, how many arms were available, and what supplies were needed.

"We learned all the mechanics of packing containers and airplanes; how agents were briefed for their missions; and how they and the containers were dropped to reception teams waiting below in the dark of night at some deserted French farm. We examined all the explosive materials these men used in sabo-taging power plants or locomotives or factories or bridges or military vehicles."

In the field, during the campaign in Normandy, "we were to operate under G-3 (plans and training officer of the general staff) to learn his plan of attack or advance, and then to propose how the Resistance networks behind enemy lines might help this plan by means of sabotaging of rear-line German communications."

Our job, Colonel Hart says, was to serve as "the link between Army or Army group commander, OSS headquarters in London, and the Resistance forces behind German lines. Our over-all purpose was to aid the commanding generals' advance into and through France."

DECEMBER 1943

25

For the United States, December 1943 marks two years since the Japanese bombed this nation into World War II at Pearl Harbor. Two years, and still the troops continue to slosh, to climb, to trudge, to hack, to drive their way through the war—as U.S. II and VI Corps do, battling at Monte Camino, Monte Sammucro, and San Pietro, Italy, in early December; as the First Marine Division does, landing on Cape Gloucester, New Britain, 26 December, and capturing the airfield by 30 December; as the Persian Gulf Command does, traversing the 636 hazardous miles from Khorramshahr on the Persian Gulf to Kazvin, delivering war supplies.

Two years, and still the planes continue their missions in support of or on raids to bomb in the Pacific, China–Burma–India, and European theaters—as in December, when the USAAF attacks Kiel, Emden, and Bremen, and as Mediterranean forces fly sorties against Turin, Innsbruck, and Augsburg, despite bad weather.

Two years, and still the vessels continue to carry troops and supplies, to sail in support, or to bombard—as six U.S. carriers and nine cruisers do, attacking Kwajalein, Marshall Islands, 4 December; as the U.S. sub *Sailfish* does, sinking escort carrier *Chuyo* in Japanese home waters 4 December; as Admiral Lee does, with his force of five battleships and twelve destroyers, bombarding Kwajalein, 8 December; and as Admiral Sherman's Task Group does, raiding Kavieng, New Ireland, 25 December.

Two years and, for many who served in World War II, it may be the first or possibly the third Christmas or Hanukkah holiday away from home.

"When the tree lights were turned on, there wasn't one dry eye among the men and women standing there, and we did not care who saw us," says Lieutenant Colonel A. George Mallis, describing Christmas Eve 1943 with Motor Transport Service 5 in Khurramabad, Iran, where he served as commanding officer, 3927th Truck Command, Persian Gulf Command.

For Colonel Michael A. Quinn at Camp Shirakawa, Formosa, spending his second Christmas as a POW, there is only one wish: "All I want is a letter. . . . Then it would really be a Merry Christmas."

11 December 1943
Mission to Emden, Germany

Lieutenant Colonel Jesse B. Edgar was a second-lieutenant bombardier, who flew thirty combat missions with 95th Bomb Group.

On 11 December, "we were awakened by the orderly at 0300 and were told briefing would be at 0430. We got up, dressed, and went to mess, kidding and joking in expectation of this, our first combat mission. We had the usual 'cackle-berries' (real eggs) for breakfast, which is the special treat given crew members when going on a raid," Lieutenant Edgar records in his diary. At the briefing, they learned their mission: Emden, Germany, population 40,000, the most-used seaport on the North Sea, with the submarine pens their target.

"There were to be 700 to 800 four-engine bombers on the mission, B-17s and B-24s, protected by several hundred fighters, P-47s and P-51s. . . . Approximately 2,000 tons of bombs were to be dropped and, if all went as expected, by tonight the City of Emden would be no more," his diary entry continues.

They took off at 0830 "loaded with ten 500-pound demolition bombs and ten 100-pound incendiaries. The ship was quite sluggish getting off but . . . slowly lifted off into the falling rain. . . . The sky soon became full of airplanes, and all the way over the Channel and the North Sea we looked for our group but couldn't find it. Everything was considerably bawled-up. No one knew just where he was supposed to be. . . .

"We caught the formation just as it turned onto the bombing run. A few small islands just off the coast sent up several bursts of flak and I seemed to just sit there and watch, not really comprehending. . . .

"The next several minutes, so much happened at an incredible speed that I didn't have time to think. I hardly had time to react. We had pulled well into the unknown group. . . . I had opened the bomb-bay doors and we were on the bombing run. As a tail-end Charlie, I did not have a bombsight but would drop on the lead plane when I saw his bombs release. . . .

"Before I realized it, two German Ju-88s were splitting right through our formation, coming in head-on. In a flash, they were through and dived just under our wing not more than twenty to thirty feet away. At the same time that they passed, I saw the B-17 ahead of us shudder as it was hit; the bomb-bay doors flew off, and other fragments fell out," including two crewmen who "were swept past us as their chutes opened. The plane began a long dive downward. At the same time, I saw two other planes drop out of formation, apparently hit. . . . George moved us over in the formation, closer to the remaining three planes left (out of six). . . .

"Suddenly, the plane on my right loosed its bombs and then another plane on my left let his go. When I saw the lead ship finally dump its bombs, I hit the toggle but the bombs didn't go out. A split second later, I hit the salvo handle and the panel lights flickered out as the bombs went away. I quickly closed the bomb-bay doors. . . .

"I didn't get to see much of what was below us. I could see the city of Emden under a smoke screen. It was my belief we had hit short of the target. George banked the ship in a turn to the right and we headed west as the group reformed. And then for the first time, I caught a glimpse of our fighter escort, P-38s and P-51s. They had just arrived on the scene. We later learned they had met some Jerries on the way over and had been delayed when they engaged the enemy fighters in combat."

September–December 1943

The *Queen Mary* to England

Lieutenant Colonel James F. Gruver was a captain with 51st Finance Disbursement Section.

Departing from the United States, his section boarded the *Queen Mary* "on a certain night in September and though the British, for safety reasons, would never permit more than 9,000 British troops aboard we later learned there were no less than 20,000 American soldiers aboard and only half that many bunks.

"The morning we arrived in Plymouth, the Germans had been over; a whole block had been wiped out and people killed. Our men were quite impressed, naturally, seeing barrage balloons everywhere and bomb-blasted Plymouth before them.

"We first set up our finance office on the outskirts of Plymouth in Plymstock. Raids came often and were heavy in the fall of 1943. The closer to D-Day, 6 June 1944, the fewer German planes were to be found.

"During our ten months in England, we watched the countrysides fill up with American soldiers living in tents, watched the vehicles and guns come into the areas, checked and camouflaged, ready for D-Day. During all these months, groups of combat men would come from the midlands, bivouac, and embark on the Channel. Several fake invasions were carried out, which kept the Germans constantly off balance."

December 1943
USAHS *Shamrock*, Naples-Bizerte-Oran Shuttle

Chief Warrant Officer Edward G. Robertson and First Lieutenant Helene Stewart (who became Mrs. Robertson) served aboard the U.S. Army Hospital Ship Shamrock, *which evacuated 12,263 patients on its first tour, 4 September 1943–March 1944.*

"I guess I will never forget this day," Lieutenant Helene Stewart begins her diary entry on 12 December. The day progresses from 0900 with choir rehearsal before church, "a nice chicken dinner," reading on the deck, a nap, and then supper, rehearsal with another choir, and an officers' and nurses' bingo party, when "at 2045, the captain announced over the loud speaker that we had received a distress signal from a destroyer. This broke up the party and we got on our working clothes."

"The boat came closer but gave no more signals," she continues. "We became suspicious, but soon they sent a boat over, carrying three badly wounded patients and said they had eighty more. It seems that this American destroyer and an English destroyer were patrolling together when they sighted a submarine this P.M. about three o'clock. They were all ready to fire on it when the sub sent a torpedo through the aft of the English destroyer with a crew of 150. (Eighty survived.) After being in the water for several hours, they were picked up and then they spotted us and now we have them. (Fifty seriously wounded.) One is near death now and they have operated on several. . . . The sub is still lurking in these waters somewhere. I trust to God that he will keep us safe."

On 13 December, Nurse Stewart continues her diary notations: "I slept very little after I went to bed at 0130 last night. All I could think of were these boys and the tragedy that they had met. I worked with Nicky down on E-2 and the boys were pretty quiet, but appreciative. Their ship went down in four minutes and nineteen seconds! Several told of the things they had ready to mail home—some to their wives, sweethearts, et cetera—for Christmas, and now on the bottom of the ocean. One boy was especially sad because he had seen his buddy jump without a life jacket and he couldn't swim, but this fellow was unable to get to him in time and he went down. And such were the stories that we listened to all morning. They were all thankful to be alive."

December 1943
Tunisia to Gioia-Di-Colle Airfield, Bari, Italy

Lieutenant Colonel Clyde Gabler continues with his diary notes.

"On 1 December 1943, the 15th Air Force Headquarters closed in Tunis and opened for business in the port city of Bari. It would be here until the end of the war. On 2 December, the Luftwaffe during nighttime hit Bari harbor and sank seventeen of our transports loaded with very-much-needed supplies. We felt it later because our spare engines were on these ships," Major Gabler records at the time.

From 14 through 25 December 1943, "the weather was not good and, sadly, we lost some pilots and planes on these missions due to both enemy action and the bad weather. . . . The loss of these five pilots threw a damper on our Christmas spirits. Some hoarded-bottles of whisky appeared to ease the pain. On Christmas Day, the mess personnel did the best they could to put some food together, somewhat resembling a holiday dinner. We still had to eat out of our mess kits.

"About this time, General Spaatz took command of the air forces in the European Theater, General Doolittle took command of the Eighth AF, and Major General Nathan F. Twining assumed command of the Fifteenth AF in Italy with 564 aircraft, 4,873 officers, and 32,867 airmen."

19–25 December 1943
Northern Adriatic Sea

Lieutenant Horace H. Jacks was a second lieutenant, serving as co-pilot when his B-17 bomber was disabled over Augsburg, Austria, 19 December 1943.

"Three engines were out and the fourth was damaged by the shooting," Lieutenant Jacks explains. "It ditched in the Northern Adriatic Sea where four other men and I boarded one of the five-man, rubber life-rafts. I then rigged a sail from the silk of my parachute," and the raft sailed south for six days. "During my time out in the sea, I was very scared, feeling that I might not be discovered or rescued. I was hungry, dehydrated, and lost several pounds. . . .

"I was thinking about my wife Sarah, wondering if she knew I was missing. I wanted to see her and to be with her." With him on that life-raft were Lieutenant James Rayson, bombardier; Lieutenant Joseph Eder, navigator; Sergeant Paul Tramble, engineer; and Sergeant Perez, tail gunner.

And then on Christmas Day, near Bari, Italy, the best of all Christmas presents arrived: a British ship to rescue them. "I then spent five months in a British hospital before being returned to the USA."

25 December

Missions from Munda, New Georgia, to Rabaul, New Britain

Lieutenant Colonel William H. Starke arrived in Nouméa, New Caledonia, at the end of November 1943.

"All through November and early December, bombers and fighters from the Fifth Air Force in New Guinea and the Thirteenth Air Force had been hitting the airfields and shipping at Rabaul, as had planes from Navy aircraft carriers. The Japanese, however, continued to bring in more planes to replace those destroyed in the air or on the ground. But Rabaul had to be neutralized: It was key to opening the route back to the Philippines!" Colonel Starke writes in his self-published *Vampire Squadron.*

"On 27 November, the 44th Fighter Squadron made a dramatic change in aircraft when it switched from the familiar single-engine Curtis P-40 to the larger, more powerful, and faster, twin-engine Lockheed P-38 Lightning. The 44th and the 339th were now the only two fighter squadrons in the Thirteenth Air Force currently flying P-38s. . . ."

On Christmas Day, sixteen P-38s escorted B-24s to Rabaul and served as "top cover," with F4Us and P-40s below, Colonel Starke writes, adding that he will always remember his thoughts that day as they approached Simpson Harbor, Rabaul. "An almost overpowering fear" seized him as he suddenly thought: *What are you doing here, Starke? . . . This is really crazy. You're going to get yourself killed today—and it's Christmas Day.*

"Every instinct" urged him "to turn the P-38 around and head back to the safety of Munda while there was still time!" Of course, he didn't do that but "hung in there—scared out of my wits—my head swiveling around as I searched the sky for bogies, and I constantly checked behind to see that I wasn't being attacked from the rear, as tail-end Charlies are usually the first to be attacked."

At the pilots' debriefing after the mission, "it was amazing and puzzling to listen to the veteran pilots describe what they saw on the airfields around Rabaul, and the number and kinds of ships in Simpson Harbor, and many other intelligence details of the mission." He claims that he was "so busy and scared" that he doesn't believe he "even saw Simpson Harbor."

"From 17 December to New Year's Eve, SOPAC planes had flown 617 individual sorties against Rabaul and claimed destruction of 147 planes against the loss of 19 aircraft," the colonel writes. "Japanese records, however, later showed they had lost only 41 planes, which further confirms this author's suspicion—based on flying many joint missions with them and afterwards at 'debriefing,' wondering if we really had been on the same missions—that claims made by some

Marine and Navy pilots in the 'tales' they told had a tendency to be somewhat exaggerated."

Winter 1943–44

Mission from Munda to Rabaul, New Britain

Captain Andrea Merrick Scheffelin submits her father's story. Then-Lieutenant Edward H. Scheffelin was a bombardier, 72nd Squadron, 5th Bomber Group, 13th Air Force.

Providing background, the Scheffelins point out that Rabaul Harbor on New Britain Island was the southernmost stronghold of the Japanese, and a Navy port, with a large, well-protected lagoon and five airstrips, complete with fighters and anti-aircraft batteries.

"Medium and light bombers would attack Rabaul during the day, and the heavies would continue throughout the night. Every ten minutes or so, a B-24 would take off. From the island of Munda, each mission was expected to take nine hours. In order to maximize their bomb payload, each plane carried only enough fuel for a ten-hour mission."

Additionally, "radio silence had to be upheld," as crews worked with "no radar, no lights, and often no moon to help guide them. On the return from one mission against Rabaul, the weather was particularly nasty. Thunderclouds 60,000 feet high were lit up like Christmas trees from lightning. They were too high to fly over, and it was too dangerous to try to fly under them. Too often those clouds blended with the ocean. Visibility was zero, and the area was dotted with tiny islands and tall mountains. Flying at about 2,000 feet, the pilot, Captain Tom Shearin, had to lace the plane around the menacing clouds. Those maneuvers caused their navigator to lose his position; they were lost," Captain Scheffelin writes.

"With only a half-hour's worth of gas left, the crew began to get concerned. All craned their necks at windows, looking for something in the soup. Finally, Lieutenant Scheffelin saw some anti-aircraft shells exploding in front of them. The navigator determined that the shells had to be coming from Rendova Island, where the United States had a small fighter base. Radio silence forbade any contact, but it gave them a position, and the plane made a beeline for Munda, home, about a half-hour away. Captain Shearin had all four engines leaned out as much as he dared.

"They entered the Munda traffic pattern. On downwind, one engine sputtered and quit. On final, a second engine fizzled out. A B-24 lands very heavily on normal landings due to the short chord length of its Davis wings. Good landing required a touchdown speed of 90 to 100 miles per hour, which also dictates that all four engines are operating.

"Somehow, Shearin made it down in one piece on only two engines. As the plane taxied to the revetment area, a third engine gave up: Shearin parked it with only one engine running.

"Had it not been for the anti-aircraft fired at them, the crew would not have known in time where they were. They would have gone down, maybe on an island, maybe on the ocean: unfriendly land and unforgiving water.

"The angel that flew with that crew did not relinquish her duty," the Scheffelins acknowledge, giving heavenly credit its due.

Winter 1943

Nouméa, New Caledonia

Commander Ethan A. Hurd was personnel officer at Camp Ducos, the living area for personnel at Naval Supply Depot (NSD), Nouméa, New Caledonia.

Commander Hurd witnessed an incident that he classifies "of epic proportion with respect to the history of events that shape the Navy or contribute to the establishment of its traditions and practices." His story comes "not from the exploits and victories of our marvelous forces in the South Pacific and elsewhere but, rather, from the gutsy, intelligent, and forward-looking action of my commanding officer (supply officer-in-command) at Camp Ducos, Commander Herschel Goldberg."

Providing background, Commander Hurd writes: "Many of the men at the NSD were recovering survivors of well-known combatant ships that were lost or badly damaged in the early battles of the Coral Sea and South Pacific. One of my first duties as personnel officer at the depot was to accomplish the return of those survivors to the States on rotation of duty in exchange for replacement personnel. This was, in fact, done, and the replacements came to us as recent draftees, largely from the rural South. They constituted a major part of the station's enlisted complement.

"Into this situation came a substantial number of seamen recently released from detention on the West Coast, their courts-martial sentences for desertion and insurrection having been commuted by the president. These were minority personnel who, while stationed at Port Chicago, California, had lived through the terror and ordeal of massive ammunition explosions at that station.

"This was the mix of personnel at Camp Ducos and the NAS when Commander Goldberg directed the desegregation of mess halls and barracks. As I recall, this was among the first if not, in fact, *the* first such action in the entire shore-based Navy."

"Only one disturbing incident occurred," Commander Hurt adds. "One night in the outdoor movie area, someone making an incendiary remark stirred a small group of the newest arrivals to make a move on the arsenal. Greeting them was the chief master-at-arms, a burly black sailor who, back home in Ohio, had been a leader on the police force of a large city. Recognizing a threat and foreseeing dire circumstances, the bos'n stanced himself before the armory with drawn .45s and, making a line in the dust with the toe of one of his brogans, issued the challenge, 'Any of you bozos cross that line is lookin' for serious trouble!'

"It took only one toe-grazing shot into the dust to cool the passion of the single daring soul who made a move to put the challenge to a test. The threat thus dissolved even more quickly than it had formed. The small group broke up, with each man going to his barracks. Nothing was heard further of this incident and it was not given any official cognizance. Camp Ducos was effectively and acceptably completely integrated. Clearly, a new standard had been set for the shore-based Navy. There was full consensus in the wardroom that we had witnessed and experienced an event of epic proportions," Commander Hurd observes.

And then, in salute to his commanding officer, he notes: "We were proud to be associated with his command. I do not know whether his exemplary action earned any official recognition within the upper echelons of the South Pacific Command or of the Navy Department, but those of us who had occasion to be aware of his further career were not the least surprised that he attained the rank of rear admiral and was appointed to serve a tour as chief of the Navy Bureau of Supplies and Accounts (now the Supply System Command), heading the entire Supply Corps of the Navy."

December 1943
POW Camp Shirakawa, Formosa

Colonel Michael A. Quinn continues his diary.

From 17 December on, when he writes the following, the journal entries are replete with comments about family and Christmas: "Colonel Rutherford received a package from home. All I want is a letter. . . . We all decorated our walls today with a few sprigs of evergreen. I made a frame around the kids' picture. Too bad I don't have a good picture of you, Mike, but I don't need one to remind me of you."

On 23 December, he records the following: "The new CO seems to be trying to help us out at Christmas. We got an issue of bread and sugar and a double issue of jam came. About six ducks are awaiting the old ax, as well as three pigs. Attended a phonograph concert tonight. . . . I got homesick when we finished the program tonight with 'Stille Nacht.'

"Christmas Eve in a faraway prison camp and my thoughts go out to you on the wings of memory," he begins on 24 December, adding that the camp commander made a little speech, told them about the Cairo Conference and wished them a Merry Christmas. "Tonight at 7:30, we had Christmas carols . . . and naturally they stirred memories that are ever present with us but are being more impressed on our minds than ever. Because it is Christmas Eve, we can stay up until ten o'clock, and smoke until 9:45."

"Again, the same old wish of a Merry Christmas to all of you," Colonel Quinn begins on Christmas Day 1943. "We had meat in the soup for breakfast, services at 9:15, and the best dinner we have had since we have been prisoners of war. At 1:30, we had sort of a field day with sack races and picnic events, volleyball between different squads and between the American officers. . . . A musical program and a couple of vaudeville skits amused us in the afternoon. Then the old reliable songs were gotten out, such as 'South of the Border,' sung in both English and Dutch, 'The Holy City,' 'Silver Threads among the Gold,' 'When I Grow Too Old to Dream'. . . . Are you taking movies of Christmas at home for me?"

On 26 December, as he concludes Book III of his journals, Colonel Quinn turns in thoughts once again to his "seven wonderful kids" and his wife: "Now at the close of Christmas, I will close this volume of letters. It is fun keeping this series going, as it keeps you always before me. So when we grow too old to dream, we will have all these things to remember and, out of this separation and sorrow, maybe good things will come."

26

"I know you folks back there are disappointed and puzzled by the slow progress in Italy. You wonder why we move northward so imperceptibly. You are impatient for us to get to Rome," war correspondent Ernie Pyle writes from the front line in Italy in mid-December 1943. "It is not the fault of our troops, nor of their direction, that the northward path is a tedious one. It is the weather and the terrain and the weather," Ernie explains simply. "It rains and it rains. Vehicles bog down and temporary bridges wash out. . . .

"Our troops are living in a way almost inconceivable to you in the States. The fertile black valleys are knee-deep in mud. Thousands of men have not been dry for weeks. Other thousands lie at night in the high mountains with the temperature below freezing and the thin snow sifting over them."

Reiterating Ernie's statements, then-Lieutenant Colonel Burton E. Parker also describes the discomforts of the Italian front. In a letter to wife Edith on Sunday, 2 January 1944, Colonel Parker writes: "Dearest Girl: I wasn't fooling on December 31 when I said we weren't yet miserable. Now we have been. About 2 A.M. on the 1st, terrific winds came again, and with it rain, then snow. Many tents were ripped to shreds and the people with their possessions soaked, frozen, and thoroughly miserable. It kept up until about 5 P.M. yesterday. . . . I got soaked, chilled to the bone, and this didn't improve my feet any."

On 22 January, upon "this terrain that old Dante could have utilized for his *Inferno*, Allied forces effected a landing at the sister towns of Anzio-Nettuno on the coast of Italy some 120 sea miles northwest of Naples," Lieutenant Colonel Curtis Carroll Davis writes. "There they established a 'bridgehead' fifteen miles long by seven miles deep—the first major, enduring occupation of Axis-dominated Europe. From this tiny toehold, the war planners hoped by pincer maneuver to capture Rome more quickly. For several reasons, their timetable lagged, and the bridgehead became home to thousands upon thousands of American and British troops, penned there until a breakthrough in late May."

The initial 36,000 troops that came ashore from 379 vessels for Operation Shingle on 22 January were augmented by 14,000 the next day. That number would reach 110,000 by the end of the campaign, described by one source as "the most brutal and prolonged battle of World War II." Churchill described it as "a story of high opportunity and shattered hopes, of skillful inception on our part and swift recovery by the enemy, of valor shared by both."

January 1944
Naples to Anzio, Italy

Lieutenant Colonel Burton G. Parker submits the WWII recollections and V-mail letters of his grandfather, then-Lieutenant Colonel Burton E. Parker, who served with Quartermaster Section, HQ VI Corps in Africa, and through Sicily, Salerno, and Anzio, where he was severely wounded. Colonel Burton E. Parker died in June 1993 at age 95, "mentally alert until the end."

In his near-daily V-mail communiqués to his wife and children in Woolaston, Massachusetts, Lieutenant Colonel Burton E. drops a few hints during January 1944 of forthcoming action. "My letters may become a little fewer than they have been, dear, as we seem to be getting exceedingly busy, and I'm not always where I can write one, so you might tell the kids not to get provoked with me if I can't hold to our old schedule," he cautions on 8 January.

On 22 January, date of the Anzio invasion, he writes: "Dearest Girl: I have been leading a very inactive [*sic*] but sometimes noisy life the past few days. . . . The reason, I am sure, will appear in this evening's or possibly tomorrow night's paper. So far, this has been a day of high nervous tension."

Lieutenant Colonel Burton G. continues his grandfather's story at this point, transcribed from a 1992 taped interview that picks up prior to departure for the invasion. He writes: "Grandfather started with the story of how the divisions he was in support of were stuck at the Volturno, due to flood water at foot of mountains and well-plotted German artillery fire-zones. Grandpa said soldiers were swept away downstream and those reaching the other side were killed or wounded by enemy fire. Under truce flag, Germans said to come get the wounded and please don't try attacking any more.

"Grandpa's divisions were pulled off the winter line and regrouped in Naples, re-equipped, and loaded out on ships for the Anzio landing.

"Grandpa said the trip north was awesome, with ships as far as you could see in both directions. The landing was with no opposing fire at all, initially. . . . He missed the boat he was to go ashore in and got on one full of trucks and jeeps that were all carrying troops.

After getting all the trucks off, . . . Grandpa [waded in], with water up to [his] chest. . . .

"Grandpa started walking north, looking for his HQ, and came to a sawmill where troops were napping on the mounds of sawdust. He found his HQ some few hundred yards away and decided he'd better start scouting around for places to establish supply dumps. In his jeep, he started toward Rome, noting likely places to set up supply stations, and came to the British sector. . . . Driving on, he came to an intersection with a sign saying fourteen kilometers to Rome. He decided to go back and tell his general the British must be about to Rome.

"Going back, he came on a British patrol whose leader asked, 'What are you doing out here?' The patrol leader said that they were the forward-most patrol. Grandpa said he told himself he was a damned fool for roaming about like that, putting himself at such risk.

"Shortly, German machine-gunners opened up on them, so they all took cover. Then, since Grandpa knew their machine-gun pattern, during a lull, he hopped in his jeep and took off. He said he never heard how the patrol fared in that engagement."

"Last night, we crawled into an old wine cellar far underground and had our first good night's sleep in some days," he writes to his "Dearest Girl" on 28 January.

22 January 1944

Anzio, Italy

Lieutenant Colonel Robert J. Morrissey landed at Anzio, a first lieutenant with 36th Combat Engineering Regiment, which made five beachhead invasions in the ETO during World War II.

"I was assigned as company commander of a company of DUKWs for the landing at Anzio," Colonel Morrissey writes. He describes DUKWs as "the seaworthy truck for ferrying supplies from Liberty ships to shore during and following an invasion."

"Having been told that we would go ashore about 0400, we found our nervous intensity mounting as we waited until 0600 when the front doors of the LST opened and the ramp dropped into the water for us to move down and float away, gaining boat power and proceeding toward shore.

"Unable to swim, I was more concerned about our safety to get ashore, since many of the men were in the same predicament. Once on the beach, my concern immediately shifted to following my orders, which were to proceed inward, cross the railroad tracks, go on to the highway, turn left and drive to a wooded area about a mile north, disburse the DUKWs, and await word for further action.

"As I (standing upright in the lead DUKW—what a target!) moved inward from the water, I noticed a number of our soldiers in the prone position firing toward the enemy. As I drew abreast of them, I sensed a number of *pings* of enemy fire close to my head.

"A soldier hollered up to me, 'Where do you think you're going, Lieutenant?'

"I replied, 'Up to the highway and north,' to which he replied, 'Hell, we haven't taken the railroad track yet.'

"Frantically, I succeeded in disbursing the DUKWs about the dunes in the beach area. We eventually found our bivouac location and worked for the duration of the beachhead carrying tons of supplies ashore."

January 1944
Salsola and Cassino, Italy

Lieutenant Colonel Clyde W. Gabler continues his diary notes.

"On 8 January, the C-47s, workhorses of the Air Force, came in again to move us," he writes. "By 9 January, both air and ground echelons were at Salsola, although our vehicles came by road and reached Foggia several days later."

During stand-down and other times, Major Gabler and available members of the Intelligence Section held study sessions with the pilots on Evasion and Escape (E&E) techniques, based on information received continually from Fifteenth Air Force HQ in Bari. "It was especially rewarding when a pilot you had instructed in E&E returned to the group," he adds.

While at Salsola, Major Gabler spent a three-day pass visiting his brother Lloyd, who was with "1st Armored Division, which was participating in the siege of the Abbey Monte Cassino."

"Our artillery boomed all night, otherwise not much activity on the Fifth Army front. At 0950 hours, saw thirty-six B-26s come over. They were engaged by enemy flak. Plenty of black bursts. B-26s made their bomb run and turned after dropping bombs on enemy lines," Major Gabler writes on 27 January 1944.

"At 1300 hours, went up to front with Lloyd in jeep. Got shelled by enemy artillery just after crossing bridge. Saw our tanks fire on Cassino."

Returning to Foggia the next day, he records on 28 January: "In one of the last missions over Austria, Lieutenant Emmet B. Gresham's P-38 was hit and he lost power in first one engine then in the other. He bailed out over northern Yugoslavia. His flight saw his parachute open. When I included this in the mission reports to 306th Wing and 15th AF HQ, I was inundated with all sorts of queries. Lieutenant Gresham was the son-in-law of Lieutenant General Carl Spaatz. By dint of luck and his wits, Gresham escaped from his captors and, with help from the partisans, was flown from an airstrip in Yugoslavia to Bari in Italy. He gave the S-2 section unstinted credit for his E&E briefings."

Winter 1943–1944
England

Lieutenant Colonel Norman N. Graber trained with the 178th Signal Repair Company at Camp Shelby, Mississippi, and served in the U.S. Army Signal Corps.

"My unit was shipped to England to train before the invasion of Europe," Colonel Graber writes. "We were stationed in a camp near an English ATS unit (Army Transportation Service), comprised mostly of women. They handled the anti-aircraft guns for the area.

"Saturday evenings, they usually invited us to their weekly dance. One such evening was interrupted by the wail of sirens—indicating that German bombers were approaching and would fly overhead on their way to bomb Bristol.

"The ATS girls put on their helmets and ran out to fire their anti-aircraft guns. The sound was deafening, as the planes flew over and the girls were firing their ack-ack guns. When the girls returned, dirty and tired, they all burst into laughter upon finding us 'brave GIs' with nothing to do—hiding under the tables for protection!"

January 1944
Missions to Germany; Life in Oregon

Colonel Ruth J. Lepschat Forsythe submits the diary of her late husband, Colonel John A. Forsythe, navigator with 379th Bomb Group, 527th Bomb Squadron, as she writes of life as a Cadet Nurse in wartime USA.

Of mission twelve to Oschersleben, Germany, 11 January, "when sixty Forts were lost," then-Lieutenant Forsythe writes: "For us, it wasn't a rough mission except for the long period of time we had to fight off fighters. After about 100 miles inside enemy territory, our fighter escort left, except for a few P-51s, and from then on we were under almost constant fighter attack. We dropped our bombs. . . . My gun went haywire, so I didn't get many shots. Flew in 524. On way home, we hit flak, which wasn't bad, at Hannover."

Of mission fifteen to Brunswick, Germany, 30 January, Lieutenant Forsythe reports: "Because of heavy contrails and clouds that we had to go through, we got separated from the group with our squadron ship, number 462. Joined 384th and dropped bombs with them. Had several tail attacks but weren't hit. Tail (Blais) and ball (Donnelly) claimed one each shot down, Fw-190. Hit very heavy and accurate flak on way home over Hannover. Also flak at Ijmuiden, Holland.

Lieutenants Adams, Bowder, Markus, Rosen, Winter, Wiley, Anderson, Torrey went down today. Because of the clouds that we went through, there were Forts everywhere. Saw several go down in flame. Fighters seem to be desperate and come up through overcast. Was rough raid and were lucky we weren't hit by fighters on tail or flak. One small flak hole."

As Lieutenant Forsythe was flying his January 1944 missions, Ruth J. Lepschat was continuing her studies in the University of Portland's four-year Cadet Nurse Corps program at St. Vincent Hospital. In between studies, exams, and floor duty, Ruth and friends found time for social activities when "the local air base sent a bus to our dorm to take us to dances at the base." They also "attended dances at the local downtown USO."

On the fashion scene, "white nylon hosiery became available long before street colors were available. We took the white hose and used tea to dye them an acceptable color for street wear and continued to wear the ugly white-cotton or lisle for duty."

May 1942–March 1944

Abadan, Iran

Lieutenant Colonel Robert Kahn arrived in Abadan 17 May 1942, a second lieutenant with Project Cedar/82nd Air Depot Group. He left in March 1944, with the rank of captain.

"We were the major delivery source of short-range aircraft to the Russians until a fly-through was developed through Alaska and across Siberia," Lieutenant Colonel Kahn explains.

"Project Cedar was initiated before the outbreak of war and was for the purpose of assembling P-39, P-40, and A-20 aircraft that were crated and deck-loaded onto tankers returning empty from the United States, after hauling oil from Iran around the tip of Africa through the Gulf Coast. As a result, we had technicians from Bell (P-39), Curtis (P-40), and Douglas (A-20). We also performed fifty-hour checks on B-25s that were flown across the Gulf of Belem, Brazil, by way of the Azores to Africa, across Africa to Khartoum, then to Cairo, Tel Aviv, and Abadan."

After the fifty-hour checks, the next step with the planes was "painting out the white star and replacing it with a red star and delivering the planes to the Russians." When Lieutenant Kahn arrived on the island of Abadan in May 1942, "the original plan was for us to have sixty days to establish the base. Upon arrival, we found crated aircraft and A-20s with only the outer wings, tail empennage, and propellers removed and boxed." With Leningrad under siege and the Russians needing planes, however, "we delivered the first assembled aircraft to them three days later, on 20 May," and operated from 0400 until 1700 without a break until 4 July 1942.

"Work on the aircraft assembly line was restricted to 0230 to 1000, after which the metal on the planes was too hot to touch. Our schedule was a little irregular: We would have a snack at 0330 and begin work at 0400, with a break around 0730 for breakfast (usually the largest meal of the day), and finish up at noon. The idea was to sleep much of the afternoon, when the heat was at its peak, and then have dinner and enjoy the *cool* of the evening. During the day, some non-shade temperatures ran 150° to 180°!

"We felt fortunate when we could get the temperature in our relatively well-insulated huts (palm fronds on the outside and three inches of mud, which was baked as hard as brick, on the roof) down to 100 at night. We would throw a bucket of water on our mattress and, attired in our shorts, would try to get to sleep before the mattress was dry."

6 January 1944
New Guinea

Major Mearle G. Eisenhart was an eighteen-year-old, "either a private first class or buck sergeant," when he wrote home from U.S. Army Headquarters Port Command, New Guinea.

"Dear Mom and Pop," young Mearle begins, and then continues as follows:

"Here it is Wednesday night about eight o'clock. The fellows in the tent went to the show tonight but I felt like writing a few letters to all on the homefront.

"Had a GI stage show here last night. Sure was good. Played some songs that I never heard before. It's been a long time since I've danced . . . guess I won't be able to when I get back. . . .

"Soon the dirt Japs will be out of the SW Pacific; then we'll see what happens. Our troops are above Madang now and headed for Wewak.

"It's a hot night tonight. A damn cuckoo bird is blowing its top outside in a coconut tree.

"Just got through with a shower and shave and also shined my shoes up. Put Vaseline on my hair and look sharp as a tack, ready to go out and do the town red, but no town. Just tents and GI trucks. Woe is me! You can bet I'll make up for lost time when I get back to the good old States. Me and millions of others.

"Chow has been swell. Steak tonight and fresh cabbage. First I've had since I left the mainland.

"Got the pipe yesterday and am smoking it now. I really don't smoke much. I hate it, but a pipe is nice at a show. It's a swell pipe.

"Haven't gotten any mail the past few days, darn it. Oh, well, it will all come at once one of these days. Never did get that picture of you folks. I mean the big one you were going to send. The fellows in the tent kiss their wives and sweethearts every night, but I'd rather kiss and say goodnight to you, Mom & Pop. Have lots of pictures of girls but still want yours. . . .

"Put $100 in the soldiers' deposit the other day toward a furlough. I will need about $150 more before I go. Hope to make part of it next payday. . . .

"I've got a lot of things on my mind that I'd like to do after this war, but time will tell. Here are some of them: finish school and go to college or stay in the Army, or travel (my one ambition is to complete my trip around the world, and one way you can do that is the Navy or Merchant Marines). . . . This place has made me change but it's made me want to see what I haven't seen and that's a lot. Have met a lot of sailors who have been all over. It does something to me.

"Old Tojo will probably never be over here again."

In a 1993 communiqué, Major Eisenhart writes that he made good on that dream of traveling, taking that "round-the-world trip in the early 1980s."

January–March 1944
Missions from Munda, New Georgia, to Rabaul, New Britain

Lieutenant Colonel William H. Starke was a second lieutenant who flew 120 [sic] combat missions with 44th Fighter Squadron, Thirteenth (Jungle) Air Force.

"The key New Britain target over which Munda- and Stirling-based P-38s flew escort during the month of January was the formidable Jap airstrip of Lakunai on the edge of Rabaul Town," Colonel Starke writes. Having flown his first mission on Christmas Day 1943, Lieutenant Starke was ready for another on New Year's Day. "Fifteen B-24s out of a scheduled twenty-one reached Lakunai Airfield near Rabaul, with an escort of forty-eight Navy F6Fs and twenty-five P-38s. They were met by heavy and accurate anti-aircraft fire, and some eighty to ninety Jap fighters attempted interception. Bomber gunners claimed twenty enemy aircraft, and the F6Fs got five," he reports.

"On a Marine F4U fighter sweep to Rabaul on 3 January, Major Greg 'Pappy' Boyington, the Marines' leading ace, was shot down and taken prisoner and spent the rest of the war as a prisoner. He had twenty-eight Jap planes to his credit before he was shot down."

On 6 January, when Lieutenant Starke participated in his fifth flight, "the 44th Squadron performed an outstanding mission. Sixteen P-38s rendezvoused with thirty-two Marine F4Us and twenty-six Navy F6Fs for a fighter sweep over Rabaul. Bad weather turned back all the Navy F6F Hellcats and all but eight of the Marine F4U Corsairs. All the P-38s reached the target, however, and ran into thirty to forty Zekes and Hamps. In a running fight that raged back and forth over Cape Gazelle, nine Jap fighters were shot down with the loss of two P-38s."

Though not known for this purpose, the P-38 Lightning was nevertheless "used repeatedly as a low-altitude interceptor and with resultant heavy losses in aircraft and pilots" during January, the 13th Fighter Command reports in its January 1944 summary of activities.

During February and March, in addition to Rabaul, "the supply centers of Vunapope, Rataval, Talili, Keravia, Ralum, and Tawai Point ammo dumps became targets for our P-38s and P-39s when these aircraft were being utilized as dive bombers."

In their New Britain and Solomons activity, the Thirteenth "was officially credited with shooting down 169 Japanese aircraft while sustaining losses of forty-three pilots due to combat, bad weather, and accidents."

January 1944
POW Camp Shirakawa, Formosa

Colonel Michael A. Quinn continues his POW diary.

"Another year gone and another one away from you, but still another year closer to you," Colonel Quinn writes on New Year's Eve, 31 December 1943. "All I can think about now is the watch parties and gatherings when we used to celebrate the coming of the New Year. The kids would have ginger ale and popcorn and everything else they could eat. . . . Well, there will be no New Year's kiss, Mike, so we will just have to imagine we had one. . . . This year, we have a great deal to look forward to, and I am doing that with hope and confidence. . . ."

He begins his 1944 POW diary entries with a wish for "a happy and prosperous New Year" to his family, and then adds: "Hope we can all be together during some part of it. As I look back on it, it really hasn't been too bad and I am certain that our country is making strides to ultimate victory but I do hope the matter of differences will be cleared up so our children will not be subject to such situations as I have been in, or worse."

After other New Year's Day comments, Colonel Quinn displays a slight hint of sadness, but ever so briefly, as he continues: "We all wished each other season's greeting, but no one felt too peppy about it. Maybe the weather had something to do with it. It is overcast and gloomy, and all of us are thinking of our own so far away. . . . As long as I couldn't be with you before the end of the year, I hoped

I would get some mail. The worst of it is, there is plenty of mail awaiting delivery some place. . . . May all the good wishes ever expressed be fulfilled with you this coming year. May God keep all of us in the future as He has in the past."

In one of his few indications that all is not always well among the prisoners, he writes on 6 January: "It is funny how this confinement takes the veneer of culture off and some individuals come out absolutely in the rough. . . . Maybe any kind of jail makes politeness unnecessary."

"Had a real hot bath today, the first in almost a year and the dirt peeled off. I got extravagant and used more soap than I have in Lord knows when," he writes on 14 January. With a "big inspection" on 25 January by the commanding officer of all POW camps in Taiwain [Formosa], there was "a conference of some of the prison officials with the senior officers. Vague promises of more food, Red Cross, letters, et cetera. . . . Why can't we get our mail? I have never known what real loneliness was until I could no longer keep in contact with you. Keeping letters from us is so senseless that it approaches downright sadism. But I will stick it out. . . ."

"Louis Dougherty has gone into the fly-trapping business," he continues on 25 January. "We are required to turn in a specified number of flies every day. So Louis goes out, works his head off, and collects. Of course, Louie cheated on this deal. He went down to the pig farm where it took no effort to kill them and brought them back to the barracks. I think the rate of pay is one candy ball for forty flies."

FEBRUARY 1944

27

It stood there overlooking the city of Cassino for more than 1,400 years, almost as much a part of the landscape as the mountain itself: the Abbey of Monte Cassino, founded in 529 by Saint Benedict as a site for religious study by his monks. It was usually a center of serenity where monks copied and preserved the works of Ovid, Virgil, Cicero, and Seneca; where paintings and manuscripts were displayed; where monks worked and prayed. This serenity, however, could be violently interrupted—as it was when the monastery was destroyed by the Lombards in 581; by the Saracens in 883; by an earthquake in 1349. Yet each time the abbey would rise again, more sturdy than before, until in 1944 it stood an edifice 150 feet high and 660 feet long, with walls ten feet thick.

During World War II, after weeks of fierce battle in the vicinity, the Benedictine Abbey of Monte Cassino would once again be desecrated, when the Allies, believing that the monastery was being used as an observation center by the Germans, decided to bomb it 15 February 1944.

"There is still much controversy about the decision to bomb the abbey, but when it was done the bomb line changed from a stagnant position to a fast-moving one, and the American and British armies once again were on the road to Rome," Major David E. Smith writes. A B-25 pilot with the 81st Bomb Squadron, 12th Bomb Group, Major Smith was among those who flew the mission that day. He notes that earlier, "on 2 December 1943, we flew two short missions from our base in Foggia, Italy, to hit targets in the Cassino area but we were forbidden to bomb within a 300-meter circle of the Monastery of Monte Cassino and were to hit roads, bridges, and military equipment. These missions continued until 15 February 1944 when a decision was made to bomb it."

"So we did it," says Lieutenant Colonel Jack W. Lloyd, a pilot on that mission. "No matter the second guessing that has taken place lately. No matter that it seems now to have been unnecessary destruction of a historic place. At the time, it was the only possible decision. Medium bombers at 1,200 feet rained bombs, left destruction, went back to base."

The *Time–Life* World War II volume *The Italian Campaign* describes the raid as follows: "Attacking in waves for several hours, medium and heavy bombers dropped nearly 600 tons of high explosives on the monastery. Between waves, Allied artillery pounded the building with volley after volley. At intervals the smoke and dust cleared, revealing the great walls in various stages of demolition. American foot soldiers, watching, wept with joy. If the men of the 34th Division had any regret, it was only that the monastery had not been bombed earlier. Inside the building, the monks and refugees prayed and died. Perhaps 300 of them—the exact number was never known—were crushed and buried in the rubble, or killed by artillery fire as they attempted to escape. The abbot and forty others survived in the depths of the abbey's crypt."

15 February 1944
Mission to Monte Cassino, Italy

Lieutenant Colonel Jack W. Lloyd was a pilot, FO, in 1943, serving with 82nd Squadron, 12th Bomb Group. Of a particular February 1944 mission he writes:

"February 1944. . . . Today's mission briefing—a monastery overlooking the advance of our troops from a high hill commanding the whole valley. Obviously a high-ground position which must be taken to allow continued advance. Many good men had been killed in the ground effort. Commanders had agonized over the decision, but finally decided to do it. It was a whole group mission, and we weren't the only Allied bombers involved. Everybody went."

Afterwards, "in the dusk, in a cold rain, the squadron commander called a meeting of all members of the squadron. Outside, up on a box, he announced, 'You have dropped your last bomb on Italy.' Pandemonium reigned. Visions of home and Stateside duty sprang to mind. Some of these men had been overseas forever, it seemed. Hooray!

"We packed up, 'roaded' over the mountains down to the toe of Italy, took ship. The *Batory*, a Polish passenger liner, took us to Cairo, where we stopped for several weeks' rest, then on to India. Nobody went home, nobody got Stateside duty. The ground folks, who'd been in Africa before, went out to India. The aircrews, who were approaching the completion of their quota of missions, found out what Catch-22 was. Later, we heard that our medium bomber group went in place of an infantry division that could not be spared from upcoming invasion plans."

15 February 1944
Cassino, Italy

Lieutenant Colonel Walter H. Johnson Sr. was a captain, 135th Infantry, 34th (Red Bull) Division.

"In the terrific, bloody historic battles at Cassino, our desperate plight was such as to appall the most seasoned of fighting men, worn to exhaustion by continuous fighting, terrible exposure, illness, and the devastating trench-foot," Colonel Johnson writes. "The countryside was a soup of rain, snow, and mud. It was an utter impossibility to 'up' sufficient food and medical supplies due to constant harassment by the enemy.

"After courageous assaults, some of our men reached the walls of the abbey only to be driven back by withering machine-gun, rocket, rifle-mortar, and artillery fire. Lieutenant General Freyberg, commanding the New Zealand Corps, decided that the abbey had to be pulverized before he would order his troops to attack it.

"Thanks to the unerring, deadly accuracy of the United States Army Air Force, the abbey was ruinously demolished. . . . Being only a few hundred yards away and in the front lines, we combat infantrymen of the famous 34th . . . witnessed that tragic bombing. The Earth shook, the Heavens roared with blasting, frightful, ominous thunder. Cassino was to resist until the middle of May. Thousands of Polish troops were to give their lives in the effort to dislodge the enemy, as did several thousand New Zealand and French troops. . . .

"After the carnage, and all the bloody and mortal fighting we had experienced in and around Cassino and the abbey, we were relieved from front-line duty and ordered to regroup and prepare to experience another living hell, 85 miles behind enemy lines. The latter part of March, we were loaded on LCIs and LCTs and transported to the hell-hole on the blood-soaked Anzio beachhead."

Winter 1943–1944—Spring 1945
Missions from Italy to Stalag Luft 1, Germany

Lieutenant Colonel M. William Mark, drafted in August 1941, took basic training and was assigned to HQ Company, 44th Division at Fort Dix, New Jersey.

After assignment to the Air Force and combat training on B-17s, heavy bombardment, he was ready for overseas, by now with the rank of second lieutenant. In Tunis, he "joined others living in tents who were part of the Fifteenth Air Force, 301st Bomb Group, 352nd Bomb Squadron. It was a detachment made up of partial crews who had survived missions from different B-17s. As a replacement, I was called upon to fill-in wherever I was needed at any hour of any day. . . .

"In December of 1943, our missions originated from Foggia, Italy. One of these raids took us to Sofia, Bulgaria. We had to cross the Adriatic Sea through unexpected heavy weather. The flying group began to break up as we searched for the target. We lost two engines and were running low on oxygen when the bombs were finally dropped. I could do nothing more than estimate our position as we fell farther behind the other planes.

"A break in the clouds revealed snow-capped mountains, indicating that we were over Yugoslavia. I charted a course for home. My co-pilot came to check on my work. He was so frightened that he told me he wouldn't let me in the life-raft if I had made an error. We were the only plane that made it back from that raid. The others had to ditch in the Adriatic or crash in Yugoslavia. My co-pilot begged for forgiveness and asked that I serve with him from that time on.

"Unfortunately, on 24 February 1944, our luck did not hold. Our B-17 bomb group, flying over the Alps to hit targets in Central Europe, experienced many enemy fighters. Since we were flying in the outer flank of the bomb group, we did our best to protect our group by firing .50-caliber guns at the enemy fighters.

"We were overwhelmed by the enemy fighters. However, our B-17 was badly damaged—in flames and out of control. The pilot signaled us to bail out, which we quickly did from over 20,000 feet.

"I was slightly wounded from the fragmentation bursts" and "the parachute harness nearly slipped off over my head during the descent, but I managed to pull the rip cord and floated down into a snowy farm field. Shortly after, the enemy home guard had surrounded me and eventually I became a POW for fifteen months at Stalag Luft I in Barth, Germany.

"The last days of my internment were especially terrifying. Hitler had ordered that Jewish-American POWs were to be segregated and made part of his 'Final Solution.' It was a race between that fate and the Russian advance. I am happy to be here to tell the tale. It was a great feeling when the Russian army freed us and gave us plenty of food. A short time later, General Eisenhower had B-17s fly us out from a captured airfield to Paris, France."

Fall 1943–Winter 1944
Missions to France and Germany

Colonel Clem R. Haulman was called to active duty in February 1941 with the 74th Coast Artillery Corps (Anti-Aircraft). In the spring of 1942, he transferred to the U.S. Army Air Force.

Second Lieutenant Haulman became a B-17 co-pilot; checked out as a first pilot and aircraft commander of a B-24; and in late September 1943, was assigned to a new B-24H bomber, "the first B-24 with a powered nose turret." He and his crew joined 506th Bomb Squadron, 44th Bomb Group, at Shipdham, England, in early December 1943.

Comparing and contrasting the planes he knew, he says: "The B-17 Flying Forts got all the good press, but the B-24 could fly longer, had more guns, and carried more bombs. They were a hot plane, though—not at all like the B-17s.

"Because of the way the B-17s could fly, higher and closer together, they could help each other out with covering fire. Not with the B-24, though. We couldn't fly real close together and we couldn't fly as high as the B-17s, so we were always in for a rough flight. This was also before the days of the long-range fighters, so we went in alone. Sometimes there would be as many as a thousand planes on a single raid. It was something to see.

"If a B-17 lost an engine or two, it could come home. There was a saying on the B-24s that if you lost an engine, just look straight down because that's where you were going to land. If you had to ditch the plane on the way back, chances are you wouldn't make it out, since the hull had a habit of collapsing in on itself when the plane hit the water.

"Still, she was a great plane. She had a landing speed that was almost as high as some of today's jets, 130 mph. . . ." Commenting that B-24 pilots were considered lucky to survive fifteen missions over Europe, Colonel Haulman cites as example, "one squadron of the 44th, the 67th, that lost all of its pilots but one, Colonel William R. Cameron, who was married to the daughter of General Joseph Stilwell." About to embark on that fearsome fifteenth, "I lost an engine on take-off and we crashed," he adds. He was hospitalized, with injuries, and returned to the States aboard a hospital ship.

February 1944
Missions to Germany

Colonel Ruth J. Lepschat Forsythe submits the WWII diary of her late husband, Colonel John A. Forsythe.

"Two things happened today. First, my promotion came through and, second, I was in a crack-up," newly promoted First Lieutenant Forsythe writes in his journal 2 February 1944. "We (Captain Gibson, assistant group operations, and Lieutenant Blue, squadron co-pilot) were leading the 527th on a practice mission. Everything went well till Blue dropped it in for a landing and the landing gear collapsed under the jolt. I was in the nose and was jolted up some as we slid about 200 yards. The chin turret was shoved up into the nose with me. The ship was quite badly damaged. Although there was a lot of gas, the ship didn't catch fire, even with the sparks caused by the sliding. It burned a little later but the gas didn't catch. We had a full load of 500-pound bombs."

"On the way in," for his twenty-first mission to Halberstadt, Germany, 22 February, "we had a few fighter attacks and some quite heavy and accurate flak at top of Ruhr. We could see ground most of the time through about six/ten clouds. Had to make a second run on target. On way home, lead ship got off course and took us over Koln where we hit very accurate flak. We came out over Holland off course and as a result were again hit by fighters. Saw Simmons get blown up by flak and Sloan get right wing shot and spin down, blowing up on way down. Colonel Preston led, and he and Major Brown both got hit by flak—hurt slightly. Got a few holes in ship. Flew with Segal as bombardier."

"We went to Schweinfurt, Germany, in a very deep penetration" on 24 February, while "twenty-third mission was to Augsburg, Germany, in a very deep penetration" on 25 February.

May 1942–March 1944
Abadan, Iran

Lieutenant Colonel Robert Kahn served in Abadan, Iran, 17 May 1942–March 1944 with Project Cedar, 82nd Air Depot Group.

Colonel Kahn writes about what he calls "problem areas encountered during his tour: dust, overenthusiastic pilots, the British, and the Russians.

Dust, or at least the pretext of dust, was the reason a much-anticipated Jack Benny troupe did not arrive on schedule to perform at the Abadan base before going on to play Khorramshahr the next night. "When the troupe flew over Habaniyah, due west of Baghdad, the British Weather Service told them they would have to land there and stay overnight because we were 'dusted in' at Abadan. Once landed, they were asked to put on their show for the RAF, which they gladly did."

The USO troupe "arrived the following morning and said how sorry they were that we had been 'dusted in.'"

Featured with Jack Benny were two actresses and harmonica virtuoso Larry Adler. Colonel Kahn notes that "Jack was not a well man, nor a young man at the time (his personal physician was traveling with him). When he found out about all of the small bases, besides the large ones he was going to play, he said that he would play all of them in the thirteen to fourteen days he was going to be there if we could get him to them. We had a four-passenger Waco and a Piper Cub, so we had six seats to take four people as passengers. They played every station and hospital and switching yard. Many times, they had to get trucks out to block a section of the road for the planes to land. Sometimes we would deliver them to a base and then there would be a special train that would take them another 50 or 60 miles to the next stop on the railroad.

"We had some 250 Russians stationed on our base, whose job was to accept the aircraft. The planes were technically on Lend-Lease. The Russians were forwarded packing slips through their channels to a Russian commander named Obreskov.

"At one time, we had more than 100 planes, mainly A-20s, backed up on the field. The Russians would not take them because, according to the packing list, such things were missing as canvas muzzle-covers for machine guns, first-aid kits, et cetera.

"Being a bunch of Reservists and young officers, we sort of made our own rules as we went along. Since Charlie Porter was the CO, he notified the British in Cairo that we had 100 A-20s, which were exactly the same as their DB-7s, and if they sent pilots, they could have them. The next day, the British Dakotas, which we call C-47s, began to arrive and, to the consternation of Obreskov, British pilots flew all 100 off, to use in the Western Desert!"

Winter 1943–1944

USS *Luce* at Kurile Islands; Camp Davao, the Philippines

Chief Warrant Officer Clifford A. Roberts served aboard the USS Dickerson *six months prior to World War II. During the war, as he served aboard other ships, his brother Hugh was confined as a Japanese POW in the Philippines.*

After the *Dickerson* escorted the first convoy to Casablanca, Morocco, for the invasion of North Africa, Mister Roberts transferred to the USS *Hobby* (DD-610) and then to the USS *Luce* (DD-522). The *Luce* was the "ship sent to Alaska to bombard the Kurile Islands," the chain of thirty-two islands extending northeast to southwest from Kamchatka Peninsula, USSR. "I was then chief fire-control-man with a very good crew of young fire-controlmen," Mister Roberts recalls. "I went to the battle-plan meeting, as it mainly concerned our assignment, guns and accuracy.

"The first raid was the only one made on a clear night, as our nearest air cover-age was 1,200 miles away. Each ship was given an area to wipe out. Our first target was the communications shack and tower because, as we were told, if they got a message out, no one would return. At the north end of Paramushiru Island was a large Japanese air base, fifty-five miles away.

"Our second raid was a small airfield. We were told not to let a plane get off the ground. They didn't. It was a beautiful raid. We operated with six destroyers and two old battleships.

"After that, we bombarded other islands, but always under cover of fog. Often, we would have to silence the guns, as we could hear Jap planes above and the flash of guns would pinpoint the ship. It was a very scary situation, as our nearest help was too far away to do any good. I was standing gunner-officer's watches, along with two officers, so I could keep up with what was going on.

"The weather was an element you couldn't depend on. It was mighty bad at times."

He acknowledges that he doesn't remember names of ships that accompanied the *Luce* to the Kuriles but "the two old battleships were four-stackers and there weren't many of them left. I think one was the *Mississippi*."

He says that, as far as he can determine, "we were bombarding the Kurile Islands the winter of 1943–44." He provides a copy of the *New York Times Index*, which records the following: "U.S. warships shell Paramushiru Island south and east coasts; hit Jap ships; planes raid Paramushiru and Shimushu; U.S. naval bombardment of Kurabu Point, Paramushiru, under Rear Admiral W. Baker's leadership" on 8 February 1944.

As for his vessel, "the USS *Luce* and crew was a ship to be proud of. It did a great job!"

From assignment in the Kuriles, the *Luce* in October 1944 went on to the Leyte invasion in the Philippines, where his brother, First Lieutenant Hugh H. Roberts, was interned as a Japanese POW.

In his one letter that described his four-year captivity, Lieutenant Roberts writes of receiving two individual American Red Cross packages on 29 February 1944. "And most of us received shoes but were not permitted to wear them until 13 November 1944," when the prisoners were sent back to Camp Bilibid, Manila.

"Very few men got shoes that fit because the Japs confiscated all the wide widths for their army. Mine are a size narrow and one-half-size too long," his letter continues.

"A lot of vitamin shots and pills came with the Red Cross [packages] and were sure a godsend. I received something over 60 B-1 shots while some cases received over 100, besides each man receiving 200 pills, which contained a 100-days' supply of all the vitamins necessary.

"About May 1944, we received a third ten-pound package of food. The protein in the packages, with the vitamin pills, helped my beriberi a lot but did not improve my eyes much, and I doubt if they ever come back because the optic nerve is dead. Of course, glasses won't help."

February 1944
POW Camp Shirakawa, Formosa

Colonel Michael A. Quinn records his glorious news for February in his POW diary.

Let cannons roar, let church bells ring, let choirs proclaim "Hosanna!" As Colonel Quinn might exclaim, "*Mirabile dictu* (wonderful to relate)," the prisoners of war at Camp Shirakawa finally receive their long-awaited mail on 22 February. For Colonel Quinn, this means twenty-two letters and cards after twenty-two months in captivity.

In his 23 February 1944 entry, he writes: "Yesterday was the day of days for the prisoners of war. How hungry we were for news and when we got our letters, some cried and some laughed. I read all of your letters about five times and showed the pictures to everybody. I feel so happy and think that everyone should get the same thrill that I do. I didn't get the letter Tom said he was sending nor did I get his or Pat's pictures. Had I gotten those, I think my cup of happiness would have overflowed. All I can say is, thank God for what I did get. The big thrill I got out of it, Mike, was that our family is working so well together. It seems to be a close corporation. That is what I have always wanted. Throughout all your letters, I read how you are all working together and for each other unselfishly. Just one family, one thought, one loyalty. May that always be so. . . ."

His entry continues with special messages to each of the children. To son Michael, he says, "Mike, I am proud of you making your own expenses. You were always an independent cuss, though. Keep it up."

On 25 February, he is still exulting, as he writes: "I have read your letters over and over again and I believe I enjoyed them just as much now as when I first got them. . . . Some of the letters brought sadness to some of our prisoners. Colonel Chase, Coast Artillery Corps, received word that his wife died last July. So today all of us offered our Mass to her memory. . . ."

In his 2 February entry, Colonel Quinn records: "Doc Worthington and Bill Braddock were stood up for pinching peanuts yesterday. Worthington got out of it all right, but Braddock was severely beaten up. As a matter of fact, they broke one of his teeth. (Note [added by Colonel Quinn in postwar editing]: Braddock was knocked down and while down was kicked in the jaw by the camp commander. Fortunately for Braddock, he was unconscious and didn't realize the severe beating he had gotten until weeks afterward when one of our soldiers who saw it described it.)"

MARCH 1944

28

Through the centuries, every parent who has ever sent a son—and now, a daughter—off to war has done so with trepidation. At least since 338 B.C. when Queen Olympias sent her eighteen-year-old son Alexander the Great off to his first battle at Chaeronea—after prayers to gods and God, after worry beads and rosary beads—there has always remained that disquieting sense of 'What else can I do?' For one brave but frightened mother from Daisy, Georgia, during the 1944 winter of World War II, that concern took the form of a letter to her son's commanding officer, asking him to look after her boy.

"Dear Captain, I have a little son who is in your Company. I, like the other million mothers, am thinking of him always. He writes me often and tells me he is well," her V-mail letter begins. "I wonder if you would do one of these little mothers the greatest favor she ever asked anyone. Would you please place your hand upon his shoulder and tell him his Mom asked you to for her. And write me just how he is. I hope he has made you a good boy. I could not ask for a better one than he has been to me. I am doing all I can for you boys. I buy every [War] Bond I can. I hope you will all be hurrying home soon to your loved ones. I pray for all of you and I know you will take good care of my boy for me. What I'd give to hold him in my arms. Hurry back and best of luck." The "little mother" then signs her name and identifies her son.

Lieutenant Colonel Joseph A. Vargas III was the captain who received that unprecedented letter. A commander whose men teased him about having the longest name in the military, Captain Vargas was with the 729th Railway Operating Battalion (ROB), which arrived in England in mid-1943. He was serving at Refresher Military Training locations in Manchester when the V-mail letter arrived 3 March. "I replied favorably to her on 6 March 1944," Colonel Vargas writes, explaining that the young sergeant "was a good dispatcher for our chief railway dispatcher, Lieutenant W. B. Gunion, and proved so during our busy train operations in Normandy, July through December 1944."

After Normandy, the 729th ROB went on to the Port of Antwerp, Belgium, where "we were under continual V-1 and V-2 missile attack" and where the sergeant was hospitalized in January 1945 at the U.S. Army hospital on the outskirts of Antwerp. "When I visited him to see how he was doing, he immediately asked me to get him out of the hospital and back to his unit. The constant V-1 buzzing was worse there than in the city," the colonel notes, for "in spite of the AA defense, some of the V-1 (buzz bombs) got through to the city and in doing so passed right over the station hospital (Buzz Bomb Alley)."

Mid-March–29 April 1944
Anzio, Italy

Lieutenant Colonel Curtis Carroll Davis, an Air Force first lieutenant, served on the Anzio Beachhead, Allied Headquarters, as air interrogator of surviving Luftwaffe flight personnel.

"I was attached to the British Air Ministry's command, dubbed 'Siz-Dik,'" for Combined Services Detailed Interrogation Center (CSDIC). While serving "on that littered landscape of shell holes, foxholes, and derelict villas," three operational missions "stand clear in my mind's eye to this moment, all of which played themselves out against the bullying background presence of *Annie*," Colonel Davis writes.

"This was *Anzio Annie*, a huge German rail-mounted gun that could hurl its projectile a good thirty miles. When one of them struck, it sounded as though some wrathful giant had taken a running jump and landed with both massive feet onto the rubble of the bridgehead. Night and day they came, almost haphazardly. But their toll claimed about 200 fatalities every twenty-four hours, with no personal hard feeling. (Today *Annie*, quite domesticated, may be viewed in the flesh at the Ordnance Museum, Aberdeen Proving Ground, Maryland)." For a more immediate visit, view *Annie* at the bottom of picture-page 6.

Colonel Davis's first memorable mission involved "the German one-man torpedo submersible" that "blundered ashore from some North Italian port—about thirty feet long, cigar-shaped, and sporting as pilot beneath its canopy a tiny teenager answering to the name of Hansi. The boy was badly frightened, and so was promptly plumped down beneath a tree whilst three or four of us Intelligence types hovered menacingly, browbeating him for information.

"But he proved a good soldier. All we learned was that his malfunctioning steed—designed to blast Allied vessels in a virtual suicide operation—was 'gesprengt (cocked or set).' It and Hansi were shipped swiftly south to British Naval Headquarters at Naples, constituting a capture that was, I believe, unique during bridgehead days."

For Colonel Davis, the second, more productive "remembered mission" took him to an enemy plane that had ditched in the Tyrrhenian Sea with an entire crew of five surviving. "But I was dumbstruck, literally, when it emerged that the craft was not a Jerry but a Savoi-Marchetti bomber of the almost non-existent Italian air force—and I spoke scarcely a word of Italian!

"Most providentially, the Royal Army Medical Corps officer attached to our POW cage was a Hungarian Jew who had studied his medicine at Rome. He obligingly worked with me as interpreter throughout a grueling two-day session which proved largely successful.

"My third remembrance seems today to have carried with it an almost teleological motif," he continues. "Among the officers with whom I maintained liaison was an RAF flight lieutenant who commanded a high-speed launch for air-sea rescue operations. I went with him on two of them. In the first, we succeeded in recovering useful documentation from the floating corpse of a German airman.

"A few days later, we battled turbulent seas in an effort to snatch from them a downed American flyer. We were minutes too late. He was dead in his life-jacket. Hindsight now instructs me that what I had witnessed was a matched pair of cavaliers canceling each other out in the grandiose morality play of global warfare."

Soon, orders arrived, and Lieutenant Davis was boarding a mail plane back to Naples and civilization but, he says, "I almost felt a twinge of reluctance at forsaking the bridgehead. For with this little plot of soil, I had evolved the most intense of relationships. Moreover, spring was, very tentatively, bedecking the landscape. Here and there, tiny blossoms poked up, half-hesitant intruders upon a terrain old Dante could have utilized for his *Inferno*. Between the *kah-rumph* of cannonading, I even thought I could detect a quavering of birdsong. Yes, I would remember Anzio. I knew, too, that each and every one of us condemned to man this very special station would never forget her either."

March–September 1944
Missions from Cerignola, Italy

Major William Allan Pearce, inducted in June 1941, served with 88th Airborne Infantry, Fort Benning, Georgia, before transferring to the AAF.

Departure for overseas from West Palm Beach, Florida, in February 1944 was for "destination unknown," but forty minutes airborne, "our pilot opened our sealed orders and read them to us over the intercom. We were going to Italy as part of the Fifteenth Air Force. We all gave a cheer when we heard that," Major Pearce recalls. On 1 March, they arrived at Cerignola, Italy, where they joined the 456th Bomb Group.

"Our home-away-from-home was squad-size tents pitched among olive trees and furnished with cots only. Each man was given a mattress cover and told to stuff it with hay from haystacks on nearby farms. Each of us was also issued a vial of chemical with instructions to break and drain it into the newly made mattresses to kill any insects!

"From 1 March until September 1944, I made fifty missions over such targets as Munich, Ploesti (three times), Vienna, Genoa, Avignon, and Budapest. . . . As radio operator, I would listen to the radio for messages from the ground, but was instructed not to transmit en route to the target. Approaching the target, I would don my flak vest and helmet and take my position at the .50-caliber machine gun at the left waist window (with a few extra flak vests on the floor to stand on). Shortly after reaching the target, we would usually pick up enemy fighter planes following us. . . . They would gradually draw closer then swoop in on us at full throttle. It got exciting then! As we came in over the target at 20,000 to 25,000 feet, they would fall back because of the anti-aircraft shells (flak). Smoke from the anti-aircraft barrage would get so dense, it was like dark clouds. Often the flak was bursting so close, our plane would tremble violently. Usually, we saw some of our planes going down. . . . Our instructions were to look for and count parachutes from these planes as they opened. Sometimes there were none. I don't remember ever seeing all ten chutes open.

"On one mission, a plane close to ours got an engine shot out. We radioed it to come in close to us for protection. Just moments later, it received a direct hit from anti-aircraft fire and exploded so completely there was practically nothing left of it. I remember seeing a propeller going one way and bits of fuselage going other ways. . . .

"Scared at times? You bet we were! But we didn't panic (like some screenplays show). There was very little conversation over the intercom. Each man had his job and did it well. We worked together as a team as if our lives depended on it, because they did! Often I would tell myself, 'I know the Allies will eventually win because our cause is just.'"

When his fiftieth mission was completed, "It was as if a great burden was lifted from my shoulders and I could look forward to life again with anticipation, not apprehension."

October 1943–August 1944

Bay of Naples, Italy

Lieutenant Colonel Frederic A. Bleyer was with 6th Port of Embarkation, which operated the Port of Casablanca, 18 November 1942–4 October 1943, when the unit sailed for Naples.

"We sat in the harbor for a few days waiting for Naples to be taken by our combat forces," Colonel Bleyer notes, and then "operated the Port of Naples until 16 August 1944 when we sailed for Marseille to operate that port."

"The 6th Port had about 500 personnel, and I was assigned to the thirty men of the Maintenance and Repair (M&R) Section. We were responsible for all the cargo-handling equipment used in loading and discharging the ships. The M&R men built their own barracks on the pier in order to be close to work, but due to nightly air raids, their barracks was hit two days after completion. Fortunately, no one was hurt.

"At first, when we had air raids, we immediately headed for the air-raid shelter, commonly known as Al's Place, since the signs pointing to the shelters said '*Al Ricovero* (to the shelter)!' After a while, we became jaded and would listen to hear how close the bombs sounded, and that would determine whether or not we got out of bed. . . .

"When we arrived in Naples, the port had been badly damaged, with demolished warehouses and cranes and sunken ships in the channels and berths. The Corps of Engineers did a fantastic job of clearing the port and building temporary structures over the sunken ships so that the U.S. ships could dock and be unloaded.

"While in Naples, Irving Berlin's *This Is the Army* visited and entertained the troops with their great show," Colonel Bleyer says. Among songs in the production were "I'm Getting Tired So I Can Sleep" and Berlin's "Oh, How I Hate to Get Up in the Morning," his WWI song written when he was a sergeant stationed at Camp Upton Yaphank, New York.

Another major show that really hit the town while Bleyer was there was Mount Vesuvius, erupting 19 March. "To us, it was a spectacular sight," he notes, "with flames shooting hundreds of feet into the air and a stream of red-hot molten lava coming down the side of the mountain. The natives were petrified, as they had been through it before, and two towns on the side of Vesuvius had been wiped out. They rebuilt, because the lava made the soil very fertile."

February–March 1944
Missions to France and Germany

Lieutenant Colonel William T. Dinwiddie was a second lieutenant who piloted thirty missions with the 569th Bomb Squadron, 390th Bomb Group.

Arriving as one of five replacement crews at Framlingham, England, in mid-February 1944, Lieutenant Dinwiddie and his crew were declared mission-ready Monday, 28 February. "The V-1 (buzz bomb) installations being built by the Germans along the coast of France were well under way and we went out to hit the one at Grand Parc," he writes in his diary at the time. "We flew as position number three in the lead element of the low squadron. Our load was twelve 300-pound bombs. We flew B-17 number 466 for three hours, thirty-six minutes. With a nine/ten thick undercast, no drop was made by the lead crew. Flak was light and we suffered no damage."

The next day, it was "up at 0300 hours" for briefing at 0400, and then "take-off at 0810 for Brunswick, Germany. Target: the aircraft engine factory. We carried ten 500-pound bombs at 21,500 feet. Since there was a ten/ten thick undercast, a Pathfinder crew led us over the target. . . . The mission was six and one-half hours long."

With a day off in between, Lieutenant Dinwiddie and crew take off 2 March for the airfield at Chartres, France, with "thirty-eight 100-pound bombs." No drop was made "because of dense clouds over the primary target; the flak was very heavy and one plane went down with a direct hit." On board that plane was a friend of co-pilot Second Lieutenant C. Jack Fleck. "It was sickening to all of us to see them go down, especially to Jack. . . . Up until now, combat is just routine, but suddenly it hit us: they're playing for 'keeps.' We could get killed out here," Lieutenant Dinwiddie writes in his diary.

"A very sad day," he writes on 8 March. "We got word that two of the other four crews that reported to the 390th Bomb Group on the same day that we did were shot down on a Berlin raid."

Later March missions take the crew to Brunswick, Germany, 15 March to target the aircraft factory; to Augsburg, Germany, 16 March, when they drop forty-two 100-pound incendiaries on Ulm, secondary target; to Augsburg 18 March, when they drop five 1,000-pound bombs on an airdrome at nearby Lechfeld; to Berlin 22 March, when they "hit a residential and industrial area, inflicting severe damage"; to Brunswick 23 March with ten 500-pound bombs on board, when they "were hit very badly. . . . and had eighteen holes in trusty old *Gung Ho*"; and to Chateaudun, France, 28 March, when they drop ten 500-pound demolition bombs on the airport and "suffer a large hole in the left wing."

One day when performing preflight routine that "required a thorough nose-to-tail inspection of the plane, both inside and outside," Colonel Dinwiddie recalls entering the radio operator's compartment to check with George, "our very conscientious and intense radio operator. Then as I started to exit, I stopped right in my tracks because there on the floor by the door into the bomb bay was a very large boulder, about twenty inches in diameter. Talk about shock!

" 'George,' I said, 'what the heck is a great big rock doing in here? Haven't we got enough trouble hauling all those bombs and ammunition and people and gasoline over there to drop on old Hitler?' He immediately jumped to attention. 'Sir,' he said, 'today would have been my brother's nineteenth birthday, but he was killed on a flight-training mission two months ago. In his honor, I was going to throw the rock out while the bomb-bay doors are open.'

" 'George, throw the damned rock,' I said. It was gone when we got back to base. I have often wondered what the Germans thought about that strange rock the U.S. Air Force was using along with those awful bombs. . . . I considered this as a very tender expression of love between brothers and hope my telling it hurts no one."

March 1944
Bougainville, Solomon Islands

Lieutenant Colonel Wilbern A. Dorris served as company executive officer and commander for twenty-one months with Company I, 132nd Infantry, Americal Division.

"On 8 March 1944, the attack for which the enemy had been preparing began, with 'the greatest concentration of Japanese artillery seen anywhere in all the battles of the Solomons, shell[ing] the Piva and Torokina Airstrips," *Maptalk* for XIV Corps Headquarters reports in September 1944.

"Sixth Division (which participated in the Rape of Nanking in 1937) attacked Hill 260. This was defended by the 132nd Infantry Battalion, immediately to the left of the 3rd Battalion that Company I belonged to. A towering giant of a banyan tree that overlooked the Torokina River supported an Americal Division outpost. Mortar and artillery observers were surrounded by the Japanese and were killed. The first battle lasted eighteen days while the Japanese clung like leeches, burrowed among the giant roots. The fighting was at such close range, only small-arms fire could be used. . . .

"Some days later, Company I was sent on a combat reconnaissance patrol to search for enemy artillery that had succeeded in making the Torokina Airstrip inoperable. The division had used support air to aggressively bomb what was believed to be artillery positions, but the artillery was still effectively firing on the airstrip."

Describing one of those artillery guns found later, Colonel Dorris says, "It had an ungainly heavy carriage with large wooden wheels and steel rims. It was as large as the Americal 105 guns. It must have been carried there piece by piece by many men. It was located on the forward slope of the hill and had been firing in the direction of the airstrip. It remained undamaged by the bombing from the air.

"The jungle was so dense that it took the infantry to find and capture the positions. The enemy was found at the end of the first day. They were in dug-in positions, some of which were connected by tunnels. . . . The enemy remained hidden until the company attacked one of the positions, and then the fight started.

"The men of the company were frustrated to make contact with the enemy so late in the day when they should have established their own perimeter of defense. To gain any advantage of the daylight that was left, I suggested to Captain Komroy that it was time to put more of the company into action to gain information."

When the CO agreed and put Lieutenant Dorris in charge of the platoon, it found "a position that stood out among the others. It had a sawed lumber floor and a thatched roof. The men threw a grenade through the roof into the position. The occupants escaped under cover of smoke from the grenade; however, the men recovered a telephone and a briefcase bulging with information that was sent to battalion Intelligence the next day."

Citing three major problems for a rifle company fighting in the jungle, Colonel Dorris mentions the need for attached medical support; the difficulty of providing a water supply; and the difficulty of using artillery. Of the first, "on this mission, the battalion surgeon and his medical team were with the company, setting up a portable hospital and operating immediately by light of flashlights when the company pulled back to a defensive position."

Concerning the second problem, "At the end of the first day, the one canteen of water per man was exhausted. A water patrol had to go outside the perimeter to search for water and return with the canteens."

On the night that he was "on the company flank, to tie in the 93rd Division Company, which had arrived with supplies and was also joining the battalion," Colonel Dorris remembers receiving the call from Lieutenant Decker telling him that Company I CP had been destroyed, that Captain Komroy and First Sergeant O'Roark had been killed, and that Colonel Franco was ordering him, Lieutenant

Dorris, to take command of the company. "Company I was the first to return to the rear area after twenty-seven days of continuous combat action. The company returned greatly reduced in strength and had to undergo an almost complete reorganization."

March 1944
Bougainville, Solomon Islands

Captain Bernard L. Patterson was a young second lieutenant, communications officer, with 2nd Battalion, 145th Infantry Regiment, 37th Division.

One week after 3rd Marines landed at Empress Augusta Bay, Bougainville, 1 November 1943, the 37th Division started landing at one-week intervals as three separate regimental combat teams. "Our regiment landed 13 November 1943," Captain Patterson writes. "Our main purpose for being there was to help reduce the large Japanese base at Rabaul on New Britain Island, about 200 to 300 miles away, and to keep Japanese planes off the small airfields on Bougainville. Our original mission was to relieve the Marines on the west and northern part of their beachhead and extend it in both directions. In December 1943, the Marines were relieved by the Americal Division, and by January 1944 the perimeter was complete and our battalion occupied Hill 700." Also by mid-January, "the fighter strip was complete and the bomber strips well on the way.

"In late February, our division patrols began to see and sometimes fight Japanese patrols," among the first contact since "the first few days after landing. The contacts became closer and closer to our positions, mutually supporting pillboxes covered with logs and connecting trenches. One Japanese patrol ran into one of our patrols and most of the Japanese were killed, with only one or two escaping. One officer who was killed had a complete Japanese field order on him, which gave their attack plans on our positions. From the diagrams, we were able to tell that they thought we had only one division on the island. The first thrust was to seize the top of Hill 700 and *stop*. This was to draw all our reserves up there to repel them. Then the main attack with tanks and infantry was to be in the flat land in front of the airstrips, so they could be destroyed.

"About 5 or 6 March, the Japanese began to shell the airstrips. They were able to chase all our planes back to New Georgia except a New Zealand fighter group. The Japanese were using artillery pieces, (approximately) 155mm howitzers. They had been hand- and mule-carried across the mountains and emplaced on the higher hill to our front.

"At about 0400 on 7 March, the Japanese attacked Hill 700. They overran the position of one of the platoons of G Company, 145th, and captured the *top* of Hill

700 and *stopped* there, as ordered. If they had come over the crest, they could have fired on 2nd Battalion Headquarters, F Company (our reserve), the H Company mortar position, and made it very hard for reinforcements to come up.

"With daylight, we counterattacked with F Company, two companies from our 1st Battalion, some engineers, and most of anti-tank company fighting as infantry only. All were finally employed in the five days this action went on.

"We had completed a road as far as the reverse slope of Hill 700 and some reinforcements came that way at night, and half-tracks resupplied us with ammunition day or night. From their positions, the Japanese could fire on about 100 yards of this road, but the half-tracks did not suffer any problems.

"On the second day after the attack on Hill 700, they attacked the 148th Infantry, 37th Division position on the flat land with tanks and infantry. Our tanks stopped their tanks and our infantry stopped their infantry with only minor damage. We had no idea how they brought tanks here. Later, after they retreated, we found a road from the north completely under the large jungle trees and 'bridges' of rocks under the water of the many streams that could not be seen from the air.

"They retreated over the mountains after leaving most of their equipment, including the artillery pieces, and about 3,000 dead on our division front. The 6th Japanese Division was demolished. We found 290 Japanese bodies on the top of Hill 700, an area about sixty yards by thirty yards. We took about fifteen prisoners, all too badly wounded to commit suicide with their hand grenades.

"Our casualties were much fewer. Ironically, many of our casualties were caused by our own grenades. The hill was so steep that a grenade had to be thrown so it landed on the top of the hill or it would roll back into our troops. After the retreat, we settled back to long-range patrolling again until we were relieved by the 3rd Australian Division, and the 37th Division went north and west for the invasion of Luzon in January 1945."

March 1944
Aboard USS *Hornet* to Palau Islands, the Carolines

Captain Kenneth M. Glass was a pilot with Torpedo Squadron Two (VT-2) aboard the USS Hornet *(CV-12), which deployed from Pearl Harbor in early March 1944 as part of Task Force 58. [This was the second carrier* Hornet; *the 1941 'Doolittle'* Hornet *(CV-8) was lost 27 October 1942 in the Battle of Santa Cruz.]*

"We pilots and others aboard were unaware where our first combat strikes would be until after we had been at sea for many days. We then learned that our mission was to mine the harbor in the Palau Islands, then occupied by the Japanese," Captain Glass writes.

For days preceding the Palau strikes, the VT-2 pilots spent their time in briefings for the mission, with a model of the harbor built "to help us determine the best approach and retirement routes for our attacks. For two days, we steamed toward the enemy stronghold undetected, but on the afternoon of the third day, Richards, while on patrol, sighted an enemy search plane. Although he gave chase in his TBF, he was unable to overtake the enemy plane or prevent a position report being sent to the enemy base. That night and throughout the following day, many bogey reports were received. During this final approach to Palau, it became clear that the enemy knew that a large American task force was at sea and coming their way. Several enemy planes were shot down by our combat air patrols. Our ships were subjected to a torpedo attack by six aircraft the night of 29 March; two of these planes were shot down and the remainder withdrew after making unsuccessful drops.

"The night before the attack, there was little sleep to be had. The uncertainty and the excitement of the impending first battle raised everyone's blood pressure a little. It was to be our first and, unfortunately, for some, the last mission undertaken. Breakfast at 0400 was difficult to stomach and, for many of us, it was only a cup of black coffee.

"Two hours before sunrise on the morning of 30 March 1944, planes from Torpedo Squadron Two and with other air-group pilots were launched from the deck of *Hornet* for their first combat strikes since arriving in the war zone of the South Pacific.

"The fighter sweep, launched in the predawn darkness, was followed by dive bombers. Then, Skipper Jack Arnold took off with Branham and me as wingmen, along with Porterfield, Lankford, and Nelson; our TBFs were loaded with mines for Palau Harbor. With the air full of planes of all types circling at preset altitudes, a cloud base at 1,500 feet, and large cumulus clouds about, rendezvous in the Stygian blackness proved difficult. After a half-hour of groping in the dark, planes began to form into groups and depart for the target. . . .

"Arriving over the target, we were greeted by Zeke fighters from above while the AA boys on Koror and Arakabesan Islands began throwing everything from 12.9 to 40mm in our direction. One Zeke hit and perforated Branham's elevator. We started the long, long chute lined with AA fire to the pinpoint target where we successfully laid our mines. We jinked all the way across the lagoon, low on the water, then climbed to the rendezvous point. After going up, we managed to avoid the Zekes by playing hide-and-seek in the clouds around the area. We returned to the carrier and, after lowering my tail hook manually, I made an uneventful landing.

"The last flight of the Palau mission was led by Skipper Arnold, with Branham, Porterfield, Nelson, and me, to further mine one of the harbors. Unfortunately, my plane didn't have enough power to remain airborne on take-off and I was forced to make a water landing a mile or two in front of the carrier. This launch disaster, as with several others, was due to the reluctance of Miles Browning, captain of the *Hornet*, to provide sufficient deck and relative wind for the take-off runs. With full weapons load, a small malfunction of the engine was sufficient cause to put plane and crew into the sea. It was unnecessary, since the torpedo bombers took off last, behind fighters and dive bombers; additional deck space was available if this highly controversial CO had chosen to provide a longer launch run. My crew—Kowal and Feenestra—and I were picked up by the destroyer *Monogham* but because of storm seas, we did not rejoin our shipmates aboard *Hornet* until two weeks later. Due to the fortunes of war, *Monogham* was to sink in a typhoon later in 1944, losing all hands. . . .

"The final tally from two days of combat had resulted in one pilot and four aircrew lost in action, five planes residing at the bottom of the Pacific, and numerous Avengers suffering damage from Zekes and AA fire. While a heavy price to pay, Palau Harbor was now closed to warships and supply vessels of the Jap fleet for an extended period of the war."

Winter 1943–1944
Milne Bay, New Guinea

Captain Samuel H. Keller arrived overseas in January 1944 with the 104th Naval Construction Battalion (CBs/Seabees).

"A noted naval authority has said, 'The ships with bases at their disposal are the ships that count.' The Seabees furnished those overseas bases, which included some of the following: piers, storehouses, shops, magazine buildings, hospitals, barracks, mess halls, laundries, hangars and aeronautical buildings, fuel storage, flying fields, recreational facilities, water supply and sewage, radio stations, and others," Captain Keller writes.

"The complement of the 104th Battalion included 1,080 enlisted men and 30 officers. The personnel were apportioned into four construction companies and one headquarters company.

"Building the structures, however, was just part of the Seabees' job. These construction men also had to be able to defend what they built and were called upon to do so in a number of instances. In fact, when the Marine detachment made its classic dawn assault on a New Georgia beach, Seabee Lieutenant Commander Robert Ryan stepped from behind some trees and extended his hand to the Marine major, saying as he did so, 'Major, the Seabees are always happy to welcome the Marines!'"

In a V-mail letter to his folks, 5 March 1944, Seabee Keller notes: "It's Sunday evening and another workday. Expect that we'll be getting Sundays off before long. Attended services this morning, held in the chow hall and fairly well attended. Rains some time every day, and walking through mud is getting to be part of the day's doings. Am sleeping in a fresh-air tent and really sleeping. Taking our atabrine [antimalaria drug] every night except Sunday, and sleep under netting. No place is closed in—even the toilets and showers open to nature. . . ."

Continuing his WWII recollection, Captain Keller reports: "The outfit had been on its first Southwest Pacific Base, Milne Bay, New Guinea, a little less than two months, and in March 1944 was loading the ship to move on to Los Negros in the Admiralty Islands. The 104th men were handling the winches and were storing the cargo. The base malaria-control officer drove out on the dock and stopped alongside the ship and left for some sort of inspection. Down came the hooks, up went the jeep, and it wasn't until three months later in the Admiralty Islands that the error was discovered. The chaplain happened to be picked up in what was claimed to be a stolen malaria-control jeep. Well, anyway, an extra bulldozer never was discovered."

March 1944
POW Camp Shirakawa, Formosa

Colonel Michael A. Quinn continues his POW diary.

Writing on "the last day of a leap-year February," Colonel Quinn records, "We may send a 100-word letter Friday, and I must start composing it soon. It is quite a job to juggle the words to get what I want to say within the limit."

Still basking in the joy of that first mail delivery since captivity, received 22 February, he transcribes the following on 3 March as the letter he will send home: "Twenty-two letters and cards received and I have read and reread them scores of times. I can't tell you how welcome they were. I haven't space to discuss them. No pictures of Tom and Pat. All others were excellent. My health is fairly good. Don't worry about me. You have all done nobly. Keep it up. Hope you heard my [radiogram] broadcast this month. I am serious about [buying] a farm. You may wait until I get home if you think best. Remember our Silver Anniversary [on 25 April]. God bless and keep you all."

On 4 March, Colonel Quinn notes: "They took movies of us watching the basketball game, buying at the PX, et cetera. I imagine they are for Jap propaganda. . . . The authorities took pictures of the Protestant services today, and they tried to get Binderman to pose for a close-up for effect. He refused and expressed his disgust at the idea of making a show of a divine service for propaganda. The air vice-marshal, Maltby, backed him up and no close-ups were taken. We haven't got anybody with sufficient rank in our outfit that has enough guts to do it. . . ."

"The rice is being cut down; no doubt because of the number of cooperatives in the 'White Detachment,'" he writes on 10 March. ". . . Louis Dougherty is now in the hospital. Lack of food principally. We have men here much younger who are put over the details, given extra food, and our own people are to blame. Those are the ones we refer to as the 'White Detachment' or 'Blond Nips.' . . ."

On 26 March, he writes: "The boredom of this existence is terrible. You've got to fight to keep interested in things and to keep from going completely crazy. The 'White Detachment' came in for an awful going over from the rest of the gang, and they don't like it. . . ."

APRIL 1944

29

"The morale is excellent in this battery I've been living with. . . . The only thing is they're impatient for movement—they'd fire all day and move all night every day and every night if they could only keep going forward swiftly. Because everywhere in our Army, 'forward,' no matter what direction, is toward home." These are the words of Ernie Pyle, Scripps-Howard correspondent and chronicler of life on the battlefronts of WWII, the man *Time* magazine praised as "a GI Boswell."

And so, in April 1944—with twenty-eight months of warfare behind them and eighteen months of fighting still to come—the troops continue their movement on all fronts and for all branches, sometimes swiftly and at other times slowly, sometimes imperceptibly forward and at other times retreating, but always, as Ernie observed, with every effort pointed "toward home."

On the various fronts, this "forward, home" movement means Air Force attacks on communications and oil targets in Ploesti, Sofia, and Belgrade in April; Task Force 58 attacks on Woleai in the Carolines and U.S. forces occupying Ndrilo and Koniniat, Admiralty Islands, 1 April; U.S. forces taking Hollandia, New Guinea, 23 April, and opening captured airfields at Hollandia and Aitape 29 April.

Spring 1944
USS *Brooklyn* at Naples and Anzio, Italy
Commander Frank A. Hanley was an ensign aboard USS Brooklyn *(CL-40).*

After the Allied landings at Anzio in January 1944, "there followed busy days of shore bombardment in support of the Anzio Beachhead, interspersed with frequent night air raids at Naples and the monotonous routines of keeping all systems of the ship operating and the personnel trained. We shared the shore bombardment duties with the light cruiser *Philadelphia* and were nearly always accompanied by the destroyers *Kearney* and *Ericson*. On one of her missions, the *Philadelphia* collided with a destroyer and earned the nickname 'The Can Opener,'" Commander Hanley writes.

"The ship was not air-conditioned, and it was so hot below decks some nights that many of the enlisted men came up and slept topside. Sometimes the setting was so romantic, what with a full moon and the perfume of orange- and lemon-tree blossoms in the air that we vowed to bring our wives back after the war. (I was one of the fortunate ones who did.). . . .

"As 5th Division officer, my area of responsibility included turret five, my GQ station, and the two catapults from which we periodically catapulted the two Scout Aircraft OS-2Us, and the stern crane with which we later retrieved them. I was also designated catapult officer, and my division was responsible for recovering the aircraft after they landed on the water-slick we created by making a high-speed turn with about 22 of rudder. The planes taxied up onto a cargo net, trailed from one end of a catapult trained out from the side of the ship, and cut their engines. A hook on the plane's pontoon snagged the trailed cargo net, and they were then in tow. We lifted them out with a crane and, if not needed, struck the aircraft below to the hangar deck by means of the elevator. . . .

"When we were not firing at the Anzio Beachhead or swinging the hook at Naples, we sometimes sailed to other ports such as Oran, infrequently to Algiers, and most frequently Palermo, Sicily, to replenish stores and ammunition, and for leave and liberty. The ship was known in the U.S. press as 'the Galloping Ghost of the Sicilian Coast.' Palermo was virtually our home port."

April 1944
Missions to Belgium, Germany, and France

Lieutenant Colonel William T. Dinwiddie was a pilot with 569th Bomb Squadron, 390th Bomb Group.

For mission sixteen to Augsburg, Germany, 13 April, "we flew old *Gung Ho* as number-two ship in lead squadron for eight and one-half hours," Lieutenant Dinwiddie writes in his journal at the time.

"On the way home, 'bandits' were spotted and we saw two of them wing up at about the two o'clock direction and head directly toward us in tandem. . . . The sweat began to roll. Our gunners answered the fire and old *Gung Ho* was shaking all over with so many of our .50-caliber guns firing at once.

"As the lead ship, a German Fw-190, flashed through the formation, we in *Gung Ho* could look into the cockpit. I still swear the German pilot had red hair.

"Then the second fighter flashed through, hot on the tail of the first and firing away. Lo and behold, it was a P-51, and here we were shooting like hell at him. We have always wondered at the tremendous amount of guts it took for the pilot of the P-51, much less the Fw-190, to fly through our B-17 formation, knowing we would be blasting away.

"Somehow, our group flew directly over Brussels and all hell broke loose. Very accurate flak—the kind that whammed against the floor of the B-17 and you knew they had our altitude pegged. We had about fifty-two holes in our *Gung Ho*, but none vital. We lost another crew (Moe Swavel) of the four that reported to Framlingham at the same time we did. We were lucky and thank God for our safe return. We are therefore the last of the five original crews that came to the 390th the same day."

Missions seventeen and eighteen, 20 and 22 April, respectively, take *Gung Ho* and crew to La Glacerie, "just south of Cherbourg on the Normandy coast of France, where the Germans were building the V-1 buzz-bomb launching ramps, supply buildings, et cetera," and to Hamm, Germany, to the "very busy railroad marshaling yard."

"We were going through flak hell and everyone was scared stiff and praying for deliverance from the black inferno," Lieutenant Dinwiddie writes of the mission to Friedrichshafen, Germany, 24 April. "At the height of the worst flak, the number-three ship in our squadron (Pilot Newell and crew) received a direct flak burst in the bomb bay. It was so close that we thought our left wing was on fire. The beautiful B-17 just folded up in the middle of a mass of flame and all ten men died right there before our eyes. We literally shook from head to toe with an all-consuming fright and a terrible sickness in the stomach. We made it through the black cloud and dropped on the secondary target at Neckarsulm, Germany. So 'shook up' was everyone that the results were poor. Eight and one-half hours total."

Heading for the airfield at Dijon-Lonvic, France, on 25 April, Lieutenant Dinwiddie and crew were on their twentieth mission; *Gung Ho* on its fiftieth. "We carried twelve 500-pound bombs on this six-hour mission," the pilot reports. "Good, tight formation and good bombing. Hit heavy flak coming back out. They almost got us. Our No.2 engine was knocked out and No. 4 had no power. Big hole in No. 2 engine. We limped home on two and one-half engines, and *Gung Ho* looked like a sieve. . . ."

While *Gung Ho* is being repaired, Pilot Dinwiddie and crew fly *Ice Cold Katy* and *Buckshot Annie* on a double-header assignment, 27 April. The first, a five-hour mission taking off at 0715 for La Glacerie, France, resulted in "darned good bombing, but terrible flak" and "a big hole in No. 3 gas tank and lots of gasoline running down wing and dripping off near No. 3 engine exhaust." The second mission took off "at 1500 for Thionville Airport, Le Culot, Belgium. Target, however, was heavily overcast, so we hit Florennes-Suzanne, France, with forty-two 100-pound incendiaries," he records in the last of his April entries.

24 April 1944
USS *Hornet* to Truk Island, the Carolines

Captain Kenneth M. Glass was a pilot with Torpedo Squadron Two (VT-2) aboard USS Hornet *(CV-12), one of eleven carriers in Task Force 58.*

"Truk, a Japanese-held island in the Carolines group, was a heavily fortified area that came under attack by Allied carrier groups on a number of occasions. At one time, it was the intent of the American forces to invade and occupy the island, but it was decided to bypass this stronghold and simply to bomb it to the extent that it would become useless to the Japanese as a base," Captain Glass explains.

"I was assigned to the second flight on the first day of our attack on that island, 24 April 1944. As we approached our objective, a layer of clouds had almost entirely obscured the island. . . . When over the target, however, we observed a hole in the clouds. Skipper Jack Arnold immediately put us in position for the dive to the target below. Anti-aircraft fire was heavy, vicious, and already taking its toll on the planes in our flight (fighters, dive bombers, torpedo bombers). We poured down through the hole in the clouds.

"As more planes dove, the Japanese concentrated their fire on this particular hole in the clouds with devastating results. Even as I pulled out of my dive after delivering bombs to the target and headed toward the rendezvous point, five of our planes had been hit and were all observed to be on fire at once. This was the heaviest enemy-firepower I encountered during my time in the combat zone.

"Throughout the day, numerous flights pounded the island. Carrier plane losses were extremely high. By day's end, twenty-five pilots and crew had been rescued by submarine. I do not know how many perished. When the submarine could no longer house additional rescued airmen below deck, survivors were told to hang on to the conning tower and the sub took them out to sea on the surface, where they were picked up by other ships.

"Scotty Scammell was a member of the flight in which I participated. As he pulled out of his dive over Truk Harbor, his plane was hit by anti-aircraft fire. He was able to make a water-landing in the lagoon, where he and his two crew members escaped from the plane, climbed into their raft, and escaped out to sea, where they were rescued by the submarine.

"We returned to Truk on one other occasion during our stay in the Pacific, but none of the other missions equaled this particular day of war's fury. The photographs and accompanying story of this daring rescue made headlines in the press for many days, both in the United States and around the world."

April or May 1944

Nadzab, New Guinea

Major William W. Turner was a first lieutenant and pilot, known as 'Pappy,' serving with Fifth Air Force, 8th Fighter Group, 36th Fighter Squadron, in New Guinea.

Arriving back in camp on "one of those bright, still, hot afternoons" in the Markum Valley of Nadzab, Major Turner recalls that his "ears were ringing from the radio and static. I was kind of beat—needed to get horizontal in the sack for a bit. I entered the tent and went over to my cot, speaking a few words to one of my tentmates (Steele Griswold) who was resting under his mosquito netting. We passed a few remarks on the day's activities; then I sat down on my cot, gave my tired old feet a fling, and plopped backwards.

"Then those damn flies came, and soon I had had enough of those buzzing bastards, so I sat up and reached up and got hold of my mosquito netting and gave it a pull and down it came, and I swept it endways and sideways until I was completely enclosed and safe from those pesty devils. I had just completed this when Griswold asked me a question. I was still sitting up and sat still while answering him; then suddenly I let my upper body fall back onto the cot. At this moment a bullet went through the tent. Again, I was sitting upright, and there was a hole through both sides of my mosquito netting that, when lined up, would have put the bullet through my temple.

"By now, I had my .45 out and was on the ground, scanning the nearby jungle. Several other pilots who had heard the shot were out also. We saw nothing, and a brief search of the area yielded nothing.

"Back in my cot, I lined up the two holes, which sighted over into a neighbor's tent. They said that they had heard something hit hard with a 'thud.' The line of sight of the two holes brought me to the tent pole in the center of their tent and there, believe it or not, was a hole and the bullet.

"I pulled out my trusty sheath knife (GI-issue, one each) and cut the bullet out. It appeared to be a .45-caliber bullet. I put it in my pocket as a lucky piece and carried it with me during the rest of my tour of duty. After all, it had had my name on it; a split second had saved me.

"I still have this bullet after all these years. I don't carry it anymore, but I don't forget those events of yesteryears and how I was spared that time and many others. 'The Lord is my Shepherd,'" Major Turner adds, in what is probably not his first prayer since the incident.

22 April 1944

Hollandia, Dutch New Guinea

Lieutenant Colonel O. T. Duggan arrived on Goodenough Island in May 1943, a second lieutenant with the 104th Anti-aircraft Artillery Battalion, Alabama National Guard.

On 4 April 1944, "the 104th AAA (AW) Battalion was put on six-hour alert" for the offensive move in New Guinea. "For the next twelve days, we packed up, practiced loading on an LST, and practiced landings south of Buna. On 16 April, we loaded up for the real thing. We left Goodenough Island about 0400 on 17 April. There were seven LSTs in the convoy. I was in command of A Battery which loaded on two LSTs," Colonel Duggan recalls.

After passing Ora Bay, the Solomons, and Lae, and picking up five transports, seven more LSTs, and six "cans" [destroyers], they passed the Admiralty Islands—""lit up like Broadway"—with benefit of P-40 and Spitfire cover on 19 April, and picked up the rest of the convoy during the night of 20 April.

"Some sight! There were more than 200 ships—eight flat-tops, five cruisers, over 100 LSTs, LCIs, and LSDs, and fifty 'Tin Cans.'

"Well out to sea, I was given maps and briefed on our destination. We were to land at Tanahmerah Bay, 25 miles north of Hollandia, Dutch New Guinea. My Battery was to be attached to the 21st Infantry Regimental Combat Team of the 24th Division. The general had asked if our 40mm Bofors guns could take out a pillbox, and I assured him that they could. We were to follow the infantry combat team from Red Beach Two to Red Beach One and on to the airstrip at Hollandia.

"April 22 was D-Day, and H-hour was 0700. The Navy had shelled the beach for an hour before we landed. Navy planes filled the air, bombing the beach and airstrip. The LCIs and other landing craft brought in troops, trucks, ammunition, gasoline, and other supplies. . . . The beach was crowded, and thirty feet off the beach the ground was deep mud."

Soon after, Lieutenant Duggan and LST 275 landed, but before they were completely unloaded, "a siren sounded for what we took as an air-raid alert. We scrambled in vain to try to find something to get behind or under on the empty deck of LST 275," where cover was scarce.

"Fortunately, it was not an air raid but a signal that General MacArthur was coming ashore. He walked to the edge of the mud. His picture was taken to record his landing and he then returned to his landing craft that carried him back to his ship in the bay. We had seen General MacArthur in person! . . .

"Unfortunately, the road that was supposed to connect Red Beach Two (where we landed) to Red Beach One did not exist. Some of the troops and equipment were transported by barge to the other beach and continued inland to the airstrip. Our guns bogged down in the mud, so we could not follow the infantry team as planned. We pulled back to the beach and set up our guns there. That day and night were a real nightmare! We were wet, muddy, tired, and hungry.

"There was small-arms fire all around us. Men of an engineering outfit were firing at 'shadows.' We heard that some of their own troops had been shot by friendly fire and their CO had their ammunition taken up. He said if they got close enough to use a bayonet, they would recognize friend from enemy.

"Since our guns were of little use at night, I told our troops to dig trenches, get in them, and not to get out for any reason. Below ground was the only safe place that night. It was wet and uncomfortable, but safe. The artillery fired over our heads all night, so there was very little rest.

"Enemy resistance on the beach was minimal and most of the troops moved on to the airstrip at Hollandia, leaving A Battery behind to provide protection of Tanahmerah Bay, where we remained until 29 September 1944. By 26 April, the airstrip was secured. Many planes were destroyed and Japanese captured. They kept coming out of hiding into the middle of May."

April 1944
POW Camp Shirakawa, Formosa

Colonel Michael A. Quinn continues his POW diary.

"Easter Sunday at a POW camp! Two years ago Bataan surrendered. . . . We had Mass and Communion, and I believe every Catholic in camp was present. Couldn't do it last year, and I hope that will be the last time I will ever miss it. . . . Mike, your card of August 13, 1942, was received yesterday and I was delighted to get it . . . ," Colonel Quinn records in his diary 9 April 1944.

"What a day!" Colonel Quinn exclaims on 18 April. "I was just thinking about our twenty-fifth anniversary when, lo and behold, my name was read off for two letters, one dated 2 February 1943, and another 22 March 1943. Now the world is all right again."

"Ordinarily, Saturday afternoons are non-work periods. However, this afternoon we were turned out for work," he writes on 22 April, adding: "Hit the scales at 135 pounds today. . . . Maybe what keeps me alive now is the fact that I was in good shape once."

"My darling Mike: Today is just as beautiful a day as it was a quarter of a century ago," Colonel Quinn writes on 25 April 1944, the couple's silver wedding anniversary. "Due to a Nip holiday, we have not had to work, so this day of days, to us at least, was not desecrated by us doing coolie labor. Tonight we are going to have one of those really tropical moons. Remember how we used to watch them in the Philippines? I celebrated our day by passing around some candy and cigarettes. That was the only celebration I could have. . . . Knowing that you are at home means more to me than you can ever realize. So many of the British and Dutch officers have no idea where their families are or how they are living. . . . Mike, after twenty-five years, all I can do is thank God for what I have. I am not complaining. Keep your chin up and keep your faith. I will do the same. Goodnight and adios. As always, Al."

April 1944
USAHS *Shamrock* from ETO to USA

Chief Warrant Officer Edward G. Robertson and First Lieutenant Helene Stewart (who later became Mrs. Robertson) served aboard the USAHS Shamrock, *one of thirty Army hospital ships in service during WWII.*

"Too much going on! I don't have any time to myself anymore. After twelve hours of duty, then choir practice. . . . and back to our room at 1030 hours, and so to bed," Nurse Helene Stewart records on 16 December 1943, in her last *Shamrock* diary entry. "I wish now, I had kept the diary," she writes in an epilogue, as she and her husband provide notes from then-Corporal William Hummrich who served with them.

From early January until mid-February 1944, the *Shamrock* continued its shuttles among the cities of Naples, Bizerte, and Mers el-Kebir, making a total of twelve trips. Arriving in Bizerte 15 February, crew and personnel "were told definitely that we were on our way home. Everyone was quite happy, as we had been out six months and it had been tiresome work," Corporal Hummrich writes. "On 17 February, we left Bizerte with a full load of [572] patients and headed back to America. . . .

On 5 March, the *Shamrock* reaches Bermuda. "All that could, got out on deck to witness the pretty sight," but "the most beautiful sight was the American air base there," with combat planes and others that would "come over the ship and tip their wings to the patients on board."

While one officer had been sent ahead to the States by plane "to make sure that everything would be in order," the *Shamrock* proceeded to Charleston, South Carolina, and up the Cooper to the Navy Yard, where the ship and its occupants were greeted with whistles blowing and everyone waving "as we passed other ships on our way up to the Army base where we were to debark our patients. Arriving there, we were greeted by the band, which played music for all to enjoy."

"Once the gangway was out, hospital units came aboard and began to separate all over the ship and then started taking the wounded ashore. I felt kind of low, as we had patients aboard who had become quite friendly and I knew I would miss them," Corporal Hummrich writes.

By 22 April—with many new crew members and soldiers replacing those who had been transferred—the U.S. hospital ship *Shamrock* departs Charleston amidst "cheers from the people about the docks and whistles from other ships bidding us good voyage." The ship and its crew are off on tour number two to provide thirty additional Naples–Oran–Bizerte shuttles in the Mediterranean area until 21 September 1944.

"From where we are, there is no road back and we have to either hold or be annihilated," Walter H. Johnson Sr. writes to the editor of his hometown newspaper on 5 May 1944 from the Anzio Beachhead, Italy. When he sent his letter to the *Catahoula News* in Harrisonburg, Louisiana, he was serving as captain with the 5th Infantry, 34th (Red Bull) Division.

"The German air corps and artillery are terrific and they have every inch of this beachhead zeroed-in," he continues. "They have been using against us their big long-range 240mm railroad guns, firing at us from 25 miles back, near Rome. . . . They have also used their secret weapon, the radio-controlled tank, but we knocked them out and stopped them cold before they got started."

As fighting escalates on Anzio in May 1944, plans and elements continue to converge in Great Britain and environs for the June 1944 Normandy landing of D-Day. Lieutenant Colonel James F. Gruver, who was with 51st Finance Disbursement Section at Plymstock, England, describes the scene: "Things were quiet all over. Everything was moving at night. The only available sign of anything out of the ordinary was the absence of military personnel in the city. All roads were marked for one-way traffic, and most of them in the direction of the Channel." He recalls that as finance officer, "in May, we were first given wooden boxes marked in code. We signed for this money by so many units. Agents were to open the boxes only when the areas were officially sealed." Even bombing missions took on a new character, with their purpose now "to isolate the battlefield and to disrupt enemy lines of communication before the invasion of Europe," according to Major Marvin M. Kraft.

In other war-related activity during May 1944, Admiral Lee's Task Force bombards Ponape in the Carolines 1 May; Monte Cassino, Italy, finally falls to the Allies 13 May; Merrill's Marauders and Chinese forces capture Myitkyina Airfield, Burma, 17 May; 163rd Infantry Regiment lands on Insoemar Island, New Guinea, and takes Wadke Airfield 18 May; and a U.S. destroyer force bombards Wake Island 21 May and Mili in the Marshall Islands 26 May.

23 May 1944

Anzio Beachhead, Italy

Lieutenant Colonel Walter H. Johnson Sr., with 135th Infantry, 34th Division, at Cassino, for two months, transferred with the division to the Anzio Beachhead in late March 1944.

"Forty-eight hours prior to the breakout, our artillery laid down an incessant, thunderous, earth-shaking barrage into the German-held impregnable fortification in the hills overlooking and encircling the beachhead. The unbelievable tempo made one wonder if Armageddon and the end of time would be as severe," Lieutenant Colonel Johnson writes.

"On D-Day, 23 May 1944, at 0400 hours, the artillery lifted and, simultaneously, hundreds of giant U.S. bombers dropped inestimable tons of blockbusters on top of the German positions. At 0430, droves of fighter planes with their guns blazing flew in close and showered the Germans with rounds of red-hot lead. At 0500, our hell on wheels, the unbelievably powerful Sherman tanks, began advancing in the direction of the enemy lines. At 0530, our time had come and we 'combat infantrymen' joined the act to do our thing.

"For two days, it was give and take as we paid dearly in lives for every inch of ground we captured. Men were slaughtered like clay pigeons in a shooting gallery. At times, as we moved through 'the valley of the shadow of death,' we walked over dead bodies. Smelling the stench of burnt and decaying flesh is something that no one should ever have to experience.

"On the third day, with fierce determination and guts, we successfully blasted our way through the German ring of steel and continued to exert relentless pressure on the retreating German army. We traveled down the old Appian Way. On the thirteenth day, the Eternal City was ours.

"Perhaps the greatest victory of the men of the beachhead was not won at Anzio after all. After the war, Germany's famous General Albert Kesselring admitted: 'If you had not pitted your strength against us at Anzio-Nettuno, you would never have landed in Northern France.' The lessons of Anzio were learned and applied to the Normandy landing. The beachhead had, at last, paid off."

Spring 1944

Cassino, Italy

Colonel Doug Hardy, captain and CO of HQ Battery, 39th FA Battalion, 3rd Infantry Division, was transferred in spring 1944 to Allied Liaison Service.

By the time of the breakout at Cassino, "a great deal of artillery support had been put in place and the fire support was truly massive," Colonel Hardy writes.

"We renamed Mount Fratello 'Million Dollar Hill,' because we estimated we expended more than a million dollars in ammunition in the taking. But if Mount Fratello is Million Dollar Hill, Mount Cassino should probably be named 'Fifty Million Dollar Hill'—more, if the Air Force bombing were to be counted. The shelling was continuous from early evening to H-hour of the attack in the morning. It was like fifty Fourth of July fireworks at one location, with lighted skies and heavy explosions continuously for about six hours. The earth shook as in a major eight-point earthquake. . . .

"The attack the next morning was eminently successful, partly due to the prodigious artillery preparation and partly due to the fact that our Allied troops in the Anzio sector had begun an attack that was progressing favorably, and the Germans could not afford to have their troops cut off by the more-northern Allied activity near Rome.

"Some of the German prisoners we took related how dazed they were by the artillery bombardment. As we traveled along the road to Rome, we were occasionally amazed to see bodies of German soldiers stacked like cordwood, indicating how precipitous had been their retreat."

May 1944
Missions from Lavenham, England

Major Marvin M. Kraft joined the 487th Bombardment Group in January 1944.

Arriving at Eighth AF Base at Lavenham, he says, "we found our ground component of the 487th already settled in. Our training flights ended with several group flights out over the ocean. These were not only for training but also for deception. German radar monitored all of our flights, so we were scheduled to fly, at altitude, a short time before an actual bombing mission but in a direction opposite the actual mission. The German air force would move fighters to bases in the path of incoming airplanes, based on radar information.

"Combat missions began with our bombing railroad marshaling yards and bridges in France and Belgium. My first mission was to Troyes, France, and I believe we bombed a bridge. The object of these missions was to isolate the battlefield and to disrupt enemy lines of communication before the invasion of Europe. . . .

"Shortly after starting to fly missions in the 487th, we received a message from the Nazi broadcasting system. The broadcast told us they knew we had arrived, they knew our tail marking, and they were going to give us what they gave the 100th Bomb Group, well-known to have been attacked and almost wiped out several times by the German air force. . . . They did broadcast good music."

As part of training in escape and evasion, as well as how to act if captured, the group was taught by American Army psychiatrists or sometimes by Americans who had escaped from German POW camps. "We were forbidden from writing a diary or narrative," since such a document "was an intelligence bonanza" if obtained by the enemy.

"We were also taught about Gestapo techniques. For instance, the Gestapo looked at the shoes one wore. We learned that our American table manners were distinctive in the way we handled a knife and fork. We learned about some of the Underground groups. We had civilian-type passport pictures taken for possible forged passports. We were given civilian-type shoes to take on missions. On missions, we also took an escape kit, with foreign money and other things we might need."

May 1944
Missions to Germany, Belgium, France

Lieutenant Colonel William T. Dinwiddie was with 569th Bomb Squadron, 390th Bomb Group.

Pilot Dinwiddie and crew are "out of the sack at 0300 and briefed for 'Big B'" on Sunday 7 May, with "ol *Gung Ho* back in action and sweating out the engines all the way." They encountered "no fighters but lots of flak" on the eight-hour Berlin mission.

Other missions in May take the crew to Laon-Athies, France, 9 May; Liege, Belgium, 11 May, when six 1,000-pound bombs are dropped into the railroad marshaling yards; Brussels, Belgium, 20 May, when the mission is abandoned because "clouds were so bad"; again to the Liege railroad yards, which were "severely damaged," 25 May; the engine factory at Strasbourg, France, 27 May, when they "hit the target on the nose, plastering it" with ten 500-pound bombs from 23,000 feet; and their last mission, number thirty, the rail yards at Troyes, France, 30 May, when they hit their target "with excellent results."

Mission number twenty-six was their "deepest penetration of the war," as they "go after the oil refinery" at Brux, Czechoslovakia, 12 May. In his journal at the time, he writes: "After finally reaching the target, we made one pass over the target but lead plane did not drop. So we circled and made another pass; still, nothing happened. With bomb-bay doors open, we were all ready to massacre our lead bombardier. So now, we flew over to the secondary target, Chemnitz, Germany, dropped our bombs finally there; then headed back.

"We flubbed around so long over there, and we had to use extra fuel, too, in number-four position, that by the time we reached Brussels on the way out, our fuel gauges on the outboard engines' red-warning light (indicating fuel getting low) had been on for some time. We could not transfer any fuel for fear of running out on all engines, so we ploughed on, but had to feather No. 2 when it ran out. We had to throttle back to minimum for just enough power to maintain flying speed and started our letdown, planning to coast downhill at least to the English Channel, which we could see dead-ahead.

"I gave the order to 'lighten the ship' (meaning to throw out loose and heavy items), and to prepare for ditching. Bombardier Charlie Pease, seeing that the Germans were firing at the formation ahead as we dropped back, decided to respond by firing his .50-caliber ammo at those Germans instead of tossing the belts out. With the problems already at hand, to add a severely vibrating B-17 nose, was more than I could stand. I had to stop it."

Heading for the nearest airport, they made an emergency landing, "limping in on two engines," at Manston, England, where the British-manned base "would only give us 100 gallons of fuel per tank, and then after a long delay. We requested permission to call our home base to report in, but British operations said they would advise them for us. They sent us to mess hall for supper. Since it was a forward base, we had our first canned peaches in six months.

"When we got cleared and took off, we flew back low-level across the Thames Estuary, tail high and at about 200 miles per hour air-speed, since the plane was so light. Ol *Gung Ho* hadn't gone that fast since she was built."

At Framlingham, "our operations went nearly berserk, since we had already been reported missing in action. . . . Our squadron thought we were gone, but in we walked like ghosts, and twice as white," Pilot Dinwiddie's journal reveals. He adds: "*Gung Ho* finally was lost on her 102nd mission, ranking her third of all the 390th B-17s."

24 May 1944
Mission to Wiener Neustadt, Austria

Lieutenant Colonel Bryant L. Smick was a pilot with the 450th Bomb Group, 723rd Bomb Squadron, flying Sweet Chariot *to bomb the airdrome at Wiener Neustadt.*

"Fifteen minutes before target time, thirty to forty Me-109s dove down on *Chariot*'s box in fierce, head-on attacks," a news article reports. Lieutenant Colonel Smick says he isn't certain whether the story is from *Stars and Stripes* or from *Sortie,* but it carries the byline of Sergeant Mortimer Metchik.

"Lieutenant Smick's ship was singled out and hopelessly crippled," the write-up continues. "The first assaults blew holes in three propellers, disabled the hydraulic lines, rendering the flaps, brakes, and turrets inoperative and tore gaping holes in the wings and fuselage. The Liberator's gunners fought a bloody forty-minute duel with the enemy fighters.

"A vicious burst of 109 fire pierced the tail and wounded Sergeant [Joseph B.] Rapoza, tail gunner. Two 20mm shells tore through his left shoulder, and at the same time, one of his guns was directly hit. But though one arm hung useless at his side and his turret system was shot out, he worked the turret manually and fired unceasingly with his one good arm until his ammunition was exhausted."

Also wounded were Sergeant Max J. Dowdy, ball gunner, who was "also struck in the arm, but clung to his guns"; Sergeant Harold E. Brown, right waist gunner, who "continued his fire after receiving his wound"; Staff Sergeant Oliver J. Russell, waist gunner, who "had been blasting away at Jerry when his guns suddenly jammed" and was hit with an impact that "spun him around." Taking over for Sergeant Brown, who was slumped at his guns and died as a result of his wounds, Sergeant Russell "destroyed two fighters before he passed out, unconscious. Altogether, these gallant gunners accounted for five Nazis," Sergeant Metchik writes. "After the fighters left, *Sweet Chariot* went on to bomb the target and was subjected to a terrific flak barrage," the article concludes.

"The plane, a new B-24 model, had around 1,500 holes through it and as a result hardly anything worked," Lieutenant Colonel Smick says. "I opted to bring it in on the skid to slow it down, so I had everyone in the tail except Ted and me. Through the grace of God, we made a perfect landing, stopping at the very end of the runway." "Ted" was co-pilot Lieutenant Theodore W. Sorenson, who later "flew for American Airlines and made major general in the Air Force Reserve. I was shot down three missions later," he adds.

28 May 1944
Lutzkendorf, Germany

Lieutenant Colonel Maurice E. (Gene) Joslyn volunteered for the Army Air Force on 3 November 1942 and served with 832nd Squadron, 486th Bomb Group, flying twenty-nine missions over Europe.

"I had eagerly volunteered, but now came the rude awakening. I passed with flying colors and was soon on my way to Fort Custer, Michigan, for shots and assignment," Lieutenant Colonel Joslyn recalls. "Never having been out of Michigan and living a somewhat sheltered life in the country—wow, what a change!"

His sixth mission, to attack military and industrial targets in Lutzkendorf, Germany, on 28 May is the one that stands out in his mind, for it was while over the target on this flight that "two bombs failed to release and six others became lodged in the control cables, rendering the rudder and elevator useless. With his controls thus frozen, the pilot had difficulty in remaining in the formation."

At this point, Lieutenant Joslyn crawled back to the bomb bay to investigate. Having to work "with speed and dexterity to prevent the control cables from snapping," he "closed the bomb-bay doors and replaced the arming pins in the bombs."

According to a newspaper account of the incident, the six bombs were passed by two crew members "along the narrow catwalk of the bomb bay to the tail of the plane where they were dropped by hand by Lieutenant Joslyn through the camera hatch. The pilot then had full use of his controls and returned the aircraft safely to base." For *Lady Lightnin'* on 28 May, Lieutenant Joslyn and crew could happily report: "*All* missions accomplished!"

18 May 1944
Myitkyina Field, Burma

Lieutenant Colonel Robert E. Finley was a pilot serving with the USAAF 4th Troop Carrier Squadron when he wrote home from Myitkyina Field.

"As usual, I start my letter with 'no mail yet.' I'm beginning to wonder if I will ever get any," he writes.

"Haven't shaved for three days but guess I will pretty soon, as I have the day off. Have been very busy lately. . . . We've been getting up at four o'clock and sometimes three o'clock in the morning and going to bed around ten or eleven at night. A few days of that will wear you out.

"I wrecked a plane a while back. We went into a Jap airfield that had been taken the afternoon before. I made a short, close approach; the Japs were shooting at me as I went in. I landed OK and turned around and started back down the field.

"As there were a bunch of bomb craters around, my co-pilot and I both were watching very closely for those that had been filled. We pulled off the runway to let another plane land and ran right into a camouflaged hole. We found out that the Japs had left places like that, hoping we would do what we did. Of course, we nosed up, but while there wasn't too much damage done, the plane won't be flown for a while.

"A lieutenant came running up and I started giving him hell for not marking this place. At the time, I thought that the field had been tested for such places as that—at least we were told so. He said, 'Hold on! We haven't tested anything! This is the test,' and he pointed at my plane.

"He said, 'You'd better get out of here; the field is under fire.' He thought he was telling me something I didn't know. Rifles were pinging, mortars and shells were chattering, and bullets were whistling, and when you can hear the whistle of a bullet, they are too damned close.

"One fellow said, 'You guys had plenty of guts coming in during a battle.' I said, 'That wasn't guts, it was ignorance.'"

In concluding, Lieutenant Colonel Finley asks friends Ed and Erma to share their letter with someone else, but to wait until "after I leave here" before show- ing it to Mother and Dad. "I don't want them to know now, for I know how they worry." Then he adds: "Write often. I'll get some mail some day."

Well, the mail finally catches up with him when he returns to Italy—not only from Ed and Erma, but from everyone else. Writing to his parents on 20 June, he exclaims: "Gosh, it is wonderful to be back. Received thirty-six letters from you, twenty-eight from Ed and Erma, three from James, nine or ten from Uncle Jim," and one each from an entire roster of relatives and friends whom he names. "Lots of magazines, candy, newspapers. Boy, it was swell. Most impor- tant was to know you are OK. . . . I'm OK. I will answer your letters tomorrow. I'm not through reading them. All in all, I received over ninety letters," their "loving son, Bobbie" jubilantly tells his folks.

March–June 1944
Los Negros, Admiralty Islands

Captain Samuel H. Keller moved on with 104th Naval CBs after two months in New Guinea.

"Los Negros has wonderful coral sand, so that the drainage problem was prac- tically nil—much different from the knee-deep mud of New Guinea," Captain Keller records. "The battalion worked around the clock almost the whole four months at Los Negros. There was a deadline of something like three weeks to meet in the construction of a landing field. It gave the battalion a wonderful feel- ing to see the last grader roll off the field at noon of the day the strip was to be finished and to see the first bomber land shortly, that afternoon. For this work and other duties at Los Negros, the unit was awarded an engagement star. . . .

"The Australians had many of the natives organized, so that a group could be hired out to build thatched roofs and siding. Some of the natives, along with a group of 104th men, built a beautiful chapel from coconut palm logs and nipa palm shingles.

"Speaking of buildings, in every camp the units always managed to have a large, framed mess hall and galley with concrete decks—sixteen-foot by sixteen-foot pyramidal tents raised off the ground on coconut logs—and with plywood decks, an open-air theater with seats and a stage, a good baseball diamond, Quonset huts for the sick bay and for various officers, a ship's service with barber shop, cobbler shop, library, laundry, and, oh yes, ice-cream machines. Well, it was almost like home—*almost!*"

May 1944
Finschhafen, New Guinea

Colonel William E. Shaklee was a first lieutenant, motor and patrol officer, with 3662nd QM Truck Company, which arrived in Australia, November 1943, and New Guinea, January 1944.

In a letter to the young lady who, after the war, would become Mrs. Shaklee, Lieutenant Shaklee writes to Rose Marie Miller of Enid, Oklahoma, on 1 May, telling her of just getting "back from the show" that started at 2000 hours, and seeing "a newsreel of the Marine landing on Cape Gloucester," followed by a World of Sports short feature narrated by Pete Smith, and then the main attraction, the movie *Jack London*. All of this played out at Heselov's Bowl, a tripartite structure featuring a stage to shelter screen and actors, a seating section, and the projection booth, all built by the battalion's special service officer, Lieutenant Heselov.

Beyond the cameras and the floodlights, there was the everyday life of the battalion in New Guinea. Describing one particular day, 6 May, Lieutenant Shaklee says that T/5 George Galmon's truck, going up North Hill, slid backward into T/5 Howard Foster's truck, knocking a hole in the radiator; Corporal Theodore Emerson was backed into, near base engineer dump, bending his truck's fender, radiator, and light guard; and Corporal Louis L. Gable ran over a hidden pipe in the mud, blowing out a tire.

For Corporal Gable, the next day was no better. "He was following a GMC DUKW 2½, six-by-six cargo when the amphibious vehicle stopped suddenly. Gable applied his brakes but they failed to work. Gable ran into the rear of the other vehicle and bent-in the radiator of his own truck." Then on 8 May, "a winchman, unloading lumber from a ship onto Corporal Myron Field's truck, dropped a load on the windshield" and "Private Clarence Wilson was run into as he started a right-hand turn into Dock 1-A" on 9 May.

It continues literally to pour upon their pool, as Lieutenant Shaklee explains to Rose Marie on 9 May: "Tonight it's raining again. Already our motor pool is a sea of mud and, at the present rate, we won't even be able to get the trucks out on the road next week. Three of them got stuck right in the motor pool today. I was mud from head to foot after hooking chains on the other trucks to pull them out. One of them took a train of four trucks to pull it out."

Somewhere, however, amidst mud and mishaps, the 3662nd was getting its work accomplished. On 31 May, Lieutenant Shaklee reports the following message received by Major General James L. Frink, commanding general, USASOS, from Commander in Chief General Douglas MacArthur: "My heartiest congratulations to you and the officers and men of your command for their splendid contribution to recent operations in New Guinea. Their indefatigable efforts and their inspiring resourcefulness in emergency were prominent factor in brilliant successes which have been attained."

Sunday Morning, Date Unknown
North Coast New Guinea

Captain Meyer A. Minchen served as a pilot in the U.S. Navy during WWII, flying B-24 Liberators out of bases in North Africa and England in night antisubmarine warfare.

In tribute to his prewar chaplain, Captain Minchen submits a recollection from Rabbi Robert I. Kahn, rabbi emeritus in the early 1990s of Congregation Emanu El, Houston, and past national chaplain of the American Legion. Rabbi Kahn was "among the first to volunteer for service following 7 December 1941, participated in a number of island invasions, and was considered a 'front-line' chaplain."

Rabbi Kahn's story centers around a certain Sunday morning that he says he has "never forgotten," when the 6th Division was protecting an offshore airfield and a major came into his chaplain's tent, announcing, "Chaplain, I need your help. I have a company of engineers on a ship offshore and we are headed toward our first combat area. My men are nervous, and I think they need some spiritual help. We sail at 1700 hours. Can you find us a Protestant and Roman Catholic chaplain and come out to our ship at 1500. Please!"

"I got on the field phone, but I knew what I would find," Rabbi Kahn recalls. "Our troops were spread out along a perimeter. In garrison, a chaplain would hold two services or perhaps three on a Sunday morning, but in a combat situation, he might have a service every hour or two all day long. Therefore, there was not a single Christian chaplain available. My assistant and I loaded up with prayer books and supplies and went out by DUKW to the ship.

"The men were gathered on an inside deck. I introduced myself and my assistant, and said, 'Fellows, I am a rabbi. I'm the only available chaplain today. I can lead you in a GI service or we can worship each according to our faith. What shall we do?'

"There was silence, but their faces told me that when a child is sick, it doesn't want a nurse, but wants its mother, and these men, apprehensive about their future, would want their mother-faith.

"So I asked, 'Is there any one here who can lead a rosary service?' There was. I distributed the rosary booklets and the men of Catholic faith knelt on the deck and recited their prayers. There was reverence in that room.

"I then announced, 'Now we'll have Protestant worship. If any of you cannot stay, feel free to leave.' Almost no one left. Most of the men who had prayed the rosary clustered at the back of the room or in the doorway.

"Again, I relied on volunteers to lead most of the Protestant worship. I could lead in the Lord's Prayer, and read the passage from Paul on love, but I asked an officer to lead the Credo, another to lead the hymn 'Onward, Christian Soldiers,' and then I asked if anyone would like to offer a prayer. One did: a prayer that was very personal and very much an expression of the heart in a time of impending peril.

"Then I announced Jewish worship. There were about twelve Jewish men aboard; they put on their service caps; we read the afternoon service, closed with a hymn.

"I gave a brief sermon on morale; I compared it to insurance, which spreads the risk but also gives security, and told them of a couple of courageous battlefield acts in my division.

"The hour was up. I gave the priestly benediction which is common to all our faiths, and after gathering prayer books, and distributing religious symbols, my assistant and I made our way to the door. One soldier put out his hand to shake mine and said, 'Chaplain, I have been listening to talk of the Four Freedoms, but I never understood what freedom of religion meant until today.'"

JUNE 1944

31

"OK, we'll go."

With uncomplicated words, after months of complicated planning, Supreme Allied Commander Dwight D. Eisenhower initiates Operation Overlord, the D-Day invasion of Normandy, France, 6 June 1944.

That simple Americanism "OK," described by one linguist as "your wonderful all-encompassing word," signals, then launches, the all-encompassing campaign that comprises 12,000 planes and more than 5,000 vessels in the largest armada ever to carry men and materiel onto the battlefields.

In the predawn hours of 6 June, 13,000 British and U.S. paratroopers land behind enemy lines in Normandy, attempting to secure bridges and other objectives prior to the beach landings. At dawn, 130,000 Allied warriors come ashore on designated beaches code-named *Utah, Omaha, Gold, Juno,* and *Sword,* along a fifty-mile stretch of Normandy's coast. By day's end, 157,000 will have come ashore; by day's end, between 2,500 to 5,000 will have died. Among the dead, about 2,200 are American; of these, about 2,000 die on Omaha Beach. "Almost everyone on the beach was dead, and I had to drag the bodies out of the way so we could get on the beach," Captain Norman H. Armour recalls of his D-Day landing on Omaha Beach.

Recording his observations when he went into combat for the first time at the Utah Beach landing, Second Lieutenant Herbert A. Taylor writes in his notebook in 1944: "It's hard to explain your feelings when you hear that high-pitched whine of a heavy artillery shell. You hit the dirt, and wonder why this had to happen to you. You feel sure you're going to be killed and you wonder how the folks at home will take it, and whether it will hurt."

Major General J. Strom Thurmond, then lieutenant colonel, was one of those GIs who got an early start. On D-Day, the future U.S. senator hit the French countryside literally, crashing in as part of the airborne assault with paratroopers on the Cotentin Peninsula.

For many of the military who did not participate in the invasion, D-Day evokes images of where they were when they heard the news. Then-Captain Jean Christy was scouting for a training-exercise site for the 50th Field Artillery Battalion in the Mourne Mountains northwest of Kilkeel, Ireland, when an old gentleman sauntered down the hill and, in lilt of Irish brogue, surprised the captain with, "I hear they landed in Normandy this mornin'."

Francis Joe Garra was a seasick private first class, draped over the rails of the *New Amsterdam*, en route to Great Britain, when the announcement came over the loudspeaker: "Now hear this: A beachhead has been established in Normandy, France, by the Allied Forces. The offense on Fortress Europe has been started."

For then-Captain Doug Hardy, who had been at Cassino and traveled the road to Rome, invasion news from Normandy seemed bittersweet. He writes: "Rome had been declared an open city and we arrived there on 5 June 1944. We felt that back home, the newspapers would be blaring with big headlines the news that Rome, the first of the enemy capitals, had been liberated. It was not until later that we discovered that our victory had rated a small article, on page thirty-eight of the *New York Times*, while the front-page headline in quadruple size declared that D-Day had arrived in France."

6–14 June 1944

St. Mere Eglise to Cherbourg in Normandy, France

Major General J. Strom Thurmond, a past president of ROA and long-time senator from South Carolina, was a lieutenant colonel and civil affairs officer with U.S. First Army who volunteered to serve with the 82nd Airborne Division.

For the Allied predawn landings, 13,000 parachutists take off—in 1,200 transport aircraft with 700 gliders—from twenty-two airfields in Great Britain the night before the Normandy beach landings, author John Keegan reports in *Six Armies in Normandy*. The paratroopers represent British 6th and 1st, scheduled to land in the Caen and Merville areas, plus U.S. 82nd (All American) and U.S. 101st (Screaming Eagles), headed for the Cotentin Peninsula of Normandy to secure bridges across the Merderet and Douve Rivers and to capture the town of St. Mere Eglise.

For these parachuting pioneers, venturing into strange countryside in even stranger craft, the burdens of battle are both figurative and literal, with gear almost equal to body weight. In a gesture that might ease one of those burdens, their supreme commander, General Eisenhower, decides "to spend the evening hours of D-minus-1 with the Screaming Eagles." According to Keegan, "his arrival at Welford was unannounced" and his appearance "created a muted sensation." One corporal "was struck by the 'terrific burden of decision and responsibility' which showed on his face and by the sincerity of his effort to communicate with his young soldiers." For those to whom he did not speak personally, there was "a mimeographed sheet bearing a farewell message." As these men left Welford in their C-47s, their commander "raised a salute to each."

With the 82nd when it departed was its commander, General Matthew B. Ridgway, who labeled the entire assemblage "the great sky caravan." Then-Lieutenant Colonel Thurmond was with the glider contingent that moved out from Greenham Common at 1852 hours on 5 June, carrying ¼-ton trucks, trailers, and personnel.

In the report prepared for Supreme Headquarters Allied Expeditionary Force (SHAEF), filed soon after the invasion, Lieutenant Colonel Thurmond and two other civil affairs officers, Major Eberhard P. Detusch and Captain John J. Knecht, record the following: "The formation of the glider column consumed nearly an hour, after which it headed across the English Channel. Shortly after 2100 hours, the column crossed the coastline of France over the Utah Beach and headed westward. At about 2120 hours, the gliders were subjected to heavy anti-aircraft fire and almost immediately thereafter were released from the towing planes."

The report notes that the three gliders carrying the civil affairs officers experienced crashes "almost identically the same as that of the others," crashing "in small adjoining fields within the German lines" and being fired upon "the moment the landing had been effected and continu[ing] thereafter." Thurmond's glider crashed in an apple orchard near St. Mere Eglise, the small town that the paratroopers were tasked with capturing that day—and which they succeeded in doing. Despite injuries from the crash, paratroopers Thurmond and Deutsch "assisted at once in the release of the vehicles from the gliders" that were "practically demolished in the landings."

The report continues: "Colonel Thurmond thereupon headed a reconnaissance party with personnel of his glider to locate a CP [Command Post] to which an effort was made to effect a rendezvous. [He] . . . made a reconnaissance of other nearby gliders, assisting their injured personnel in getting to the rendezvous."

As Major Deutsch and Captain Knecht continued to gather personnel from other gliders, Colonel Thurmond sent word that "a tentative rendezvous had been established near the CP of a Battalion of the 4th Infantry. . . . The group thereupon proceeded by jeep and on foot. . . . The enemy fire had remained continuous but was somewhat less intense. The wounded were carried in the vehicles taken from the gliders."

Lt. Catherine Piraino (Emig Strong) receives orders of the day from Brig. Gen. Charles H. Barnwell, USA, Pacific Theater, 1943 or 1944.

1st Lt. Carlos E. Dominguez, USAAF, flew daily missions over Atlas Mountains for Gen. Eisenhower during North African campaign, 1943.

Ground crew accepts kudos on *Gung Ho*'s 50th mission, April 25, 1944, as Capt. William Dinwiddie, USAAF, looks on with pride.

Lt. Cmdr. George F. Heckler, USNR (Ret.), as Ph 3/c, covered departure parties for NAS ABSECON VF-13 in Atlantic City between October 1943 and March 1944.

Signal officer Lt. Col. James C. Smith, USMC, commends Navajo "code talkers" for their role in maintaining communications at Peleliu, November 1944.

1st Lt. Joseph S. Drewry Jr., at Fort Ord, Calif., prior to the invasion of Kiska, August 15, 1943. He was a "mule skinner" with the 602nd Field Artillery Battalion (Pack).

Lts. Maury Herman, Norm Williams, Marc Fountain, and Oscar DiEdening flew out of England in 1943 as crew of the *Royal Flush*.

Lt. Cmdr. Jacob Brouwer, USNR (Ret.), then ensign and skipper of LCT (L) 513, Utah Beach.

Maj. James L. Peacock Jr., AUS (Ret.), then captain, Shore Control Team 5, Utah Beach.

Lt. Col. Herbert A. Taylor, AUS (Ret.), then lieutenant, 1st Engineers, Special Brigade, Utah Beach.

D-Day Veterans

These officers were among almost 157,000 GIs who landed in Normandy, France, on D-Day, June 5, 1944. Operation Overlord was under way. The strike against Fortress Europe was a tactical surprise. On that day the Allies suffered between 2,500 and 5,000 killed.

Maj. Gen. J. Strom Thurmond, USAR (Ret.), then lieutenant colonel, St. Mere-Eglise.

Maj. Gen. J. Milnor Roberts, AUS (Ret.), then captain, tactical aide to CO, Omaha Beach.

Humphrey Bogart and Lauren Bacall—interviewed by broadcaster Jack Brown—salute GIs via Armed Forces Radio Service during World War II.

Marines advance across Tinian Island in the Marianas in pursuit of Japanese, July 1944.

Lt. Col. O. T. Duggan recalls that Japanese planes left at Hollandia in mid-1944 were source of souvenirs.

Marine fighter pilot Lt. Carl P. Writer on Okinawa, 1945.

In eight successive waves, U.S. Marines landed on Okinawa April 1–4, 1945, meeting mild resistance. But that was to change when they turned south.

Flight officer Marvin Kraft's bomber group flew a mission on D-Day but cloud cover prevented a bomb drop.

By June 1945, Joe Garra was a sergeant with the Army's Co. B, 3rd Section, 744th Tank Battalion.

GIs inspect German Quad 20mm captured in central France.

Capt. Cecil C. Ellzey, liaison pilot with 28th FA Bn, returns to his aircraft near Huertgen Forest, Stolberg, Germany.

Platoon led by Lt. James J. Ahern clears cave of Japanese on Iwo Jima, April 1945.

Burial detail works under direction of Chaplain H. P. Abbott at Ousseltia, Tunisia, January 1943.

Lt. j.g. Ken Glass, then VT-2 pilot on the *Hornet* (CV-12), retired as captain.

1st Lt. Gretchen Hovis, USA, served with 50th General Hospital in France, July 1944 to 1945.

Lt. John H. Wilson Jr., USA, witnessed brutality of Nazis at Gardelegen, Germany, April 1945.

Twin Ensigns Wesley and Warren Craig, pictured in October 1941, would find life in idyllic Hawaii disrupted by Japanese.

Then-S/Sgt. William A. Pearce, front left, poses with B-24 crew, 756th Bomb Group, 15th Air Force near Cerignola, Italy. They completed 50 missions unscathed, says Major Pearce.

Capt. Fred E. Bamberger stands astride FW-190 at Bolzano Airport, Italy, April 1945 when Luftwaffe South commander surrendered to the 12th Air Force.

Ens. Jeanne Gleason, USCG, in June 1944. She retired as captain in 1973.

Capt. Vivian Reese Harned, USCG (Ret.), was a storekeeper 2C in New York City in 1944.

Pfc. George R. Woltman, USA, was a personal bodyguard to Gen. Douglas MacArthur.

Lt. Lester Kurtis,
754th Tank Battalion,
Bougainville, Solomon
Islands, November 1944.

Col. Ruth Lepschat Forsythe,
USAFR (ret.) as a Cadet Nurse
in 1944.

2nd Lts. Geraldine Wells
and Gladys Gussendan,
Army nurses, on Saipan,
November 1944.

V–E Day 1945
found a happy
couple, Joan
McCurrah and
fiancé Robert J.
Greenwald, at
the celebration
near the Arc de
Triomphe. Then a
captain, he retired
as a colonel.

Then Capt. Walter
Johnson was one
of the GIs who
retired this flag
in Rome.

Capt. Joseph S.
Frelinghuysen landed in
North Africa in 1942, was
captured, but escaped.

GIs of the 135th Infantry, 34th Division, captured *Anzio Annie*, German 280mm railroad gun, at Civitavecchia, just north of Rome, June 7, 1944.

Mascot Kelly, stationed on Saipan in mid-1944, exhibits the jaunty look of a bluejacket.

Capt. James F. Gruver and Capt. Antell had $$ in the bag on payday after D-Day.

Lt. John G. Brosky, USA, scans horizon of Guadalcanal, Solomon Islands, for the 300 Missouri mules maintained on his manifest in late 1942. He retired as a brigadier general, PaANG.

Class 396, Ft. Benning Infantry School, December 1944. Among January 1945 graduates is Maj. Gen. Evan L. Huffman, AUS (Ret.), right front, who would later serve as president of ROA 1981–1982 and then as executive director from June 1986 to January 1994.

Coast Guardsmen on loan to U.S. Coast and Geodetic Survey flew this modified Army Air Force B-17, mapping missions in the Artic toward war's end. They operated out of Point Barrow, Alaska. Photo courtesy of Rear Adm. Bennett S. Sparks, USCGR (Ret.), right, president of ROA 1982–1983 and deputy executive director July 1988 to April 1991.

Golden Gate Bridge was a sight to behold for our GIs returning from Manila, September 5, 1946, aboard USAT *General Brewster*.

Army Col. And Mrs. Michael A. Quinn and family celebrate Christmas in 1947. He was a POW of the Japanese for 40 months.

Later that night at an 8th Infantry aid station, Thurmond received first-aid treatment for his glider-crash injuries, "a severe contusion of his left knee and laceration of the left knee and both hands." He was treated again the next morning at a medical station of the 82nd Airborne Division. Captain Knecht's injuries to hands and knees were slight. The severe chest and back injuries sustained by Major Deutsch "were later revealed to have consisted of fractured ribs and a strained back."

In the course of one day's activity, Colonel Thurmond and the regular civil-affairs officer "located the billet of the German lieutenant general who had commanded the 91st German Division and who had been killed in action. The records found in the billet, of great importance and considerable volume, were promptly reported to G-2 and by them to Corps Headquarters for handling." Continuing on with the 82nd Division through the capture of Cretteville on 8 June and Picauville on 13 June, Colonel Thurmond returned on 14 June to Army Headquarters where he resumed civil-affairs duties.

6 June 1944
Omaha Beach, Normandy

Major General J. Milnor Roberts, former executive director of ROA, was a captain serving as tactical aide to Major General Leonard T. Gerow, commander of the invasion of Omaha Beach and of the U.S. Army's V Corps. He provides the following account:

"The first real feeling I had about D-Day was on the evening of June 5, when we left Portland Naval Base in England, bound for the beaches of Normandy. Looking at the rest of the men on board the USS *Carroll*, I could not help but think that by the next night half of these guys would be dead. I hadn't thought to consider myself among them, but I guess you never do.

"At about 0530 on 6 June, the naval bombardment of the German defenses began. Battleships, cruisers, and destroyers opened up with everything they had.

"While the *Carroll* sat five miles out to sea with the rest of the transport ships during the bombardment, the GIs began to board LCVPs that would take the men ashore. Once we received word to go in, the LCVPs broke for the beach in a ragged line. That is when your heart stops, and you just stand there watching them speed toward the shore.

"The LCVPs caught fire as they got in close enough for the German guns to be in range. First we were hit with 88s (three-inch anti-aircraft guns fired like field guns, point-blank) about a mile out. Then came the automatic weapons, machine guns and such, at about 600 yards. It was like a summer thunderstorm; a few drops at first, then everything all at once. Only this was lead.

"Confusion quickly set in as we were pounded by 88s about 200 yards from shore. The captain of our LCVP was killed and the crew panicked. We got hung up on a sand bar about 100 yards out and we were catching the full force of the German guns. Though we should have backed up, the ramp was lowered. We had gone as far as that boat was going to take us. We were now on our own.

"Someone yelled, 'This is it!' and we went scrambling into the water. The water was deep, deeper than we had expected. Men who had been cramped and seasick inside the landing craft were now splashing about in the water, the zip and snap of sniper-fire cracking in the air around them. We were overloaded and top-heavy with equipment, and some of the men who had instinctively inflated their life preservers began to capsize and drown.

"By this point I was terrified. It was tough to move and I was having trouble breathing, with the water almost up to my mouth. To get ashore, we had to hop along with the waves. Fortunately, I had decided against inflating my life vest, and I eventually made it to the mangled shore, which was littered with the bodies of my fellow soldiers.

"The 29th Infantry was suffering about a 30 percent casualty rate for the day, a little over ten hours into the invasion that began at dawn. Some estimate that about 2,700 men were dead by the time my feet hit the water that afternoon. When we landed, much of the 352nd German Division had been pushed back from the beach, but there were still many lingering German snipers remaining in the hills surrounding the beach. Dug-in along the little pathways in the tall grassy hills beside the bluff, they were firing at soldiers approaching the shore. As the bullets whizzed by, I quickly scrambled for some cover, trying to get off the beach as quickly as possible.

"Running for cover, I passed an Allied amphibious tank that had caught fire. I could hear the men screaming from deep inside the tank, but there wasn't a thing I could do about it. With feet wet and facing intense fire, I charged up a ravine only to find myself face to face with a sniper. I drew my carbine and pulled the trigger, but nothing happened. The salt water and sand had fouled the weapon to such an extent as to make it unusable. Diving into a nearby abandoned foxhole, I attempted to fix my gun. Luckily, the sniper soon disappeared, and I was able to continue toward the top of the bluff.

"Once I reached the top of the bluff, I turned to look out over the English Channel. The largest armada of battleships, cruisers, destroyers, and merchant vessels ever assembled anywhere on Earth could be seen stretching all the way to the horizon. The awesome sight of that power and force, assembled, literally, to save the world, was simply unforgettable. For the Germans, this sight would prove to be the sign of their ultimate defeat. The landings on D-Day would come to be regarded as the beginning of the end of World War II.

"After making it through that first night, hiding in a ditch and under fire from snipers, artillery, mortars, and bombings, the worst seemed to be over. I was assigned to make contact with an element of the reserve unit back at the beach when I came upon a soldier I had recognized. He was on his knees, dead, behind a sea wall, shot right in the forehead. The bullet had penetrated right through his helmet. I had just met the soldier the night before the landing. We were the same rank, the same age. We had similar training and backgrounds. For all intents and purposes, we were interchangeable; we just had different assignments. Not until then did I feel the real power of all that had happened.

"Looking back on my fallen comrade, I could not help but think that it could have been me. It has really stuck with me all of these years."

6 June 1944

Omaha Beach, Normandy

Lieutenant Colonel William D. Sink submits WWII notes from his late father, Brigadier General James D. Sink. Enlisting as a private at age nineteen in 1941, he served with HQ and HQ Company, 116th Infantry, 29th Division, until discharge in 1945 as captain.

"Those of us aboard the *Charles Carroll* arose about 0200 hours while the ship was still in motion and had early breakfast," with anchorage some twelve miles out, Captain Sink writes at that time in recording D-Day activity of 116th's forward element of the Command Post (CP). "Massive aircraft flights could be heard off in the distance toward the Cherbourg Peninsula. Flashes of light in the sky and the roar of distant artillery indicated anti-aircraft fire. The wind was coming up, and the waters beginning to run rough . . . about 0530, H-hour being 0630."

At 0600 hours, it was time to load into LCM-10–2-DG. Proceeding slowly through rough seas, the craft reached the British control ship *Prince Baudwin* "to be told that our wave had departed and to return to our parent ship for instructions." Back at the *Charles Carroll*, their craft was ordered "to proceed to land on our own. Meanwhile, H-hour had come and gone.

"During movement toward shore, the waters were running so heavy that it was necessary to roll out an overhead canvas cover to keep the men dry. The rolling and heaving brought on several instances of seasickness. Helmets were used to catch the vomit which was washed out over the sides of the craft. Those who were in a position to see over the high sides of the craft saw a number of men floating in the channel with life preservers on. No attempt was made to pick up any of them. Ashore, landmarks were almost obscured by smoke from many fires seen burning.

"About 0730, radio contact was made with Major Jackson, regimental S-2, in the command party with Colonel Canham, about the advisability of landing on time at 0740 on Dog Green Beach at Vierville. . . . It was about 0750 when Major Jackson radioed to come on in.

"The ramp had been unlocked and prepared for dropping in front on Dog Green Beach when one of a pair of LCIs immediately to our right front seemed to explode and be enveloped in flames." It was later learned that the craft, LCI-81, carrying the alternate headquarters group of the 116th Infantry and an engineer outfit, exploded when "charged flamethrowers on the decks . . . were hit by artillery fire."

After turning the LCM out to sea without comment, the young ensign was talked into landing some minutes later, though "he set a new course for land which proved to be some 2,000 yards to the east of the designated beach and east of the Les Moulins draw in the general vicinity of the west boundary of the 16th Infantry. The time by now was about 0800. . . . There were few signs of landing activity on the right toward Les Moulins. This beach had its share of the dead, the dying, the wounded, and the disorganized when LCM-10-2-DG came in."

Aware of the misplaced landing, most of the officers "scattered on the beach, seeking information to help clear up the situation. Everything seemed to be completely disorganized and confused. There was little evidence of concerted action to move off the beach and inland over the bluff facing the sea. The confusion was further compounded by additional boats coming in and disgorging cargoes of vehicles and personnel on the already-crowded beach.

"Around 0900, LCI-12-1, carrying the regimental security platoon and elements of the 104th Medical Battalion, beached nearby to the east of the Les Moulins draw. This was another misplaced landing."

Lieutenant Kelly of the Regimental Security Platoon and Captain Sink decided to "get the men off the beach and move toward the initial CP objective of the regiment which was located south of Vierville. . . . After notifying key noncoms of both boat teams to round up the men and get going," the two commanders "crossed the beach road, breached the barbed wire obstacles, and proceeded to climb the cliff." As they "crested the bluff and came out into the open in the field at the top," they "came under small-arms fire and hit the dirt immediately."

Looking to the rear, they saw Corporal Lefwich and his wire team "coming over the top of the bluff"—only it wasn't the entire team. "The file was out and only six enlisted men from the party were still with the lead." While two men were dispatched to "find the column and have the missing men move up," the six men atop the bluff, "noting a hedgerow," took up position behind it to "await the rest of the men."

"Moving from the protection of the hedgerow to a vantage point to better observe the village of Vierville sur Mir," the captain and Lieutenant Kelly "came under machine-gun fire from the village of St. Laurent to the immediate front." Simultaneous with the firing, a voice was shouting: "For gosh sake, get down before you get killed." It was Colonel Lawrence Meeks, 3rd Battalion commander, who had just arrived with the leading elements of his battalion. "It was at this point that Colonel Meeks issued his first order to his battalion to move against St. Laurent, a mission that was to occupy the balance of the day. The time was approximately 1000 hours. . . .

"At the end of D-Day, Colonel Canham was in his designated command post with most of his staff. He knew where the rest of his headquarters company was located. Evidently, he had made up his mind what he would do come morning."

6 June 1944

Omaha Beach, Normandy

Captain Norman H. Armour was with 467th AAA Battalion, First Army.

"We were well-trained in amphibious landing and chosen to land on Omaha Beach early D-Day morning to provide anti-aircraft defense," Captain Armour writes. "The assault engineers went in first to blow up the underwater obstacles, followed by the infantry, most of whom were killed. Then our battalion of AAA guns mounted on half-tracks went in. Only half of our vehicles made it.

"The German pillboxes above us on the cliffs were firing their 88s and machine guns, causing great destruction to our landing crafts. They were finally silenced by the accurate fire of the 16-inch guns on the battleships offshore.

"There were several valleys between the cliffs, but these were blocked by big antitank ditches, and covered by German 88s and MG fire. A U.S. tank equipped with a bulldozer blade finally filled-in the ditches. Our units helped knock out the 88s, and after being on the beach for ten hours, we finally made it to the top of the cliffs.

"This beach landing was especially difficult because of the high cliffs, and the Germans had an infantry division there on assault maneuvers. We did not see any German planes during the entire day, but a few bombers were sent over at night to bomb us with their butterfly anti-personnel bombs.

"When we got off the beach, we expected to see Hitler's Tiger tanks but they were at Calais, as he thought the main invasion would be there, which was lucky for us. . . . Lieutenant General Omar N. Bradley, invasion commander of U.S. Ground Forces, said, 'Every man who set foot on Omaha Beach that day was a hero.'" Acknowledging this tribute, Captain Armour replies, "Thanks, general."

4–6 June 1944

England to Utah Beach, Normandy

Lieutenant Colonel Herbert A. Taylor was a second lieutenant with Provost Marshal Section, 1st Engineers Special Brigade, 4th Division, First Army.

What do service members do as they sit for "several days aboard a small LCI," waiting to go into battle? For the men with Lieutenant Taylor, "the only way of relieving boredom had been to play cards or feed the sea gulls, and you soon grow tired of each. The ship's barber had done a rushing business, and the robber was charging two shillings. . . . It was something to break the monotony or else we wanted an invasion haircut in case we were heroes and had our pictures taken." Lieutenant Taylor recorded his impressions in his notebook less than a month after D-Day 1944, "when memory was fresh."

"As we moved down the river, there was a feeling of separation from reality that is hard to explain. . . . It was hard to realize as we talked and joked that within less than twenty-four hours, we might be fighting for our country and for our lives and that not all of us would be present at the final victory. . . .

"The channel was a bit rough during the night and when breakfast time came around, I would have preferred not to eat, but a captain in the medics insisted that everyone eat something. I managed to get down some cereal, bacon, and coffee, and it was a good thing because my next meal was to be about fifteen hours later. . . .

"No German planes were sighted until we were within a mile or so of the beach. . . . However, our ship was now within range of their 88mm guns. . . . The blast of our big naval guns behind us was almost deafening. What a pounding that area took! . . .

"We transferred to small LCVPs while still a quarter of a mile out. . . . The boat grounded about fifty yards out and the end opened for us to go out. You've heard men say how they were the first out on similar occasions. Well, I was last out. The water was about chest-deep, and I remember struggling to keep my feet in the choppy surf. The next thing I remember is lying flat on my stomach next to the sea wall about a hundred yards or so away, trying to make myself as small as possible. We were taking a pounding from artillery and bombs. There was no strafing at this time. Our air support was very good. . . .

"During a lull in the firing, we went back to the beach and reported to Lieutenant Colonel Shinberger, the provost marshal, at traffic headquarters. . . . My first assignment was to straighten out a traffic jam caused by trying to move heavy vehicles over an inadequate road. . . . All along the edges of the fields bordering the roads were German signs, printed signs, indicating the presence of mines. We later learned that a large number of these signs were for the benefit of their inspecting officers and . . . did not necessarily mean that the area was mined. However, we couldn't afford to take chances. As soon as possible, engineers were put to work demining the roads and fields."

Reporting back to Colonel Shinberger, Lieutenant Taylor was ordered to make a reconnaissance of the area. Cautiously, he hiked several miles to a little French town where he joined up with a paratrooper lieutenant and three of his men who were trying to contact others from their outfit on the other side of town.

As the men moved up the road, they were fired upon by snipers along the way; by a sniper from a two-story house at a juncture in the road; and then by a "German machine gun firing spasmodically" in their direction. . . .

"We moved on down the road about a hundred yards, stumbling over dead Germans and paratroopers. . . . It was now quite dark and we took over an old stable for the night. We took stock of the situation: plenty of small-arms ammunition, grenades, and two machine guns; a bazooka, but no rockets."

When planes flew over about dawn, dropping food and equipment, "two men at a time went after the kits while the rest of us stood guard. Those K-rations tasted plenty good.

"At the same time, gliders full of more airborne troops were landing by the dozen. . . . One of them caught a wing on a tree in the field next to us and crashed. . . . Only two had received minor injuries. The rest were either seriously injured or dead. Miraculously, a medical officer appeared on the scene and went to work. . . .

"Tearing a page out of my notebook, I made out a report, sent it back to the provost marshal by messenger, and continued my reconnaissance of the area. This concluded my first twenty-four hours on French soil. As one of my paratrooper friends said, 'If anyone ever wisecracks to you about an MP never seeing combat duty, tell him this little story.'"

Mid-May–6 June 1944

England to Utah Beach, Normandy

Major James L. Peacock Jr. was a captain in charge of Shore Control Team No. 5, working with 2nd Battalion, 12th Infantry, 4th Division, for the Normandy landing.

"About 25 May, we are briefed on the operation. I go to several conferences. . . . We get maps of all ports, plenty of G-2 information and plenty of aerial photographs," Captain Peacock records in a notebook compiled while hospitalized in December 1944.

"About 2 June, we march in the hot sun and load an LCI in Plymouth Harbor. We get set and sit and sweat it out. We see the *Augusta, Arkansas,* a bunch of APA (*Chase, Dickman*), and APC. We hear of *Gooseberry,* a code name for sinking ships to form a breakwater.

"On 4 June, we start out, get to mouth of the harbor and are turned back. We weren't too excited; I didn't feel scared. Why, I don't know. . . .

"On 5 June, we start again and are on the way. We check equipment and find batteries dead in one radio. We have two good radios though. We are near the Isle of Wight when I'm about knocked out of my bunk by an explosion. I go topside and see a destroyer dropping depth charges. We go on and nothing happens.

"On 6 June, I get up at 0300 to see the bombing of the coast and the bombardment. All I can see is a bunch of flashes. We are to land at H-plus-240; H-hour is 0630. At daybreak, we begin to see shell-splashes around our convoy; they miss us though. We pass through the transport area and watch the unloading. . . . We see the large ships firing at coastal and inland targets. We are out about 1,000 yards and can see the church steeple in St. Martin de Varreville. We watch the beach and don't see much activity; we see shell-bursts but no heavy shelling. We are to load into LCMs and land in them. . . . I get off the boat, wade in, but notice Taurville can't get radio on his back. I wade out to help him. I get in about twenty yards when I get hit near top of my boot by a shell-fragment. I see it coming like a fast baseball.

"We hit the dirt, then run like heck for the sea wall. I stumble and fall in the road; a medic shows up. I give Sergeant Crutchfield my map and 536 radio and tell him, 'I'll come up as soon as my leg is bandaged.' My leg bleeds but doesn't hurt. I hobble to aid station; they dress it (I didn't want any morphine).

"There was plenty of shell-fire on the beach. I had a ringside seat from the aid station but was too scared to look up much. Ammunition trucks, et cetera, are being hit quite frequently and there is a heck of a racket all the time, but it was miraculous how few men were hit and killed. . . ."

"Trucks and jeeps hit an occasional string of mines and are demolished. We hear small-arms fire up the beach and know that the 22nd Infantry is catching it. . . .

"I see Colonel Luskett come in; he was riding in a half-track. The Germans start dropping some big stuff on the beach, probably 150mm, but we were behind the sea wall and didn't get hit."

Taken by jeep to an LCT that is under fire, Captain Peacock hobbles into the water and is pulled aboard, where he waits for about an hour before departing for an LST equipped as a hospital ship. Given a tetanus shot, penicillin, and a candy bar, he tries to sleep in a bunk but "there's racket, bombs fall, and small craft bump the side of the ship.

"Finally, we leave the transport area at about 2000 hours 7 June and go by convoy to Southampton, arriving 1000 on 8 June. . . . I'm sent to 110 Station Hospital and after about one or two days, they find out my leg is broken." With his leg in a cast and with a series of colds, fevers, and foot infection, he spends until 28 December in various hospitals.

After the war, he returned to his home in Tifton, Georgia, where Vice Admiral William W. Outerbridge was also residing. "Admiral Outerbridge was [then-captain and] skipper of the *Ward* that fired the first shot of WWII and sank a small Jap sub shortly before the Pearl Harbor attack," the major says. While lunching with him and others one afternoon, Major Peacock mentioned the D-Day crossing when he had been awakened by a destroyer dropping depth charges. "To my surprise, the admiral spoke up and said: 'Let me finish that story.' He said that it was his destroyer; that there was only one sub about that day and that the sub escaped by going under the small vessels of the invasion force."

6 June 1944
Utah Beach, Normandy

Lieutenant Commander Jacob Brouwer served as captain of USS LCI (L) 513.

LCI (L) 513 was one of hundreds of landing craft that "floated in a slow procession down the tranquil Dart River the first week of June" to form up in "locations prescribed by the convoy diagrams" for Operation Overlord, Lieutenant Commander Brouwer writes.

"Our huge impatient armada waited, treading water, in the choppy, foam-flecked channel twenty-four long hours. We mustered our edgy crew and read them a pep message from General Eisenhower. It was much like a coach sending his team into a game. We gave an overall description of invasion plans and wished our men well.

"As dawn broke through a cloudy sky on the 6th, our ship stood sloshing in enemy waters, within sight of the distant shore. All men topside, including me, were weighted down by awkward, sticky anti-gas clothing. Gas masks hung from our necks, ready to be slipped on at the first sign of a Nazi counterattack.

"With startling suddenness, formations of American planes zoomed from behind us and swept down the beaches, dropping bombs. Navy Big Berthas belched fire and smoke, and seconds later the air reverberated with deafening explosions. Rows of small amphibians, a variety of flat-bottomed boats, sliced into the wave-lashed beaches. Rocket boats a few hundred yards offshore arched trajectories of fire into Nazi fortifications. German howitzers spit lead at us from beyond the low coastal hills. . . .

"Operation orders had us scheduled to beach at 1030, four hours after the first shot. We sat, idling, in formations of threes, waiting. A control ship lined us up like race horses. Our ship lunged forward.

"Another command ship blinked a message, halting us temporarily. Messages seemed to come from several directions, helter-skelter. The last one spelled out: DO NOT BEACH. UNLOAD TO LCMs.

"A small vessel pulled up on each side. Scrabble nets were flung over the sides. Our engineers, doctors, and specialists in electronic equipment lowered themselves down the nets. They sloshed ashore to secure the beach. Men and vehicles landed without opposition.

"Our orders were to retreat ten miles to the transport area. Heading back out to sea, Weise, Spitaleri, and I studied the beach with our binoculars. Jeeps and tanks, with their human cargo, seemed to be spilling out on the sands without trouble. Bustling small craft retreated from the shoreline, puttering back to large ships for troops that now were landing in an uninterrupted procession. From my vantage point, it appeared that the invasion was going well. We stole away with a sense of relief into the obscurity of the channel night. . . .

"Young Spitaleri had the watch, and relieved me. I was nicely tucked into bed when the jangling of General Quarters' bells and sirens jarred me awake. . . . I rushed to the bridge to hear Spitaleri still screaming over the public address system. Never had I seen the young officer so agitated: 'The sonovabitch almost got us. That was too damn close for me. Did you see that plane dive straight for us? That damn ship in front of us showed a blinker light. The German saw it, dropped right down through the cloud cover. Skimmed down our whole row of ships! Did you hear the explosion? The bomb dropped off the port side, only a couple hundred yards from the ship ahead.' His words were rushed.

"'Let's secure General Quarters, Spitaleri,' I advised. 'We'd only give away our position by opening fire. He won't be able to find us in the darkness anymore. I just hope every ship remains blacked-out now.' Nobody showed another light.

"By mid-morning our ships pulled into Portsmouth Harbor, stringing into the Calshot docks. Being at home in England gave us a warm, safe feeling.

"On the dock I met Archie, an acquaintance who commanded another LCI. He told of having his bow battered by underwater obstructions at Omaha. He expected orders to dry-dock up the Dart River, and seemed relieved to be out of the conflict. I envied him in a way, but expressed condolence."

6 June 1944
Mission to Caen, France

Major Marvin M. Kraft, a twenty-year-old flight officer with 487th Bombardment Group, Eighth Air Force, at Levenham, England, flew his fifth mission on D-Day.

In preparation for D-Day, "we had begun practicing night take-offs and landings. On D-Day itself, we took off at about 0300 or 0400 and circled until dawn. The plan was to then bomb Caen so that the German panzer divisions could not reach the beaches. Fortunately or unfortunately, this did not happen," Major Kraft writes.

"Like so many things on D-Day, snafus began immediately. England was completely blacked-out, as it had been for years. Only coded beacons could be seen flashing below. We had been given the wrong flimsy for the codes. The splasher radio beacons were being meconed, a type of jamming where the enemy receives your signal and rebroadcasts it after amplifying it a million times. Jamming was intense on all radio signals that night.

"Bomber groups were assembling all over the sky. We couldn't locate our group, so we joined with another group and flew over France. The sky had begun to cloud over as we circled. Cloud cover was complete and in several layers below us. We could not drop our bombs. We flew over France for hours trying to find a hole or target of opportunity. Finally, low on gas, we flew back to England.

"Our plane had to land at a P-38 fighter base on the southern coast; we were almost out of fuel. Very fortunately, the fighter group needed our bombs desperately, and the bombs were immediately loaded onto fighters and used on enemy installations around the beaches. We watched the P-38s take off.

"The P-38 fighters had used up all of their bombs, or almost all, before we arrived. They had been heavily engaged in flying across to France below the clouds at almost tree-top level in support of the landings. Very few bomb groups were able to get below the clouds to drop bombs. Fighters supplied most of the air support for the invasion that morning."

Major Kraft says that "many things went wrong with the invasion," but "the D-Day landings succeeded because of the sheer weight of men and materiel thrown across the channel, and because the German army, navy, and air force was by then so weak."

"We in the Eighth Air Force had been working hard to destroy the German air force by bombing their factories. This made them use their fighters against us. We wanted them to send up fighters so our fighter-escorts could shoot them down. The Royal Air Force was bombing at night, but they had the same idea."

May–18 June 1944
England to Cherbourg, France

Colonel William M. McConahey went overseas with the 90th Infantry Division aboard the Dominion Monarch, *which left New York Harbor 23 March 1944, in a convoy of sixty vessels heading for Great Britain.*

"We would land on D-plus-two; the place of landing was the Cotentin (Cherbourg) Peninsula; the objective was Cherbourg; the 4th Division was going in first, and the paratroopers would land behind the beaches," Colonel McConahey explains in his book *Battalion Surgeon*. He points out that the 90th Division, although part of the Third Army, was attached to the First Army for this invasion. Soon after D-Day, on 18 June, he was assigned as surgeon of the First's 2nd Battalion, 357th Infantry Regiment, remaining with the infantry until transfer to field artillery in October 1944.

In his book, Colonel McConahey describes a series of motivational talks given by their leaders at various times before the troops left England. The men heard Major General Lawton Collins, commander of VII Corps, to which the 90th was attached; they heard then-Lieutenant General Omar Bradley, commander of the U.S. First Army for the D-Day landing, who impressed them with "his sincerity, quiet confidence, and genuine friendliness" as he gave his "fatherly sort of talk"; and they heard then-Lieutenant General George Patton, commander of the Third Army, in what Colonel McConahey calls "the most fiery, 'fightingest' harangue I have ever heard."

"It was a harangue, all right, but it was masterful. The language was far from parlor English, for he cursed and swore at a great rate, but he really . . . incited men to a high fighting pitch." As he records a string of Pattonisms the colonel adds, "'Old Blood and Guts' really lived the part."

But then there was another speech on "one certain, warm, quiet evening in May . . . [when] our beloved and respected regimental commanding officer, Colonel Sheehy, addressed us. The silver-haired colonel, who soon was to lead us into battle, arose and said in a quiet, dignified voice, 'Gentlemen, we have heard these last few days what to do if we are captured. It even sounds like fun to be captured and to escape, but that's not the case. Let us resolve not to become prisoners. We are here to fight and win a war, not to give up to the enemy. Let us be known as a fighting regiment, rather than as surrendering cowards. Fight always, then, and don't surrender. It isn't so bad to die.'

"Within twenty-four hours of his first action, the gallant colonel was dead, cut down by Kraut machine-gunners while he was at the front of his men; and before the Normandy campaign was over, the majority of the officers who heard his words that spring evening were dead or badly wounded."

May–June 1944
Taunton, England

Lieutenant Colonel Peter O. Sykora was a captain, 94th Troop Carrier Squadron, 439th Troop Carrier Group.

Things began "to hum back at the air base," yet there still remained "the feeling that this could be but a dress rehearsal," Lieutenant Colonel Sykora recalls.

"As supply officer, I suddenly found myself with gallons and gallons of black and white paint that I had not ordered. I kept insisting on trying to return it to the air base central supply. . . . I was finally told point-blank just to keep it and store it. . . .

"Now things were moving at even a faster pace. Airplane crews were briefed, and then held in enclosures to secure information. Suddenly, the little things that were so important, and normally so unavailable, were available. Candy bars and cigarettes were free for the asking. Pistols, carbines, rifles, and plumbers' nightmares (submachine guns), all were being cleaned or exchanged. . . .

"The unwanted paint was brought out of storage and the wings of all aircraft painted with black and white stripes to clearly identify them as friendly aircraft. There was not to be a repeat of earlier invasions when the Allied Forces mistakenly fired on their own aircraft.

"Paratroopers and glider infantry were on the air base and, like the aircraft crews, all busy preparing for what was to come. Now, even more than before, there was the feeling that this was it. The secrecy of the past months was about to end. The invasion of Normandy was about to begin. D-Day was here."

May–August 1944
England to St. Mere Eglise, Normandy

Lieutenant Colonel James F. Gruver was a captain with the 51st Finance
Disbursement Section in Plymstock, England.

Having been given wooden boxes marked in code in May 1944, "we signed for this money by so many units" and "the contents remained a secret," Lieutenant Colonel Gruver writes. "Finally on Saturday, we were told payment would be made on Monday [5 June].

"On Sunday, we opened the boxes for the first time and were surprised to find French francs of the same type used in Africa. We had had the same type in the office all the time and didn't know it.

"We paid each man $4.03 in invasion currency. Many thought it was a dry run, as before, so they kept their British money. Then, at last, everyone realized it was the 'Real McCoy'! From that moment on, we were swamped with business. Some wanted to send their money home, some put it in soldiers' deposits at 4 percent interest, and some really got patriotic and purchased War Bonds. . . .

"Two days later, we packed and left for France ourselves. We took our money along as personal baggage on a Liberty ship. Kept a guard on duty twenty-four hours a day. From the Liberty ship, we transferred to an LCT, then to the beach with 'No Loss.'

On 4 August, "we set up a tent at St. Mere Eglise (lines then were north of St. Lo). The Germans were still shelling Carentan just a few miles south of us. We used German-captured office equipment and boxes until our equipment arrived from the beach. . . . It wasn't until two months later that we became reassigned to a rear-echelon Seine Base Section."

5 June 1944–28 March 1945
China–Burma–India Theater

Lieutenant Colonel Donald T. Means, navigator-bombardier, test-flew in combat
the first B-29 Superforts with 678th Squadron, 444th Bomb Group, 58th Wing,
20th AF.

"We took off from Gander, Newfoundland, 7 April, using almost all of the 6,000-foot runway. We climbed to 9,000 feet and flew most of the night between cloud layers. Finally, on 12 April, we arrived at Charra, India, where we faced extreme heat, humidity, monsoons, and malaria," Lieutenant Colonel Means recalls.

"Security was a problem in India," what with civilian Sikhs who worked on roads near the runways, Japanese sympathizers in the area, and "even the local police highly suspect. The secret Superfortress was too big to hide. We even told General Chennault's escape and evasion (E&E) specialist that our planes were B-17s. Tokyo Rose radioed that the Japanese knew all about us and that they would bomb us on a certain day. That day arrived. No bomb attack."

June 5, 1944, was the day set for "the first-in-history B-29 Superfortress combat mission, a rehearsal for the first land-based combat operations against the mainland of Japan. The target for us was the railyards of Bangkok, Siam [Thailand].

"The four-bladed propellers strained to lift 134,900 pounds of aircraft, crew, bombs, and fuel. We carried eighteen 500-pound bombs to be dropped on the railroad repair-shop. We had left Karaghpur, India, at about dawn and on the way to bombing altitude of 23,000 feet, we began to get a compression loss on No. 3 engine. Because of this, we dropped back, lost our formation, and at about 1130 hours dropped our bombs on the target and headed home for India.

"Soon after that, No. 1 engine ran out of fuel and quit. Japanese fighters looked us over as we turned due north toward Kunming, China, which was some 250 miles nearer to us than our base in India. We made a slow let-down; chopped up our radar set, which had malfunctioned; threw overboard tools; put a .45-caliber bullet through the brains of the secret Norden bombsight and tossed it out; jettisoned the empty bomb-bay tank; and threw out other items that could lighten the load and save gasoline.

"By 1445, we had crossed the Mekong River and were about 120 miles south of Kunming. We soon made plans to abandon ship. We actually bailed out near Yuchi, China, about 56 miles from Kunming," with four of the crew going out the nose wheel-well, and eight, including the author, departing from the bomb bay. "Actually, our right gunner rode the plane down and was killed.

"Some of us landed in rice paddies. I landed on a gravestone and fractured my left ankle. Hours later, with the help of local Chinese military, we arrived at the China Inland Mission, Yuchi. The missionaries were German, British, French, and Polish. We made contact with a nearby American radio station to relay a message to General Chennault's headquarters for help. They must have smiled at our claim that we were a B-17 crew, not B-29.

"That night in the mission, I slept with my .45 pistol at ready. After all, there were Germans in the mission and this young American had been, a year before, imbued with anti-German and anti-Japanese sentiment. . . .

"General Chennault's E&E crew soon arrived with a jeep and hospital wagon and drove us to his headquarters. On the way, we stopped at the American Army radio station, my first visit to one. Our guide, Chennault's E&E man at this time, told us about Operation Overlord, the invasion of Europe. And so, on 5 and 6 June 1944, we hit the enemy from both ends, East and West [besides entering Rome, capital of Italy, on 5 June].

"On one mission against Japan, we had an engine fire over the target. I drew a course for Vladivostok, but fortunately we extinguished the fire and flew home on three engines. Unfortunately, other B-29s had been forced to land at Vladivostok. There, our friends impounded the crews, delayed their return to friendly units, and copied their B-29 aircraft (the copy became a Tupilov).

"By November 1944, B-29s of the Twentieth Air Force from the China–Burma–India [CBI] Theater had bombed targets in Siam, Japan, China, Sumatra, Manchuria, Formosa, Burma, and Malaya. Between combat missions, we flew numerous trips across the Hump to help supply our bases in China with gasoline, bombs, and other supplies.

"From our bases near Chengtu, China, the flight to Japan and return was about fifteen hours. A round-trip from India to Singapore was about eighteen hours.

"We left the CBI Theater after having flown twenty combat missions and thirty-six combat/operational/supply missions over the Hump. The last combat mission for us was on 28 March 1945."

June 1944
Maffin Bay, New Guinea

Lieutenant Colonel Charles R. Keefe was a captain serving with the 63rd Infantry Regiment, 6th Infantry Division, which left Hawaii January 1944 en route to Milne Bay, New Guinea.

"After observing blackout regulations for the previous six months, we looked in awe upon Milne Bay at night—lighted up like Coney Island, yet the nearest outpost to the Japs at the time," William L. West writes in a unit history, which continues: "We disembarked on 2 February, and thus began our year of living in the hell that is New Guinea. . . ."

"Then it was on to the first combat at Maffin Bay, New Guinea, near Wakde Island" on 8 June, Lieutenant Colonel Keefe says. "The battle to take Lone Tree Hill took several weeks. Actually, it was heavy jungle on a steep hill, mostly coral rock. The 'Lone Tree' came from the sketchy maps available; it had one tree shown on the hill! Actually, solid jungle!"

"When we landed, the beachhead was about three miles long—and 100 yards deep!" Mr. West records, adding: "It was at this time that the names of Lone Tree Hill, Hill 225, and Hill 265 were engraved in the history of the 63rd. It was here that Radio Tokyo—through a charming personality known as Tokyo Rose—broadcast that the 63rd doughboys were 'blood-thirsty Americans!' And it was here that we defeated the best that the crack 36th Japanese Division could put up against us. Some of the first Japs seen were Imperial Marines—six feet tall—all dead. It was almost impossible to see a live Jap, so well were they concealed.

"We were constantly harassed by snipers and the entire push was over a hill of solid coral. We couldn't dig in, so we built bunkers—on top of the ground. We found out that the Japs' tactics were anything but orthodox, so we played them at their own game. The division lost 150 KIA and over 700 wounded. Jap losses were likely over 1,000."

8 June 1944

Mission near Waigeo Island, north of Dutch New Guinea

Lieutenant Colonel Paul R. Sciortino was a first lieutenant, 17th Reconnaissance Squadron (B), 71st Reconnaissance Group.

On 8 June, Lieutenant Sciortino participated in the strike against a Japanese naval task force carrying reinforcements to the island of Biak, New Guinea, where troops were still engaged with the enemy and where an American airstrip had been established.

"There must have been hundreds of thoughts running through my mind that fateful morning of 8 June 1944 when our squadron of ten B-25 bombers set out to intercept a Japanese task force," he writes. "The one thought I can remember clearly is this: We were not trained to attack naval vessels. We had been trained to perform low-level bombing and strafing missions."

"Although greatly fatigued by loss of sleep from enemy bombing raids, the ground echelon labored diligently and efficiently the night before the mission to load bombs and ammunition and to put the aircraft in perfect mechanical condition," the 17th's Unit Citations read, and then continue: "Contacting the enemy naval task force the next day off Waigeo Island north of Dutch New Guinea, the ten crews of the 17th Reconnaissance Squadron (B) discovered that it was composed of four destroyers and two cruisers protected by ten aircraft. Although an attack on six heavily armed warships by a single squadron was almost suicidal, the B-25s without hesitation were formed into two-plane elements and descended to minimum altitude. . . .

"In order to divert the intense anti-aircraft fire from the other B-25s, one of the two-plane elements headed for a cruiser. Both of these planes were shot down by the withering anti-aircraft barrage but this action enabled the other B-25s, dropping 500-pound and 1,000-pound bombs, to destroy or sink all four of the destroyers and force the cruisers to turn back. A total of three B-25s were lost in this engagement and five were seriously damaged, while the escorting P-38s accounted for six enemy aircraft. . . ." Major William G. Tennille and Captain Sumner G. Lind were the two who sacrificed their lives "so that the rest of us could accomplish our mission," the colonel notes.

After the task force was discovered and its size ascertained, Lieutenant Colonel Sciortino recalls, "I remember hearing our squadron commander, Major William Tennille, order us to break off into preassigned formations and that he would attack the first vessel. From then on, everything seems hazy. However, I do recall that as we made our bombing run I was on my knees in the nose of our aircraft praying.

"I must have opened the bomb-bay doors, dropped the three bombs, and closed the bomb-bay doors instinctively. I vividly recall raking a destroyer and the barge it was pulling with my flexible .50-caliber machine gun. I can still see men jumping over the side. It wasn't until our pilot, Lieutenant Archie Trantham, turned the aircraft, after we had safely got beyond the range of the Japanese guns, that I could look to my right and see at least one vessel sinking.

"It still strikes me as some sort of miracle how the remaining six of our ten aircraft spotted one B-25, and it was this aircraft that guided us safely to our base of Wakde. The pilot of that aircraft was First Lieutenant Glenn H. Pruitt, and the navigator was Major William Boone Smith." From contemporary newspaper accounts of their mission, fighter cover was identified as having come from the 475th Fighter Group.

Lieutenant Colonel Sciortino believes that "there were two surprises in this mission: One, the Japanese, because we had the daring and courage to attack them; and two, us—because we pulled it off."

16 June 1944
POW Camps Davao to Cabanatuan, the Philippines

First Lieutenant Hugh H. Roberts continues his POW diary-letter, written from Bilibid Prison, Manila, the Philippines, 26 November 1944.

"We left [Camp Davao] 16 June 1944 and returned to Cabanatuan," Lieutenant Roberts writes, in describing yet another move for the POWs. "We were loaded into trucks at Dexecol [probably Dapecol, abbreviation for Davao Penal Colony], tied up with ropes and blindfolded to prevent escape. We were loaded aboard ship so crowded that only one-third of the men could lie down at a time. Then we were issued our fourth and last ten-pound Red Cross box. The stealing was terrible. My box was not complete to start with.

"When we anchored off Zamboanga, an officer dove overboard and escaped, so we were all put below decks where only about half of the men could sit down, and when a man fainted he couldn't fall. When this happened, the Japs would let two men carry him up on deck till he recovered, but the men had to go back. The air was sure foul down there.

"Many of the men thought it would only be temporary and left their Red Cross food above, and the Japs kicked it around the deck, overboard, and bayoneted much of it. We were permitted to go above deck single-file for food, and eight men at a time to relieve themselves; otherwise we stayed below for three days and nights till we reached Cebu. At Cebu, we went ashore and lay out in the ashes of an old Spanish fort, without blankets, for three days. We got one bath there and I got my hair all cut off and a shave. That helped. There were 1,100 of us; the rest stayed on Mindanao building an airport.

"After being there three days, we left on a freighter that had brought coal to Cebu. We had to lie in the coal dust on the steel deck below decks without blankets. It was hot and the air was foul, but everyone could sit down and most men could lie down. About twenty or thirty of us crawled through a small hatchway to a vacant hold and had lots of room and better air, though it was dark, as it was the third hold below decks. Our baggage was in the fourth and so we got something to sleep on, too. My shirt still has coal dust in it [as he writes at the end of November 1944].

"On ship, we were reduced to one-half-pound rice and a little thin soup daily in two meals, and once they cut one of them off for punishment. We each received two to three quarts of water per day for everything. This policy applied on both ships.

"At Manila, we lay out in the harbor three days, until a man died from the conditions, before they unloaded us on 27 June, and we stayed that night here at Bilibid. The next day we were loaded in boxcars and went by railroad to Cabanatuan where we were on three meals again and permitted to rest four or five days before being put to work. We received about three-fourths pound of rice and some green vegetables. When we worked, we got a little extra for dinner and supper. It started off with four to eight ounces of rice but dwindled as time went on, changing to corn, and then to cassava. No deduction for cobs or peelings," he informs his family in that single, comprehensive letter from Bilibid that covers his period of imprisonment, 9 April 1942–26 November 1944.

JULY 1944

32

While the war that was fought "in division, corps, and Army headquarters . . . was one of maps and lines and pins and shifting troops here and there . . . , the war I saw was one of mud and discomfort and suffering and death and terror and destruction," Colonel William M. McConahey says in the introduction to his book *Battalion Surgeon*, written in 1945 and published privately twenty years later. A professor emeritus of medicine in 1994 at the Mayo Medical School, Rochester, Minnesota, after almost thirty-seven years on the Mayo Clinic staff, Colonel McConahey served as surgeon for 2nd Battalion, 357th Regiment, soon after landing with the 90th Infantry Division on the Cotentin Peninsula of Normandy on D-Day-plus-2. On 9 June, the 90th was sent in to relieve part of the 82nd Airborne, with orders to attack at dawn.

"It was brutal up there, and what a slaughter!" the young surgeon writes of those earliest days in Normandy. "The wounded poured back in dozens, and I've never seen such horrible wounds, before or since—legs off, arms off, faces shot away, eviscerations, chests ripped open, and so on. We worked at top speed, hour after hour, until we were too tired to stand up—and then we still kept going. How many lives we saved by the hundreds of units of plasma we gave I'll never know. The 1st and 3rd Battalion aid stations were working together here, so four physicians, two chaplains, and all our technicians were working constantly.

"It was a bit 'hot,' too. Machine guns and rifles not far away made quite a din; stray bullets continually whizzed by the aid station, and mortar and 99mm shells hit uncomfortably close. . . .

"Late in the afternoon, word came to Tony [Dominski, captain and one of the nine in the 90th's medical detachment] and me that our battalion was to be pulled out and marched around to attack the strong point from the flank," Colonel McConahey continues. "I have never forgotten the expressions on the faces of those officers as they were again ordered to lead their exhausted, battered companies into another futile, costly assault. Their tired, old-looking, lined, bearded faces, their bloodshot eyes, their torn, muddy clothes, and their grim lips told the story. . . .

"So it went for five wild days and nights—attack, attack, attack, again and again and again, with bloody losses each time. During those five days we treated about 150 men a day in the combined 1st and 3rd Battalion aid stations. For five days and nights I did not wash, I did not shave, I did not sleep, except for a rare, brief catnap, and I hardly ate, except to gulp part of a cold K-ration when things slowed up now and then. How the litter bearers lasted I do not know. The long litter hauls through that rough hedgerow country were tough. . . .

"One bit of mute evidence of the tremendous number of wounded men treated in our station was the huge pile of discarded weapons outside. . . . Garand rifles, Tommy guns, bayonets, trench knives, Browning automatic rifles, pistols, helmets, packs, blankets, and so on. These represented the less seriously hurt boys; the stretcher cases usually came in without such equipment. Their weapons were left where they had fallen."

That day in Gonfreville, 25 July 1944—"the beginning of our breakout in Normandy," when he watched "the air show" of 3,000 American planes "bomb and strafe enemy positions" and when the 357th was to put on their "drive to take Periers"—he records as "the beginning of a rough day for us," the day that he felt himself "slipping."

"The enemy resistance was fanatical, and after a full day of bitter fighting we had advanced only 300 yards," he writes. "Casualties were heavy and bad, and all of us in the aid station were exhausted by the continual stream of wounded. We had more than the usual number of men with combat exhaustion, too— those pitiful men who sit rigidly in the station shaking and crying, with faces and wide eyes filled with horror. . . .

"It was during this day that I felt myself slipping. I thought I couldn't stand to see many more bleeding, mutilated American boys, to see and smell the rotting bodies of the dead, to hear and cringe under the crash of shells and to see the screaming men with combat exhaustion. I had to get a hold on myself that day to keep on going. Whether I might have become a victim of battle exhaustion myself had this kept up I do not know, but the next day the enemy collapsed in front of us and our race across France soon began."

July 1944
St. Lo, Normandy

Lieutenant Colonel William D. Sink submits the WWII memoirs of his late father, Brigadier General James D. Sink, a captain with HQ and HQ Company, 116th Infantry, 29th Division.

"During operations on the 13th in support of the 2nd Battalion [astride Martinville Ridge just east of Martinville], tanks of the 747th Tank Battalion received an order in perfectly good English to withdraw. Lieutenant Colonel Stuart G. Fries, battalion commander, happened to be at the 116th CP when he received word of the deception and was fortunately able to countermand the order given by the Germans before any serious disruption could occur. The fighting on the 12th and 13th was extremely hard. Casualties were high and little ground gained," Captain Sink records at the time.

On 17 July, "the 3rd Battalion jumped off at 0430 in a column of companies. Major Howie had made it clear that only two men in the platoon were authorized to fire in emergencies and that main reliance would be upon bayonets and hand grenades . . . The objective of the attack was stated to be relief of the 2nd Battalion at La Madeleine. By a combination of skill, luck, and morning fog, the 3rd Battalion slipped between two German companies to reach La Madeleine by 0600 hours. . . . As Major Howie was issuing his orders for the attack, a mortar shell hit nearby, killing him instantly. . . .

"At 1800 hours, a serious counterattack threat menaced the two isolated battalions so an air strike was called. The planes were in the air and over the two battalions in the target area about 2100 but failed to locate the units on the ground. A query from regiment indicated the units had failed to carry front-line marking panels. It was suggested that white undershirts and copies of the *Stars and Stripes* be used. These markings were picked up by the 506th Fighter Bomber Squadron, which shortly afterwards came in with telling blows and broke up the threat.

"The air attack was so devastating and broke up the attack so completely that a number of Germans ran forward to surrender rather than stay in it. The event proved to be one of the first outstanding examples of close air-support in the war and resulted in the rules being rewritten. The regiment learned something, too. From then on, it was SOP [standard operating procedure] for each front-line soldier to carry a section of a cerise front-line marking panel to display under such emergencies."

"The battle of St. Lo proved to be almost as costly as the initial engagement on Omaha Beach to Headquarters Company," Captain Sink summarizes. "More than 25 percent of the effective company strength became casualties during this operation. . . .

"One had to be at St. Lo to appreciate the ordeal the men went through. The incessant pounding of the artillery and mortar-fire was dealt with by remaining underground most of the time, venturing out only when absolutely necessary. . . . Most men had a week's growth of beard when relieved on 19 July. Cheeks were sallow, eyes listless and sunk back in their heads. . . .

"From 19 to 28 July, rehabilitation of the company [at Les Cables] proceeded at a rapid pace under the influence of rest, food, and relaxation. Cheeks filled out again and color came back. Eyes took on a sparkle and looked normal again. . . . The company sent a delegation to participate in the dedication of the 29th Division Cemetery at La Cambe. Most of the company dead were buried there. All was well when the regiment was alerted to move out to participate in Operation Cobra, the St. Lo breakthrough scheduled for 28 July."

June–July 1944

Cotentin Peninsula, Normandy

Colonel William M. McConahey, battalion surgeon, continues his story.

With orders to move out about midnight Friday, 9 June, to relieve part of the 82nd Airborne Division and attack at dawn, "our long march to the front began," Colonel McConahey writes. "On we marched in silence for three hours, through the ruins of St. Mere Eglise, past our own flashing, roaring artillery guns and closer and closer to the enemy. Even today [as he writes, one year after the invasion], the memory of that dark night seems like a nightmare.

"About 0300, we halted . . . and started to dig foxholes, but in a short time moved out again as the first streaks of daylight appeared."

After finally crossing a stream where "a Kraut 88 . . . kept slapping in shells smack across that bridge," he reports: "And there I was in battle. But what confusion! I can't remember any clear-cut facts, but I can never forget . . . the mass of milling soldiers, the sharp crack of enemy shells, the stinging odor of cordite on my eyes and nose, the many burned-out tanks strewn along the road and in the fields, and the dead German and American soldiers in great numbers. . . .

"I was getting desperate; I had to find a spot for an aid station soon, for I knew the casualties would be coming back shortly." As the battalion attacked and moved and repositioned, stations were set up again and again—first in a farmhouse where "88s ripped over"; then a mile or two into the "badly smashed" village of Amfreville, "in a building the Germans had used for a dressing station"; into an old farmhouse, partially occupied by men of the 82nd Airborne; and then a little old French house, and all in the first "five wild days and nights," before moving back to Amfreville 14 June.

In July, the 90th Division made its "historic and bloody assault on the heavily fortified enemy position in the Foret de Monte Castre," known as Hill 122; the 358th Infantry made its "ill-fated and tragic attack on 'the Island' in an effort to straighten the lines"; and for about ten days they "sat on the north side of the Seves River, under constant enemy shell fire."

It was at "the Island," a fortified bit of ground in the swampy Seves River, that "three chaplains of the regiment did a wonderful and courageous deed. After the attack collapsed, many of our wounded men lay helplessly in places too close to the German positions to be reached. The chaplains walked out in full view of the enemy, carrying a white flag of truce. Then they proceeded to pick up all the wounded soldiers they could find and to bring them back. For several hours they worked directly in front of the enemy, but no shots were fired at them."

July 1944
St. Lo, Normandy

Colonel Jean W. Christy, with 50th Field Artillery Battalion, 5th Infantry Division, heads with them from Belfast in a five-ship convoy 7 July 1944.

On 9 July at about 1000 hours, sighting the Normandy coast and seeing "signs of the fighting that has been there, we wonder at the absence of enemy aircraft, but realize why when Thunderbolts (P-47s) appear everywhere in the sky, and land and take off from a field right on the shore," Colonel Christy writes.

"The sea just north of the entrance of the Carentan Canal is crowded with ships. It stretches for miles, ships jumbled together within a few hundred yards of each other. The landing was made on an iron causeway that the engineers had constructed into the sea. We didn't even get our feet wet.

"All of the division personnel then marched, with full pack, five miles to Transit Area B, where units organized. Then they marched to the 5th Division concentration area about twelve miles away, a mile or so north of Montebourg.

"It all went smoothly. Someone had done a lot of preparation. Along the twelve-mile hike, there were even mile markers with signs giving encouragement, like 'Sherman was right.'"

Their orders were "to relieve the 1st Infantry Division in the line north of St. Lo. The 50th was to relieve the 33rd FA. The division was to move out at 1000 hours on 13 July.

"I confess that I entered the battalion area with trepidation. I was in awe of these men of the 1st Infantry Division. They had made the invasion of North Africa when we were back in Iceland. Then they had participated in the invasion of Sicily. Just a month before, they had come ashore on D-Day and had been fighting ever since. I visualized them as grizzled combat veterans, with hard, piercing eyes, and leathery, wrinkled faces. To my surprise and amazement, we found them to be young men about the same age and disposition that we were."

After being filled in and shown around, "we were finally in combat" when "C Battery registered its guns at 2028 hours, the first artillery of the division to fire. . . . A total of 80 rounds was fired before midnight. Our ammunition allotment was set at 500 rounds per day for the time being.

"Some officers from the 7th remained with us for another day to show us all of their installations. . . . Captain Whitney took me on a tour of the battalion observation posts. We were hampered wherever we went by the hedgerows around each small field. The fields were rectangular, on average perhaps a hundred yards or so on a side. The hedgerows were centuries old, and consisted of a dirt embankment two to four feet thick and about four feet high with tall shrubs and small trees growing on the top. Sometimes there were two fields side by side with a ten- or fifteen-foot space between their adjacent hedgerows, [making] it extremely difficult for attacking forces to make any headway.

"On the evening of 18 July, we received our first instructions for the big push, which was to allow us to break out of the beachhead in Normandy." However, "the situation changed abruptly when Captain Paul Rennord was wounded on 20 July," with plans changing almost daily: from 22 July to the 23rd, then to 25 July. "Then we learned that Operation Cobra was again postponed," Colonel Christy says. It reminded him of the old first sergeant of C Battery back at Fort Custer in 1941 who told him, "Lieutenant, it goes like this: Order, Counterorder, Disorder!"

On the afternoon of 24 July, "there was a regular dogfight in the battalion area—P-47 Thunderbolts, Focke Wulf 190s, and Me-109s. . . . Later we learned that for some reason Field Marshal Hermann Goering himself, commander of the German Luftwaffe, had all of his planes on the Western Front make this one last desperate attack on the Allied beachhead. Actually, he didn't have more than a few dozen planes left. . . . From that day on, the German air force was never a factor in the ground war."

On 26 July, "the town of Vidouville was taken, or rather passed through, at 1130 hours. . . . We fired a lot of artillery that day, starting with preparation fires on Vidouville prior to the attack."

On 31 July, Colonel Christy records: "After vicious fighting for five days, suddenly the Germans just weren't there any more. There were a few isolated riflemen left behind whose purpose was to keep us from catching on to the truth too fast, but the opposition had just melted away. A disengagement from full contact in battle is recognized as one of the most difficult operations there is. The German 2nd Parachute Division, however, did it almost flawlessly.

"The 2nd Infantry Regiment moved forward quickly on 31 July. The 50th FA Battalion displaced forward into the position area reconnoitered the day before. . . . Orders came from Artillery headquarters to turn our new position into an assembly area, and stay there. . . .

"It was now obvious that the 5th Infantry Division was being withdrawn from the attack in preparation for the formation of the Third U.S. Army."

July 1944–April 1945
Carentan to Commercy, France

First Lieutenant Gretchen L. Hovis joined 50th General Hospital at Camp Carson, Colorado, in July 1943 and went overseas with the group 29 December 1943.

After more drills and classes in England, and taking over an evacuation hospital in Glasgow, Scotland, the 50th and the 289th left for France in mid-July 1944. Initially bivouacked four miles from the front, "we were located at Carentan," where "the Germans were trying to bomb a bridge one-half mile from us. The main road (the Red Ball Highway) for supplies, tanks, artillery, and personnel went past us, so we heard a lot of noise from the heavy convoys, from the anti-aircraft next to us, and from the planes overhead! We saw chandelier flares, falling planes, and smoke at St. Lo, not far away. It was scary!" First Lieutenant Hovis declares.

"On 25 July, 3,000 planes that bombed St. Lo flew directly over our area. We watched for five straight hours and we thought they would never stop coming. It was an awesome sight."

By 14 August, their hospital was ready. Patients arriving "could hardly believe the clean sheets and blankets on their beds, hot meals, and American girls!"

"We lived in tents and learned to fix fires, chop wood by flashlight, shower usually in cold water, read and write letters by candlelight, and when we had no fuel except that for the patients, realized that warmth was a luxury. We had a sad experience when one of our nurses, ill with pneumonia, died 5 October 1944 and was buried in an American cemetery at St. Mere Eglise, France. Tears streamed down our faces as we attended the funeral and watched as our friend Joy, wrapped in the American flag, was lowered into the ground."

On 18 November, the 50th moved near Verdun and Metz, "in the combat zone once more, to hear the Jerries anew," into a building that initially had no fuel or lights. "Our entire hospital wards were in buildings that were formerly a French Cavalry post. Patients were admitted 4 December 1944 and at one time [we] cared for over 2,300 patients. In addition to our many wounded GIs, we treated Russian, Italian, and German patients."

July 1944
Missions over Normandy

Colonel Cecil C. Ellzey was a pilot with 28th FA Battalion, 8th Infantry.

"'Fun-flying' [over Great Britain] suddenly changed to scary, serious flying the morning of 4 July 1944 when I took off from Ibsley Air Base, west of Southampton, England, leading a flight of ten L-4s over the English Channel, destination Omaha Beachhead along the coast of Normandy. This flight of liaison planes consisted of observation aircraft of the 8th Infantry Division, 28th Field Artillery Battalion, commanded by Lieutenant Colonel F. J. Chesarek. The 8th relieved the 82nd Airborne Division in the line near La Haye-du-Puits on the western side of the Cotentin Peninsula," Colonel Ellzey relates.

"On my first day of flying, I was hit over La Haye-du-Puits, with a bullet passing through the pants leg of my observer, Lieutenant Paul R. Dumas, of Rumford, Maine, and stopping against my back after penetrating my backpack parachute. Normally, I wore a seat-pack chute, but for our flight across the Channel we were provided backpacks, the reason never questioned because it saved my life. The angle of the bullet path would have exited through my heart."

In the breakthrough at St. Lo, Colonel Ellzey says, "our division played an important role in crossing the Ay River near Lessay to secure the western end of Lessay–Periers–St. Lo Road to allow the armor and infantry divisions to break out and reach Rennes in just under four days.

"During this breakthrough, I was able to follow the leading armor element and report their location to my battalion commander before division and corps knew exactly the location of the forward elements. South of Avranches, my plane was attacked by two Fw-190s; two bullet holes through the stabilizer. I returned to our field of operations with the radio in the lap of my observer, Lieutenant Dumas, since it broke loose from its anchor."

Colonel Ellzey describes the L-4s (Piper Cubs) as "air observation posts for the field artillery through the war on all fronts." The "unarmed single-engine plane, commonly referred to as the 'Flying Grasshopper,' was well-adapted for aerial observation, reconnaissance, and general administrative flights behind the front lines" and "could operate from small fields and most roads. The after-action reports at cessation of hostilities concluded that the liaison aircraft had a great impact on the effectiveness of field-artillery fire throughout World War II on all fronts."

July 1944
Normandy, France

Lieutenant Colonel Norman N. Graber served as troubleshooter with the Army Signal Corps.

"It was dusk, raining, and the dirt roads were extremely muddy. Our convoy was on the move and MPs were at crossroads to point the way and keep us out of mined fields," Lieutenant Colonel Graber writes. "I was in the cab of one of the vehicles and was able to see mud spraying up on the MPs as the vehicles passed. Suddenly, I saw and recognized one of the MPs as a friend from Brooklyn and just had enough time to call out his name as we passed.

"I never located him again in France, but in 1964 I saw him in New York. It was so strange seeing him again in those surroundings and in a suit, shirt, and tie. We were both quite happy and emotional. I told him, finally, that it was I who called his name twenty years ago in Normandy. It's hard to describe his expression and excitement—and relief—upon finding and being able to identify the voice that called his name that dark, hectic afternoon back in 1944."

June–December 1944
Normandy to St. Lo, France

Lieutenant Colonel Paul C. Scott was a Tech 4 with the 56th Finance Disbursing Section that accompanied HQ First Army from Omaha Beach through France, Belgium, and into Germany.

"Shortly after D-Day, we loaded our personnel and equipment into three 6x6 trucks and headed for Southampton where we drove onto an LST. Rough seas forced us to remain in the harbor for two nights," Colonel Scott recalls. "On 30 June, all our troops were paid in full—less the $4.03 previously paid," in England, just prior to the invasion.

"Of particular interest to me was the bombing of St. Lo. At the time, our tents were pitched on high ground about ten miles from St. Lo. As we had been told, the first wave of what was to be 5,000 planes [sources say "more than 3,000"] came over at noon heading for St. Lo. To confuse the German anti-aircraft guns, the first wave dropped strips of aluminum foil, some of which fell like snowflakes on our position. At the appropriate time, the lead bombers dropped a line of smoke trails, which were to be the guide for the many waves that followed to start dropping their bombs. Unfortunately, the wind kept moving these smoke trails toward the friendly lines. When the smoke cleared, it appeared that more damage may have been done to our own troops than to the enemy. Among the casualties were two high-ranking generals who had come from Washington to observe the bombing, one of whom was the Chief of Army Ground Forces, Lieutenant General Lesley J. McNair. [Sources list General McNair as being killed 25 July "while observing carpet bombing during Operation Cobra."] "The next day, the same [number of] planes, having reloaded their bomb racks in England, returned at noon and pulverized St. Lo. . . .

"The 56th Finance Disbursing Section continued to pay its troops on the last day of each month, including December 1944 when we were forced to withdraw 100 miles during the Battle of the Bulge."

July–December 1944
Cherbourg Peninsula, France

Lieutenant Colonel Joseph A. Vargas III was a captain with the 729th Railway Operating Battalion (ROB), which arrived in England in mid-1943 and, with the 756th R Shop Battalion, assembled 29,000 railway cars before landing in Normandy in July 1944.

"Up to D-plus-41, Military Railway Service units reconnoitered and surveyed the French rail lines to be used," and by "D-plus-45, ferrying of rail equipment from England to France was begun," Colonel Vargas's records reveal. By November 1944, "American military railways in Europe are hauling more than 10,000 tons of freight daily," *Railroad Trainman* magazine reports at the time.

These goals were achieved while men and trains were "strafed, bombed, and sniped at," as trains drove "through the blackout without headlights," as brakemen signaled "by swinging the glowing butts of cigarettes or the tiny flames of cigarette lighters," and one night as a determined captain and four enlisted soldiers hand-poured "2,100 gallons of fuel from five-gallon cans into the tanks of three diesel engines." They loaded and hauled the cans in a "3/4-ton weapons carrier from a dump five miles away." In another case, "a single key switchyard in France was cluttered with charred and rusting junk of 1,300 locomotives and freight cars when the engineers arrived. But two tracks were repaired and the trains got through," the magazine article reports.

According to Timetable No. 1 of the U.S. Army Military Railroad, Cherbourg Peninsula Division, effective Monday, 17 July 1944, trains were moving on 48.6 miles of double-track between Cherbourg and Lison; a 46.8-mile stretch between Cherbourg and Montebourg Junction; a 43.7-mile stretch between Sottevast and Coutances; and a 42.7-mile stretch between Carteret and Carentan.

"By mid-August 1944, the 729 ROB was hauling loaded trains (mainly ammo and POL—petroleum, oil, lubricants) along the branch railway to the east (St. Sauveur, La Haye-du-Puits, Lessay, Periers, Coutance, Avranches, Fougeres, and to Le Mans)," Colonel Vargas writes. "These loaded trains on single track were moving slowly and stopping because the U.S. Army Engineer Battalions and our Company A track and bridge teams were still rehabitating the rail line. . . . The first trainload of ammo hauled by a 729 ROB train crew arrived 17 August 1944, 1300 hours, at the First Army railhead at Le Mans, France. This was at a time when the First Army and Patton needed all the POL and ammo they could get for the drive to Paris."

"At Le Mans, French railroad men told them that they would be lucky to clear two trains a day. They got twenty-seven through," the November 1944 *Railroad Trainman* reports.

"During a peak twenty-four-hour period of rail operations in Normandy around mid-September 1944, the 729th ROB handled 52 loaded trains involving 102 different train and engine movements. When the day's work was over, the train dispatcher's sheet was nearly ten feet long," Colonel Vargas declares.

Spring–Summer 1944
Watford, England

Colonel Boaz L. Brandmarker was a first lieutenant, CO, 839th Signal Service Company (Special), comprising twenty officers and 200-plus enlisted men.

"Our mission was to keep all the communication lines open for the Normandy invasion and to remain in contact with the continent, a job we were doing since 1942," Colonel Brandmarker writes, pointing out that "a detachment from his company did land in Normandy."

"The use of SCUD missiles during the Gulf War of 1990–91 brought to mind our own experiences with rockets and missiles," he says. "It was summer 1944 in Watford, where the days lasted until past 2300 hours, when the Nazis decided to launch a rocket attack, directed toward London. These rockets were nicknamed 'buzz bombs' because the motor sounded like a lawn mower and could be heard and seen from the ground. Many were intercepted by the RAF and were shot down in flight. Those that got away continued until they ran out of fuel and came down, and whatever was hit exploded, causing loss of life and property.

"There was no air-raid siren to warn you, as they were coming over quite regularly. Our soldiers could hear and see the buzz bomb, but when the motor cut out there was a scramble for cover because it would be coming down and explode.

"This went on for a couple of weeks when a new and more dangerous menace came in the form of the large and high-flying V-2 bomb, which in this case was like a missile. It flew very high, gave no sound or warning, and these V-2s were hitting London itself, with loss of life. It was a very unnerving experience . . . and you couldn't stay in an air-raid shelter all the time. These bombs could not be destroyed by the RAF (too fast), nor was anti-aircraft effective.

"The success of the invasion put a stop to these rocket attacks," the colonel adds.

High on his list of other wartime recollections, the colonel singles out "Hubert," the GI cartoon character who gave him and many other veterans of World War II a few bright moments. In submitting a 1945 British paperback with reprints of *The Best of Hubert*, Colonel Brandmarker notes: "I clipped most of these and others to brighten my time. And they surely did."

The cartoons were the creation of then-Sergeant Dick Wingert, who began his military career with the 34th Infantry Division at Camp Claiborne, Louisiana, and began submitting cartoons to the Belfast and, subsequently, the London edition of *Stars and Stripes*, where Hubert put on weight and evolved as "a gold-bricking GI who goofs off." When Sergeant Wingert was discharged in 1945, Hubert also became a civilian and continued in syndication into the early 1990s from Richard Wingert's home-base in Nashville, Indiana.

16 June–9 July 1944
Saipan, Mariana Islands

Colonel Martin E. Nolan, a second lieutenant, commanded a rifle company during the siege of Makin Island, November 1943. By June 1944, he was on Saipan with the 27th Division as operations officer.

"For the 3rd Battalion, 165th Infantry Regiment, the Saipan battle began on D-plus-1 [16 June] at 1800 hours with a radio message for its commander to report aboard the regimental command transport to receive orders to land immediately, on beaches secured the previous day by the 2nd and 4th Marine Divisions," Colonel Nolan writes.

In the three weeks of combat that remained before Saipan was secured, there were "flashes of high tension or sometimes almost comic relief," among them, the following:

"A Marine amphtrac driver who adopted the battalion when he found it occupying the positions held by the 4th MarDiv the day before and kept it supplied with ammo, water, and food for three days until the transports returned.

"A reconnaissance into the foothills of the wooded, rocky slopes of Mount Tapotchau, where alongside a ridge-line trail, the body of a Marine rifleman lay, seeming almost to be asleep, except for the gaping wound in his side. He might have symbolized all the young men at war, his helmet off, with flame-red hair and a freckled face serenely at rest, looking like he might have seen seventeen summers before this one.

"A telephone message in the middle of the night that motors could be heard approaching. The disbelief when one round from a 37mm AT gun stopped an 'assault' by one lone motorcycle and sidecar, ridden by a Japanese staff officer who had no inkling that the Americans were so far in the rear of his units' main defenses.

"The incredible sight of 500 or 600 Japanese infantrymen in full uniform withdrawing from the Tapotchau area across flat, open terrain, four abreast and dog-trotting easily, individual and crew-served weapons on their shoulders. The column disappearing unharmed over a ridge-line and down into what was later called Hara-Kiri Gulch.

"Suicidal attacks, continuous after dark, by small groups of Japanese coming up the cliff trails, with front-line company commanders calling mortar and artillery supporting fire on top of their own positions to break up these attacks. Brief, intense firefights against infiltrating Japanese within the perimeter, illuminated by fires from battalion mortars and naval support ships. Finally, at first-light the next morning, the view over the Tanapag area, littered with bodies from a *gyokusai* [final suicide] attack by 4,000 or 5,000 Japanese against two infantry battalions. At first, the sense of a scene frozen in time, like a Matthew Brady photograph of a Civil War battlefield.

"Finally, the unreal sight and sound of a Japanese soldier in full uniform, seated on a rock in the middle of half-a-dozen GIs, smoking a Lucky Strike and saying in pure Brooklyn English: 'Boy, am I glad to see you guys!' Returning to Japan for a short visit with his grandparents, he had instead been granted the honor of serving Nippon. In a war where prisoners were seldom taken, it was a final, bizarre but memorable note at the end of the battalion's combat action on Saipan."

13 July 1944
Mission from Biak Island to Halmahera Island

Major Richard H. Wright arrived in New Guinea, November 1943, a second lieutenant with 71st Reconnaissance Group. He was lead navigator, 17th Squadron, and flew sixty-three missions.

"With a flight of six B-25Ds, Captain J. C. Wise (who was a brigadier general in the early 1990s) took off on 13 July at 0600 hours from Biak Island, in the Schouten Islands about 100 miles north of New Guinea," Major Wright records, from the perspective of navigator for Captain Wise.

"The combat sweep was directed west toward the head of New Guinea, Halmahera Island, and the Celebes Sea. Around 1030 hours, a Japanese transport, about Liberty-ship size, was sighted off the east coast of Halmahera Island. Captain Wise separated from the flight and attacked the ship. He flew over the ship at mast height, strafing, and dropped the stick of four 500-pound bombs.

"Our crew sank their ship, but they sank our plane, a plane which had already accounted for five other Japanese ships and a Japanese airplane. The deck guns from the ship—probably 22mm—crippled the B-25 by shooting off the hub of the left engine propeller so that it could not be feathered," making it necessary to ditch the plane in the ocean.

Exiting from the cockpit roof, "I stepped out on the left wing and slid off into the ocean, the oil from the propeller having made the wing slick. When we hit the water, Sergeant Price pulled a lever" to inflate a rubber raft. "With everyone shouting at him to get the oars out, the metal collar that hooks the oars together tore a hole in the raft so that, instead of having a five-man raft, six men now had a two-and-one-half-man raft."

"In the meantime, the other five B-25s started to drop supplies to us. You should be there when a Gibson-Girl radio goes by your head at 250mph. We signaled to them to stop, which they interpreted to mean 'drop more.'"

Soon after the forced-landing at sea, "word was received aboard the USS Wright (that's right!)" on Tuesday, the 13th, and "one of the Catalinas based on board took off and landed at Woendi, with plans for a night search." However, "it could have been Friday the 13th," because, by the time the Catalina was ready for take-off, "the radar went out, the communication system wouldn't work, the gyro pilot refused to function, and the weather got very bad."

After repairs at Woendi, the *Gardenia Special*, commanded by Navy Lieutenant George Favorite, took off on 14 July, sighted the downed airmen at around 1230 hours, "set the Catalina down in ten-foot swells" and took the six aboard, twenty-six hours after they had ditched. Rescued along with Lieutenant Wright and Captain Wise were the co-pilot, Second Lieutenant F. W. Watkins, and Staff Sergeants P. C. Price, R. R. Manes, and H. J. Salerno. Rightfully happy that the USS *Wright* had "made it all possible," navigator Wright at the time promised to name his first child Catalina.

July 1944
Sansapor, New Guinea

Lieutenant Colonel Charles R. Keefe was a captain, 63rd Infantry Regiment, 6th Infantry Division.

After battle at Maffin Bay, "all elements of the 63rd were relieved by the 167th Infantry on 16 July and, after a very brief rest, we embarked for the next stop in New Guinea—a place called Sansapor—only 600 miles from the Philippines," William L. West writes in a unit history.

"The 63rd Division mission was to establish a beachhead so that a bomber airfield could be constructed in the jungle. Aircraft based there bombed targets in Halmahera, Borneo, and the Philippine Islands," Lieutenant Colonel Keefe explains, as the historian continues:

"Here again, the campsite was hacked out of heavy jungle growth. Our fight at Sansapor was mostly with disease. The dreaded scrub typhus was ever-present, as well as the threat of malaria and other jungle skin-ailments. Sansapor, however, was located between two densely populated Japanese garrisons—and our patrols were daily cutting their escape route.

"Withal, there was ample time for the sack, or to swim, or engage in other athletics. Because of the intense heat, training could only be held in the early morning. So here we baked—until the middle of September, when we began an intensive refresher-training program, at the end of which we were ready for the campaign for which we had waited three years [to retake the Philippines]."

July 1944
POW Camp Shirakawa, Formosa

Colonel Michael A. Quinn begins Book V of his POW diary.

On 1 July 1944, Colonel Quinn writes: "A new book, a new month," and then he uses one of his oft-repeated phrases, "and one month closer to you. I hope to the Lord I can finish this book at home with you." Later in the month, on 22 July, he records: "We had a showdown inspection today. Several diaries were taken, but they looked mine over and threw them back. I don't know if they couldn't get anything out of it. It is quite possible that they couldn't read it. I know you would say that, so I am going to beat you to it."

Other July 1944 entries tell of the continued pressure on prisoners because of their "no more work" vote. "We are constantly harassed with night roll calls, 'no cards,' 'no music,' 'no amusements,' and they are cutting down rations and limiting all meat," he summarizes on 8 July.

The arrival of Red Cross items on 14 July includes "some prayer books and books of a religious nature for all denominations. The Catholic prayer book was written by Fulton J. Sheen, and all of a sudden we were ordered to turn them in because they contained sentiments that were objectionable to the Nips. I don't think around a half-dozen people in camp had read it up to that time, but everybody started reading it. The dedication that apparently riled them—'Dedicated to Mary, Mother Immaculate, Gracious Protectoress of the United States in humble petition of thy land which was violated on the eve of thy great feast [8 December, observed by Catholics as the Feast of the Immaculate Conception]. Victorious and inviolate again may be that feast when the false god of the Rising Sun sets and the double cross untwists itself and we who have fought to make others free are ourselves made free in the glorious liberty of the children of God.' Now everybody has a copy of the dedication."

AUGUST 1944

33

As Allied troops prepare for the 15 August 1944 invasion of Southern France, in an operation code-named *Dragoon*, their counterparts elsewhere in Europe are entering conquered cities as heroes. While their landings are initially labeled *invasions*, the men who make them are generally being greeted as liberators, not invaders, as they march into Rome on 5 June 1944, into Paris on 25 August 1944, and through many of the towns and villages en route to these capitals.

"The wild, happy, riotous welcome the people gave us made us forget a little about the bitter days in Normandy," Colonel William M. McConahey comments about entry into Le Mans the morning of 9 August.

"The road was lined with happy Frenchmen who waved and cheered, and women who threw flowers and kisses," Colonel Jean W. Christy says of his 8 August route through Guille, Ballots, Craon, Segre, and St. Clement on the move toward Angers. "They waved and called, '*Vive l'Amerique.*' It was a great experience being a victorious warrior cheered by an appreciative crowd."

For Colonel Tommy R. Gilliam, however, there would never be another welcome quite like the one he received "somewhere southeast of Vidouville." He recounts that moment:

"As the advance guard company for 1st Battalion [2nd Infantry Regiment, 5th Infantry Division], I was leading my company as we were pushing on in a forced march to support the British on the Vire River. We were marching at midnight through a heavily wooded forest on a one-lane dirt road, with men on each side of the road, two to three yards apart. First Sergeant Tom Miller, a dedicated Regular Army soldier, was across from me, and both of us were tense in the blackness of the woods, not knowing if we might encounter enemy positions. There was only the muffled sound of men marching in route step on the dirt road, the clanking of weapons and equipment, until we heard another sound—hands clapping quietly in applause as we approached a small clearing.

"There was no moon, but in the darkness we could make out the shapes of civilians lining both sides of the road, men and women and children, not talking, some crying, apparently from a village in the forest, and as we came abreast of them there were no sounds other than the increased applause. In the eerie still-ness of the woods, it was our first welcome from the French people.

"As we continued marching through the area, a little blonde, petite girl—maybe five years old—came up to me and, taking my hand without a word, walked for a hundred yards or so and then stood waving as we disappeared from view. It was an unreal and emotional incident in a brutal war. We had many other welcomes, with kisses and fruit and flowers and wine—but none were as heart-warming as the one we received in Le Foret Militaire somewhere southeast of Vidouville," Colonel Gilliam affirms.

About the time that Colonel Gilliam was experiencing that haunting moment in the French forest, Colonel Joseph S. Drewry Jr. was experiencing moments that would forever haunt him, but in an entirely different manner. For him, arriving by glider with the paratroopers in Southern France, 15 August 1944 will be remembered as a day when "gliders were landing on top of each other" and when "men were screaming in pain [and] many were killed."

"Some of us went back to try to rescue some of the men in the gliders," he writes. "The medics were outstanding. We did what we could but many of the men were killed in the landing, as equipment broke loose due to the impact. I saw one glider in which a quarter-ton trailer had broken loose and literally cut each member of the crew in half as it spun around in the glider." These were members of the 442nd Regimental Combat Team, with whom then-Lieutenant Drewry had worked previously in Italy.

15 August 1944
La Motte, Southern France

Colonel Joseph S. Drewry Jr. was a first lieutenant with 602nd Field Artillery Battalion (Pack).

"My unit, the 602nd FA Battalion, was pulled out of the line in Italy in July 1944 for some unknown reason. We went into bivouac near Velletri, Italy, where physical conditioning was the watchword. Rumors circulated that we, a mule-pack artillery unit, were to participate in an airborne operation," Colonel Drewry writes.

On 23 July, "we mounted trucks and headed for Marchigliano Airfield, near Rome. Here we drew airborne equipment and reorganized into a Glider Artillery TO&E [Table of Organization and Equipment]," the 602nd Field Artillery Battalion, Airborne, "the third name-change in our unit's life."

"For two weeks, we concentrated on airborne tactics, physical conditioning, loading and lashing loads in the CG4A (Waco) gliders, and finally in the space of two hours took our two qualifying glider rides. We were now airborne-qualified, all in less than two weeks.

"We were still in the dark but on 12 August, we were advised of our future destination—La Motte in Southern France, Operation Dragoon. . . . On 15 August, all hell broke loose. Just after midnight, troops began moving about in full-battle regalia. Tension began to mount and, before dawn, C-47 aircraft took off, loaded with paratroopers headed for Southern France. At about 1000 hours, we began loading our equipment, making sure it was properly tied down in the glider. On completion of the loading, we flaked out in the shade of our assigned gliders and waited, and waited, and waited—all kinds of thoughts going through my mind: *Were all of my people healthy? Do they have their weapons? Do they have their basic ammunition load? Were the howitzers loaded and lashed properly? Am I sure of my mission?* . . . I was too busy to think about home, my personal safety, trivial things. This was the real thing.

"As battery officer, I had charge of the six-gun firing battery, so before take-off, I conducted one last-minute inspection and wished my men a happy landing. The Air Force flight leader was bitching about having to tow gliders. I quickly reminded him that he at least had a way to get back to base.

"At 1605 hours, I felt the tug of the nylon tow rope as we began our taxi down the runway. After a few seconds, we began to be airborne above our tow plane and were soon followed in the liftoff of our C-47. Due to the length of the trip—a two and one-half hour flight—each C-47 towed only one glider. Airborne at last and traveling at approximately 150 miles per hour at a height of 3,500 feet, I began to relax for the first time in many hours. . . .

"En route, one glider slipped down into the prop wash of the tow plane and completely disintegrated, dropping men, equipment, and glider parts into the Mediterranean Sea. Later in the flight, I saw another glider cut loose from its tow plane and plunge into the sea.

"As we approached the shore of Southern France, I could hear small-arms fire and the unmistakable 'splat' of projectiles piercing the fabric of the Waco. It was then I learned of another place to wear my steel helmet.

"About 1830, I detected the outline of my assigned landing zone (LZ). Two problems: We had already been cut loose by our tow plane and the LZ was not large enough to accommodate all the gliders that were supposed to land there. In fact, it was full when we got there. Seeing this, my glider pilot (GP) panicked. He did not know what to do. There we were in a descent, no power, and not the slightest idea of where to land. I grabbed the right arm of the GP and, while vigorously shaking him and yelling to him, saw an empty field about a quarter mile away. He gained composure and headed for the new field, not knowing what we would encounter in the probably unsecured field. The GP made an outstanding and, believe it or not, a smooth landing.

"Even before the dust and the noise of the landing had subsided, we evacuated the Waco and ran like hell for the protection of the nearby woods. Lucky for us! In less than two minutes, this field too became overrun with gliders, one landing directly on top of our evacuated Waco. None of the gliders in either the primary LZ or *my* LZ could have flown again. The carnage resulting from the landing was almost indescribable. Such a waste of young men! I will never forget the sights of this airborne landing. Somehow my battery survived with only nine men injured. Fortunately, I was not one of them.

"In spite of all of the confusion and mayhem of the landing, we were in position and ready to fire by 2030 hours that day, exactly 365 days to the day from our amphibious landing on Kiska Island in the Aleutian Chain."

He and his battery operated from an initial position around the towns of Frejus and La Muy. Though "things continued to be confused" after landing, "we were moving much faster than had been planned and we received more help from the French Forces of the Interior than was anticipated. Our mission, along with the paratroopers', was to secure certain critical road and railroad intersections to prevent the German movement of troops to block the Allied seaborne landings that were also taking place at this time."

Just as they joined their supported infantry units to begin an eastward move late in the afternoon, they were told "to remain on standby. There were explosions all around, some caused by us, some by the Germans, and some by the French, who by that time were openly working with the invasion forces. We managed to down a K-ration or two.

"Next morning, bright and early, came an aerial supply—hundreds of C-47 aircraft dropping bundles of supplies and ammunition. Many of the bundles were free-dropped but the ammunition bundles were equipped with chutes that did not always open. In fact, one such chute exploded on impact, killing one of our men. After gathering the supplies, we headed farther inland to the town of Draguignan. Here we met some resistance and set up for a perimeter defense. . . .

"We stayed in position 16 and 17 August, waiting for a link-up of the beach landing-forces. About midmorning, we saw our first beach forces and made contact about half an hour later. We had performed our mission. The Germans were unable to reinforce the beach."

18 August 1944
Mission to Toulon Harbor, Southern France

Colonel Frank M. (Mike) Furey was a pilot, 321st Bombardment Group (M), 57th Bomb Wing.

"On 15 August 1944, U.S., British, and French amphibious forces made landings on the southern coast of France in an area between Marseille and Nice," Colonel Furey writes. "For eleven days prior to the landings, the 321st Bombardment Group (M) and other units of the 57th Bomb Wing flew missions against German gun positions and road- and rail-bridges in a softening-up campaign.

"On 18 August, the 321st was called upon to attack Toulon Harbor, which was designated a 'heavy bomber' target because it was ringed with a heavy net of anti-aircraft guns. Reconnaissance planes came back with pictures of a 702-foot battleship (*Strasbourg*), a cruiser (La Galissonniere class), a destroyer, and a submarine.

"As our group approached the target, we were greeted by a very heavy barrage of flak, and it continued right through the target area. I was flying squadron (448th) lead, with Colonel Richard H. (Snuffy) Smith, group commander, as co-pilot." A news article from the 321st's publication at that time reports that "no less than eighty-two heavy anti-aircraft guns protected the harbor at Toulon and it seemed that all of them opened up on 321st B-25s."

"With Lieutenant Bob Joyce as my bombardier, we had a perfect run and laid a pattern of bombs right on the targets. The submarine was sunk, the cruiser capsized over on its side, and the battleship was gutted by fire and completely disabled," Colonel Furey reports. "Of the seven members of my crew, only Bob Joyce escaped being wounded. Both the colonel and I, plus ten others, were hit by shrapnel from the flak, but not a single bomber was lost" from the twenty-seven on that mission.

August 1944
St. Raphael, Southern France

Colonel Henry H. Fantus was a lieutenant, 4136th Quartermaster Company.

Bombarded from the air for several days and from the sea by battleships at dawn on 15 August 1944, the shores of Southern France were hit by invasion troops at 0830, Colonel Fantus writes. "They met little resistance, except in one small area, and advanced quickly inland. At 1030 hours, a QM Service Battalion of about 1,000 troops (five separate companies) was landed to supply the labor necessary to unload supplies needed to support the combat troops over the beaches.

"Because of the lack of resistance, the swiftly moving Army immediately needed gasoline (POL—petroleum, oil, lubricants) in large quantities. Unfortunately, the supply ships were loaded based on statistics gained from the Normandy invasion, with Class V (Ammunition) and Class I (Food) given higher priorities than Class III (POL). This caused quite a problem on the beaches. Class V and I supplies had to be unloaded as quickly as possible in order to get at the Class III.

"The situation became so critical that the combat units' supply trucks lined up, waiting to take fuel back to their units. By the third or fourth day, the division QM was draining all vehicles in order to be able to have enough fuel for two trucks to return to the beaches to obtain enough POL to fill up all the vehicles in the division train. Then those vehicles could get to the beaches and obtain enough POL to allow the combat units to advance."

To aid in unloading freighters waiting offshore, "Seabees erected floating docks. Gasoline in five-gallon cans was lowered in cargo nets directly into amphibious vehicles (DUKWs), which drove over the beach to the Class III dumps operated by QM service companies. There the cans were transferred directly onto the waiting vehicles of the combat units.

"Other supplies were offloaded onto LCIs, which plied between the ships and the floating docks. The QM service troops transferred these supplies to trucks that took them to any handy spot and dumped them, without any semblance of order. One such place was a small, unused airfield near St. Raphael. When the entire coast was finally secured and regular dock facilities were available, the temporary dumps had to be cleared out. . . .

"The 4136th did such an excellent job at St. Raphael, it was given the assignment to handle Class I supplies for the area and subsequently for Nice. There, it became the Class I issue point for combat troops battling in the Alpes-Maritimes and for the United States Riviera Recreation Area (USRRA), the spot in Nice where combat troops were brought directly from the combat area. Here they were issued clean uniforms, quartered in luxury hotels with clean sheets and hot showers, feasted with food prepared by French chefs, and freed from Army discipline for the period of their stay. Nice was off-limits to all officers except those whose duties required them to be there. A GI paradise, to say the least!"

May–August 1944

USAHS *Shamrock*, North Africa to Italy to France

Chief Warrant Officer Edward G. Robertson and First Lieutenant Helene Stewart Robertson continue their Shamrock *story with diary notes from then-Corporal William Hummrich.*

Departing for its second tour from Charleston, South Carolina, 22 April, the *Shamrock* arrives in Bizerte in early May, takes on a load of wounded, and heads for Mers el-Kebir, near Oran. "June 5 finds us carrying a load of patients, all Germans, to Oran where they will be exchanged for our own wounded in the enemy hospitals. The following day brought us news of the invasion of Northern France. We told the Germans about it but they still believed that they were in possession of Africa," Corporal Hummrich comments.

There were a few more trips until mid-July and then a week of rest in El Truk before returning to Naples. "We didn't stay in Naples long as there were twelve hospital ships there, including ourselves. We were sent to Palermo, Sicily. The thing we noticed about Naples this time was that the harbor was loaded to the gill with all kinds of ships. They were putting numbers on them as we left and that spelled invasion to us."

On 15 August, when the invasion was made known, the *Shamrock* was just 100 miles from Southern France. "On the morning of 16 August, we arrived along the pretty coast of France and took on our first patients at about 0130 as land mines blew up all along the shore," the corporal continues. "We took on 114 wounded that day and just as soon as they came on they were checked and put down for immediate operations. The two regular operating rooms and a third one set up in the first-aid station kept all our doctors and nurses busy. Also, we had with us a group of surgical teams that deserve a great deal of credit for their work.

"We left that evening about 1900 hours as it began to get dark, and no sooner had we left when an air raid began. You could look down the line and see the anti-aircraft guns firing at the planes and just spin your head around as the shore group followed them along. It was a pretty sight and showed how quickly the Americans had set up their positions.

"Meanwhile, the battleships and cruisers shelled Toulon as destroyers put up a smoke screen. We took our patients to Naples and turned once more to France. Our patients this time were French and we took them to Oran, Africa."

August 1944
Mayenne, St. Suzanne, and Le Mans, France

Colonel William M. McConahey, battalion surgeon, continues his story.

In late July, soon after their month-long battle in the Foret de Mont Castre or Hill 122, "our morale reached a low ebb. We were dazed by the shattering battles of the preceding weeks and by the wholesale slaughter and mangling of so many comrades. We were tired and dirty and uncomfortable, and we could see no end to this miserable existence. If we were going to have to keep on battling our way yard by yard clear to Berlin, it would take us a decade," Colonel McConahey writes.

"And then the electrifying news spread through the ranks like wildfire that General Patton was in Normandy. All sorts of quotations said to have been his words were repeated over and over. 'Patton says he'll be in Paris in a month.' . . . 'Patton says he'll be in Berlin in ninety days.' How many of these declarations he actually made, I don't know, but we had a long way to go yet—farther than any of us thought. . . .

"Then the 90th got orders to take off, to strike out boldly to capture Le Mans, far to the southeast. We were just to keep going, not worrying about enemy troops on the flanks and behind us. Just keep going! . . .

"Thus began a strange and weird type of warfare. From that time until we ran out of gasoline at Metz, it was a race of long spearheads across France. We never knew where the Krauts were, how many there were, or what we'd run into. We simply kept smashing ahead. It was all very confusing, but the Germans were more confused than we were. . . .

"The 357th spearheaded the drive to Le Mans. The regiment was motorized, and started out early in the morning of 5 August. . . . By late afternoon we had reached Mayenne, which we took that night after a sharp fight. . . . I set up an aid station in a small barn near the building in which the battalion command post was located, and waited for the rest of the medical personnel and equipment to arrive. . . .

"About an hour after dark a German staff car with three officers (one a medical officer) drove right into the center of the town without realizing that it was held by the Americans. When they discovered this and leaped from the car, a burst from a .50-caliber machine gun instantly killed two of the officers and cut the car to pieces. Miraculously, the medical officer was not hit. . . . He knew a little English and I knew a little German, and so we were able to converse a bit. It seemed strange to be sitting outside in the dark in a French town talking with a German physician, while the sounds of fighting echoed around us and low-flying planes growled by in the inky sky above."

And so, they "just kept going"—on the way to Le Mans—until they reached the town of St. Suzanne, where the 1st Battalion "had been attacked from the rear by about 500 fanatical, screaming paratroopers. . . . When our battalion arrived, it attacked the attackers, and until the middle of the afternoon we fought around St. Suzanne," until ordered to "keep going toward Le Mans." Late on the night of 8 August, "the leading elements of our battalion entered Le Mans, and the next morning we marched through it in triumph."

August 1944
Angers, France

Colonel Jean W. Christy continues his 5th Infantry Division account.

"On 1 August, the 2nd Infantry Regiment advanced rapidly, and by 1030 hours the 2nd and 3rd Battalions were on the River Vire. It looked as though we had made a complete breakthrough of the German positions. In fact, it seemed that the Allied forces had broken out of the beachhead all across the front," Colonel Christy writes. "I was still acting as liaison officer at Division Artillery headquarters, and all of the activity there was concentrated on planning to pull the 5th Division out of the action in preparation for the about-to-be-formed Third Army."

Drawing on information from the battalion journal, the colonel continues: "The division was to march through Toregni-sur-Vire, St. Lo, and Marigny, to an area near Champrepus. . . . The road was jammed and the march was slowed considerably. . . . The march was jerky until after we passed St. Lo. That town was a battered shambles. . . .

"We were passing through country which had been ours but a few days. . . . The French here were returning to their homes. They all smiled and waved enthusiastically. For the most part, their homes and fields were scarcely touched. Some were not so fortunate. One woman, I believe, evoked the pity and sympathy of us all. She stood sad-faced and dejected before the heap of dusty stones and rubble, which was all that remained of her home. Blank-faced, hardly seeing us, she raised her arm and waved as we passed. . . .

In Angers, which became ours on 11 August, "the 2nd Infantry found a warehouse with 9,400 cases of an after-dinner liqueur called *Contreau,* which the German army had confiscated. The 2nd Infantry confiscated it in turn. Division Headquarters didn't quite know what to do about it, and called Third Army supply. Third Army, in essence, said, 'Keep what you can use and send the rest up here to us.'

"The Contreau was rationed out among the 5th Division units. Few of the men, and not too many officers, had any idea what an after-dinner liqueur was. In A Battery of the 50th, the first sergeant blew his whistle one evening after mess and announced, 'Liquor Call!' The men came running with their canteen cups outstretched. Every man in line got a half-canteen-cup of Contreau, a liqueur usually served in a small glass about the size of a man's pinky finger. The next evening the first sergeant again blew his whistle and announced, 'Liquor Call!' This time, two men showed up. It ended up that quite a few cases of Contreau went on up to Third Army."

By mid-August when they were again almost off their 1/50,000 maps—and using road maps until Third Army would airdrop more—"we were presented with the answers to two questions. We had been concerned about the one, and completely uncomprehending of the other.

"Question One: We had known for some time that we were the units farthest out in front and on the right of the advance. Vaguely, we wondered who was securing our right flank. Someone got a copy of *Time* magazine in the mail, which had an article that informed us that the Eighth Air Force was guarding our right flank. Somehow that didn't fill us with confidence, because our understanding was that the Eighth Air Force was deeply involved with other activities.

"Question Two: We had heard various stories about a big German tank attack at a town behind us called Falaise. Our tank forces counterattacked, as we understood it, and a fierce battle raged in the 'Falaise Gap' for several days. From the maps in *Time* magazine, we learned that we were the ones that the Germans were trying to cut off. If their attack had succeeded, we would have been isolated far out ahead of the rest of the Allied forces."

August 1944
Angers, France

Colonel Tommy R. Gilliam continues his story.

"My regiment, the 2nd Infantry Regiment, relieved the 16th Infantry Regiment, and my Company B relieved Company G, commanded by Captain Dawson, who was one of the heroes of the Normandy landing on Omaha Beach. Two weeks later, we jumped off in the initial phases of the St. Lo breakthrough," Colonel Gilliam writes.

"I commanded a company that did not have a noncom with less than three years' service or a private with less than a year's service. The majority of my noncoms and senior privates had been with the unit since the Louisiana maneuvers of 1941. In the first two days of the St. Lo breakthrough we faced a determined enemy in the German 9th Paratroop Regiment, and in that two days I lost seventy-nine men and two officers, killed or wounded in the vicinity of Vidouville and Haut Vidouville.

"I never again had another company that could match the fighting ability of that group of men. Probably a third of them were of Polish descent, coming from Hamtramack, Michigan, which was near the home station of the battalion when the draft began. However, we had many from Kentucky and West Virginia who had come to us at Fort Custer, Michigan, in the fall of 1941. . . .

"Relieved of our mission of supporting the British, we bivouacked in a field for replacements and resupply and began to have our first payday on French soil, when the word came to 'saddle up,' as we had just been the first division assigned to General George S. Patton Jr.'s Third Army, and we began the mad dash across France that was to lead us as part of the XX Corps to the gates of Metz in four short weeks.

"In forty-eight hours we had crossed the base of the Brest Peninsula and were attacking the German garrison at Angers. The motor march was memorable in the miles and miles of dead horses and men and shattered equipment of various German units that had been caught on the road by our Air Force. And it was memorable in the fact that we captured [thousands of] cases of Contreau liqueur in Angers, each bottle stamped across the front, 'Reserved for the Wehrmacht.'

"On we went, racing abreast of the 4th Armored Division. We were not a motorized division per se and only one truck company was assigned to the division, but we improvised. A platoon of men could ride on a platoon of tanks or a platoon of tank destroyers. You could get seven to ten men on a jeep and trailer. Two rifle squads could ride on the kitchen truck. Anybody left over was sent to ride with the artillery on their prime movers. In this manner, we moved 30 to 40 miles a day, three battalions abreast, a couple of miles between battalions, and by early afternoon we were off our maps—with sharp but conclusive firefights through Chartres, Etampes, Fontainebleu, Epernay, and on to the capture of Reims and finally Etain and Verdun.

"And then the C-47s supplying our gas were pulled for Montgomery's ill-fated Arnhem attack and we were grounded a few short miles from Metz, which was undefended at the time. We didn't even have gas for our kitchen ranges. We felt strongly that if we had been provided with gas we could have stormed right on into Berlin—the enemy was fleeing in utter confusion.

"A week later, we received gas again and took off for Metz and an ambush at Amnavillers—and a five-day battle on the outskirts of a now-defended Metz that cost my unit a total of 218 men and five officers killed or wounded—but that is another story that takes up September and continues into October, November, and December, when Third Army crossed the lines of communication of the First Army to help raise the siege of Bastogne—without me. I was wounded 9 November at Louvigny in the final assault on Metz and spent the next three months in hospitals in France and England, rejoining my unit shortly after the crossing of the Sauer River, in the vicinity of Diekirch and Ekternach on 19 February 1945, the third anniversary of the date we sailed from the United States in 1942."

August 1944
Le Mans, Normandy

Lieutenant Colonel Dwight M. Gowdey served with 1303rd Engineer General Service Regiment.

The battalion received word 25 June that it was assigned to the Third Army, arriving on Omaha Beach 19 July and setting off on foot to bivouac at Quettetot. According to Colonel Gowdey's diary notes from that period, the regiment "started to improve the area a little" until ordered to move on, "about five miles south of Coutances." There, with the arrival of the rest of the regiment by 3 August, the regiment started several jobs—"a flight strip, clearing the route through Coutances, and widening a by-pass." The move on 4 August took them to Les Chambres, where "the Germans were bombing the main road nearly every night and we were kept busy fixing the craters. We (Company F) also built our first PW camp just north of Avranches at about this time."

On 7 August, they moved to La Croix Avranchin where "Company D got into the first of its combat roles. They started out to clear the road to St. Malo and came upon a combat engineering company that had been ambushed. They helped extricate them and then withdrew. . . . Also, we started to drain the dam west of St. Hilaire, so that if the Germans bombed it the flood wouldn't wash out bridges at Pontabault. . . .

"Although an Engineer General Service Regiment was not normally attached to a Corps, it proved to be one of the reasons why Patton was able to continue across France as fast and as far as he did," the colonel contends. "The combat engineers would bridge the rivers with tactical bridging (mostly Bailey) and then move forward. In the other armies, this bridging would be left in place until it could be replaced by communication zone engineers. Since there was a limited supply of bridging, this meant that when it was used up, the Army had to stop until it could get replacements.

"In the Third Army, the general service regiments would replace the tactical bridging with fixed bridges, and then move the tactical bridging forward to the combat engineers so that the Army could continue to move ahead. Normally, this would be done by providing a by-pass and then replacing the bridge. Sometimes a by-pass could not be provided and this meant disrupting the route for days at a time while the bridge was replaced.

"On 31 August at Cloyes, Company A, under Lieutenant Robert Bolle, initiated the procedure of building a fixed bridge underneath the Bailey, so the main supply route would not be disrupted. This meant that the only interruption to traffic was for the few minutes required to remove the Bailey and to put the final decking in place. This practice became standard in the regiment and throughout the Third Army wherever possible."

One day while waiting along the highway as a unit passed by, the colonel says that he started talking to a Frenchman. "He remarked that 'the Germans are soldiers, but you Americans are only armed working men.' But, we had the Germans on the run," Colonel Gowdey adds.

August 1944
Cherbourg, France

Chief Warrant Officer Sidney Bowen, assigned to the 494th Anti-aircraft Artillery Gun Battalion, Battery, landed on Utah Beach, France, 16 July.

"We have moved again," T-5 Bowen informs wife Isabel in a letter dated 4 August. "Beard and I are living in a German ammo cellar. It has a cement top, bottom, and side. The roof is sodded over like a farmer's root cellar. . . . Meanwhile, it has been backbreaking: sandbagging, digging-in our heavy equipment, and covering all with camouflage netting.

"Hydrangeas literally cover this crown of land overlooking the beach. I stood among them, and the flower heads are as large as my head; and the shrubs, my height. They appear in yards everywhere. Rambling red roses are profuse, and dahlias thrive in a riot of size and color. The hydrangeas are in shades of pink to purple even on the same bush.

"The homes in this area are usually built of rounded fieldstones, and the fences are either fieldstone or hedgerow. The hedgerows consist of dense-growth shrubs, thick and thorny and capable of all the concealment necessary when the Germans held them on the defensive."

"We all went blackberry picking," he notes on 10 August. "Even eating as I picked, I wound up with a half-helmet liner of berries to carry back to camp."

He ends his letter with his perpetual "YELH" [Your Ever-Loving Husband] and signature.

After moving again and setting up "for air defense of this position," he writes to Isabel on 27 August, "The German position we took over must have been a backbreaker for the Germans. They had dug-in and had even sandbagged their huts. The soil here is like digging into one of Dorothy Chudinski's cakes."

21 August 1944
Mission to Brest in Brittany, France

Colonel Cecil C. Ellzey, liaison pilot with 28th Field Artillery Battalion, 8th Infantry Division, arrived on the Omaha Beachhead near St. Laurent-sur-Mer, Normandy, 4 July 1944.

In August, "during the Brest operations, I was called upon by the division artillery commanding general, Brigadier General James A. Pickering, to penetrate the air space of the front lines and draw enemy fire, be it small arms or artillery, since the front was too quiet and our forward ground observers were concerned about what was taking place, with some thought that the Germans had withdrawn in Brest," Colonel Ellzey writes.

"Their suspicion was entirely wrong because only a short distance beyond the front line, 88s opened up and bracketed the aircraft. Lieutenant Paul Dumas [observer for then-Lieutenant Ellzey] was able to deliver counterbattery fire. Also, the forward observers were able to pinpoint some targets. . . .

"My experiences in Europe were somewhat unique inasmuch as World War II was an introduction to the employment of light, slow-speed aircraft, primarily for artillery-fire observation. . . . General Pickering was a veteran of World War I, with horse-drawn-artillery experience. He did not readily accept the concept of air observation for artillery counterbattery fire and did not hesitate to tell me. Shortly after joining the division near Yuma, Arizona, he had admonished me (an old-fashioned chewing-out) during desert maneuvers, referring to us (L-4 pilots) as boys with a new toy. However, once in combat, his perception changed and we appreciated his support because he did not hesitate to call for special missions, some with great risks. In fact, before departing Kassel, Germany, to return home, he told me that he was taking me to the Pacific Theater as his air officer, which would be a promotion to major."

1944
England and France

Colonel Harold R. Hennessy was assigned to the London G-5 Section, Military
Government, SHAEF, in Public-Health Planning on General Eisenhower's staff.

With offices in the old American Embassy in Central London, "I was hard at
work—sometimes seven days a week. . . . Finally, D-Day arrived and the great
invasion became operational," Colonel Hennessy writes.

After numerous delays, "I finally reached Paris. The Germans had just
departed and the confusion in the great city was terrible . . . Our huge headquarters was located near the great Paris Arch," where he serves as chief of public
health section, HQ , G-5 Section, Military Government and Civil-Affairs Communication Zone, ETOUSA.

There was "almost daily contact with the French government office of the public health minister," dealing with public-health problems. Generally, during mili-
tary-action months, this consisted in applying "principles of disease-control to
the community, rather than to the individual." Pertinent public-health information was also made available to the military medical service.

Another job of the civil-affairs public-health officers was the weekly compilation and analysis of data, prepared by each base section, concerning communica-
ble diseases "and the insurance that immediate control steps were taken by the
civilian medical or health authorities." Weekly, this epidemiological report was
sent to SHAEF's health officer.

"After troops landed in France on D-Day, local public-health requirements
were met by civil-affairs detachments operating under the supervision of the
fighting armies," Colonel Hennessy says. With progress of the troops, Advance
Section Communications Zone, Normandy Base G-5, took over. Eventually, it
was extended to other base sections, reaching from the Mediterranean to the
North Sea. "It was indeed a very efficient operation."

Writing of another "very efficient operation," Colonel Hennessy recounts an
experience that pays tribute to his wife, Helen Lounsberry Hennessy, and all of
the "brave military wives and families who were left alone Stateside."

"It was about mid-March 1942. Helen was giving a piano lesson to our oldest
daughter, Virginia, when the Quartermaster at the Presidio called. It was then
about 0730 hours. My family had only about one-hour advance notice of the
upcoming official station-transfer/move. . . .

"That same day, at about 1800 hours, Helen Hennessy, together with four
small children entrained with bags, bundles and boxes, school records, dolls, and
other such items from Oakland, California, for Salt Lake City. . . . Just before

going to sleep on the train, Virginia asked her mother if the piano lesson could be completed someplace else. Helen said, 'Yes,' and in a few minutes Virginia was sound asleep."

Basically, without skipping a beat, life and piano lessons went on—for the Hennesseys "in an old, empty fraternity house located near the rapidly expanding military base," just as it did for other families who somehow always managed to "pick up the pieces," as well as the beat, before, during, and after each transfer.

Returning from overseas in 1945, survivor-soldier Hennessy found his family at home, but not where he'd left them. "The fraternity house in Salt Lake City had been put up for sale" but "rising to this sudden situation, Helen, . . . over the telephone and sight unseen, made arrangements to purchase a house in Los Angeles, and then in a day or so moved the family there."

"The last item to be moved from the old house in Utah was the window service flag," that minibanner displayed by many families to indicate household members in service. Each blue star on the banner signified an active-duty relative; silver star, an overseas member; and gold star, a deceased member.

August 1944
Mission to Ploesti, Romania

Major Robert J. Lagasse submits the recollections of his brother, Lieutenant Colonel Harvey Lagasse, who died in 1991.

Then–First Lieutenant Harvey Lagasse and his B-24 crew arrived in Foggia, Italy, in the spring of 1944 to join the 459th Bomb Group. After a few orientation flights around the area, all were ready for their first mission. "It was a 'milk run' over northern Italy," Lieutenant Colonel Lagasse writes. "We discovered later that the type of mission we flew as our indoctrination was few and far between. . . ."

Soon thereafter, the lieutenant joined his crew, and others, being briefed for their next mission. "There was a huge map of our area of operations. . . . We followed the black line from Cherignola, across the Adriatic Sea, through Yugoslavia and into Romania and, of all places, *Ploesti*.

"The Ploesti oil fields and cracking plants were the worst targets in the theater of operations and we won it for today's work," he records. "Ploesti was the target first subjected to low-level bombing from Africa [1 August 1943], and using the Liberator. The mission was a disaster because of a navigational error. We were never sure of that information, but everyone who spoke of Ploesti told the same story. . . ."

"Activity on the ground and in the air proved . . . that this was to be a maximum effort, probably involving approximately 800 bombers. Some of the bombers carried 'R,' which was a high-explosive bomb more powerful than the conventional TNT. Others carried clusters of incendiary bombs that exploded with tremendous heat and left many fires on the target."

After takeoff, they "encountered some light flak over Yugoslavia" and "were steadily climbing to reach bombing altitude of 24,500" when they "crossed the Yugo border into Romania and all hell broke loose," as fighters came at them from the sun.

Lieutenant Colonel Lagasse continues: "Screams came over the intercom: 'Bandits at three o'clock!' Two coming in at nine o'clock; they're after the belly tank. God, the sky is full of those bastards. I shouted to the nose-gunner: 'They're coming in at twelve o'clock low.' I braced myself for the onslaught, but it never came. Apparently, the pilot was after the belly turret and the burst went below us.

"Then I saw an Me-109 coming in at two o'clock. I screamed a warning to Joe and hit the deck. The burst came into the nose, behind the nose turret and above me, and exited just in front of the pilot's legs. I was beginning to believe that we could never survive these attacks when the fighters broke off the engagement. This meant just one thing: We were within range of the flak, and intelligence was correct: there were hundreds of anti-aircraft guns down there. The explosions were huge, with an ugly array of blacks, reds, and yellows.

"We were approaching the initial point (IP). . . . As I was watching the lead plane, I felt a tremendous explosion and turned to see the bomber on our right wing explode. They apparently took a direct hit in the bomb bay. The bombardier was blown out of the plane without his parachute. It was at that fleeting moment that I vowed never to fly again with a chest chute. . . .

"It's extremely cold at 25,000 feet but I was bathed in perspiration. The sky was one big mass of explosions. The old B-24 rocked and shuttered. I couldn't believe we could get out of this in one piece. I had my hand on the salvo lever and my eyes glued to our lead plane when a burst of flak exploded under our starboard wing, forcing the ship into a very undesirable bank. Harry responded instantly and leveled off just as the bombs were released by the lead ship. I immediately released our load and yelled, 'Bombs away!' The formation executed a steep bank to port and after executing a 180 turn, we were heading home, back through fighter alley once again.

"There were Ju-88s, Me-109s, and Fw-190s all over the sky. They passed through our formation at such great speed that they appeared to be a group of black-crossed blurs. They raised hell with us until we were out of their range.

"The Adriatic looked beautiful and the vineyards we called home were a sight to behold. We landed, kissed the good Italian earth, and said a quiet prayer. Our ship was a real mess. It looked like a sieve; our starboard had minimal damage. Apparently, it was concussion that forced us into that bank over the target. When I told the guys in the crew what I had observed when the bomber on our right wing exploded, we all went to supply to draw the backpack-type parachute."

1944
North and Central Burma

Lieutenant Colonel Harry H. Leonhardt was liaison to the 22nd Light Infantry Division of the Chinese army, training in India and ready to reclaim Burma from the Japanese.

"It was quite an experience, for I spoke not one word of the Chinese language and there was not one of the Chinese who spoke English. But it is amazing what can be accomplished if both sides are in earnest and try.

"The initial forward movement went very well. Then we got into situations where a company or battalion would be assigned to a flanking area that would be inaccessible by motorized vehicles. Our rations and ammunition would be delivered by air-drop.

"We had white-cloth panels about two feet wide and eight or ten feet long. For the drop, the task was to find a place where the pilots could find these panels, displayed in a certain precoded shape. . . .

Initially, "parachutes were used to lower the cargo to the ground," but wind would sometimes cause the chutes to drift off too far to be found. "Then it was discovered that free-drop could be used." On the free-drops, "ammunition did quite well, but sometimes we would have to dig it out of the ground. . . . Most of the time it would be as far in the soil as the diameter of the packing crate."

Rice, however, went against the grain. "After some experimenting, it was decided that the best method to package would be to put about 150 pounds of rice in a burlap bag and sew it up really well. After that, it was placed in a larger bag that was securely closed. When the rice hit the ground, the inside bag would burst, but the outer bag held."

"When we got to the eastern side of Burma, where the terrain was more rolling and the vegetation was not so dense or tall, it was not so difficult to clear an area large enough for the supply planes to land. The last such place I recall was about 3 miles from the joining of the Ledo Road with the Burma Road."

15 August 1944
Kumisanger, New Guinea

Captain Robert W. Teeples went overseas with Company C, 128th Infantry, 32nd Division, in April 1942, participating in the five-month battle of Buna, New Guinea, at Saidor and Aitape, and then at Kumisanger, with the Sixth Army Alamo Scouts.

In a V-mail letter on 15 August 1944, then-Sergeant Teeples explains to his folks in Black River Falls, Wisconsin, why they have not heard from him: "It has been some time since I've written to you but I've been helping to lick the Nips again." He elaborates: "On Father's birthday [6 August 1944], we made the push [on Kumisanger]; on Violet's birthday [10 August], we were still pushing; and on my birthday [his twenty-sixth, on 14 August], we finished, so you see I had quite the celebrations on our birthdays. It was on Mom's birthday [3 March 1944], you know, that I made a landing [in northern New Guinea] and so won the Silver Star.

"I'm sure looking forward to seeing you folks soon. I've had a pretty rough go over here, but I'm not kicking. God has brought me through and I have faith in Him seeing me home safely. I've gotten my quota. I've settled some old scores for pals I lost."

In a letter on 26 August, from the hospital with "the fever again," he comments: "They can talk about the mud in Italy and the cold in Alaska, but New Guinea takes the prize. Well, at least we ought to be getting out of here pretty soon, as we've got the Japs pretty well cleaned out. I shouldn't be complaining but if a man couldn't complain to his folks, he couldn't complain to anybody. Anyway, I've got the best folks in the world and it will be the happiest day in my life when I can put my arms around them again.

"I was just thinking that I could eat a whole quart of those dill pickles, with ham-and-tomato sandwiches, and about a quart of milk to wash them down with. . . . I'll always be thinking of you and making plans for when I see you."

SEPTEMBER 1944

34

"No man is an island, entire of itself; every man is a piece of the continent, a part of the main." The words of John Donne somehow convey, if any words possibly can, why "the death of one man diminishes every other man," and why we continue to be saddened several hundred years after a civil war by the loss of men and boys and potential families or still grieve for lives lost and futures unfulfilled as we read or listen to the stories of World War II and all of our other wars.

Death gone unmourned seems to belie nature. Yet for the many who die in warfare, sadly for both the deceased and their compatriots, there is often no time to mourn at that moment. For surviving families, while there is grief, there is often the emptiness of not knowing the circumstances of the loved-ones' deaths.

In memoriam to the many U.S. military men and women who have died during our nation's history, here is one soldier's loving testimonial after the death of his friend and fellow soldier. The eulogy is written by Private First Class Harold Noak in a letter received by Major Robert W. Anderson after the death of his brother, Private First Class Russell N. Anderson, on the road "to take Metz," 11 September 1944. Like his father, who was awarded the *croix de guerre* by the French army in World War I, Private Anderson was also with the ambulance corps in France. He and Private Noak were with Company B, 110th Medical Battalion, attached to the 35th Division.

In his two-page, typed letter, Harold Noak reconstructs for Major Anderson a timeline of friendship from their day of first meeting until Russell's death. Written on the third anniversary of Pearl Harbor, as its author was recovering from wounds received in the same incident that took his friend's life, the letter bears a title: "The Story of the Passing of an Unsung Hero: Russell Anderson."

He was "rated as one of the best in the outfit" as an ambulance driver and "was loved by all his comrades and the squadron officers," Private Noak writes. "I noticed these qualities in Russell Anderson, which were very pronounced and which made him one of the best-loved men in our outfit: His sense of humor and pleasing personality, his calmness of judgment and his willingness to serve his buddies. I lost the best buddy in the outfit."

11 September 1944
En Route to Metz, France

Major Robert W. Anderson submits the letter of tribute to his brother.

"I became acquainted with Russell Anderson of Detroit Lakes, Minnesota, on 3 March 1943 while en route from Fort Snelling, Minnesota, to Camp Luis Obispo, California," Private First Class Harold Noak begins his letter, as he tells of boot training together; mutual friends from Detroit Lakes; arriving together in England on the *Alexandria* 28 May 1944; and billeting together in Liverpool and Bodmin. He continues: "We became inseparable companions and enjoyed basketball games, football games, shows, and other entertainment afforded soldiers. He, like many, had a picture of his sweetheart with him and often talked about her. . . .

"We shoved off from near Southampton during the early morning of 6 July 1944 and landed on the beach near Cherbourg, France, then proceeded to St. Lo on 9 July. During all of this time, I was very close to Russell. Being a stretcher-bearer, I went to the lines to carry back the wounded to the First Aid Station, from which Russell and the other drivers would take the wounded back to the beach, which was approximately 20 miles. . . .

"After St. Lo and the breakthrough, our outfit continued south through Le Mans, Orleans, Sens, and Troyes. I might say that Orleans was captured by our division. During all of this time, Russell kept his ambulance going night and day, hauling back the wounded after we brought them to the clearance station. . . .

"We had one rest period near Orleans for one week, billeted in a large hospital. While there, Russell and I took in movies and other entertainment. Our outfit was then ordered with Patton's Army to take Metz. This particular day was 11 September 1944. It was a beautiful day and we got an early start. We did notice that the Germans were shelling the highways with artillery, located on a ridge toward which we were moving. All of us were scared.

"Ten other medics and I were in the ambulance driven by Russell Anderson and his assistant. . . . As we approached a little town in the valley (I don't remember the name of it) the Krauts commenced laying down fire directly on the road. . . . Orders were given to scatter and all of us in the ambulance, including Russell and his assistant, Ralph Heckmeyer of Nebraska, flopped alongside a three-story building. We had no sooner run for cover than shrapnel burst right over us. It blew up the ambulance and I felt a burning feeling in my arm and knew I was hit. . . . I thought Russell was dead and that he, Heckmeyer, and Jack Benivento of New Haven, Connecticut, had apparently been killed instantly.

"The outfit behind us rushed over to where we were. They picked up Russell, as it appeared that there was some life in him, and they placed him on a stretcher in an ambulance [with] the other wounded. . . . On the way I learned that Russell was dead. It was at the collecting station, at about one o'clock in the afternoon that I found Russell's stretcher and I noticed they had a blanket over him.

"As to myself, shrapnel had struck me in the arm below the elbow and had shattered the bones. I have a scar where the shrapnel went through my helmet and struck me on the left side of my forehead," Private Noak says, explaining that he spent months in hospitals in England and the States. As he writes, with his arm in a cast, he is on convalescent furlough. His letter concludes with his previously mentioned accolades to Russell, a listing of others in their outfit, plus his final comment: "Russell, George Jesse, and I were usually always together."

September 1944
Metz, France

Colonel Jean W. Christy continues his 5th Infantry account.

Entering World War I country in early September 1944, members of the 5th Infantry Division returned to towns familiar to their division counterparts of 1918. Further impediments this time, besides the Germans and the weather, were "the infamous shortage of gasoline" and a shortage of maps.

On 6 September, "although we still had no gasoline, we began planning for a move to a division area east of Metz, a major city in the Saar Valley going back to A.D. 600 in the time before Charlemagne," a city that "had never been conquered by assault in the history of warfare. It is surrounded by a ring of underground fortresses," Colonel Christy writes.

"That afternoon we did get some maps. There were fourteen sheets of 1/100,000 scale maps, not the 1/25,000 we needed for artillery fire. We got ten or twelve copies of each, but we really needed twenty copies. It was enough for planning purposes, but not for operations.

"Bad weather and the Germans had kept us confined to our small beachhead," in the area "generally south of Metz and along the top of the high ridge formed by the hills east of the Moselle," but on 20 September, "the 5th Division began a coordinated attack to move east and attack the city from the south.

"It was a wet, misting day, and the infantry wore their GI raincoats when they jumped off. Lieutenant Colonel Blakefield led his 1st Battalion across the open, muddy field. Shortly after our preparation lifted, and his men were strung along out in the open, German mortar fire began to come in. There was nothing to do but keep the men moving.

"There are several underground forts around Metz, and Fort Driant is the largest. On our left, it had been by-passed as the division moved eastward. It reaches several stories underground, and has its own water well deep inside. It also has gun turrets placed on its roof so that they blend into the hilltop. We didn't know about the gun turrets until later.

"During the attack up to the Seille River, we began getting numerous reports of our artillery rounds falling short and endangering our own troops. Every artilleryman's nightmare! Thorough and methodical checking uncovered no possible reason that our friendly fire could have fallen short. Our friends in the infantry had trouble believing us until, later, we learned that the guns of Fort Driant had been firing at our troops from the rear. By nightfall, the 2nd Infantry was on its objective. On our left, the 10th Infantry was still fighting for the town of Pournoy, its objective."

In the midst of the battle at Metz, the battalion journal records the following for 22 September 1944: "Bing Crosby, the movie star and crooner, was in the division area today, putting on a USO show for the troops. We were not informed about it until it was too late to go."

17 **September 1944**
Mission North of Eindhoven, the Netherlands

Colonel Frank C. Morris flew a replacement C-47 and crew over the North Atlantic Ferry Route in July 1944, and soon joined the 83rd Squadron, 437th Troop Carrier Group, Ninth Air Force.

"My first combat experience was on Sunday, 17 September 1944. I was a second lieutenant flying as co-pilot with my flight leader, Captain Walter Rudolph. Our plane was a C-47, the *Expendable You*; our mission, the infamous Operation Market Garden. We were leading a four-ship, trailing-right echelon, towing single CG-4A gliders. We were one of about 450 aircraft in a sky train that dropped three divisions—U.S. 101st and 82nd, and the British 1st Airborne—in about fifty minutes into DZs and LZs (drop zones and landing zones) in Holland. It was the largest airborne drop in history," Colonel Morris asserts.

After taking off from a base near Ramsbury in the Wiltshire plain of southwest England, "we released our gliders into an LZ north of Eindhoven near the Maas River Bridge. We flew about thirty-eight to forty miles over German-held territory. We didn't need a navigator; one could just follow the crashed and burning airplanes on the ground. Most of the flak burst just above us. Thank goodness, the Jerries didn't have proximity fuses and could not fuse the shells to burst at our altitude, which was nearing about 800 feet. We usually released gliders at 500 feet and 95mph.

"As we flew over the enemy, I watched the planes in our element by turning my head slightly to the right. They trailed out to the right and behind us. Suddenly, the fourth ship lurched upward at a sharp angle and then spiraled off to the right, out of sight. A few minutes later, the third plane exploded in a big orange ball of fire and then plunged to earth.

"We two survivors continued on to our landing zone and released our gliders. Upon reaching the LZ, there were many German tanks with the 88mm gun muzzles pointing up at us and firing. The tanks were in set positions behind rows of trees adjacent to a road that was one boundary of the LZ. We immediately surmised that they must have been forewarned of the mission. Years later, we read that a double-agent spy had sold out to the Germans and they did indeed know we were coming!

"All the way in to the LZ, P-47s were strafing and bombing German gun positions. It was thrilling to watch them dive almost vertically and clobber the Wehrmacht. We could not be aggressive; all we could do was hope we didn't get hit, and cheer on our fighter bombers.

"Our two planes made it back to England unscathed, but our group lost twelve of eighty aircraft, with the deaths of many great guys and with several badly wounded. The 53rd Carrier Wing lost twenty-nine aircraft. It was a Black Sunday indeed for us!"

Calling Market Garden "a great disaster," the colonel gives his reasons: "Field Marshal Montgomery dreamed up the mission probably as an ego trip to divert attention from a troop carrier hero, General George S. Patton, Third U.S. Army commander. . . . The weakest link in the whole operation was the dependence on British armor to advance down the dike roads to join up with the airborne holding the bridges and to sweep across the Rhine at Arnhem. A freshman ROTC student with only rudimentary knowledge of tactics could have foreseen disaster. The dike roads are the highest terrain in Holland! The Germans simply let a couple of tanks advance and then blasted the next few to halt the whole column. The armor never reached Arnhem.

"Our group flew resupply missions to drop parabundles to the airborne troops near the Rhine bridges. We had no further casualties.

"About 27 September, we flew into Brussels and evacuated survivors of the British 1st Airborne. Of a total of some 8,000, fewer than 2,400 reached safety. The rest were dead or captured. I'll never forget those tired, dirty, ragged, bloody, hungry men. Many were walking wounded with the look of having been to hell and back. . . .

"We went on to participate in the relief of the 101st at Bastogne, probably the overall best mission I can recall. We also participated in the airborne assault over the Rhine near Wesel where we dropped units of the 17th Airborne Division in their first combat role. On the latter flight, our ship was shot down and our crew captured for nine hours until units of the airborne took control of the command post where we were being held. We were up on the front for about five days and then were evacuated across the Rhine in a DUKW, skippered by the only sailor in Navy uniform that we saw in a year in the ETO."

18 September 1944
Mission South of Nijmegen, the Netherlands

Major Frederick D. (Dusty) Worthen was a bombardier with 93rd Bomb Group, 328th Squadron, Eighth AF, when he participated in his third mission, Operation Market Garden.

"Early in the morning on 18 September, we were called for a mission briefing. This would be our third mission and would be a resupply effort to American ground troops that had made a parachute drop and glider landings in the Groesbeek area south of Nijmegen, the Netherlands. This was one of three major drop zones," Major Worthen writes.

"By midday, we had formed up and were on our way across the Channel at maybe 1,000 feet. We made landfall over Schouwen Island, Holland, little knowing that some twenty missions later we would make an unscheduled visit to this very spot.

"We then let down to about 50 to 100 feet. The view along the route to the drop zone was incredible. Crashed C-47 planes, burned outlines of crashed gliders, gliders nose-up or on their back—a general mess.

"As we neared the target, the small-arms fire became intense. We were hit several times. One slug stopped in the backpack parachute of our tail gunner.

"The drop plan was to fly in at 50 feet, pull up to 400 feet at the target marker, and drop the cargo. Due to smoke and haze, the fast speed at a low altitude, and other uncertainties, the accuracy of the drop was unknown. We did, however, see what looked like Germans picking up supplies. After 'cargo away,' we gained a few thousand feet and headed home, along about the same course we followed in. The downed aircraft from this altitude were just as grim as before. We lost two planes on this mission and apparently it was not too successful a venture at that. We never found out what it was all about."

In the Cornelius Ryan book *A Bridge Too Far*, "about four pages were devoted to this air mission and the part played by the B-24s," Major Worthen points out. "Our part was small compared to what the ground forces went through during Operation Market Garden, but it was a bit gratifying even after all these years to learn that in the Groesbeek area 80 percent of our supplies were recovered by the U.S. troops, while in the other two areas it was less than 50 percent and about 12 percent recovery."

Summer 1944
Mission to Czechoslovakia

Major Robert Lagasse submits the recollections of his late brother, Lieutenant Colonel Harvey Lagasse, who was with 459th Bomb Group at Foggia, Italy, in 1944.

After their August missions to Ploesti, Romania, and "a tough target in and around Avignon" in support of the invasion of Southern France 15 August, then-Lieutenant Harvey Lagasse and crew get their fourth assignment 22 August: the Blechhammer North oil refineries in Czechoslovakia.

"We took off in a flight of ten bombers, and en route seven turned back to Italy because of fuel consumptions. It was just our luck we had a plane that was good on fuel, so we and two other 24s continued on to the target," Lieutenant Lagasse records. "I received a real rapid promotion on that flight. I became the lead bombardier with a tremendous force of two bombers. . . . There were fighters, nothing like those in the Ploesti raid but enough to scare the hell out of anyone.

"We reached the initial point and I began to synchronize on the target, made some slight course corrections and shouted, 'Bombs away.' The other bombers dropped their bombs on my release. We made a sharp turn to starboard and were hit by a flak burst on our inboard port engine. . . . We headed for home with one engine on fire. The co-pilot feathered the prop and activated the fire extinguisher. . . .

"Harry was straining to hold the opposite rudder to compensate for the loss of one engine" when, "well into Hungary, over Lake Balaton, seven German fighters jumped us." Responding to Harry that "it would be about twenty minutes" to make it to Yugoslavia and "a pretty good chance," Lieutenant Lagasse was interrupted by shouts from the nose gunner and the ball-turret gunner: "Two bandits coming in at twelve o'clock low!" and "One of those bastards at four o'clock low" and then, "Christ, they're all over the damn place!"

"Tom, our left-waist gunner screamed over the intercom, 'O God, they got Bill. There's blood all over the bulkhead. O Sweet Jesus, he has a big hole in his chest. Lieutenant, he's dead. God, Bill is dead!'

"The fighters made another pass and we could hear screams of pain that sounded like Frank in the ball turret. He screamed again, 'I'm hit! O Mother of God, I'm hit!'

"With great strength and determination, and bearing excruciating pain, Frank climbed out of the turret and bailed out at about 10,000 feet. . . . I recall saying a silent prayer that he would be found by someone who would assist him. . . .

"The fighter attack continued, and on one pass an Fw-190 hit us on the port side and knocked out the inboard engine and it caught on fire. . . . An Me-109 came in at about two o'clock high and opened up on the nose. A burst of fire from his wing guns cut into the nose and missed my legs by inches, cutting my parachute bag to shreds. Harry dropped down to 1,000 feet, but with two engines, we couldn't hold that altitude and we dropped to 800 feet, and Harry screamed, 'Get the hell out of here. Bail out!' Joe and I bailed out through the nose-wheel door. . . . I pulled my ripcord and my chute blossomed and at that moment I hit the ground, somewhat shaken but apparently intact. I looked skyward and saw our P-51s all over the sky. We must have just reached fighter range. It was too late for us but they sure gave those German fighters some real grief.

"I landed in a garden with bean poles and, according to my training, I was supposed to bury my parachute so it could not be seen from the air. The effort was in vain for when I turned around I saw about thirty-five people with weapons, ranging from beat-up old shotguns, small-caliber rifles, several pistols, and the remainder of the group carried axes and pitchforks. I recalled the number of rounds in my .45 automatic and it was not thirty-five, so I lifted it from my shoulder holster with two fingers and dropped it on the ground." *[Colonel Lagasse's story continues in later chapters.]*

September 1944
Angaur, Palau Islands

Major Alfred E. Peloquin served with the 726th Amphibian Tractor Battalion, which was assigned to the 81st Infantry Division for the invasion of the Palau Islands.

"Down in Australia, there's a strange animal called the duck-billed platypus. It is equally at home on land or water. It has a beaver body, a duck's bill, and it lays eggs. On 26 January 1944, the War Department hatched an oddity called the 726th Amphibian Tractor Battalion. In many respects it has been as unique as that mammal which lives Down Under, with one exception—it never (officially) laid an egg." Thus begins the 726th's unit history by an unknown author who provides a story about "a bunch of young men who went overseas with a collection of Rube Goldberg machines called Landing Vehicles Tracked," those "armor-plated floating vehicles, powered by an airplane engine, propelled on land and water by caterpillar-type tracks, and bristling with fire power."

The 726th departed Seattle aboard the USAT *Shawnee*, 7 June 1944; the group left Pearl Harbor, 8 August, in a medium convoy headed southwest—with seven of the LSTs carrying the 726th Amphibian Tractor Battalion that had been reinforced by eighteen amphibian tanks of Company D, 776th Amphibian Tank Battalion.

"Four days later, the convoy lay at anchor off the palm-fringed shores of the Solomon Islands." To the scarred beaches of Guadalcanal, "on 30 August and 1 September, the 726th made its final dry run. . . . Tokyo Rose announced cheerfully over short-wave radio that a big convoy was assembling at Guadalcanal and her people were prepared to give it a warm reception. We laughed—but how the hell did she know?

"On 4 September, we were back on our LSTs, to participate in the Palau Island operation. We were to take the 81st Infantry ashore to capture Angaur Island, useful to the Japs for its huge phosphate deposits, radio station, and lookout points. Meanwhile, the 1st Marine Division was to precede us by landing on seven-mile-long Peleliu, an important airbase. . . . It was important to gain the Palaus, we learned later, in order to make the waters of the Western Carolines secure for the forthcoming Philippine campaign. . . .

"September 17, and the weatherman was on our side. . . . The clear eastern sky turned pink, then golden, and little more than a mile away was low-lying Angaur, shadowy and foreboding. Ships were everywhere and the dawn of Fox Day was greeted by the guns of tensely waiting naval vessels: LCIs, sub-chasers, DEs, destroyers, cruisers, and battlewagons. All hell broke loose. It was a thousand July Fourths rolled into one. Naval guns spoke and the hostile shores shuddered. Then planes roared upon the scene knocking out known Jap positions. They dropped jellied gasoline firebombs, new in the Pacific, and great pillars of flame smothered their targets. The island became a smoking volcano. We shook our heads in awe of the preinvasion bombardment. Could any Jap live through it?

"Meanwhile, LSTs had opened their bows and out rolled the tractors, loaded with infantry and ready to go in. The tractors went into formation and the first wave began its water march toward shore. . . . As the tractors neared the beach at 0830, the Navy advanced its shelling to targets inland. The tractors rolled up to the beaches, safe. And crew members and infantry were greeted by scenes of unforgettable devastation. . . .

"On Red Beach, Company A tractors were met by scattered small-arms and mortar fire, while on Blue Beach, Company B observed some mortar fire. But on neither beach was resistance strong enough to slow the landing. . . . The invasion beaches had been chosen well and the Japs had been caught with their pants down. On any beaches other than Red and Blue, they would have given us hell."

"I guess the things I remember most about the war years are the apparent total confusion of a battle while establishing a beachhead and the camaraderie that developed within my platoon," Major Peloquin writes. "Subsequent to establishment of beachheads, our unit was assigned various support duties, such as unloading ships, clearing out ammunition dumps of duds and damaged ammunition through ocean disposal, and with flame throwers mounted on some of our tractors, working with the infantry in ferreting Japs out of caves."

21 September 1944
USS *Hornet* to the Philippines

Captain Kenneth M. Glass was a pilot with Torpedo Squadron Two (VT-2) aboard the USS Hornet *(CV-12), one of eleven carriers in Task Force 58.*

"Air Group Two's final weeks aboard *Hornet* were spent attacking shipping, installations, and targets of opportunity throughout the Philippine Islands. As part of the task force, we were back attacking the Philippines for the first time since the Japanese occupied the island nation early in the war," Captain Glass reports.

"We ranged far and wide over Mindanao, Davao, and Luzon as we hit targets during flights that lasted more than six hours. Fighter opposition was spotty. What few enemy planes did appear were either shot down or chased away by our fighters. We did have to be concerned about anti-aircraft fire, though.

"On my second mission over Manila Bay, 21 September 1944 (Manila was a city of 650,000 in those days), we were assigned to bomb dock installations. I had been assigned as flight leader of a group of nine torpedo planes (TBFs). One of the planes was piloted by Ensign Reiser, with two crewmen aboard. He was assigned to fly on my wing.

"We made our approach over the harbor at 14,000 feet, and immediately encountered heavy flak from Japanese anti-aircraft batteries. The flak bursting around us was so intense that the smell filled the cockpit. Just as I was maneuvering into position for my dive on the target with the other eight planes, my wingman received a direct hit from an anti-aircraft burst. His plane caught fire and began falling to the ocean below.

"I immediately went into my dive, to lay my bombs on the docks. During our dive, my turret gunner was in a good position to watch the stricken plane. Two of the crew escaped, as two parachutes were observed opening. The third man apparently went in with the plane as it crashed into the ocean. Unfortunately, no word was ever received as to the fate of the two who escaped from the plane. Many of us believe they were shot while hanging from the parachutes as they descended. Such executions were common practice by the Japanese at this time.

"My luck was with me that day, since I'm convinced that burst was meant for me as flight leader of the group."

21 September 1944

POW Camp Cabanatuan, the Philippines

First Lieutenant Hugh H. Roberts continues his POW diary-letter written from Bilibid Prison, Manila, 26 November 1944, several weeks before his death.

"The most beautiful sight I ever saw came on 21 September when about 100 American planes flew over to bomb Clark Field. They shot down a Jap plane near us. We did not know they were American planes till then," POW Roberts writes.

"The planes also bombed a Jap convoy in which [there] were 1,200 British and Dutch prisoners," the lieutenant continues, in a chillingly prophetic description of what would be his own fate a few months later. "Only sixty have been picked up. The Japs then started preparing to take us to Japan and they took one shipload out on November 12. with it my best friend, Lieutenant Ben F. Vansant, of Mount Victory, Kentucky, and if I fail to show up I wish you would contact him or his folks."

OCTOBER 1944

35

"We, and a certain general, had returned to the Philippines," Chief Warrant Officer Fourth Class David L. Wischemann declares triumphantly, writing of the 20 October 1944 invasion of Leyte. He was an electrician's mate third class, aboard LST-18, which left Humbolt Bay, Hollandia, Dutch New Guinea, in the late afternoon of 12 October, with "ships of every description."

"As far as you could see ahead, there was nothing but one vast black-gray mass of ships. When the ships of the Third and Fifth Fleets joined us (about three days out), there was said to be 600 ships in this invasion force. It was seven days from Hollandia to Leyte Gulf and, of course, we were to enter the gulf at night, in the dark of the moon, 19 October 1944," he reports.

Also sailing with that armada was then–Private First Class George R. Woltman, a personal bodyguard to that "certain general," the supreme commander of the Southwest Pacific Theater, General Douglas MacArthur. "After being in New Guinea for two years, our unit was alerted to break camp and we boarded a ship within hours," Mr. Woltman writes. "Each morning at sunrise we picked up more ships in our convoy. All around, on the third day, U.S. troopships and Navy ships could be seen from close by to the horizon. At that time, we all were informed of our invasion [objective] of Leyte Gulf in the Philippines. What we couldn't understand was why we did not go to Mindanao where the Japs had thousands of troops. MacArthur's strategy was to cut them off by sea and air and that's what happened. Many perished."

According to Mr. Wischemann, "The Army Rangers had taken a small island at the entrance to the gulf and had signalmen on the island signaling, by flashing light, instructions to our ships. Here was this mass of ships and at some prearranged point each ship blew its horn and made a 90 degree turn to port. I wondered at how much surprise we were to the enemy, with all this ruckus. As we found out later, the destroyers had been in Leyte Gulf for three days before our arrival, shelling the beach and sweeping mines.

"The Navy guns bombarded the beach all night, and we all were about 300 yards from the shore. The ships then started to unload their troops at Tacloban, Red Beach, and the 77th Division went in on White Beach, an area three miles down the beach. No enemy action for at least twelve hours. Then the Japanese planes and the torpedo bombers came within everyone's sight and it was some experience to witness 600 ships firing at one time into the dusk and to see all the tracer bullets lighting up the sky. The torpedo bombers would come in low and sank some of our ships, because if we fired on them we would strike our own ships, being that we were so close. Their losses were heavy."

"We approached our beaching area about daybreak," Mr. Wischemann continues, "just as the Navy started bombing and shelling with aircraft, battleships, cruisers, and destroyers. I had never experienced anything akin to this in my life. For two hours there was nothing but a continual roar of ear-splitting explosions, and gun smoke so thick you could not see land. I could not see how any living thing could have survived that shelling.

"As the bombardment lifted, the first-assault infantry waves headed for the invasion beach," he adds. Within a few hours, so too did Supreme Commander MacArthur, who later broadcast to the Philippine people their long-awaited news of his return.

October 1944
Leyte Gulf, the Philippines

Chief Warrant Officer George R. Woltman was one of six men recruited in October 1942 to serve as bodyguards to General Douglas MacArthur.

About the time of the invasion of Leyte, "Admiral Halsey was proceeding north on the east side of the islands, and it was detected that the main Jap naval force was on the west side, coming through the Surigao Strait and heading south in Leyte Gulf to turn the tide on the American forces there," Mr. Woltman writes. "Admiral Halsey's forces were contacted, and he reversed his direction to the gulf, [but he] did not arrive in time.

"I witnessed PT boats going up to the Japanese ships and firing their torpedoes and sinking them. But our losses were heavy, too. Out of about eight PT boats, only three returned to base during that conflict. They did a marvelous job. They held the Japs off until Admiral Sprague's task force arrived through the San Bernardino Strait. The Japs reversed their course.

"Admiral Sprague's force saved the invasion force; we were informed at that time to unload and arrived on the beach. At that time, it was dark and a typhoon hit the gulf. The winds were very strong and rains heavy, and the next morning many Corvette ships were up on the beach. Most of the Japs had gone for protection in the mountains after our heavy naval shelling."

During his six-month period in the Philippines, until April 1945, Mr. Wolt-man says, "the enemy continued with bombing every night and with dogfights during the day, but we had air superiority not long after the Philippine invasion. The new P-38 fighters were splendid."

As for General MacArthur going ashore in the Philippines, rank does not always 'come first.' Mr. Woltman says that it was he—6 foot 5 inch, 180-pound Private First Class Woltman—who first tested the waters as he waded ashore to check whether the beach was safe when the general made good his promise to return to the Philippines.

September–November 1944
Leyte Gulf, the Philippines

Chief Warrant Officer Fourth Class David L. Wischemann, electrician's mate third class in May 1944, was just turning nineteen when assigned to LST-18.

In Leyte Gulf with the invasion fleet, "as word was passed to me to 'open the bow doors and lower the ramp,' I watched with much apprehension, through a one-inch bulletproof window as the ramp lowered and sunshine gradually began to flood the tank deck. . . .

"The first rig out of our ship was a bulldozer that U.S. Army Engineers had retrofitted with a steel plate around the operator's seat, complete with eye slits cut on all four sides of the cab. He immediately started building a sand fill-up to our ramp, so that the trucks and other equipment on our ship could exit to the beach."

Describing the effects of the "hellacious bombardment" that "rained down on that beach," Mr. Wischemann says: "The invasion area was a shambles. Many of the palm trees were cut off about halfway up by the shellfire from the fleet. Apparently the five-inch shells from the destroyers just cut through the trees without exploding. The Navy bombers would pass overhead (they sounded like a bunch of bolts rattling around in a fifty-gallon barrel), dive, go out of sight behind the trees, and you would hear and feel a series of explosions. Then, up they would come into the sky again. Hell itself was being delivered to the enemy."

And now, on Leyte beach, "there were trucks, tractors, equipment of all kinds, people everywhere milling around on that beach, and slowly ambling down the whole length of this bedlam was a carabao cow and her calf, completely unaware of our great contribution to the liberation.

"Mobile equipment rolled off the 18 at once; then the unloading of the tank deck was next. Part of the standard cargo were 300 barrels of high-octane avia-tion fuel and 300 artillery rounds, which were stored against the after-bulkhead in the tank deck. This same bulkhead was the forward part of the crew's quarters, just below the officers' quarters and just above the main and auxiliary engine rooms. When the tank deck was unloaded, we all were just a little less nervous."

Toward evening, as Electrician's Mate Wischemann and crew members "wandered into the forward area to an abandoned, enemy machine-gun nest, looking for souvenirs," a soldier on the same mission asked: "Hey, you sailors off the LSTs on the beach?" When they replied *yes*, he informed them: "You know they are under attack!"

"It must have been a mile back to the ships and I'll bet I did it in two minutes. I saw the bow doors and ramp, ran right into the ship, ran up to the weather deck, and something didn't look right. It wasn't right; I was on the wrong LST. I really took a lot of ribbing for this.

"We were under attack from artillery, and word was passed for all LSTs to make fog. This was to cover the unloading operations at night, and those old fog-makers on the stern of our ships were really effective. We heard that the cruiser *Honolulu*, our bombardment cover, was hit this night, but none of our group even had near-misses.

"The soldiers unloaded all night and early the next morning, 21 October. Our ship retracted from the beach and headed toward the mouth of Leyte Gulf to make up the first convoy going south to pick up more troops and cargo to resupply the beachhead. It was lucky for us to be in the first convoy out, because the war in and about Leyte got quite hot the next couple of weeks.

"Our convoy headed back toward New Guinea with only three or four sub-chasers and patrol craft for escort, and as the days went by we heard about the naval engagement with a part of the Japanese fleet in the Surigao Strait. Word came down from the radio shack that our escort ships might have to go back and help fight the battle, if things turned bad for our forces. Aboard ship, all rumors originate in the radio shack."

Praising "the defense that these small ships of our Navy put up against a vastly superior Japanese battle group," Mr. Wischemann adds: "Many an American male lived out his normal lifespan because of the devotion and bravery of our little Seventh Fleet off the eastern approaches to Leyte Gulf."

In the two weeks that it took the *18* to return to Leyte, "the Japanese land-based bombers in the Philippines had had a field day bombing the supply ships in the harbor, the troops and the supply dumps on land, and the airfields under construction. The rainfall had been torrential, slowing down almost all construction of the airfields, so that our land-based planes could not be used in close support of our forces."

On their return they also saw some of the damage from the first Kamikaze suicide planes: "A Liberty ship with its bridge half blown away and a destroyer barely afloat (the main deck almost awash), with a repair barge alongside and with many pumps going full bore, trying to keep her afloat." Another Kamikaze victim was "one of our Coast Guard–manned sister ships, LST-28, which had a Kamikaze plane crash into the after-gun tub, killing and wounding the men on the stern."

September–October 1944
Ulithi Atoll and Peleliu, Caroline Islands

Major Alfred E. Peloquin was with the 726th Amphibian Tractor Battalion, assigned to the 81st Infantry Division.

After the 17 September invasion of Angaur in the Palaus, "there was another job to be done. Ulithi Atoll was Jap-held and it was needed as a naval anchorage. Colonel Switzer gave the troop-landing job to Company A, plus a Headquarters and Service Company detachment," which shoved off 20 September on four LSTs, according to unit history.

Because the Japanese had already evacuated, "unopposed landings were made on Falalop, Asor, and Mog Mog Islands, with tractors holding their fire and friendly natives coming out to greet the Americans. The islands were a pleasant surprise, clean and beautiful, lacking nothing of a typical Hollywood version of the South Seas except pretty women," the history continues. "Life at Ulithi was a pleasant diversion—except for the typhoon. It was a typhoon of typhoons. Hardly man or tent stood up against it. . . . But it's an ill wind that blows nobody good. To the men of Lieutenant Stevenson's 1st Platoon, it came as a blessing in disguise. An LCT was driven aground nearby and its large refrigerators of perishable foods had to be consumed or spoil. The Navy shared with the Army, and when the CO's runner came up to find out how the platoon had weathered the gale, he found everyone feasting like kings on ham, chicken, turkey, and fresh fruits."

Meanwhile, "on 23 September, Company B and a portion of Headquarters and Service Company moved to Peleliu to assist the 321st Infantry Regiment and the 1st Marine Division. . . . First impressions were much like those at Guadalcanal—except that Peleliu's vast destruction was freshly wrought and the sick smell of death hung in the air. The battalion was attached to the 8th Amphibian Tractor Group of the 1st Marines, and immediately our reinforcing tractors began hauling much-needed ammunition and supplies from ships to front-line positions. . . .

"Probably the most hazardous of any assignments given LVT [Landing Vehicle, Tracked] crews was that of flame-thrower details. The Navy had developed a $2^1/_2$-ton flamethrower of deadly potentialities, and tractors were about the only available vehicle that could carry it to front-line areas for use in mopping up Jap caves.

"On 26 September, [a threesome] went with a Marine detachment to give the thrower its baptismal use. They encountered engine trouble and were relieved by Corporal Preston Aishton and his crew of T/5 Arthur Middleton, Corporal Mitchell Parrish, and Corporal Robert Hilber. This crew operated in conjunction with Marine advances. In many cases, they spearheaded attacks in the taking of successive hills."

Working with the Marines, and until the infantry took over, four crews "made repeated flaming assaults on 'The Five Brothers and Sisters.' After these key positions had been wrenched from the enemy's grasp, [there were] the final advances of the fight for Peleliu which proceeded through Death Valley and over the 'China Wall' into Hell's Pocket. . . .

"While the flamethrowers were busy . . . , other tractors of the battalion were . . . clearing the Japs from nearby small islands . . . Ngesebus, Kongauru, Ngabad, Garakayo, Gorokottan, Ngergon, Kayargel. The 726th tractors visited them all."

"By 26 November 1944, when Peleliu was declared secure, . . . we had helped the 81st Division run up a tally of 3,249 Japs dead and 180 taken prisoner" on that seven-mile-long island, Colonel Peloquin's anonymous author reports.

In *The Two-Ocean War*, historian Samuel Eliot Morison writes: "Considering that the capture of Peleliu and the adjacent small island of Angaur cost almost as many American lives as the assault on Omaha Beach, it would seem that CINCPAC here made one of his rare mistakes. . . . [Colonel Nakagawa's] garrison was exterminated, but he had cost the Marines and Army 1,950 lives."

October 1944
Longueville, France

Colonel Jean W. Christy continues his 5th Infantry Division account.

Along the Seille River near Longueville and Cheminot, "the rains continued on into October, and there was a real test of how well everyone's slit-trench home had been built. The log- and dirt-covered roof of the fire direction center leaked a little, but was repaired by readjusting the tarps which made it waterproof," Colonel Christy records.

When visibility cleared on 4 October, "a little enemy activity was again picked up," as well as the first game of the World Series, on Armed Services Radio, when the Saint Louis Browns defeated the Saint Louis Cardinals 2–1 in the opener. "We managed to listen to all seven games of the World Series," won by the Cards 3–1 on 9 October.

Battalion records for a "very quiet" 12 October indicate that the "ammunition allotment was cut to 260 rounds, then to none at all." The same allotment continued 13 and 14 October. "We didn't know the reason" for the serious ammunition shortage, "but thought it might have to do with the effort up at Fort Driant." When enemy forces "began to show signs of thinking that they could move freely about without being shot at," battalion records for 15 October reveal the plan of action: "Company A of the 736th Tank Battalion is going to shoot for us. They have twelve tanks with 75mm guns and four with 76mm guns. There are no range tables for the 76s; the company just got them.

"We put them into position as two six-gun batteries and one four-gun battery. We are doing the fire direction for them." The tank-battalion support continued until about 19 October, when "we learned that we were to be relieved by the 95th Infantry Division and go into a rest area near the town of Mercy le Haut, northwest of Audun le Roman."

"As in any new situation, we all explored the town and surrounding areas as quickly as possible," Colonel Christy says, as he recalls a general-purpose dry-goods store, housed in a weather-worn, wooden structure. "When the proprietor saw the 5th Division troops come in, he took one look at their Red Diamond shoulder patches, dived under his counter, and came up with a dusty box. It was full of Red Diamond pins about a half-inch long. He had ordered them in 1918, and *that* 5th Infantry Division had moved on before his order arrived. The box had been on the shelf under his counter for twenty-six years. Now he blew off the dust of time and sold all of those Red Diamond pins in less than four hours, as the word spread and a steady stream of soldiers beat a path to his door.

"I bought one of those Red Diamond pins to take home to Peggy [his wife]. She still wears it on her charm bracelet. It fascinated our grandchildren when they were little."

October–December 1944
Cherbourg, France

Colonel Lester B. Cundiff was a second lieutenant, a chemical-warfare service replacement officer, who went ashore on Omaha Beach two months after D-Day.

"After a few weeks in the replacement depot, I was sent to Cherbourg and attached to the 398th Engineer General Service Regiment. . . . [as] camp commander for a POW camp to be set up to provide workers for rebuilding the Port of Cherbourg," Colonel Cundiff writes.

"My German-speaking interpreter and I accompanied the guards on the truck, sent to get the 250 German prisoners we expected. Imagine my surprise to find we were getting 247 Russian prisoners, none of whom spoke English and only a few of whom knew a few words of German. Also assigned to us were three prisoners from India, none of whom spoke English, and who spoke three different dialects," the colonel says, explaining that the Russian POWs had been captured on the Eastern Front and the Indians in North Africa. "All had been put to work by the Germans, building the Atlantic Wall."

Colonel Cundiff recalls that "language was my problem for three days until Sergeant John Zohovetz, from Nevada and of Russian ancestry, was assigned as my interpreter."

"On the first evening, I was too busy to go to dinner at the mess and I was busy with various visitors until about 2100 hours. . . . I was about to sit down on my bunk and open a K-ration when I heard a knock on the door." Opening it, "I saw the small Mongolian self-appointed mess sergeant standing outside with a dish of stew he had saved from their meal. '*Loot-nant, soupe?*' he asked. It was a delicious stew. He, or someone among the prisoners, had obviously been aware of my every move that afternoon and evening and knew that I had not eaten. . . .

"These Russian prisoners were extraordinarily cooperative. Their attitude was that now they could help the Americans defeat the hated Germans. . . .

"After a few weeks, the regimental commander decided that we should get 250 more prisoners, so we moved the prisoners to a larger compound and requisitioned 250 more Russians. No more Russians were available, so we were issued 250 German prisoners, who had to live in the same compound and cooperate with the Russians. We were sitting on a powder keg. Fortunately, no serious incidents occurred before we turned in the Russians and got another 250 Germans."

October 1944
Near Omaha Beach, Normandy

Chief Warrant Officer Sidney Bowen was a T-5, with 494th Anti-Aircraft Artillery Gun Battalion, Battery.

"Tomorrow the men who have not received absentee ballots from their respective states will be allowed to vote by secret ballot. The ballots, in turn, will be forwarded to the states of residence," Sidney writes on Sunday, 8 October, to wife Isabel.

"The mud has attained the consistency of chocolate fudge and, for the time, leggings have been authorized as wear in lieu of overshoes. Overshoes keep your feet dry but are clumsy and weighty when caked with mud."

"I made two trips to Cherbourg proper, one to take a shower and the other to sightsee a German flying-bomb site. . . . Nothing I could tell you about the place would differ from the newspaper accounts of the wrecked port. German POWs are unloading cargoes from ships and doing hard labor under the supervision of American Negro troops," he tells Isabel on 12 October.

"I have no cold or other ailments of any kind, just a big yearning for you. . . . I need you like Barnum needs Bailey," Sidney signs off in one of his October letters.

Fall 1944
Mission to Berlin, Germany

Lieutenant Colonel Norman L. Stevens Jr. was the lad who would rather 'fight than write' [see December 1942 story]. And he did.

"For most of us in the Eighth Air Force, when the briefing curtain went up and the target designation was Berlin, there was a great surge from the bottom of the stomach to the top of the throat. Berlin was defended with over 700 very accurate anti-aircraft 88s. It was a fierce target," Lieutenant Colonel Stevens recalls.

"The first mission taught me that everyone on the crew had to do his job. This was disconcerting to me, as to navigation, for I always wanted to know where I was in case I had an in-flight problem. Then I could mentally adjust where I might be able to get to, depending on the degree of the problem.

"One time, we were coming back from a target. . . . I was very busy in the cockpit, and I pushed the intercom and said, Pilot to navigator, what is our position?' Without hesitation, the navigator snapped back, 'Navigator to pilot, we are five miles from *Unter den Linden*.' I said, 'Roger. Thank you, navigator.'"

"About twenty minutes later, it hit me like a ton of bricks. My navigator had discovered one of my idiosyncrasies: It was important to my morale and well-being to know exactly where we were at all times."

Sitting there, thinking "what a smart little navigator Stalnaker was," Lieutenant Colonel Stevens says he suddenly realized: "*Unter den Linden* is the main drag in Berlin, and we were probably 400 miles from Berlin. I didn't laugh then, but I've laughed many times since."

September–October 1944
Mission to the Netherlands

*Lieutenant Colonel A. Ray Kubly arrived in England 1 August 1944, assigned to
7th Squadron of 34th Bomb Group, 3rd Bomb Division, Eighth Air Force.*

"After training with other crews, all B-17 replacements and the old B-24 crews
were assigned their first combat mission," Lieutenant Colonel Kubly records.
"Sunday, 17 September 1944, we were to bomb the German flak batteries that
surrounded the city of Arnhem, the Netherlands, to eliminate or reduce the
losses for all the paratroops and gliders that were supposed to land in the big
Market Garden Operation.

"After flying seven missions to Germany, we were assigned to bomb a synthetic oil refinery near Meresberg, Germany, on 7 October."

Taking off about 0400, they rendezvoused with others until "about 500
planes were involved. All went well until we started our bombing run. It seemed
we just started straight and level when black puffs of smoke started popping
around us.

"Suddenly, we left the formation, as our plane was hit several times. We
started to drop altitude while smoke and fire were coming out of one engine.
Then we lost two engines! No. 1 engine was 'feathered,' and with the fire extinguisher our pilot was able to put out the fire. No. 3 engine propeller could not be
feathered and was wind-milling from the air speed.

"We decided to try to make it to Eindhoven, Holland, which was then in Allied
hands and was free. Our friendly P-51s came up alongside us to escort us back
to Holland, where some English Spitfires watched us for a short while, so the
Jerries wouldn't shoot us down.

"I was up in the nose of the airplane doing navigation. We were still losing
altitude. . . . Our pilot called . . . to prepare for ditching. We couldn't lower the
wheels. The hydraulics must have been damaged. . . . Wiley Moore [ball-turret
gunner] said, 'Everyone bail out!'

"I pulled my emergency cord immediately after clearing the plane. My forward velocity was so fast that my chute opened horizontally behind me. . . . As I
was swinging in the air, I heard some rifle shots. . . . Next thing I knew, a sharp
sting went through the right calf of my leg. I knew I was hit, as I could feel the
warm blood running down my leg."

After landing in a ditch along a county road, "I was pulling my chute together
[when] two Jerries came running up with their rifles, pointing at me, yelling,
'Comrade! Comrade! For you the war is over!' I then knew I was a POW."

Taking his first-aid kit from his belt, Lieutenant Colonel Kubly recalls that he sprinkled sulfa powder on both bullet holes that went in and out of his right leg, put compresses on, and taped the wounds. "The two Germans then formed a basket with their hands and carried me to their headquarters about one-quarter mile away. We had bailed out right over a German front-line staging area. There must have been over 100 German troops in that immediate area.

"Shortly, they brought up my pilot, Jim Helby, on a stretcher. He was shot in the back and was bleeding internally. He kept on asking for a doctor. None ever came. . . . Jim Helby died that evening. Wiley Moore was brought up with a broken leg from his parachute landing. I never did see any of the rest of the crew. My understanding was they were taken right to a POW camp in Germany. Later that afternoon, a German lieutenant came over and said that [waist gunner] Hubert Betterton was killed. His parachute never opened. . . .

"That night I was taken with wounded Germans to a front-line first-aid station. We were only five to ten miles behind the front lines. . . .

"The next morning, a German truck picked up all of us wounded (all Germans except Pappy Moore and me) and, without any lights, we headed for Utrecht, Holland, and the Saint Antoninous Hospital, which the Germans had taken over from the Dutch Sisters. It was filled with 300 to 400 wounded Germans and about 20 wounded Allied POWs: English, Canadian, Polish, Dutch, American, and some other nationalities. We were all considered 'litter patients,' since we couldn't walk. Otherwise, you would go right to a German POW camp. . . .

"Then came 26 October 1944. Just a few days before, a Dutch engineer, named Mr. Dekker, came to us and asked if any of us would like to escape. . . . After much talk and consideration, six of us wounded decided we would take the chance." The six included Pappy Moore from Asheville, North Carolina, and the author.

"Our plans were to go to the basement of the hospital and crawl through the heating-system inspection tunnel. All we had to do was follow the 'hot' uninsulated steam pipes to the main furnace room. There were civilian clothes to change into in the tunnel. The Dutch Underground people met us with bicycles outside the main furnace building. It all went like clockwork. By the time Corporal Schultz, our German guard, came around for a bed check, we were safe with three different families around Utrecht. After our escape, the Germans made several attempts to find us with road blocks and house-to-house searches. Thanks to the Dutch people, they never did find any of us." *Lieutenant Colonel Kubly's story continues in the next chapter.*

28 October 1944
Mission to Munich, Germany

Major Onan A. Hill was a radar navigator, 353rd Bomb Squadron, 301st Bomb Group, 5th Wing, stationed with Fifteenth Air Force, Bari, Italy.

A "lone-wolf mission to Munich, Germany, flown on the night of 28 October 1944" was "a memorable flight for a number of reasons," Major Hill writes. Though not the first mission flown at night, "I don't recall one that started so late."

"This was a flight I had misgivings about before we took off. The pilot who was assigned to fly this mission was one who had had several misadventures, . . . [that] caused crew members to be a bit superstitious. There isn't much doubt that he was a good pilot.

"The flight to Munich had barely begun when the azimuth stabilizer went out on my radar set. Were we jinxed? I reported the failure to the pilot and we discussed whether the flight should be aborted. I told the pilot that I thought I could find and bomb the target without the azimuth stabilizer, but it would entail some difficulty.

"I am sure that this pilot was aware of the reputation that he was acquiring. And being a proud individual and knowing that pilots who aborted missions, even with sufficient justification, were often looked at askance, he decided to continue. He could have aborted the mission and placed the onus on me. After all, I was the one who encountered the difficulty with the radar set. He did not choose to do so.

"Over the target, we encountered something that none of us had seen before. The Germans were shooting something that made a giant burst of flame when it exploded. For instance, a burst of ordinary flak, in the daytime, looks like a puff of smoke about a foot wide and maybe two feet long. . . . But what they were shooting at us made an orange burst of flame as big as a house. Fortunately, they were lousy shots and, except for it making the plane rock, we flew serenely through.

"On the way home, we were cruising along through the cold moonlight when we were jumped by a night fighter. All we were sure of is that he was shooting at us because we could see the tracers just as well as he could. Someone in the nose of the aircraft (I was in the waist) screamed: 'These GD guns won't work.' The pilot growled, 'Shut up down there,' and cocked that B-17 on one wing like it was a P-51 Mustang, and dived for a cloud bank several thousand feet below. For whatever reasons, we did not see him again.

"After everyone calmed down, someone came on the intercom and inquired: 'Who said that about them guns?' Again, the pilot interposed: 'Let's let the matter drop.' He went up about three notches in my estimation then and there. He had sensed the panic in the voice that had screamed about the guns. And he had told him to 'shut up' to keep the panic from spreading. Now that the incident was over, he recognized that panic as a source of embarrassment to one of his crew, and he put a stop to it. . . .

"Debriefings were common occurrences after a mission, but after this mission it was almost a grilling. We actually had to go to 5th Wing Headquarters. They were particularly interested in the giant orange bursts of flame. I think that they thought the Germans may have had a new weapon they were testing on us. We never heard any more about it and, as far as I know, no other crews had a similar experience. Someone suggested the Germans may have been shooting a 155mm howitzer at us. Sounds reasonable to me. That would account for their inaccuracy when they had to elevate the barrel high enough to fire at an airplane. I am just speculating. For all I know, the barrel of a howitzer may not even elevate that high."

Summer–Fall 1944
Hungary

Major Robert J. Lagasse submits the recollections of his late brother, Lieutenant Colonel Harvey Lagasse.

When their B-24 was hit over Czechoslovakia 22 August, then-Lieutenant Harvey Lagasse and crew bailed out near Lake Balaton, Hungary. The hostile crowd of about thirty-five farmers pushed him to the town square and "were shouting many things that I didn't understand. However, when one of the men came out of the crowd with a rope in his hand, I understood. I just couldn't believe my eyes," he writes. "I was terrified of that angry crowd and their rope. They made a noose and placed it over my head and pushed me in the direction of a group of trees, all the time chanting something about *Terrorfleiger* and *Luftgangser*. . . .

"One of the men threw a rope over one of the branches, and several others joined in hauling me up. I felt my neck stretching and although I fought, I knew it was in vain. . . .

"Then I heard shots, and my captors released the rope and I fell to the ground. I looked up in disbelief to see one man (the *burgermeister*) in civilian clothes and three others in uniform."

Led down a dirt road to a large building, probably the town hall, the lieutenant was pushed into a semicircular room where he "was shocked to see the ball-turret gunner lying in a pool of blood. He was screaming in agony."

Taking out the first-aid pack, "I laid the sulfa medication on the floor while I administered the morphine. When the shot took effect, Frank quieted down some and I turned to administer the other medication; it had been stolen. I stood up cursing and swearing at them for taking the medicine when I felt a pain in the back of my head and I passed out. When I awoke, it was dusk. I was in the back of a hay wagon and chained to the slats. . . . Apparently, when I blew my stack one of the soldiers had hit me in the back of the head with his rifle."

After a long and bumpy ride to what seemed military barracks, and a night sleeping on the floor, Lieutenant Lagasse was awakened the following morning by a rifle nudge from a Hungarian soldier, given "a piece of black bread spread with lard and paprika," and pushed out the door to another hay wagon. "There in the hay wagon was the body of our waist-gunner, Bill. He had a large wound in the center of his chest, apparently from a 20mm round, usually fired from the German Me-109. The nature of the wound assured me that Bill had not suffered any pain." After conveying to his captors his concern about Bill's interment, he "saw Bill buried" and "was given a few minutes to pray for him."

Then, once again: another wagon, more dirt roads, and a town with a very old prison. "My captors shoved me into a dark cell and there they were—my crew! Everyone was in good shape and all anxious to know about our two missing members. . . .

"We remained in the filthy, damp dungeon for two nights and as we left we were handed a piece of black bread to take with us. . . . In spite of the secrecy, there were people out to throw stones and rocks at us and yell *Luftgangsers* and *Terrorfleigers*."

Destination this time: initially, "an old run-down platform by a single railroad track" and then, after a day-long train ride, the Budapest railroad station, where "we walked down the platform through a not-too-friendly crowd to some stake and platform trucks. . . . The thing that bothered us most about our transportation was the fact that the trucks were Fords."

Taken to an old Hungarian prison, Lieutenant Lagasse spent an indeterminate number of days in solitary confinement "in a deep, damp dungeon." After several interrogations by German SS officers and subsequent returns "to the slammer," he and his crew were reunited and "herded into boxcars," heading "north, into Naziland" and eventually Sagan.

Colonel Lagasse writes of "an interesting event" during his first interrogation. "When I refused to give the *Hauptman* the information he was seeking, he leaned over his desk and said: 'You fool, do you think I know nothing of you? You enlisted in the Army in August in 1940 and in 1941 you were ordered to active duty with orders to report to a new camp named Blanding in the state of Florida.' The *Hauptman* scared the hell out of me as he took me through my entire military life. I couldn't imagine where he received all those facts. I learned later that from the day I enlisted, the German Intelligence prepared a file on me in a huge facility outside Berlin, and everything that was published in the local newspaper was forwarded to Germany through the German bunds formed in the United States and smuggled into Germany through the South American states.

"When I was shot down and captured, the enemy took my 'dog tags' and forwarded the information on them to the intelligence organization in Berlin. An intelligence officer was assigned to my case," as well as other cases, and the information obtained was used "for its shock value on the new POWs."

1943–1944
ETO to Africa to CBI

Lieutenant Colonel Henry M. Hawthorn was a pilot with the 81st Fighter Group, 91st Fighter Squadron, in North Africa, Sicily, Italy, and China, June 1943–June 1945.

Lieutenant Colonel Hawthorn describes the moves of his first year with the 81st as going from Africa, "where everything was brown except for the olive trees, which were OD, olive drab," to "the little green island" of Sicily, to "the mud puddle" of Italy.

In Africa, "for the most part we flew training missions—gunnery, formation, just wheel-spinning."

In Italy, at the airfield near Naples, there were "long, boring flights over convoys and harbors" until January 1944, when "the older men were going home and we got a new CO, Pappy Chandler, and some new pilots. Pappy was a tall, bald, don't-give-a-damn type guy. . . .

"And since we were turning over all our equipment to a new outfit, we had to get some new planes. . . . Our first stop was Algiers. [where] we gassed up and headed for Casablanca.

There, "we took possession of the planes, still 39s but newer than the old junkers we had in Italy." Soon after returning to Naples, "we gave our ships away to another squadron and loaded aboard C-47s for the flight to Tunis to await transportation to India. Karachi (now Pakistan) would be our next home, where we were to get P-47s. . . .

"When we got to Tunis, we off-loaded our stuff and one of the guys from the 93rd Squadron thought it would be a good time to have an old 328th Group reunion. We had it at the Casino," where "the food was very good, but we brought our own bread and butter," bartered from the Navy.

As the airmen toasted comrades who were no longer around, "the Bey of Tunis [Sidi Mohammed Lamine] was throwing a party at the next table, so when we were ready to leave we asked him if he would like to have the remains of our bread and butter. . . . He accepted it with thanks and away we went, out into the night. . . .

"The next day, I took three or four of my pilots (I was a flight commander by that time) and went riding around Tunis. We drove past the old Roman aqueduct. . . . Along the way we passed the Bey's palace, so [we] drove in to look around. We were rather taken aback when a couple of the old boy's guards in their green and tan uniforms, and with their rifles bearing the three-sided 'pig sticker' bayonets on the muzzles, stopped us and motioned for us to get out of the jeep. Who's to argue? Then some joker came out of one of the buildings and asked, in excellent English, if we had been in the group at the Casino the night before. I told him that I had been there. He told us that the Bey would like us to come in and have a bite to eat and a drink. (He was a Muslim and didn't drink, but had good wine for guests.)

"So we went in and met the old boy. In the course of the conversation, we learned that he had replaced the previous Bey because he was pro-Allies.

"Instead of chips and dips and small hors d'oeuvres, he had some native and French tidbits brought out," Lieutenant Colonel Hawthorn recalls. "One of the small bits was escargot. The name didn't mean anything until I saw the plate. Snails! The same things we saw eating the crops when we moved from Bone to Sfax. But we were stuck, so—after he very graciously showed us how to spear them from the shells with the long gold needles, probably, and rightly, assuming that a bunch of Yanks from an uncultured country didn't know how to do it, we ate. And they weren't bad; in fact, they were good.

"All in all, we had a very good (and different) afternoon with the old boy. He was a most gracious host. We were sweaty and dusty from riding in the jeep and our shoes weren't shined, but he treated us as honored guests. That was probably the high point of all the things I did in Africa." After several days of "bumming around," and stops at Bengazi, Cairo, and Abadan, the crew was off to Karachi and duty in the China–Burma–India Theater.

October 1944
Camp Shirakawa, Formosa

Colonel Michael A. Quinn continues his POW diary entries, his last from Camp Shirakawa.

After writing of squads quarantined for typhoid, Colonel Quinn continues on 30 September: "All general officers except the British are to leave here tomorrow, destination unknown. Also, reason for move unknown. In fact, nothing known."

On 1 October, he records: "The generals left today. We don't know where but believe they are leaving the island by air. . . . Because of the quarantine, Father Kennedy had Mass on his side of the fence. We stayed on the other side."

"Twenty Britishers left today. Luggage allowance raised from ten to thirty kilos. All were warned to wear heavy clothes the second day out," he writes on 3 October, adding on the 5th: "The second group of Britishers leaves tomorrow."

"This morning we were notified that all colonels would leave on the 10th or 12th for a cold climate, destination unknown. Colonel Van der Steen of the Dutch NEI gave me a pair of long drawers. He assured me he had an extra pair. . . . We are all on edge now trying to pack our stuff. There is no limit on our luggage so far, so more than likely, we are going by ship," he records 7 October.

Essentially, these are the entirety of Colonel Quinn's journal entries for October 1944, his briefest during forty months of captivity.

NOVEMBER 1944

36

Enemy fire is a given during wartime. There is other firepower, however, often fatal to its victims: that olympian of oxymorons known as "friendly fire."

For eighteen-year-old U.S. Merchant Marine Raymond Thompson, his enemy zoomed in as eighteen Japanese Kamikazes in three waves of three, six, and then nine planes over his Liberty ship SS *Leonidas Merritt* and other ships in San Pedro Bay, Leyte, in the Philippines, 12 November 1944. Two of those suicide planes struck the *Merritt* that day in separate attacks.

From diary notes written at the time, now–Brigadier General Raymond Thompson provides impressions as he assisted the purser in tending to the wounded: "It was surprising to see just how brave these wounded men acted. They kept back tears and did not holler out in pain. One soldier had his left leg torn off just above the ankle and he lay there on the deck, waiting his turn and only speaking when he wanted someone to watch out for his leg. . . .

"Another soldier, with blood pouring from a huge wound in his abdomen, told me he was going to vomit and wanted a pan. I told him to let it go on the deck and he did. 'I'm sorry, sir,' he said. He died a few minutes later."

For POW Lieutenant Hugh H. Roberts, the known enemy had ruled his every breathing moment for thirty-two months in prison camps throughout the Philippines, but the newer enemy came as *'unfriendly* fire from friends,' when U.S. planes target an unmarked vessel transporting POWs to Japan 15 December 1944. Lieutenant Roberts was among the approximately 4,000 American POWs killed during World War II as transfer was being made in unmarked Japanese ships.

While correspondence from Chief Warrant Officer Clifford A. Roberts does not mention the name of his brother's ship, the Purple Heart citation with date of death as 15 December makes it likely that it was the infamous *Oryoku Maru*, a 7,000-ton passenger vessel referred to as "the hell ship" by prisoners. According to ROA member Lieutenant Colonel Mariano Villarin, who interviewed eight of its survivors, the ship carried "Japanese guards and about 2,000 civilians, including women and children, who were mostly prewar residents of the Philippines" and 1,619 Allied POWs. He speculates that "the *Oryoku Maru* was probably the last ship to leave Manila for Japan with a human cargo."

"With the landing of the American forces on Leyte in October, the Japanese high command, after three years of war, was not about to lose face by giving up to the liberating forces approximately 3,000 Allied POWs still remaining at various camps throughout the Philippines," Lieutenant Colonel Villarin writes in *We Remember Bataan and Corregidor*. "Had the Japanese had the foresight to identify the *Oryoku Maru* as a prison ship, they would have had a safe passage to Japan, prevented the loss of a valuable ship, and saved the lives of hundreds of their citizens as well as hundreds of POWs in the holds."

The 1,619 POWS aboard the *Oryoku Maru* had been herded from Bilibid Prison and crushed into the holds of the ship on 13 December, about to begin a forty-nine-day voyage that would diminish their ranks to 400 and subject them to profanations that would include four attacks by bombs, rockets, and machine guns by fighter planes from the carrier *Hornet* and others from Task Force 38 on 14 December; machine-gun spray by Japanese patrol boats as POWs attempted to swim to shore in Subic Bay; three more attacks with rockets, bombs, and strafing on 15 December when the ship burst into flames and finally sank; encampment and exposure to the elements for five or six days in the tennis-court area near the bay for 1,333 who actually made it to shore, many naked and most starving and dehydrated; transfer aboard trucks to the provincial jail at San Fernando, Pampanga, 20 and 21 December; transfer by boxcars, where they stood shoulder to shoulder for an eighteen-hour ride to San Fernando, La Union, on Christmas Day; a three-mile march to a schoolhouse and their Christmas meal of "half a cup of rice and one-third canteen cup of water"; a two-and-one-half-mile march to Lingayen Beach and encampment for three days before being relegated to two freighters, the *Enoura Maru* and the *Brazil Maru*.

The two ships arrived at Takao, Formosa, New Year's Day 1945, and lay at anchor for nine hopeless, hungry, thirsty days for the POWs—with those on the *Brazil Maru* being transferred to the *Enoura Maru*—when further horror struck on 9 January.

"In its last air strike in support of the invasion [of Luzon], Task Force 38 dropped over 200 tons of bombs on Formosa, primarily to destroy enemy airfields and aircraft. . . . They destroyed few planes—the Japanese did not have many left—but did sink or damage a number of ships at anchor. One of these was the *Enoura Maru*," E. Bartlett Kerr writes in *Surrender and Survival: The Experience of American POWs in the Pacific, 1941–1945*.

The above paragraphs are mere skeletal outline, literally and figuratively, of the *Oryoku Maru* POWs and their movements, from information in both Lieutenant Colonel Villarin and Mr. Kerr's books. Both authors provide horrifically painful details of conditions and atrocities and loss of life during each segment of the *Oryoku Maru* tragedy, which the former labels "a gruesome and hideous tale that unfolded in large-scale suffering, torture, bloodshed, horror, and lingering death."

When the *Brazil Maru* arrived 29 January 1945 at Moji, Japan, 500 of the original 1,619 POWs were still alive. "Of this number, over 100 were so weak and unhealthy that they died within the next few weeks. Fewer than 300 survived to be liberated when the war ended," writes Kerr, whose own father was a victim of the *Oryoku Maru* bombing.

Among prisoners who died en route aboard the *Brazil Maru* were Major Thomas Smothers and Maryknoll Father William T. Cummings. Major Smothers, a West Pointer, was the father of show business personalities Tom and Dick Smothers; Father Cummings was the chaplain wounded during Japanese bombing of U.S. Hospital #1 on Bataan who reputedly said, during one of his Bataan sermons, "There are no atheists in foxholes." His prayerful calm in soothing and ministering to other POWs during imprisonment, and particularly during their hellhole captivity, has been praised by many survivors.

12 November 1944
Leyte, the Philippines

Brigadier General Raymond Thompson was that young Mariner aboard the SS
Leonidas Merritt when it was hit by two Japanese Kamikazes.

"Under cover of a thick Navy smokescreen, the first merchant convoy entered San Pedro Bay, Leyte, on 24 October 1944, four days after the initial Army landing. We were the lead ship, carrying Matson landing mats, to build or rebuild airfields, and parts to build bridges. As civilian merchant seamen, we felt important, contributing to helping General MacArthur keep his 'I shall return' promise. We did not know what was in store for us," Brigadier General Thompson exclaims from a fifty-year perspective. After unloading the landing mats, the *Merritt* was ordered to anchorage to await unloading of the bridge parts and other cargo.

On 12 November, "all-clear was sounded at 0745 and, after our first leisurely breakfast in a long, long time, word reached us that MacArthur had declared Leyte 'secure,'" Mariner Thompson records in his diary at the time. "I went swimming this morning with some of the other boys. Nude. When I was ready to come back on board at 1115 hours, I was pulled up on the cargo net on the number five winch. . . . I walked back aft, still naked.

"All of a sudden, we heard the *rat-tat-tat* of a machine gun and the cry: 'Watch out! It's a Jap!' We immediately hit the afterhouse for cover. We had no sooner gotten under cover when the ship was rocked by a terrific explosion. Debris was flying all over, some of it flying off the fantail. Someone yelled: 'Our ready box is hit!' That was the wrong thing to say as it nearly caused a panic. . . .

"Zep [a Navy Armed Guard] gave me a pair of pants and I ran forward to see how I could help. There was a scene I hope I never see again. The passageways and forward deck were crowded with wounded and dead seamen, Navy Armed Guard, and Negro soldiers from the port battalion that had been unloading us. Some were without legs and others had big holes in their bodies. Fires were everywhere. The purser . . . was working feverishly to help some of the men. He called to me to help him and I applied tourniquets to those men whose wounds were bleeding profusely, laid wet towels underneath those who had been burned, and poured sulfa on some of the wounds."

We had very little in the way of medical supplies to help the wounded on that day, Brigadier General Thompson interjects, pointing out that "merchant ships did not have doctors aboard, nor medics, and carried only a small first-aid chest."

"We cannot understand why an alarm was not sounded so that we could have been ready for them," he resumes in his diary. "There is nothing recognizable on our foredeck except the forward gun tubs, which somehow escaped injury. All but two of the booms are down and the winches are torn out of place; the deck is shot full of thermite holes and shrapnel holes.

"The Navy gunners went on GQ during the afternoon and, after the dead and wounded were removed on barges and DUWKs, I resumed my post as the loader on the No. 8 20mm," the diary notes continue. "Six more suicide planes came in at 1715 hours. Our forward gunners concentrated on several planes, and none of us saw, until too late, a Jap single-engine bomber which came in from dead ahead, strafing, and hit No. 3 boom, causing its 550-pound bomb to explode. The plane itself hit the fore part of the bridge house and the engine went through three steel bulkheads and dented a fourth before it stopped. It hit on the chief engineer's room on the port side, leaving a hole big enough for a truck to drive through.

"There were more casualties, dead and wounded, scattered across the fore-deck and monkey bridge. Navy gunner S. B. Collins, manning the No. 4 20mm, lost both legs, but crawled his way out of the fire. 'Well, I guess they got them,' he told me, pointing to his missing legs. 'Oh, well, I can't wait till I kick the side of my horse with my wooden ones!' He's from Texas. What courage!"

Writing hours later "when the shooting stopped," Mariner Thompson notes: "Everybody did a lot of talking just to let off steam, but they also were preparing for the next attack we thought certain would come. The ship was badly damaged, but not in danger of sinking. Every last man on this ship stood up well and is doing his part to ensure an early victory for us. A lot of credit must be given the boys in the Navy Armed Guard. . . .

"Much credit must also be given to the Merchant Marine. We're sometimes called 'draft dodgers.' That's a laugh! Most of the men are in their forties and fifties, some in their sixties. Even prisoners who have had sea experience have been paroled from jail . . . to return to their previous jobs on ships. . . . I can never let it be said that the men of the Merchant Marine do not go through as much hell as the boys in the so-called 'armed service.' The Japs are after our shipping and, from what I hear, it's tougher in the Atlantic, where the Nazis have been sinking ships right and left. We will carry supplies all over the world to our fighting men and no amount of Axis guns or powder can stop us!"

"Fortunately," Brigadier General Thompson observes in 1994, "a 1988 act of the U.S. Congress gave World War II veterans' status to those who served in the Merchant Marine."

26 November 1944
Bilibid Prison, the Philippines

Chief Warrant Officer Clifford A. Roberts submitted the POW diary-letter of his brother, First Lieutenant Hugh H. Roberts, which he began writing 26 November 1944 from Bilibid Prison.

"Four days ago, the Japs moved a general and his staff into camp for protection from bombing and we were issued a truckload of cassava (an edible tree root that tapioca is made from that tasted like Irish potatoes) and for two days we got about four ounces for supper," he writes in his lengthy and only letter. "The men all decided the Yanks were just around the corner and we would all be free Thanksgiving, but the cassava was a four-day issue and the cooks gave it all to us because it won't keep four days. Now the men are all downhearted because we only get rice, and also there has been no tobacco in camp for a month and many men suffer more from that than from hunger. Some even trade their food for tobacco."

"I was brought to Bilibid on November 13 on the way to Japan but air raids sank all the boats as fast as they could bring them in, so they have failed so far to get us out," First Lieutenant Roberts writes in what become prophetic terms. "I think they have given up trying but they act by instinct instead of reason.

"Today is November 29 and tomorrow is Thanksgiving and I sure have a lot to be thankful for, being alive and American troops only 200 miles away. . . .

"This letter is getting bulky. I think I will close it. It is up to date anyway." He signs it: "With lots of love, Hugh."

Concerning his brother's diary-letter, Mr. Roberts says that "one other letter reached the States," but it was a duplicate of the one the family had already received.

In another of those palpable ironies of the First Lieutenant Roberts story, a picture of him appears almost a year after his death, accompanying an article about the fall of Bataan and Corregidor, written by General Wainwright and published in the Washington, D.C., *Evening Star* 18 October 1945.

"Someone in Seattle, who knew Hugh, saw it and called our mother and sent her the article. It supposedly is the only picture smuggled out of the area during the war," Mr. Roberts writes. The photo caption reads: "Pfc. Avon Sherman and First Lieutenant H. H. Roberts eating doughnuts, one of the dietary staples for General Wainwright's hungry defenders of Bataan."

For First Lieutenant Roberts who, minus food, had survived his five-day, 60-mile march from Bataan to San Fernando, the November 1944 transfer to Bilibid was his fourth since arrival at POW Camp O'Donnell in mid-April 1942. With U.S. troops in the Philippines and with his brother Clifford as close as the other side of the island aboard the destroyer USS *Luce*, First Lieutenant Roberts died 15 December 1944 when American planes targeted the Japanese ship transporting him and other POWs to Japan.

September 1944–June 1945
Missions to Guadalcanal, the Philippines, and Okinawa

Lieutenant Colonel Carl P. Writer graduated from college, was commissioned into the USMCR, and married his high-school sweetheart, all on 24 November 1943.

After training on the F4F Wildcat and the F4U-1 Corsair, Second Lieutenant Writer shipped out for Guadalcanal in September 1944 on CVE-85 *Shipley Bay*. On 23 September 1944, "Bougainville, Able-Charlie Beach, was the first hop."

Second Lieutenant Writer "joined VMF223 with three friends, all still around. We went a long way together. It was an alphabetical thing: Weston, Wozniack, Writer, and Zorn. We were at the fighter strip, Piva North. Flew patrol, bombing, strafing, escorting SBD to Rabaul."

On Sunday, 1 November, Lieutenant Writer participated in "a four-plane bombing mission on a village on Duke of York Island, off Rabaul," where they strafed an airfield. He was "shot down, landed in the water, and was picked up by a Dumbo Navy PBY out of Green Island." By 9 November, he was "back on flight status."

"The squadron stood down to go to the Philippines, where suicide planes were giving the Navy a bad time. Left on 8 January 1945. Flew up Bougainville, Emerin, Hollandia, Biak, Peleliu (still fighting there), and on to Samar, the Philippines," where their first flight was 15 January on a convoy cover, "strafing and providing close air support for the Army." In June, it was on to Okinawa, from where they flew their first mission 15 June 1945, "intercepting suicide planes about 100 miles out."

24 November 1944

Saipan

Major Geraldine Wells was an a U.S. Army nurse, second lieutenant, who left Hawaii with about ten other Army nurses to join their unit, the 176th Station Hospital on Saipan.

"It was the day after Thanksgiving, Saipan, 1944" when the nurses arrived, "packed along with cargo in a C-47, or C-54, sitting in bucket seats," Major Wells writes. "It was at the break of dawn; we were peering out the tiny windows, trying to get a glimpse of the island where we had arrived. Our thoughts were on '*What is it like to nurse battle casualties? Would we perform at our best? How long would we be here?*'

"Suddenly, there were two long runways! Planes were lined up all along them! Just as suddenly, they began to take off, alternating runways! We watched these perfect take-offs, with precision timing, seconds apart. Our cargo plane circled and circled. . . . I can't remember that anyone said a word. We just watched. Then we landed. A young airman came running out to our plane with outstretched arms: 'Ladies, welcome to Saipan! You have just seen history made. This is our first big airstrike on Tokyo!' They were B-29s!

"As I've reflected on this sight over the years, lumps still come in the throat! I witnessed not only our U.S. Air Force on a super mission; I had witnessed a nation on a mission. . . .

"The air missions were with us daily during my tour of duty on Saipan. At dawn, we could hear the planes take off. At dusk, we could hear and sometimes see them return—motors sputtering, wings or another part of the plane tattered. Always the question: '*How many have returned?*'

"My first night on Saipan, my tentmate and I were suddenly awakened with, 'Halt! Who goes there?' We both sat up, with the stark realization of where we were: in a battle zone! We had come almost around the world for this!

"Most of our battle casualties were from Iwo Jima. They were so young! Once, before a hospital-ward inspection, I suggested to a young blond Marine that he shave. His reply came: 'Lieutenant, I have never shaved but once before in my life.' I believed him."

November 1944

En Route to Metz, France

Colonel Jean W. Christy continues with his 5th Infantry Division account.

In November 1944, with the weather continuing rainy and cold, "the Third Army under General Patton mounted an all-out assault on the city of Metz to wrest it from the Wehrmacht. The city had never been taken by assault in the history of modern warfare, going back before Charlemagne in the A.D. 600s. It is probably just as well that most of us were unaware of this historical fact," Colonel Christy comments, as he details activities recorded in the battalion's "Record of Events." Spelling or numerical errors may be the result of referring to a fourth-carbon copy, he says.

For the assault on Metz, "the attack jumped off on time," 9 November. "At 0600 the 2nd Battalion passed through the 3rd, and crossed the Seille River on foot-bridges between Longueville and Cheminot, and south of Cheminot. . . . Cheminot fell without resistance. Only one man was in the town, and he came out with a white flag. The 2nd Battalion occupied its objective rapidly.

"The 1st Battalion crossed the Seille River south of Cheminot . . . to a point south of Louvigny. In the afternoon they assaulted the town. . . .

"Lieutenant Clegg, from an organic OP, did a lot of shooting at the Germans, trying to evacuate the north end of Louvigny. Our fire was so effective that some of the enemy were observed to raise their hands and walk back . . . to surrender. . . ."

On 11 November, "as the 6th Armored approached the river, the bridge at Ancerville was blown." They crossed the next day on a bridge between Aube and Sanry. They occupied Sanry, then the division objective, Vaucremont.

Notes for the 13th record: "Three counterattacks—all at Sanry" and "low on ammunition on hand. Trains have been sent for more."

On 14 November, "the whole division has begun to move north . . . , meeting relatively little resistance. Last night . . . there was fighting in the streets [of Sanry]. The tanks bounced 75mm shells down the street, ricochet fire. The American troops stayed inside and any moving thing out in the streets was fired on. This morning there were an estimated 100 Germans dead."

On the 15th, "during the attack, Lieutenant Clegg was captured. He was firing a mission on a counterattack. . . . We heard him say on the radio, 'Cease firing, I am captured.'

"The 6th Armored has . . . moved out of the bridgehead. The 1st Battalion has a detachment in Ancerville. . . . We hear that it has been put up to General Patton: We can either hold the bridgehead (over the Seille River) and hold the line we are on—or we can give up the bridgehead and move forward. He is to make a decision."

Notes for the 16th indicate "3rd Battalion . . . moved forward under our plastering and took their objective easily. They are very tired. . . . We hope to get our positions close enough to town [Christy says 'Fontay' but questions the spelling] to get the men in out of the weather and give them a chance to dry off. The men, particularly the infantry, are beginning to have trouble with 'trench foot' due to the wet and cold."

In his own notes, Colonel Christy observes: "Trench foot became such a universal problem that General Patton issued orders that, throughout the Third Army, clean, dry socks for each man would be brought up daily with the food rations. The intention was for the men to be able to change into dry socks each day."

On 17 November, "overshoes were issued. It is the first time the men have had overshoes since we left Ireland." That same evening, orders were received from division for the plan to take Metz. At 0830 on 18 November, Fort St. Quentin fell, the last fort between the division and Metz.

After the "1st Battalion made contact with the 90th Infantry Division, closing the ring around Metz" on 19 November, "we were firing into Metz," journal records proclaim. On 20 November, "the gap around Metz is completely closed. . . . During the day, E Company took some 800 prisoners, Germans trying to escape out of the trap."

"And so Metz fell," Colonel Christy adds. "We all heard about how, soon after, General Patton had visited our 5th Infantry Division headquarters and our division commander, Major General Stuart LeRoy (Red) Irwin. Patton had put his hand around the division commander's shoulders and said, 'Thanks, Stu. Thanks for Metz.'

"In all honesty, however, it should be noted that the 80th Infantry Division, the 90th Infantry Division, the 95th Infantry Division, the 10th Armored Division, and any number of Corps and Army artillery battalions, engineer battalions, and other support units also participated in taking Metz."

November 1944
En Route to Metz, France

Colonel William M. McConahey, battalion surgeon, continues his story.

"Early in November, the 90th Division was replaced by the 10th Armored Division (fresh from the States) and we pulled back for a two or three days' rest. When that happened we knew that General Patton had another tough job for us, and we weren't kept waiting long," Colonel McConahey writes.

"The 90th was to cross the Moselle November 9, so several days before that, the division moved secretly at night to the point of attack near Cattenom and got 'under cover.' All the division symbols on our helmets and uniforms were covered, as were the '90s' on the vehicles. Our artillery battalion's command post and aid station were in one of the large underground forts of the Maginot Line, and there I lived for about ten days. It was quite an interesting place, with its moats, steel doors, disappearing machine-gun turrets, gun ports, thick concrete walls, deep subterranean rooms. . . .

"The weather as usual was terrible—cold, muddy, and pouring rains. The mud was worst of all. I knew how the infantry would be feeling. . . . There is a strange, disquieting feeling of being alone—alone with the enemy and with death.

"Before daylight the morning of 9 November, the attack began. Our infantry crossed the river in rubber assault boats (in a cold, drizzling rain) without previous artillery preparation, catching the Germans by surprise. By daylight our boys had a good toehold on the east bank, and by nightfall all three infantry regiments were across.

"But then nature hit us a crack. Because of the heavy rains, the Moselle River began to rise and within a few hours we had the worst Moselle flood in fifty years. When the first infantrymen slipped across the river before dawn, it was a swift-flowing stream a couple of hundred yards wide, but by evening it had become a raging torrent nearly a mile across, over which the engineers were unable to put a bridge. As a result, the infantrymen were really 'on their own.'"

Isolated, without "overcoats, raincoats or blankets," with "no overshoes" and with little food or ammunition, "those boys stood fast against the fury of desperate counterattacks, threw back the enemy, and advanced across the heavily mined fields in the face of fanatical resistance.

"The key to the enemy defenses in this area was Fort Koenigsmacher . . . , a series of steel and concrete strongpoints built into the top of a commanding hill . . . [with] underground passages, dozens of machine-gun emplacements, anti-tank ditches, four disappearing 150mm artillery pieces. . . . But it fell to the undying courage and determination of the infantry. Some of the boys of the 358th

Regiment fought their way to the top of it, poured burning gasoline into the ventilators, blew open the massive steel doors with composition C and routed out the *Boche*. . . .

"Still the raging river prevented help from getting across to the hard-pressed combat soldiers. The artillery cub planes dropped medical supplies, composition C, and blankets to the troops. . . . At last, however, the river began to recede, and the engineers started to work on two bridges: one in our area at Cattenom and one down the river several miles where the 359th Infantry had crossed."

After the bridge at Cattenom was completed and the 344th Field Artillery crossed that night, "the infantry pushed ahead fast, and we moved frequently in order to give them close support." In one of the towns that was captured, lost, then recaptured again by the Americans, "German dead littered the streets. . . . When I walked across the field I had trouble walking around or stepping over the bodies. . . .

"Two days later we made contact with the 6th Armored Division. The 5th and 95th Divisions had entered Metz and the battle for that fortress was over. For the first time in history, Metz had fallen to an attacking force."

November 1944
Drusenheim, France, to Germany

Lieutenant Colonel Romolo D. Tedeschi was with 128th Supply and Evacuation Regiment in Aversa, Italy, in April 1944.

After paratroop training in Rome, Lieutenant Colonel Tedeschi says, he was temporarily attached to the 50th Parachute Battalion in Marseille, destined for Leyte in the Philippines. However, with the surprise German advance in France, he was assigned in November as platoon leader, Heavy Weapons Platoon, Company A, 314th Battalion, 79th Infantry Division, stationed near Drusenheim, France. On reporting, some of the men "reminded me that I was the seventh officer to head the platoon since D-Day, the other six having been killed in action." He told them that he "wasn't planning on being killed in combat by those damn Germans."

"In addition to flushing out the Germans from the town, part of our mission was to rescue the so-called 'Lost Battalion' of the Rainbow Division. We accomplished both following heavy fighting, which included dangerous house-to-house fighting. . . .

During the latter, "we found many French villagers cowering in their cellars, . . . fearful that the Germans might return. Looking for the Germans, I walked down a driveway and cautiously walked to a door into the cellar, and there they were—six Germans, ready and waiting. I fired a blast with my .30-caliber rifle and ran back up the driveway, just ahead of two grenades, yelling to my men. The Germans would not surrender, but started running away from the house. I ordered my men to shoot the officer, since it was obvious that the other men wanted to surrender. Once the officer was killed, the others surrendered.

"We chased the Germans out of town and took a holding action during which our battalion found itself surrounded by a division of paratroopers fresh from Norway. Our artillery had been diverted to another sector, meaning that we could not have any artillery support until late the next day.

"Surrender was inevitable. Personnel from some of the other companies came to my headquarters. There were more than sixty men in the house. I had them all burn and destroy whatever weapons they had before surrendering. Unhappily, I destroyed my weapons: a .45 pistol, .45-caliber grease gun (submachine gun), and my .30-cal folding stock rifle, as well as my parachute wings.

"The Germans came house to house, ordering us to surrender. We had no choice and no communication from headquarters. I was concerned for the safety of my men, as well as the safety of a friendly French Resistance fighter. We helped him escape, giving him a white sheet as camouflage in the snow. . . . We were then marched to the Rhine River, onto boats, and to the German headquarters for interrogation. We were treated well by the German soldiers and given a bowl of hot barley, most welcome on a cold, snowy winter day. A German sergeant came to us speaking perfect English, asking how we all were doing. He was an American from Egg Harbor, New Jersey, who had been drafted by the Germans while visiting his mother early in the war.

"We, twenty-six officers, were then taken across the Rhine River and moved east to Germany's interior to a German headquarters where we were held for questioning." When a German captain inquired why they killed German prisoners, the captives "immediately denied any such shootings."

"We hoped that we had convinced him," Lieutenant Colonel Tedeschi continues, "but we were then marched out about two miles to a wooded area and brought to a halt. I was certain that we were to be shot on the spot. I recall praying very hard that this would not happen. I still believe that God intervened, for the few German soldiers guarding us suddenly turned us around and marched us back to headquarters." *[Lieutenant Colonel Tedeschi's story continues in March and May 1945 chapters.]*

November 1944

Near Peulis, Belgium

Chief Warrant Officer Sidney Bowen was with the 494th Anti-Aircraft Artillery
Gun Battalion, Battery.

"I sent my laundry out with a kid who visits us regularly. His mother did it
up beautifully last week; every hole was patched with a precision that made me
feel guilty at the price I paid," T-4 Sidney Bowen writes in one of his near-daily
letters to wife Isabel in November 1944.

"Along with several other anti-aircraft gun battalions, we were assigned positions in a checkerboard pattern between the V-1 launching sites and the Port of
Antwerp," he notes on 16 November as he describes how "the scale of the German attack assumed staggering proportions when the Germans diverted all their
V-1 bomb attacks from England to the Port of Antwerp," upon realizing that "the
destruction of the port facilities was essential."

"Had a bit of excitement late in the afternoon," he writes on 18 November.
"We picked up an incoming V-1, and we locked on the target. Our 90s opened
fire, and we could trace the paths of the projectiles racing toward the V-1. The V-
1 took a body hit and shot straight upwards as it reached our site. We kept it on
the PPI [pre-positioned indicator] screen and then observed that the target had
reversed in flight and was headed rapidly downward toward us. We were preparing to jump out of the radar when the V-1 abruptly leveled off at approximately
the altitude of the incoming pattern, but due to some malfunction of the gyro-
scope control, headed back toward the direction of the German launching site. A
chorus of cheers from everyone climaxed this unprecedented event," Sidney tells
Isabel in the letter that ends with "millions of paper kisses."

"We knew it was Thanksgiving Day by the deluge of food," he writes on 23
November. "I'll try to list the works: roast turkey and dressing, mashed potatoes
and gravy, cranberry sauce, peas, bread and butter, peach pie, an apple, and coffee. The birds were not cremated Army-style. They had been taken to a local bakery and roasted in their bakery ovens."

November 1944

The Netherlands

Lieutenant Colonel A. Ray Kubly, shot down and wounded on mission seven,
escaped from the Netherlands hospital where he had been held prisoner.

Crediting the Dutch Underground with arranging the first phase of his
escape, Colonel Kubly describes Pegasus I, "The Great Escape," that took place
22 October when 130 U.S., British, and Canadian military, plus three Russians,

were provided with fresh uniforms and weapons, led through German front-line positions from Ede to Renkum, and taken down to the Rhine to cross to the south bank in assault boats, as agreed upon in a plan with Second Army.

The escapees had been participants in Operation Market Garden, the airborne invasion of Arnhem, the Netherlands. Most were "English escapees that the Dutch Resistance gathered in the area around Ede." The three Russians "disappeared as suddenly and as mysteriously as they appeared."

On 14 November, "we all had a little party . . . in Leersum prior to our departure for another attempt to go through the front lines. This was to be Pegasus II.

"Jack Murrell and I were then led by two girls to the home of the Idenburg family. . . . While there, a German patrol came through the area looking for anyone suspicious. Jack and I hid under some evergreen trees where we could see the Germans' feet as they walked by. . . .

"We ended up in the woods between Ede and Otterlo where Gerit Van Ee was our Underground guide. We were issued English uniforms and ordered to hide in the woods for the arrival of Major Maquire and his other Underground friends. . . .

On 18 November, "we got going after dark. . . . Each one of us tied a cloth rope to our belt behind our back so we could hang on to each other and not get lost. The experienced English Rangers and airborne fellows were up front, while we 'fly-boys' brought up the rear. We were all excited because they said we would be across the river by midnight and be drinking wine! We were to cross the Rhine between Renkum and Wageningen. . . .

"After walking across fields and down through fire lanes in the woods, we heard a voice calling, 'Halt!' All at once, someone yelled, 'Germans!' Then machine-gun fire erupted up in front of the group. We threw our English sten guns in the woods and ran as fast as we could in the direction we had been coming from. Our idea was to get back to the wooded area and try to contact the Underground again.

"From about fifty men that started out, forty or more were taken POW, with eight being wounded and one killed. As far as we know, Jack Murrell and I were among the few to have evaded capture. . . .

"At daybreak, we were extremely thirsty, hungry, and tired. An old farmer gave us some warm milk and some kind of hot porridge. He showed us where to cover up with some hay and we slept all day in the barn."

Upon waking, the two took off in search of Underground contacts. From the home of the Donkers family, they were guided to "a little country guest hotel named *Leperkoen*, owned by a Mr. Schreuder," where they remained in the attic for about ten days, when temperatures fell below freezing. Their next stop, for four days, was at the home of the Barneveld postmaster, Dries Klooster, whose two young sons were used "as couriers and for other Underground activities." By the time the Germans came looking for them in the Klooster home, escapees Kubly and Murrell were on the outskirts of Barneveld at the home of Cor Lof.

"The time between 5 December to late February 1945 went slowly as the Battle of the Bulge was going on nearby. We saw lots of air battles when the sky was clear. Cor Lof and family, plus Jan Mulder and Kasper Reinstra, were our contact with the Dutch Underground." *[Lieutenant Colonel Kubly's story concludes in the March 1945 chapter.]*

1944

Rome, Italy

Lieutenant Colonel Carlos E. Dominguez was with AFHQ Intelligence, Algiers and Oran, as officer courier to General Eisenhower, and then in Psychological Warfare Branch (PWB).

After a brief period in Sicily and nine months in Naples, the PWB office moved to Rome, where it remained for one year. Lieutenant Colonel Dominguez recalls being handed his assignment—"a pile of old yellow papers, about people," presented to him in December 1943 in Algiers—by Mr. C. A. Ralegh Radford, deputy director of PWB. . . .

Conferred upon the young officer, along with the yellow papers, was the title "Mr. Personalities" and the challenge to "learn how to get along in Italian" in three months. This meant that as chief of *Who's Who*, from beginning till end of the Italian Campaign, he was responsible for having and supplying information on Italian political and military personalities to all Allied forces and embassies.

He started out with "no help (except one American sergeant), no typewriters, no furniture, and no office," and was the only American in the Intelligence Section of PWB. "I began to make acquaintances and to establish good relations with other Intelligence groups in our area of operations to the point that I was able to borrow, on a temporary basis, help, typewriters, some furniture, et cetera." Finding an empty fifth-floor office, which nobody wanted because it was a walk-up, Lieutenant Colonel Dominguez says he became "sort of a scrounger," determined to prove that Americans could perform the mission assigned.

When Director Radford showed up in Rome one day and finally found the American's office, he left with commendations for the seven he found working there. "The next day I was called down to the second floor where our 'high command' was located and was asked without any preambles what I needed. I even got a telephone installed in my office."

Fortified with supplies and personnel, including two British refugees fluent in eight and five languages, respectively, PWB plunged into "gathering and evaluating all information possible" from "newspaper editors, local police files, existing *Who's Who*, liberated and occupied Italian newspapers, radio monitors, visiting partisans, and our own agents who may be college professors, students, or patriots."

Lieutenant Colonel Dominguez notes that "when the German Front began to collapse in Northern Italy" and plans were made to transfer his D Section to Milan, he began to realize the potency of work accomplished when "both embassies as well as most of the Intelligence groups around Rome began to protest not only by personal visits and telephone calls but also in writing."

"In view of the interest shown for our files," Lieutenant Colonel Dominguez and Mr. Radford decided that while "the files belonged to the Allied Forces and all original documents had to be sent to Caserta, Italy," both British and American embassies should have copies. Arrangements were made to have them microfilmed and copied.

"The original files were in a wooden box, marked *Secret* all over. It measured $60 \times 28 \times 14$ and weighed 450 pounds." At war's end, when that file "contained dossiers on over 22,000 Italian personalities," he "lugged this box around, from office to port of embarkation, and from the ship in New York to Washington, D.C.," where he spent three days answering questions about its contents.

October–November 1944
POW Camps, Formosa to Manchuria

Colonel Michael A. Quinn continues his diary entries from his new camp in Manchuria.

On 7 November, one month after his 7 October journal entry from POW Camp Shirakawa in Formosa, Colonel Quinn resumes his journal writings from his new camp, Hoten, at Chen Chia Tung, about 150 kilometers north of Fengtien (formerly Mukden), Manchuria. For eight printed pages in his book, he describes the month-long odyssey that takes 250 prisoners "from the subtropics to the subarctic in one jump," as they travel what would be the equivalent of about 1,500 air miles in everything from narrow-gauge gondola and trains, to ships and street cars that resembled "'goat' cars—one truck, four wheels."

Notified of the move at 2000 hours on 8 October, the POWs leave camp at 0400 on 9 October after being provided "rice and soup for breakfast and an extra rice ball for the noon meal." Taken by gondola to a larger town, they entrain for Tiahoku, arriving there about 1740.

"We were hustled aboard a ship, the *Oryoko Maru* [the ship that would be bombed 15 December], and were jammed into a space about one-third of normal requirements. The hold we were in was a watertight compartment," the colonel writes.

From Fusan on the 11th, "at about 2130, we entrained and were under way. . . . We had excellent meals while traveling, and once drew apples, the first in about three years. Lord, how good they were! We crossed the Yalu River about noon on the 13th. The weather was growing colder . . . so we were issued a blanket and fur-collared overcoats and some captured uniforms. I drew a pair of Scots plaid trousers, a Gordon Highland outfit with a cutaway Highland jacket. . . . Snow and ice on the 13th, and on the 14th we arrived at our new camp."

For the colonel, there are reunions with two who had left POW Camp Karenko, Formosa, in April 1943: Governor Tjarda of the Netherlands East Indies and Colonel Quinn's old boss, General Wainwright. But transfers, yet again, compel him to write on Thanksgiving Day, 30 November: "Went to say good-bye to General Wainwright. . . . This is the only time I have ever seen Skinny bitter, and he really was. . . . Wainwright doesn't look good at all. He is emaciated and seems to have lost a tremendous amount of weight. He never had too much to spare anyway. It seemed to me that I could see a deadening of his spirits. . . ."

In the few nontravel notes that he includes in his November writings, Colonel Quinn mentions that Red Cross packages are in "but no action taken on their distribution." He adds: "We hear that Franklin D. Roosevelt has been reelected, though, and that makes Harry Truman vice-president. The last time I knew of him he was a major in the Field Artillery in Missouri."

EDITOR'S NOTE: *Dual dates of 23 and 30 November for Thanksgiving in the preceding stories reflect what was wryly referred to as the Republican and Democrats' Thanksgivings. Since Lincoln's proclamation in 1863, the last Thursday in November had been traditionally observed. In 1939, President Roosevelt introduced the third Thursday celebration, in effect for several years, ostensibly to provide merchants with a longer season for holiday shopping]*

DECEMBER 1944

37

For U.S. troops in December 1944, fighting ranges from the bitter-cold Ardennes in the ETO to rain- and sun-soaked Pacific Islands, where ships and troops are already converging for the January invasion of Luzon. For American service members and civilians, it will mark the fourth of the Christmas and Hanukkah holidays of World War II. While some military personnel observe the occasions for a few brief moments, others are barely able to acknowledge their passing.

In a requiescat for about 750 men, Colonel William C. Hollis writes in his diary on Christmas Day 1944 from Cherbourg, France: "It was a sad day here and was sadder for the families in the USA, but they didn't know that their sons had died on Christmas Eve." He refers to members of the 66th Division, 262nd and 264th Regiments, who died when the Belgium liner *Leopoldville* was torpedoed in the English Channel by German sub U-486, five to eight miles from Cherbourg Harbor.

At Saarlautern, Germany, on Christmas Day, Colonel Jean W. Christy remembers the special announcement to 1st Battalion, 2nd Infantry Regiment, when time-of-attack orders are changed for the fourth time at 1100 hours. "To hell with it! We're going to have a hot Christmas dinner, and *then* we'll attack," Battalion Commander Lieutenant Colonel Bill Blakefield declares.

Off the island of Biak, LST-18 had just finished loading high-octane gas, artillery ammo, cargo, and troops for the invasion of Luzon when "word was passed that anyone wanting to attend Christmas Eve services would be allowed to go ashore that evening." It was a beautiful night with "millions of fireflies in the air," Chief Warrant Officer David L. Wischemann recalls. "Somehow, I attended a Catholic Mass, and understood not a bit of what went on [with liturgy then in Latin], but I enjoyed it anyway."

In Chengtu, China, a twenty-two-year-old pilot with the Twentieth Air Force hears "White Christmas" from "the fella in the next tent," who plays it "over and over and over." Lieutenant Colonel Nick J. Soulis recalls that "on a pillow wet with tears," he was thinking of the white Christmases in North Dakota and wondering "when the war would end and when he would quit playing 'White Christmas.'"

24 December 1944
Cherbourg Harbor and English Channel

Lieutenant Colonel Arthur R. Hummel was one of four officers and eight non-coms aboard S.T. 539, part of 357th Harborcraft Company, when the call came to assist the Leopoldville.

Lieutenant Colonel Hummel remembers 24 December as "a stormy, windy day," with "ship and barge movements minimized in the harbor." S.T. 539, an 85-foot, 600hp diesel Army tug, was standing by a freighter when at "about 1630 to 1700 hours, . . . we received a radio message from the control tower to stand by to possibly go to the relief of a stricken craft," he writes in a 1955 report of the *Leopoldville* disaster.

"We knew that it would be rough in the channel. . . . My guess estimated about a twenty-foot sea. . . . We were subjected to violent pitching, throwing our stern and propeller clear of water and causing the ship to vibrate violently momentarily until the engineer could cut power. Our forward motion was slow and seemingly an eternity before we reached our destination. . . . I would say about an hour to an hour and fifteen minutes were involved. . . .

"As we approached, we could see the troops lining the rails. . . . I found that I had my hands full just trying to keep clear of other craft in the area since it seemed that each wave and wind would carry the tug about 300 feet.

"[T]he liner was sitting pretty well but all of a sudden she started to sink lower. . . . Not too much time had elapsed since we had arrived—I would say not over thirty minutes—and I don't believe that we could have gotten in close enough to her bow to have secured a towing hawser without having crashed into her. She did sink rapidly and we could see troops jumping as the water approached the decks. . . .

"As soon as she went under, we moved in toward the mass of men. . . . The entire crew began to pull the survivors aboard. . . .

"We were amazed at the gear these troops had on, overcoats, packs, web equipment, and the like. . . . It required about three of us to pull each man in but some of the survivors, pulled in early, assisted the crew later in rescue work. . . . Some men were so far gone or frozen that they couldn't help themselves to safety and were lost. . . . We counted the preservers left the next day and although I can't recall the exact number, I do know we had over sixty jackets," Lieutenant Colonel Hummel reports.

Summarizing his conclusions about loss of life in the *Leopoldville* disaster, he cites excessive gear loading down the troops; the Belgian liner's antiquated life-jackets that were "not of sufficient buoyancy to hold weight"; and the fact, reported by his CO and other officers ashore, that officers and crew of the *Leo-poldville* were in Cherbourg Harbor "about the time of our departure from the scene" in S.T. 539.

Lieutenant Colonel Hummel's 1955 report was written in response to a magazine advertisment requesting information about the incident. His and other replies served as basis for the book *A Night before Christmas* by Jacquin Sanders.

Listing other factors contributory to the loss of many lives, Mr. Sanders cites the Christmas holidays and concomitant absence of many of the ship's key personnel and also crew members from potential rescue vessels in Cherbourg Harbor; language barriers and frictions among British, Belgian, and Congalese crew; little communication between American officers and non-English-speaking crew and, reputedly, the captain; malfunctioning public address system in certain areas of the ship; only fourteen lifeboats for more than 2,200 soldiers and 230 crew; the initial delay in sounding the distress signal; and a fifty-minute snafu in relaying requests for assistance when, because of differing radio signals, the distress had to be sent via Southampton to Cherbourg.

24 and 25 December 1944
Cherbourg, France

Colonel John M. Hollis submits an excerpt from the WWII diary of his father, Colonel William C. Hollis, who was with G-3 section of HQ 4th Port located in Cherbourg, France.

On Sunday, 24 December 1944, Colonel William C. Hollis records the following in his diary: "Went to St. Clements. At 1800, went with DeBush to see troops come ashore. There, got word of the damaging of Belgian ship *Leopoldville* by mines or torpedo. Went to Navy landing on Avant Port. About forty injured were carried ashore. Later went to end of Gare Mereline where tugs, et cetera, were bringing walking and stretcher cases ashore. About twenty dead were laid out. They all seemed to have died of exposure. A doctor examined their eyes and listened to their hearts.

"Left dock about 2400 and returned to the hotel. The dining room had been cleared of tables and benches and was filled with men sleeping on the floor. The 280th Station Hospital was filled. The dispensary had about twenty, and other hospitals had some. Went to room of Lieutenant Colonel Arumdel, who had prepared an Xmas spread of cake, sandwiches, punch, et cetera. He brought in the ship's captain, first mate, surgeon, and we all talked. The captain said it was a mine and it blew up aft in the most crowded section, then one deck fell in. The rescue boat took one hour to get there even though it was only 8 miles out. A British destroyer took off at 0600. The wind had dropped, though waves were very high."

November and December 1944

Moselle and Saar Rivers

Colonel Martin Lifschultz writes of two river crossings as an infantryman with 2nd Battalion, 358th Infantry, 90th Division.

In early November, for their first river-crossing, he and his men were given the mission "to cross the Moselle by assault boats and capture Fort Koenigs-macher." In a heavy rainstorm on election night, they moved by truck "to within 200 yards of the river at Cattenom" and "heard on shortwave radio that President Roosevelt had been reelected," Colonel Lifschultz recalls.

After crossing safely, "on our second day, we moved up to the high ground overlooking the river, and prepared for the attack on the fort. Company A of the 1st Battalion was the first to reach the fort. They poured gallon after gallon of gasoline into the fort's ventilators and ignited them with white phosphorous grenades. Our G Company positioned itself behind the fort. The German defenders, blackened by smoke and flames, desperately rushed out the rear of the fort. They were captured by our company."

For the second river crossing, "on 5 December, we received orders to cross the Saar in the vicinity of Dillingen, Germany. We approached the point of crossing under heavy artillery fire. The light rain that had accompanied us as we moved on turned into a heavy downpour. Kowalski and I approached a steep hill that led to the river's edge. We started down. Men were sliding in the mud, unable to get any kind of foothold.

"I slid down the hill about twenty-five feet into a tree. I discarded the four mortar shells I was carrying. I continued by sliding on my back, lost my carbine as I went down, and discarded my extra clips. Twenty-five more feet of sliding brought me to the river bank. There was a narrow footbridge to cross. On the other side, I could see the Protestant chaplain shouting encouragement to the thin line of GIs making the crossing.

Once across the river, "I joined a small group of men from A Company," who "loaned me an M-1 rifle. We approached a house, from which we could hear German soldiers speaking to one another. A corporal from our group yelled out: '*Deutches soldaten, kommen Sie rauch mit Hände hoch!*' They were the professionally trained troops we had fought in France.

"I caught up with my unit several days later. . . . While holding a defensive position in one of the many German pillboxes lining the banks of the Saar, we heard the startling news of von Rundstedt's counterattack in what was to become known as the Battle of the Bulge."

Late Fall 1944
Vosges Mountains, France

Colonel Lorenzo D. Atkinson served as captain with 772nd FA Battalion.

As the Allied Army mounted its offensive in late November and early December, our mission "as a Corps Artillery separate battalion was to cross the Vosges Mountains (4,500-feet elevation) and provide supporting artillery fire to the American 79th Infantry Division, which was to move over the mountains and across the plain to a position near Limburg and Haguenau," Colonel Atkinson writes. "The 79th was to move through a northern pass while our 772nd FA Battalion followed an armored division through another southern pass. The 79th was to be in position between us and the retreating Germans.

"It started snowing the night we moved out. The higher we got on the crooked mountain road, the deeper the snow got. Fortunately, there was an armored unit in front of us breaking trail. Over the mountains, down on the plain, we came to a major road junction and saw that the armored column and our lead battalion (containing our command-and-control elements) had headed southwest toward Strasbourg. All road signs pointed the same way but the map and compass indicated another road to the east. After discussion, I made a 'command decision' and ordered the column to follow the new route. Later we found that the Germans were switching signs as they retreated in front of us.

"So, here we were at midnight, in the middle of a blinding snowstorm, chasing the rear elements of an armored panzer unit through the night. Every so often, our lead elements, part of an anti-aircraft unit assigned to protect us, would encounter small-arms fire, or light artillery, which the .50-quad unit or the 90mm would open up on in return.

"By morning, we arrived at our assigned position and found ourselves faced with small-arms, light-cannon, and mortar fire from across an open field 500 to 1,000 yards wide. The 79th Infantry was no place to be seen. Establishing a front line was not the mission of a field artillery battalion, but we had no choice.

"Placing our guns in a ditch behind some railroad tracks, we leveled our tubes point-blank across the tracks and fired at anything that fired at us. Our projectiles weighed about fifty-five pounds and had the fragmentation of a 155 round. Firing soon came to a stop, as the Germans probably thought they were facing a medi-um- or heavy-tank unit. Our .50-caliber and .30-caliber machine guns were posi-tioned between and at the end of our string of twelve artillery pieces. We did have firepower!

"Within three days, the 79th was able to complete its move through the snow-clogged roads, and our missing headquarters battery rejoined us, together with the service battery. With the infantry in place between our guns and the enemy, we were able to point the tubes toward the Rhine River and begin destroying bridges over which the Germans were fleeing. But then the Battle of the Bulge began. In a couple days, we were pulled back over the icy mountain roads to help 'pinch off' the penetration. The temperature had dropped to a $-4°$ during this period."

December 1944
Mission to France

Lieutenant Colonel Bart Hagerman was a twenty-one-year-old private first class, serving as 60mm mortar gunner in Company D, 193rd Glider Infantry Regiment, 17th Airborne Division.

"The 17th Airborne trained in England until the Germans initiated the Ardennes Offensive," on 16 December, Lieutenant Colonel Hagerman writes. "On 18 December, with the realization that this was no minor counterattack, the 17th Airborne was alerted and moved to a marshaling area on 19 December."

By noon the next day, the men were tying down equipment in their C-47s. "We then attended briefings all afternoon. It had been reported that German paratroops had been landed in the area of the Reims Airfield, where we were to land, and that our landing would be a tactical one.

"Our unit had been trained to fly into combat by glider and most of us were also jump-qualified, but no one had ever mentioned a tactical landing in powered aircraft! We were a bit apprehensive, but we bent to the task of learning what we would have to do.

"Fog socked in the field the first day and the operation was cancelled," with gear off-loaded and planes then loaded for an equipment drop to the encircled 101st Airborne at Bastogne.

"Finally, the weather cleared on 23 December. We loaded our gear again, tied it down, and late that night took off for France," landing at Reims Airfield in the early hours of Christmas Eve as snow began to fall.

"The German paratroop threat failed to materialize, although the airfield was strafed by a lone German fighter plane. We dashed from the C-47s into the woods, expecting to find a German behind every tree. Instead, we found more snow and a two-hour wait that seemed to set the stage for the weeks of bitter-cold combat that awaited us."

The men left the woods, marched a few miles, and were loaded onto trucks for Camp Mourmelon near Reims. "We spent the rest of that day readying our equipment and drawing additional ammunition. We should have known our stay here would be a short one. Sure enough, before dawn on Christmas Day, we were awakened to a breakfast of C-rations and the news that we were moving up on the line. A great Christmas present!"

The 17th was assigned to set up a defensive line at the Meuse River, Lieutenant Colonel Hagerman says, as a last-ditch effort to stop the German drive aimed at the port of Antwerp. "When the drive was slowed short of the line, the 17th Airborne was moved up to join the American counteroffensive to drive the Germans back across the Rhine."

16–23 December 1944
Mission to France and Belgium

Colonel Robert W. Creamer served as assistant group operations and liaison officer with 435th Troop Carrier Group.

When word arrived before sunrise on the morning of 16 December from 53rd Troop Carrier Wing, the aerial supply group at Welford Park, England, began loading forty-five C-47s with combat resupplies, "intended for airdrop to the 101st Airborne Division somewhere in the area that would become known as *the Bulge*," Colonel Creamer writes. With the mission considered urgent, but "exact coordinates of the 101st not yet known," the group was ordered to proceed to an airfield near Liege, Belgium, to await briefing from SHAEF Forward HQ.

"I was ordered to load a jeep in the group commander's aircraft, the *Brass Hat*, and precede the group to the continent, contact SHAEF Forward, and be ready to brief the group upon arrival," but "the mission did not develop according to plan. SHAEF Forward HQ did not have the foggiest notion where the 101st Airborne might be because the tactical situation was very fluid. We were ordered to proceed to Chateaudun, France (A-39) to refuel and await orders for a next-day resupply of the 101st.

"Our arrival at Chateaudun was well after dark and by the time we were all parked and headed to the mess hall for a late supper, all of France was fogged in. The 435th slept in their aircraft the next few nights—a cold, wet, miserable experience, but not nearly as rough as we knew it was for the 101st Airborne. The very dense fog persisted."

On the morning of 19 December, fog was heavy, "but toward noon the fog lifted, intermittently revealing low clouds from which a light, steady drizzle fell. The visibility varied from one-half to two miles. Lieutenant Colonel Bob Lewis, mission commander and CO of the 76th Troop Carrier Squadron, received word from the group to return to Welford Park if at all possible.

"To accomplish a contact as early as possible with Welford, we climbed to 10,000 feet MSL [mean sea level or elevation above average sea surface]. Welford Park weather decoded as zero-zero, light rain, fog, and drizzle. Lieutenant Colonel Lewis's voice came in loud and clear when we advised a no-go for the group and that we would return to A-39. The news: 'A-39 ceiling and visibility zero-zero.' And then as sort of an afterthought, 'Advise your intentions.'

"I advised Lieutenant Colonel Lewis we were proceeding to Welford Park" where, with careful and tedious coordination between navigator and crew, "a Category III Landing was made in 1944, years before its time. The 101st Airborne Division was resupplied at Bastogne, 23 December, and I was along."

22 December 1944–8 January 1945

Trier to Luxembourg City

Colonel Harold J. Salfen was a first lieutenant, forward director of Post #3, known as "Ripsaw 3," attached to 312th Fighter Control Squadron, during the Battle of the Bulge.

"Here in a tiny trailer, smaller than a modern kitchenette was unfolded the whole drama of this greatest day in the air war since 1940." So begins the United Press story datelined "Ninth Air Force Control Station, Western Front" with the byline "Walter Cronkite."

"Somewhere out over the German lines this morning, an artillery observation patrol of Piper Cubs—little two-pilot sport planes that used to rattle around the airports back home—skipped in and out of the clouds looking for the enemy," the write-up continues

Two pilots, First Lieutenant Ellis E. Thompson of Fairfield, North Dakota, and Second Lieutenant Bernard B. Mackell of Pittsburgh, Pennsylvania, were given equal credit for sighting the enemy that day—"a column of tanks, half-tracks, buses, and trailers that stretched through the woods down a dale and up and beyond a hill." One of the pilots yelled: "There are trucks and tanks up here—millions of them. Let's have some air, quick."

Ready to give them air, and quickly, was Flight Officer William Stephens of Glendale, Arizona, who took the call and information; radioed 'Red Leader' to inform, "I have a target for you"; and then called in other flights of Thunderbolts. The date was 22 December; the location, the German-Luxembourg border region, as the column headed from Trier toward Luxembourg City.

"Flight after flight was steered to the target and flight after flight crackled out success reports, logging through ether the greatest day in the air war," Cronkite's story concludes.

And that's the way it was, as Yank fliers, under the direction of Ripsaw 3, ripped into 3,000 Nazi vehicles. Colonel Salfen reports that the men of Ripsaw 3 "stayed in Luxembourg City during the Battle of the Bulge and directed the aircraft that destroyed incoming German tanks and infantry. Additionally, Ripsaw 3 moved along with the advancing Third Army, directing aircraft as well as intercepting enemy planes. The tiny trailer that Cronkite describes had thirty-six swastikas painted on its side, indicating direct kills controlled by Ripsaw 3."

3–17, 24 December 1944
Saarlautern, Germany, and Ritzing, France

Chief Warrant Officer Francis Joe Garra was now a sergeant with Company B, 3rd Section, 3rd Platoon, 774th Tank Destroyer Battalion.

"They considered Metz 'in the bag' though we were not in the city. We edged toward the Saar River to the Siegfried Line. Artillery fire started to come in. We stalled and then moved forward," Mr. Garra writes.

"On this drizzly, dreary night, intermittent firing of all kinds was heard: artillery fire without a pattern. Flames from fires could be seen in all directions. We were briefed but didn't know what was going on. We were told that we would dig-in along the Saar River bank and support an infantry attack on Saarlautern with direct fire on pillboxes, personnel, and opportune targets. . . .

"We approached, very carefully, that part of Saarlautern on the west bank. Our platoon went into position . . . spread out about 600 yards along the river. A road was in front of us and then a steep hill or ridge behind that. We were in a bad position. The ridge acted as a backboard for fire coming in, and the trees caused many tree bursts.

"The drizzle stopped and it started to clear. We now could see the stars and the moon. This was about 3 December. We started to dig-in. We dug all night, and before dawn we had the gun in position, slit trenches and the ammo lined up. We had a halfway decent field of fire to the front but poor traverse coverage. A limb obscured our fire and DeWitt went down and chopped it off. He came back with a big black eye, but we had a better field of fire. Now we could see where we were. River bank to river bank was less than a thousand yards. A railroad track ran along the river on the other side and freight cars were lined up all along the tracks. Pillboxes were built in the hillsides, in depth as far as you could see. We knew that every building, barn, factory, and haystack was also a pillbox.

"We were instructed to keep our fire above the freight cars. We started to fire as we had on many other occasions. We stopped to let the gun cool off, and then they let us have it. Eighty-eights, artillery, and mortar, not to mention small-arms fire. We headed for the slit trenches. . . .

"This was our introduction to fourteen nights and thirteen days of the roughest going I ever experienced." When sections to right and left pulled back, "that left our section in position and functioning. Up till then we dreaded the night; now it couldn't come soon enough. . . .

"When we had fire missions, we . . . always drew counterfire. Nobody knew how many rounds were coming in every day. We were told to count them. I counted at about the rate of twenty-five or thirty rounds a minute. They wouldn't believe us, so they reported 5,000 rounds a day coming in. I knew it was more. . . .

"One morning, Staff Sergeant Shep Fields came out to our gun position. While we were talking, he mentioned they couldn't figure where the enemy was getting all its ammunition for their counterfiring. I mentioned that during the nights there was a lot of activity across the river by the freight cars. I told him: 'Shep, I have been ordered to keep our fire over the railroad tracks but the next time, I'm going to fire at the freight cars, starting at our right.' He told me: 'OK, and I'm going to have Jack Best's section fire on them from the left side.'

"We soon had a fire mission and we fired at the freight cars. Sergeant Best did the same from the other end. When we raked those cars one end to the other, all hell let loose. The cars were loaded with ammo and caught fire and the rounds started to explode. It was like the Fourth of July, shrapnel and fragments going in all directions. We went to our slit trenches so we wouldn't get hit. It took a day and a night for the ammo to burn out. After that, we never received the terrific fire as we did at first. We were more or less neutralized but enemy fire dropped off too."

"We headed south 24 December 1944," with Patton's Third Army, assigned to guard his flank. "There was heavy snow falling and late that night we reached our gun position in a desolate field. No buildings in sight except a castle a few miles away near Ritzing. It was the Castle Schloss Mandern. I threw my bedroll down on the snow and crawled in. The beauty of this scene impressed me. I thought of my wife and family back in Yonkers and the Bronx.

"The snow stopped and the sky cleared. The moon and stars were shining. I watched the largest and brightest star move slowly across the sky, heading for the castle. The sky might have looked like this in Bethlehem 1,944 years ago."

24–25 December 1944
Saarlautern, Germany

Colonel Jean W. Christy continues his 5th Infantry Division account.

On 8 December, "Fort Driant fell, just half an hour before the 2nd Infantry turned the area over to the 87th Division," battalion records reveal. "The fort was commanded by Lieutenant Colonel Richter who destroyed every weapon in the fort before running up the white flag. He volunteered, out of a clear blue sky, the statement that if we intended sending his men and officers to Russia, he'd have them shot where they were."

Colonel Christy adds: "Upon hearing of the fall of Fort Driant, Colonel Worrell E. Rolfe, commander of 2nd Infantry Regiment, hastened to the scene. Deep inside the fort, he accepted the sword of Lieutenant Colonel Richter who said, 'I surrender. Your gun [Long Tom, 155mm] has ruined my fort.' Then he made his protest against sending his men to Russia."

Assigned as liaison officer number-one on 14 December, Colonel Christy writes that he traveled with the 1st Battalion column on 17 December to "relieve units of the 95th Infantry Division" at Saarlautern, where "the 1st Battalion inherited a situation of house-to-house fighting. The Siegfried Line ran right through the town, utilizing the buildings there, and the Saar River, as obstacles to our advance. Pillboxes were concealed in buildings, shops, houses, and even coal piles in the town, and were usually detected only when they opened fire on our troops. The only option open to Blakefield was to batter away from house to house, pillbox to pillbox, to clear the enemy."

With Patton heading to Luxembourg "to mount an attack on 22 December, 5th Division received orders the afternoon of 21 December to "get to the fighting in Luxembourg by morning the next day. Heroic measures were called for. Orders came to turn our vehicle headlights on, and drive our overloaded trucks as fast as possible over the snow-covered and slippery roads.

"Snow was piled hip-deep along the narrow, two-lane roads. We had now been overseas for almost three years [including eighteen months in Iceland], during all of which we had observed a rigid blackout. To be so brightly lighted as we hurtled through the night to meet the specter of the most serious enemy threat of the war, so far, went against all of our training and indoctrination. It was downright scary."

Just after dawn, the battalion reached its destination, 20 miles northeast of Luxembourg City, with the German drive stalled at Bastogne, "about 20 miles to our northwest." The battalion's "first rounds were fired in Luxembourg at 0640 hours on 22 December, a little more than twelve hours since the battalion had been firing in the Saar, almost 100 miles away."

"On Christmas Eve, 1st Battalion had reached its objective, consolidated its position, and established a perimeter, and a warning order was received from regiment for an attack the next day, Christmas Day," Colonel Christy continues.

"It was time to think about our Christmas presents. The problem was to find a more suitable place to open and enjoy them than a snow bank in the dark woods. I called my liaison section together and, with our bags of presents, we walked a short way down a road and across a snowy field to a house set alone back in a wooded area. . . .

"A middle-aged man answered my knock. He was more inquisitive than frightened when he saw four strange soldiers in the night. Fortunately, he spoke English. I explained [our mission]. With some reluctance, he invited us in. . . . Then he rejoined his family at supper in the adjacent dining room. Although the windows were covered for the blackout, there was a tall Christmas tree in the living room. The four of us settled down around the tree and took turns opening our presents. . . .

"When they had finished their meal, the man and his wife and their three young teenagers joined us in the living room. We sang carols together for a half hour or so. Then, about nine o'clock, we excused ourselves, thanking the family profusely for their hospitality. We found ourselves wishing each other a 'Merry Christmas' as we parted, and then suddenly became aware of the obvious incongruity of the situation.

"We were silent as we went back through the dark and snow. . . . I joined the infantry staff in the planning for the attack on Christmas morning."

On Christmas Day 1944—that day when General McAuliffe uttered "Nuts" to surrendering his 101st Airborne troops at Bastogne and that day when Lieutenant Colonel Blakefield uttered his "To hell with it" commentary—1st Battalion, 2nd Infantry Regiment feasted on "roast turkey with stuffing, mashed potatoes and gravy, green beans, and pumpkin pie. I don't know where it came from," Colonel Christy says, "but the guys in supply had done things right this time. . . . The men had a hot Christmas dinner, served in mess kits, while sitting on a variety of snow banks. The attack jumped off in mid-afternoon."

24–25 December 1944

Ardennes Mountains, Lammersdorf, Germany

Lieutenant Colonel Gordon Wallace was a sergeant with Anti-Tank Company, 309 Infantry Regiment, 78th Infantry Division.

"The evening meal was over, and seven or eight of us were hunched in a circle around a small campfire toasting our hands and feet. It was Christmas Eve in the Ardennes Mountains and darkness had set in early. The warmth of the fire dispelled the cold, but it could not drive away the thoughts we all entertained about loved ones at home and happier Christmases we had known in a past life," Lieutenant Colonel Wallace writes.

"These men had just been through eleven days and nights of combat in what became popularly known as the Battle of the Bulge, and they had survived without harm to either mind or body. They were lucky. Thirteen hundred of their fellow soldiers in the infantry regiment of 3,000 that jumped off into the face of the von Rundstedt counteroffensive early on the morning of 13 December 1944 were not so lucky; they were casualties of war. It was, in fact, this severe mauling at the hands of the German enemy that forced our withdrawal from action along the Siegfried Line on the day before Christmas to a relatively safe haven in the forest several miles from the front line, where we were to regroup our forces and receive replacements."

Into this setting, "a runner from the company command post came with a message for me to report at once to the company commander. The captain, not unaware of the drama which he was helping to unfold, brought me to full and alert attention with opening words: 'Sergeant Wallace, I have a wonderful Christmas present for you.' Then, after proper pause for effect, he continued: 'I have just received orders to transport you to rear-division headquarters at the earliest possible time. My information is that you are being returned to the United States to study Japanese at the University of Michigan. So get your gear together and be prepared to leave some time tomorrow.' Then, with understandable curiosity, he asked, 'How in the hell did you pull that off, sergeant?' I told him—but that is another story.

"The word spread like wildfire across the division bivouac area that a GI was actually leaving the Western Front and being sent back to the States with a whole skin. I became an instant celebrity. All morning long on Christmas Day, GIs drifted in from various units to talk to me and see for themselves that such a person really existed. In reality, I was more than a celebrity. I was a symbol. Without exception, these men were happy for me. What had happened to me demonstrated to them that what seemed impossible could happen, and this renewed their hopes that some day they, too, would escape from the bloody and bitter world which had engulfed them. I was living proof that it could happen."

November–December 1944

France to Luxembourg

Lieutenant Colonel Richard J. Frederick was a first lieutenant, maintenance and supply platoon leader, 131st Ordnance Company, Heavy Maintenance, FA.

Proceeding by truck convoy to the Montebourg vicinity, the 131st was assigned to the Third Army but remained in the staging area awaiting further assignment plus replacement of equipment lost in off-loading. "On 10 October, this organization was attached to 69th Ordnance Group," departing 24 November by convoy from Valognes for the 495-mile trip to Champigneulles and assignment to the 14th Ordnance Battalion, Lieutenant Colonel Frederick reports. "Our maintenance assignment was the 6th Cavalry Group. Our mission was to attach ring mounts for .50-caliber machine guns to the turrets of the scout cars equipped with the 37mm cannon to afford additional firepower against ground and air attack.

"On 23 December, the unit departed Champigneulles en route to Rodange, Luxembourg, . . . [where it] set up shop in a steel-rolling mill. During this period, the unit serviced artillery units of the III and VIII Corps, as well as the 6th Cavalry Group and other miscellaneous units. The large number of units being serviced and the inclement weather . . . presented many problems in supply and maintenance."

In the midst of the "snow, slush, fog, and icy roads" encountered during the Battle of the Bulge, Lieutenant Colonel Frederick recalls that "one of the 155mm gun battalions was experiencing short round range. After examining the gun books for rounds per tube and the tubes themselves, having the loaders place a round in the breech, muzzle depressed, I could see snow through the tube. It was obvious that the lands had been shot out, causing the short rounds." He requisitioned "six 155mm gun tubes." The supply and artillery officers "departed with jeep driver and three Jimmies [simple, rugged trucks] and drivers for base ordnance in Paris" and returned in two days with two tubes per truck.

"To prepare them for installation, they of course had to be cleaned and the cosmoline removed from the interior of the tubes. The temperature being so cold, the only way they could be cleaned was to have them placed on the side of a hill, breech on the down side, pour gasoline in the tubes and set them on fire, burning out the congealed cosmoline. After this was accomplished, the tubes were reloaded on the trucks and transported to the artillery battalion location where, with the aid of our ten-ton wrecker and the one in the artillery battalion, they were installed."

December 1944

Near Mirecourt, France

First Lieutenant Dorothy C. Berry Holmgren, an Army nurse with 58th Station in Tunis from the spring of 1943, joined 21st General Hospital in May 1944, serving with it in Italy and France.

"Our unit, 21st General Hospital, was caught in cross fire . . . several days after Christmas during the Battle of the Bulge," First Lieutenant Berry Holmgren writes.

"I was off duty and in the nurses' quarters and saw it happen. Three patients in a nearby building were hit and got Purple Hearts. No one was killed. One colonel said, 'We're in position to be hit some more before the battle moves.' There was a big uproar from our patients, so German prisoners and the nurses and doctors moved into one of the large buildings and were surprised [to find] German-speaking nurses and doctors."

This multinational system began when "a detachment of German prisoners was sent to work at the hospital and German casualties were treated." According to an article in the *St. Louis Globe-Democrat* at the time, "Soon a 'hospital within a hospital' was set up when six German doctors and forty-nine German nurses began to care for the prisoners."

The article reports that the 21st received its first patients in France 21 October and "in the next few weeks admitted an average of 135 patients per day." A newspaper article 22 March 1945 notes treatment by the 21st of its 50,000th patient.

"Personnel numbered 244 nurses, 178 officers and 22 temporary, and 1,031 enlisted men. We had 2,000 beds with 2,000 in tents, if needed. We traveled in 2½-ton trucks and ambulances," and as a result, "I saw little of France," First Lieutenant Berry Holmgren comments.

26–28 December 1944

Sadzot, Belgium

Lieutenant Colonel Philip R. Bradley served with 289th Regimental Combat Team, made up of the 289th Infantry Regiment and 897th Artillery Battalion.

"We were put into the line of combat to support and reinforce the 3rd Armored Division at Grandmenil, Belgium. We advanced against second-rate troops until we took the ground above Sadzot," Lieutenant Colonel Bradley writes.

"During the night of 26 December, the first-rate troops of the 12th SS Panzer and 2nd SS probed our defensive positions. . . . When the German probes reached C Company, that company retreated, then counterattacked, having lost some killed, wounded, and captured. They regained their positions. They found five of their men—each having been captured, shot in the head, and boots taken. These men were murdered by the SS troops.

"On the night of 27–28 December, the enormously superior strength of the SS troops attacked. Our entire regimental front was hit. . . . C Company was penetrated. . . . As the commander of 1st Battalion 289th became aware that C Company had ceased to exist as an effective fighting force, he, Major Henry Fluck, ordered an artillery officer, Captain Kastenbader, to place artillery fire closer and closer to what had been C Company's line. We did not know that part of C Company was still fighting. We did know that hundreds of Germans were pouring into the forest that was behind us, and into Sadzot and Briscol.

"We brought the artillery fire into the forest itself. The artillery shells, exploding within the trees, rained shell fragments onto the German SS *and* our own men. . . . C Company Platoon Sergeant McClure and his men, unbeknownst to us, were still fighting. To this day, [they] thank us of the 897th Artillery for having brought our fire with extreme accuracy to their front and to their rear, so as to kill the Germans who were about to overwhelm them. Captain Kastenbader's shooting (fire direction) was an example of exquisite skill in the employment of artillery in a close-support situation. The 897th Battalion fired 4,300 artillery shells that night. Those shells were fired by a mere twelve guns. . . .

"At first light on 28 December, Captain Kastenbader sent me to reconnoiter the forest and identify the flanks of A and B Companies. . . . The forest floor above Sadzot was littered with German dead. . . . The number seemed to me to be upwards of 500. But such a high number seemed impossible. . . . Only later did we learn that we had been attacked by two regiments," the 2nd and 12th SS.

24–25 December 1944
Stalag XIIA, Limburg, Germany

Commander John F. O'Connell provides the diary of his late brother, Lieutenant James J. O'Connell.

After sixty days of battle, then-Private O'Connell had been send to rest at Echternach, Luxembourg, with eighty officers and men of Company E, 12th Infantry, 4th Division. That's where they were captured when the Germans broke through.

"Dazed and heartily disheartened," the GIs walked from their shell-blasted wine cellar 20 December, after five days of fighting, to face an enemy that was armed with submachine guns, giant bazookas, flamethrowers, and electrically detonated Tellar mines. There were also two King Tiger tanks with long-barreled 88s, two 88mm field pieces, several more Tiger tanks, and armored cars. "It had taken all this, five days to capture the town from a company of infantrymen armed with rifles and a few machine guns!" Private O'Connell exclaims.

En route to Stalag XIIA after interrogations, the new POWs were marched from Echternach across the Our River, to "the depths of the Siegfried Line," through "mountainous and densely wooded country of Eifel Province to Irrel; trucked to Wittlich and Koblenz; marched again, 10 miles from Koblenz, because "tracks had been blown up the night before during one of the RAF night raids"; entrained at Niederlahnsahn for Limburg; and marched, for an hour, to their camp.

Moving down the prison street, "we were surprised to see wrecked buildings and the huge bomb craters which had characterized the residential areas of Koblenz and Limburg. Could it be that our fliers had gone so wrong as to bomb a prison camp in violation of the Geneva Convention Treaty? . . . We learned the answer: British Lancasters had been over the night previous and had bombed Limburg's residential sections and railroad yards. Then, mistaking the camp in the dark (which was a scant 200 yards from the railroad tracks—in violation of the Geneva Convention), they had unloaded the rest of their eggs upon the helpless prisoners. The guards' barracks had received a direct hit and the American officers' compound was demolished. Over seventy American officers had been instantly killed—none escaped. What was more horrible, several trainloads had spent the terrible night of bombing locked in their prisoner cattle cars. . . . Deserted by their German guards, the poor fellows in these death traps were left to face the blazing death from the sky without a chance of escape. . . . Some of our number were recruited that night to go to work the next morning (Christmas Day) picking up the battered remains of those in the blasted officers' barracks. . . .

"With the tragic news of the bombing to haunt our dreams, we were led away to our 'sleeping quarters'"—two sections of barracks "good for 200 men," where over 800 were now crowded in triple-tiered bunks. "We were not even accorded the privilege of these body-heated barracks, but were led elsewhere. It was a fearfully cold night (about 10 F) and snow, blown by a biting wind, had already begun to blanket the ground. We were placed in our shelter—a series of long tents with a narrow flooring of straw. . . . After an hour of futile attempts at sleep, we spent the remainder of the night punching each other and running up and down to keep warm.

At "dawn's early light, it was Christmas morning. . . . It was a day of consolations, for early in the afternoon, Mass was celebrated for us in the tents by a German priest. . . .

"Since the day held such a deep significance for all Germans, it was the signal for 'extra' holiday rations. We had a cup of American coffee and our daily ration of black bread (one sixteenth of a loaf) for breakfast. For lunch, we had a mess kit of pea and turnip soup (the peas, however, were as hard as marbles). For dinner, we had a cup of tea and for each two men, a box of prunes or raisins. (Nothing has *ever* tasted better than that shared box of prunes!) We wondered how this could be a departure from the regular prison fare."

24–25 December 1944
Stalag Luft III, Lower Silesia

Major Robert J. Lagasse submits recollections from his late brother, Lieutenant Colonel Harvey Lagasse.

"The days dragged on and the cold, howling winds became unbearable, especially for those of us shot down during summer months and still wearing lightweight uniforms," then-Lieutenant Lagasse writes.

"The holiday season was upon us. It was the time of Hanukkah and Christmas. Christmas Eve morning dawned bright and beautiful. It seemed as though God had provided the first gift of Christmas in the form of a beautiful blue sky and the soothing warmth of the sun. . . .

"The prisoners of Stalag III had built a place where the POWs could gather, and we all took advantage of that gathering place on Christmas Eve. The weathered, leaky old walls reverberated to the strains of "Silent Night," "The First Noel," and even "Jingle Bells." To us in Stalag Luft III, He was born again. . . .

"We returned to our barracks and I spoke to the Boy Jesus and thanked Him for our Christmas Eve . . . and I asked Him to remain with us during our ordeal. I rolled over to sleep and dream of Christmastime in the past, then, behold, the day was complete, for there outside my barracks was a beautiful, gently falling snow. I fell asleep dreaming of a white Christmas and those I loved at home so many, many miles away."

As Christmas Day was ending, Santa appeared, in "a small wagon pulled by two of our *kriegies* dressed as Donner and Blitzen," to distribute mail and packages that had been held out by the mail officer, even for those who had not been in camp long enough to receive items from home. "Yes, Santa came to that remote camp and rekindled in each of us a hope that had dimmed with each passing day."

8 December 1944
Missions from Sansapor, New Guinea

Brigadier General William G. Hathaway was a second lieutenant flying B-25 aircraft with 70th Squadron, 42nd Bombardment Group.

In late 1944, the mission of medium-altitude bombardment was changed "to the distinctly more hazardous one of 'on-the-deck' strafing." The new assignment "brought us into much closer contact with the enemy, flying close formation, managing guns and bombs, and avoiding ground fire, offering opportunities heretofore not experienced," Brigadier General Hathaway explains.

"We took off for the target [Goeroea, Halmahera] at early dawn, 8 December 1944, with instruction to cross the target line abreast while strafing and dropping parafrag bombs on gun emplacements. [Parafrag bombs were small fragmentation bombs attached to small parachutes to allow bombers to move to safer distance before detonation.]

"Fortunately, the weather was clear and we had been well trained. The bad news was that there were more guns than we had been briefed, but there was no way to turn back so we, in all our derring-do, drove across the target area with guns blazing and bombs dropping. Things happened so fast, we didn't have time to be scared. . . .

"The parafrags successfully descended on the gun emplacements but all the guns were bearing on our incoming route. Successful as it was, our first strafing mission gave us a new realization of our own mortality.

"The low-altitude missions were successful and we became more experienced, albeit we garnered a few more gray hairs. There were other missions flown by many brave young men, some of whom did not return. . . . We think of them fondly."

25 December 1944
New Guinea

Colonel Stan W. Carlson was with the U.S. Army Infantry, Headquarters, 123rd Infantry Regiment, 33rd Division.

"There was little promise of a pleasant Yule until we decided that we would do our best to celebrate this great event," Colonel Carlson recalls. "For Christmas

Day, we asked our colonel to cease combat patrols and to maintain only necessary security. He agreed.

"Our officers and soldiers contributed food from their parcels from home to
provide a festive table. Our cooks baked enough bread for two slices each. We
had Spam and sardines, canned fruit, such as peaches and pineapple. There was
the well-known 'battery acid' lemonade and our chefs had baked a large cake and
decorated it. We had nuts and candy.

"After the meal, we sang Christmas carols, accompanied by the chaplain's
wheezy organ. As dusk approached, we had a movie in our jungle 'theater' with
its coconut-log seats.

"We had invited Navy men from the nearby anchored ships, and at dusk they
gave us a real surprise. The sailors had strung lights to outline a ship—all blue
bulbs. As darkness descended, the lights went on and the outlined ship was
beautiful to behold. For a few brief hours, the war seemed far away and all of us
knew the true meaning of 'peace on earth, good will toward men.'"

December 1944
Manus Island, Admiralty Islands

*Colonel Frank D. Slocum was a quartermaster second class on the USS LSM-313,
which was rendezvousing with other ships at Manus Island for the invasion of
Luzon on 9 January 1945.*

After practicing landings on Bougainville and the coast of New Guinea, "we
picked up a contingent of first-wave Army combat troops of the Americal Division who would hit the beach in their amphibious tanks, followed by tank
destroyers," Colonel Slocum writes.

Heading to Manus Island, however, "our rendezvous was marred by our first
loss. While riding darkened ship, one of the tanks in the well deck started to
burn. I was on the conning tower with Signalman Max Bradley of Roscommon,
Michigan, when we heard the screams of someone trapped inside. We both ran
down the ladder and jumped on the tank. Just then, an Army man named Pep-
pard crawled out of the hatch and calmly warned us to jump, as the tank would
explode. We all jumped, but one look at the man was enough to tell us that he
was severely burned over all his body and was in total shock despite his calm
conversation.

"Permission was obtained to leave the convoy, along with an LST that had a
doctor aboard." Despite little light and choppy water, "the doctor . . . made it over
by a bos'n chair. There wasn't much he could do even with blood plasma . . .

until we reached Manus Island," where the patient was transferred to a hospital, but died."

Quartermaster Slocum was "selected to go ashore to pick up supplies and also to check if any mail was being held," since LSM-313 had not received mail in five months. Having to wait for supplies, the detail stayed over for the Christmas Eve, gathering "in the huge outdoor amphitheater," where members heard their first radio news in some time and saw the movie *Since You Went Away*. "Traditional Christmas carols were sung by the choir and, for the thousands attending, it was a time to weep without shame since everyone else was doing the same. We were all aware that our comrades were dying up north, and we missed our loved ones. . . .

"I can't recall how or why we were singled out, but I know that the small LSM-313 group met with the chaplain after the service behind the screen of the stage. We were treated to fresh-baked rolls, complete with a jar of homemade jam. I don't think I will ever forget the taste of those rolls."

7 December 1944
Leyte, the Philippines

Major Thomas A. Warthin was a surgeon with Headquarters Fifth Army Air Force Service Command.

When the Japanese attempted "to wreak havoc on all our air bases on Leyte by a combined paratroop and land attack" on the anniversary of their success at Pearl Harbor, all did not go as planned, Major Warthin writes, with "the ground attack jumping off ahead of schedule by infiltrating in the early morning the light perimeter defense to the west of Burauen, an important town already holding the headquarters of the Fifth Air Force and the advance echelon of the Wisconsin General Hospital. This early morning attack alerted all the area between Burauen and Dulag, so that the air attack that followed in the afternoon was almost totally destroyed before doing any significant damage.

"Two Jap troop carriers of the DC-2 type, carrying eight paratroopers planning to land at Dulag, were shot down well short of the strip. There were also two aiming for Tacloban. One made it and destroyed six airplanes in its kamikaze landing. The thirty other carriers flew up the road toward Burauen, dropping strong, tall paratroopers from the northern island. Unfortunately for them, Jap Zeros had made it a habit to strafe the road early each morning, and, to prevent this, 50mm ack-ack had been placed along every mile or so. Two aircraft burst into flame as they passed over our unit and crashed just beyond. As apparently ordered, the paratroopers made for the road, set up machine guns and began firing blindly down the road. It was shamefully easy to sneak up on them in the thick foliage and cut them down from the side.

"As it grew dark, a truck from a black quartermaster trucking unit located near the San Pablo strips roared into our area. Black units at that time were not issued arms and these men needed and deserved them. We were happy to 'lend' them carbines and my .45 pistol. Later, most of the weapons were returned and we received excellent trucking service when we moved on to Mindoro the next month.

"Sixth Army sent a regiment of the 13th Airborne the next day to clear out the remainder of the ground and air attackers cornered in the San Pablo area. After five days, there were no survivors or soldiers willing to surrender. Papers recovered from the dead indicated that there had been 450 airborne and 400 ground personnel involved. They had fought bravely, but were uncoordinated and without imagination, giving us insight into the disintegration of the Japanese war machine."

7 December 1944
Mission to Mukden, Manchuria

Lieutenant Colonel Nick J. Soulis was a pilot with 58th Bomb Wing, 444th Bomb Group, 677th Squadron, stationed in Chengtu, China.

"Just finished briefing and trying to get some shut-eye before a midnight take-off on a B-29 mission to Mukden, Manchuria," Lieutenant Colonel Soulis recalls. The target would be an aircraft factory; the early morning temperature was −40 degrees.

"First Lieutenant H. W. Mather of St. Joseph, Michigan, was piloting 411 in the 'Purple Heart Corner' of the B-29 formation," with then–First Lieutenant Nick Soulis as co-pilot, according to a story at the time by Corporal Ralph Zahnizer in the *Jamestown* [North Dakota] *Sun*. Near their target, a reception of Jap fighters awaited. "As the bombardier . . . took over for the bombing run, a Jap Nick slipped through the formation and blazed away with all guns from one o'clock. No. 1 engine of 411 was hit and hit hard," the write-up continues.

Lieutenants Mather and Soulis "struggled but could not 'feather' the crippled engine. After 411 fell from 24,000 feet to 6,000 feet, the Japs swarmed in for the kill—thirty to thirty-five strong. The interphone hummed like a party line as the gunners called out fighters at every hour of the clock. . . .

"'Roaring Richard' Hayton went into action. . . . He saw his tracers finding their mark but still the Nip came in. . . . Just as the crew thought the Jap was going to hit them, he pulled up, missing them by yards; then dropped to the other side where Crase saw the pilot abandon his burning Tojo. . . . Another Jap came in on Hayton who poured lead until the plane peeled off, caught fire and exploded. . . .

"An hour passed and still guns smoked and tracers gleamed as gallant 411 withstood the onslaught. Ammunition was running low, the lower aft turret already empty. . . . Major J. L. Martin left the formation to look for . . . the 411 crew who had flown most of their missions with the major. After a long search, Major Martin and Captain B. J. Sisson located 411 and moved in to aid the wounded Superfort. The sons of heaven . . . showed their tail and scampered for safer skies."

After mapping the way "toward the nearest emergency field," and with cover from Martin and Sisson, the crew relaxed and Lieutenant Mather landed. "Bomber Command confirmed thirteen of the crew's claims," the account reports. Staff Sergeant Hayton, who through "technical misunderstanding" was listed as "Private" Hayton, was credited with "three enemy aircraft destroyed and eight damaged in less than an hour." For this, Sergeant Hayton was *promoted* to private first class.

December 1944
POW Camp Chen Chia Tung, Manchuria

Colonel Michael A. Quinn continues his POW diary.

Settled in for about two weeks in his new POW camp at Chen Chia Tung, Colonel Quinn writes in early December of being so ill that he couldn't hold up his head, couldn't hold his food down, and hadn't been walking recently. He writes, too, of near–zero-degree weather and putting his overcoat over himself when sleeping until heavier clothing is finally issued, including pajamas, "the first in three years."

To his family on Christmas Eve, he writes: "I will fly back to you in spirit, and while you are so far away, I don't believe you were ever nearer." On Christmas Day, he writes, "A Merry Christmas to all of you from me. . . . I hope my absence will not darken your Christmas, because I am still with you. . . . Today we really celebrated. I splurged with three cups of coffee, and jam and buttered toast for breakfast. It was impossible to get a priest for services, so we had religious services our own way. . . . The commandant wished us all a Merry Christmas. They issued sugar and coffee from the Red Cross supplies. We had some grease in the beans at noon today, and tonight we had more than I could eat. Here's what we had: vegetable stew with 100 pounds of meat, side dish of fish, Yorkshire pudding, apple pie, corn bread, and started all over again with coffee. Smoked Camel cigarettes all day, and life wasn't so bad. We may stay up until ten o'clock tonight. . . .

"Ted Lily brought out his old guitar, and we sang all the ditties that seemed to go with the good times . . . 'Clementine,' 'Red Sails in the Sunset,' and 'South of the Border.' All in all, it was a pretty good time and gave us a chance to enter into the real spirit of Christmas. After all, if we can believe that Christ left His home and came down to us, we are not so badly off. When thinking it over, I am not very much grieved at my lot."

JANUARY 1945

38

"War-weary" might be the term that best describes moods on battlefront and homefront for the United States in January 1945, with the country heading into its fourth year of World War II. For soldiers and civilians alike, days seem as eternities, while everyone wonders when the war will ever end.

On the homefront in early 1945, newspaper columnist Paul Gallico writes, there were "shortages that pinched the nation more and more—meat, cigarettes, liquor, apartments, cabs, hotels, railroad seats, eggs, radios, coal, oil." In his 1946 essay, intended to update returning service members on what happened while they were gone, Gallico also labeled early 1945 "a filthy winter for weather, the worst in fifty years, with freezing, stinging cold and blizzards that tied up rail transportation and disrupted the movement of coal, food, and troops."

In Europe, it was equally a filthy winter for *war*, especially in the locale of "the largest land battle fought by U.S. forces"—that relentless struggle now known as the Battle of the Bulge, fought in the Ardennes Mountains of Belgium and Luxembourg from 16 December 1944 until late January 1945.

"Every time I rode in my jeep during the entire winter, my feet became numb with cold, for I literally rode with my feet on a cake of ice," Colonel William M. McConahey writes. "The sandbags which had been put on the floor of the jeep for protection in case we hit a mine became thoroughly soaked in the fall rains. When the weather turned cold, the soggy bags froze solidly and remained frozen until spring came."

January 1945
Near Bastogne, Belgium

Colonel William M. McConahey, battalion surgeon, continues his story.

"All along we had known that sooner or later the old 90th would be sent up to the Ardennes battle where the fighting was so bitter and so difficult, and soon we got our orders. We were to move secretly and attack the enemy by surprise," Colonel McConahey writes. "We drove more than 100 miles that day in heavy snow and terrible cold . . . to a little town in Luxembourg a few miles northeast of Bastogne, Belgium, . . . and got set for a surprise attack at dawn on 9 January.

For many days, the 26th Infantry Division had been battering against crack enemy troops on this southern flank of the salient without progress. They assured us that the 90th would be lucky to advance 100 yards.

"At dawn, our boys jumped off, and by dark they had driven the Germans back 2¹/₂ miles. We caught them by surprise, for so successful had been our secret move that the enemy did not know that a fresh division had come into the line. The next six weeks were as miserable as any we ever lived through. The bitter cold, the deep snow, the howling blizzards, the mountainous terrain we were fighting across, and the bloody, bitter fighting made it a hell we'll never forget. . . .

"One titanic battle I still remember. Our artillery battalion was in position around Bras, Belgium. . . . The Krauts were ordered to retake Oberwampach at any cost, so during the night they threw all available SS troops into a violent counterattack. For twenty-four hours the battle flamed and swirled in the cold and snow in and around the town. Wave after wave of screaming, fanatical enemy soldiers accompanied by tanks and tank destroyers smashed at our men. Point-blank tank duels, street fighting, bayonet encounters, and heavy artillery fire made Oberwampach a village of horror and sudden death; but our boys held firm and the Germans could not crack our line. . . . During this twenty-four-hour period, the 344th Field Artillery Battalion fired nearly 3,500 rounds of ammunition, the most it ever fired in a twenty-four-hour period. Bringing up ammunition to the spitting howitzers over the snow-clogged country roads was a tremendous task for the service troops, but the ammunition got to us."

January 1945
Diekirch, Luxembourg

Colonel Jean W. Christy, serving as commander of A Battery by late January,
continues his account of the 5th Infantry Division.

During the first two weeks of the new year, in the Battle of the Bulge, "the 5th Infantry Division had driven the enemy back across the Sauer River, and now assumed a defensive posture, containing the Germans within the 'Bulge' they had made," says Colonel Christy. "The 50th Field Artillery fired harassing and interdiction missions, as well as on observed targets, and developed delaying positions for use in the event of a strong enemy counterattack. The 1st Battalion patrolled aggressively to locate mine fields and other enemy positions, and to capture prisoners. As much information as possible was gathered in preparation for the push that we all knew was coming. The weather was terrible; ice, snow, and freezing cold were a constant factor."

Ordered to attack across the Sauer River at 0300 hours on 18 January in the direction of Diekirch, "the soldiers of 1st Battalion assembled in the bitter cold night and filed off to their appointed places. They were a motley-looking crew, covered with tablecloths, bed sheets, shawls—anything white to furnish camouflage in the snow. We had no 'snow suits' issued to us, so the men did the best they could with what they could find. I stood with members of the infantry staff, watching as they trudged off looking like a band of gypsies."

Among that band was "newly promoted First Lieutenant Bob Massonet, the forward observer from A Battery, who passed by and stopped to talk. 'Why do we have to go at night, Jean?' he asked. 'Bob, you've done this before,' I answered. 'You know that we wouldn't even make it down to the river in daylight.' He wasn't reassured and, shaking his head, followed the infantry down the hill into the darkness. His radio operator, Private First Class Merlin Johnson, smiled his little smile, shouldered his radio, and trailed after him."

In the midst of the action, a soldier with a red cross painted on his helmet approached then-Captain Christy, handed him a small, folded piece of paper, and told him: 'We evacuated one of your guys, and he asked me to give you this.' It was a scrap torn from a pocket notebook. A message was scrawled in pencil: 'Jean, Bob is at 317. Private First Class Merlin Johnson.'

"Later we found Bob Massonet's body at the location of Concentration 317. Merlin Johnson, though wounded, thought to send a message about his fallen buddy. I never learned the extent of Merlin's wounds, or whatever became of him."

Five cold, snowy days and nights, and hundreds of lost lives later, "except for a few stray units and a stream of troops fleeing to the east, the Battle of the Bulge was over."

January 1945
Rodange, Luxembourg

Lieutenant Colonel Richard J. Frederick was a maintenance and supply platoon leader, first lieutenant, with 131st Ordnance Company, Heavy Maintenance, FA.

While in Rodange, Luxembourg, from late December through 31 January, during the Battle of the Bulge, "the artillery and automotive sections had the heaviest workload," Lieutenant Colonel Frederick reports. "The artillery section changed six 155 gun tubes in the field for the 731st FA Battalion; fourteen 4.5 gun tubes in the field for 176th FA Battalion; and gave a six-month check on five 8-inch howitzers in Rodange for the 578th FA Battalion."

In the automotive section, duties included servicing assigned units as well as numerous vehicles that broke down along the road. "The extremely cold weather was a contributing factor to the maintenance problems. Cooling, fuel, and brake systems were affected by the cold, and many jobs were brought in with these problems," Lieutenant Colonel Frederick recounts.

In the small-arms sections, "maintenance was performed in the company shop, although contact parties were frequently sent out to make spot repairs in the field. The cold weather caused many weapon failures, in that cosmoline left in parts of weapons was not usually removed and cleaned thoroughly by using units. This would harden in the weapon and cause malfunction."

At first attempting to do all service work in-shop, the instrument section soon sent roving contact parties to check "field-artillery control instruments in the field and made spot repairs. Direct exchange was used when defective, unrepairable instruments were obtained. The main cause for instrument failure was the extreme cold, causing the freezing of the condensation collected in the instruments."

While the ten-ton wreckers of the service section "were constantly kept busy with recovery work," this section's other functions included "improvising and fabricating parts for all sections within the company." These included "trail and body spades for heavy artillery pieces, firing pins, obturator spindle plugs, a towing device for the eight-inch howitzer, and tow bars for wreckers and prime movers."

For the supply section, this period covered the German breakthrough in Belgium, when "quantities of major items, tools and equipment, and spare parts were lost. Requisitions were submitted and processed in overwhelming numbers. . . . The critical items at this time included tires and tubes, brake fluid, and antifreeze."

January–March 1945
Colmar Pocket, Alsace France

Colonel Edwin K. Adam was eighteen when he headed overseas, as an infantry heavy-weapons crewman.

Completely re-outfitted "with clothing, individual equipment, and a brand-new M-1 rifle (full of cosmoline)," Edwin Adam joined his new unit, Company A, 1st Battalion, 15th Infantry Regiment, 3rd Infantry Division, about 13 January 1945. "At that time, there was almost two feet of snow on the ground and it was very cold, especially at night," Colonel Adam recalls.

"On 22 January, the division began the assault into what is known as the Colmar Pocket, one of the most difficult battles that the 3rd fought. It took sixteen days to defeat and drive the Germans out of the area. It was during this battle on 26 January that Lieutenant Audie Murphy earned the Medal of Honor for his action in riding a burning TD and firing its .50-caliber machine gun, killing or wounding fifty enemy and beating back the enemy attack. Audie was assigned to Company B.

"When we reached the Colmar Canal, we were down to about one platoon of soldiers. The division had captured twenty-two towns and taken 4,016 prisoners, with 713 killed and 297 wounded. The division suffered 317 KIA, 1,410 WIA, and 323 MIA, with total battle casualties of 2,050.

"After a short off-line rest, we then prepared for attack across the Rhine and by 17 March were at the Siegfried Line. Being pinned down where we could not assault the line and, receiving enemy AT gunfire, our regimental exec, Lieutenant Colonel Keith Ware (later major general and Chief of Information, killed in Vietnam), along with one of our tank destroyers, circled around the gun and knocked it out. After the Siegfried Line, the Germans fell back fast and the 3rd moved on anything with wheels or tracks."

20 January 1945
Hatten-Rittershoffen, Alsace, France

Colonel Stephen Popadich was a private, Company B, 125th Engineer Battalion, 14th Armored Division.

On the afternoon of 20 January, squad leader Danielson said, "'Baum and Popadich, pack up your machine gun. You won't be on outpost at this spot anymore. Lieutenant Eddington has another job for you.'

"At 3rd Platoon CP, the lieutenant said: 'Our platoon has a job tonight and I need a dozen men. A few nights ago, Company B laid a large mine field about 1¹/₂ miles long, on the outskirts of Hatten-Rittershoffen. Last night, the 2nd Platoon opened up a 150-yard gap in the mine field. This morning, our tankers were going to make an attack. Two of the tanks got as far as the gap and were immediately knocked out. The spot is zeroed-in by Jerry machine guns and artillery. We've got to close this gap so the Jerries can't get through it. Then the division will withdraw to a better position.

"'The mines are under a tree on one end of the gap. I'll pick up the first mines and pace off the distance. Sergeants Needham and Davis will follow with their mines [and spread them] in the correct pattern. Baum and Startz will follow.

After they place their mines, Popadich, you and the other six men will carry mines until the gap is closed.' . . .

"Rork drove blackout to the aid station in the next town. When we got there about 2030 hours, the skies were clear; it was very cold and the moon was full. It seemed as though it were daylight. It would be suicide to go out and lay the mines. The lieutenant said, 'Let's all get into the cellar and wait for the moon to go down before we start.'"

As the moon went down about 0200, the lieutenant led his men, who fol-lowed at ten-yard intervals. . . . Several Jerry flares "lit the surrounding area as if it were daylight," and then died down. Half an hour later, the men "reached the tree where the mines were. . . . The two knocked-out tanks were now behind us. . . . The crews lay in the tanks. Someone had tried to rescue them but was spotted and killed. Everyone was tense. . . . We pulled our rifles over our heads and on our backs so that our hands would be free to work. It was very cold and it was impossible to work with gloves. My hands were frozen, yet a sweat was rolling down my face. I prayed and repeated to myself a couple hundred times: 'Holy Mary, Mother of God, pray for us sinners, now and at the hour of our death.'

"We worked quickly and quietly. In about an hour the gap was closed. About five minutes after we passed the house at the edge of town, another Jerry flare went up and lit the area where we had been working. Thanks to a thorough briefing by Lieutenant Eddington, our training, some luck, and the grace of God, our mission was completed successfully."

Winter 1944–1945
Bischwiller to Luneville, France

Lieutenant Colonel Elmer H. Puchta was a captain, commanding 3360th
Quartermaster Truck Company, attached to 36th Infantry Division.

"In late December 1944, Seventh Army Transportation ordered us to work the railhead at Haguenau. I found an abandoned factory in Bischwiller, which had garages and usable buildings," Lieutenant Colonel Puchta writes.

"After reporting our new location, I became curious as to the location, know-ing that Bischwiller was only eight kilometers from the Rhine River. I checked in the G-3 office and to my chagrin found that there were no units between us and the Rhine. I was told that it was a quiet sector and that a recon squadron patrolled the Rhine bank two or three times a day. It was a funny feeling know-ing that a QM truck company was the point for the Seventh Army in that area.

"Shortly after the first of the year, I received a call in the middle of the night ordering me to evacuate the area, as there were reports of German paratroopers landing north of us. We immediately prepared to leave and I took off to find a new site. I shall always remember members of the French Forces of the Interior, directing traffic in Bischwiller while the Americans vacated the area.

"The trip was a nightmare. Driving under strict blackout, we were frequently stopped at roadblocks manned by nervous MPs. One time, I heard what sounded like a tank closing on my rear. I pulled off the road, and a large tracked vehicle, towing the barrel of a 240mm gun, roared past. The driver wasn't stopping for roadblocks.

"We finally settled in Luneville, France, where we spent the rest of the winter assigned to Seventh Army Transportation. As a separate company, we would get many special assignments. There were times when I had trucks spread from Brussels to Marseille."

20–21 January 1945
Niedermodern, France

Colonel Walter D. Rice was a private first class and first scout in a rifle platoon, Company I, 409th Infantry, part of the 103rd Infantry Division.

"In a defensive position near Climbach, in Northeastern France" after the Battle of the Bulge, "our unit was ordered to withdraw to the Moder River in Alsace and assume a defensive position along that line," Colonel Rice recalls.

"Accordingly, on the night of 20–21 January 1945, we executed this planned withdrawal, breaking contact with the enemy and executing a thirty-kilometer march over roads coated with two or three inches of ice. On one of my many falls that night, an earlier injury to my knee, which had healed, reopened and bled for the remainder of the march.

"Upon arrival in the village of Niedermodern, about noon on the 21st, our squad settled-in in the home of a French family for rest and warmth. The home was the scene of hastened activity as the mother and children were preparing to evacuate to Saverne while the father was to remain. As I sat exhausted in the kitchen of that home, I rolled my trouser leg and long-john leg up above my knee. As the teen-aged daughter passed by, I asked her in my best high-school French, *'Pardonnez moi, Mademoiselle, mais avez vous quelque chase pour cet?'* and pointed to my bloody knee. She hurried off, calling, *'Maman, ici est un blessant.'* Her mother came and tenderly washed and bandaged my knee. They soon left and we saw them no more, although we stayed in the vicinity for about a month. My knee healed nicely."

As postscript to his story, Colonel Rice says that when the four towns of Niedermodern, Pfaffenhofen, Uberach, and LaWalck observed the forty-fifth anniversary of their liberation and invited 103rd veterans to return, he and his wife were among 120 who joined in the celebration.

Having told his wife beforehand that he "would like to return to that house," Colonel Rice exclaims, "Sure enough, as we rode through Niedermodern one day on our bus, I recognized 'my house.'"

On 21 May 1989, "my wife and I, accompanied by a young English-speaking Frenchman, visited the house. The middle-aged husband asked me to describe where I was seated during the dressing of my knee. . . . When I described the bench, he nodded and motioned for me to follow him. He led me to the kitchen and showed me where the bench had been located. He was eleven years old in 1945 and remembered the event. We sat around the parlor table with his family for two hours, fellowshipping over wine and pretzels. Sadly, his mother and father have been deceased for a number of years. His sister lived in another town."

1 January 1945
Stalag IIIA, Luckenwalde, Germany

Commander John F. O'Connell provides the POW diary of his late brother, Lieutenant James J. O'Connell.

After internment at Limburg's Stalag XIIA for the Christmas period, the eighty POWs were transferred to Stalag IIIA, Luckenwalde, arriving there on the day of New Year's Eve. "Our first taste of prison life here took place immediately after our arrival, at the bathing and delousing buildings," then-Private O'Connell writes.

"After our bout with the German god Cleanliness, we were herded once again across the road to the prison *kanteen*. . . . Here, we were greeted by some of the finest fellow-prisoners we ever encountered in our captivity, the English and Irish captives of Dieppe and Dunkirk [captured respectively in August 1942 and May–June 1940]. These swell fellows, besides their cheerful words of encouragement, had chipped in their tea, milk, and sugar rations, as well as some cakes from Red Cross parcels, to welcome us in style. . . . An English captain made a short speech after the feast, welcoming us and telling us to keep our spirits up, for it couldn't last much longer with the enemy."

"In time for the celebration of New Year's Day," the POWs "all received double rations of black bread, potatoes, tea, and oatmeal (barley soup) during the day. It is peculiar how popular the subject of food became in our midst. Talk centered upon 'places to try' in various states. Food, food, and more especially, the really most-expensive and elaborate of foods was indeed the general topic in the Stalag. It is surprising how much better one felt, too, after such an enlightening discussion."

January 1945
Stalag Luft III, Sagan, Germany

Lieutenant Colonel George T. FitzGibbon, who served with the 82nd Fighter Group, was a POW from the time of the 1943 invasion of Sicily.

"In January 1945, we knew from our hidden radio and BBC news that Joe Stalin's armies were not very far away and were pushing toward us, so it was no surprise when we heard and saw light of artillery fire at night. About 2030 hours on 27 January, we were told to get ready, as we'd be leaving camp soon. It was about 20F, and we'd just had six inches of new snow," Lieutenant Colonel Fitz-Gibbon writes.

"In preparation, I took a khaki shirt, sewed up the bottom with my mom's sewing kit, sewed the sleeves to the back, and had something of a knapsack. I wore everything I could: both pairs of my prized long-johns that my mother had sent me, two pairs of socks, woolen pants, shirt, Eisenhower jacket, pullover hat, and gloves. Into the knapsack went extra socks, cigarettes, bread, margarine, cheese, part of a big Hershey bar, plus I carried one blanket. I managed not to freeze anything in the next five or six days.

"After being up most of the night, we set out on foot in the snow at 0530 hours on 28 January. We walked all day with periodic breaks, during which I nibbled on some of my goodies. That night, I slept in a cold, cold stable and shared blankets and body heat with Victor J. Grabowski of Racine, Wisconsin. He was a good chap, but far too bony!

"Off again for another all-day jaunt, but this time we were put in a factory for the night—way too much heat and we couldn't sleep. One extreme to the other!

"The third and fourth nights, we were in the haymows of small barns and in high heaven. We were dead tired and had been provided with no food except for a bowl of broth. On the fifth day, we arrived at the railroad station in Cottbus and were loaded into boxcars. We were given some soup, the contents of which were questionable, but we'd have eaten anything at this point. We had walked 45 to 50 miles in the dead of winter with practically no food, and thought we had really accomplished something.

"We were 10,000-strong, led by Colonel Delmar T. Spivey who, when offered a cup of coffee by a German housewife, declined unless she had coffee for all 10,000 of us. He retired as a major general. We were then transported to a large POW camp at Moosburg, near Munich. There we remained until liberation in April 1945."

28 January 1945
Stalag Luft III, Lower Silesia

Major Robert J. Lagasse submits recollections by his late brother, Lieutenant Colonel Harvey Lagasse, whose POW story continues.

On a "bitter-cold and very still night," 28 January 1945, a distant bugle sounded "adjutant's call," the call "established within the compounds for emergencies, to alert all prisoners," and soon "word came down the corridor, 'We're moving out,'" Lieutenant Colonel Lagasse writes. "The silence was broken by the unmistakable sound of artillery fire, the first we had heard, coming from the east, and we knew then that the Russian Front had moved very close to Stalag Luft III. . . .

"At three in the morning, [a] biting, snow-laden wind from the west easily penetrated the thin clothing worn by the prisoners. . . . The hours went by and I could think of nothing but the bitter cold. . . . The pace of the march had slackened to a crawl and finally, for the first time, the column was halted for a short rest. We dropped in our tracks, and I muttered a quiet prayer for the strength to rise again. . . . It was now five in the morning. The wind howled across the open country as we were ordered to move out.

"Time passed; I don't know how much time, but in that confused span the recollection of prisoners falling by the road, too weak to go on and too exhausted to care, was vividly etched in my mind.

"Upon arrival in a town called Friewaldau [sic], [where] we were to be given shelter, we were told that [the building] was full and we would have to wait. The blizzard raged around us and we began a desperate search for wood to start a fire. . . . I was amazed to see thousands of prisoners; some were just lying in the snow while others were wandering through the mass of humanity with wide, disbelieving eyes."

The wood supply lasted thirty minutes; the wait outdoors, two hours. "When we entered the large room, the warmth encompassed my entire body, and I fell into a deep, troubled sleep. . . .

"During our rest period, we found that we had marched thirty kilometers in twelve hours and now, on 28 January 1945 at 1900 hours, we were to continue the march.

"It was dark and the blizzard had not slackened. . . . The column moved along for two hours and finally halted for adjusting packs, wrapping feet with pieces of cloth, stuffing pants legs into frozen boots, and helping each other for the next long haul. The order came and we were on our feet once again. . . . The only sound was the shrieking wind and the crunching of snow under the heels of thousands of combat boots. . . . Suddenly, this monotony of sound was broken by a sharp crack, then another, and instinctively each prisoner dropped into the snow. . . . The column was a mass of confusion; guards shouted orders; men ran in all directions, some falling with a scream as the bullets from our unknown assailants found their mark."

Back on the road, "the march became a nightmare—men fell asleep while still walking, others fell exhausted into the deep snow." After another rest in a barn, a twelve-kilometer march to Mascau where the POWs were billeted for two days, and a twenty-five-kilometer march to Spremberg, they were loaded into old 40& 8 boxcars and moved to Dresden where, horrified and imprisoned fifty-three men per car, they sat out a bombing raid as "bomb after bomb fell in a seemingly endless succession" before the all-clear sounded. "Two days in a cramped, rotten, stench-filled boxcar, and we arrived in Nuremberg. . . . We walked a few hundred yards and entered the gates of Stalag XIII."

28 January 1945
Mission to Germany

Major Frederick D. (Dusty) Worthen was a bombardier with the 93rd Bomb Group, 328th and 329th Squadrons, stationed at Hardwick, England, since mid-August 1944.

"I flew twenty-three missions over Germany, with varying degrees of danger, enemy anti-aircraft fire, and luck," Major Worthen says of his six months of flying B-24s. Starting out on 28 January for Dortmund, Germany, in the industrial Ruhr Valley, Major Worthen recalls making landfall "at 22,000-feet altitude over the Zuider Zee in Holland. . . . About halfway along the bomb run, with heavy flak in the area, we lost an engine on the left side of the plane. . . . We could not keep up with the formation, so we dropped out of our position, still trying to 'feather' the propeller. Determining this could not be done, we reversed our course" to return to England.

"As we approached the Zuider Zee, we lost the second engine on the left side. This propeller also would not 'feather.' With the amount of drag and the angle of the list, and losing altitude fast, the pilot concluded that we could not make it back to England. This was my first realization that we might be in serious trouble."

As the plane flew south off the coast of the Netherlands, "the navigator and I decided to vacate the nose position. . . . As I crawled onto the deck, I couldn't believe what I saw: The pilot and co-pilot each had both feet on the right rudder peddle and they were still having a hard time keeping the plane in a safe flying attitude. It was scary. . . .

"When we reached the Hague in Holland, we got several bursts of flak. At about the same time a third engine began to falter. We headed for the nearest land, which was Schouwen Island in the Schelde Estuary, the coastal waterway inlet to the city of Antwerp. . . . The decision was made to bail out over Schouwen.

"Parachuting was taught by lectures only. This was a first for all! . . . We must have been at about 1,000 to 1,500 feet. I jumped and counted to ten in about two seconds. . . . I pulled so hard my whole arm flew above me. . . . I was trying to figure out how to pull the chute out from the backpack when all of a sudden it opened, with it and me in a horizontal position. . . .

"I could hear the plane still flying nearby (on autopilot). It seemed that it was coming back at me. Then I saw it below, heading for what looked like a light-house near the coast. It dipped a wing, hit the ground, cartwheeled, and blew up in a huge ball of flame. After looking around a bit to see what to do next, I realized that we were being shot at by small-arms fire from the troops below.

"I saw some of the other chutes landing when I finally realized I was getting close to the ground and was coming in backwards. . . . I received a bad sprained ankle, and a small bone was broken. I landed in the snow in the lowlands, below the dikes. I buried my chute in the snow. Immediately thereafter I saw troops coming over the horizon. I sat down on a rock and ate a candy bar I had in my pocket. As the troops neared, I could see the German insignia on their uniforms," Major Worthen writes, in the first installment of his POW story.

9–15 January 1945
Lingayen Gulf, the Philippines

Lieutenant Colonel Donald G. Robbers was a member of 6th MP, 6th Infantry Division, which landed "about two hours after the first wave" in the invasion of the Philippines.

"The convoy that took us here was really a monstrous thing," then-Lieutenant Robbers informs his wife in a letter written 14 January 1945.

"I got up about four o'clock the morning of the invasion to watch the perform- ance. It was a perfect night to sneak up into position. It was real dark and cloudy, so the Japs could not spot us. Then, about dawn, the Navy started shelling the shore. . . . Big sixteen-inch guns firing salvo after salvo. They kept us below decks for a while but I had my head out a porthole watching. . . . Then, just before the hour, the bombardment increased in tempo and it was deafening to hear. . . . All this time, all the boats were unloading men and vehicles, and the water seemed alive with small craft. The way everything went so efficiently was a miracle. . . .

"We arrived into our area about noon and everything was quiet as far as the enemy was concerned. The natives were really glad to see the Americans. . . .

"I did not sleep very good the first night here. The ground was pretty hard. Then, too, we slept in the middle of a Philippine village. The natives had two stud horses that broke loose . . . [that] would run through our area and chase the boys into their foxholes."

Continuing his letter on Monday, 15 January, Lieutenant Robbers writes: "When we first landed, [the Filipinos] were all dressed pretty ragged, but every day they start to dress better. The Japs took most everything that they had but most of the people were smart and buried all their valuables. One woman had a nicely pressed print dress and told us when the Americans left she buried it until we would come back. . . .

"Yesterday, Sunday morning, we were roused from our sleep by the ringing of church bells. It sounded almost like being at home. . . . The chaplain had services, so I managed to get to go to Mass."

9 January–2 February 1945
Lingayen Gulf and Onward, the Philippines

Colonel William M. Enright was a twenty-year-old, going into his second campaign with the 37th Infantry Division, in the fifth wave at Lingayen Gulf.

The landing at Lingayen Gulf went as planned, Colonel Enright reports, with J-hour at 0930 having been "preceded by an air umbrella of bombers and fight- ers. At J-minus-three, the naval guns ceased firing. There were no Japs on the beach. A few Filipinos greeted the troops. The first objective was the town of Binmaley, a welcome sight after two and one-half years of jungle fighting. The Jap dive bombers came over around noon and crashed into the battleship *New Mexico* and an Australian cruiser. There were several casualties. Jap air attacks continued sporadically throughout the day.

"Our battalion occupied the municipality of San Carlos on 10 January. It was good to hear so many Filipinos speak English and to see many women and children.

"On 12 January, 5 miles south of San Carlos, our 3rd Battalion made contact with ninety-three Japs. After softening up the enemy position, our rifle company attacked and killed twenty-three Japs and captured three. The rest dispersed. We had only three wounded in this attack. We were now 29 miles inland from the beach.

"We were heading south toward Manila. Without heavy resistance, we moved along the dusty roads and across the muddy rice paddies of Central Luzon. On a 13-mile road from Camiling to Paniqui, we encountered twenty-one bridges, all in need of repair. As we later found out, fifty-one bridges had been destroyed between Lingayen and Manila.

"We met small resistance on 18 January, and with the help of a flight of fifteen Mustangs, most of the Japanese garrison were killed. We kept heading south. Each day, there were more long, hard, hot miles covered. The medical officers were busy doctoring hundreds of blistered and bruised feet. We were walking on one-third feet and two-thirds guts, one medical officer commented.

"On the night of 23 January, a fifty-man patrol from Company C, 148th Infantry, encountered Japs in the barrio of San Felipe. The patrol found them in a house and with the aid of a rocket launcher, they killed twenty.

"The 129th Regiment was assigned the objective of Clark Field, Fort Stotsenberg, and the high ground overlooking these objectives—the 129th on the right and the 145th on the left. The Japs had the area heavily mined. There were a total of 1,349 mines removed. The Japanese had superior observation and their counterbattery fire destroyed two 105 howitzers of our division artillery. The battle for Fort Stotsenberg was settled by 31 January, and Army Commander Lieutenant General Walter Krueger raised the U.S. flag. Clark Field was captured 2 February. There was a total of 782 counted enemy dead."

11 January 1945
Luzon, the Philippines

Chief Warrant Officer Fourth Class David L. Wischemann was a nineteen-year-old electrician's mate third class who arrived at Milne Bay, New Guinea, in June 1944, assigned to LST-18.

After a month in Hollandia, Dutch New Guinea, on much-needed ship maintenance, "we moved up to Biak to take on troops for the invasion of Luzon. . . . We finished loading on 24 December, and pulled out to sea with five or six other ships," heading into "D-Day-plus-2 on the beach at San Fabian in Lingayen Gulf," Mr. Wischemann reports.

Explaining that "old *18*" was among the first LSTs built, he adds: "Our ship was just one solid mass of rust—hadn't been painted since she left the States—therefore a person could understand someone else thinking we were expendable. So we were told to go in first, that the beach was very shallow a long way out, and it would be necessary for the Army to construct a very long sand causeway in the water out to our ramp.

"Our CO had a few faults, but ship-handling was not one of them. About 5 miles out, he called down to the engine room for 'flank speed.' The engine room turned on everything it had, and the 'Old Bucket' started shaking and rumbling, with every weld in her straining at about nine knots. About a half mile from the beach, you could feel the ship bump on the bottom, then go some more, and then more bumps; this repeated itself until we were right up on the beach, and I lowered the ramp down on dry land. The Old Man didn't want to spend any more time than was absolutely necessary in this spot. . . .

"As soon as we beached, destroyers and cruisers started long-range shelling of targets inland, firing right over our group of ships, and every so often, there would be a 'short' round."

In keeping with "the old Navy/Coast Guard law that states, 'Always call special sea detail, or move a vessel, just as the crew sits down to a meal,' the first lieutenant came into the mess deck just as we sat down to supper the second night at Lingayen Gulf and stated: 'The soldiers unloading the ship are dead-tired. If we don't help them finish unloading, we'll have to spend another night on this damn beach. We have to do it before dark because they won't let us retract after sunset.' No one said a word; we just all went into the tank deck and began loading trucks with a passion. . . . Everyone was throwing 100-pound sacks; trucks were moving as we loaded them. Word was passed to the bridge that the last truck was off the ship just as the sun was setting. The Old Man put the *18* in reverse with bow doors open and ramp down; soldiers were jumping off the ramp onto the beach and we were still throwing supplies off the ramp as the ship backed out to the open water and away from the night-time enemy shelling."

January 1945
En Route to Lingayen Gulf, the Philippines

Lieutenant Colonel Teri Friedman Reid submits a tribute to her deceased uncle, Sergeant Sidney Sherman, veteran of Sixth Army, 1878th Combat Engineers.

Sergeant Sidney Sherman and his engineer buddies "had built the airstrip on Biak . . . and defended it against Japanese counterattack. On 7 January 1945, they embarked on the *Kyle B. Johnson* for the invasion of Lingayen Gulf, the Philippines," Lieutenant Colonel Friedman Reid reports.

In the diary of his voyage with the invasion fleet from New Guinea to the Philippines, Sergeant Sherman relates "'the misery of storms at sea, seasickness, and moldy rations,'" as well as the scenic beauty of Mindoro Island, which they passed on the morning of 11 January.

"On 12 January, the tone of his diary changes dramatically as he writes of the events of the previous evening: 'Three Kamikazes hit our ship at 1930. We were in the death position of the convoy on the outside, in front. They hit the starboard side at a hatch; all the boys in B Company were killed. They gave me a fire hose to hose the body parts off the deck of the ship; we fell out of the convoy to fight the fires and caught up later.'

"He concludes his diary the night before he landed in Lingayen Gulf, after which he would fight 150 miles through the jungle to liberate Manila and Baguio. His final entry reads: 'There is a lot I haven't put in my diary, but I will always remember. I miss my wife and baby son so much.'

"I am so very proud of my uncle Sidney Sherman," Lieutenant Colonel Friedman Reid declares, "as well as my Uncle Sol Kaplan, who fought in the Battle of the Bulge, but preferred not to relive his memories of that time in his life. I feel that I honor them by continuing a tradition of service to our country."

January 1945
Luzon, the Philippines

Lieutenant Colonel Charles R. Keefe was a captain with 63rd Infantry Regiment, 6th Infantry Division.

"The 6th Infantry Division left Sansapor, New Guinea, about 400 miles south of the equator, on 29 December 1944. Cannon Company of the 63rd Infantry was on an LST with our six self-propelled 105mm howitzers," Lieutenant Colonel Keefe writes.

"New Year's Day found us en route to the Philippine Islands for the initial landing on the main island of Luzon at Lingayen Gulf. On 7 January, we had our first experience with the Kamikaze, suicide, piloted planes. . . . Several escort ships were hit over a three- or four-day period.

"The landing was made on 9 January against light initial resistance on the beach. The main Jap positions were on the high hills and mountains beyond the beachhead. The resistance strengthened as the units moved inland.

"Initially, the 63rd Infantry (less the 53rd Field Artillery Battalion) was with corps reserve. The regiment was given the mission of clearing any enemy resistance on the high ground and hills on the left of the beachhead toward the town of Rosario. This proved to be a bloody job, and the area became known as Purple Heart Valley. For the first ten days, the bulk of supporting artillery fire came from the six 105mm howitzers of Cannon Company. We would sometimes refer to fire requests as 'OK, fire one truckload.' The ravine near the company position was filled with empty shell cases.

"The battle for the hills surrounding Purple Heart Valley concluded at the end of January 1945 with about 1,000 enemy dead. The 63rd Infantry regiment suffered 103 KIA and 486 wounded. The regiment joined the rest of the 6th Division on the route south toward Manila and other major battles."

25 January 1945
En Route to Manila, the Philippines

Captain Bernard L. Patterson was a first lieutenant, weapons platoon leader, Company F, 145th Infantry, 37th Division, when the division landed 9 January at Lingayen Gulf.

On 25 January, "about 8 or 9 miles north of Angeles, east of the edge of Clark Airfield, as we approached the barrio of Dau, we had our first enemy contact of the day," Captain Patterson recalls. "A small group of six to eight Japanese soldiers who were armed only with a pole charge, no rifles, were discovered in holes by the road, waiting for our tanks to approach. . . . They were to place the charge against the side of a tank and explode the charge. The explosion would kill the bearer but hopefully would destroy the tank."

Tanks, however, were far to the rear because the Japanese had destroyed many bridges. Having met the pole-charge men where the road narrowed, leading platoons of E and F Companies then "spread out in the open fields on both sides of the highway" where the road straightened.

"Advancing slowly, just behind leading platoons for about 1½ miles, this appeared to be a route march. Suddenly, a Japanese tank appeared about 300 yards ahead. It must have been a shock to the Japanese gunner. So many targets—American soldiers on both sides of at least one-half mile of the straight highway. The tank fired one shot straight down the middle of the road. The shell ricocheted off the pavement near me and exploded far to the rear. . . . Before the tank could fire again, all our soldiers were in the roadside ditch or farther away. The tank fired once more and that shell exploded across the road from me and caused a few casualties. The tank then turned back toward Angeles."

With "our entire company now in the fields," and not having heard another enemy shot fired all day, "we approached the high ground, near the area where the tank had appeared. There was a line of trees stretching all across the high ground. . . . We were about 150 yards from the trees when a large Japanese flag began waving back and forth near the trees. We stopped our advance.

"A Japanese officer stepped out from the trees, shouting in English, and slowly walked out in the light. He continued shouting and began to walk toward us. Japanese soldiers began to stand up at the edge of the trees, in the open. Their rifles were at trail (butts on the ground), and at least two machine guns were in sight on the ground. There were forty to sixty soldiers.

"First Lieutenant Floyd Roegner, company executive officer, began to advance toward the Japanese officer [who] was saying something about 'meeting his fate.' They were about 30 yards apart when a foolish man on our right told the foolish man next to him to shoot the Japanese officer. He tried, but missed. The Japanese officer turned and jogged back to his lines. . . . The Japanese soldiers sank out of sight. Lieutenant Roegner turned and walked back to our lines. Later, he said he was expecting one of those machine guns to stitch him up the back, but not a shot was fired.

"Not a Japanese soldier was in sight, so Captain Paulak, our CO, ordered us to move out. We started and then lots of shots were fired. We had three killed and ten to twelve wounded in about two minutes. We stopped and dug-in and waited. Captain Paulak was one of the wounded and was evacuated with the rest. After the intense fire stopped us, very little firing occurred. Lieutenant Roegner took over the company, but in his report of the day's actions, he ignored the strange encounter with the Japanese officer, so it never made our division history.

"That night, the Japanese withdrew toward Clark Field and Fort Stotsenberg. We moved toward the Japanese position, which was a low, road ditch. Just behind the trees, a road led west to Clark Field. We marched into Angeles unopposed. After Clark Field and Stotsenberg were secured, we resumed our drive for Manila."

"For fifty years I have wondered," just as Major Roegner has, whether that officer wanted "individual combat or to surrender his troops," Captain Pattererson confides. "I think we were lucky to have run into that Japanese officer. If another one had been in charge, we could have lost a lot more men than we did."

30 January 1945
Loi Kang Ridge, Burma

Lieutenant Colonel Albert T. Willis Jr. was a replacement company commander, Mars Task Force, made up of the 5332nd Brigade, consisting of 475th Infantry and 124th Cavalry.

"The 475th Infantry had entered the Nawhkam area 18 January after following a jungle and mountain trail from Myitkyina some 300 miles to the north," Lieutenant Colonel Willis writes. "Of secondary construction, the Burma Road became of primary concern in weaving a pattern for survival as a lifeline to China. Constructed by the British, occupied by the Japanese, fought for by the Chinese and Americans, it became for one day a place of victory and defeat.

"We sent patrols to 'The Road' every day to plant mines and set booby traps in the hope of harassing the retreating Japs. . . . We set the traps during the day. The Japs disarmed them at night. Just like a game, a deadly game—with control of The Road going to the winner."

As company commander of 2nd Battalion, then-Captain Willis went along "with a patrol from Easy Company as an observer" on 30 January. "We skirted the drop zone. . . . It was 1000 hours and the sun was hot and bright. We proceeded through the high cane grass and unused rice fields with extreme caution. A thousand yards ahead lay The Road. . . .

"The point of the patrol halted a little farther on and signaled the platoon leader forward. . . . A lieutenant had reported to the battalion commander that a dummy field gun made of logs had been observed in the area. He was right: There it was, looking for real like the biggest field gun we had ever seen in Burma. What a crazy war! Dummies guarding The Road!"

On a small knoll overlooking The Road near the 76-mile marker, "we suddenly saw in the direction of Namhpaka a lone Jap soldier heading south on The Road and trudging along it like any ordinary hitchhiker back in the States. The platoon sergeant's M-1 dropped him in his tracks practically on top of the 76-mile marker. The game was on and we were leading 1–0. . . .

"We held the patrol perimeter tight for a few minutes to see what effect the shot would have as the sound was absorbed in the soft brown Burma hills all around us. Nothing happened. We eased the patrol onto The Road and set about our business. . . ."

Selecting a different route to return, the patrol was instructed by battalion "to investigate some hostile movement in a wood atop a good-sized hill to our left flank. . . . The patrol leader dispatched one squad under cover of 60mm mortar fire. . . . The rest of the patrol took cover and observed, with the patrol leader directing the mortar fire by his radio. It started out just routine, with the mortar shells dropping ahead of the squad, now advancing as skirmishers up the gentle slope.

"Suddenly, and without warning, a round fell short and burst in the midst of the squad, and a bit of shrapnel buried itself in the belly of one of the infantry-men, killing him instantly. The fire was lifted as the squad reached its objective to find nothing there. The game was tied up now, 1–1, by a foul ball stamped with the words 'Made in the USA.'

"The body of the infantryman was gently carried back to the patrol and onto Loi Kang Ridge. I carried his Tommy gun back with me, with its picture of a girl taped on the stock and the name 'Phyllis' carved under it.

"Back on Loi Kang Ridge, I looked back toward the 76-mile marker, not any-more with awe, curiosity, or pride, but this time with only disgust. . . . The Road lay like a thread between the Burma hills, a dirty thread splotched with red."

January 1945
POW Camp Hoten, Chen Chia Tung, Manchuria

Colonel Michael A. Quinn begins Book VI of his POW diary.

Colonel Quinn greets his wife and seven children on New Year's Day 1945: "My thoughts were of you all back home. . . . All I could do is to remember you in our religious services today, which I did."

"As a rule I hope I am not envious of other people for their good fortune. But when some Americans received radios [messages relayed by ham radio opera-tors] today and I didn't, I must frankly confess, I was very envious. I know that you did send all the messages you were able to, but it is just my luck not to get any," he writes on 6 January

Among his news for 11 January, he says: "We have rumors that we are to be asked to comment on our reaction to treatment during the war. As far as I am concerned, they will not even get the satisfaction of a complaint from me."

On 13 January, the colonel reports: "We are authorized to write home, but here's the joke. All letters must be typed in duplicate. We must furnish the type-writer. There is only one in camp, and there is no carbon paper and no fresh typewriter ribbons."

On 29 January, he turns over to the library his May 1939 copy of *Fortune* mag-azine, wondering whether any copy "was ever read more than this issue." He muses about "sending it back to the publishers" as a "real souvenir." Then, in a postwar comment, he says that he did so, and that the magazine was on display in *Fortune*'s World War II museum.

2–5 January 1945
SS *Leonidas Merritt*, Homeward Bound, Rebound

Brigadier General Raymond Thompson was a young U.S. Merchant Mariner returning home aboard the unescorted SS Leonidas Merritt, *heavily damaged by two Japanese Kamikazes, 12 November 1944. The ship made it back to the States on 2 January—and 5 January 1945.*

"Our ship still looked like a shipwreck when we sailed into San Francisco harbor this morning but we were looking forward to a big welcome, some ice cream, and a telephone call home," Mariner Thompson writes in his diary on 2 January 1945. "We were disappointed. A Coast Guard cutter intercepted us as we neared the Golden Gate Bridge. We were ordered to stop engines and a captain came aboard. He inspected the damage on the foredeck with our captain and marveled at the pieces of plywood we had used to board up gaping holes in the bridge-house and the deck where the two Kamikazes had struck us."

Brigadier General Thompson explains that "both planes flattened forward masts and booms, and huge holes were burned into the foredeck in an attack that cost many lives. One of the suicide planes had hit the fore part of the bridge-house and the engine went through three steel bulkheads and dented a fourth before it stopped. It was difficult to walk on the deck, although we had cleared most of the debris during the thirty-six days it took us after we left Leyte to reach San Francisco," he writes from a fifty-year perspective.

"That Coast Guard captain kept shaking his head side to side. 'I can't let you into San Francisco harbor,' he finally told our skipper. 'You're a menace to navigation!'

"A menace to navigation? Holy cow! We thought he was kidding, but he wasn't. We were stunned when he told us we'd have to take the Liberty ship to Portland, Oregon, where the shipyard there might consider scrapping her or maybe try to make repairs. But he offered to send aboard some fresh vegetables, milk, and ice cream, and within a few hours we were underway again. It took us four days to go the short distance to Portland, where we received a much warmer welcome."

Mariner Thompson recorded it thus in his diary on 5 January 1945: "We sailed down the Willamette River with all of our signal flags flying on the aft section of the ship. We couldn't fly them forward because of the loss of the masts, booms, et cetera. But we want to make a good impression. I guess we're doing just that. Hundreds of people are lining the shores, waving to us. It feels good to be home!"

FEBRUARY 1945

39

"The sixty-seven Army nurses imprisoned in Santo Tomas Internment camp in Manila, Philippine Islands, were still performing all the nursing duties for the internee population of approximately 5,000 civilians" on 3 February 1945, says Lieutenant Colonel Hattie R. Brantley, one of the nurse-POWs who were imprisoned there. "Rations had been reduced below half since the preceding September when American bombers had returned to the area," bombing the port sector and vicinity. The internees were "half-starved, half-sick," and "life was at a low-ebb in the prison camp."

"Just after dark on this February evening, the smell of gasoline permeated the atmosphere, and an increase in gunfire in the city was heard," she recalls. "Blackout had been the rule for months, so, in the darkness, no one could guess what was happening. But toward midnight, a Sherman tank crashed through the bamboo gates of the prison camp and approached the main building with lights ablaze. Excitement reigned! With sword drawn, the Japanese commandant charged the tank as it neared the building. The turret came up and a rifle aimed at the onrushing figure. He disregarded the command to halt, and a bullet drilled him right between the eyes.

"Pandemonium!" she exclaims. "The truth that the Americans had returned was too much to comprehend" for those confined in the university-turned-prison of Santo Tomas, many there since the fall of Bataan in April 1942.

On the days after that Sherman tank crashed into the internees' Santo Tomas quarters, two battalions land on Corregidor in Manila Bay 16 February; U.S. XI Corps completes capture of Bataan area of Luzon 21 February; and fighting ends on Corregidor 26 February. On Iwo Jima, Task Forces 52 and 54, along with B-24s, bombard the Japanese-held island 16–18 February and two divisions of Marines from V Amphibious Corps land in Operation Detachment 19 February.

At about the same time, on the Western Front in the ETO, the Siegfried Line is broken north of Echternach by VIII Corps 18 February; US XX Corps completes battle in the Saar–Moselle area 22 February; and First and Ninth Armies begin the Roer offensive 23 February.

Post–9 January–February 1945
Manila, the Philippines

Lieutenant Colonel Louis C. Rosenstein was S-4 on the brigade staff of Brigadier General Henry Hutchins, U.S. Corps of Engineers, commanding the 4th Engineer Special Brigade, Sixth Army.

Once General Walter Krueger's Sixth Army made its 9 January landing in the Lingayen Gulf area of Luzon and secured the beachheads, "about 120 miles of Japanese-held rugged terrain lay between the advancing American forces and their objective, the capital city of Manila," Lieutenant Colonel Rosenstein writes. "At the same time, the Sixth Army had to protect its flanks and rear from remaining Japanese forces on the island. This required the coordinated efforts of all Sixth Army units and presented enormous logistic-support problems, as all supply had to come through the Lingayen Gulf Beachhead.

"As the American forces fought their way south toward Manila, there was little time to think of means to feed the teeming population of Manila and the huge American force, once the city had been captured. The stubborn and fanatic Japanese defense required the full attention of all concerned. . . . During that bloody assault, however, one far-sighted general was very much concerned with future support. Brigadier General Henry Hutchins was actively reconnoitering for a location. . . .

"The only possible area he found was a very shallow, poor beach that was entirely blocked from roads by a strong, high stone seawall. Without hesitation, he brought in the heavy bulldozers from the shore battalion of one of his regiments to break down the wall in places and to construct an artificial beach capable of handling various sizes of beach landing craft, trucks, and track-mounted cranes that could handle supply to Manila until such a time as the elaborate harbor facilities could be repaired or replaced. . . .

"By the time Manila was fully occupied, after desperate battles, its entire port system had been totally destroyed by the Japanese, and for months the starving population, as well as the U.S. Army, depended upon supplies, food, et cetera, brought in across the artificial beach built by General Hutchins' bulldozers for the use of landing craft, ferrying in cargo from ships anchored offshore.

"Long after the city had been captured, there were strong pockets of Japanese resistance that had to be blasted out, but there was a good supply of food and other necessities for the American troops and the almost-starving population, thanks to the foresight and initiative of Brigadier General Henry Hutchins, U.S. Army Corps of Engineers."

12 January–February 1945

Manila, the Philippines

Major John R. Edwards served through New Guinea, the Philippines, Okinawa,
Korea, and Tokyo with 3rd Air Cargo Control Squadron.

"We arrived on D-plus-3 [12 January] on Luzon on board an LST with our
equipment and personnel," Major Edwards writes. "While we waited to land, I
recall a captured, U.S. rail-mounted artillery gun firing salvos at our ships. It was
housed in a concrete bunker on rails. The Japs would roll it out, fire a round,
and return it to the bunker. Fortunately, their range calculations were poor and
they did little beyond harassment. A fighter bomber located it and rendered it
inoperable.

"We went ashore with a combat engineer company to Lingayen, where they
activated an airstrip for our cargo planes and fighters. Rifle and sniper fire from
the hills north of the strip was silenced by naval bombardment from battlewagons offshore. We set up operations, called our C-47 and -46 birds in, and with
aid of quartermaster truck companies started loading and shipping air freight to
areas as needed.

"One unforgettable shipment I shall always remember was a group of POWs
from Clark Field in Manila to be airlifted to hospitals and finally home to the
United States. They were walking or on stretchers—gaunt, fragile, ill, and crippled from death marches, starvation, neglected medical treatment, and mistreat-
ment in POW camps. I can never forget these soldiers who fought so valiantly
until captured—the vacant look in their eyes, heroes from a living hell."

3 February 1945

From POW in the Philippines to Home

Lieutenant Colonel Hattie R. Brantley, who served with Field Hospital #1 at
Cabcaben and at Little Baguio, and was interned at Santo Tomas since the fall of
Bataan, continues her story.

When that Sherman tank crashed through the prison's bamboo gates, bringing freedom on 3 February, nurse Hattie Brantley was on duty in the hospital. "It
was some time before one of the returning Americans came to the ward where I
was on duty. He was a correspondent who had left Manila in 1942, leaving
behind his wife, who became interned. She was a patient in the hospital, and he
came to visit," Lieutenant Colonel Brantley recalls. "I will never forget how he
looked—so big, and strong, and healthy, skin shining, and smooth, ruddy com-
plexion." By contrast, "we, having lacked food and medicine for so long, were
thin, pale, and wrinkled, with sallow complexions. He looked like a Greek god

by comparison. Also, his vibrant actions, whereas we had moved like zombies for so long! What a sight for sore eyes!"

"General MacArthur had made good his promise to return, and indeed, the 1st Cavalry had stormed the prison camp gates and entered to set up resistance in the camp grounds. And so began the Battle of Manila, 1945 style!

"The Army kitchen quickly provided food, and most of the internees became ill from eating too much, but it was so good! Food, cigarettes, and a ready supply of medicine seemed almost too good to believe.

"It was several days before the Army nurses were evacuated, being flown in a C-47 taking off from Dewey Boulevard to land in Leyte for the first look, feel of freedom in three years. New uniforms were issued, three meals per day provided, and one promotion in rank for the entire complement of nurses, after having served on Bataan, Corregidor, and enduring the years of imprisonment and degradation by their Japanese captors."

"Freedom isn't free," Lieutenant Colonel Brantley attests, "but this group could thoroughly appreciate and receive, and say with fervor and conviction: 'God bless the USA.'"

February 1945
Bilibid Prison, Manila, the Philippines

Betsy Herold Heimke, wife of Major Karl F. Heimke, spent three of her teen years as a civilian POW of the Japanese before being rescued by the 1st Cavalry from Bilibid Prison.

Responding to Lieutenant Colonel Hattie Brantley's rescue story when it appeared in *The Officer* magazine, Mrs. Heimke writes: "I was saddened to learn that the brave and courageous soldier, company commander Captain Rogers, lost his life. I owe him my own life. I was an American fifteen-year-old teenager in that Bilibid Prison (with my parents and older brother) who was among the 456 civilian POWs in Bilibid and one of the very happy individuals who was liberated that memorable 4 February 1945."

She explains that the civilians had not been at Bilibid during the entire period: "The American and Allied civilians were moved from Baguio, where they were interned at Camp John Hay and Camp Holmes for three years. On 28 and 29 December 1944, the Japs trucked them, like cattle, to Bilibid Prison in Manila. Adjacent and contiguous to their compound were approximately 811 emaciated and mostly bed-ridden military POWs, remnants of the Bataan Death March, Corregidor, and other places in the islands.

"During the night of 5 February 1945, our two groups were temporarily evacuated by our glorious liberators from Bilibid to an old shoe factory, Ang Tibay, about 5 miles north. This feat was miraculously executed without loss of life to the new ex-POWs. This brief and exciting encounter gave us our first opportunity to talk and visit with these gallant souls and to learn the fate of many of our own friends, husbands, fathers, and sons who had 'joined the military' after 8 December 1941. The Japs were dishonest and reluctant to share this important news with us. These brand-new reports were both happy and sad. I humbly give a heartfelt 'Thanks' and 'God Bless' to all the brave GIs whose heroic efforts made our freedom possible."

4 February–3 March 1945
Manila, the Philippines

Captain Bernard L. Patterson was a first lieutenant, weapon platoon leader, Company F, 145th Infantry, 37th Division.

"About 0200 on 4 February, we entered Manila after crossing the last small river north of the city, the Tuliahan, on a footbridge made of planks and empty fifty-gallon gasoline drums, because all bridging materials had been sent to General Wainwright's old 1st Cavalry Division so they could get to Manila first. A task force from the 1st Cavalry had entered Manila on 3 February and liberated the Santo Tomas Internment Camp of American civilians but then was cut off and our division had to rescue them," Captain Patterson writes.

Continuing toward the Pasig River after daylight, Company F "advanced down Juan Luna Street and was greeted by large crowds of happy Filipinos who offered wine and whiskey as we walked rapidly onward. As we approached the Estero de la Reina, a small stream, and the Tondo district, we came under fire from a 20mm anti-aircraft gun that was firing straight down Juan Luna Street. We had no casualties and I saw no civilian injuries. . . .

"We had advanced about three blocks without contact with any Japanese when we noticed an increase in civilians running toward our lines, followed by lots of smoke, and soon we could see fire. The Japanese had set Tondo on fire, as well as other areas north of the Pasig River. The wind was driving the fire toward us and, as we had no fire-fighting equipment, we retreated back over the Estero de la Reina Bridge. The small stream stopped the fire from crossing to our area.

"Other units in our division had liberated Bilibid Prison with hundreds of prisoners, mostly Americans and Australians, with a few Dutch soldiers, and made contact with the cut-off task force of the 1st Cavalry on the same day. On 5 February, we recrossed the bridge and advanced toward the Pasig River. The entire area had been burned; now, just smoldering ruins remained. About six blocks from the bridge, we passed Tondo cathedral, where large numbers of Filipinos had sought sanctuary when the fighting started, now an empty shell of a building. The Japanese set it on fire when they burned Tondo and shot the Filipinos as they sought to escape, with very few survivors."

After two weeks spent clearing the Japanese from the area between Highway 3 and Manila Bay, "2nd Battalion then returned to a position north of the Pasig River for the onslaught on Intramuros," the old Walled City. At 0730 on 23 February, "our artillery and other divisional artillery began to increase fire on Intramuros. At 0830, the artillery fire was lifted and at exactly 0830, F Company's 2nd Platoon, led by First Lieutenant Jim Ryan, took off at a dead-run to cross the 200-yards-plus from the post office steps to Queqon Gate. They went through the gate and into Latron College building in less than two minutes. . . .

"Inside Intramuros, F Company had a zone three blocks wide and eight blocks deep to the west wall of Intramuros and by sundown had made contact with the wall except for a small area with several pillboxes. . . . Late that afternoon, we fired some mortar rounds at the pillboxes. . . . Right away, a white flag came out of the hole followed by eighteen to twenty unarmed Formosan labor troops, our only prisoners in Manila.

"The following day, we completed our mission and made contact with other American troops west of the wall. The 2nd and 1st Battalions, 145th Infantry, and 3rd Battalion, 129th Infantry, all a part of the 37th Division, had captured Intramuros. . . .

"The battle for Manila ended on 3 March 1945, almost thirty days after General MacArthur had announced the capture of Manila," Captain Patterson says, adding that "the liberation of Manila was the only time in the war against Japan that a major city had been seized by American troops."

15–16 February 1945
Corregidor, the Philippines

Major William W. Turner was captain and pilot, 36th Fighter Squadron, 8th Fighter Group, which provided cover for C-47s carrying paratroopers in the invasion of Corregidor.

On 15 February, "planes from the 36th Fighter Squadron had reported to a spotter plane over Corregidor for any targets in the area," Major Turner reports. "They had been covering the landing on the Bataan Peninsula and still had 500-pound bombs available. I remember that the spotter had reported that a large coastal gun in a revetment was still operational and needed to be worked over.

He indicated the target. I made the first dive-bombing run at it. He then assessed the damage and said, 'You got a direct hit on the breech. That gun is out for good. We won't waste any more on it.' He then picked out other targets for the rest of the planes to work over."

The date selected for the invasion of Corregidor, 16 February, "turned out to be an overcast day with moderate winds. As I recall, each plane carried twenty-four paratroopers. I led the squadron (sixteen P-38 Fighters), and we picked up the twenty-four C-47 planes just north of our base (San Jose, Mindoro). We all headed for Corregidor some 150 miles away. . . .

"The ground assault was to be accomplished, in part, by dropping paratroopers on top of the high portion, which offered only two small adjacent areas—no room for a mass drop. To make conditions worse, a strong wind was blowing across these two areas.

"Upon arriving over the target, the C-47s broke formation and formed into a single long line and made a large circle. Then one plane at a time would fly over the drop area and discharge the paratroopers. At first, due to the crosswinds, many of the men missed the drop area and were carried over the cliffs, some even into the pounding surf below.

"General Douglas MacArthur's Silver B-17 was there observing the operation. . . . After some discussion with the drop forces, the planes started coming in at a minimum drop altitude, allowed more for the wind drift, and dropped only six men in a pass. . . . It wasn't long until the ground below was polka-dotted with chutes and many brave men. . . .

"Paratroopers are special men. . . . They ride to the ground supported by a bunch of cloth. They are sitting ducks as they float down. They hit hard when they land, then have to find their squad, organize, assess the situation, move on out, and fight like hell. I have great respect for them and the crews of the unarmed C-47s. Gentlemen, I salute you," Major Turner writes in tribute.

16 February 1945
Corregidor, the Philippines

Major Paul J. Cain staged on Goodenough Island for the invasion of Hollandia, New Guinea, and served as CO of Company I, 34th Infantry Regiment, in the retaking of Corregidor.

"On 16 February 1945, after loading on landing craft, we crossed North Channel of Manila Bay for landing on South Beach, bottom side on Corregidor, while 503rd Paratroops landed by parachute topside. On trip across channel, we witnessed a 100-plane B-24 bomb attack on the island, leaving a big cloud of dust, which completely covered the island," Major Cain reports.

"With fire-support from Navy gunboats and landing crafts, we got on beach. Found beach heavily mined. Our mission: To clear South and North Beach area and make contact with 503rd on our left; K and L Companies to move to top of Malinta Hill as rapidly as possible, to our right. Japanese had heavy machine guns in caves on either side covering beach. Navy kept two light cruisers offshore for fire-support. They did a good job of quieting the machine guns. . . .

"After clearing mines from a portion of beach area, a platoon of tanks . . . quickly quieted snipers firing at us from inside Malinta Tunnel and from a storage building in north dock area. First night in, with help from Navy flares, we directed mortar fire on enemy pulling a *banzai* attack on our troops atop Malinta Hill. . . .

"Second day, Company I killed forty Japanese in caves. . . . Third day in, Company I replaced Company K, which had lost its CO and a number of other casualties, while being pushed off a portion of Malinta Hill. We were two days getting that area back.

"I couldn't help but recall a briefing by two naval officers, advising us that one of the laterals on Malinta Tunnel was filled with torpedo warheads and if they decided to blow it, it would likely leave only a channel across the island where Malinta Hill stood. Seventh night in, Japs blew the tunnel. No channel, but a squad of infantry lost three men in a rock slide into the ocean on south end of hill. . . ."

Major Cain credits the Navy "with support fire and the Air Force with bombs and napon [*sic*] that knocked out Japanese communications so they could never put together a coordinated attack. Later, Intelligence told us there were over 20,000 Japs on the island, and we landed with 5,000 troops."

7 February 1945
Echternach, Luxembourg

Colonel Jean W. Christy continues his 5th Infantry Division account.

After reconnaissance, "the 50th Field Artillery Battalion finally found a position southwest of Echternach that was suitable to support the attack east across the Sauer River," Colonel Christy writes. The attack "jumped off at 0300 hours," 7 February 1945.

"Determined German resistance had been anticipated. In addition to the obstacle of the river, the ground rose sharply from the river bed into high hills and bluffs, which offered excellent defensive positions. Pillboxes of the Siegfried Line, only 150 yards back from the river, were concealed there. Tanks and entrenched infantrymen were interspersed between the pillboxes, and mine fields were laid in front of them."

"To make matters worse, although it was wintry cold, an early thaw had turned the Sauer from a normally placid stream into a swollen river with a violent current. The high water actually covered some of the German barbed wire and other obstacles, hiding them from our assault boats.

"The initial assault was met by grazing fires from machine guns and rifles, and by mortar and artillery fire. The swift and treacherous stream capsized some of the boats. Enemy fire sank others. The barbed wire and obstacles under the water caused the destruction of other boats. The heavily weighted infantrymen, unable to shed their equipment and swim clear, were swept into the undertow and drowned. More than sixty perished this way.

"The 10th Infantry made a second attempt shortly before 0800 hours, and was met by the same conditions. All but two out of twelve boats were sunk. A total of only eight men made it ashore. Although under heavy mortar and machine-gun fire, they held the 5th Infantry Division bridgehead for twenty-two hours while artillery shells from both sides crashed around them. Then help came.

"The 417th Infantry, in its first combat mission, fared better. General Patton notes that it was probably because they didn't realize how dangerous it really was. . . .

"In order to make progress, our troops had to overcome the obstacles of the pillboxes. They were concealed in various ways: one was discovered hidden inside a barn, and another inside a regular house. Our infantry quickly became adept in locating pillboxes and neutralizing them. . . .

"The 11th Infantry got troops across. The 10th got a whole battalion across. The 80th did well in its assault. And we had a bridgehead."

During the crossing of the Sauer on 13 February by General Patton and General Eddy, XII Corps commander, "one of the better General Patton stories of the war" materialized, which the general mentions in his memoir *War As I Knew It*.

"The way I heard it," Colonel Christy says, "was that it was early morning, and there was a heavy mist rising from the river, completely concealing the already partly submerged bridge. A surprised infantry soldier guarding the bridge on the far shore looked up to see General Patton walking across the river. Believing what he thought he saw, he told everyone that Patton had walked across on the water."

February 1945
Diekirch, Luxembourg

Colonel Tommy R. Gilliam, who landed with his unit at Normandy on D-plus-33, continued with them until wounded 9 November 1944 at Metz.

"I rejoined the 1st Battalion, 2nd Infantry, 5th Division, on 19 February . . . three years to the day since I had sailed from the New York Port of Embarkation for overseas [to Iceland]," Colonel Gilliam recalls. Taking command of C Company, he stayed the first night at the Battalion CP. "During the night, a Nebelwerfer rocket barrage hit the field next to the house and I woke up trying to get in the six-inch space under a bureau in the room. None of my reflex actions had been lost while I was in the hospital replacement-depot pipeline!"

"We had some short, fierce firefights, and then the enemy began melting away. The engineers threw a footbridge across a small river, either the Kyll or the Prum and we crossed at midnight. Waiting to cross, I was behind B Company in an open field on a bright moonlit night and I had a premonition that caused me to draw the company up alongside B Company. About ten minutes after we completed this move, a heavy Nebelwerfer rocket concentration hit the field where we had been. Crossing the river, we attacked a town at daybreak, capturing the German company defending it, asleep in its barracks. . . .

"Arriving on the high ground, we set up our attached heavy machine guns to control the road down which the German unit soon appeared, retreating in good order in a route march formation. As our machine guns opened up, they couldn't run up the hill to surrender fast enough and soon we had 200 men and eight officers as prisoners—but we couldn't evacuate them until dark, as the return route was still under German artillery observation and fire. My men were digging their foxholes and decided the prisoners needed some exercise, so they put them to work digging the holes.

"About this time, a Germany artillery captain, impeccably uniformed—riding pants, polished boots, swagger stick and map case under his arm, and monocle in his eye—came up the hill and in heavily accented British English announced he was a *Hauptmann* in the Wehrmacht, gave his name and serial number, and said he was surrendering under the Geneva Rules of Warfare and was placed with the German officers. The same platoon sergeant decided that if the men's holes were being dug by the prisoners, then the officers should dig the holes for the American officers. They jumped to with alacrity, all except the artillery captain, who informed us that under the Geneva Convention, officers were not required to do labor. The sergeant put his .45 muzzle next to the *Hauptmann's* temple and said, 'I said, dig!' 'Yah, Yah,' cried the captain, grabbing a shovel, 'I dig, I dig!'"

January–March 1945
Biron to Stetternich to Dusseldorf, Germany

Colonel George W. Irvine was a lieutenant colonel commanding the 324th Field Artillery Battalion, "armed with tractor-drawn 155mm howitzers, the general support artillery of the 83rd Division throughout combat in Northern Europe."

"From Rochefort, we leap-frogged along the northern shoulder of the Bulge, moving to Biron on 1 January, to Harre on the 4th, to Hierlot on the 7th, and to Verleumont on the 12th," Colonel Irvine writes. On one of these moves through the snow-covered foothills, we came to a long, steady, uphill grade on a paved road covered with ice. The cleats on our thirteen-ton tractors would not do anything except slip and slide. However, our little quarter-ton jeeps with four-wheel drive did have traction. We found that by putting a jeep with a tow chain in front of each tractor, they were able to gain forward momentum, and we made it over the hill and into our next firing position. From there, we moved to Petite Langlir and finally on 22 January to Chene-Al-Pierre.

"We were transferred back to Ninth Army on 3 February, for the final time, and the XIX Corps, going into position at Durboslar on 7 February, reinforcing the 29th Division along the Roer River, west of Julich. In Operation Grenade, the 29th crossed the Roer on 23 February. We crossed to Stetternich on the 28th and were pushed through the 29th for a drive with the 2nd Armored Division.

"We reached the Rhine in the vicinity of Neuss, across from Dusseldorf, on 2 March, and fired our first rounds across the Rhine at about 1100 hours. Three German 88mm guns were found, together with about 4,000 rounds of ammunition, and for two weeks we fired them at targets around Dusseldorf."

February 1945
Luxembourg, France, and Germany

Lieutenant Colonel Richard J. Frederick was a maintenance and supply platoon leader, first lieutenant, with 131st Ordnance Company, Heavy Maintenance, FA, since September 1944.

On 1 February, the company moved 115 miles from Rodange to Dombasle, France, where it was attached to U.S. Seventh Army and then to the 19th Ordnance Battalion. While awaiting an area to set up shop, the company "did only collection-point work and operated as a fourth-echelon shop only" from Chau-fontaine, France. "Our chief operation was repair and combat-loading of half-tracks and scout cars, which came to us practically in a state of salvage. We usually could restore one good vehicle from four or five wrecks."

Another move on 20 February took them 110 miles to Lintgen, Luxembourg, where control reverted to 12th Army Group, Third Army. "This began our fast movement out of Luxembourg and across Germany in support of XII Corps.

"While at Hildburghausen, Germany, we replaced some of our tools and supplies, metal cutting saws, heads for our milling machines, wrenches and sockets, and abrasive materials. All of this was obtained from an abandoned Haenel aircraft cannon plant, with the permission of the U.S. Military Government office in Hildburghausen."

1945
France, Germany, and Austria

Major Robert L. Kasting submits a history of his deceased father, Robert Francis Kasting, staff sergeant and pharmacist with the 117th Evacuation Hospital in France, Germany, and Austria.

Major Kasting's father was inducted into the Army in August 1942 with "about 500 from the Louisville, Kentucky, area." After three months' training at Fort Bragg, the 117th departed New York City on the SS *Mariposa* with three other evacuation hospitals. Mr. Kasting told family members, "We were assigned to the Seventh Army and left for Epinal, France. Now we were ready to go into operation. We followed the Seventh across France and into Germany, treating the wounded and sick of the 100th Division, which was in front of us."

A press release at the time from Sixth Army Group, France, reports: "This 400-bed hospital, following the advance of U.S. Seventh Army troops in General Jacob L. Devers's 6th Army Group, has treated over 5,000 patients during three months of combat operations in France. Fifty-six percent of all admissions were surgical cases and 44 percent medical."

"Attesting to the skilled medical-care wounded Americans receive on the Western Front is one surgical achievement of the 117th Evacuation Hospital—fifty brain operations without one death," the write-up notes.

Winter 1944–1945
Trier, Germany

Colonel Thomas F. Royals was a Ranger, 417th Infantry Regiment Combat Team, taken prisoner at Trier 20 January 1945.

"There was snow on the ground that January, quite a bit of snow," Colonel Royals recalls. "I was used to cold and snow, as I grew up in Chicago where we always had snow in January. However, this snow looked different. On the hills, there were red spots all over, and more red spots than white near foxholes. The German 88s had zeroed in on some of the foxholes and the men inside had died. . . .

"As the shelling has stopped, you know it is time. Rifle in hand, bayonet in place, we go down the hill as they come up—face to face, knife to knife, and soon it is over. (Not the way it's supposed to be.) You can no longer stand or fight, having been shot, knifed, and bayoneted. You cannot see, as the blood is all over your face and going down your leg. For once, the snow will help. You can wash your face and use the cold icicle-like snow to stop the bleeding. With the help of some of the men, you can get down the hill to the area where the German troops are ordering you to go. Wait! Two of the men cannot move. The Germans say they will take care of them. As we move around the hill, we hear two shots. Two great Americans lie dead. The Germans did take care of them! We wonder if we will be the next.

"The fact of being captured is so overwhelming a disaster that for a little while one's mind fails to grasp its significance. . . . Like every soldier who enters battle, I had foreseen the possibilities of death and of incapacity from wounds, but I had never for one moment thought of capture."

After "some medical patches" and their "longest day" at a German aid station, the POWs move out at nightfall on their "long walk to the Rhine River from Trier." They stop at a small farmhouse, where "we waited until the SS trooper takes us one by one through a passageway to a small room in the house. The SS officer tells me, 'For you, the war is over.' . . . At Speyer on the Rhine, I am placed in a German hospital to have wounds treated. After two days, my intern helps me escape—the wrong way across the Rhine and back into German hands!

"We move out and I, once again, join my own men at a holding area. We move at nighttime and walk from 1800 hours until 0400 the next morning, with a break every two hours. . . .

"About 0200 one night, it is cold and rainy, mud and snow on the road, and we are dragging one foot after the other. The German guards are moving along with us and they are just as tired, but their dogs keep everyone moving. At the end of the line, the dogs nip at the people who fall behind. Then somewhere up the line (there are 200 or more of us) comes a voice singing 'God Bless America.' First one and then another picks up the tune and soon all the men in the entire column are singing at the top of their voices. We sing loud and clear, and we will show these Germans they cannot beat us. We laugh, we cry, but we are not defeated. Survival is a personal thing, but also a group effort." *[Colonel Royals' story continues in the April 1945 chapter.]*

40

"At about this time," mid-March 1945, "the enemy became very disorganized. German troops began surrendering wholesale. The chase was on to the Rhine River," Colonel Jean W. Christy writes. "German forces fled toward the Rhine, hoping to reach the east bank before the Americans did. Rapidly moving American armor and infantry columns crisscrossed the area, cutting the Germans off. The Eighth Air Force bombed and strafed. American artillery continually fired interdiction missions on the fleeing columns. The retreating enemy had American armor and infantry constantly nipping at their heels.

"A wild eight days followed, during which we covered more than 100 miles as the crow flies. The odometers on the trucks probably registered more than twice that as we swung back and forth to cut off the flight of enemy units. The 50th Field Artillery displaced at least ten times, often twice or more a day. Prisoners were taken by the thousands, as bewildered and confused enemy forces found themselves surrounded and cut off from their homeland. . . .

"From 20 March on, we drove straight for the Rhine River, in some cases passing German units as we went. . . . While we had been fooling around and mopping up and taking prisoners, Patton had other forces sweeping far out in front. Supplies and equipment had been pushed up as close to the Rhine as possible in preparation for a crossing. Naval Unit N-2, consisting of twelve LCVPs and their crews, was attached to Third Army. They had practiced at Toul, back in France, especially for this crossing of the Rhine.

"The 5th Division closed up on the Rhine River in the vicinity of the city of Oppenheim in the late afternoon of 22 March. It was obvious that the 5th Infantry Division was about to conduct an assault crossing. Everyone knew that a day or so would be taken up in planning. Everyone knew that a day or two would be needed to assemble supplies and equipment before the assault could start. Everyone was wrong! In the midst of their preliminary planning, the three infantry regiments were informed that the 5th Division would begin its crossing at 2230 hours that night, 22 March, after just arriving that afternoon."

Late February–Early March 1945

Bitburg, Germany

Colonel Tommy R. Gilliam concludes his story, after rejoining Company B, 1st
Battalion, 2nd Infantry Regiment, 5th Infantry Division.

In reserve, near Bitburg, "we jumped off, as the division advance guard,
through the astonished 10th Infantry lines, riding in 2½-ton trucks. Through the
day, we were harassed by a German SP firing at our column, and after dark we
halted and detrucked to get the battalion order: 'No knowledge of enemy strength
in the area. No friendly troops on our right or left. . . . Capture the town of
Schwarzenborn and then move on one-half mile and seize the town of Eisen-
schmitt. Lay sound-power wire for backup commo as you go. Any questions?
Move out.' . . .

"As we approached the town around midnight, we could see a German
armored car burning in the street. There was a large farmhouse on each side of
the road." Then-Captain Gilliam and the A Company commander each seized
his designated house, "and I sent two platoons forward to take the next house.
All combat veterans, they forgot all they knew and went into the basement of the
house for a cigarette. A Jerry Tiger came roaring up the road and turned the
muzzle of his 88 and fired on that house, and the two platoons came streaming
back in disarray. In a short time, A Company's house was burning and I called
battalion and received permission for the three companies to move back to the
river line. But the Jerries had moved into our rear and surrounded us. . . . Of
course, our sound-power phone wire had been cut. Shortly after that, B Company
came under heavy mortar fire and broke and ended up in my house."

At about 0500, "my radio went out and I was at the window trying to get it
going again when a Tiger roared down the road, overran my bazooka team and
shoved the muzzle of his 88 in the house I was in and started firing. The first
round went off in the attic. The second round went off in the room I was in and
it blew me out the window. I landed on my hands and knees [but] I knew I had
a platoon in the back of the house and I had to get them out of there.

"The Jerries had pulled in for the final attack and, as we pulled out, I was the
last one out, still directing artillery fire on the enemy, as my runner had grabbed
the radio and it began working again."

Back at battalion, "the CO said, 'Rough night, Tom.'

"'Colonel,' I replied, 'that's the third time I've ended up senior company commander, battalion 1,500 yards to the rear, no knowledge of troops on my right or
left, and just getting the hell kicked out of us. Of the troops who landed on Utah
Beach on July 9, Bussolati and I are the only company commanders left in this

division as far as I know, and Bussolati is home on forty-five-day leave. I want a staff job or a leave home. Blackie Russo, the motor officer, and I are the only officers in this battalion who sailed with it in 1942.

"'Tom, the Old Man says you are his best company commander.'

"'Colonel, I'm going to be a dead company commander if this keeps up,' and I turned on my heel and walked out of the CP. We retook the town the next day, but we lost 117 men up there that night.

"Less than three weeks later, I was on orders to return home for a forty-five-day leave. But that three weeks included the second crossing of the Moselle, the closing of the Trier pocket, the crossing of the Rhine at Oppenheim, the capture of Frankfurt am Main, and the memorial service for President Roosevelt aboard ship."

7–11 March 1945
Near Remagen, Rhineland–Palatinate, Germany

Brigadier General John W. Barnes was a captain and battalion operations officer, 51st Engineer Combat Battalion. He provides his story of building the ponton bridge across the Rhine:

"On 7 March 1945, Brigadier General William M. Hoge's Combat Command B of the 9th Armored Division reached the Rhine River at Remagen and found the Ludendorff Railroad Bridge still standing. Acting on his own initiative, he seized the bridge and started crossing his command over it to establish a bridge-head on the far shore. His action was flash-reported through channels to General Eisenhower who immediately supported his initiative by ordering the concentra-tion of engineer units and resources in the vicinity to prepare additional crossing sites for a major offensive into Germany.

"The 51st Engineer Combat Battalion received orders on 8 March to construct a twenty-five-ton heavy ponton bridge with equipment provided by the 181st and 552nd Engineer Heavy Ponton Battalions. As the S-3 of the 51st, I was responsi-ble for planning, preparing the orders and instructions to accomplish the task, and to staff supervision of the construction activity. The site selected for the bridge was from Kripp to Linz, two small towns opposite each other on the Rhine, about one and a half miles upstream (south) of the Ludendorff Bridge. . . .

"By the morning of 10 March, the 51st had moved forty miles from its previ-ous location to the site, and all of the resources needed were on hand. Construc-tion began at 1600 with preparation of approach ramps on both shores, but was interrupted periodically by enemy artillery and sporadic small-arms fire until smoke pots were found and used to prevent enemy observation of activity at the site. However, all during construction and until an expanded bridgehead had been established on the far shore, sporadic unobserved enemy artillery fire continued to harass the bridge site. Several engineers were wounded during construction; six were killed, including the commander of the 552nd Heavy Ponton Battalion. The Germans even fired several V-2 rockets from launchers in Holland, the only time they ever fired onto German soil. They caused no damage.

"Construction continued on into the night and the next day. The bridge was built in parts, with four groups working simultaneously on four-boat rafts, mostly by feel in the dark. By 0400 the next morning, 11 March, fourteen four-boat rafts had been completed and were ready to be assembled together as a bridge. When the rafts were in place, they were reinforced with pneumatic floats between the steel pontons, so that the bridge could take the weight of thirty-six-ton Sherman tanks. A total of sixty pontons and fifty-seven pneumatic rubber floats were used.

"As the four-boat rafts were maneuvered into position, they constantly extended the bridge from the near shore, increasing the pull on the anchors holding them in place. Triple anchors were then used, but as the bridge extended farther out into midstream, they too started to fail, and the engineer power boats were not strong enough to hold the bridge in place while anchors were being set. At about this time, we discovered that the Navy had some LCVPs in the area and we requested their assistance. Ten LCVPs came to the rescue and were able to hold the bridge against the current until we could install a one-inch steel cable across the Rhine immediately upstream of the bridge, to which the anchors for each ponton were attached. This solved the problem of holding the bridge against the current, estimated to be nearly ten feet per second. Remaining four-boat rafts were connected to the anchor cable, eased into position, and connected to the ever-extending bridge until the far shore was reached.

"Finally, at 1900 on 11 March, twenty-seven hours after starting construction, the 969-foot heavy ponton bridge was completed. It was the longest floating bridge ever constructed by the Corps of Engineers under fire. Traffic started at 2300, with one vehicle crossing every two minutes during daylight hours. During the first seven days, 2,500 vehicles, including tanks, crossed the bridge.

"At the same time that we were building our bridge, one of the other battalions in our Engineer Combat Group constructed an M2 steel treadway bridge for lighter vehicles immediately downstream from the Ludendorff Bridge. The two bridges provided two-way traffic across the Rhine, with heavier vehicles crossing our 51st heavy ponton bridge on the way to the front, and returning lighter vehicles crossing the 291st treadway bridge. This enabled closing the Ludendorff

Bridge for repairs, which were not completed before it collapsed from fatigue ten days after its capture."

22–24 March 1945
Rhine River, Germany

Colonel Jean W. Christy continues his 5th Infantry Division story.

After the Rhine River crossing on 22 March, "the 2nd Battalion, 2nd Infantry, with me as the liaison officer, now constituted the division reserve. It also was assigned to guard the bridge base and other key installations on the near shore of the crossing site. . . . The treadway bridge was completed and was in use by 1600 hours 23 March. The next morning, 24 March, it was carrying a steady stream of trucks with supplies and personnel across the river. Periodically, the traffic flowing east was interrupted and, when the bridge cleared, the west-bound vehicles were given their chance to use the one-way bridge."

Deciding that "it would be wise for me to cross the bridge and find the 50th Field Artillery . . . , I got my jeep and driver, and we went to the bridge entrance. With just a single vehicle, we soon found a space in the bridge traffic and started across. The thought of more German air raids on the bridge was still scary, so I was instantly concerned when the line of vehicles came to a stop when we were only about halfway across. Remembering my Fort Sill training that 'a good motor officer goes to the head of the column,' I swung out of my seat to start forward on the bridge to find the problem.

"As I left my seat, my eye caught sight of an ivory-handled revolver on a hip about thirty yards ahead. That could mean only one thing: General Patton was there. The problem being explained to my satisfaction, I sat back down and waited. . . .

"The traffic moved forward again. As each vehicle passed the group of ranking officers, everyone saluted like crazy and did an eyes-right to see who all was there. In addition to General Eddy, I saw Major General Walton Walker, commander of XX Corps, and a couple of other generals and [others] whom I didn't recognize.

"And there, out on the end of the ponton, was General George S. Patton. In full view of the world at large, with his pants unbuttoned and his knees flexed, he was making bubbles in the Rhine River. He had announced to one and all as we crossed France and Germany that he wanted to do it. And now he was doing it with apparent pleasure."

In postscript, Colonel Christy recounts obtaining a photo, in the 1980s, of Patton at the Rhine. He notes: "Remember that this was a one-lane bridge, and that I was going from west to east when I observed General Patton. . . . In the photo, the buildings directly behind the general's head are ones that I recognize as those that the 2nd Battalion, 2nd Infantry, was using for its headquarters at this time. That means that we are looking at the west bank of the river. That means that the vehicles in the picture must have been going from east to west.

"That means that this obviously is not the scene that I saw. The Old Fraud, always with a watchful eye for public relations, must have reenacted his actions for the war correspondents' cameras. They were all aware of his often-stated desire to do this. When they heard that he had, and asked him about it, he probably repeated it for their benefit."

24 March 1945
Mission to Wesel Area, Germany

Colonel Frank C. Morris, who participated in Operation Market Garden, September 1944, flew as co-pilot with 83rd Squadron, 437th Troop Carrier Group, in Mission Varsity.

"Mission Varsity was an airborne assault across the Rhine near the town of Wesel, Germany. The 437th Troop Carrier Group's mission was a double-glider tow of C-47s towing CG-4A gliders involving troops of the 17th Airborne Division in their first combat drop. The 17th was to land and establish a bridgehead from which Army units would advance and seize and hold the north flank of the Ruhr basin," Colonel Morris explains.

"We were approaching the LZ at 500 feet above the terrain. Crew Chief Al Perez was watching the gliders from the astral dome, alert to give the cast-off signal, when he saw a flak-burst halfway between our plane and the gliders. Seconds later, he saw a burst just aft of the tail section. Shortly after, we received a direct hit on the belly of the center section that destroyed the tank selector valves, cutting off fuel to both engines. We were on fire. It became terribly quiet and we had only seconds to respond. The gliders cast off when we were hit. . . .

"The pilot, Captain Walter Rudolph, and I both kicked the opposite rudder pedal and simultaneously moved the controls. . . .

"In just seconds, we missed a row of sixty-foot-tall trees and just cleared electric-train control wires about eighteen feet high, and then belly-flopped across a newly plowed farm field for about 450 feet. We came to a stop about sixty feet from a three-story building, which was a German army command post! A great no-power belly-landing. . . .

"The crew staggered to a small hedge next to the command post. Several German soldiers appeared and ordered the crew inside. We were searched, they took our guns, and we were led downstairs. . . . We could hear the Germans firing at our planes and we could feel the building shake when our artillery shells landed nearby. . . . We dressed Perez's abdominal shrapnel wound and splinted the broken wrists crudely with sticks and shoe laces.

"After about eight hours, a German colonel appeared and ordered Rudolph to come upstairs with him. A small 17th Airborne unit had the place surrounded and the German wished to surrender. Rudolph took the officer's gun; we got ours back, and we were soon herding fifteen Germans to the PW stockade about two miles away. Before we arrived there, we had over fifty prisoners, as the airborne troops mopped up the area. We then turned over the Germans to the stockade people, got our two crewmen to an aid station, and joined the glider troops in the defense perimeter. . . .

"After five days, we were evacuated across the Rhine in a DUKW, manned by the only navy sailor we had seen in the ETO. After a short ride in trucks to Helmond, the Netherlands, we were flown back to A-58 near Paris for a joyful reunion with our squadron. It was great to be alive! A little later, in April, we enjoyed a rest leave of five days on the French Riviera—American beer and wiener roasts on the beach at Cannes!"

26 February–26 March 1945
Mission to Berlin, Germany

Colonel Floyd A. Peede flew his twenty-ninth mission 26 February, piloting one of three chaff planes, with his B-17 group "leading all of the Eighth Air Force to a single target—Berlin."

Entering Germany north of Bremen, "with the 70-knot tailwind, we were just short of the IP in two hours when we received instructions [to] begin the chaff run. While inbound to the target, the engine with 150mag drop blew a cylinder head and began pumping oil overboard," Colonel Peede reports.

"The tachometer broke when the engine went through 4,100 rpm. . . . While the crew donned chutes and stood by the escape hatches, I tried to control the bucking airplane that seemed destined to disintegrate itself from the sheer vibration of the runaway engine. I tried to make the runaway prop leave the engine. . . . The vibration that had seemed to last forever soon stopped. Then I realized the prop shaft had sheared from the engine crank shaft but the prop stayed on the engine. Again, I tried to make the prop leave the engine. . . . I kicked rudder, pulled the elevator quickly, and even tried steep turns. Part of the engine and cowl fell off, but not the prop.

"Not wanting to become German POWs, we decided to turn to an easterly heading and look for a place to land in Poland or Russia."

Continuing for fifteen or twenty minutes, "we came to a double-track railroad" and flew 200 feet above the tracks until "a bright white flare appeared off our right." With guidance from "some people on the ground [who] were holding a strip of cloth to indicate the landing direction," Pilot Peede made a "normal landing" on the snow-covered, dirt landing strip of the burnt-out civilian airport at Lodz, Poland.

After convincing "the Russian base commander we were *Amerikanski* and had bombed Berlin," Colonel Peede says that he inspected his plane and discovered that "the vibration had popped several hundred rivets in the wings and fuselage and buckled the aluminum skin and cracked it in many places. We were lucky the plane held together as long as it did."

After preliminaries over shared American cigarettes, "our Russian hosts treated us all as though we were officers and pilots," sharing their cots, their German schnapps or vodka, and their meals, consisting "primarily of fried pork, sauerkraut, dill pickles, and black bread. We found out later how fortunate we were to be with a combat unit" that had food in supply.

"On the tenth day after our arrival at Lodz, the Russians received orders over their radio to transport us to Warsaw" for a 500-mile trip to Poltava on a nonpriority basis. . . . The trip lasted eleven, nearly food-free, days.

Thirty days later and thirty pounds lighter, the airmen arrived back in England to the surprise of fellow crewmen who hardly recognized their crewmates, carried as "missing in action."

22 March–Summer 1945
Mission to Ruhland, Germany

Chaplain (Major) Ralph F. Bates was a lieutenant/pilot, 817th Squadron, 483rd Bombardment Group.

Heading for Ruhland's oil depot, south of Berlin, in that "gigantic attack force of perhaps 1,000 bombers," the crew experienced moderate but accurate flak as it approached the target. "No sooner had we dropped our bombs than we were shaken up again. A terrifying explosion rocked the ship! I switched to intercom and heard the boys calling, 'Fighters, six o'clock!' All of our 50mm machine guns that could face the rear safely were rattling; we could see an Me-262 swinging swiftly overhead, going by at twice our speed. More shaking, more fighters, firing 30mm cannon that exploded as they contacted the trailing edges of our wings. Violent explosions rocked us. . . . We could see others of our formation going down. Amid the chaos, however, we were able to bag one Me-262, and another probable," Major Bates writes.

"Our right wing started dipping dangerously; gunners were shouting, 'Fires— both wings!' We were going down! Worse, we were unable to control the plane, which was in a dangerous flat spin. . . . Fires were spreading rapidly on the trailing edge of the right wing; a large fire burst out in the left wing. . . .

"Now down from 25,000-feet to 15,000-feet altitude and spinning lazily, we realized that the thrust of the two good left-wing engines was increasing the spin, so we let up on the power and set the trim tabs as far as possible for a left turn. Thank God, we started to level off. Meanwhile, we were able to get a little power out of No. 3 engine. . . .

"We headed for the nearest friendly country, Russian-occupied Poland, following a double-tracked railroad. The fires in the wings were now subsiding, and we were holding steady at 5,000 feet. . . . Having flown for an hour and a half since the attack, "we soon spotted an airfield where a number of small airplanes were parked. . . .

"In preparing to land, our right wheel wouldn't go down! To add to the peril, when I lowered the flaps a huge section of the right flap, or what was left of it, simply fell off! Immediately, the plane lurched down to the right. With the wings leaning dangerously to the right, we landed hard on the very wheel that Flight Engineer Brewer (seriously injured) had just manually cranked down with great effort! . . . When we finally rolled to a stop, all we could do was lift our hands in thanks to God. . . .

"We stayed in a makeshift barn-turned-into-barracks for three days, being treated well by the Russian military. This, while they arranged for us to be transferred to what turned out to be a former 'shuttle base' near Poltava, Ukraine, USSR. We camped in the chapel until the end of April, along with several other American crews. . . . The Russians never said why we couldn't return to Italy any earlier. We played cards with each other, and volleyball with our hosts, and enjoyed good meals in the military clubs. We finally returned to our base in Italy via Iran, Egypt, and Greece, arriving on the very day our base was proclaimed non-operational. The war in Europe was over."

January–March 1945
POW Camps, Germany

Major Frederick D. (Dusty) Worthen, B-24 bombardier, continues his POW tale.

"After interrogation, there was confinement, when the guard outside his cell repeated in English the perfunctory lines that many a prisoner heard: 'It looks like this is the end of the war for you.' Of course, this meant to me that the end was soon to come," Major Worthen comments. "Late in the afternoon, they took us all outside and marched us up to a solid brick wall with half a dozen or so armed German soldiers standing in a row about twenty-five feet away facing the wall. I knew this had to be the firing squad. However, we walked right past the wall and into the officers mess hall for something to eat (talk about negative thinking!).

"When it got dark, they took us down to a pier, put us on a boat, and we ended up in Rotterdam an hour or so later. Then began our trip to Germany. We traveled by wood-burning trucks, trains, streetcar, and on foot. . . .

"On the second day, we went to Dortmund, our mission target of January 28, which had apparently turned out to be successful. We had to walk through part of the town, since the railroad system was out of commission. If it hadn't been for our guards, the local civilians surely would have killed us. Gradually, we felt a friendship toward the German guards."

From Frankfurt and then Oberursel, where the new POWs were in solitary confinement for ten days and "English bombers came over and dropped the big blockbusters," it was on to Wetzlar, as "P-38s were dive-bombing the Leica camera factory right next to the base," and then to Nuremberg to a camp on the edge of town. . . .

"On 20 and 21 February, there were maximum-effort bombing missions over Nuremberg by the Eighth Air Force. It was devastating to the town. Bombs hit close to our camp but caused no problems for us. . . .

"On 4 March, the English bombed Nuremberg at night. An ammo dump in town continued to blow up for two days. All the time we were here, we could hear the American artillery and knew the front lines were approaching."

27 March 1945
Oflag XIIIB, Hammelburg, Germany

Lieutenant Colonel Romolo D. Tedeschi, taken prisoner in November 1944, continues his story.

"We heard guns firing in the distance and had been hearing 'latrine rumors' that the Americans were on the way to our camp. Late that afternoon, American tanks appeared over the hill, firing at the camp's guard towers, which were demolished," Lieutenant Colonel Tedeschi recalls. The fifty tanks and half-tracks, a 4th Armored Task Force, had fought their way sixty miles into German territory intending to rescue five hundred American POWs who, they believed, "were to be executed by the Germans.

"It was also rumored that another purpose was to rescue Lieutenant Colonel John Waters, General Patton's son-in-law. The tankers were surprised and shocked when they were told that there were over 1,000 POWs at the *Oflag*.

"Following a brief skirmish with German guards, the prison camp's commandant, General Von Goeckel, asked our Colonel Goode to protect his family from any harm and then surrendered to Goode. In a brief surrender ceremony, the German general, Colonel Goode, Lieutenant Colonel Waters, and several staff officers marched to open the front gate, carrying the American flag as well as a white flag of surrender. Suddenly, without warning, a German corporal appeared and shot Colonel Waters, who was immediately carried to the camp infirmary. He was eventually evacuated to a hospital. The wound was serious but he did recover.

"We POWs were told by the tankers that we had a choice of riding back sixty miles to the American lines with the task force, remaining in camp, or trying to walk back to the American lines. Three of us from my unit in the 79th decided to ride the tanks back through enemy territory and hopped on the lead tank. . . .

"As the task force began leaving the camp, our light tank was struck by a German bazooka fired from a wooded area. We were knocked off the tank and hopped on another, even though it was rather crowded by this time. A few miles later, the second tank blew a track. We persisted and climbed on a third tank to continue on a wild journey in the darkness. Meanwhile, the Germans were searching for the task force with their Tiger tanks. I recall stopping in a small village [where] a German civilian called out *Brot* and threw me a loaf of German bread. . . .

"When it became obvious that we could not escape the encircling German tanks, the task force decided to stay and fight. We were told that we could remain with them and fight—if we had weapons—or return to the prison camp on foot. Without weapons and weak from malnutrition, most of us walked back to camp, led by Colonel Goode. As we approached the camp, we saw some buildings were burning. . . .

"Some of the POWs had decided to walk to friendly lines—either American or British. . . . I understand that those men who walked north to the British lines made it safely while those who went west were captured. I was placed on one of the trains headed for Nuremberg while those POWs who had been shipped out on [an earlier] train were killed as a result of American planes strafing and bombing. Again, there were no markings on the trains to signify to our Air Force that American POWs were being transported."

Winter 1945
Reims, France

Lieutenant Colonel John S. Smith was assigned as captain, Rail Transportation Section of OISE Intermediate Section, SOSETOUSA.

"The American Army had liberated a large number of Russian nationals from German prisoner-of-war camps and brought them into France. Since they had to be fed and housed, it was decided they would be excellent personnel to use as guards over our prisoner-of-war camps for Germans," Lieutenant Colonel Smith explains. He was among about a dozen officers who oversaw one of the Russian companies, tasked with building a camp "of ten- to fifteen-man tents to house the Russians within an existing German POW camp in the stadium in the city of Reims."

"I was given a detail of about twelve German carpenters who were to construct the camp. By a strange coincidence, the chief carpenter of the group was Sergeant Johann Schmidt. Prewar, he had been a builder in Germany, and a very efficient one," Lieutenant Colonel Smith recalls. "Sergeant Schmidt gave me a list of the materials he had figured he would require. . . . In practically no time, the camp was completed, [and] less than a weapons-carrier load of scrap lumber had to be hauled off."

One afternoon, "a young Russian private, well oiled with French champagne and wine, approached me, and proceeded to tell me in Russian what he thought of me in particular and Americans in general. I knew his remarks weren't complimentary, but I ignored him."

The Russian in charge of the unit, "Captain Pogolorev, heard the private lambasting me. . . . He listened for a few seconds, then proceeded to hit the private, knocking him to the ground. Before the private could stand up, Captain Pogolorev stomped him three or four times with his boot heel, then pulled the private to a standing position, and told him to leave the camp immediately. Captain Pogolorev went into the orderly room, found the private's name on the roster, and drew a red line through it. When he drew that red line, he gave the private a dishonorable discharge from the Russian army, took his Russian citizenship, and banished him from ever returning to Russia. I still think he did the private a tremendous favor."

After about three months of duty with the Russians, Captain Smith was transferred to Headquarters, 10th Military Labor District, in Nancy, France, where he supervised the personnel records of 35,000 Italian and approximately 50,000 German POWs until November 1945.

March 1945
Mission to Amsterdam, the Netherlands

Major James W. Hall was a B-17 ball-turret gunner, 96th Bomb Group (H).

"In February and March 1945, food was so scare in the Amsterdam, German-occupied pocket that it was reported civilians were dying from starvation by the hundreds daily," Major Hall writes. "In March 1945, a temporary 'truce' was reached between the Allied Command and the Germans that would allow the Eighth Air Force to air-drop food to the civilian population."

Loaded with bags of flour and cases of tinned, dried, and powdered foods in the bomb bays, and with their "full complement of gunners," the B-17s were to go in, single file, at 100 to 150 feet, "in varying altitudes to try to eliminate the hazards of propwash."

Since "B-17 aircraft had a ground speed at that altitude of 125mph, we would be sitting ducks for ground and artillery fire if the Germans did not abide by the 'truce agreement.' . . ." All of the air crews were wary, tense, and distrustful of the German army on those first two or three food missions.

"While the food-drop was under way, I was to observe the impact on the ground and to report the results. Because parachutes were not used, the cases broke open on impact and containers of food became dangerous missiles; bags of flour burst and became 'smoke' bombs; A large part of the first mission's delivery was lost for human consumption however, I did not see anyone get hurt, in spite of flying cans and debris. The second and subsequent missions had modifications, such as strapping to the cases and parachutes for the flour, so the food delivery was more successful. . . .

"Eighth Air Force Command sent a major from Intelligence to go as an observer. He was assigned to fly on our ship. Immediately after the food drop, he directed our aircraft commander to pull out of the agreed flight route so that he might see anything about the German positions that could be of value. Our aircraft commander argued but did comply when given a direct order.

"On our course alteration, the Germans immediately opened fire with 88 tracer fire in our direction as a warning. Our aircraft commander then told the Eighth Air Force Intelligence major to 'stuff it' when he was ordered to ignore the German fire. We returned immediately to the normal aircraft traffic flow and hence to safety in England."

Summarizing the eight missions, Major Hall adds: "The Eighth Air Force was credited with saving thousands of lives as a result of these humanitarian flights. The German army did not violate the truce, and it expired at the predetermined time without any casualties, to my knowledge."

12 March 1945

From the Netherlands to Freedom

Lieutenant Colonel A. Ray Kubly, shot down and captured 7 October 1944, concludes his POW escape story.

During February and March, "a new route through the Biesbosh (a marshy area forming the mouth of the Waal River into the North Sea) was developed and many individuals were taken successfully through," Lieutenant Colonel Kubly writes.

"Mick Tapson, an Australian Mosquito pilot, was leading our group of four to cross a dike near Vianen. . . . Mick got past the German checkpoint, but John Sjursen (of the Canadian army), who was right behind, got stopped. I was next in line but when I saw what was happening, we rode our bikes *Hell Maal Schnell-footsie,* which means 'Get the hell out of here!' The last I saw of John was when he was taking off his farm coveralls and showing his army uniform. . . . Jack and I got back with the Underground group at Vreeswjyk. Mick went on and completed the crossing.

"In a few days, another attempt would be made," from a farm "near Schoonhaven where we crossed the Rhine River without any problem" into an area that was still in German hands, guided by new contacts from the Underground. "We biked to Sliderecht. . . . After a wait for a dark, moonless night, the Underground said we were going through the Biesbosh and would be free by midnight. [We] set out in a small rowboat with a Dutch guide. We had to be very quiet as there were German patrols watching for any activity. This was the front line! . . .

"After we made the crossing, someone yelled, 'Halt!' I remember yelling, 'Don't shoot. We are Americans!' The Canadians informed us, 'You are now free!' What a wonderful feeling. They took us to their headquarters for a wonderful welcome. Some wine showed up and we toasted our new freedom. This was 12 March 1945."

After interrogation by the British and Canadians in Antwerp, Belgium, "we flew to Paris and spent another few weeks being interrogated by the American Intelligence service. After completing this activity, I was sent to the Eighth Air Force Headquarters to lecture on escape and evasion tactics at other Bomb Groups in the 3rd Bomb Division."

With the war's end soon after, "happy days are here again," Lieutenant Colonel Kubly exclaims. "I returned home by ship to Boston and returned to the home farm."

March 1945
Luzon, the Philippines

Colonel Bert D. Miner was completing special training at Fort Ord, California, when the 25th Infantry Division landed on Luzon 11 January 1945. About sixty days later, he was there also.

"I joined Love Company, 161st Infantry, just in time to participate in the battle for what became known as 'Winch Hill' and 'Banzai Ridge.' The terrain was extremely rugged and covered with caves, trenches, and other planned fortifications. It was like fighting through the Rocky Mountains," Colonel Miner explains.

"The day after I joined Love Company, it was sent back into the line. Both sides of the trail leading to our positions in the line were covered with dead bodies wrapped in mattress covers. I thought at the time, I had better adjust quickly to death or it will destroy me mentally. . . .

"We were dug-in on the reverse side of the ridge. The Japanese were positioned a few hundred yards to our front on another ridge parallel to ours. We were warned repeatedly to keep our heads down because of snipers. One newcomer just had to take a look and was shot right between the eyes. The rest of us took the warning to heart.

"Each morning, a two-man detail picked up all the canteens in our squad and went to company headquarters to fetch water for the day. Also, each morning the Japanese shelled our positions with artillery and mortars.

"My turn on the detail came the third day. The other soldier and I strung all the canteens on our belts for ease of carrying. While we were filling the canteens at company headquarters, the morning shelling began. We instantly hit the dirt and stayed there until the shelling stopped. Then we finished filling the canteens and returned to our positions. On arriving there, I saw that the foxhole I had shared with another soldier had taken a direct hit. There was nothing left of him. I thought, it could just as easily have been me. It shook me to the core.

"Over the next couple of months, I was engaged in fierce and bloody combat, even hand-to-hand, to dig the Japanese out of their caves, trenches, and other fortifications. In one of these fierce trench battles, I met a future brother-in-law. He wielded a Browning automatic rifle (BAR) to make the Japanese keep their heads down while I lobbed hand grenades into the trenches. Finally, we actually jumped into and raced along the trench, eliminating the last defenders who were hiding in small holes they had dug into the sides of the trench.

"It was a dirty business that still conjures distinct images in my mind over forty-five years later. Yes, I was wounded. Fortunately, it was not debilitating."

March 1945
Cebu, the Philippinenes

Chief Warrant Officer David L. Wischemann was an electrician's mate third class, assigned in July 1944 to LST-18.

In March 1945, *LST-18* "moved to Ormac City, on the western side of Leyte, to load part of the Americal Division for the invasion of Cebu Island in the Central Philippines," Mr. Wischemann writes. "It took about twenty-four hours to load the troops and supplies, then at dusk we retracted from the beach and dropped anchor about a mile out. . . . The five new LSTs beached and added their combined bow waves to Ormac City. After the ships were loaded, the tide was not high enough for them to retract, and they had to stay loaded, on the beach, an additional day to await higher water.

"After the other ships joined us at anchor, we understood that each of our LSTs was to pull either an Army crash boat or an LCM (Landing Craft Medium) to the Cebu invasion. Assigned an LCM for the *18* to pull, our CO refused to do this. He stated that 'the towing bits are too far aft on an LCM to be safe,' but accepted a crash boat to tow instead. . . .

"During the night, our convoy encountered a bad storm, and our tows began to take quite a beating. One LCM, with a truck and seven-man crew, was pulled beneath the waves and went to the bottom. The LST tug merely cut the towing line and proceeded on in convoy. Our Skipper had been right. . . .

"The enemy resistance at the beach was negligible, but later the Americal Division encountered bitter resistance from the Japanese in the hills." On the return to Cebu with more troops and supplies to reinforce the Americal Division, "we were able to pull right up to the docks" and could see "what a beautiful city this was" and why it was considered "the Riviera of the Philippines."

"After we unloaded, we pulled out into the harbor, by a small island, and dropped anchor." Since there was no blackout at the time, a movie was scheduled. "About halfway through the show, a firefight broke out on shore—machine guns, artillery, tracers. The whole battle raged about three or four miles away. The movie was stopped. . . . The firing went on for a time then suddenly quit. We resumed the movie. I have never been able to forget that there we were, watching a movie, and people were being torn apart with shell-fire."

19 March 1945
Aboard USS *Adams*, Okinawa

*Captain James E. Beemer began his Navy career in 1940. His first ship was the
USS* Saratoga, *in the convoy to Iceland and Greenland when the USS* Reuben
James *was sunk 31 October 1941.*

After duty in Australia, New Guinea, and the Timorese Democratic Union,
Captain Beemer says, "my tour of duty on the USS *Adams* began when I was
transferred to Bath, Maine, as chief electrician's mate, to commission the ship
in October 1944. . . . My duty aboard was chief in charge of the ship's electrical
system and my battle station was in charge of damage control during the invasion of Okinawa."

According to a 1945 newspaper account of the invasion, the *Adams*

sailed for Okinawa with a task force of fifty ships consisting of minesweepers and
various supporting ships, charged with the job of clearing mines and buoying channels for the invasion of that island scheduled for April 1.

On the evening of March 23, the ship had its first contact with the enemy, when
the task force was attacked by Japanese planes. During the next week there were
enemy planes in the area almost continually and the *Adams* was attacked by at least
twelve, six of which were definitely destroyed by her anti-aircraft guns and two
more "probables."

At sunrise on March 28, a Jap plane was hit off the port bow and crashed into
the sea twenty-five feet from the *Adams'* bow. Parts of the plane and the pilot's body
landed on the deck and the forward part of the ship as high as the open bridge. The
ship was forced to retire for emergency repairs.

After being patched up, the ship returned to duty and on April 1 (D-Day), and
while patrolling southeast of Kerama Retto, another badly damaged plane, her
bomb racks loaded, hit the water just astern of the ship and exploded under the
fantail, doing considerable damage to the aft section of the vessel and jamming
rudders in hard right position. While circling in this condition, the *Adams* was
attacked by two other suicide planes, one of which was destroyed by the *Adams* and
the other by the destroyer, USS *Mullaney*, which came to assist from a nearby patrol
station.

On April 12, the *Adams* left Okinawa for San Francisco on her historic journey,
arriving there on May 7.

The news clipping provided by Captain Beemer was from the 27 December
1945 edition of the *China Press*, Shanghai's English-language newspaper. Refer-
ence to the *Adams'* historic journey and reason for the write-up are made clear
in the story's opening paragraph:

The USS *Adams* (DM-27), which arrived in Shanghai recently from Formosa, has the distinction of being the second ship in the history of the U.S. Navy that has managed to travel a distance of more than 7,000 miles (Okinawa to San Francisco) without rudders. This amazing feat was accomplished in April after the *Adams'* steering gear was put out of commission by a Japanese suicide plane at Okinawa. During the long journey, steering was done with the ship's engines.

No name is provided for that other "rudderless ship" mentioned in the story.

Winter 1944–45
Angaur and Peleliu, Caroline Islands

Captain Sheldon A. Jacobson was a staff medical officer to the admiral
commanding the Western Carolines submarine areas in the last year of the war,
with headquarters on Peleliu.

"I have seen a garbled version of this incident somewhere, but this is what actually occurred," says Dr. Jacobson in preface to his story. "On the nearby island of Angaur, also in our hands, there was a disused old dovecote. Near it, one of our patrols one day picked up a square of paper, about a square-inch or so in size. On it were tiny markings. The paper had obviously not been lying in the rain. Evidently, a Japanese observer was transmitting by carrier pigeon.

"The paper was handed to Intelligence. The Japanese-language officers said it was a Korean code, and they could not read it. The Korean-language officers said it was a Japanese code. Then someone had a brain wave, and showed the paper to me. I translated it for them.

"The language was Hebrew. It was devotional material, the inside of what we call a *mezuzah*, used at every Jewish home and by some of our Jewish troops as a sort of amulet. Since there was no Jewish chaplain attached, on another occasion, I joined with Jewish enlisted men to say a prayer at each of the graves of our co-religionists who had fallen at the Battle of Peleliu.

"I also joined with them—there were many—for the celebration of Passover that spring. They ran the whole ceremony, and beautifully. I was very proud of them," says the medical officer who cracked the code at Angaur.

41

"And then came the Holocaust, which shook history and by its dimensions and goals marked the end of a civilization. Concentration-camp man discovered the anti-savior." These are the words of 1986 Nobel Peace Laureate Elie Wiesel who as adolescent, survived Birkenau, Auschwitz, Buna, and Buchenwald concentration camps, where family members perished; who as young man, "under the seal of memory and silence" [his words], waited ten years before he would allow himself to write or speak of the atrocities; and who as elder—mystic and messenger—wears the burdensome crown of "conscience of mankind."

For American troops arriving upon the horrific scenes at the extermination camps in April 1945, however, there was the immediacy of reports to be written and letters being sent home, trying to describe in human terms the inhumanity they were witness to upon arrival into the very depths of hell.

"What a cesspool of suffering and torture and human degradation," Colonel William M. McConahey writes of the Flossenburg concentration camp in Bavaria on 24 April 1945, the day after its liberation by American troops. "One who has not seen it cannot visualize it in his mind, and I am sure that one who had not lived through the never-ending days and nights of terror in such a place cannot possibly comprehend a fraction of its misery. Flossenburg normally held 10,000 to 15,000 tortured souls, but when we got to it, all but 1,500 of the inmates had been herded farther inland.

"I have never before or since seen such wild, delirious joy as that shown by these pitiful 1,500 at their deliverance. Great holes had been torn in the barbed-wire fences by the madly happy prisoners when they first saw American troops. . . . Liberty had been long in coming and was not to be delayed another instant."

"In the four years of Flossenburg's operation, between 60,000 and 100,000 miserable souls died there in agony," Colonel McConahey writes. He adds: "It should be remembered by all Americans that . . . [a]t the war crimes trial in Nuremberg it was testified that at Flossenburg Concentration Camp on Christmas Eve, December 1944, fifteen American paratroopers were hanged by the SS beside gaily decorated Christmas trees at a sadistic 'Christmas party' for the inmates, who were compelled to watch the exhibition."

Colonel A. Lewis Greene, who provides recollections of his arrival at Dachau, also submits an official report describing conditions at Buchenwald, located on the north edge of Weimar, when on 12 April "U.S. armor overran the general area in which the camp is located." The report, authored by Brigadier General Eric F. Wood, Lieutenant Colonel Charles H. Ott, and Chief Warrant Officer S. M. Dye, describes their inspection the morning of 16 April 1945.

When U.S. administrative personnel and supplies reached the camp on Friday, the 13th of April, the surviving inmates numbered 20,000. The camp's mission is described as "extermination factory. Means of extermination: starvation, complicated by hard work, abuse, beating, and tortures, incredibly crowded sleeping conditions . . . , and sickness (for instance, typhus rampant in the camp; and many inmates tubercular). By these means, many tens of thousands of the best leadership personnel of Europe (including German democrats and anti-Nazis) have been exterminated. . . . The recent death rate was about 200 a day. Fifty-seven hundred had died or been killed in February; 5,900 in March; and about 2,000 in the first ten days of April."

Item 9 in the report describes the Medical Experiment Building: "Block 41 was used for medical experiments and vivisections, with prisoners as 'guinea pigs.' Medical scientists came from Berlin periodically to reinforce the experimental staff. In particular, new toxins and antitoxins were tried out on prisoners. Few prisoners who entered this experimental building ever emerged alive."

Item 10 describes The Body Disposal Plant: "It had a maximum disposal capacity of about 400 bodies per 10-hour day. All bodies were reduced to bone ash, thus destroying all 'evidence.' All gold-filled teeth were extracted from bodies before incineration. . . .

"For a period of about ten days in March the coal supply for the incinerator ran out. Awaiting the arrival of a new supply, bodies to the number of about 1,880 [or 1,660; numerals are blurred] were allowed to collect in the front yard, stacked up like cordwood. . . . So a truck detachment, and a fatigue detail of internees, was organized. The bodies were loaded in the trucks and hauled out of camp. The fatigue detail dug one huge burial pit, threw the bodies into it, filling it except for one end, and covered the bodies. Then the SS shot all the members of the fatigue detail, threw their bodies into the vacant end, and covered them up."

As the world of 1945 gasps in collective shock and pain at the enormity of the deaths in the extermination camps, Americans grieve also the loss of two specific individuals: their troops' commander in chief, President Franklin D. Roosevelt who died on 12 April, and their boys' adopted comrade-in-arms, correspondent Ernie Pyle who was killed by a Japanese sniper on Ie Shima, 18 April, three months after arriving in the Pacific Theater to describe the war there for the folks back home.

3 April 1945
Meiningen, Germany

Major Russell L. Foss was a sergeant with 3rd Battalion, 5th Infantry Regiment.

On arrival at the German political prison camp, "we found that most of the prisoners were in 'skin-and-bones' physical condition," Major Foss recalls. "Our battalion set up its kitchens and made soup to feed the masses."

Among the masses was a POW from Banffshire, Scotland. He was "the only one who spoke English and he seemed very anxious to communicate with his parents. The only way I could figure to accomplish this was to have him write a letter that I would send via our company postal system, which we did," Major Foss writes.

In a letter of gratitude on 18 June 1945, the POW's father writes to Sergeant Foss:

On 3 April, you liberated my son James. . . . As we had not heard from him for nearly three years, we had almost given up hope of ever seeing or hearing from him again. . . .

Words can hardly describe our feelings at the good news, and the joy of knowing that he was alive and well, and on behalf of my wife and myself, I wish to thank you with all my heart for saving Jim's life and for the joy you were the means of bringing to our home. No words of mine can describe our gratitude to you, so I will . . . wish you all the good things that this world can bestow upon you, a safe return to your home, and the prayer of two people, well on in life, that you may long be spared and that you will be very happy always.

Like one family's own military honor roll, the letter continues:

Our eldest son was severely wounded in Burma . . . and has since had his left leg amputated. He was a captain, Gordon Highlanders, attached to the 10th Gurka Rifles, and went to India in 1941. Our second son was a pilot officer, RAF, and was killed over Frankfurt in November 1943 when his Lancaster bomber was shot down. We have another son in India; he is a junior engineer on a Seiner [a fishing vessel, often called into service during WWII] and is well as far as we know. You will understand that James knew nothing about this when you rescued him from certain death.

"In closing, may I say that we will never forget you although we have not had, or are not likely to have, the pleasure of meeting you," the letter ends. And they never did meet, nor continue to correspond. "I have written to his family but have never received a reply," Major Foss adds.

29 April 1945
Dachau, Germany

Colonel A. Lewis Greene was a captain, Seventh Army, when he entered Dachau, outside of Munich, 29 April, the day after its liberation.

On seeing the horrors of one of the Nazi extermination camps, where millions of Jewish and other citizens of Europe died, then-Captain Greene writes home to family on 30 April 1945, describing World War II Germany as "as nation of gangsters."

"To see the remains of some of the slave labor camps—what was becoming of this 'mad nation'!" he exclaims in his letter. "This is not the nation we all believed to be lovers of art, beauty, and culture. Quite the contrary. It is a nation of gangsters, no better than Dillinger.

"Aside from all this, the nation has gone sex mad. To count the sexual perverts is impossible. . . . My friends and I are still in a daze." Providing one example, he continues: "There was a factory we came across, back near Mannheim, where the Germans had women work in the nude. They'd beat them with cat-o-nine-tails and use them for sexual satisfaction whenever so desired. Women who became pregnant were cremated. Sickly women were also killed."

Germany's first concentration camp, Dachau was set up on the grounds of a former ammunition factory 22 March 1933, soon after the Nazis seized power on 30 January. A 1990s brochure from the present-day Dachau Museum and Memorial Site provides the following information:

Political opponents, Jews, clergymen, and so-called 'undesirable elements' were to be isolated here as enemies of the National-Socialist regime. In 1937, the camp originally planned for 5,000 persons proved to be too small. The prisoners had to build a larger camp which was completed in 1938. The camp office files show a total of more than 206,000 prisoners, registered between 1933 and 1945. In addition, however, many prisoners were taken to Dachau without being registered. The exact figures are unknown.

When the crematory outside the prisoners' compound proved to be too small, "a larger *krematorium (Baracke X)* had to be built by prisoners in 1942," the brochure continues. "Prisoners selected for 'gassing' were transported from Dachau to the Hartheim Castle, near Linz (Austria) or to other camps."

"This isn't the nation of Germans we knew. We should never show them any mercy for these atrocities. *All* Germans can never be forgiven," Captain Greene wrote in his letter fifty years ago. Today, he has tempered his feelings toward Germany but says, "I'm worried about the Skinheads, the resurgence of Naziism."

In the 1990s, "since there are still doubters that a Holocaust existed," Colonel Green says that he speaks to church and service groups. He has also shared information on Dachau with Emory University's Center for Research in Social Change, Atlanta, Georgia.

April 1945
Gardelegen, Germany

Colonel John H. Wilson Jr. was a first lieutenant with 599th Ordnance Ammunition Company. He was one of five black officers in the unit commanded by a white captain.

Arriving overseas in January 1944, the 599th was tasked with loading ammunition for the impending assault on Fortress Europe. "Our unit landed on Omaha Beach, France, on 6 June 1944—D-Day—in Patton's Third Army," Colonel Wilson writes.

"We remained with Patton until he broke out in northeast France at Metz, along the Moselle River. The 599th subsequently was transferred to the U.S. Ninth Army and became the most forward Army Supply Point until American forces reached the Elbe River in late April 1945.

"On our way to the Elbe, we arrived in a German town called Gardelegen. It was here that my unit and I witnessed the Holocaust firsthand. The Germans had packed more than 500 slave laborers in a brick barn and barred the wooden doors. With American forces bearing down on the town, the Germans saturated the doors with kerosene or gasoline and set the barn ablaze. Those laborers who forced the burning entrances were mowed down by machine-gun fire. It was a tragic sight. The odor of burned flesh is one I'll never forget.

"I had picked up a 16mm camera and film in the rubble of Dusseldorf before my company had crossed the Rhine. Taking the camera in hand, I panned the charred remains of the slave laborers, stacked three and four feet high in the barn. The victims came from many nations. (The film remains in my possession, albeit in poor condition. That's okay by me. I still must contend with the stench of the slaughter that hasn't left me. I do not need a graphic reminder.)

"The next morning, the senior officer in the town, an infantry major who was acting as the burgomaster, ordered all civilians out of their homes. They had to bring with them shovels and spades. The men were ordered to dig six-foot-deep trenches and bury the bodies in the proper manner. Women and children of the town watched the procedure. A month later, the war in Europe ended."

For gallantry in action at La Haye Pesnel, France, on 7 August 1944, then–First Lieutenant Wilson was awarded the Silver Star. His citation notes that he "personally organized and evacuated enlisted men under his command from an Ammunition Depot while the depot was being bombed and strafed by enemy aircraft." In that same incident, the Bronze Star was awarded to four men in the company, the Purple Heart to six.

In another commendation for the mission assigned 20–23 August 1944, Colonel L. M. Bricker praises the company "for superior work performed." The letter notes that "average tonnage handled was 20.7 tons per man per day," which was "3.4 times the expected normal handling capacity."

April 1945
Near Nordhausen, Germany

Lieutenant Colonel Albert C. Fritz served with the Medical Corps in Europe, arriving in Normandy on D-plus-20.

"I was with First Army through various engagements, including Huertgen Forest and the Battle of the Bulge," Lieutenant Colonel Fritz writes. In February 1945, he received a field commission to second lieutenant MAC and was assigned to 354th Infantry Regiment, 89th Division, Third Army.

"Near Nordhausen, we came across a work camp where slave labor was employed. The camp built pilotless aircraft and the rockets (V-1s and V-2s) that poured down on the troops, especially toward the last months of the war. The workers were chained to platforms in the caves and worked until they dropped.

"One of the things that I remember about our visit was when a Polish-speaking lieutenant with our group got into a conversation with some of the Polish inmates who cleared a spot on the table and served us some vodka, which they had fermented from beets. Such conviviality in the midst of hardship made an impression on me. After V-E Day, our division was put in boxcars and sent down to St. Valery, France, where we operated Camp Lucky Strike, processing RAMPS (released Allied military prisoners) until 29 October 1945 when we returned to the States."

April 1945
Frankfurt am Main, Germany

General Wayne C. Temple was a staff sergeant with 3431st Signal Equipment Installation Detachment, 3352nd Signal Service Battalion of Army Communication Service, Plant Engineering Agency, based in Paris in 1945.

"During the first part of April in 1945, two teams of ten men each were hand-picked from my unit for a secret mission," General Temple relates. "But what was so important about Frankfurt am Main, our destination? It was a gutted city with only the I. G. Farben complex still standing intact. Why would anybody want another small air base here? . . .

"We bitched among ourselves when forced to labor both day and night. Quickly, the antenna poles went up, the International diesels began to roar, and the T-4 transmitters crackled. . . . When my fellow cable-splicer, Robert F. Drescher of Hibbing, Minnesota, and I examined the huge roll of lead cable on its reel, we discovered to our horror that it was in several pieces. No single piece would reach from the generator area to the tower. . . . Well, we were good cable splicers but when we unwrapped the sealed chest of equipment from Stateside, there was no wooden lead dresser to shape the splicing sleeves, nor even any sleeves! Furthermore, the furnace had no solder pot. Nor was there any stearin, which we used as a flux. A typical snafu. . . .

"After a search of several houses back in Frankfurt, we 'requisitioned' some candles to use in place of stearin and headed back. On the way, we spotted a German helmet which the original owner now had no earthly use for. . . .

"To fashion splicing sleeves, we cut lengths of lead from cable covering and soldered them together. We slipped the sleeve over one end and spliced the wires carefully and then drew the 'sleeve' over the splice. With a common hammer, we beat the end of the sleeve down upon the cable sheath and prepared our solder. We fired up our splicing furnace and placed the helmet on top. Gradually the temperature of the solder rose. Drescher quickly filled his pouring ladle and wiped a perfect joint on one end of the lead sleeve, and I wiped the other. Mission accomplished.

"In just a few days, we had installed a complete airfield. Our radio men checked out the installation, and we fell into our bed rolls for the first full night's sleep in four days. Then we waited and waited. Only fighter planes came and went. . . . Finally, the control-tower operator received a call from a C-54 requesting landing instructions. This message ended with the statement that the pilot had VIP aboard and wanted to land as quickly as possible."

Soon after the plane landed, "General of the Army Dwight David Eisenhower appeared in the doorway with a big grin on his face. No fuss, no fanfare, no previously planned ceremonies—that was the way it was when Eisenhower used this little strip. . . .

"No, the I. G. Farben buildings were not going to be a hospital. Those white buildings were to become the new site of Supreme Headquarters Allied Expeditionary Forces. When I questioned out loud why the general had chosen this little strip, an aide to the general replied, 'He did not want to hinder operations of a new fighter base where it might be necessary to scramble a squadron into the air at a moment's notice.' That was typical of General Eisenhower, whom we all admired and loved. He was truly a soldier's soldier."

17 April 1945
Degnershausen, Germany

Lieutenant Colonel David D. Silberberg was a first lieutenant in Intelligence with 47th Infantry, 9th Infantry Division, when he returned to the Harz Mountain region—where he was born in 1921, which he left in 1936, and where he reeled in his "cache of the day" in April 1945.

While wrecked vehicles along the roads were commonplace, "one truck caught my attention outside Degnershausen," Lieutenant Colonel Silberberg recalls. "It was lying in a ditch, with papers scattered all around. I picked up one of the papers and saw that it was signed by von Ribbentrop, the foreign minister of Nazi Germany."

Aware that he had discovered something worth investigating, he returned to Degnershausen to find someone to talk to. "The mayor had left town," he says, "but a villager told us that trucks had been bringing stuff to this area for two years. Every able-bodied person had been ordered to help unload and store the material."

With Sergeants Herbert Schader, George Novak, and Charles Mangum of Intelligence, First Lieutenant Silberberg went to the "storehouse," a 500-foot-long landmark known as the Chateau Degnershausen, owned by a baroness who immediately handed him a note saying that she was anti-Nazi. She informed him that a baron was on the lower level, the Baron von Griesheim. His first words were, "Please, don't shoot." With hands raised, "he pointed to a window sill where he'd put down his pistol and holster. I still have them both." Pointing out that the Chateau was crammed with files, he exclaims: "I couldn't believe what I saw. There were documents signed by the Kaiser, by Bismarck, by the famous generals of World War I. A number of papers were signed by Hitler, including one telling the commanding general in Paris that he was to obliterate the city." Also on the premises were the archives of the German Ministry of Foreign Affairs from 1929 to 1942.

Under questioning, Baron von Griesheim told First Lieutenant Silberberg of two other nearby hiding places, Chateau Meisdorf and Castle Falkenstein, located under good cover, deep in the mountains. Though there was little danger of air strike to these retreats, there was, however, the order from Berlin that those in charge were to burn everything. "I told them to pass the word to stop any burning or we would deal with them in a way they wouldn't like," Lieutenant Colonel Silberberg recalls.

At Chateau Meisdorf, where a few documents had been burned, "we found the official records covering World War I, from 1914 to 1918." At the fortress-like Castle Falkenstein, discoveries included archives from the Franco-Prussian War, World War I, and hundreds of crates of paintings, sculptures, and art objects. "We opened a couple of them. They were from the Berlin Academy of Arts and the Royal Museum," Lieutenant Colonel Silberberg says. The Berlin Academy collection proved to be that of the entire Library, intact.

The following morning after notifying his superiors, who assigned a company of MPs to guard the treasure trove, First Lieutenant Silberberg continued on with the 9th toward Berlin, about 100 miles northeast. Two days after the discoveries, Generals Dwight Eisenhower and George Patton were photographed at Chateau Meisdorf inspecting the treasures. "So important was this capture of archives that fifty C-47s were requested to fly the massive files to safety and further examination," the 9th U.S. Infantry Division history reports in *Eight Stars to Victory*.

April 1945
En Route to the Elbe and Tangermunde, Germany

Lieutenant Colonel David Saltman was with 6th Tank Destroyer Group Headquarters, a unit of XII Corps, Ninth Army, as liaison officer with 5th Armored Division, "in the final drive east to link up with the Russians."

"I volunteered for Combat Command A (CCA)," Colonel Saltman recalls, and "about noon on the second day, CCA sprang into action. With a deafening roar, every tank and armored vehicle started its engines and CCA passed through to take the lead in the offensive. When the column halted at night, explosions were seen everywhere. It seemed that the Germans were blowing up many bridges to hinder our advance."

On the third day, "at 2300 hours, I got worried that we were running out of gas in the vehicles' fifty-gallon tanks, so I ordered them refilled while still on the move. Riding on the cobblestone roads, our vehicle swayed from side to side. Half of the gasoline went into the tank and the other half spilled on the floor. . . .

"Our progress was rapid. We stopped at an airfield temporarily and German planes flying low overhead were amazed when met with a hail of machine-gun fire. We knocked them out of the sky, bagging six enemy planes in two hours.

"We reached our final objective at the Elbe River at Tangermünde, where a fight began for the bridge across the Elbe. At that time, I turned on my radio, a huge device on which we hand-cranked the controls to reach a desired frequency. My intention was to report the situation to Corps HQ when I heard a deafening explosion. The bridge had been blown from the east bank.

"We liberated 500 American prisoners and some British. Some of the British POWs had been captured five years earlier. Many of the Americans had been captured in North Africa. There were 1,200 other captives who had been evacuated by the Germans to the east side of the Elbe before the bridge was blown. Enemy artillery fire, which was heavy the first day, began to taper off. The Germans were squeezed by U.S. troops on the west and the advancing Russians on the east. This time, we took many German prisoners and collected all weapons.

"General Eisenhower had ordered all troops to stop at the Elbe River and go no farther. . . . And wait we did. Day after day, I walked up to the bank of the Elbe River looking for the Russians. All was quiet, with no Russians in sight. It was a week to ten days later that the Russians finally reached the east bank of the Elbe River."

March–April 1945
Dusseldorf to the Elbe and Barby, Germany

Colonel George W. Irvine was a lieutenant colonel, commanding 324th Field Artillery Battalion, which was "armed with tractor-drawn 155mm howitzers."

Transferred back to Ninth Army for the final time on 3 February, the 324th Field Artillery Battalion "reached the Rhine in the vicinity of Neuss, across from Dusseldorf, on 2 March, and fired our first rounds across the Rhine at about 1100 hours," Colonel Irvine reports. "Three German 88mm guns were found, together with about 4,000 rounds of ammunition, and for two weeks we fired them at targets around Dusseldorf.

"On April 1st, we had an unhappy April Fool experience. We were reconnoitering for gun positions near Hamm, and I had given each of the firing batteries a goose-egg. A German patrol was still in a farmhouse in Battery A's area. They captured three of our men, including the first sergeant, and then departed. One of our sergeants returned a day later with several of his captors who wanted to surrender to us.

"At this time, we were starting a race toward Berlin. The 2nd Armored Division was on our left and about a day ahead of us. Part of our division was motorized with a quartermaster truck company. Much of the rest used captured German vehicles of every description. The *Stars and Stripes* newspaper nicknamed our division 'the rag-tag circus.' My battalion surgeon commandeered a small two-wheeled trailer about two feet wide. When we crossed a river on an engineer bridge, consisting of two sections spaced for normal vehicles, with a gap in between the tracks, he had to walk behind his jeep, lifting the body of the trailer."

From Hamm, the battalion moved through an entire German alphabet of towns—Wadersloh and Paderborn to Halberstadt, Wegeleben, Wespen, and towns in between—"firing across the Elbe on 13 April. We had detoured through the 2nd Armored area on 7 April to utilize their bridge over the Weser River. We occupied as many as four positions in one day, took a few prisoners, but fired relatively few rounds. We fired our 50,000th round on 14 April.

"We crossed the Elbe River on 14 April, at Barby [where] we stayed, 55 miles from Berlin, and waited for the Russians to come and meet up. We fired our last rounds on 28 April, and on 29 April we moved back to start occupation duty. Initially, we operated a transient camp for displaced persons, at Schneidlingen. On 6 May, we started military government at Helmstedt, which later became the entry point between British and Russian occupation zones. V-E Day came on 8 May."

April 1945
Missions over Apennines and Po River, Italy

Lieutenant Colonel Earl M. Amundsen was a pilot, 5th Photographic Squadron, at Peretola Airdrome and then Pisa to pioneer nighttime photographic-reconnaissance missions.

Then–Second Lieutenant Amundsen flew daytime missions over Italy in the P-38/F5A Lightning fighter until April. On 2 April, he flew his first of sixteen night missions to the Po Valley in the B-25/F10 Billy Mitchell medium bomber. At the beginning of April, his squadron wrestled with three key unanswered intelligence questions:

"How were supplies from Germany getting through the Alps into the Po Valley," since "German-controlled highway and railroad passes through the Alps were considered impassable and there was no Axis ability to airlift supplies?

How were the Axis Forces able to move these supplies across the Po River," since "every bridge along the Po had been destroyed for many months? And "why weren't many apparently serviceable Axis fighter and bomber aircraft being flown?

"Daily reconnaissance missions confirmed that there were numerous bombed-out sections of highway and rail lines throughout the Brenner Pass. Some repairs were under way, as seen in daily photo coverage, but not far enough along to warrant scheduling heavy bomber attacks. . . .

"We had two B-25/F10s to cover the length" of the Po River, about 600 miles with its bends and twists. "Each of the two F10s . . . carried cameras with photoelectric lenses and twelve white-phosphorous bombs in the bomb bay. Three bombs were dropped at each assigned target. . . .

"Allied engineering and intelligence . . . believed that it would require most of the night hours to assemble a pontoon bridge across the Po River . . . [and] insisted this would not leave enough hours of darkness to move the quantity of supplies that was being accomplished. They were undoubtedly right if a pontoon bridge is assembled for the first time." But "they did not consider the *repetition factor.*"

Sent on rest leave 24 April, Second Lieutenant Amundsen was on Capri when the war in Italy ended on 2 May, a few days before it ended with Germany. Returning to his squadron, he "began to learn the truth," answers to the key questions: "German engineering had fabricated temporary rail sections and rail-bridge spans that were lifted into place with giant cranes at dusk each evening. Just before dawn each new day, the temporary spans were lifted out and concealed. The daily photographs that showed slow progress in highway and railroad damage-area repairs was an Axis sham to convince Allied Intelligence that the Brenner Pass was impassable.

"The repetition factor was also involved in moving supplies across the Po River. Pontoon bridge sections were connected with long cables that could be pulled by steam winches to assemble the pontoon bridge in an unbelievably short time at dusk. As dawn approached, the cables would be unwound so that the pontoon sections could float downstream and be camouflaged along the river banks. . . .

"The Axis Forces also had semipermanent pontoon bridges that were submerged a foot or so below the river surface to make them difficult to observe in either day or night photographs. These bridges could be used as soon as darkness set in.

"Intelligence reports in early May 1945 also provided the answer to the third question: . . . The Axis Forces had run critically short of experienced pilots. What a blessing for the Allies."

Late April 1945
POW Camp, Moosburg, Germany

Lieutenant Colonel George T. FitzGibbon, with the 82nd Fighter Group, was captured 10 July 1943 in the invasion of Sicily.

Moved from Sagan in late January 1945, Lieutenant Colonel FitzGibbon says he was confined in Bavaria near Munich in late April 1945. "Our underground radio people reported that Patton's Third Army had Nuremberg surrounded and that some of his armored infantry had moved south, toward Munich. I think it was 28 April, as I was walking around the camp with a friend, when I spotted something moving out of the woods to the north. It turned out to be a Sherman tank, and soon there were six of them. At about the same time, small-arms fire began in the woods adjacent to our camp. We immediately took refuge in a long trench we had dug in the event we needed cover.

"Some Hitler Youth were firing machine guns from the church steeples in Moosburg. Our tanks began firing on the churches and soon leveled them. The small-arms fire continued for a couple hours. One POW got a bullet in the leg; a couple of the braver guards were shot, though most had taken off earlier. It all began about 0930 and by 1230 hours, the American flag was flying over the village.

"Soon a Sherman tank came through the front gate into our camp and created bedlam. Guys climbed all over the tank—terrific excitement. My thoughts turned to getting out of there pronto.

"Allowing 30,000 POWs loose in the countryside all at once was ridiculous, of course, so we could visualize another two weeks there. Our own MPs were around the perimeter quickly. My friend Red Hansen, from Iowa somewhere, suggested we had been there long enough and that we should attempt a breakout that very night. We made a successful escape (my only one), but we had the feeling that if we got discovered, the guards would not shoot—that makes a big difference!

"We walked until daybreak and then managed to get some rides in U.S. jeeps and such. Each time, however, we had difficulty proving ourselves. We looked terrible, filthy dirty, in mostly British army clothes, no insignia, no identification, and we got asked many questions about the Yankees and Dodgers, sometimes at gunpoint.

"We got to Nuremberg in two days, found the airfield where the Gooney Birds (C-47s) were bringing in supplies from Le Havre and going back empty. We gave the big sell to the ops officer, got a cot for the night, and flew to Le Havre the next day.

"Upon our arrival, a band was playing, and some nice Red Cross girls met us, gave us coffee and sweet smiles, loaded us into buses, and off we went to Camp Lucky Strike. There, the attendants took our measurements, took our clothes and threw them away, deloused us with huge spray guns, sent us to the showers, greeted us with new underwear, uniforms, shoes, et cetera. What a treat!

"We were debriefed by Intelligence, brought up-to-date on the war, received an advance on pay, had a physical exam, and were put on a strict schedule of five meals a day, very limited portions. Soon I was on a troopship heading home. Upon arrival, and after clearing the military base, I got to a barbershop where I got a shave, haircut and shampoo, and was treated like a hero. Soon I was wildly greeted by my family, and for George FitzGibbon, the war was over."

April–May 1945
POW Camps, Germany to Freedom

Colonel Thomas F. Royals was a Ranger with 417th Infantry Regiment Combat Team when taken prisoner at Trier, Germany, 20 January 1945. He concludes his story.

"One day after we had been separated from the larger group, we enter a POW camp at 1500 hours at Ludwigsburg. About 1600, they start to pass out food, however, we are not included in the rationing for this day," Colonel Royals recalls. "I am the last one and a tank trooper brings me over to his far corner to share his food with other crew members. They are a bit away from everyone else because they are black. To them, I am just a man who needs help. They are from the famed black tank-destroyer group that made history in Europe.

"On Easter Sunday, we moved out toward Munich near the small town of Gmünd in the Schwäbisch area where we are placed in a small camp. There are Punjab Indians, French and Italians, and a Polish doctor. Across the road, there is a group of two hundred Russians who are used for slave labor. . . .

"As the Germans begin their retreat toward Munich, our survival plan is put into action. In the old schoolhouse that served as our POW camp was a deep cellar, entered only by moving certain sections of floor under our beds. . . .

"On the last evening, all moved to the cellar and our guards left the compound on their own. Later that night, we could hear the SS troops shouting at the Russian POWs across the road. The SS troops went through our area, and our medic who spoke German said the SS troops thought we had been moved.

"As the dawn came, so did an eerie silence. We moved slowly and found nothing of the German troops. An Indian Punjab sergeant and I went into the town and at the main square came upon an American tank. The men's first words were, 'What are you doing here, and where are your guns?' After understanding we were POWs, they gave us some rifles and food—good ol' American C- and K-rations. We led them and two more tanks back to the POW camp where more food and rifles were passed out to our people.

"With a few rifles, we were left on our own while the tanks moved on. Some of the Resistance fighters identified themselves, and we told them we needed a truck. A large pick-up truck was found. A tank came through and gave us some gas and, with the few things we owned, the Americans, the RAF and Indian men climbed in the back of the truck, and I drove on, with the Polish doctor giving directions toward the Rhine River.

"As we moved on, singing, we came to a roadblock of American infantry troops. They could not believe their eyes—a bunch of crazy Americans, Indians, and English, all yelling and singing at the same time. . . .

"As we moved to the middle of the Rhine bridge, our truck ran out of gas and the MPs told us to move the truck or they would put us in jail! We all laughed as we pushed the truck into the river. An MP found transportation to the ex-POW camp. We were indeed back in Army control on the 8th day of May 1945.

"From Mannheim, we were transported to the coast of France to a camp for ex-POWs called Lucky Strike. As we headed toward our tent-camp area, I heard American music. It was Armed Forces Radio, and Kate Smith was singing our favorite song, 'God Bless America,'" the anthem that had sustained Colonel Royals and two hundred prisoners months earlier as they were marched for days and nights through cold and rain, mud and snow.

Winter–Spring 1945
Luzon, the Philippines

Colonel Bert D. Miner joined Love Company, 161st Infantry, in March 1945 and participated in the battles of Winch Hill and Banzai Ridge.

"I advanced to first scout when the man in that position was badly wounded. I was therefore the lead man when we were ordered to push forward one morning to scout an area," Colonel Miner writes. "We left our positions and started up a steep trail on this tree-covered mountain, . . . always seeking to take the high ground. . . . The trail led upward and then opened into a small grassy clearing."

Arriving at the clearing, "I stopped briefly to survey the area for any move-ment or anything unusual. On the far side, the slopes of two mountains came together in a V-like gorge. The gorge was filled with boulders and a stream flowed out of it into the clearing. Beyond the stream and near the mouth of the gorge sat a huge boulder (seven- or eight-feet tall and just as wide). At the boul-der, I could get a much better view of the gorge and the mountain slopes up from it.

"I crossed the clearing quickly, waded the stream, stepped up on the far bank and moved to the boulder. After only a moment's hesitation, I stepped to my right from behind the boulder. As I did so, I came face to face with a Japanese soldier from the other side of the boulder. Instantaneously, I was firing my M-1 rifle at him from the hip and sprinting back to the stream. I dropped on my stomach in the water and up against the bank. I could hear the bullets hitting the bank above me and see and hear them hitting the water beyond me. I lay there until enough smoke was dropped on the Japanese positions to cover my withdrawal to a more secure position. I was not injured in that battle but others in the squad were."

Winter–Spring 1945
Villa Verde Trail, Luzon, the Philippines

Captain Robert W. Teeples served with 128th Infantry, 32nd Division, in New Guinea and as a Sixth Army Alamo Scout in New Guinea and on the Admiralty Islands.

In battle for the Villa Verde Trail in the Philippines, Captain Teeples recalls arriving "at a triangular-type piece of ground," at night during a rainstorm, and digging two-man foxholes. During the night, the Nips threw grenades at us and lobbed mortar rounds into our area. Our company sustained a heavy loss of per-sonnel that night but my platoon had the fewest casualties, so we were the ones picked for the reconnaissance patrol in the morning. . . .

"It had commenced to drizzle again as the patrol moved out, and the wetness on the red clay from the foxholes made the uniforms glisten against the green foliage—like walking bull's eyes. . . .

"As the Browning automatic rifle (BAR) man's assistant climbed onto the pla-teau, a shot rang out and he fell back over the edge. Almost immediately, another shot rang out and the BAR man grabbed his throat and ran toward me. As he ran, he began to cry, fell down on his knees, onto his face, and lay still. By this time, the two scouts and I were flat on the ground as a Japanese machine gun had opened up on us from the high ground to our left. I crawled to the BAR man and felt for his pulse, but he was gone.

"Now another machine gun started firing on us from a position on our right flank, and the twigs and branches were snapping all around us. The Japs started to drop occasional mortar rounds on the plateau and I realized we would have to withdraw. I motioned for my scouts to come back, but kept firing at the Jap positions to give them some cover. A bullet ricocheted off the helmet of the first scout but otherwise they made it back safely. I tried to drag the BAR man's body toward the edge of the plateau but his ammunition harness kept catching in the brush. I managed to drag him almost to the edge when I was knocked out by a mortar round."

Given a battlefield commission as second lieutenant in May, Captain Teeples was later injured and returned to the States in August 1945.

13–15 April 1945
En Route to Mindanao, the Philippines

Colonel Charles B. Gwynn arrived in the Southwest Pacific Theater in early 1945 with the 655th Field Artillery Battalion.

"I must admit I was lucky to activate, train, command, and take into combat an 8-inch howitzer battalion. In my opinion, it was the best field-artillery piece developed during WWII. It was a massive twenty-ton weapon towed by a twenty-ton tractor. It fired a 200-pound shell nearly ten miles. The trail spades, the jacks, rammer staffs, et cetera, were in the hundreds of pounds, requiring rugged cannoneers," Colonel Gwynn rhapsodizes.

On 12 April, the day President Roosevelt died, "my field artillery unit had just been combat-loaded and buttoned up aboard an LST in the San Rogue Harbor south of Tacloban, Leyte, Philippine Islands, ready to move out for the X Corps invasion of Mindanao.

"The LST was part of a large convoy passing through the historic Surigao Strait, the Sulu Sea, west of the Zamboanga Peninsula and through the Basilan Strait for the invasion landing on the west side of the island near the Pollock Harbor about 15 April. On D-Day, I went ashore with my three-quarter-ton command vehicle, transferring successively from the LST to an LCI, LCM, LCVP, and finally the last one hundred yards in shallow water.

"A few days later, I was on the beach awaiting the unloading over the beach of my twelve howitzers when I met and talked with Major General F. R. Sibert, X Corps commander, and Admiral Thomas Kincaid, commanding the 7th Fleet, which convoyed us and saw us safely ashore."

21 April—15 May 1945
Mount Pacawagen, the Philippines

Captain Bernard L. Patterson was serving as 2nd Battalion ammunitions officer, 145th Infantry Regiment, 37th Division, guarding Manila.

On 15 April, the 145th Regimental Combat Team was attached to the 6th Division to assist in an attack against the Kobayashi Force holding the mountains about fifteen miles east of Manila. "At 0200 hours on 21 April, the 1st and 3rd Battalions of the 145th attacked the Japanese positions on the west slope of Mount Pacawagen, a horseshoe-shaped mountain, attacking to the east. After the west leg of the horseshoe was taken, the attack would continue across the top and down the east leg of the shoe," Captain Patterson writes. "The Japanese had more artillery and mortars here than any place our regiment had been before. . . . The artillery piece would be pushed to the mouth of the caves, fire a few rounds, and then pulled back into the caves. Only a direct hit would damage them.

"We bulldozed a road to the top of the mountain at the southwest end and, assisted by bulldozers, pulled the 145th Cannon Company's M-7s to the top of Mount Pacawagen. . . . The grade up the side of Mount Pacawagen was a 45 angle and higher. The only vehicles besides bulldozers that could climb it were jeeps and trailers. . . . All food, water, and ammunition at first had to be hand-carried from the bottom of the mountain to the units on top. Antitank, service, regimental, and battalion headquarters companies supplied the carriers, with as many Filipino men as we could get. . . .

"Wounded were brought out the same way, in reverse—hand-carried, four men to a litter, sometimes over a mile, then by jeep (all equipped with litter racks) to the battalion aid station. However, to get off the mountain, the wounded were placed in a trailer and pulled down by bulldozer. . . .

"By 30 April, most of the top of Mount Pacawagen was taken. . . . The regiment soon completed the capture [but] . . . the Japanese never just fell back to another position. You had to dig them out of their holes all the way down the mountain. For several days, this was the next task, before we could take Mount Biniayan and the Sugarloaf.

"The 2nd Battalion's objective was the Sugarloaf, a steep, rocky mountain. It was taken with more ease than Mount Pacawagen, as was Mount Biniayan. . . . Both crests were secure by 9 May 1945 and Wawa Dam was in sight just down the mountain. Those of us who were high enough could see Manila celebrating V-E Day with fireworks, just twenty miles away. We weren't ready to celebrate yet. Wiping up on these two mountains was rougher than taking them [but] . . . it was completed by 15 May 1945."

1 April 1945

USS *Oconto* en Route to Okinawa

Lieutenant Colonel Bernard J. Jochim served as E Division Officer, electrical
assistant to the chief engineer, on the USS Oconto (APA-187), transporting 25th
Division troops to Okinawa.

Listing activity as *Oconto* headed into Easter Sunday and Okinawa, young Jochim records at that time: "0000 midnight, Easter Mass for all Catholic men; 0500, Dawn Alert (Condition One)—breakfast for Army troops; 0545, arrive at outer transport area—lower all boats; 0600, call Army boat teams; 0815, twelfth wave leaves transport area. . . .

"Bombardment of the beaches was continuous by the destroyers and battle-wagons and aircraft. The area was crowded with ships—APAs, AKAs, men-of-war, and small craft loaded with troops and supplies. The sea was rough and the small craft had problems as they circled in waves, awaiting orders to head for the beaches.

"The Kamikazes were busy at times. They would fly in low among the ships to avoid being shot at. . . . The appearance of Kamikazes always triggered the use of smoke generators by all the ships to conceal their locations. . . .

"Personnel on topside were all instructed to be on the lookout for enemy swimmers. They would approach ships by hiding under floating debris (boxes, et cetera) to attach explosives to a ship's hull. This was a different kind of warfare than I had in the earlier part of the war," when "I served on board the USS *Gudgeon* (SS-211) during her first six war patrols. It was a new experience being able to see and hear and smell the action—different from the so-called silent service, which was not always so silent. The *Gudgeon* was later lost on her twelfth war patrol, with all hands."

7 April 1945

Mission from Iwo Jima to Japan

Colonel Douglas B. Moore was a first lieutenant and pilot with 78th Fighter
Squadron, 15th Fighter Group, December 1943–August 1945.

When eighty-two P-51s of the 15th and 21st Fighter Groups arrived at Guam 13 February, "we in the 15th then flew to East Field on Saipan while waiting for the Marines to take Iwo. They went ashore on the 19th. . . . On 6 March, the 47th Squadron flew from Saipan to the captured and repaired South Field on Iwo Jima," Colonel Moore reports.

"The engineers had filled in the holes on the airstrip and cleared off the debris of battle and it was in good shape but wasn't paved. The Japanese occupied most of the north end of the 3¹/₂-mile-long island, and we could stand on our airstrip and see the front line. We immediately started flying support missions for the Marines and maintained a Combat Air Patrol. . . . We also conducted missions to the Bonin Islands northeast of Iwo Jima. . . .

"The day finally arrived for our first very-long-range fighter mission to Japan. . . . 7 April 1945, [escorting] 100-plus B-29s of the 73rd Bomb Wing on a mission to Tokyo. Their target was the Nakajima aircraft plant. . . . I was pleased to be assigned to fly the wing of our squadron commander, Major Jim VandeHey. . . .

"The strike force crossed over the Japanese coast at about 1045 and we dropped our wing tanks over Yokohama as we were intercepted. . . . The B-29 strike force of 103 aircraft was stacked up from 12,000 feet, and we were 18,000 to 20,000 feet. The 15th Fighter Group was protecting the front of the bomber stream. None of us who were there will ever forget the sight and radio chatter involved, as we were intercepted by a large Japanese force that some estimated to be over 200 aircraft.

"The first enemy aircraft I saw was a twin-engine Nick, not more than 500 feet directly above us. I called it out to Major VandeHey and then tried to climb up behind him but he started a left-descending turn toward the bomber stream and the best I could do was fire a burst at him which was then about out of range. . . .

"The B-29s lost three, two to flak and one to fighters. The Mustangs lost one over the target and another pilot bailed out on the way back to Iwo due to low fuel; he was picked up by an air-sea rescue destroyer. The P-51s claimed twenty-two destroyed, six probables, and six damaged.

"My logbook shows that I flew seven hours, fifteen minutes during that first mission," Colonel Moore reports. "The 7th Fighter Command fighters on Iwo conducted a total of fifty-one very-long-range missions before the war ended in August 1945. The missions changed from escort to fighter strikes, as the Japanese intercepts of the bombers dwindled and the B-29s conducted more of the night fire-bombing missions."

7 and 13 April 1945

Iwo Jima

Lieutenant Colonel James J. Ahern was a lieutenant with Company F, 147th Infantry Regiment.

In a letter on 7 April to Mary Eells, the young lady who would become his wife a year later, Lieutenant Ahern informs her: "Yesterday, I made a reconnaissance and came across a spot where I noticed a lot of Jap activity. . . . About 0100 hours, we saw five of them coming up the road. When I gave the order to fire, the machine gun did not fire. Neither did the M-1 rifle or submachine gun. I picked up a grenade and threw it. Then the machine gun opened fire. . . . What a feeling when everything fouled up."

Writing of another night, when shots rang out over his head and grenades hit next to his position during five attacks, "I kept saying to myself, 'Lord, you made the night too long.'" In his letter of Friday the 13th, he reports: "Yesterday, I formed a patrol; picked up several hundred pounds of TNT and a flamethrower. The Japs were holed up in a cave in the face of a cliff. . . . I placed a charge down in the opening and we blew it. It opened a terrible-sized hole. We fired a few bazooka shells in there; then we tossed a few smoke grenades into it. I took the flamethrower and worked the cave over.

"After the cave cooled down, we walked or inched cautiously into the cave. . . . I looked to the left of the cave and saw a Jap. I did think that he was dead. Nevertheless, I threw three shots into him. The third shot must have hit him. He raised his head, opened his eyes, and pulled the pin of a grenade he had in his hands. I put a couple of more shots into him and ran like hell. The grenade went off just as I reached the entrance. . . .

"So I worked the cave over again with the flamethrower. I decided to enter again. We reached the spot where we saw the Jap the first time. I'll be a son-of-a-gun if he didn't fire at us with a pistol. So my sergeant and I ducked behind a rock, [then] I with the flashlight and pistol and he with a Tommy gun opened up and we blasted the Jap. We finally closed the cave with a large charge. . . .

"Then we went to another cave. . . . I threw in a smoke grenade in hope of smoking the Japs out. As I did, the Jap tossed the grenade back at me. I received many phosphorous burns. A little later, the Jap tossed it back at me again and once more I was burned. I became angry and decided to blow a larger entrance into the cave with twenty-seven pounds of TNT. . . . I put the flamethrower on my back. It weighed close to 100 pounds. . . . As I ran up to the cave, a Jap tossed a grenade from the cave. I did not duck quick enough, for a fragment of the grenade hit my wrist and took a little skin off. It really only grazed me. I got the flamethrower working and let them have it. . . .

"As I was working on the second cave, I had the wind blowing from my back. The next thing I knew I was completely enveloped in flames. My clothes were set on fire. I rolled down the slope off the wall of the crevice and fell about twenty feet. I beat the flames out with my hands, with the sergeant helping out. As a result of the weight and my fall, I strained my knee; a few burns and a banged-up back."

After all of this detail, he adds: "Now don't go worrying, I am not in the hospital. I will be back to duty in a few days. . . . Your prayers are helping out."

April 1945
POW Camp Hoten, Manchuria

Colonel Michael A. Quinn continues his POW diary.

At POW Camp Hoten in Chen Chia Tung, Manchuria, April 1945 marks three years of captivity for most of the prisoners. April also brings more dust storms from the Gobi Desert, more trench-digging in case of air raids, more requests to "volunteer" to farm, with promises once again that food raised would be theirs, and the more encouraging news of Allied victories nearby and in the ETO. The men learn this from Japanese newspapers that one of the POWs is now able to translate.

On 15 April, Colonel Quinn writes: "Had a long talk with Drake tonight about reports. It is Drake's idea not to cause any trouble in his reports. My idea is to tell the truth and shame the devil. Of all the QMs I have ever met, I believe General Drake is by far the smartest. There is one thing about him that I didn't like. He wouldn't scrap with higher authority. . . . The food debacle on Bataan is directly traceable to the fact that none of Drake's recommendations regarding supply had been taken by the USAFFE staff, and Drake wouldn't go to MacArthur over the heads of general staff. Anyway, after this talk, Drake agreed with me that if these reports should be of value to anyone in the future, they can only be of value if they are truthful."

On 25 April, their twenty-sixth wedding anniversary, Colonel Quinn writes a love letter to wife Mike: "My Darling: I wish I could express my love to you as I really mean it today. . . . Today, the only way I could remember our wedding anniversary was to read the Nuptial Mass. Now in retrospect, the beauty of it was greater than ever before."

42

"And so it is over. The catastrophe on one side of the world has run its course. The day that it had so long seemed would never come has come at last. . . .

"First a shouting of the good news with such joyous surprise that you would think the shouter himself had brought it about. And then an unspoken sense of gigantic relief—and then a hope that the collapse in Europe would hasten the end in the Pacific."

So begins a rough draft of the V-E Day column that correspondent Ernie Pyle was preparing for the end of the war in Europe. It was found on his body the day he was killed by a sniper's bullet on Ie Shima, 18 April 1945, about three weeks before V-E Day, 8 May 1945.

In their accounts for May 1945, some ROA contributors share their shouts of "joyous surprise" at the good news; others tell of involvement to help "bring it about." For service members in the Pacific Theater, however, there are three additional months yet to come of what Ernie Pyle, in his V-E Day story, calls "the companionship . . . of death and misery," the "spouse that tolerates no divorce."

1–8 May 1945
Volary, Czechoslovakia

Colonel Jean W. Christy continues his account of the 5th Infantry Division.

"With Berlin having fallen to the Russian armies, the Ruhr pocket cleaned up, and the U.S. First Army holding a firm bridgehead across the Elbe River linking up with the Russians, there remained few sectors of German resistance in Europe. There was no organized defense in existence any longer, yet certain Army groups continued to fight on because they didn't have any orders to do otherwise. Fate and the U.S. Army commanders decreed that the 5th Infantry Division should be in on the curtain call of the Wehrmacht, in its Czechoslovakian 'last ditch' stand," 5th Infantry Division history records.

Of events between 4 and 6 May, Colonel Christy reports: "By this time, our infantry units had reached the place where the borders of Germany, Austria, and Czechoslovakia meet. There was a small concrete monument marking the exact spot. Our imaginative soldiers quickly found that it was possible to stand with one foot in Czechoslovakia, the other foot in Austria, and puddle on Germany. And a lot of us found the time to do just that.

"It was at about this time that we all became very much aware that the end of hostilities was now quite near. Rumors flew about meetings at SHAEF Headquarters back in Reims, France, between General Eisenhower and German army generals. An alert came down on 5 May to watch for a German white monoplane that might be flying over. This airplane would be carrying German officers for the truce talks, and was to be protected."

Division history picks up the story on 7 May: "Vicinity of Volary, Czechoslovakia. On road to carry 3rd Battalion forward at 0730. Plans changed at 0815 and closed into present position at 1215 on six-hour alert pending orders from Corps. Received word, through channels, at 1900 of unconditional surrender by Doenitz of all German forces at 070141—official end of hostilities to be 090001. Defensive precautions still to be carried out."

"And so the war in Europe came to an end," Colonel Christy comments. "More accurately, arrangements had been made by SHAEF and the German general staff for the fighting to be brought to a close. As we had learned so well, it takes time for information to be disseminated throughout the many echelons in an army. That was why the official end of hostilities was set two days after the signing."

The last entry in the 50th Field Artillery Battalion's "Record of Events" is the following: "8 May 1945: Officially declared as V-E Day. Taken very quietly by men and officers with a feeling of a job well done. In way of celebration, all former officers of unit invited to a party with present officers. A very good celebration."

"And what a party it was," Colonel Christy exclaims. "I have no idea how the word got out so quickly, but a real crowd showed up—some from more than a hundred miles away. . . .

"The crowd began to assemble shortly after dusk. . . . Old friends were together again, the strong punch flowed, and new stories mingled with the old ones. . . . By midnight, the mere mortals among us began to drift away to bed. The real party guys stayed on longer; some stayed up all night, sitting by the light of Coleman lanterns, talking quietly, retelling old stories, remembering mutual adventures."

4–6 May
Vörgl, Austria

Colonel Walter D. Rice was a sergeant with 3rd Platoon, Company I, 409th Infantry, 103rd Infantry Division, when it was involved in its last combat action after having captured Oberammergau and Garmisch-Partenkirchen, Germany, and Innsbruck, Austria.

"Our platoon was quartered in the town of Schwaz awaiting orders," says Colonel Rice. "Those orders came shortly after noon 4 May. Under the command of First Lieutenant Willard W. Hebert of Lake Charles, Louisiana, we mounted the tanks and headed out. . . .

"At about 1930 hours, we came to the town of Vörgl, finding it to be occupied by infantry and tanks from the XXI Corps. I had posted one of my men as security for our tanks and had returned to our quarters. Sitting down to enjoy the luxury of removing my boots, I was interrupted by the sentry that I had just assigned to guard duty.

"He said, 'There's a Kraut out here and he wants to talk to the lieutenant.' I went out and met the man, who was a corporal in the Wehrmacht and who spoke fairly good English. After questioning him, I went in and wakened First Lieutenant Hebert . . . [who] instructed me to bring the German to him.

"The German corporal saluted Lieutenant Hebert and told him that his *Oberleutnant* had sent him to talk to the American commander. The message was that a thirty-man SS detachment in the surrounding mountains had called, demanding to know how many *Panzerwaggens* we had in town, and that the SS would attack the next morning. He went on to say that his *Oberleutnant* did not give the information to the SS. Further, his instructions were to tell us that they knew that our men were tired, so the Wehrmacht would guard our tanks that night, and that if the SS attacked in the morning, the Wehrmacht would help to fight them. He then saluted again and departed.

"Sure enough, Wehrmacht soldiers 'walked post,' guarding our armor all night. Of course, our people maintained security as well from covered positions nearby.

"When morning came, the SS attack did not materialize. Under orders from division headquarters, we turned control of the town over to the XXI Corps and returned to Schwaz.

"On 5 May 1945, the following message was received from Headquarters, Seventh U.S. Army: 'To be broadcast by the Seventh Army radio every fifteen minutes until 2000; thereafter, every half hour: All troops of German army Group G which opposes the Seventh U.S. Army have been ordered by their commander to surrender by 1200 tomorrow, 6 May. Forward units of the Seventh Army are directed to remain in place and cease further combat at once. By Command of Lieutenant General Patch.'

"Great was the rejoicing among our group of 'dogfaces,' though it was tempered with the memory of our comrades who were not there to enjoy it with us."

7–8 May 1945
Czechoslovakia

Colonel William M. McConahey, battalion surgeon, continues his story.

"Finally it came: the long-waited-for news. I was standing in the command post about ten o'clock on Monday morning, 7 May. One of the telephones rang. An officer answered it, and then turned to us and said: 'The war is over!' No one cheered. No one fired off his gun. The news was too big for that—too awesome. We simply stood there looking at each other and saying, 'The war's over at last!' Then the telephone rang again, and we received the division orders. We were to remain in place, take any Germans prisoner who came in, and not fire unless fired upon," Colonel McConahey writes.

"That afternoon Peter Wendl and I drove to Suscice . . . , to locate the division artillery aid station. On the way, we passed from the Sudetenland into old Czechoslovakia, and it was like going from night to day. Instead of a cold, silent, hostile populace, we found crowds of cheering, flower-throwing, rejoicing people waving Czech flags. What a welcome we got in Suscice! It was like being in France, only more so. I think every citizen must have been out in the streets cheering us, their liberators, and laughing, waving Czech, American, and Russian flags, throwing flowers and so forth. . . .

"The next day, 8 May, the battalion moved to Schihebetz, a little town in old Czechoslovakia, and what a great welcome we received! The people were deliriously happy to see us, and they treated us like honored guests. They had a village ceremony of thanksgiving for their deliverance from the Germans, at which they presented our battalion with a little Czech flag. . . . The town band gave concerts in the public square; they had native dances in the open each evening; and they all did everything they could to make us happy. I had a room in a local house for my aid station, and the family . . . helped us all they could, baked cakes and cookies for us, and cooked chickens for us. I soon came to love the friendly, moral, hard-working Czech people."

V-E Day, 8 May 1945
Marseille, France

*Lieutenant Colonel Norman Wiener was with 40th TC Traffic Battalion, 6th
Major Port.*

"On V-E Day, high rank did not know what to expect in the reaction of French
civilians. Would they attempt to 'invade' our warehouse? Break windows? Steal
badly needed supplies? I was assigned to ride a jeep on the main street. We had
no trouble. Only extremely happy civilians, joyous at the end of a long and painful war."

V-E Day, 8 May 1945
Reims, France

*Lieutenant Colonel Harvey Lagasse, lieutenant with 459th Bomb Group, had just
been released from a German POW camp.*

"A gang of us went into town with an advance for some of our back pay. We
found a bistro and ordered champagne, of course. It was like nectar from the
gods. French girls swarmed into the bistro, kissing everyone in sight and, let me
assure you, I was in sight. Everyone danced in the once-Nazi-held streets. Later,
in the midst of this beautiful turmoil, we sang 'God Bless America,' and those
happy French people joined in as best they could. That night was one I will never
forget."

V-E Day, 8 May 1945
Ulm, Germany

*Lieutenant Colonel William P. Tait Jr. served as captain with 285th Quartermaster
Truck Battalion.*

"Shortly after dark on 8 May 1945, suddenly, shooting surrounded us and the
sky was bright with tracer bullets and flares, noisier and brighter than we had
ever seen. . . . As I approached our office, I noticed several soldiers firing their
rifles into the air. Coming within earshot, I could hear the excited men shouting:
'Germany has surrendered! The war in Europe is over!'"

V-E Day, 8 May 1945
Near Ulm, Germany

*Lieutenant Colonel Donald W. Caman served with 3rd Platoon, 100th Cavalry
Reconnaissance Troop, 100th Infantry Division.*

"On V-E Day, though I didn't know it was that at the time, I was picking up
POWs from a field of thousands guarded by a couple of GIs with a .30-caliber

MG mounted on a $1/4$-ton—location, somewhere southeast of Ulm. The Germans fought to get on those trucks; they didn't want to be captured by the Russians. You would be surprised how many standing POWs you can jam into the back of a $2^1/_2$-ton. We were on the road to the rear when we heard the war was over."

V-E Day, 8 May 1945
Schierstein, Germany

Major August T. Savoy served as theater chief of transportation, HQ, Marine Operation Division.

"When the war ended, I was with an engineer unit building a pontoon bridge across the Rhine. . . . The colonel toasted our victory and asked who was on the night shift."

V-E Day, 8 May 1945
Okinawa

Lieutenant Colonel Alanson H. Sturgis Jr, a captain and naval gunfire spotter, served with 2nd Battalion, 307th Infantry Regiment, 77th Infantry Division.

"One day early in May, we were out of combat, and were behind the line . . . when we heard a request for nomination of targets. At 1200 hours on that day, a TOT (time on target) mission would be fired by every gun, ashore and afloat, on twelve selected targets, to mark 'Victor Easy [V-E] Day.' That was the first news we'd had of the German surrender. The general reaction was to the effect, 'Well, maybe *now* we'll be getting some help out here.' . . .

"I have no idea how many pieces fired on that mission. The Army had calibers from 75mm howitzers up to and including eight-inch pieces; the Navy guns ranged from the five-inch guns on the destroyers through cruisers with six-inch or eight-inch guns to battleships with sixteen-inch batteries. . . . It looked as though the whole ridge-line was picked up and put down again in a cloud of smoke, dust, rocks, and trees. I can't imagine what the Japanese thought was going on. . . . As I remember, their resistance was just as stubborn afterwards as it had been before. Still, it really was a sight to be remembered for a long time."

16 May 1945
Regensburg, Germany

Colonel Raymond O. Ford was a colonel on the general staff of General Bradley's 12th Army Group in Wiesbaden as World War II wound down.

On 15 May 1945, "I received a call from my boss, General Moses, Bradley's G-4, that he wanted me to meet him the next day at a conference at Patton's Third

Army Headquarters in Regensburg," Colonel Ford writes. "I met General Moses at 1100 on the airstrip, and he said that General Patton had been called back from leave in London and that he and Bradley had spent the night with Eisenhower in Reims.

"A group of officers had assembled, and at about 1145 a plane arrived with Bradley and Patton, our host, who said he would take the generals to his quarters for lunch and told his chief of staff to take the others to the officers' mess" prior to all meeting in the war room at 1330 hours. The Russians were in Czechoslovakia a week earlier, when the Germans surrendered. Patton had wanted to capture Prague, but had been forbidden to cross the boundary. In Yugoslavia, communist activity had arisen under Tito.

"General Bradley opened the conference saying that in view of the tension in the area Eisenhower wanted our recommendations in case the Russians attacked us. Patton in his high-pitched voice replied, 'Let's attack the SOBs.' This was not the approved solution, but we delayed the redeployment of five divisions for thirty days until the tension diminished. I have often wondered how history would have changed if we had adopted Patton's solution."

Spring 1945
Bolzano, Italy

Colonel Fred E. Bamberger served in North Africa in 1943, with the 90th Photo
Recon Wing in Italy, and with HQ 12th AF as staff photo officer.

When the commander of Luftwaffe South, in Bolzano, Italy, indicated his wish to surrender to the commanding general of the Twelfth Air Force, then-Captains Bamberger and Thomas J. Hallahan were sent from Peretola Airfield, near Florence, to work out arrangements at the operating HQ of the 88th Division.

"It was an eerie feeling to walk down the main street of Bolzano surrounded by thousands of German troops, who eyed us curiously, and we were constantly returning the salutes of many of these soldiers," Colonel Bamberger recalls. "All at once, Tom and I found ourselves in front of a magnificent chateau, and in front of the entrance gate were two American MP sergeants. . . . [The chateau] . . . had been taken over by SS General Karl Wolff, commanding general of the German Storm Troopers. Even as I was talking to the sergeants, he appeared and strode forcefully through the entrance gate. He was in truth the total archetypal Nazi."

Recognizing him as the highest-ranking German officer in the area, "both Tom and I saluted him smartly. At this point, he took out a monocle, put it to his eye, and stared through it directly at me. After a very long and deliberate moment, he removed the monocle and proceeded to walk on by as though we never existed. . . . Anger overtook protocol. I yanked the Colt .45 out of my shoulder holster, pulled back the hammer, and shouted '*Achtung!*'

"I immediately sensed that hundreds of eyes were riveted on me. . . . Hurriedly, I turned to one of the MP sergeants and asked, 'Do you speak German?' He quickly nodded and replied loudly, 'Yes, Sir.'

" 'Tell the general he has failed to return the salute of two American officers.' General Wolff again resorted to using the monocle to coldly scrutinize me and then spoke tartly to the sergeant: 'Advise your *Kapitan* that I only salute officers of equal rank.'

"I understood what he was saying, but I did not let him know that. After the sergeant had duly informed me, it was now my turn: 'Remind the general that he is on the losing side and that an American captain now outranks any German officer. I am also the direct personal representative of Major General John K. Cannon, commander of the United States Twelfth Air Force, and I now request that General Wolff surrender his pistol to me, which I will properly present to my commander.'. . .

Staring at the still upraised .45 with the hammer still cocked, the general slowly unbuckled his holster with its contents and thrust it at the sergeant. "I then spoke again: 'Sergeant, remind the general, again, we are waiting for him to return our salutes.' Now looking fixedly at me, he pressed his lips together and suddenly clicked his heels sharply, raised his arm stiffly, and screamed, 'Heil Hitler.' I slowly lowered the .45 and nodded to the sergeants: 'That looks like the best we're going to get. You can inform Herr General Wolff he is now dismissed.'

"Tom and I, along with a lot of Germans and Italians, watched in studied silence as the now-disarmed Teuton Tiger stalked quickly back into the chateau. I now secured the .45 to a safe position and returned it to its holster. The MP sergeants waited . . . and then both of them saluted smartly. 'I think this is what you were looking for, Captain, and I might add, Sir, that I was never as proud as I am at this very moment to be an American soldier,' the one said. I never will forget that moment nor the look on their faces when I returned their salutes and replied easily in German, 'I feel the same way!' "

Spring 1945
Mission to Linz, Austria

Lieutenant Colonel Norman L. Stevens Jr. was the book-report dropout turned Eighth AF drop-in. [See his December 1942 story.]

"As the war was winding down in Europe, Patton was screaming eastward. He overran a German prison camp that was full of French soldiers. Patton radioed back to England to get these French officers out of his hair, and that came down to Colonel Stann, my squadron commander, and two other pilots, myself and 'I forget the other guy.' Each plane took skeleton crews and flew for Linz, Austria," Lieutenant Colonel Stevens writes.

"We hadn't been on the ground thirty seconds before this horde of French officers came in at a trot toward the three B-17s. . . . The take-off was a little long but very successful. We gained altitude and headed west as quickly as possible.

"I became verbally acquainted with a Colonel Le Spirit. We talked in French and English, off and on, and he said that he had been a prisoner for five years. When we came to the Rhine, I told Colonel Le Spirit to tell the rest of his officers that we were now crossing the Rhine and we are in France. All of the Frenchmen began to have tears in their eyes.

"I asked Colonel Le Spirit what he would like to see in France, and he said, 'What every Frenchman would like to see, the Eiffel Tower.'

"I said, 'Colonel, you will see the Eiffel Tower like you have never seen the Eiffel Tower!'

"When I got to Paris, I dropped down to about 500 feet and approached the Eiffel Tower and then did three complete 360 turns around the Eiffel Tower. There was not a dry-eyed Frenchman in the bunch, and it made the trip well worth it!"

March–25 May 1945
POW Camps to Freedom

Lieutenant Colonel Romolo D. Tedeschi concludes his POW story.

After confinement at Oflag XIIIB, Hammelburg, and rescue on 27 March, POW Tedeschi and his group were recaptured and sent to a POW Camp in Nuremberg. From there, hundreds of POWs from "all the nations fighting the Germans" began "a long, arduous forced march south through Bavaria" to their final camp, in Moosburg. "We had to scrounge for food from the friendly Bavarian farmers and kept warm at night by sleeping in their enormous haystacks. . . . We were surprised at the kindness of these Bavarians who allowed us not only to eat their potatoes but also gave us eggs in exchange for cigarettes.

"One day during the march, our column was spotted by two American fighter planes, one of which started a strafing run at us. In the middle of the run, he must have realized that we were not the enemy and wagged his wings at the second plane as a signal to pull up. Unfortunately, however, this happened after he had dropped a bomb and strafed with machine-gun fire, from which a few of the POWs were injured, but not seriously. From that day on, American planes flew daily escort over the marching column. . . .

"We finally arrived in Moosburg after over four weeks on the road. . . . A week after our arrival we heard firing in the distance and the rumble of tanks. . . . That afternoon, the tanks attacked the guard towers, which offered little resistance to what turned out to be units of General Patton's Third Army. When the Germans were subdued, Patton drove up in his jeep, wearing his famous ivory-handled pistols and looking larger than life. He asked us what we needed or desired most. Food, and especially bread, was our top priority, of course. The next day, we were given fresh GI bread and it tasted like angel-food cake.

Red Cross personnel appeared that afternoon offering coffee and doughnuts to anyone. . . . Two of the Red Cross personnel turned out to be close friends of mine from Aversa, Italy. I recognized them, but they had difficulty recognizing me. I had lost considerable weight and had grown a beard. When they finally realized who I was, they burst into tears and hugged me. That night, they returned to their quarters in Munich and telephoned my ordnance unit in Aversa, announcing that I was alive and well.

"Following a change of clothing and burning our lice-infested clothes, we were flown to Camp Lucky Strike in Le Havre, France, and from there shipped on a Victory ship to the United States, about 25 May 1945."

29 April—8 May 1945
German POW Camp to Freedom

Commander John F. O'Connell provides the diary of his late brother, Lieutenant James J. O'Connell.

"Russian army attacking environs of Rheinsberg, as German army retreated through the town," Private O'Connell records in his diary 29 April 1945. A group of American POWs, volunteers at the *Carmol Fabric* (drug factory), were return-ing to the compound when "Russian Yak planes commenced strafing the town, dropping antipersonnel bombs in the streets. During their three passes, we nar-rowly escaped by flattening ourselves against masonry walls and buildings. Then we discovered that our own main building had been hit by bombs and strafing. . . . Troops of Russian Cossack Cavalry began entering Rheinsberg. . . . We all stood up simultaneously and gave ourselves up to the Russians. Drinks were poured and we all shook hands."

On the morning of 30 April, "we were marched to the town square. Here were assembled the various POW and slave-labor contingents from France, Italy, Russia, Poland, Yugoslavia, and the USA, as well as the new German prisoners. At this assembly point, we were set free by the Russians and told to head for Odessa, Russia. This location was some 3,000 kilometers southeast in the Russian Crimea! Well, no way were we undertaking that journey, with the American GIs camping on the Elbe River, some 125 kilometers to the west. Today's march covered about 25 kilometers," to the Dannenwalde Railroad Station.

On 1 May, the POWs march 13 kilometers to Gransee, "on the main road south to Berlin," and "spent the night in a former German Hitler *Mädels* Barracks. It was furnished quite luxuriously—even had a moving-picture theater and radios in all the rooms. They had a well-stocked wine cellar and the bunch celebrated with champagnes and German wine—plus a hot meal on the Hitler *Mädels*!" [Hitler *Mädels* were German girls selected by the Nazis to bear children of selected SS troops for the good of the fatherland.]

From Gransee, it was 31 kilometers to Neuruppin on 2 May, and 22 kilometers on foot, plus 36 kilometers on bicycles (confiscated from a German refugee caravan) to reach Kyritz east of the Elbe River on 3 May. "We spent the night with a Russian army unit, which had taken over a castle property. They slaughtered and cooked a suckling pig for the four of us. Tonight's feast consisted of delicious pork, chicken, applesauce, Russian rye bread, wine, and a toast with cognac! All around us was complete desolation of all types."

"This morning," on 4 May, "we peddled our bikes 41 kilometers to Perleberg," Private O'Connell records. "We reached Wittenberg about 4 P.M., met a group of American GIs from a Searchlight Platoon of the 84th Infantry Division, joined their unit for the night and experienced our first trip through a real GI chow line in over five months!"

On 5 May, the POWs were driven about 60 kilometers to 19th Corps Headquarters in Klotze and "on the Autobahn some 120 kilometers to Hildesheim . . . [and then] to the Rhein-Main Airport." On 6 May, "receiving fine treatment at this post where they are constantly (it seems) handing out cigars, cigarettes, chewing gum, and candy. I went to a movie today for the first time in six months," he writes.

Appropriately, his last entry is dated Tuesday, 8 May, V-E Day. "War ended at 0241 today," Private O'Connell records. "We were flown by C-47 to Nancy,

France. Passed over the city of Cologne, Germany, and noted the huge Gothic-style cathedral in utter ruin. The trip covered 300 miles and took two hours. We arrived in time for the V-E Day celebration in Nancy. Crowds of cheering people greeted us as our trucks of liberated prisoners joined the victory parade through the city. We detrucked at Nancy's railroad station and took the train to Epinal, 60 kilometers south of Nancy, the site of the RAMP Center."

Winter–Spring 1945

German POW Camps, Then Freedom

Major Robert J. Lagasse submits recollections by his late brother, Lieutenant Colonel Harvey Lagasse.

After their own Death March from Stalag Luft III, Lower Silesia, in the bitter cold of January 1945, the surviving POWs finally entrain for the trip to Stalag XIID in Nuremberg. At the Nuremberg camp, which bordered the railroad yards, "our fighters buzzed the compound very low and very slow. The German 88mm was worthless at that altitude and the 40mm was the only threat, and I never saw one of our fighters hit by the 40s," Lieutenant Colonel Lagasse writes.

"Strong rumors ran rampant that General George Patton and his Third Army were rapidly approaching Nuremberg. The excitement in the camp was electric. Men laughed, men cried, men danced, and some even gathered their meager belongings in wild anticipation. Most of us didn't sleep that night. . . .

"Then," the next night, "we heard it way off in the distance, barely audible. It was unmistakably artillery fire. Everyone was on their feet. There was wild anticipation until it happened for the second time: 'adjutant's call.' This could only mean one thing—another forced march to prevent our liberation by General Patton's Third Army. Our anticipation was correct. . . .

"We formed in a column of threes as before and moved out smartly," marching to Feucht and then to Ochenbruk, where "we observed some of our Thunderbolts dive-bombing the town we had just left. Apparently they were after the panzer outfit. Our column was eight miles long, I was told, and those POWs at the end of the column were killed in the bombing."

In Polling, the German guards permitted the POWs to sleep in barns in the area. "This was a far cry from the winter march. We crawled into the new-mown hay that smelled so sweet and was without the curse of bedbugs and lice. I laid back and tried to remember all the events of the past. The one experience that evaded me most was the details of the winter march. I tried to remember the names of those we lost on the march but it all became a total blur. . . . I fell into a deep sleep, a glorious sleep without dreams, without nightmares, and most of all without filthy insects crawling over me. . . .

"It was then that the rains came. The roads became a mass of mud and we were drenched and cold. . . . When we arrived in Neumarket we saw a spectacular sight: There were at least 1,000 bombers, B-17s and B-24s, all converging on Nuremberg."

After torrential rain, thunder, and lightning delays at Berching, the POWs set out once more, this time sighting "some P-47s in the air. They apparently thought we were German troops and strafed the column and dropped bombs on us. . . . We all removed our tee shirts and whenever we stopped we made a big sign with the shirts spelling *POW*.

"The P-47s came in the following day and spotted our sign; they wiggled their wings and headed for home. . . . They were with us every day after that incident."

Nine days after leaving Nuremberg, the POWs arrive at Stalag VIIA in Moosburg, north of Munich, where they are housed by the hundreds in a huge tent. Upon awakening Sunday morning, then-Lieutenant Lagasse attends service in a field, returns to his tent to lie down, and suddenly sees holes appear in the tent. "I couldn't understand until I realized that they were bullet holes. I jumped to my feet and screamed at everyone, 'The camp is under attack. It must be Patton.'. . .

"We watched a church tower where there were a couple of snipers taking potshots at the incoming troops. . . . All hell broke loose and the church tower disappeared, from artillery fire and small-arms fire. . . . There was cheering as we pressed against the fence. . . . We were all screaming, laughing, and crying when, all of a sudden, a complete hush came over the prisoners. Coming down the dusty road, standing in front of his jeep was 'the boss.' Yes, indeed, old 'Blood and Guts' had come to visit just as we felt he would. . . .

"General Patton looked down on the ragged, unkempt, starving mass of men before him and I was close enough to see compassion and anger in his eyes. He spoke to us about conditions in the camp, the progress of the war, and plans to return us Stateside as soon as possible. He said, to the best of my recollection, 'You will soon be out of this garbage dump and on the way to the USA, and if any one of these bastards treated you inhumanely, I want his name, and let me assure you that the man you soldiers name will be doing guard duty in front of my headquarters regardless of his rank.'

"Apparently, someone in our group turned in the name of a *Hauptmann* (captain) who went out of his way to make life miserable for us. A short time later, we were loaded in 2¹/₂'s and, as we passed the general's headquarters, our *Haupt-mann* was walking 'tour' in front in his bare feet. What a guy!

"We arrived at a farm and waited in a barn for our planes to come. . . . The day finally came. . . . We heard them off in the distance, the unmistakable drone of twin-engine aircraft. It had to be our C-47s. . . .

"We landed in Reims, France, and were housed at a former residence. . . . Everything was clean, everything was neat, everything was glorious! . . . I received some very pleasant news. We were to be allowed to go into town for a very special reason. This was V-E Day."

En route home aboard a Liberty ship, "we were told that there were a number of German U-boats on radio silence for many months that had not received word of the surrender. . . . Some time during the next evening, we were all relaxing on deck when we heard *whoop, whoop, whoop* from our destroyer escort. . . . A U-boat surfaced close to our ship and made signs of surrender. The crew was taken aboard one of the destroyers and told the captain that their ship was disabled and that is why they surrendered. I heard later that the U-boat captain, when shown proof of the [German] surrender, used a secret frequency and code word to reach many of the other U-boats to tell them of the surrender. . . .

Finally, "I saw beautiful Cape Cod with its beautiful sand dunes. I saw Boston off in the distance and, unashamed, I sank to my knees to thank God for my deliverance and the deliverance of those great people I had come to know under those terrible conditions in Germany. I stood, to once again behold the spectacle before me, and my eyes strained to take in all I could. I raised my hands and my eyes to heaven and proudly exclaimed: 'God, I'm home!'"

25 May 1945
Mission to Impasugono, Mindanao, the Philippines

Lieutenant Colonel Herbert H. Hirschkoff was a second lieutenant, 63rd Troop Carrier Squadron, 403rd Troop Carrier Group, when assigned as co-pilot on his first C-47 combat mission.

Lieutenant Colonel Hirschkoff writes of taking off from Dulag Airstrip, Leyte, with pilot/forward observer Harwood (Zeke) Hellen, a crew chief, radio operator, four droppers, and cargo of 5,100 pounds of food rations, bound for the area of Impasugono. After a stop at Del Monte airstrip, they were directed to remnants of the 31st Division of the Eighth Army, "desperately needing this shipment of K-rations. . . .

"The first 400 pounds of rations was dropped on the target routinely. At that moment, the port engine lost power and fuel pressure went to zero." Lieutenant

Hirschkoff immediately began single-engine emergency procedure when "the propeller mechanism failed," which "caused an excess amount of drag on the airplane, making it almost impossible to hold the port wing up."

After both pilots "applied full right rudder and full aileron in a vain attempt to level the wings," Lieutenant Hirschkoff attempted "to restore fuel pressure by frantically pumping the wobble pump, which proved to be fruitless." When turning on the cross-feed valve "only caused the starboard engine to lose fuel pressure, orders were given to 'jettison cargo.' Four minutes after the engine failed, the wing hit the ground and crumpled. The plane ground-looped, shearing the tail section and ripping off both engines." After the impact, the pilots "cut all switches, shut off the gas cocks, escaped through the upper hatch," and went to the aid of their crew, "trapped in the fuselage and buried under loose boxes of cargo."

Determining that they were behind enemy lines, the pilots destroyed all confidential material, set the plane afire, and began walking toward the drop zone. They noticed that they were "being given air cover by three SBD dive bombers from Malaybalay air strip on Mindanao. The bombers strafed the downed airplane to spread the fire faster." As the crew proceeded, "the last man in line saw two of the Marine SBDs collide and crash. The remaining Marine bomber buzzed the group in order to point them in the right direction. Walking well over three hours, crossing swamps and ravines, and fighting high bushes and grasses" that were cause of great pain, the crew finally came upon "a small detachment of American troops, and safety."

May 1945
POW Camps, Manchuria

Colonel Michael A. Quinn continues his POW diary.

"Well, the heat is on and no mistake," as a result of the prisoners' refusal to work, Colonel Quinn records on 4 May 1945. "We are supposed to salute all officers, soldiers, and civilian guards who wear armbands. If anyone should 'abscond,' the vigilante guard will be severely punished as accessory. This is Japanese wording and Japanese sense of justice. I try not to let their stupidity drive me to hatred, as hatred is too expensive a hobby for anyone in my condition. . . . Tomorrow, flour is cut and our bread rations are cut 50 percent. . . . They even cut the coal allowance, so we can't get hot water for our bath."

"Lots of excitement here today," Colonel Quinn relates on 13 May. "We have noticed such a friendly attitude on the part of the Nips in contrast with their former manner that we feel that things must be happening. Today we were notified that we will leave this camp for another one, destination unknown. . . . There are only two reasons for this move that we can figure. First, there may be a Russian threat on Manchuria, or the war is over. Naturally, we are hoping for the latter. . . . We hear that President Roosevelt died on April 12, as a result of assassination."

"If these persistent rumors of Germany being out of the war are true, I wonder what these people will do?" he ponders on 16 May. "We are being overfed now and can't eat all we get. . . . The local glee club, which consists of everybody, had a songfest tonight. So the old songs were trotted out and were as good as ever. I wonder what the war songs in this war have been? You ought to have some good ones."

The POWs depart camp Sunday, 19 May, after reveille at 0400 and breakfast of "cornmeal and bread" at 0700. Not permitted to take any of their Red Cross food, the prisoners travel for twenty-four hours, subsisting on three rolls and one-half cup of water. "About 1000 hours Monday . . . in the railroad yards of Mukden, Air Vice-Marshal Maltby called for an interpreter . . . to take a message to the CO to the effect that we were being starved, suffocated, and denied water. . . . About noon, we received another roll but no water," Colonel Quinn reports.

As the POWs settle in at Camp Mukden, "who showed up but Bob Lawler, captain, CAC, son of old Pappy Lawler, who was the CO of the 112th QM Regiment when I was an instructor at the Ohio National Guard." There are reunions with more old friends and updates on others—some of whom have died and one, Father Duffy, whose death had been reported but who is "here and alive. Physically, his condition is terrible, but the old rascal still has the spirit."

"Ran into two of my enlisted men from Bataan. As far as I can find out, I have lost twenty-six officers out of forty-two and at least 50 percent of my enlisted men. . . . With Memorial Day just around the corner, we had memorial services by a Catholic and a Protestant chaplain this morning. . . . This camp has about 1,300 to 1,400 men. Haven't had a chance to see them all yet."

EDITOR'S NOTE: *Colonel Quinn wonders about the war songs back home. Up-tempo songs included "Let's Remember Pearl Harbor," "Praise the Lord and Pass the Ammunition," "Don't Sit under the Apple Tree," and a Spike Jones rendition of "Heil in the Führer's Face." Ballads at the time included "The White Cliffs of Dover," "I Don't Want to Walk without You," "I Left My Heart at the Stage Door Canteen," "When the Lights Go on Again," "You'll Never Know," "I'll Be Seeing You," "I'll Walk Alone," and "It's Been a Long, Long Time."*

43

"Being an air-combat veteran of the Pacific Theater aboard B-29s in 1945, I notice in many historical accounts that the media film footage seems to jump simply from the conquest of Iwo Jima to the atomic bomb, March to August 1945," says Lieutenant Colonel Richard B. Vogenitz.

"Many students of history know well that we had a tremendous air bombardment of Japan in progress. It was called *Air Offensive Japan*. Men and whole crews were losing life and limb every day. Navy air was very involved, as well. Thus, by means of a long bombing campaign, carried out day and night by the same type aircraft, the B-29 Superfortress, we were preparing the home island of Japan for an invasion by the Allied land forces in the autumn of 1945. We thought it might be very healthy and thoughtful of the Japanese if they would surrender to our air power alone. It may be that there were some indications toward such a surrender in the historical records. It never came to pass until the two atomic bombs were used," he observes.

General Curtis LeMay began sending missions from the Marianas to Japan in November 1944. Because bomber losses were high in daylight raids, he proposed low-level nighttime bombing using fire bombs. More than 300 Superfortresses inaugurate the plan the night of 9 March 1945 in a spectacular three-hour raid on Tokyo that destroys about 250,000 buildings, nearly 25 percent of a sixteen-square-mile area.

"The death toll is at least 80,000 and probably as many as 120,000 [later confirmed as 130,000 by Japanese authorities, says historian Martin Gilbert]. It is the most damaging air attack of the war including the atomic attacks on Hiroshima and Nagasaki," according to *The World Almanac Book of World War II*, which is the source of statistics in the following paragraphs.

The fire bombings continue throughout April 1945, with Tokyo, Kawasaki, and Nagoya targeted, along with home-island airfields where many Kamikazes are based. In May, as Pacific Fleet carriers attack Japan, the Superfortresses—in armadas of 400 and 500 planes—drop 24,000 tons of bombs. Targets include Tokyo, Nagoya, Otake, Oshima, and Tokuyama. In June, the B-29s pinpoint aircraft plants, naval bases, and airfields. Again, Tokyo and Nagoya are bombed, as are Osaka and Kobe.

While the firestorms continue throughout Japan, that firestorm known as the Battle of Okinawa continues, until, finally, the island is captured on 22 June. Of the "enormous number of casualties among the Marines on Okinawa," Martin Gilbert writes in *The Second World War: A Complete History*, "on average, an American rifleman could expect to fight for only about three weeks before becoming a casualty. In many front line companies, every soldier was wounded, and their replacements then wounded in their turn. Some replacements were killed before they could fire a single shot." The United States counts casualties at 12,500 dead and 35,000 wounded. The Navy reports 36 ships sunk and 368 damaged; the Air Force, 763 planes lost. Among the Japanese, there are 120,000 military and 42,000 civilian deaths. And, in a rare occurrence, 10,755 Japanese are taken as prisoners.

Spring–Summer 1945
Missions from Mariana Islands to Japan

Lieutenant Colonel Richard B. Vogenitz was a staff sergeant and B-29 left waist gunner aboard P-24 Liberty Belle II, *with 61st Bomb Squadron, 39th Bomb Group, 314th Bomb Wing.*

"One day, the officers of our crew came into our Quonset hut. We came to attention and were put 'at ease' promptly. The pilot indicated that we worked well together as a crew. He asked whether we would now volunteer for an extra fifteen missions when our usual quota of thirty-five was completed—to cover the invasion," Lieutenant Colonel Vogenitz recalls.

"Captain Gordon A. Anderson of Minneapolis, the aircraft commander, said: 'Take a few minutes to talk it over and decide.' He later said that he had seen no hesitation; that we had all stepped forward to take on the extra missions. (Captain Anderson's brother was pilot of the first *Liberty Belle*, lost over Germany.)

"Among his comments, our captain told us: 'We will be going in at 750-feet altitude with some bombs and lots of ammunition to hit the human horde we expect to see at the shoreline. Also, before you decide, please remember that we will have brothers and cousins, our countrymen and Allies, in the waves hitting the beach. There will be nurses and doctors among them. We *must* get a foothold and then gain more airfields.' . . .

"Our co-pilot, Lieutenant Herbert Snow, who had survived a bailout over Schweinfurt, Germany, and trekked to freedom, explained, 'It will be D-Day Japan, and we have plenty of fine examples from D-Day Normandy to go on. We believe that the Twentieth Air Force will mostly operate from Okinawa.' We were then in the Mariana Islands. "Later, hearing these plans discussed by air crews,

I came to realize that the expectation was that our ground-invasion forces would meet a much-depleted Japanese force on the terrain of a bomb-saturated land."

Among his own missions, Colonel Vogenitz recalls the Twentieth Air Force attack 1 June 1945 against Osaka, second-largest Japanese city in population and industrial production. "On this day, we went in over target nearly last and had to bomb the edge of a 40,000-foot smoke cloud. Lots of fighters nearby. We went through the smoke cloud and nearly stalled out."

1944–Mid-1945
Saipan, Mariana Islands

Lieutenant Colonel Clifford W. Potter Jr. was a storekeeper third class, with U. S. Navy Leon 8 E-I, U.S. NSO Navy 324.

"During late 1944 and 1945, I recall that Tanapag Harbor, Saipan, Mariana Islands, was a very busy place. I was stationed there to help issue fresh provisions to the fleet to help the Navy in the invasions of the Philippines, Iwo Jima, and Okinawa," Lieutenant Colonel Potter writes.

"I still remember when I looked up into the sky one day and saw the first formations of B-29s as they began to arrive to use the Mariana Islands as a base to bomb Japan. I was so excited that I wrote home and told my parents and later, after the war, found out that each word describing B-29s was blacked out for security.

"I can also remember watching the B-29s fly out in early morning formation to bomb Japan and later observing them coming back alone at sunset, and the sadness I felt when one of the damaged aircraft would crash on landing.

"Then there was the day after we had bombed Iwo Jima. I was standing in the chow line, at noon on a clear day, when I observed a Japanese reconnaissance float plane, either a Judy or Jill type, suddenly appear over the harbor on Saipan and drop a parachute with a wreath attached. The aircraft was quickly shot down by a Hellcat. I was never able to find out the significance of this feat and whether the wreath was to honor the dead on Saipan or Iwo Jima. I was impressed by this very brave deed, as the Japanese must have known they would not survive.

"Toward the middle of the summer of 1945, we began to hear hushed conversations from pilots and crew members of the Navy and Air Force about some kind of big explosive device to use to bomb Japan and end the war. This information was difficult to believe until we found out that this was indeed the atomic bomb, which was used to bomb Hiroshima and Nagasaki by B-29s from the Marianas."

7–13 June 1945
Okinawa

Lieutenant Colonel James J. Ahern, with 147th Infantry Regiment on Iwo Jima, got word in May that he would join Company F, 96th Division, 381st Infantry Regiment, on Okinawa.

"In less than twenty-four hours" after getting word, "I was in the front line of Okinawa," Lieutenant Colonel Ahern writes. When he arrived, "there were only ninety men in lieu of authorized strength of 180 and one officer in lieu of six. We actually battled day and night. There were no periods that one could get more than two hours on duty and two off duty once night began."

In the midst of the fray, he begins a letter to the young lady who would become his wife, written in tiny script on borrowed paper over a six-day period. After preliminaries, he confides to Mary: "I don't know what to tell my Mom. Honest, I hate like the devil to lie to her. I won't tell my family where I am until this operation is over. . . .

"Frankly, I'm worried, Mary, and really praying. So with your prayers and mine, our Blessed Mother will help me make the right decision and bring me through all right. My morale is still tops. . . . Now, if I could only receive a letter from you, I would be walking on air. . . .

"The mud is terrific. I slushed along in it and in one spot it was above my knees. I stopped and couldn't lift my feet. I pulled so hard and I fell flat on my face into it. I really cussed. Miserable wasn't the word for it. My carbine was all fouled up with the mud. That night I dug me a hole, crawled into it and tried to sleep. Mosquitoes had a feast on me—and it was cold." Promising "to try to be home for Christmas," he closes with: "I'll end up now so I can dig into a nice can of meat and beans."

He continues the next day: "This morning just before dawn, I was pulling my watch and was thinking of you and a thought came to my mind: 'I wonder when that Jap 40mm is going to open up.' Damned if he didn't, just before the thought left my mind. I took cover and sweated it out. Twice before while I was day-dreaming of you, the same thing happened. . . ."

"At the rate we are going, it will be some time before I get to mail this," he writes on the third day. "For the first time, I'm really worried, Mary. I have a feeling that something will happen to me today or tonight. Better say a few more prayers. Just in case this will be my last letter, there are a few last things I wish to tell you. Yesterday, I received Holy Communion, so I'm squared with God. And lastly, I'm sure that I could make you very happy for a lifetime."

"It seems that I have gotten another reprieve because I'm sound in body," he reports the following morning. "I am praying the weather will stay fair. Rain and mud sure do make fighting a war more difficult. Am trying to figure just what day of the week it is."

"Another day and another reprieve. Someone's prayers must be keeping me safe," he continues on day five. "I am in a very awkward position; a foxhole is my home and my wallet is my desk. . . . It is warm today and I'm loaded down with my pack and rations. An artillery shell damn near made hash out of me, just now."

"Good morning," the last paragraph of his letter begins. "If it weren't for the fact that my sergeant's wife has a good habit of enclosing an envelope, stamp, and paper, I would probably have to put this letter away for a week. I darn near got it last night during an attack. Take care of yourself, Mary," he signs off. He was medical-evacuated from Okinawa in July 1945 and remained in Stateside hospitals until November 1945.

3–9 June 1945
Iheya and Aguni, Ryukyu Islands

Major Alfred E. Peloquin was with 726th Amphibian Tractor Battalion, assigned to 81st Infantry Division for the invasion of the Palau Islands, September through October 1944.

Leaving the Palaus "with a feeling of relief on 17 April," the 726th "began loading upon the USS *Windsor*, destination Saipan," battalion history begins.

"Orders soon came through telling of our next job. We were attached to the 8th Marine Regimental Combat Team, given whatever new equipment we needed, and on 24 May left Saipan behind, loaded on eleven LSTs. We were to bring Marines ashore for combat landings on two little islands near Okinawa, Iheya and Aguni, both needed for radar-observation purposes.

"The ships stood offshore from Okinawa for a few days, while everyone was more or less worried about Jap bombing and Kamikaze raids. But the Japs either did not see our little convoy or were not interested, for the few who got through tried for bigger game at Naha and Buckner Bay.

"The morning of 3 June found our ships lying off Iheya, a few miles northwest of Okinawa. There was the usual shelling, strafing, and bombing—much lighter than the fireworks display back on the Palaus. The amphtracs rolled ashore, not knowing what to expect but fearing mortar and shellfire from the high hills overlooking the beach. But there was no resistance. The small Jap garrison had left some weeks before, having attempted to go by boat to Okinawa to reinforce troops there and (according to rumor) having had their boats sunk by our planes while en route.

"The natives began to emerge from their hiding places in the hills, amid much bowing and pleas for mercy. We found them to be unarmed, peaceful, ragged, and hungry for both food and cigarettes. . . . There was a similar occupation job to perform on Aguni Island, to the south, which was accomplished without opposition on 9 June."

14 June–10 July 1945
Kiangan, Northern Luzon, the Philippines

Lieutenant Colonel Charles R. Keefe was a captain, 63rd Infantry Regiment, 6th Infantry Division.

The twenty-five-mile drive was on to seize Kiangan, headquarters of the Japanese 14th Army, "high in the mountains of Northern Luzon, where General Yamashita, supreme commander of the Philippines, was making his last stand with a force of approximately 35,000 men," regiment history records.

"On 14 June, the assault echelon of the regiment left the town of Bagabag near the junction of Highways 4 and 5 in the Cagayan Valley, and secured a bridgehead over the swift-moving Lamut River. . . . Moving up along the highway, one could see hundreds of carabao carts and trucks of all descriptions strewn all along the road—the result of a strafing attack by our Air Force. The air was fetid with the smell of death, and flies were present by the thousands.

"The push up the highway was a difficult one, due to impenetrable bamboo growths, canalized approaches, and narrow defiles, and further hindered by tenacious groups of enemy, ranging from isolated groups to well-organized rifle companies, which ambushed our supply trains, suicidally *banzaied* our positions night after night, and delayed our advance further by establishing well-entrenched road blocks. A probational officer captured by our units identified one of his units as the Sukegawa Independent Provisional Infantry Company, made up of officer candidates such as himself and of patients discharged from hospitals. . . .

"The first determined resistance met was from Lane's Ridge, running north from Santo Domingo across old Highway 4 to new Highway 4. . . . The enemy defending this strongpoint was the Suzuki Infantry Battalion. . . . Their fighting spirit was most superior in the initial phase of our attacks on their positions. The interlocking lanes of fire were skillfully sighted. This too was the first instance where we had encountered enemy who traversed their machine guns rather than firing them in fixed positions. An 81mm mortar captured by our troops was only fired by the Japs when our own artillery and mortars fired. The Japs dropped but one or two rounds, thus giving the appearance of our own rounds falling short. These Jap tactics caused some unrest among our troops and some delay ensued each time in checking all firing data. . . .

"Fighting tenaciously in the defense of the mountain approaches to Kiangan, the enemy employed a complicated network of defensive positions situated on commanding ground and thus effecting a strong zone of fire against our attacking troops. . . . Individual holes were dug from a depth of six to ten feet; a step, halfway up, provided a convenient perch for the occupant, while the floor of the hole was enlarged into a semblance of a tunnel, leading a few feet to the rear and offering adequate protection from our artillery and mortar barrages. These pockets of resistance were suicide defense positions.

"Determined and fanatical infiltration tactics under concealment of darkness were used extensively by the enemy. In these Bushido tactics, use was made of demolition charges. Our supply train was constantly subject to enemy . . . ambush teams [that] included riflemen, automatic weapons, and demolition men, the latter being armed with satchel and pole charges. Bamboo thickets along the road offered excellent hiding places for these groups."

1942–1945
The Philippines to Japan to the Philippines

Lieutenant Colonel Mariano Villarin, second lieutenant in the Philippine Army and a survivor of the Bataan Death March, was imprisoned at Camp O'Donnell until late 1942.

"During the enemy occupation of the Philippines, the Japanese military administration started a program of 'spiritual rejuvenation,' in which they shipped to Japan Filipino hostages (they called them 'students') in groups of twenty or thirty at a time. In our group of twenty-seven students, the Japanese decided to include ten military personnel, survivors of Bataan and Corregidor who had been taken prisoner. They wanted to cleanse from our system the remaining vestiges of American influence. . . . Our group underwent a rigorous 'brainwashing' for two months before sailing for Japan.

"As part of their program to convince us of their armed strength and to win us over, the Japanese took us on psychological sightseeing trips to military installations and war plants. Being in the military ourselves, we were unusually observant, since one of our objectives was to collect intelligence information, which we later turned over to General MacArthur's G-2 office during the liberation of the Philippines. . . .

"Postwar records disclosed that China-based B-29s bombed Kyushu Island a few times in June and July 1944, four being shot down in one raid over the Yawata Iron Works. One of the Flying Fortresses that had been shot down was put on display in downtown Tokyo. Our Japanese 'honcho' took us to the Ginza to view the parts of the wrecked B-29 and the gear worn by its occupants."

"After sixteen months, the Japanese thought that we had been sufficiently 'Japanized,' so they repatriated us while they retained the civilian hostages," Lieutenant Colonel Villarin adds. In his book, he details being reunited with his family, who had not heard from him in six months; joining up with a guerrilla organization north of Manila under Captain José Abueg and serving as his intelligence operative; and meeting up with "the first American patrol from the 32nd (Red Arrow) Division" after two weeks of hiding in the hills of Binaga.

"The mess sergeant gave us Spam, which we ate ravenously to the surprise of the GIs who had had their fill of it for two years. As soon as they knew that I had been to wartime Japan and I spoke Japanese, and that I had valuable intelligence information, they provided me with transportation to Manila. I got home only to find that my sister had passed away—another innocent victim of the ugly war. . . .

"I reported to G-2 GHQ, in the city hall building. I met with Colonel Fred Munson, chief of the Battle Orders Division, to whom I explained all the intelligence detail I knew about Japan."

14 May–June 1945
Occupied Eastern Bavaria

Colonel William M. McConahey concludes his battalion surgeon story.

After V-E Day, "although none of us knew what the ultimate plans for the division were, we did know that for a while we were to be occupation troops in Eastern Bavaria," Colonel McConahey writes. "The battalion convoy rolled into Maxhütte about an hour before sundown on the evening of 14 May. . . .

"For some time the battalion was busily engaged in getting things organized . . . [such as] deposing the local Nazi *Burgermeister* and finding a non-Nazi to put in his place, establishing guard posts, getting road patrols started, studying the local economic situation, regulating the great number of wandering displaced persons (foreigners from all over Europe), screening and checking the hundreds of demobilized German soldiers who were dejectedly trudging across the country on the way home. . . .

"The two most pressing problems were presented by the displaced persons and the demobilized soldiers. All over Germany were these millions of foreign slaves, whom the 'master race' had brought in to work in the fields and factories.

Now they were free, but did not know where to go or what to do. First they were gathered into nationality groups and then, as fast as transportation could be arranged, they were taken to large collecting points set up by the Army. From there, they were sent home.

"Some of the displaced persons posed a special problem. These were the ones who feared the Russians and whose countries were now under Russian control—the people from Estonia, Latvia, and Lithuania, and some of the Poles. They could not go home, under penalty of death. We did the best we could for them. We found them places in which to live and got them food and clothes.

"The great hordes of demobilized German soldiers were another problem. . . . As they entered our *Kreis* (district), they were all checked. . . . If they proved to be ordinary Wehrmacht soldiers, they were given papers and sent on their way, but if they were found to be SS men or war criminals, they were arrested and sent to higher headquarters.

"Obviously, SS troops were not fit to be allowed to return to civilian life, so they were all picked up and put in camp. Many of them, knowing they were marked men, threw away their SS uniforms and tried to pass themselves off as Wehrmacht soldiers. But there was one telltale mark. All SS troops had had their blood types tattooed on the inner surface of the left upper arm, and so it was a simple matter to order an SS suspect to remove his shirt and to look for this mark. Some recently had had this mark excised or had burned it off with a lighted cigarette, but this left a scar. All those with scars in this location were held for further questioning by some of our Intelligence interrogators.

"This checking of the defeated soldiers was a tremendous task for they were wandering across Germany in every direction by the millions. . . . We had no place in which to house them while they were being held for checking, and so they were all gathered together in a grove of trees on the edge of Maxhütte, where they pitched their tents and remained under guard until they were released or sent to higher headquarters. Getting food for them was quite a problem, but we were able to draw rations for them from German army food supplies captured by our Army."

June–July 1945
Passau, Germany, and Homeward Bound

Colonel Jean W. Christy continues his story, as the 50th FA prepares to head home.

"After the surrender of the German units, the 5th Infantry Division was moved south and dispersed through an area along both sides of the Danube River, more or less centered around the city of Passau," Colonel Christy writes.

"The 50th Field Artillery battalion was stationed in the city of Passau itself, and had few assigned duties. Although a training schedule was prepared, the classes were light and were a review of the basics. Much of the men's time was spent in doing maintenance of equipment but the overall atmosphere was one of well-deserved relaxation, and we found ways to adjust to this new situation. . . .

"The days passed with an unaccustomed lack of urgency. There was card playing, of course, but a lot of reading and talking also. A few of the officers may even have had a drink as we passed the time in the evenings. . . .

"By the middle of June 1945, there were strong rumors that we were about to go home. They became real one evening . . . [when] the battalion commander, Lieutenant Colonel Calhoun, sat down next to me and informed me that I was to lead the battalion advance party back to the United States. . . .

"My responsibilities would include, after a homecoming leave, reporting to our new duty station and drawing all of the buildings and much of the equipment that our battalion would need. I would have everything ready for the arrival of the battalion so that the officers and men could move right in and begin training promptly. An additional, but important, job for me was to find and rent whatever housing I could locate for the twenty-one married officers of the battalion. It was anticipated that we would go to Camp Campbell, Kentucky, [and] . . . immediately begin training to take part in the imminent invasion of Japan. . . .

Sailing from Le Havre about 30 June on a Liberty ship, "we crossed the Atlantic Ocean in just five days. The ship's loudspeaker played music continuously, all the current favorites, hoping to please the anxious and lonely soldiers. By the end of the five days, I never wanted to hear 'Sentimental Journey' ever again. . . .

"We entered New York Harbor on the 4th of July, and were given the full treatment. Our ship passed close by the Statue of Liberty, and fireboats sprayed countless streams of water high into the air. Ships and tugs blew their horns and whistles to welcome us home."

May and June 1945 to 1947
Czechoslovakia, Germany, USA

Chief Warrant Officer Fourth Class Francis Joe Garra was by now a sergeant, Company B, 3rd Section, 774th Tank Destroyer Battalion.

"The war in Europe was over and we were relaxed and thankful that we had made it this far. We were so busy, I wondered how we did it. We had guard duty, a quota of houses to search, vehicle maintenance, POW camps to operate, checkpoints to watch," Sergeant Garra recalls. "We also had the Displaced Persons camps.

"The British troops took over our area and we reluctantly left to head for Czechoslovakia to the village of Ausergefelde in the Baumerwalde. When the Russians took over the jurisdiction of Czechoslovakia, we headed west, with stops at Virnsberg and Nuremberg. Our relations with Russians (*Communists* would be a better word) were not harmonious at Ausergefelde. Patton wanted to continue eastward until we at least kept Poland from being enslaved by the Russians. I wish we had.

"After World War II, back in civilian life, there was something missing. I joined the Reserves in 1947, the 325th Tank Battalion. The battalion needed more enlisted men. I talked Sal Mingacci into joining as our supply sergeant. I never failed to mention that we were sticking our necks out and could be recalled to active duty. Sal joined and he recruited his brother-in-law Jimmy Vasta, his nephew Jimmy Benincasa, his uncle Sale Valente, and his uncle's landlord Joe Scalise. Sure enough, in 1950 we were recalled to active duty. Sal was a very unpopular man in Brooklyn at that time."

June 1945
POW Camp Mukden, Manchuria

Colonel Michael A. Quinn continues his POW diary.

"The Nips authorized services, so we had Mass and Communion, but no sermons are allowed," he writes on 3 June. "Lots of rumors about our activities in this part of the world. Hope they are true," he notes on 9 June. "We had to turn in our woolen uniforms the Japs issued us, and then they sold them back to us today for 29.18 yen. They will be delightful souvenirs."

On 14 June, their mutual birthdays and his fourth in captivity, he writes to his wife: "Happy Birthday to you, Mike. Many Happy Returns of the Day. May we spend the rest of ours together. . . . Say, girls and boys, do you realize I am a half-century old today? I am saying it because I lived in the most eventful half-century in the world. . . . I hope we get as much enjoyment out of the next fifty years as we have had in the last."

Colonel Quinn's entry on 30 June, his last in Book VI of his journals, takes up three and one-third printed pages in his book, as he summarizes thoughts and feelings, news and activities before beginning Book VII: "I have been thinking so much of you at home lately that I am becoming impatient to be with you again. I am wondering what the children are doing. Are they the kind of kids we want them to be? What are their plans for the future? Good gosh, Mike, you had a tremendous job. I haven't the slightest doubt but that you carried it all well. . . .

"We have 1,235 POWs in camp and we have a library of 1,240 books, all old. . . . No papers or broadcasts of any kind are available. (Note: We did manage to get Jap newspapers, but I did not write that down in these notes.) . . . Cards are a pastime, but now they are wearing out, and we have gotten none in about a year. . . .

"We discuss plans for homes, places we have been, and places we want to go to. We take the world apart and put it back together. Then we take it down again. . . .

"Some have delusions of grandeur that they will stay on active duty. . . . As to my military future, I have no illusions. Mine is behind me. Physically, I doubt if I could take it. . . . One very pompous individual says that he is as good as he ever was. I have no doubt about it! He wasn't worth a damn before the war and won't get any better now, and I doubt if he could be any worse. . . .

"Somebody has said the world runs by contrast. Without vice, there would be no virtue. Without thirst, we would never appreciate water. Without starvation, we would never appreciate food. So now I can look to this separation, and without it, I don't believe we would ever have known how much we meant to each other. Your own, Al."

June 1945
Home Again, USA

Major Philip Rose was a young B-24 pilot who flew thirty-five missions with the Eighth Army Air Force, 14th Wing, 392nd Group, 578th Squadron, autumn 1944–mid-May 1945.

For the World War II series, Major Rose sent an audiotape that he had prepared in recent years for his B-24 crew, describing their thirty-five missions. When asked to select from the tape and provide a written version of his "most memorable experience," he submits what is probably the definitive story on the youthfulness of the men who fought and won the war. It is his "welcome back home" story:

"As per your request, I will give you my favorite story. It might not be what you want but it does tell a lot about the times. Also, it is not an unusual story, as many of my friends—my co-pilot, for example—could tell similar ones.

"As a B-24 first pilot, I picked up my crew of ten men in Kansas, staged in Idaho, then flew thirty-five missions in the 392nd BG (H) from Wendling, England. We dropped 200,000 pounds of bombs on Germany. Hundreds of our finest fighting men flew my wings into combat.

"Then, after being sent home on leave, I went into the Department of Motor Vehicles to get my driver's license. There I was, in my Pinks and Greens, with four Battle Stars, six Air Medals, and a DFC. This lady in the DMV looked at my application and said, 'Lieutenant, you can't get a driver's license without your parents' consent until you are twenty-one years old.'"

JULY 1945

44

In July 1945, Japan is bombarded by U.S. bomber forces, by American and British carrier forces, and even by leaflets dropped on eleven cities 29 July, telling residents that their cities are targets for U.S. bombings. For six of the cities, the leaflet warnings materialize the next day. Targets for bomber forces during July include Akashi, Osaka, Kure, and Kumamoto.

On 10 July, 1,022 planes from U.S. carrier forces bomb Tokyo. U.S. carrier strikes also include north Honshu and south Hokkaido 14 July; steel works at Kamaishi 14 July; iron and steel works at Muroran 15 July; shipping in the Tsugaru Strait 15 July; and, in conjunction with British Task Force 37, the Tokyo–Yokohama area 17–18 July.

In other activity, far removed from but very closely associated with Japan, the first atomic weapons test takes place 16 July at Alamogordo, New Mexico. Truman, Stalin, and Churchill meet at Potsdam, proclaiming the Potsdam Declaration on 26 July that calls for unconditional surrender of Japan; and the U.S. carrier *Indianapolis*, after delivering the atom bomb to the Mariana Islands air base, is torpedoed and sunk by a Japanese submarine between Tinian and Guam 29 July. The disaster is noted only after the ship is three days overdue. Eighty-four hours after the ship went down, 316 survivors are rescued from among the 1,199 who had been aboard.

1 July 1945
Balikpapan, Borneo

Lieutenant Junior Grade Robert H. Mugalian was a line ensign commanding USS LCT-373, one of ten taking Australian Matilda tanks to the beach in the sixth wave of Operation Oboe II.

"General Douglas MacArthur's last major effort of the war and the final operation of the 7th Amphibious Force was the assault and occupation of Balikpapan, Borneo," Lieutenant Mugalian writes. "It was an Allied operation in which U.S. Navy and Coast Guard were to transport the 7th Australian Division of 33,000 men to the beaches. Borneo, with its 30,000 defenders, had provided 42 percent of Japan's oil in 1942. MacArthur also felt that the assault would reveal new defense techniques of the Japanese that would be employed to resist the Allied invasions of the home islands, scheduled to take place in the fall of 1945.

"The 200-ship armada left the staging area of Morotai, 800 miles from Balik-papan, at 1500 hours 26 June 1945. . . . We arrived off the Klandasan coast in the waters east of Balikpapan, tied up ramp to ramp to our towing LST while our A Squadron (21st Brigade) of Australian 3 medium Matilda tanks with officer and troops was transferred to our tank deck.

"The primary beaches had been swept by frogmen, although the waters and beaches were heavily mined, including magnetic mines laid earlier by the Allies. . . .

"With the 20mm gun crews at quarters, buckled with helmet, life preserver, and .45 on station at the conn with my executive officer Ensign James Engels, we headed for the line of departure 3,000 yards from the beach. . . . Black smoke from the bombardment was evident as we steamed over mineswept waters. . . . There was intense reaction to the landing from enemy coastal batteries, although air opposition was light.

"After discharging our tank squadron, we performed lighterage duties. The following day, we rounded Rocky Point and entered Balikpapan Bay. As we headed north toward the town, I was standing on the tank deck, my executive officer at the conn. A member of my crew said, 'Skipper, what is that coming toward us?' I do not know exactly how he saw it, but I turned my head left and I saw the copper rotating band of the coastal gun projectile, reflected brightly in the sunlight, passing about thirty feet to our portside. The projectile then hit an LST to our stern. At this point, all vessels were ordered by signal to reverse course from town until the well-hidden coastal gun could be silenced: another instance when our number wasn't on this one."

7 July 1945
Kita, Iwo Jima

Major Robert P. Wright was a flight officer, with 4th Emergency Rescue Squadron, AAF.

"On 7 July 1945, an Army OA-10A on which F/O [forward observer] Wright was a co-pilot was called to search an area in the vicinity of Kita, Iwo Jima, for a downed P-51 pilot. The survivor was located at 1745, too late to be reached by surface craft before dark. A difficult open-sea landing was made and the survivor was brought aboard safely. Great difficulty was encountered in restarting the port engine, making it necessary for F/O Wright to climb out to the wing of the pitch-ing aircraft and help start the engine manually. The take-off was successful and the survivor returned to Iwo Jima. . . ." So reads Article 2 of the recommendation for oak leaf cluster that was signed by Lieutenant Colonel William C. Lindsay Jr., 2 September 1945.

"The name of the pilot we rescued was Harold Collins, a captain in the Air Force," Major Wright comments. He adds: "Although the citation and recommendation for the award were prepared, they were never submitted for final approval due to the fact that the war ended and the administrative staff was more concerned about getting home than submitting the paperwork."

With his story of the rescue, Major Wright submits write-ups that describe rescues by PBYs and B-17 Dumbos. An article in the 6 August 1945 issue of *Time* magazine states: "One of the incredible things about Americans, according to the Japanese, is the great trouble and expense they endure to rescue one man. But to Americans, a comrade's life is more than a unit of supply. To save a life, they frequently tie up many valuable ships, daily risk planes and submarines."

"Between June 1944 and June 1945 the Navy alone saved 2,100 of its pilots and crewmen," the story notes. According to *Time*, "The capture of Iwo Jima last March [1945] provided an ideal Dumbo base. Nowadays, the rescue planes leave for their assigned areas as regularly as the bombers and fighters take off."

July 1945
Luzon, the Philippines

Major General Robert L. Shirkey, with U.S. Army Alamo Scouts, had just returned to Sixth Army HQ from a mission behind Japanese lines, "very near General Yamashita's headquarters in the mountains of northern Luzon."

Awaiting transportation to Subic Bay rest camp on Bataan Peninsula, with visions of "chicken, ice cream, Coca-Cola, and other delicacies, much to my disappointment, a messenger came to me and said that I was to report to General Krueger's G-1 section," Major General Shirkey recalls. "Upon reporting, I was briefed and was given explicit instruction on how to operate and employ my task force of two gunboats, two LCIs, and 200 guerrillas who were placed under my command.

"Leaving Sixth Army Headquarters that evening with my Alamo Scout team, we met the task force and guerrillas at Infanta, which is on the east coast of Luzon. The next morning, we sailed out of Infanta to our objective, Palanan Bay. Arriving late in the afternoon, we completed our plans for landing the guerrillas early the next morning, [when] we gave the beach a terrific bombardment. After the bombardment, I gave the guerrilla commander the order to land his troops. However, I met with the reply that the guerrillas would not land unless the

'American officer' would accompany them. Hurriedly, I grabbed my rifle and said, 'Let's go!'

"Upon getting ashore, I was once again told that the guerrillas would not go unless I led. Inasmuch as I had 110 going-home points, I did not relish the job of first scout because most generally he was the first person to get injured. But I led. . . .

"That evening back aboard ship, a Filipino came out and gave a report of a group of Japanese who were headed for the beach area. . . . When I asked for volunteers from the scout team, it seemed as if everyone was eager for a good ambush. Deciding to wait until the next morning to go ashore, we left very early and disappeared into the dark, dank, swampy jungle. . . .

"Starting [the next] afternoon and with the aid of Negritos, we located them just before dark. We made camp for the evening about 500 yards from them, as it was too dark to ambush them then. It was agreed upon that daylight would be about the best time to spring the trap. But much to our surprise, we found that they were early risers and had already started on their journey. . . . Immediately picking up their trail, we followed them all morning. . . .

"As we were in dense jungle, plus the fact that it was raining and overcast, it seemed as though our chance would never come. . . . Finally, however, it stopped raining and cleared off. The Japs halted on the bank of a stream to bathe, wash their clothes, and rest. . . . I briefed my men on the plan of action. . . . After getting within about twenty or even forty yards, I started firing. Four Japs, who were nude, were sunning themselves. They were side by side and perpendicular to my front, thus making a wonderful target. The other two Alamo Scouts, on either side of me, picked off the rest. Two who managed to escape surrendered shortly afterward."

July–September 1945
From France to Belgium to Home

Chief Warrant Officer Sidney Bowen served with 494th Anti-Aircraft Artillery Gun Battalion, A Battery.

"Here it is, two days before we are scheduled to leave for Replacement (Repl) Depot 19, APO 176," Sidney writes to wife Isabel on 1 July 1945. "Beard, Jones, Werner, and I left camp about 2:30 P.M. after making the rounds, bidding our ack-ack buddies goodbye." On 6 July, he enters his plea: "Don't cease writing to me. Just write letters and stack them for my return. . . ."

Finally, on 7 August, Sidney et al. depart Antwerp for the United States on the SS *William T. Barry*. In his last letter to Isabel from Camp Beale Separation

Center, California, Sidney provides details of his last days in service, 2 and 3 September, and then concludes: "I am writing all this down to complete my 'saga' because it will be a cold day in hell before we have to communicate on paper again. I am going to hand-deliver this last separation letter, personally, to be received but not read until after a million warm and real kisses. Most affectionately, from Your Ever Loving Husband, Sidney."

Abiding by those declarations of love and fidelity that abound in his wartime letters, "ever loving husband Sidney" cared for his "dearest Isabel" through seventeen years of Alzheimer's, until her death in 1996 at age eighty-eight. She died on the couple's fifty-sixth wedding anniversary.

July–October 1945
ETO to USA

First Lieutenant Gretchen L. Hovis went into France with the 50th General Hospital in mid-July 1944, serving at Carentan and Commercy, France, through the battles of St. Lo and the Bulge.

"After V-E Day, we were still busy but gradually the patients were evacuated back to hospitals in the United States. We had a lot of extra time then, so we sunbathed, walked the countryside, and at night didn't have to worry about blackout curtains!" First Lieutenant Hovis recalls.

"In August, I was transferred to a hospital in Luxembourg. There we swam often in a pool, and took trips to Bastogne, Spa, St. Vith, and Malmedy. They looked like the majority of French towns we saw—not much left of any of them—unbelievable sight! . . .

"I was transferred back into the 50th GH and was very happy! Soon we were on our way home. We stayed in Verdun for ten days late in August 1945 and then boarded a train with three other groups of general hospital nurses and were on our way to Marseille. . . . We arrived in Marseille 9 September and never saw so many nurses at one time—2,300 waiting patiently. We had a lot of fun at the staging area—swimming, tennis, archery, shows, and forming long lines to buy Coke and ice cream, all fun activities. . . .

"October 15 was our lucky day. We walked the gangplank on to the *George Washington* and left Marseille that night. . . . We walked the deck during the days, played cards, saw shows, and planned for our future in civilian life. . . .

"On 25 October, we all were on deck trying to sight land but it was so foggy we couldn't see a thing until we were on the Hudson River that night and saw the Jersey shores and car lights. We were anchored all night and were out on deck at 0530 to watch the ferry boats and barges—and glided by the Statue of

Liberty. That was the biggest thrill, and we all had tears streaming down our faces. After debarking, we were whisked away in buses where we had our first carton of milk since we left the States. From Camp Kilmer, we were sent to separation centers (I went to Fort Dix, New Jersey) and on to our homes throughout the United States. . . .

"When I left the train in Toledo, . . . I sat on my luggage until [my parents] found me . . . and then I was really home! On our way to Gibsonburg, I handed my mother a list of food requests. . . . It seems I craved desserts and soups and, of course, my mother complied, as I knew she would. It was wonderful to be home again!"

July 1945
POW Camp Mukden, Manchuria

Colonel Michael A. Quinn begins Book VII of his POW diary.

"We cannot help feel the refusal of the Nips to furnish us with any news is because they have no news that is good for them to report. From past experience we knew when things were going their way, we received plenty of news . . . ," Colonel Quinn writes on 2 July. On 3 July he notes: "From news we hear, the income tax is pretty high. I wonder if you are paying it, because under the law I am exempt because I am still on duty in the Philippines. (Note: When I returned to the States, I was informed by the Internal Revenue Department that I wasn't exempted from income tax while in prison camp, as I had left the Philippine Islands and therefore the law did not apply. As though I had any choice about leaving.)"

"We hear that 1,200 planes flew over Tokyo several days ago. . . . I should have no love for the Japs, but the thought leaves me thunderstruck. If people only realized how terrible the war is on so many innocent victims who have nothing to do with the causes, they might learn from it; but they never do," he observes on 13 July.

"Our food has been cut again and now we get two rolls a day, and our bean ration is halved. Occasionally a few potatoes are available and they help out. . . . General Drake gave me a copy of a letter that General Homma of the Japanese army delivered to Bataan to be delivered to General Wainwright. . . . (The only thing of any note was that International Law will be strictly adhered to by the Japanese forces and that 'your excellency and those under you will be treated accordingly.') I think the thing that made General Wainwright maddest about this was that they threw this down on us from the air in empty beer cans with long streamers attached. General Wainwright's only comment was that they might have sent a couple of full cans," Colonel Quinn relates on 19 July.

"No church services today, as it is not a holiday. These people are beyond me. They must face the world after all this is over. . . . They have gone out of their way to make the world antagonistic toward them. Look at the treatment accorded prisoners of war, and I don't imagine internees are treated very much better. Brutality; starvation; lack of ordinary, simple medication; withholding letters, coming or going; mishandling of Red Cross supplies; absolute indifference to anything like health, recreation, and surroundings; and even cutting off religious services. At other camps, the plea was 'no chaplains.' However, here there are three priests and two ministers. I give up trying to figure it out," he writes on 29 July.

July 1945
Home Again, USA

Colonel Jean W. Christy—with 50th Field Artillery Battalion, 5th Infantry Division. from Iceland to Ireland to the ETO—is finally back in the States after forty-two months overseas.

After welcome-home greetings from ships and tugs in New York Harbor on the 4th of July, "we were taken immediately to Camp Shanks, New York. Here we were processed to be sent on our way to whatever military installation was closest to our home," Colonel Christy writes.

"Here, also, we got spruced up to look our best. We changed from the brown wool uniform shirt and trousers that we had worn overseas for three and a half years to summer cotton khaki. I hadn't worn a khaki uniform since Fort Sill in the summer of 1941.

"Also, for the first time, we were able to obtain the various ribbons and other decorations that we were entitled to wear. Overseas stripes were a recent innovation, one allotted for each six months served overseas. We were entitled to seven of them for our long service, and we quickly sewed them on our sleeves.

"Dressed in our new khakis, a large 5th Division contingent went to the PX barber shop. Here we were greeted by an unexpected reaction. As we passed, the rest of the soldiers stopped and stared as they saw our overseas stripes. Most of the returnees had two or three. . . . One of them spoke, expressing what they all were thinking. 'Holy Cow!' he exploded. 'These guys must have been *born* overseas.'"

After haircuts, "we went to make our phone call home. We went into a very large room, the size of a basketball court, with numbered telephone booths all around the walls. After what seemed an eternity, my name was called and I was directed to one of the numbered phone booths. I picked up the receiver, and Peggy [his wife] was on the line. I could actually hear her voice. It was an overwhelming moment. Strangely, neither of us could think of much to say after we had waited so long. I told her that we were coming by train to Camp Atterbury, just outside of Indianapolis."

After an overnight trip and arrival at Camp Atterbury, "the processing began again and orders were prepared for each of us to take thirty days of 'Recuperation Leave.' Midway through my leave, we spent most of one week visiting the Camp Campbell, Kentucky, area. One of my responsibilities was to find housing for the other married officers in the battalion. . . . We began making commitments on all the decent places to live in that we could find, writing checks for earnest money on Peggy's checking account. . . . We used up more than $500 but I never had any doubt that each of the officers would repay me when they arrived. . . .

"We found a nice apartment for ourselves in Hopkinsville, Kentucky. . . . We arranged that we would move in on 10 August 1945. It was our first home together."

July–August 1945
Sioux Falls, South Dakota, and New York

Lieutenant Colonel Norman L. Stevens Jr. survived a December 1942 book report and then many missions over Europe with the Eighth Air Force. He tells yet another story of surviving.

"In late July, early August of 1945, our group was stationed in Sioux Falls, South Dakota. The purpose of our stay at Sioux Falls was to regroup and go to the Pacific. The atomic bomb, later that month, changed those plans and a million others," Lieutenant Colonel Stevens writes.

"The base at Sioux Falls had a B-25 that was used by various personnel to get from point A to point B. One day, Lieutenant Colonel Bill Smith, our deputy group CO, came to me and said, 'Lieutenant, I am going to go to New Bedford, Massachusetts, this weekend, and I would like to have you go.' I said, 'Colonel, do you want me to go as a pilot or as a passenger?' He said, 'As a passenger.' I said, 'That being the case, colonel, with all due respect, I would like to decline.' He asked, 'Why?' I said, 'Well, I have been trying to get a date with a beautiful blonde by the name of Joanne Bolin ever since we got here, and I have a date with her this weekend, and if you don't need me as a pilot I would prefer to stay here.' He said, 'I don't need you as a pilot. And good luck.'

"History now records that Bill Smith took off with a couple of the other fellows from the group and left them at Teterboro, New Jersey, and he proceeded to New Bedford. He visited his wife and newborn baby and then took off [28 July] with a sailor hitchhiker and his aircraft engineer and headed back to Teterboro to pick up his two passengers that he had dropped off two days previously.

"The weather was almost below minimums and the colonel was trying to stay below the weather when he came down across lower Connecticut and lower New York and into Manhattan. In my opinion, he confused the East River with the Hudson River. When he saw the East River, because of the bad visibility, he thought that he was across the Hudson and headed south toward Teterboro. When he did this he inadvertently started flying down Manhattan and before he could make a correction he slammed into the Empire State Building. He, the engineer, and the sailor hitchhiker of course were killed instantly." Newspaper accounts of the event record that eleven in the building were also killed. Twenty-six were injured. Since the crash occurred on a Saturday, the usual 15,000 who might have been in the building were not at their jobs.

"That blonde in Sioux Falls, South Dakota, saved my life," Lieutenant Colonel Stevens acknowledges.

AUGUST 1945

45

Bombs fell in surprise attack on Pearl Harbor 7 December 1941, and quickly World War II began for the United States. Forty-four months later, bombs fell, in surprise of design and magnitude, on Hiroshima and Nagasaki, 6 and 8 August 1945, respectively, and quickly World War II was over for the United States, for its Allies, and for Japan. And so it ends, almost as it began, with reverberations that would resound throughout the centuries.

Like December 1941, August 1945 would become a month of *firsts* and *lasts*, *beginnings* and *endings*. Bombs dropped on Hiroshima and Nagasaki would be the first (and, the world continues to pray, the last) atom bombs ever to be used in warfare. They brought an end to the war, to further battles and bombings, to countless other deaths, to imprisonment for the POWs. They brought the beginnings of peace, after six dreadful and death-full years of worldwide war; beginnings to occupation and eventually democracy in Japan; beginnings once again for many families whose lives had been put on hold. For others throughout the world, however, war had brought the ultimate end: to family, to dreams, to life.

From among ROA's valiant World War II participants or from their faithful family members, come remembrances of some of those *firsts* and *lasts*, *beginnings* and *endings* for August 1945.

6 and 19 August 1945
Okinawa and Ie Shima

Colonel Jack R. Amos—in New Caledonia and on Guadalcanal since April 1944—served as duty officer of A-3 Section, HQ Fifth AF, near Motobu Airstrip, Okinawa.

On the night of 5–6 August, "just after midnight, a TWX was received from 20th Bomber Command, General Twining. In essence, it stated that no aircraft would be within a 200-mile radius of the primary, secondary, or ternary targets that the 20th BC had scheduled for 6 August 1945. Also, no aircraft were to fly in any clouds within a 200-mile radius of these three targets for two hours before or six hours after TOT (time over target)," Colonel Amos reports.

"Realizing that the Fifth AF had targets for our aircraft to hit that were near these designated targets of 20th BC, I woke Colonel Johnny R. Allison, the A-3. Colonel Allison studied the teletype and conferred with General Whitehead, CG Fifth AF.

"I was instructed to relay the same information to our fighter and bomber commands. Very shortly after the TWX was sent, two of the fighter group commanders were on the telephone with me, stating that they had pilots down in the water near these targets because of their air activity on 5 August. The pilots, who were in the water, were scheduled to be picked up by Dumbos (PBYs), with the aid of their fighters providing air support.

"Since I could not give them any relief, they flew over from Ie Shima and again Colonel Allison was awakened. He finally agreed for them to continue their rescue operations, providing they could be out of the designated areas not later than one hour before TOT. The fighter planes strafed the shore batteries as the Dumbos picked up the four pilots (in three different places) and provided air cover for the PBYs back to Ie Shima.

"That day, 6 August 1945, a new weapon was unleashed upon the city of Hiroshima, Japan. A solo B-29, the *Enola Gay*, dropped the first atomic bomb."

"On the morning of 19 August," Colonel Amos continues, "I went down to Motobu Airstrip on Okinawa, looking for a way to get over to Ie Shima. This is the day that the surrendering Japanese envoys were instructed by General Douglas MacArthur to land at Ie Shima, and from there they would continue by American transport planes to meet with him in Manila.

"I saw Colonel Gerald R. Johnson, one of the leading aces of the Pacific war, getting ready to take off in a C-47. He let me ride with him to Ie Shima.

"Instructions were given that the Betty bomber would be painted white with green crosses and that the pilots would use the code name *Bataan*. The two aircraft landed at 1000 hours as per instructions. Japan had objected both to the painting of their aircraft white with green crosses and the use of the word *Bataan* as their recognition signal. However, General MacArthur assured them that they would do both.

"Also, General MacArthur had issued orders that no personnel who were less than six-feet tall would be at the Ie Shima Airstrip, or Clark Field, or his Headquarters, where the Japanese surrender envoys could see them during their visit."

8 August 1945
Kyushu, Japan

Lieutenant Colonel Everett H. Krippner and wife Virginia, a former sergeant and
Link Trainer instructor, submit an account of what might have been the last
Japanese fighter plane shot down.

Then-Lieutenant Krippner piloted B-24J, 11th Bomb Group (H), Seventh AF, which left Okinawa for Usa Airfield, Kyushu, 8 August 1945. "The weather was good. The crew of nine was in good spirits. Why not? Japanese fighter opposition was nil and anti-aircraft ineffective. It was assumed that there was no threat. However, upon turning to the thirty-second bomb run, two Japanese Tojo-type fighters attacked the formation, dropping phosphorus bombs toward the lead flight," the Krippners report.

Technical Sergeant Joseph A. Reres, radio operator and gunner, in his report, described the incident as follows: "Approximately two minutes before *bombs away* at 081010, a phosphorus bomb burst was observed at one o'clock high over this formation. Shortly afterward, an enemy fighter identified as a Tojo was observed by crew members of AP #280, lead A/C of the 98th Bombardment Squadron (H) formation, at about three o'clock and slightly high. The Tojo had apparently just executed a near-vertical climb and appeared to be at the stalling-out point within approximately 250 yards from AP #280.

"At this time, F/O Walls, navigator, called on the interphone to the waist gunner and Sergeant Reres answered by saying, 'I got him.' Top turret gunner Staff Sergeant Miller immediately opened fire but missed. Almost simultaneously, Sergeant Reres took up the firing from his right-waist-gun position then saw his tracers entering the Tojo's fuselage and flames shooting out as the fighter began diving toward the sea."

Along with five other crew members who, in the words of the report, "saw the Tojo burning and smoking as it fell toward the sea apparently out of control" was "Sergeant Lee J. Freiberg, combat cameraman. . . . [who] also took pictures from just before [the time] when Sergeant Reres began firing at it until the fighter had fallen approximately 400 yards."

"I was scared to death," Colonel Krippner recalls. "My hands and feet were shaking so badly that I had to concentrate very hard on flying the airplane.

"We are still wondering: Was it the last Japanese fighter plane shot down just before the war was over?" Though 12 August 1945 is the date recorded for the last B-24 missions, "there appears to be no documentation that any other enemy warplane was destroyed."

V-J Day, 14 August 1945
Okinawa

Lieutenant Colonel Thomas P. Loftain was a Seabee, third class petty officer, with
139th NCB, which built an amphitheater overlooking Okinawa's Awase Airstrip
and Buckner Bay.

The Bay was "formerly called Nakagusuku Bay and renamed after Lieutenant General Simon Bolivar Buckner, who was killed in action 18 June 1945, just three days before the island was officially secured," Lieutenant Colonel Loftain explains.

"It was the evening of 14 August and many of our battalion were sitting in the amphitheater watching the movie *The Clock,* starring Robert Walker and Judy Garland. All of a sudden, tracer anti-aircraft shells lit up the sky from a solitary ship anchored in the bay. Then a second ship at the opposite end of the bay commenced firing. Then it seemed that every ship in the bay, and there were hundreds of them, started firing. Then the AA batteries on the land joined in, and all hell broke loose.

"We were accustomed to frequent Kamikaze attacks, and our loudspeaker squawked 'gas attack.' Everyone ran for their gas masks, which were in the most inaccessible places. Mine was buried at the very bottom of my duffel bag in my tent. One of my fellow Seabees decided he needed it more than I and grabbed it away from me. My .45 automatic did some fast convincing. I ran to the nearest Okinawan burial cave and spent the rest of the fireworks display there. When the fireworks subsided, I emerged to find that the war was over."

14 August–15 October 1945
Mindanao, the Philippines

Colonel Charles B. Gwynn was with 655th FA Battalion, attached to X Corps
Artillery, on R&R near Davao at war's end.

"From April to July 1945, the 655 Field Artillery Battalion (eight-inch howitzer)—which I had activated, trained, commanded, and took overseas to the Southwest Pacific—had fought through the campaign on Mindanao in the southern Philippines. Just before 1 August 1945, the battle ended," Colonel Gwynn writes.

"We were ordered into bivouac, and set up a tent camp beside Libby Airdrome, south of Davao. While enjoying rest and recuperation, we were under orders to be moved by LST with all our equipment up to Clark Field outside of Manila, Luzon. We were to prepare and train with Sixth Army for the November 1945 first-wave invasion of Kyushu, the southernmost island of Japan.

"In camp near Davao on 14 August 1945, the unit had just finished evening chow when over the radio came the word that the Japanese had surrendered unconditionally.

"Throughout the battalion, there was an individual sense of joy, and relief, especially because it voided the 'blood bath' anticipated during the initial invasion of Japan. Great shouting and commotion broke out. I immediately called the battery commanders together. All carbine and pistol ammunition was collected to prevent indiscriminate shooting or someone getting hurt who had survived combat.

"Immediately after V-J Day, X Corps troops started the task of rounding up all of the Japanese. Those left had been pushed way back and scattered into the hills, mountains, and what the maps labeled 'unexplored land,' thick, tropical jungle. The problem was to get them to accept the fact that their emperor had unconditionally surrendered. Radio broadcasts brought a few in. A mimeographed flyer written in Japanese was produced. Assisting, I flew our Piper Cub liaison planes all over the easterly portion of Mindanao dropping the leaflets. In some areas deep in the jungle, the Japanese soldiers had started crops of corn and vegetables.

"The leaflets described areas and road junctions where the soldiers could be picked up. Our 2^1/$_2$-ton trucks went to designated places every day to make pickups. It was slow work but eventually over 30,000 were brought in. They were placed in stockades of 10,000 each. The assortment was divided roughly as follows: 10,000 civilians—men, women, and children; 5,000 Jap marines, Korean and navy personnel; 15,000 Jap soldiers. All were well treated and fed, clothed, and had tents to live in. By 15 October, the evacuation of these people back to Japan was under way.

"About 8 September, I went with Colonel Matthews of the 167th Infantry Regiment of the 31st Division, way up into the jungles of central Mindanao at Tamogan to accept the surrender of Major General Tamochika, chief of staff of the 35th Imperial Japanese army. It was a simple, solemn occasion. I got the autograph of the general and a samurai sword of some other Japanese officer."

14 August 1945
Negros Island, the Philippines

Lieutenant Colonel Henry T. Capiz was a nineteen-year-old, drafted out of high school in 1944, who served with the 503rd Parachute Regimental Combat Team in the Philippines.

Though the campaign for Negros Island was officially over in June 1945, the 503rd "continued to skirmish with the remnants of 17,000 Japanese defenders into August." On the morning of 14 August, Private First Class Capiz was sent with his platoon into the central region of the island on a search-and-destroy mission. "We must have hit one of their camps because we received some really intense small-arms fire as we entered the valley," he says. Backed into a clearing at the top of a hill, the troops radioed for supplies, only to watch as the anticipated parachutes dropped and drifted over to the Japanese positions.

"Boy, were we mad," Colonel Capiz recalls. "By that time, we were hungrier than hell and thirsty, too. So we called for more supplies. When the crates landed, they broke open and spread our supplies all over the place."

·Holding their position and digging in for the night, the troops awaited the usual night infiltration of Japanese troops. They never came. Instead, at 2300 hours, a radio message came, telling them the war was over. "You've never seen a happier bunch of guys. Some even went so far as to light up cigarettes."

The next morning, upon requesting permission to pull out, the troops were told to continue fighting until further orders. "We were angry," Colonel Capiz notes, "and did as little as possible, not wanting to be killed on the last day of fighting. We finally got orders to pull out about noon. We made it back to camp in record time that day, and had some Filipino beer and whiskey to celebrate."

On the island in the following days, "6,000 remaining Japanese defenders surrendered, after Nisei troops in the regiment convinced them the war was over. Most were half-starved and many were sick."

July–October 1945
USS *Nicholas* in the Pacific, off Japan

Commander Douglas Perret Starr was a sonarman second class who served aboard USS Nicholas *(DD-449).*

"I was one month over eighteen years old when I joined USS *Nicholas* at Mare Island Naval Shipyard, Vallejo, California, in mid-December 1943. Twenty-one months later, *Nicholas* and I had fought in eleven battles and island landings and sunk two Japanese submarines, and I was not yet twenty years old. All in all, it was a grand adventure; I would not have missed it for the world," Commander Starr comments.

"The destroyer *Nicholas* was the lead ship in Admiral William (Bull) Halsey's Third Fleet, which was patrolling well at sea off Japan in July and August 1945, awaiting word to invade the Japanese home islands, an operation the 300 officers and crew knew would be their toughest fight of the Pacific war.

"The high command had forecast that the Japanese people would repel to the death any invasion of their sacred soil by infidels and had estimated 1 million United States casualties.

"In addition, *Nicholas* had been at sea fifty-one days, twenty-one days past the time stored food had run out, and *Nicholas* was on short rations. Two weeks earlier, we had drawn dry stores by breeches buoy from the battleship *Iowa*. For two weeks, we had been eating nothing but weevily bread, beans, and rice, moldy beef, green pork, and, of course, drinking coffee.

"All in all, we were a salty crew who had been through invasions and countless convoy runs from the Marshalls to Okinawa. None of us was eager about it, but we figured we could handle the Japanese home island, too. Then came the word that atomic bombs had been dropped on Hiroshima and Nagasaki. Nobody cheered, but we all knew that, for all practical purposes, the Pacific war was over.

"On our fifty-second day off Japan, Admiral Halsey addressed the Third Fleet by radio, saying that the shooting was ended and that all hands should stand down. However, he warned, it remained possible that suicidal Japanese aircraft might yet attack the fleet. If that happened, he said, 'shoot them down, not vindictively, but in a friendly sort of way.'

"The next day, *Nicholas* picked up pilots and interpreters from the Japanese gunboat *Hatusakura*, delivered them to the battleship *Missouri*, and led the Third Fleet into Sagami Harbor at the foot of Mount Fuji.

"The Pacific war was, indeed, ended. *Nicholas* was going home but not yet. *Nicholas* spent the next two months collecting emaciated prisoners of war from Japanese camps and returning them to hospital ships in Tokyo Bay for return Stateside."

Mid-August–October 1945
Honshu, Japan

Colonel Thomas J. King Jr. was a second lieutenant, Army Corps of Engineers, who went into Japan "early" and served with 1409 Base Depot at Fukuoka, Kyushu, Japan, until 1946.

"I went into Japan at Wakayama, Honshu, as part of the central invasion force, Operation Olympic, second wave on an LST boat from the Philippines about three months ahead of the planned invasion-time set for November. I merely just stepped off the boat 'like a tourist,' except, since I had low points, I stayed nearly a year," Colonel King points out.

"Several months later, I saw the result of the Hiroshima bombing. We were transferred to the southern main island of Kyushu on a trooptrain that went through the western edge of Hiroshima at nighttime under a brilliant moonlit, clear sky. Everything looked so deadly quiet. I remember the bowl-like skyline over a three- or four-mile length, with trees and buildings on the edge of the bowl sloping down to the center, which was mostly flat to the ground. Our train never stopped, maybe slowed down some. . . . To my knowledge, no one was allowed in the 'hot' area for miles around. Truly, they paid dearly. However, don't forget the Japanese started the war with us, using a sneak attack on Pearl Harbor. . . .

"They estimated one-half million casualties/deaths in the combined U.S. and Allied invasion force and $1^1/_2$ million casualties/deaths to the combined Japanese military and civilian population. So, I thank President Truman and his people for the tough decision he had to make. Again, I say I am glad I went into Japan in 1945 the way I did rather than the way my entrance had been planned. I, my children, and grandchildren are here today because of the atomic bomb."

June–V-J Day, 14 August 1945
Admiralty Islands, New Guinea, and Hollandia

Chief Warrant Officer Fourth Class David L. Wischemann was an electrician's mate third class, on LST-18.

"As June 1945 rolled around, we were informed that a complete overhaul of our ship was to take place, at Manus in the Admiralty Islands. This, of course, was to prepare us for the invasion of Japan," Mr. Wischemann relates.

"We immediately entered a floating dry dock so large that we had another LST beside us, a Liberty ship astern of us, and a destroyer ahead of us. These dry docks were towed to war from the United States in three sections and joined together at their destinations.

"Radar was installed on the mast, the engines were overhauled, all systems checked, eight more 20mm ack-ack guns installed, and old 18 was completely painted with a new coat of jungle-green.

"August had us moving to Wadke, on New Guinea, to pick up Australian and New Zealand troops for Borneo. Just before we left Wadke, the scuttlebutt told of a *bomb* being dropped on Japan, but as usual you took it for what it was worth, about 99 percent nothing. We then proceeded to Hollandia for water and supplies, before going on to Borneo.

"As was usual, after morning chow, I took a breather on the fantail before I 'turned to' at 0800. Suddenly, I heard the word passed: 'The War Is Over!' There is no way anyone could explain the feeling, or loss of feeling, that went through me and millions of other guys at that moment of truth.

"Hollandia Harbor erupted into one solid uproar. Every pyrotechnic device known to man was fired, and when that was gone, *they* started shooting 20mm and 40mm guns in the air. This went on all day and into the night, and when this was mixed with certain fermented juices, it became prudent to celebrate below decks."

15 August 1945
Southwest Pacific, en Route to Korea

Major John R. Edwards was aboard an LST, bound for Korea in August 1945 to establish another air-resupply mission.

"There were rumors of Japan being bombed and the possibility of its surrender. We were under way without running lights, as was customary of task-force ships under war-blackout conditions. We were allowed topside under no-smoking order," Major Edwards recalls.

"I shall ever remember the ship's lights coming ablaze and the convoy commander's words over the speakers of Japan's surrender, after which we returned to blackout conditions, as a precaution against enemy ships or aircraft not aware of their country's surrender.

"There were cheers and, I am sure, prayers of thanks. My thoughts were of thanks that the war had ended, pride in our country and our forces, and somber thoughts of comrades parted or lost, the almost-fear, but the desire, to return home to families and friends, not knowing just how we would adjust to civilian life, peace, and the future."

15 August 1945
Iheya Shima, Ryukyu Islands

Major Alfred E. Peloquin was with 726th Amphibian Tractor Battalion, attached to 8th Marine Regimental Combat Team for the landings on Iheya and Aguni in May 1945.

"I believe my unit, the 726th Amphibian Tractor Battalion, holds the distinction of being the last American military unit to take an enemy hit in World War II," Major Peloquin writes. "On the evening of 15 August, shortly after sundown and some twelve hours after the war had been declared ended, two Japanese pilots made what was then thought to be kamikaze crashes on the island of Iheya Shima, northwest of Okinawa. One of the crashes occurred in our battalion area."

The battalion's unit historian records it thus: "Spirits were particularly high the evening of 15 August, for the Jap emperor had just acknowledged acceptance of peace terms. But our celebration was a bit premature, for two Jap suicide planes, shortly after sundown, chose our island to make their last grandstand plays. One crashed in a ball of fire down on the beach, doing no damage. The other landed near battalion headquarters, and the flying fragments of bomb and exploding plane severely wounded T/5 Andrew Barstow and T/5 Charles Kniola. Barstow died that night of his wounds; Kniola was a long time recovering."

19 August 1945
Ie Shima, Ryukyu Islands

Lieutenant Colonel Robert J. Lather was a first lieutenant, armament officer, 413th Fighter Group. His P47Ns flew missions over Japan and Formosa supporting Tenth Army on Okinawa.

"The war with the Japanese was unofficially over, but everybody was on pins and needles. We were wondering if . . . the Japanese [were] stalling for more time to better fortify their home islands against an expected invasion. We did not know it at the time, but later learned that the invasion of Japan was scheduled for 1 November 1945, and that our fighter group was slated to be one of the first ashore after ground forces had secured an airfield," Lieutenant Colonel Lather writes.

"On 19 August, there were rumors that a party of Japanese was going to land on our island (Ie Shima, a small island off the coast of Okinawa) on their way to Manila to discuss surrender terms and procedures with General MacArthur and his staff. I decided to go and see what was going on.

"There were hundreds of service people gathered around the end of one of our airstrips. There were barricades and numerous Japanese aircraft.

"I had not been there very long when, sure enough, a Japanese Betty bomber, painted white with green crosses, came into sight. The pilot made a smooth landing and taxied up to the end of the runway where I was standing. Doors opened, and Japanese military officers, with swords, briefcases, et cetera, stepped down from the plane. One member of the aircrew stood up through the hatch over the cockpit to survey the crowd. The Japanese even carried flowers as a gesture of peace.

"The Japanese were met by officers from MacArthur's headquarters, along with Japanese-American interpreters. They were whisked away to board a C-54 to continue the flight to the Philippines to discuss the surrender terms with MacArthur's staff.

"After seeing all of this, it was easier to believe that, very possibly, the war was really over. That was something we had been looking forward to for almost four years. Now that the end was in sight, we could allow ourselves to dream of that land so far away, the beautiful United States of America."

6 August 1945
En Route to Marseille, France

Colonel Lester B. Cundiff was a lieutenant, 225th Chemical Base Depot Company at Depot C-913, Montebourg, France, from December 1944 until it was deactivated.

"Shortly after V-E Day, the 225th was moved to Le Havre, then in July to Camp New Orleans, south of Reims, to prepare for shipment to the Pacific," Colonel Cundiff notes.

"Our trucks and other organizational equipment had been made ready and were in convoy toward Marseille when the atomic bomb was dropped on Hiroshima. That morning, one of the sergeants (who always seemed to get the word first) looked into the officers' tent and announced: 'We've dropped a bomb on Japan so big that it's tilted the island to a 45° angle and all the Japs are rolling off into the ocean.' His exaggeration notwithstanding, we were delighted to hear the news and the later rumor that we would still go to the Pacific, but now a new sign under the 'On to Tokio [sic]' sign proclaimed 'Viva the Good Ol' USA.'

"Soon the 225th and all other CWS service units in the ETO were ordered to Liege, Belgium, where reorganization and deactivation began. Major John M. Appel (later major general) was in charge of transferring all the men with the highest point counts into certain units to ship back to the States. Those with fewer points were transferred into other units to go home later. Still others with very few points were given assignments to units or agencies that would stay for a year or more. Those who wished could volunteer to stay, which I did, planning to go home a couple of months before the 1946 fall semester at college."

August 1945
POW Camp Mukden, Manchuria

Colonel Michael A. Quinn, even with the end of captivity in sight, maintains his POW diary.

Finally, on 17 August, after nearly forty months as a POW of the Japanese, Colonel Quinn can at last proclaim: "My dearest ones: The news of all times came in today at 8:15. General Parker called for an assemblage of all officers in camp and asked us that there be no demonstration about the news he was about to impart: 'The war is over' and an armistice is in effect between Japan, the United States, England, and the Netherlands. We are still to remain prisoners of war but the feeling is entirely different. Last night, Private Honiker, a soldier from my outfit in Bataan, came in about suppertime and told me the whole story. He said the war was over at 9 A.M. yesterday morning and that six delegates to take care of us arrived by plane and parachuted to the ground and they were in camp now. . . . Nobody would believe it; it was simply too good to be true. Last night, camp discipline went all to hell. Smoking all night long. Everyone in a daze. . . . There is to be a Mass of thanksgiving tomorrow and I will be there. Yesterday Floyd Marshall was buried. Isn't that irony? Just the time his funeral was being held, the armistice was signed. His last words just before he died were, 'The war will be over soon.' I am not going to try to tell of the frenzy around here; I can't."

"What an evening," Colonel Quinn declares on 20 August. "A concert was scheduled for 7:00 P.M. this evening, and the three national anthems were sung. . . . Later we were told to report for a talk by the Russian commander. . . . Through an American who was used as interpreter, he talked about the glory of the Red army and finally wound up with this statement—'I now declare you free men.' . . . The Russians stated that they would disarm the Japanese oppressors. . . . The Nips were paraded. The men laid down their rifles, literally. Then the officers laid down their sabers, after which the Russians armed the American guards with Nip rifles, making a little speech to each soldier. . . . The Japanese officers and men were then forced to pass in review before all of us, under command of American guard detail. One man started to give the Bronx cheer as the Japs passed, and the whole gang turned on him. . . . It was a supreme humiliation of this war that we had to be rearmed by Russians who came in at the very end and had no effect on the outcome of the war."

"We have been notified that we will leave here by air beginning within three to five days. First to leave are the sick in order of rank," the colonel reports 22 August. "We have Mass here every day, and I am going to make up for lost time. . . . Our soldiers now guard the Nip prisoners. . . . This food is something we can hardly believe. Chicken soup today at noon and eight hogs were killed for the evening meal. That makes about six months' supply of meat à la Jap."

"I went to Mukden this afternoon," he writes again on 26 August. "Driving through town, I saw twin Gothic spires and told the rickshaw coolie that's where I wanted to go. . . . It was the cathedral of the French Catholic mission at Mukden. The bishop is a Frenchman by the name of Blois. . . . The nuns are of Chinese, Japanese, French, Polish, and one of Irish descent. The latter was Mother Superior. . . . You have to hand it to those people for courage. During all the years of war, they kept up the work of the convent. . . . They had tried to come to our camp, but that was disallowed."

"Bishop Blois invited me to lunch yesterday, and I brought Ken Hoeffel," he notes on 28 August. "Can you imagine after all these years, sitting down to a table with a white tablecloth, napkins, chinaware, knives and forks? Formerly,

our food had been carried to us in baskets. Yesterday we were served from plat-
ters. The meal was simple, the company excellent, and after lunch the bishop
invited us to go to the chapel for a few moments of meditation."

"Colonel Richards, Air Force, left this morning with fifty-eight others," Colonel Quinn reports 30 August. "Yesterday a bunch of B-29s came over to drop
supplies by chute. Considerable damage was done by parcels breaking away from
their chutes and crashing through roofs. Fortunately, nobody was hurt."

COUNTDOWN TO V-J DAY, 2 SEPTEMBER 1945

46

Convinced that further battle would reduce Japan to ashes, Emperor Hirohito, the Imperial Son of Heaven of Great Japan, refuses to yield to Imperial Conference voices on 14 August 1945 that urge "one last battle." He accepts the terms of the Potsdam Declaration and Radio Tokyo announces the decision 14 August, East Longitude date, at 1449 hours. Word reaches U.S. President Harry S. Truman 14 August, West Longitude date, at 1550. He announces the joyous news from the White House at 1900 and declares a two-day holiday.

On 15 August, at 1000 hours, Admiral Chester Nimitz, commander in chief of the Pacific Fleet, orders the Navy to "cease all offensive operations against Japan." In celebratory salute at 1100 hours, the flagship USS *Missouri* blows its whistle and sounds its siren for a full minute, under orders from Admiral William F. Halsey, commander of the Central Pacific Fleet. At 1600 hours on Japanese radio, via a message recorded the previous day, Hirohito speaks to the people of Japan who hear for the first time ever the voice of their god-emperor. He informs them that the enemy "has begun to employ a new and most cruel bomb, the power of which to do damage is indeed incalculable. . . ." For this reason, "we have ordered our government to communicate to the governments of the United States, Great Britain, China, and the Soviet Union that our empire accepts the provisions of their Joint Declaration." On the same day, President Truman appoints General Douglas MacArthur supreme commander for the Allied Powers. The general immediately directs the Japanese government to order "immediate cessation of hostilities" and to send "competent" representation to Manila to discuss the surrender and occupation.

On 16 August at 1600 hours, Japanese Armed Forces are commanded, by imperial order, to cease fire immediately. On 19 August, two Mitsubishis, Betty bombers, arrive on Ie Shima carrying a sixteen-man Japanese delegation that is transferred to the C-54 that will take the men to Manila and MacArthur.

On 27 August, ships of the U.S. 3rd Fleet and British Pacific Fleet begin to anchor in Sagami Bay at the foot of Mout Fuji—with U.S. battleship *Missouri* and British battleship *Duke of York* among them. At 0600, the 4th Marines stream ashore. C-47s, unloading paratroopers, begin arriving at Atsugi Air Base near Yokohama.

On 28 August, Colonel Charles Tench, a member of General MacArthur's staff, arrives at Atsugi with a contingent of 150 men. On 29 August, the *Missouri* and *Duke of York* arrive in Tokyo Bay off Yokohama.

On 30 August, landings begin at forts at the entrance to Tokyo Bay and at Yokosuka naval base. Lieutenant General Robert L. Eichelberger, Eighth Army commander, arrives at Atsugi to prepare, with trepidation and two hours' lead time, for the arrival of General MacArthur at the airfield that has served as training base for Kamikaze pilots, 300 of whom are still in the vicinity. Nearby, on the Kanto Plain of Tokyo, there remain twenty-two enemy divisions of 300,000 well-trained men. Undaunted and against the advice of staff who call the plan "a gamble," the general lands on Atsugi Airfield in C-54 *Bataan* at 1405. (Churchill would later comment: "Of all the amazing deeds in the war, I regard General MacArthur's landing at Atsugi as the bravest of the lot.") With corncob pipe in hand, the general, ever the dramatist, takes two steps down from the plane and two puffs on his pipe. To the sound of martial music from a paratrooper band, he deplanes, greets the small group of officers assembled, and sets off for the New Grand Hotel in Yokohama with his entourage to make final arrangements for the surrender signing—in what General Courtney Whitney, his chief aide, describes as "a ramshackle motorcade" with "a fire engine that resembled the Toonerville Trolley" leading the procession. The fifteen-mile route is flanked by more than 30,000 Japanese soldiers, at parade rest, with bayonets fixed and backs toward the motorcade, the same gesture of respect reserved for their emperor.

By Sunday, 2 September, 258 Allied warships are at anchor in Tokyo Bay for the formal surrender aboard the USS *Missouri*. Displayed on a bulkhead, overlooking the scene, is the flag carried into Tokyo Bay by Admiral Perry in 1853. Flying from the *Missouri*'s flagstaff is the flag that flew over the Capitol in Washington, D.C., on 7 December 1941.

At 0803, high-ranking officers and Allied representatives, delivered by the destroyer *Buchanan*, board the *Missouri*. At 0805, Fleet Admiral Chester Nimitz comes on board. At 0855, the eleven-member Japanese delegation arrives, brought by the destroyer *Lansdowne* and launch, and then piped on board. The entourage is headed by Japan's new foreign minister, Mamoru Shigemitsu, representing the government, and General Yoshijiro Umedzu, chief of staff of the Japanese army, representing the Supreme Command. The remaining nine—

three each from the Foreign Office, the War Department, and the Navy Department—include Toshikazu Kase, secretary to Shigemitsu; Admiral Sadatoshi Tomioka, chief navy planner for Imperial General Headquarters; Colonel Ichiji Sugita, who served as interpreter at the surrender of Singapore in 1942; and Lieutenant General Yatsuji Nagai. Among civilians in the group, dress is formal morning attire, with top hats. Among U.S. military aboard the *Missouri*, dress is casual, with collars open at the neck. The atmosphere is frigid and silent.

At about 0900, a chaplain's invocation and a recorded version of the "Star-Spangled Banner" introduce the proceedings. General MacArthur appears, in uniform, with collar unbuttoned, and minus his medals and ribbons. Arriving with him are Admirals Nimitz and Halsey. The general takes his place at the microphone to begin the ceremony, with U.S. Lieutenant General Jonathan M. Wainwright and British Lieutenant General Sir Arthur E. Percival standing nearby—both Japanese prisoners of war since early 1942, both recently released and flown in from POW camps in Manchuria.

In a brief statement, General MacArthur says:

> We are gathered here, representatives of the major warring powers, to conclude a solemn agreement whereby peace may be restored. . . . It is my earnest hope—indeed the hope of all mankind—that from this solemn occasion a better world shall emerge out of the blood and carnage of the past, a world founded upon faith and understanding, a world dedicated to the destiny of man and the fulfillment of his most cherished wish for freedom, tolerance, and justice.

At 0904, in the presence of General MacArthur, Foreign Minister Shigemitsu, who had been quietly advocating peace for about a year, is the first to sign the surrender document. General Umedzu is next, signing for Imperial General Headquarters. At this point, General MacArthur affixes his signature, accepting the surrender on behalf of the Allies. Admiral Nimitz then signs for the United States; Admiral Sir Bruce Fraser, commander in chief of the Eastern Fleet, for Great Britain; and then representatives from the Allied nations of China, the Soviet Union, France, Canada, Australia, New Zealand, and the Netherlands.

After the signings, General MacArthur adds: "Let us pray that peace be now restored to the world and that God will preserve it always."

At 0925, the formal ceremonies end. The sun appears—as do 450 carrier aircraft and hundreds of U.S. Army Air Force planes, in roaring salute as they fly over the USS *Missouri* and the other ships moored in peace in Tokyo Bay.

Stateside, it is the night of 1 September. An entire nation is tuned in to the radio description of the surrender and then hears General MacArthur begin a speech that he has spent much of the previous night writing and rewriting, a speech that Senator Arthur Vandenberg later tells him "was the greatest since Lincoln's Gettysburg Address."

"Today the guns are silent. A great tragedy has ended. A great victory has been won. The skies no longer rain death—the seas bear only commerce—men everywhere walk upright in the sunlight. The entire world is quietly at peace. The holy mission has been completed," he begins. "And in reporting this to you, the people, I speak for the thousands of silent lips, forever stilled among the jungles and the beaches and in the deep waters of the Pacific which marked the way. I speak for the unnamed brave millions homeward bound to take up the challenge of that future which they did so much to salvage from the brink of disaster. . . ."

In a plea to find recourses other than war, he continues:

If we do not now devise some greater and more equitable system, Armageddon will be at our door. The problem basically is theological and involves a spiritual recrudescence and improvement of human character that will synchronize with our almost matchless advances in science, art, literature, and all material and cultural developments of the past two thousand years. It must be of the spirit if we are to save the flesh.

"And so, my fellow countrymen," he concludes, "today I report to you that your sons and daughters have served you well and faithfully. . . . Their spiritual strength and power has brought us through to victory. They are homeward bound—take care of them."

Among the intent listeners to the ceremony and MacArthur's speech on that momentous evening is President Harry S. Truman himself, who addresses his "fellow Americans" as soon as the broadcast is over. "The thoughts and hopes of all America—indeed, of all the civilized world—are centered tonight on the battleship *Missiouri*. There on that small piece of American soil anchored in Tokyo Harbor, the Japanese have just officially laid down their arms," the president tells his radio listeners. "They have signed terms of unconditional surrender. . . . To all of us there comes first a sense of gratitude to Almighty God who sustained us and our Allies in the dark days of grave danger, who made us to grow from weakness into the strongest fighting force in history, and who now has seen us overcome the forces of tyranny that sought to destroy His civilization. . . ."

After specific tributes to all who aided in the war effort—from FDR and the Allies to those who gave their lives and those who worked in factories and on farms—the president proclaims "Sunday, September second, 1945, to be V-J Day," even though citizenry throughout the world had already proclaimed their own V-J Days with celebrations on 14 and 15 August 1945. President Truman concludes: "From this day we move forward. We move toward a new era of security at home. With the other United Nations we move toward a new and better world of peace and international good will and cooperation. . . ."

In ceremonies that same evening in Tokyo Bay, aboard the British flagship HMS *Duke of York*, Navy military gather—commemorating, singing hymns, and observing, literally and figuratively, the setting of the sun upon the Japanese Empire.

SEPTEMBER 1945 AND BEYOND

47

Word came at last that on 2 September 1945 "the final surrender papers would be signed on the deck of the battleship *Missouri* in Tokyo Bay," says Lieutenant General James V. Edmundson. He was a U.S. Army Air Force pilot on Tinian in the Marianas, anxiously waiting, when "the announcement came out that the Twentieth Air Force would fly a 500-plane show-of-force mission at low altitude over the ceremony. This was the mission that everyone wanted to fly."

Few, however, could be more eager to fly that September 2nd mission than Edmundson. Involved in the war since day one, when he was wounded by a bomb fragment at Hickam Field when Pearl Harbor was bombed, he participated in the Battle of Midway, May and June 1942; went with the 11th Bombardment Group in July 1942 to take part in the Guadalcanal campaign for nearly a year; and, after training in "a short, intensive" B-29 program in Kansas, was off to the China–Burma–India Theater as squadron commander, 468th Group, one of four in the 58th Wing, the initial wing of B-29s. "When our group commander was shot down over Singapore, I took over command of the 468th," which moved to Tinian early in 1945, Lieutenant General Edmundson writes.

Continuing his account of the mission over the *Missouri*, he says: "I received a phone call in my tent that my boss, General Roger M. Ramey, commander of the 58th Wing, wanted to see me at once. He said, 'Eddie, I just had a call from General LeMay, down on Guam, and he told me that my 58th Wing had been in the war longer than any of his other wings. He considered us his best wing and he has chosen us to lead the show-of-force mission over the *Missouri*. Now, I'm telling you, Eddie, your group is the best group in my wing, so the 468th is going to lead the parade and I'm going to fly with you.'

"I set General Ramey up with one of my best crews to lead the mission and I flew deputy lead on his wing. It was quite a day! The sky was full of B-29s, but I'm sure they had a better view of it all from down below than we did. There were two things about the mission that struck me at the time: the tremendous, historic event that was taking place beneath us in Tokyo Bay [and] the amazement at being able to fly around over downtown Tokyo at 1,000 feet altitude and not have anyone shooting at us."

At about the same time the official surrender was taking place aboard the *Missouri*, individual Japanese garrisons were surrendering throughout the Pacific Theater: the Marcus Island garrison on 31 August; garrisons on Truk in the Carolines, Pagan and Rota in the Marianas, and the Palau Islands, 2 September; 2,200 Japanese on Wake Island and forces from the Ryukyu Islands at Okinawa, both on 7 September.

And with those surrenders came the long-dreamed-of homecomings. "They are homeward bound. Take care of them," General MacArthur advised his fellow countrymen at the peace-treaty signing aboard the USS *Missouri*.

July–Postwar 1945
Tinian to Tokyo Bay to USA

Lieutenant General James V. Edmundson was commander of the 468th Group of B-29s at West Field on Tinian in early 1945.

"Operations during the closing months of the Twentieth Air Force campaign against the Japanese Empire were at an intense pitch," Lieutenant General Edmundson recalls. "Missions went out virtually every day. The average mission strength was about 500 airplanes. Groups would mount an effort about every two to three days. . . .

"During this period, the Japanese ability to defend themselves had fallen off drastically. . . . The only thing left to do was to make the Japanese admit they had lost. . . .

"In July, my good friend and flying-school classmate Paul Tibbets and his 509th Group arrived on Tinian. . . . It was obvious that the 509th was a special sort of outfit. It had only one B-29 bomb squadron and its B-29s were equipped with reversible electric propellers, instead of the hydraulic propellers the rest of us had. . . . Paul visited my group a couple of times to sit in on mission briefings and interrogations and I visited his outfit several times. I saw some of the special facilities provided for the 509th, like that pit that was used to load the oversized bombs they carried, but nobody, including me, had the wildest idea about the nature of those bombs until Paul returned from his Hiroshima strike on the afternoon of the 6th of August. Three days later and it was Nagasaki's turn. We all kept our fingers crossed. . . .

"Meanwhile, our war went on as usual. On 14 August, I led forty-five B-29s of my group against the naval arsenal at Hikari. It was a successful mission with little opposition, except for intense flak over the target. The aiming points were well-covered and we lost no airplanes. We were on the way home when a radio broadcast was received stating that the Japanese had accepted the terms of unconditional surrender and that the war was 'over—*repeat*—over.'. . .

"For the next few days, everything seemed to be in slow motion. . . . I initiated a program of training missions so the crews wouldn't lose their touch. . . . Our only real activity was flying missions to Japanese POW camps, where Americans were imprisoned, and dropping packs of food and medicine by parachute. There was a lot of personal satisfaction in flying these missions and we were amazed that we never got shot at."

After his mission over the *Missouri* on 2 September, "it was all downhill," the lieutenant general reports. "A point system was developed to determine who were the most deserving people to go home first. A project called 'Sunset' was announced, in which our airplanes would all be flown back to the States. My group, having spent a year in the CBI Theater was set to go home almost intact. . . . We worked for days painting and polishing our airplanes so that we would look like a real outfit when we got back to the States. . . .

"The 468th arrived back in Sacramento, California, with all of our wonderful crews and all of our shiny B-29s, and found we were in the middle of a frantic demobilization frenzy. Before we could climb down out of the cockpit, some guy came climbing up through the nose wheel-well with a handful of papers. 'Sign these,' he said, 'and turn in all of your equipment, and tomorrow you'll all be civilians.' We were dazed, but we followed this guy into the building where there were three processing lines: For those who wanted out of the Army in a hurry, those who wanted out even faster, and those who wanted out yesterday. What a shock! I had a tough time explaining that I was a Regular Army officer and I wasn't about to turn in all my equipment, sign their damn papers, and walk out of there in a pin-striped suit. I shorted out the circuit. They didn't know what to do with me.

"'What happens to my airplanes?' I asked, as they were trying to process me. I was told not to worry about them; they would be left in a backyard corner of the field and someone else would figure out what to do with them later. There's no hurry, I was told, since nobody wants them anymore.

"'What about my outfit?' I asked. I was told that I no longer had an outfit, and to forget about it.

"'Where do I report for duty?' was my last question. I was told that I had an automatic sixty days' leave and to go home. Eventually, I was told, someone would probably send me some orders and tell me what to do.

"In just one lousy morning back in the States, my group had taken more hits than it had during its many months of combat. My people were scattered to the four winds, my beautiful B-29s were headed for the scrap heap, my proud outfit had ceased to exist, and I had been placed on indefinite hold. It was a glum homecoming for a conquering hero."

August–September 1945
Japan

Captain Armand E. Breard submits the recollections of his father-in-law, Colonel Arthur "Chap" Turner, chief of counterintelligence operations, Eighth Army.

On 30 August, "we landed at Atsugi Airfield, about twenty miles out of Yokohama and Tokyo, at 0920 hours, I-time. I was among the first there. Our plane was integrated with planes bringing in the advance elements of the 11th Airborne Division," Chap writes on 2 September 1945 from Yokohama to "Mary dearest," his wife.

"There were Jap naval guards around the field and as I walked toward the empty hangar which was our Eighth Army control point. I was very surprised to receive salutes. . . . Planes were landing on the field at three-minute intervals with troops and equipment, but it was just a routine show. . . . General MacArthur and his party flew in; a band played. . . . As General Eichelberger came in to the control point, six men walked in, looking sort of lost. One of them had no left leg, and was walking on bamboo crutches. . . . They had been prisoners of war of the Japanese in a camp at Kobe, quite a distance. They had learned of the surrender and the planned landing of American troops at Atsugi, so they walked out of the prison camp, bummed their way on passenger trains, and made it to us at Atsugi. . . . We gave them some boxes of K-rations and they said it tasted like Christmas dinner." Colonel Turner says that after sitting around the airfield most of the day as the MacArthur party was routed to Yokohama, "we finally got transportation into the city in an old charcoal-burning bus (the Japanese had run out of gasoline)."

Among postwar duties, the colonel says, "we had pinpointed the people we would be arresting, including some Germans, but the direct orders from MacArthur were to do absolutely nothing until he gave the word. That was understandable; he wanted enough troops on Japan to give us a good fighting chance in case there was a hitch in the surrender terms. . . .

"One morning, I received a direct order from the general's chief of staff. He said, 'Arrest Tokyo Rose.' I knew where she was (right above the general's own office making a recording for some Signal Corps people). We took her in custody, on tiptoes, and arranged the next day for the Japanese police to guard her in her apartment in Tokyo. . . . She was later moved to a brief prison stay, was freed, and did not stand trial as a traitor until she came back to this country. I liked the young woman. Her broadcasts, which I had listened to in New Guinea and the Philippines, were entertaining rather than traitorous. You see, Iva Toguri D'Aquino was an American citizen who stayed in Japan after the Pearl Harbor attack, but actually did nothing to harm American operations.

"There was another order that was far more difficult: 'Get Homma,' the infamous Japanese commander who had ordered and supervised the long American Death March from Bataan to torture in prison camps. . . . We knew that Homma was surrounded by a dedicated group of Japanese soldiers and the most we could muster to rush his home in the country were forty-five men—no chance at all. We did know, though, that he was a vain man and liked publicity. We arranged with an American correspondent to lure Homma into Tokyo, in civilian clothes, on the pretext of an interview. The thing worked. The minute Homma arrived, he was arrested and soon shot before a firing squad (he should have been hanged instead).

"Still another order: 'Get Tojo.' In his small house near Tokyo, we found Hideki Tojo, the arch–war criminal, where he tried to commit suicide with a small pistol when he learned the Americans had come to get him. Captain Jake Wilpers of the 308th CIC detachment literally broke down the door to Tojo's house, stopped the suicide attempt, and got Tojo to a 1st Cavalry Division ambulance where prompt American medical attention saved Tojo for the trial that resulted in his being hanged."

7 September 1945
Okinawa, Ryukyu Islands

Lieutenant Colonel Kenneth G. Jenkins was a captain, G-2 Section, Tenth Army HQ, on Okinawa.

On Okinawa, 7 September 1945, "unconditional surrender of the Japanese empire to GI Joe was now to become a reality for those in the Ryukyus Area," the report proclaims. A copy of the report, "Surrender of the Ryukyus," was provided by Lieutenant Colonel Jenkins who had found it, along with a copy of the surrender document, on his desk "in the G-2 Quonset a few weeks after the ceremony." He believes that the report was probably written by some member of General Stilwell's personal staff, "with the thought of being incorporated into a Tenth Army Headquarters staff unit history."

On Okinawa the day of the surrender, at 0600, Old Glory was raised—not a new Old Glory but an *old* Old Glory, the one that had flown over General Joseph

W. Stilwell's U.S. Army Headquarters in Chungking from May 1942 until the general left China.

"At 1030, the [Tenth Army] Headquarters area was a swarm of humanity. . . . No one wanted to miss a second of the ceremony. . . . The growing tension was relieved a bit when the band broke the silence with a few marches and 'Roll Out the Barrel' and 'The Old Gray Mare.' . . .

"Among American officers who were invited were Lieutenant General James H. Doolittle, Eighth Air Force; Vice Admiral J. B. Oldendorf, commander of Task Force 95; Major General DeWitt Peck, 1st Marine Division; Brigadier General Lawrence J. Carr, Seventh Bomber Command; and Major General Gilbert X. Cheves, Island Command 14. . . .

"At 1130, General Stilwell marched out of his headquarters building and down the path to the table. . . . Lieutenant General Toshiro Nomi [commander Japanese forces, Sakishima Gunto] stepped forward and sat at the little table where he signed six copies of surrender. . . . A typical gem of American humor was heard by some of the spectators in the rear: 'Just like the Army—original and six copies.' Major General Toshisada Tokada [commander Japanese army forces, Amami Gunto] and Rear Admiral Tadao Kato [commander Japanese navy forces, Amami Gunto] signed in quick succession." General Stilwell then "affixed his signature, after which, formation after formation of silver-winged bombers and fighter planes roared overhead in precise formation." As the Japanese officers were taken from the area, "General Stilwell spoke quietly, merely thinking out loud: 'There go the war lords of the Pacific.'"

Autumn 1945
The Philippines to Korea

Lieutenant Colonel Charles R. Keefe was a captain, 63rd Infantry Regiment, 6th Infantry Division.

On 15 August 1945, when World War II ended, elements of the 63rd Infantry were still up in the front line on Luzon, according to regiment history. "As a unit of the 6th Infantry Division, we are the proud holders of the Pacific record of days of continuous combat, a total of 219 consecutive days of fighting. The cost of these laurels was not light, however, as the regiment had almost 1,400 battle casualties on Luzon, including 303 dead," the regiment's anonymous historian reports.

"Early in September, the regiment moved again, this time to San Fernando, La Union, Philippines, where preparations for the move to Korea were started. On 5 October, loading began, and on 10 October, the regiment sailed. . . . During the voyage, the regiment had a few days of rough seas caused by the typhoon that hit Okinawa, [8–12] October 1945. On 18 October, the regiment landed at Inchon, Korea, and immediately entrained for the trip to Cholla Pukto Province where the Fighting 63rd began its first occupation mission. . . .

"First-priority mission of the regiment was to disarm and evacuate to Japan all Japanese army and navy forces in its zone. This important job was done rapidly and efficiently and was completed by November. . . . At the same time, the regiment took over the job of guarding vast stores of Japanese army supplies and equipment, including everything from airplane engines to horseshoe nails. After inventorying these stores, the 63rd began the difficult task of destroying all warlike supplies and equipment. . . .

"Another important mission was the handling of all displaced persons in its zone. By 10 December, 98 percent of the 30,000 Japanese civilians residing in the regimental zone had been evacuated to Japan. The regiment also fell heir to the task of guarding the large amount of Japanese private and government-owned property in the area, pending its final disposition. Early in December, the port of Kunsan was designated as a main port of entry for Korean repatriates returning from Japan and China, and by 31 December, over 35,000 Koreans [had] been processed through the port."

September–October 1945
POW Camp, Manchuria, Then Home, Finally

Colonel Michael A. Quinn completes his diary, with entries on his last days as a Japanese POW after forty months in captivity.

"Supplies are coming in by plane, and our food is picking up rapidly. So will I," Colonel Quinn proclaims on 2 September, from the liberated POW camp at Mukden, Manchuria. "We were informed last night that those in good physical shape are to go home by ship and that we may be here at least a month. . . ."

Aboard the USS *Relief*, 13 September, en route from Formosa to Okinawa, Colonel Quinn updates his journal, with details of his last bit of socializing in Manchuria with newfound friends among the Catholic community, including Catholic nuns, Bishop Blois, and Bishop Raymond Lane, a Maryknoll missionary from Boston.

"I just got back from Mukden in time to throw my stuff in a truck and start back to the station where we arrived about 1400 hours [10 September] . . . , got under way at 1950, and what was supposed to be a twelve-hour trip turned into a twenty-five-hour trip. . . .

"About 2100 hours Tuesday [11 September], we arrived at the quay at Dairen. . . . Mattresses, clean sheets, and soft pillows. . . . I saw towels piled up a foot thick. I took a shower bath and felt so good, I took two more. No limit on soap and no limit on water, which was hot as could be. Then stepped into clean pajamas. I have never known such joy in being clean in my life. Then they topped it off by a cup of hot coffee. We had already retired when, lo and behold, we were ordered out again to eat a steak dinner. Had more coffee and went to bed about midnight. . . . I am putting on weight—143 pounds and it isn't fat; very solid. We have ice cream daily—my weakness. . . ."

In his last journal entry on 17 September, Colonel Quinn records: "Came in Buckner Bay some time Saturday. . . . There are more ships in this bay than I knew existed. There must be thousands of them. . . . Yesterday, a typhoon started up, and we pulled about five miles east of the islands and were forced to stay there most of the day. . . . In the shuffle someone aboard stole my camera. There has been a report of a lot of pilferage on this trip. . . ."

After two weeks in Manila visiting old friends, Colonel Quinn "boarded the *Globester* on its first trip around the world, with stops at Guam, Kwajalein, and Hawaii," and then twelve hours later, he says, "I was able to look out of the window of the plane and see the one woman on the strip at Hamilton Field [California]—*my wife.*"

EDITOR'S NOTE: *In a sidebar to the Quinn POW story, Major Michael Quinn relates that his father had the option, when leaving the Philippines, of sending some of his belongings back to the States by ship. He had a steamer trunk filled with personal items and souvenirs collected during his tours of duty that had been in the possession of a Filipino friend, who had buried the trunk for safekeeping during Japanese occupation. Originally, Colonel Quinn planned to include his POW journals in that trunk but—to borrow yet one last time again that favored expression of his—mirabili dictu (wonderful to relate), decided against it, choosing instead to take his diaries with him by plane. Later, upon retrieving his trunk, he discovered that it had been ransacked by Navy personnel aboard ship and many of his treasures taken. One can only surmise what might have happened to his journals had they been in that trunk.*

1942–1949
Japan, the Philippines, and USA

Colonel Mariano Villarin, a second lieutenant in the Philippine Army and survivor of the Bataan Death March, had been imprisoned at Camp O'Donnell until late 1942, when shipped to Japan with Filipino hostages for "spiritual rejuvenation."

During that period in Japan, "one day our Japanese 'honcho' took a small group of former POWs to Radio Tokyo as part of the indoctrination," Colonel

Villarin recalls. "I sneaked back to Radio Tokyo a few times after, because I wanted to talk to three Allied POWs who had been screened and found to have radio broadcasting experience; they were now forced to work for Radio Tokyo on anti-American propaganda, at the risk of death. One of them introduced me to Tokyo Rose (Iva Toguri D'Aquino), a Los Angeles-born Nisei who was stranded in Tokyo when war broke out. I saw her actually speaking into a microphone and broadcasting anti-American propaganda, followed by nostalgic American music. I wrote it down in my diary."

After the war, in 1949, Colonel Villarin was "subpoenaed to appear in a San Francisco federal court after word went around that the FBI was looking for the hostage who had kept a diary in which Tokyo Rose was mentioned. I never thought that that diary, which was used as an exhibit in court, would make me a witness for the prosecution in the trial of Tokyo Rose in 1949. In court testimony, I repeated her statement before a microphone: 'Why do you have to stay in the foxholes of New Guinea while your girlfriends back home are running around with other men?' She was found guilty and was sentenced to ten years in prison and fined $10,000.

"Tokyo Rose served only six and a half years of a ten-year sentence. In January 1977, President Gerald Ford, on the strength of a petition submitted by the Japanese-American League, pardoned Mrs. D'Aquino, thus restoring her U.S. citizenship, which she had lost when she was convicted in 1949. The pardon also vindicated the woman who supporters maintained was simply a victim of strong anti-Japanese feelings in the immediate postwar years," Colonel Villarin writes in *We Remember Bataan and Corregidor*.

In summarizing the Philippine story, Colonel Villarin adds: "The appalling figure of 29,000 Filipinos and 2,000 Americans who died in Camp O'Donnell will remain etched in the memory of those of us who survived. For these war crimes, including the atrocities committed during the liberation of the Philippines in 1945, Generals Masaharu Homma and Tomoyuki Yamashita were tried, convicted, and executed in Manila.

"A total of 1.1 million Filipinos died during the three years of ruthless enemy occupation of the Philippines. In Manila alone, 250,000 innocent civilians were killed and their houses burned by the retreating Japanese as the American liberators under MacArthur 'returned' to recapture Manila.

"World War II had recently ended when General Jonathan Wainwright stopped at the Madigan Army Hospital near Fort Lewis, Washington, to visit with some thirty former POWs liberated in the Far East. In a voice heavy with emotion, he told them, 'We knew we were an outpost and that outposts must be sacrificed when no help could get to us. Yet you fought down to the last ditch. If we had been prepared, none of you would be here because there would have been no war . . . no Pearl Harbor, no attack on the Philippines. There never would have been a Death March from Bataan. . . . You are heroes. Every one of you is a symbol of what must never happen again.'"

ACKNOWLEDGMENTS

To Colonel Norman S. Burzynski, for steadfast support and advice during pursuit of publication into book format of *The Officer*'s World War II series; Rear Admiral Bennett S. Sparks, USCGR (Ret.), and Major General Evan L. Hultman, AUS (Ret.), for sparking publication approval from ROA; Major General Robert A. McIntosh, USAF (Ret.), for granting ROA's permission to publish; Commander Paul Hewett for obtaining California contributor permissions; Lieutenant General Dennis M. McCarthy, USMC (Ret.), ROA executive director, and Eric Minton, editor of *The Officer*, for cooperation with Fordham University Press in the final stages of publication; Richard Berger, for his weight-lifter's nudge to "get that book published"; Catherine Buzzanell Rea for continual rays of encouragement; Anne Dorsey for friendship that transcends indexing pagination; and to the Kelly Family—husband Richard, our children Christopher, Gregory, Maria, Martin, Matthew, and Regina, and spouses—for serving always as cheerleaders: *Aciu* (thank you) from the depths of my Lithuanian heart. To Fordham University Press, its director Robert Oppedisano, and the Press board of directors for recognizing the value of preserving a valuable segment of World War II history, my profound gratitude.

Contributor Acknowledgments

Material quoted from the following ROA contributors is excerpted or abridged, with permission from authors or a family member, from the books or manuscript listed.

Abbott, Chaplain H. P. *The Nazi "88" Made Believers.* Dayton, Ohio: Otterbein Press, 1946. Self-published and out of print.

Bowen, Sidney. *Dearest Isabel: Letters from an Enlisted Man in World War II.* Manhattan, Kan.: Sunflower University Press, 1992.

Chester, Alvin P. *A Sailor's Odyssey: At Peace and at War 1935–1945.* Miami, Fla.: Odysseus Books, 1991. Quoted with permission of author, publisher, and Destroyer Escort Sailors Association. Available at $19.95 (includes shipping and handling) from DESA, P.O. Box 3448, Deland FL 32721–3448.

Frelinghuysen, Joseph S. *Passages to Freedom: A Story of Capture and Escape.* Manhattan, Kan.: Sunflower University Press, 1990. Available at $15 (includes shipping and handling) from Joseph Frelinghuysen Jr., P.O. Box 270, Gladstone, NJ 07934.

Gabler, Clyde W. *What Did You Do in WWII, Grandpa?* Manuscript, transcribed from author's wartime notebooks, for distribution to family and friends. Copyright 1991.

McConahey, William M., M.D. *Battalion Surgeon.* Copyright 1966 by William M. McConahey. Published privately in Rochester, Minn., 1966, for limited distribution. Second printing, 1974. Third printing in paperback; copyright date not available. Available from eBay or Amazon.

Quinn, Colonel Michael A. *Love Letters to Mike: Forty Months as a Japanese P.O.W.* Self-published by Vantage Press, New York, 1977. Permission to excerpt from First Edition obtained from Major Michael H. Quinn. Second Edition published by Circle Q Press, Steilacoom, Wash., copyright date not available. Available at $20 (includes shipping and handling) from Michael H. Quinn, 12419 McGinnis Road, Danville, OH 43014–9690.

Starke, William H. *Vampire Squadron: Story of the 44th Fighter Squadron, 13th (Jungle) Air Force.* Self-published and out of print. Copyright date not available.

Villarin, Mariano. *We Remember Bataan and Corregidor: The Story of the American and Filipino Defenders of Bataan and Corregidor and Their Captivity.* Baltimore, Md.: Gateway Press, 1990. Available at $12 (includes shipping and handling) from the author at 1910 Harding St., Long Beach CA 90805. While some material for *The Officer*'s World War II series was written specifically for the magazine, most of Colonel Villarin's write-ups were excerpted from his book.

Photo Credits

Cover Photo: INFO to COME

In general, permissions for photos are from ROA contributors themselves or from their family members. For certain photos, credits are as follows for the picture pages:

Page 2, Navajo code breakers, Defense Department Photo (Marine Corps).

Page 3, Bogart and Bacall, National Archives photo.

Page 4, Marines on Tinian, National Archives photo. Marines on Okinawa, courtesy of Lt. Col. Kenneth Radnitzer, USAR (Ret.).

Page 5, Quad 20mm, courtesy of Lt. Col. Roland L. Stewart, AUS (Ret.).

Page 10, *Anzio Annie,* courtesy of Lt. Col. Walter H. Johnson Sr., USAR (Ret.); Mascot Kelly, courtesy of Cmdr. Esmonde F. O'Brien Jr., USCGR (Ret.).

Page 12, the USAT *General Brewster,* courtesy of Maj. Taylor W. Millner, USAR (Ret.).

SELECTED BIBLIOGRAPHY

Army Times, editors of. *The Banners and the Glory: The Story of General Douglas MacArthur*. New York: G. P. Putnam's Sons, 1965.

Associated Press, writers and photographers. *World War II: A 50th Anniversary History*. New York: Henry Holt, 1989.

Blair, Clay, Jr. *The U.S. Submarine War against Japan*, vol. 2 of *Silent Victory*. Philadelphia and New York: Lippincott, 1975.

Churchill, Winston S. *The Grand Alliance*, vol. 3 of *The Second World War*. Boston: Houghton Mifflin, 1950.

———. *The Hinge of Fate*, vol. 4 of *The Second World War*. Boston: Houghton Mifflin, 1950.

———. *Triumph and Tragedy*, vol. 6 of *The Second World War*. New York: Bantam Books, 1962.

Dear, I. C. B., and M. R. D. Foot, eds. *The Oxford Companion to World War II*. Oxford and New York: Oxford University Press, 1995.

Department of Defense (U.S.) 50th Anniversary of World War II Commemoration Committee, various publicity materials.

Gansberg, Judith M. *Stalag: U.S.A.* New York: Thomas Y. Crowell, 1977.

Gilbert, Martin. *Road to Victory, 1942–1945*, vol. 7 of *The Churchill Biography*. Boston: Houghton Mifflin, 1986.

———. *The Second World War: A Complete History*. New York: Henry Holt, 1989.

Hunt, Frazier. *The Untold Story of Douglas MacArthur*. New York: Devin-Adair, 1954.

Keegan, John. *Six Armies in Normandy*. New York: Viking Press, 1982.

Kerr, E. Bartlett. *Surrender and Survival: The Experience of American POWs in the Pacific, 1941–1945*. New York: William Morrow, 1985.

MacArthur, Gen. Douglas. *Reminiscences*. New York: McGraw-Hill, 1964.

Manchester, William. *American Caesar: Douglas MacArthur 1880–1964*. Boston: Little, Brown, 1978.

Mayer, S. L. *The Biography of General of the Army Douglas MacArthur*. Northbrook, Ill.: Bison, 1981.

McCutcheon, Marc. *The Writer's Guide to Everyday Life: From Prohibition through World War II*. Cincinnati: Writer's Digest, 1995.

Meacham, Jon. *Franklin and Winston: An Intimate Portrait of an Epic Friendship*. New York: Random House, 2003.

Merriam-Webster's Geographical Dictionary, 3rd edition. Springfield, Mass.: Merriam-Webster, 1998.

Morison, Samuel Eliot. *The Two-Ocean War: A Short History of the United States Navy in the Second World War*. Boston: Little, Brown, 1963.

National Archives World War II Commemorative Committee. Various publicity materials.

Nichols, David, ed. *Ernie's War: The Best of Ernie Pyle's World War II Dispatches*. New York: Random House, 1986.

Reserve Officers Association. World War II commemorative calendars, 1991–95.

Sanders, Jacquin. *A Night before Christmas*. New York: G. P. Putnam's Sons, 1963.

Time-Life Books, eds. *WWII: Time-Life Books History of the Second World War*. New York: Prentice Hall, 1989.

Truman, Harry S. *Year of Decision*, vol. 1 of *Memoirs*. Garden City, N.Y.: Doubleday, 1955.

Young, Brigadier Peter, ed. *The World Almanac Book of World War II: The Complete and Comprehensive Documentary of World War II*. New York: World Almanac, 1981.

Sources for Chronology: Churchill, *The Hinge of Fate*; Dear and Foot, eds., *The Oxford Companion to World War II*; Gilbert, *Road to Victory, 1942–1945*; McCutcheon, *The Writer's Guide to Everyday Life*; Meacham, *Franklin and Winston*; Time-Life, eds., *WWII: Time-Life Books History of the Second World War*; Department of Defense 50th Anniversary of World War II Commemoration Committee; *Merriam Webster's Geographical Dictionary*; Reserve Officers Association, World War II commemorative calendars, 1991–95; Young, ed., *The World Almanac Book of World War II*.

Sources for Chapter 46, V-J Day Countdown: *Army Times*, eds., *The Banners and the Glory*; Associated Press, *World War II: A 50th Anniversary History*; Blair, *The U.S. Submarine War against Japan*; Gilbert, *The Second World War: A Complete History*; Hunt, *The Untold Story of Douglas MacArthur*; MacArthur, *Reminiscences*; Manchester, *American Caesar*; Mayer, *The Biography of General of the Army, Douglas MacArthur*; Morison, *The Two-Ocean War*; Truman, *Year of Decision*; Young, ed., *The World Almanac Book of World War II*.

ABOUT THE EDITOR

Carol Adele Kelly (née Consavage) graduated from the University of Pittsburgh with a B.A. in journalism. She served as editor of two Pittsburgh suburban weekly newspapers, and then on the staff of the *Pittsburgh Catholic* newspaper.

With marriage to Richard M. Kelly, Carol exchanged newspaper deadlines for family deadlines, as the couple raised their six children. When the youngest ones entered high school, Carol began freelance work: editing prayer books and liturgical references by the Reverend Lucian Deiss, C.S.Sp., French Bible scholar and composer; and serving as editor of *Disabilities Digest* and of a community monthly newspaper.

For the past twenty-three years, she has freelanced for *The Officer* magazine, serving as project officer and copy editor, with the World War II and Korean War series among her editorial assignments.

INDEX

Contributors are listed in the Index with names in capital letters; they are identified by last known rank and place of residence. In service information, the addition of R *after branch indicates* Reserve. ANG *indicates Air National Guard; it is preceded by the two-letter state abbreviation. Picture pages are referenced at the end of lines with* "pp" *plus page number in italics.*

World War II: The Global, Human, and Ethical Dimension

G. Kurt Piehler, *series editor*